THE REMEMBERED VICTORY

HONORING THE FALLEN HEROES OF THE KOREAN WAR

This limited edition commemorative book was published under the direction of the **Korean War Veterans Memorial Foundation** by Remember My Service Productions, a division of StoryRock, Inc.

RememberMyService.com

The Remembered Victory: Honoring the Fallen Heroes of the Korean War

In accordance with the "Korean War Veterans Memorial Wall of Remembrance Act" enacted by the Senate and House of Representatives of the United States of America in Congress assembled on October 7, 2016, a Wall of Remembrance is to be constructed at the Korean War Veterans Memorial in Washington, D.C. A list of names, the eligibility criteria of which is determined by U.S. Secretary of Defense and the U.S. Secretary of the Interior, is to be included on the wall. The names included are members of the Armed Forces of the United States who died in the Korean War. Additional information on the Wall of Remembrance may include other information about the Korean War and names from Korean Augmentation to the United States Army, the Republic of Korea Armed Forces, and other nations of the United Nations Command who were killed in action, wounded in action, listed as missing in action, or were prisoners of war.

No federal funds were used in the construction of the Korean War Veterans Memorial Wall of Remembrance. The memorial was privately funded by donations made to the Korean War Veterans Memorial Foundation in honor of all who served during the Korean War.

This publication based upon *Korea Reborn: A Grateful Nation Honors War Veterans for 60 Years of Growth* was originally published (first edition) in 2013 by Remember My Service Productions, a division of StoryRock, Inc. Unless credited otherwise, all photographs and copyrights herein are provided by the Republic of Korea's Ministry of Patriots and Veterans Affairs and the United States National Archives and Records Administration (NARA).

Visit us at: www.RememberMyService.com

The Remembered Victory: Honoring the Fallen Heroes of the Korean War
Remember My Service Productions
p. cm.

ISBN: 978-1-7322976-9-2

THE REMEMBERED VICTORY

HONORING THE FALLEN HEROES OF THE KOREAN WAR

We honor and remember the men and women who made the ultimate sacrifice in defense of freedom for the people of the Republic of Korea. This book is dedicated to the families of the fallen and Korean War Veterans.

Because of

SEOUL 1953

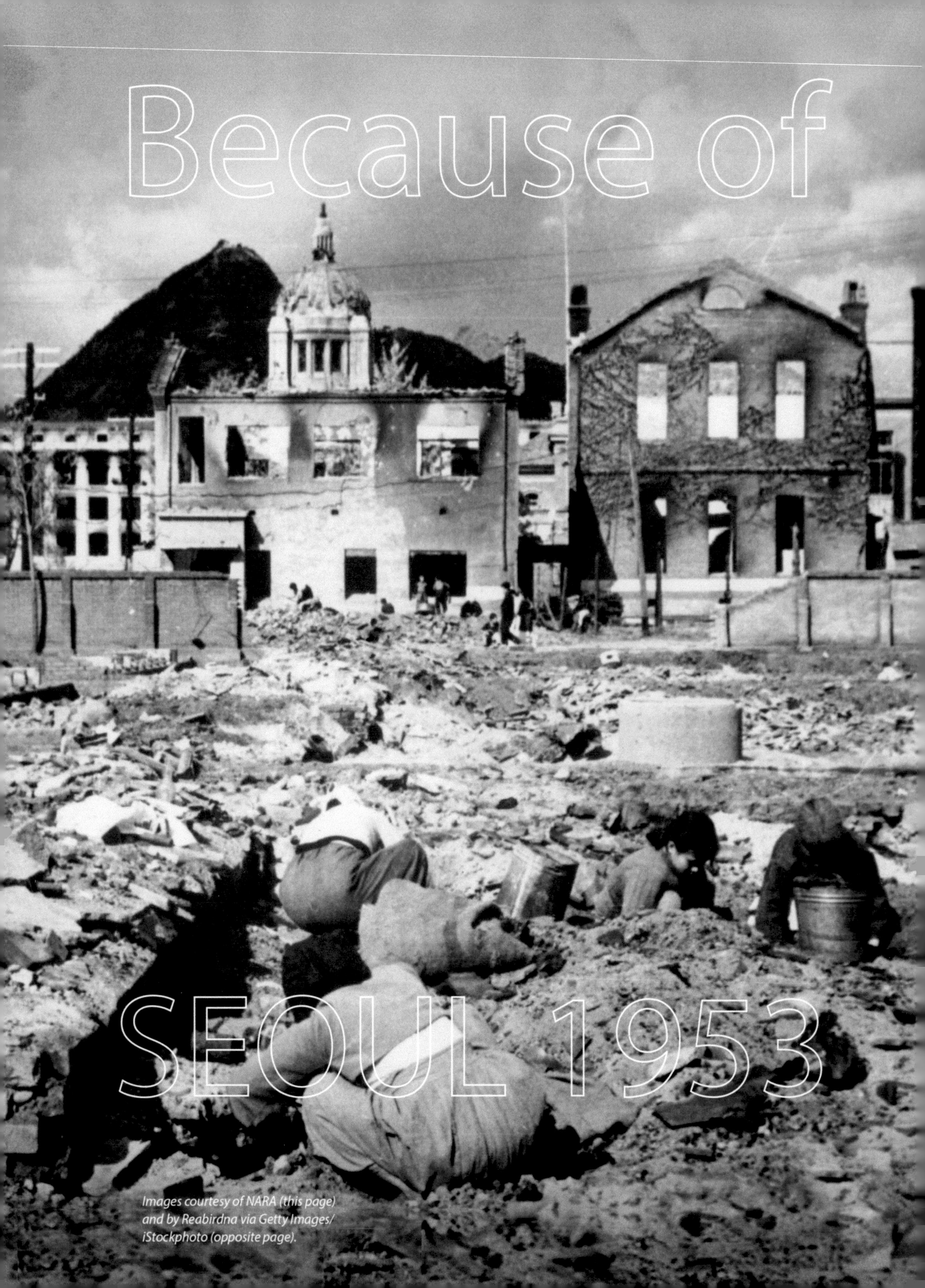

Images courtesy of NARA (this page) and by Reabirdna via Getty Images/iStockphoto (opposite page).

your service
SEOUL TODAY

THE REMEMBERED VICTORY

HONORING THE FALLEN HEROES OF THE KOREAN WAR

TABLE OF CONTENTS

To the Korean War Veterans and the Families of the Fallen:

I am honored to be the Chairman of the Korean War Veterans Memorial Foundation, whose mission is to honor the veterans who served during the Korean War and the families of the fallen, to preserve and upgrade the beautiful Korean War Memorial on the Mall in Washington, D.C., and to add a Wall of Remembrance to the existent Memorial.

The last two years have been momentous ones for the Foundation, in that the dream of adding the Wall of Remembrance to the memorial will become a reality. As you view this Wall of Remembrance, we all should understand the cost of war in human sacrifice, the strength of the Republic of Korea and United States Alliance, and that "Freedom is Not Free."

This project of renovation and building the Wall of Remembrance has been a total collaborative effort with many organizations, including the architects, the building contractor, the National Park Service. the Department of Defense, and the foundation.

As you can see in the following pages, many organizations and individuals have contributed to this project; however, without the generous support of the Korean government and the Korean people, this project could not have been accomplished. Their contribution demonstrates the gratitude of the Korean people for the preservation of their democracy.

On behalf of the foundation Board of Directors, I welcome you to the Korean War Memorial. Lastly, I welcome and thank each Korean veteran to your Memorial. And to the families of the fallen who have a loved one listed on the wall, you have our deepest gratitude.

General John H. Tilelli, Jr.
U.S. Army (Retired)
Chairman, Korean War Veterans Memorial Foundation

CHAPTER 1

Dear Honored Korean War Veterans,

For almost 70 years, SK has driven innovations that improve and strengthen our world.

These advances would not have been possible, however, without the sacrifices of the Korean War veterans and their loved ones. The heroic deeds of these Americans live on in the hearts and memories of the Korean people, and we are honored to express our gratitude for their service through this commemorative book.

The Remembered Victory honors the legacy of the brave 1.8 million Americans who fought to protect the freedom of the Korean people. As a result of the tremendous courage of these service members and their families, South Korea has grown into a dynamic economy that enjoys a vibrant democracy. All this while the enduring friendship between the United States and South Korea continues to flourish. At SK, we believe that this partnership is crucial to maintaining peace and stability and expanding economic growth globally.

With this book, we honor, remember, and commemorate the Korean War veterans who defended the universal values that the people of South Korea enjoy today. And we pay tribute to the trusted partnership between the United States and South Korea that helps safeguard our collective prosperity and security.

With gratitude,

Chey Tae-won
SK Group Chairman

SK

Tourists walk along the path next to the Korean War Memorial in West Potomac Park, just south of the Reflecting Pool. *Image courtesy of iStockphoto/Getty Images.*

CHAPTER 2

The Korean War Veterans Memorial, Washington, D.C.

Southeast of the Lincoln Memorial on the National Mall resides the Korean War Veterans Memorial. A short walk South from the reflecting pool, this solemn monument is dedicated to service members of the U.S. Armed Forces who served and sacrificed during the Korean War. This Washington, D.C., landmark was dedicated on July 27, 1995, and was designed and financed privately under the direction of the Korean War Veterans Memorial Advisory Board composed of Korean War veterans appointed by President Reagan.

The memorial commemorates the 5.8 million American service members who served during the three-year period of the Korean War. This war was one of the most hard-fought conflicts in our nations's history, with over 36,000 U.S. service members and over 7,100 Korean Augmentation to the United States Army (KATUSA) having died during the war. Of these, 8,200 are listed as missing in action or lost or buried at sea. Another 103,284 were wounded during the war.

The Korean War Veterans Memorial Foundation is the organization originally entrusted to take care of the memorial in perpetuity. The foundation's additional responsibilities include helping with the coordination of ceremonies and other events honoring Korean War veterans hosted at the memorial.

The memorial is free and open to the public 24 hours a day. The memorial consists of five parts: The Statues, The Mural Wall, The Pool of Remembrance, The United Nations Walkway, and its newest feature, the Wall of Remembrance. The muralists, sculptors, and architects worked closely to create a memorable compilation of three-dimensional and two-dimensional artwork comprising this beautiful memorial.

The Statues, located on the west end of the memorial, includes 19 stainless steel sculptures. Each is approximately seven feet tall and represents an ethnic cross section of America. This hauntingly beautiful display was sculpted by Frank Gaylord of Barre, Vermont, and cast by Tallix Foundries of

Lights illuminate the sculptures at Korean War Veterans Memorial in Washington, D.C. *Image courtesy of iStockphoto/Getty Images.*

Visitors and statues that represent a squad on patrol are reflected in the polished granite of the Mural Wall. The Korean War Veterans Memorial in Washington, D.C. *Image courtesy of iStockphoto/Getty Images.*

Section of the granite wall at the Korean War Veterans Memorial. National Mall, Washington, DC. The word 'Freedom' is part of the sign inlaid in silver: 'Freedom Is Not Free.'" *Image courtesy of iStockphoto/Getty Images.*

Beacon, New York. The statues illustrate an advance party of troops with 14 Army soldiers, three Marines, one Navy member, and one Air Force member. The statues stand in patches of juniper bushes, separated by strips of polished granite.

The Mural Wall consists of 41 panels, eight inches thick, extending 164 feet. The wall appears as an isosceles triangle, with the tip intersecting a circle over the Pool of Remembrance. Designed by Louis Nelson of New York City and fabricated by Coldspring, a stone manufacturer in Minnesota, the mural depicts members of the Army, Navy, Marine Corps, Air Force, and Coast Guard and their equipment, and is based upon over 2,400 images from the National Archives. The reflective quality of the Academy Black granite creates the image of a total of 38 statues, symbolic of the 38th parallel and the 38 months of the war.

At the far end of the memorial in its circular centers sits the **Pool of Remembrance**. This reflective pool, thirty feet in diameter, encircles the "Freedom Is Not Free" wall and alcove, at the base of which are numerically listed the names of troops killed in action (KIA), wounded in action (WIA), missing in action (MIA), and prisoners of war (POW). The Pool is surrounded by a wide walkway with benches and encircled by carefully manicured trees.

To the left of the Mural Wall is a **United Nations Walkway** with engraved markers commemorating all 22 nations that contributed troops to the United Nations efforts in the Korean War.

The newest feature at the memorial is **the Wall of Remembrance**. Legislation signed into law on October 2016 by President Barack Obama authorized the establishment and construction of a wall to be incorporated into the existing Korean War Veterans Memorial. The Wall of Remembrance memorializes the names of over 36,000 American servicemen and 7,100 Korean Augmentation to the United States Army (KATUSA), who gave their lives defending freedoms and lives of the people of South Korea.

All funding for the wall was made possible through generous donations of the American and Korean people. The construction of the Wall of Remembrance and refurbishment of the entire Korean War Veterans Memorial project began on March 15, 2021, and was dedicated on July 27, 2022.

The newly refurbished memorial stands as a testament to the service and sacrifice to all of the heroes of the Korean War—a lasting reminder that freedom is not free.

Convoy of DUKWs (six-wheel drive amphibious trucks), carrying American and ROK Marines, move to Han River in offensive launched against the North Korean forces in that area (September 20, 1950). *NARA photo.*

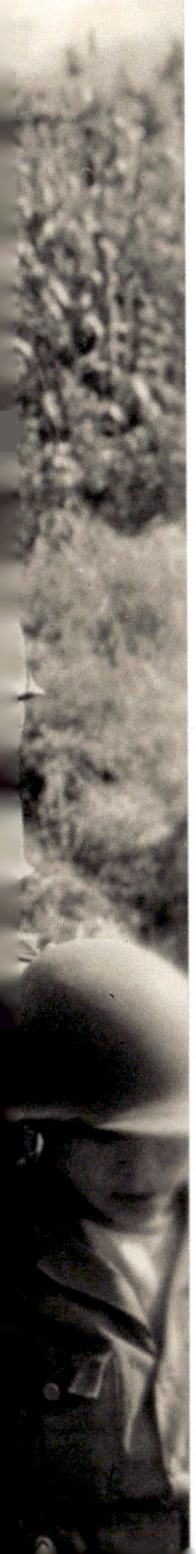

CHAPTER 3

Families of Korean War Fallen:

We recognize that you have made lifelong sacrifices, and you have our deepest condolences.

The addition of the Wall of Remembrance to the Korean War Veterans Memorial will hopefully bring a sense of peace and demonstrate the sincere appreciation for your loved one's ultimate sacrifice.

The sacrifice of each Korean War Veteran made in defense of freedom saved South Korea from the grips of North Korea's communist regime and helped enable the vibrant democracy it is today. Their legacy is millions of Koreans who live in freedom in South Korea and all over the world. We will never forget that freedom is not free.

More than 36,000 Americans and 7,100 Korean augmentees were killed in action, and many more were wounded for the sake of freedom. The Wall of Remembrance displays the names of the fallen and is a reflection and recognition of a grateful nation.

Words from President Lincoln's letter to a family of the fallen of the Civil War ring true today: "I feel how weak and fruitless must be any word of mine which should attempt to beguile you from the grief of a loss so overwhelming. But I cannot refrain from tendering you the consolation that may be found in the thanks of the Republic they died to save."

May the United States and the Republic of Korea alliance borne in battle survive forever and be committed to freedom.

The Statues at the Korean Warm Veterans Memorial, located adjacent to the Lincoln Memorial. *Image courtesy of iStockphoto/Getty Images.*

CHAPTER 4

Korean War Veterans Memorial Foundation

Engraved on the Korean War Contemplative Bench in Arlington Cemetery is this quote by Herman Wouk: "The beginning of the end of war lies in remembrance."

The Korean War Veterans Memorial is a living manifestation of those words. The foundation that oversees the memorial continues to honor the veterans of the Korean War by caring for, and adding to, the Memorial. The latest monument added to this beautiful memorial is the Wall of Remembrance, which will honor the fallen military personnel of the United States and the Republic of Korea.

As a nonprofit, tax-exempt organization, the Korean War Veterans Memorial Foundation is entrusted with maintaining the Korean War Veterans Memorial in our nation's capital, and assisting with ceremonies at the memorial honoring all those who served during the Korean War.

Legislation was passed in October of 2016 that gave the foundation additional responsibility raising the funds necessary to build and establish the Wall of Remembrance, a new monument to Korean War Veterans to be incorporated within the existing Korean War Veterans Memorial in Washington, D.C. The Wall will become the permanent home to the names of those who died fighting for freedom during the Korean War. The entirety of funding for this new ambitious project has come from the generous donations of the American and Korean people.

The United States and the Republic of Korea share a long history of friendship and cooperation based on shared values and interests. This alliance was set in motion by the invasion of South Korea on June 25, 1950. After approximately three years of fighting, an armistice was signed on July 27, 1953, ending the active conflict. Over 36,000 American military personnel and 7,100 Korean Augmentation to the United States Army (KATUSA) gave their lives defending the people of South Korea from aggression and ensuring their freedom.

The Korean War Veterans Memorial Foundation is dedicated to their memory and to ensure that their sacrifice is remembered with the sacred memorial maintained in their honor. To this end, the Foundation helps to educate the more than four million people who visit the memorial in Washington, D.C., each year. The Wall of Remembrance will become the permanent

Close-up of the Mural Wall at the Korean War Memorial. The Memorial Wall has 2,400 etched images taken from photographs from various aspects of the war. *Image courtesy of iStockphoto/Getty Images.*

The Mural Wall at the Korean War Veterans Memorial contains 2,400 etched images depicting various aspects of the war. *Image courtesy of iStockphoto/Getty Images.*

The Foundation Board

Board of Directors

General
John H. Tilelli, Jr.
U.S. Army, Retired
BOARD CHAIRMAN

Lieutenant General
Bernie Champoux
U.S. Army, Retired
VICE CHAIRMAN

Colonel
Richard W. Dean, II
U.S. Army, Retired
VICE CHAIRMAN

Thomas S. Kim
BOARD MEMBER

Colonel
Louis Berman
U.S. Army, Retired
BOARD MEMBER

Sunny K. Park
BOARD MEMBER

Annelie Weber
BOARD MEMBER

Colonel
William Weber
U.S. Army, Retired
CHAIRMAN EMERITUS

Maryland First Lady
Yumi Hogan
HONORARY MEMBER

Staff

Lieutenant Colonel
James R. Fisher
U.S. Army, Retired
EXECUTIVE DIRECTOR

Michel Au Buchon
BOARD SECRETARY
and TREASURER

home to the names of those who died fighting for freedom for the Korean people.

The foundation's tireless efforts to raise funds for the memorial and the new Wall of Remembrance have involved nationwide publicity efforts, grassroots lobbying, and solicitation of donations. The foundation continues to seek funding from various sources, such as families, fraternal military unit organizations, corporate entities, and grants.

The Korean War Veterans Honor Roll pays tribute to every veteran who served in the Korean War, including those who made it home. While their names are not on the memorial's Wall of Remembrance, they are never forgotten. Listing on the honor roll is a free service of the foundation. However, your tax-deductible donations in honor of the listed veteran, though not mandatory, will help us maintain this site and would be most appreciated.

Board members of the foundation actively participate in many fundraising events and devote 100 percent to their efforts to this important cause without remuneration. None of the donations for the new Wall of Remembrance were used for administrative costs.

The foundation and its board is honored to have participated in this latest effort to plan, build, and dedicate the Wall of Remembrance. The opportunity to honor all those who served and sacrificed in the Korean War is a meaningful and solemn undertaking. The Korean War Veterans Memorial and the Wall of Remembrance is a lasting testament to freedom and the heroes who fight for it. ■

Soldier statue at the Korean War Veterans Memorial. Statues represents all branches of the armed forces. The nineteen statues each stand seven feet tall. *Image courtesy of iStockphoto/Getty Images.*

CHAPTER 5

[114th Congress Public Law 230]
[From the U.S. Government Publishing Office]

An Act

[[Page 130 STAT. 947]]
Public Law 114-230
114th Congress

To authorize a Wall of Remembrance as part of the Korean War Veterans Memorial and to allow certain private contributions to fund that Wall of Remembrance. <<NOTE: Oct. 7, 2016 - [H.R. 1475]>>

Be it enacted by the Senate and House of Representatives of the United States of America in Congress assembled, <<NOTE: Korean War Veterans Memorial Wall of Remembrance Act. 42 USC 8903 note.>> SECTION 1. SHORT TITLE.

This Act may be cited as the ``Korean War Veterans Memorial Wall of Remembrance Act''.
SEC. 2. WALL OF REMEMBRANCE.

(a) Authorization.--
(1) In general.--Notwithstanding section 8908(c) of title 40, United States Code, the Korean War Veterans Memorial Foundation, Inc., may construct a Wall of Remembrance at the site of the Korean War Veterans Memorial.
(2) <<NOTE: Lists.>> Requirement.--
(A) <<NOTE: Determination.>> In general.--The Wall of Remembrance shall include a list of names of members of the Armed Forces of the United States who died in the Korean War, as determined by the Secretary of Defense, in accordance with subparagraph (B).
(B) Criteria; submission to the secretary of the interior.--The Secretary of Defense shall--
(i) establish eligibility criteria for the inclusion of names on the Wall of Remembrance under subparagraph (A); and
(ii) provide to the Secretary of the Interior a final list of names for inclusion on the Wall of Remembrance under subparagraph (A) that meet the criteria established under clause (i).
(3) Additional information.--The Wall of Remembrance may include other information about the Korean War, including the number of members of the Armed Forces of the United States, the Korean Augmentation to the United States Army, the Republic of Korea Armed Forces, and the other nations of the United Nations Command who, in regards to the Korean War--
(A) were killed in action;
(B) were wounded in action;
(C) are listed as missing in action; or
(D) were prisoners of war.

(b) <<NOTE: Applicability.>> Commemorative Works Act.--Except as provided in subsection (a)(1), chapter 89 of title 40, United States Code (commonly known as the ``Commemorative Works Act''), shall apply.

[[Page 130 STAT. 948]]

(c) No Federal Funds.--No Federal funds may be used to construct the Wall of Remembrance.

Approved October 7, 2016.

LEGISLATIVE HISTORY--H.R. 1475:

HOUSE REPORTS: No. 114-433 (Comm. on Natural Resources).
SENATE REPORTS: No. 114-336 (Comm. on Energy and Natural Resources).
CONGRESSIONAL RECORD, Vol. 162 (2016):
Feb. 24, considered and passed House.
Sept. 19, considered and passed Senate, amended.
Sept. 21, House concurred in Senate amendment.

Korea becomes an independent nation. President Syngman Rhee speaks at the ceremonies of the inauguration of the newly formed government of the Republic of Korea (Seoul, Korea, August 15, 1948). *NARA photo.*

CHAPTER 6

Setting the Stage

When World War II ended in 1945, few realized that another war was beginning. It would take five years for the conflict in Korea to gain international attention—and participation—but it started when the Empire of Japan, which had occupied Korea for more than three decades, was defeated in World War II by the Allies. In order to accept the surrender of Japanese forces in Korea, the Americans occupied Korea south of the 38th Parallel, and the Soviet Union occupied the peninsula north of the Parallel.

In theory, the two countries agreed to temporarily occupy the country as "trustees" establishing a Korean provisional government that would ultimately lead to a free and independent country.

Wary of the "domino effect" (the concern that if one state in a region were controlled by the Communists, surrounding countries would soon follow), the United States began to watch Korea closely. President Harry S. Truman persuaded the United Nations to assume responsibility for Korea. The United Nations called for general and free elections to be held in both halves of Korea. The Soviet Union refused to cooperate, and the die was cast: a Communist state with Soviet support was established in North Korea, while a democratic movement gained favor in South Korea.

Kim Il Sung, a major who had led a Korean contingent in the Soviet army, returned to North Korea from Manchuria to lead the new communist government. With the backing of both the Soviet Union and China, he planned to unify the two Koreas by military force. Meanwhile, under U.N. mandate, the democratic Republic of Korea was being formed in the south, with Syngman Rhee elected as its first president. This move toward freedom hadn't come easily, however; some quarters of Southern society opposed the new state, resulting in upheavals throughout the country.

The end result? North Korea's military forces and supplies grew substantially, while in South Korea, both human and equipment resources were dramatically depleted in the civil unrest. Although there were attempts to unify the two countries, tension grew and cross-border raids and skirmishes at the 38th parallelbecame commonplace. When North Korea launched an attack on June 25, 1950, the Republic of Korea forces were under-prepared, under-supplied, and outnumbered.

Brig. Gen. Courtney Whitney; Gen. Douglas MacArthur, Commander in Chief of U.N. Forces; and Maj. Gen. Edward M. Almond observe the shelling of Incheon from USS *Mt. McKinley* (September 15, 1950). *Photo by Nutter, U.S. Army.*

Jacob A. Malik, Soviet representative on the U.N. Security Council, raises his hand to cast the only dissenting vote to the resolution calling on the Chinese forces to withdraw troops from Korea (Lake Success, New York, December 1950). *USIA photo.*

The Beginning of the Cold War

The term "cold war" was first used by English author and journalist George Orwell in an essay titled "You and the Atomic Bomb," published October 19, 1945, in the British newspaper *Tribune.*

Orwell wrote about the impact of the threat of nuclear war, predicting a nuclear stalemate between "two or three monstrous super-states, each possessed of a weapon by which millions of people can be wiped out in a few seconds.... Few people have yet considered its ideological implications—that is, the kind of world-view, the kind of beliefs, and the social structure that would probably prevail in a state which was at once unconquerable and in a permanent state of 'cold war' with its neighbors."

Orwell used the term a second time when writing an article for *The Observer,* which was published March 10, 1946. In that article, Orwell observed that, "after the Moscow conference last December, Russia began to make a 'cold war' on Britain and the British Empire."

In 1947, American financier and presidential advisor Bernard Baruch delivered a speech where the term was used to describe the post–World War II tensions between the United States, its Western European allies, and the Soviet Union: "Let us not be deceived: we are today in the midst of a cold war."

That same year, the term became more widely used and recognized when Walter Lippman, a newspaper reporter, wrote a book called *The Cold War.*

It is generally accepted that the Cold War began near the end of World War II, with an uneasy truce declared between the United States and the Soviet Union. The United States and its Western European allies were committed to a system where individual countries were led by democratic governments, and differences were resolved by international organizations. With a history of invasion and incredibly high casualties, the Soviet Union wanted to increase security by controlling the governments of the countries that bordered it. The United States and its Western European allies watched warily as the Soviet Union began to establish Communist governments in several Eastern European countries that had been liberated by the Red Army.

The Cold War reached its peak in the years preceding and throughout the Korean War. During this time, the Soviets unsuccessfully blockaded the Western-held sectors of West Berlin (1948–49), the United States joined with its European allies to create the North Atlantic Treaty Organization (NATO), a unified military command aimed to resist the Soviet presence in Europe (1949), the Soviets exploded their first atomic warhead, ending the American monopoly on the atomic bomb (1949), and a Communist government came to power in China (1949). Finally, Soviet-backed North Korean armies invaded South Korea, launching the Korean War.

The sustained state of political and military tension between the United States and Soviet Union continued for several decades. The Cold War was waged largely on propaganda, economic, and political fields, but military clashes—largely indirect, such as in Vietnam and Afghanistan—took place too. In 1991, the Soviet Union collapsed, as its various satellite states rose in mostly peaceful revolts, leaving the United States as the sole superpower.

Pres. Harry S. Truman is shown at his desk at the White House signing a proclamation declaring a national emergency in Korea (December 16, 1950). *USIA photo.*

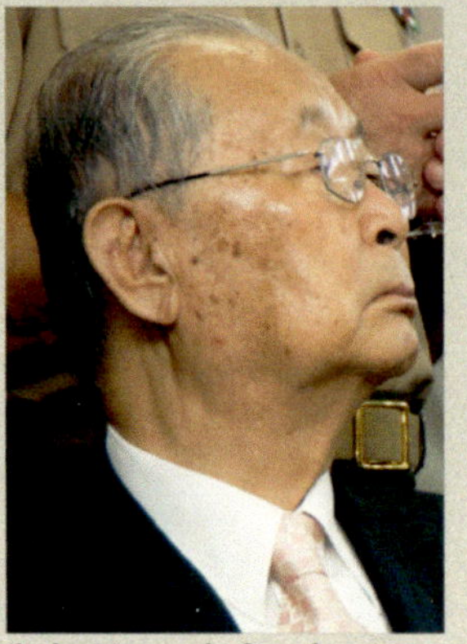

ABOVE: The late General Paik during and after the war.

"I shall be at the front. If I turn back, shoot me."

At the outset of the Korean War, a then-29-year-old Colonel Paik distinguished himself as the commander of the ROK 1st Infantry Division. During the battle at Dabudong (a.k.a. the "Bowling Alley"), Paik's First Division bravely counterattacked a ridgeline previously lost to the attacking North Korean Army. Paik famously inspired his troops by telling them, "We are going to turn around and kick the enemy off our ridge, and I shall be at the front. If I turn back, shoot me."

Being at the forefront of leadership had always been a trademark of Paik Sun Yup. In November 1951, the ROK 1 Corps (later named Task Force Paik) mounted a campaign against guerilla activity in the Mt. Jirisan region of southwestern Korea. Dubbed Operation "Rat Killer," the troops under Paik's command (now promoted to a general) captured or killed an estimated 25,000 guerillas by March 1952.

In July of the same year, General Paik was appointed ROK Army Chief of Staff, the highest position in the ROK Army. At only 32 years old, he commanded ten Army divisions, which would grow to 20 divisions by 1953.

General Paik Sun Yup became Korea's first officer to attain four-star rank, and would later command the First Field Army, serve a second appointment as Army Chief of Staff, and finally serve the remainder of his career as Chairman for the ROK Joint Chiefs of Staff. He retired from military service in 1960 and began his second career as a diplomat, serving as ambassador to China, France, and Canada. Following his diplomatic service in 1969, he served as Minister of Transportation until 1971. Thereafter, he served as president of two national policy companies.

Before his death in July 2020, General Paik had become a distinguished author and respected voice for veterans' affairs. With a lifetime devoted to public service and to his family, Gen. Paik Sun Yup will remain an iconic figure in the history of the Rupublic of Korea.

Gen. Douglas MacArthur inspects troops of the 24th Infantry on his arrival at Gimpo Airfield for a tour of the battlefront (February 21, 1951). *USIA photo.*

United Nations flag waves crowd waiting to hear Dr. Syngman Rhee speak to the United Nations Council in Daegu, Korea (July 30, 1950). *Photo by Sgt. Girard, U.S. Army.*

Korean refugees prepare to board an LST during the evacuation of Hungnam, while other refugees unload some of their meager belongings from an oxcart and load them on a fishing boat (December 19, 1950). *U.S. Navy photo.*

United Nation forces recross the 38th parallel ahead of pursuing Chinese forces (1950).
Photo by USIA.

Choosing the 38th Parallel

As World War II drew to an end, leaders of the winning countries (United States, United Kingdom, and the Soviet Union) gathered together at the Potsdam Conference to discuss the details of a peace treaty officially ending the war. As part of that treaty, the 38th parallel (a popular name given to 38° N Latitude) was chosen as a separation between South and North Korea.

The line roughly divides the peninsula in half. According to the agreement, the Soviet Union was to accept the surrender of Japanese forces north of the line, while the United States was to accept the Japanese surrender south of the line.

Initially, the 38th parallel was intended to be a temporary division of the country, while the United States and the Soviet Union assisted the two Koreas in establishing one country and one government. The onset of the Cold War, however, created entirely new circumstances, which ultimately led to the Korean War.

Miss Mo Yun Sook, famed Korean poet, telling how she escaped the Communist-led North Koreans when they captured Seoul by hiding in the mountains until the U.N. forces liberated the city (November 8, 1950). *Photo by Cpl. Robert Dangel, U.S. Army.*

Cpl. John W. Simms of Bradbury Heights, Maryland, bids his wife, Ann, and their 9-month-old son, John Jr., goodbye as he leaves for Korea (1950).
Photo by The Washington Post, USIA.

CHAPTER 7

The War Begins

As early as 1949, Kim Il-Sung had approached Soviet leader Joseph Stalin, asking for support to invade the South. Unconvinced that North Korean forces were prepared, and concerned about the response of the United States, Stalin refused. During the next year, however, numerous Korean veterans returned from China after serving in the People's Liberation Army, strengthening North Korean forces. By mid-1950, Stalin was on board, and the Soviets provided additional armaments.

Before the sun rose on June 25, 1950, North Korea began a thunderous artillery attack along the 38th parallel. More than 50,000 soldiers poured across the Imjin River, heading toward Seoul. Another 54,000 soldiers attacked several cities located strategically along the way.

It took only three days for the North Korean troops to reach their destination, wreaking havoc and destruction in their wake. Once in Seoul, however, they were unexpectedly stopped—temporarily. The badly beaten Republic of Korea forces made a desperate stand to protect their capital city, forming a defensive line along the Han River. Knowing they couldn't hold off the enemy for long, the Rhee government sent out a frantic plea for help to the United States.

Initially, President Truman ordered Gen. Douglas MacArthur to oversee operations to provide the Republic of Korea with munitions and evacuate U.S. citizens. President Truman also turned to the United Nations, which had called for the invasion to stop the day it started.

The United Nations Security Council passed a resolution calling on member states to provide military assistance. As a permanent member of the United Nations, the Soviet Union could have vetoed the resolution, but the country had boycotted the Council after the United Nations recognized the Republic of China, which had relocated to Taiwan after the Chinese Civil War. Because the Soviets weren't there, the resolution passed with little resistance.

The United States quickly deployed nearby military forces stationed in Japan, but the lack of preparation was evident. U.S. soldiers fought valiantly alongside their Republic of Korea counterparts, but inadequate weapons and manpower meant the North Koreans continued their relentless advance southward into the Korean peninsula.

A stunned world—including an American public—watched as a fledgling democratic country, along with its U.N. allies, came dangerously close to being destroyed.

Sgt. Jim Ecerett, of the Lowell Main Recruiting Station, gives prospect Carville Berehman the R-2 and R-3 enlistment papers (June 12, 1950). *NARA photo.*

Signing Up to Fight

On a wave of post-patriotic enthusiasm following victory in World War II, a new generation of young men and women were eager to fight in the Korean War. Some were drafted; others signed up. Many had little or no idea what they were getting into—they just knew they wanted to serve.

"Not quite a year after we graduated from high school, a whole group of us got drafted at the same time," recalls Bill Hartsock, a sergeant in the U.S. Air Force. "We were bussed up to Des Moines, and we all took our physicals. They told us that if we wanted to enlist in something other than the Army, we would have 30 days to make the choice. Some of us flipped coins . . . that's how I ended up in the Air Force."

Willie B. Harris, who retired as a Command Sergeant Major in the Air Force, enlisted in 1949 because it was a tradition. "I had three brothers in World War II," he notes, "and when I was old enough to realize, you know, I had a dream to be an airborne soldier." Harris recalls that his first experience "wasn't very nice. The second day I was detailed for KP, which is kitchen police, and I must have peeled about 2,000 pounds of potatoes."

Robert L. Cornwell was a senior in high school when he and his buddy started talking about serving. "We decided we might like to go to the Navy. Then one Saturday he came in and I was playing pool, and he said, 'Let's go to Burlington and enlist.' I said, 'OK,' and so we went." After boot camp, Cornwell was assigned to an LST, "an amphibious ship that will run up onto the beach, drop a ramp, and unload directly onto the beach." He immediately got seasick. Despite that shaky beginning, Cornwell earned several Korean service medals. "One of my most memorable experiences was when we went above the 38th parallel, into enemy territory, and spent two weeks being a target and trying to draw fire from the shoreline so we could find out where they were."

Log-lifting combines physical exercise with team work. Recruits are kept outdoors most of the time (September 16, 1950). *NARA photo.*

Boot Camp: An Introduction

Boot camp is a universal military requirement regardless of the branch of service. The intense introduction to military life is an experience no service member forgets.

"When I was in boot camp at Parris Island, they were really adamant about everybody being a good marksman with the M-1 rifle. Of the 10 or 11 weeks, three of those weeks were solid weeks spent out on the rifle range," remembers Rexford Early, who served as a Marine during the war. "The first week just snapping in the different positions and blank firing. The second week we actually got live ammunition and you practiced and shot, and at the end of the third week, everybody had to qualify. We had to rapid fire, we had to slow fire, and the last 10 rounds of qualification was 500 yards, now that's five football fields. If you didn't qualify, they made you march all the way back to camp . . . about eight or ten miles."

Early continues, "I don't care how cocky you are, how tough you are, how smart you think you are, they whittle your ass down to nothing. They make you think you are the lowest thing that ever walked on the face of the earth . . . . But after a few weeks, they start building you up. By the time you graduate, you think you're the toughest, meanest son of a gun that ever wore a pair of low cuts. And that's the psychology . . . you're going to do things that you might think are humanly impossible or you might be scared to death, but you're going to do them because you're not going to let your buddies down."

The most memorable moment of the war for Early was graduating from boot camp. "My DI, who had kicked me, hit me, cursed at me, yelled at me, and threatened me, stuck out his hand, pinned the globe and anchor on my collar and said, 'Congratulations, you are now a Marine, and I would be proud to serve with you.' That was a hell of a compliment . . . that was the proudest moment of my life."

Pfc. Paul Rivers, 23rd RCT, 2nd Infantry Division, looks for enemy snipers in a burning village as U.S. troops launch an offensive against the North Korean forces in the Yeongsan area (September 16, 1950). *NARA photo.*

The UN's First Military Deployment

South Korea and its allies fought under the UN flag. The United States was, by far, the largest non-Korean contributor of troops to the UN side, but 15 other nations also dispatched troops. The following nations contributed combat forces:

> United States, United Kingdom, Australia, Netherlands, Canada, New Zealand, France, Philippines, Turkey, Thailand, Greece, South Africa, Belgium, Luxembourg, Columbia, and Ethiopia.

Sweden, India, Denmark, Norway, and Italy also contributed medical support units. Non-U.S. forces played leading roles in many of the Korean War's most critical battles. For instance, the dramatic last stand of the British Gloucestershire Regiment during the Battle of Imjin River and the Australian, New Zealand, and Canadian victory at the Battle of Gapyeong in April 1951 gave UN forces the time they needed to retreat to prepared positions north of Seoul, saving the Korean capital from capture by the Communist Chinese.

Fresh and eager troops, newly arrived at the vital southern supply port of Busan, prior to moving up to the front lines. (August 1950). *USIA photo.*

CHAPTER 8

Standing Strong in Busan

It took only a few weeks for the North Korea People's Army to occupy almost all of South Korea. The mood was frantic when U.N. troops dug in their heels at the Busan Perimeter. This desperate stand at Busan gave the U.N. forces invaluable time to gather the men, equipment, and political support necessary to not only stop the southern progress of the North Koreans, but to begin moving northward and recapturing lost ground, including Seoul.

U.N. troops, led by Lt. Gen. Walton Walker, had endured weeks of heartbreaking losses. With time, Lieutenant General Walker was hoping to build up stronger forces so he could mount an offensive against the enemy, but in Busan, time ran out. The U.N. forces knew they had to hold on to Busan, the last open deepwater port in the Republic of Korea. Vital manpower and equipment from the United States and Japan were arriving by ship daily, and critical airfields were also located there.

On July 29, Walker issued a "stand or die" order, stating, "There will be no more retreating, withdrawal, or readjustment of the lines or any other term you choose .... I want everybody to understand we are going to hold this line."

Forces came mostly from the U.S. Marine Corps, the U.S. Army, the Republic of Korea, and the British Army. The desperate, heroic battle continued all along a 140-mile defensive line that protected the vital port of Busan. The battle became known as the Battle of the Busan Perimeter.

For six weeks, these stubborn soldiers refused to give in, fighting off repeated attacks. By this time, North Korean troops were spread thin along a line of devastation from the 38th parallel, through Seoul, and south into the perimeter. Their supplies were running low, and they had suffered terrible casualties. Nevertheless, they continued to attack, launching a carefully planned offensive that included simultaneous attacks in as many as five locations.

However, things were finally coming together for the U.N. forces, which for the first time enjoyed an advantage in troops, equipment, and logistics. The U.N. troops broke out all along the front on September 16, the day after the U.S. X Corps made a surprise landing at the port of Incheon and quickly captured the city just 35 miles west of Seoul. The Battle of the Busan Perimeter was over. Within days, the shattered North Korean forces were retracing their steps, heading north in defeat, with U.N. soldiers in hot pursuit. ■

Task Force Smith

Task Force Smith arrives in South Korea. *NARA photo.*

The first units of the 24th Infantry Division arrived in Japan on June 30, 1950. Task Force Smith, named after its commander Charles Bradford Smith and comprised of 504 men, was poorly equipped and understrength: Most of the task force were teenagers with no combat experience and only eight weeks of basic training, and only a third had combat experience.

By July 1, Task Force Smith had established a headquarters in Taejon and began moving north to oppose the North Korean Army. The task force was one of the first of many small units with the mission to take on the initial advances of North Korean troops to buy time for more U.S. units to arrive.

Tasked with stopping the North Korean force along the highway from Suwon, Task Force Smith engaged a North Korean tank column, during which the first American casualty of the war occurred. Despite ineffective artillery, the task force was able to hold the line for three hours before a disorderly withdrawal to the northern outskirts of Osan.

The Battle of Osan was the first U.S. ground action of the war. With a 40 percent casualty rate, the battle showed that U.S. forces were unprepared for war and their equipment was insufficient to fight the enemy. Though badly defeated, Task Force Smith was able to accomplish its mission and delay the advancement of North Koreans for seven hours. Three months later, U.S. and U.N. forces would take Osan, culminating in a complete defeat of the North Korean Army in the South.

"When you get to Pusan, head for Taejon. We want to stop the North Koreans as far from Pusan as we can. Block the main road as far north as possible. Make contact with General Church. If you can't find him, go to Taejon and beyond if you can. Sorry I can't give you more information—that's all I've got. Good luck, and God bless you and your men!"

—Maj. Gen. William F. Dean's orders to Colonel Smith

One Soldier—All the Protection We Had

Bernadette Reider had received basic nursing training when she signed up for the Army Nurses Corps. "I already had two brothers in the service, so I decided to go and do what I could," she recalls. She served in the Korean War, working at hospitals near Busan: "I remember arriving in June of 1950, and we were the first hospital there in Busan. We were on a ship that had arrived from Japan, and there was one man, a soldier sitting up on a hill there with a machine gun, and that was it, that was all the protection we had. So then we disembarked and set up our hospital in an old school, and I'll tell you it was full of fleas. Everybody was just covered with bites; we stayed there a couple of weeks, and then we moved to another building which was a lot better.

"My most memorable experience was when another nurse and I took a train up country to pick up the wounded. It took us two days to get there; we had one car hitched onto the engine. My goodness, when we got there, everyone was running around, and all we had time to do was run from our train into the other one, and then we took off. The North Koreans were almost there, and if we hadn't gotten there when we did, we probably wouldn't have gotten out. We had no medical supplies on the train, and there was nothing we could do .... We had five cars full of wounded ... the fighting was so heavy, and there were so many casualties; they just kept coming and coming."

Members of the 89th RCT disembark from USS *General M. M. Patrick* at Busan, Korea (July 31, 1950). *NARA photo.*

Marines use scaling ladders to storm ashore at Incheon in the amphibious landing on September 15, 1950. The attack was so swift that casualties were surprisingly low. *Photo by Staff Sgt. W.W. Frank, U.S. Marine Corps.*

CHAPTER 9

The Incheon Landing

Combined with the breakout from the Busan Perimeter, the daring landing at Incheon, a port near Seoul, marked the turning of the tide in the Korean War. With this successful surprise landing, U.N. forces began a strong push eastward, first recapturing Seoul, then continuing to pursue retreating North Korean troops.

General MacArthur had started planning a landing behind enemy lines in early July and set a target date of September 15. Concerns about the landing were valid. Military chiefs of staff worried that by dividing troops between Incheon and the Busan Perimeter, defeat in both places was possible; the Incheon beach was only accessible six hours a day because of tide patterns; the approach to the port was narrow and could be protected by mines; and even if the landing were successful, Incheon resources might not be able to support the operation.

MacArthur reassured naysayers with all the positive points of the landing: The vast majority of North Korean troops were fighting in the Busan Perimeter; the enemy didn't expect an attack at Incheon, so thus would be unprepared; and the recapture of Seoul, only 20 miles from Incheon, would represent a significant moral and military victory. The plans for the Incheon landing moved forward.

After preliminary maneuvers, troops began landing on three different beaches on September 15, unloading vital equipment and overpowering any resistance. Although sporadic fighting took place, all three beaches were captured by the end of the day. On September 19, the troops captured Gimpo Airport, the largest airport in Korea and a strategic location essential to success. Next, they headed for Seoul.

While the landing on Incheon was swift and relatively easy, the march and recapture of Seoul was slow and laborious. Troops took 11 days to travel 20 miles, meeting resistance along the way and giving the North Koreans time to fortify the city. Once the soldiers entered the capital, they engaged in house-to-house fighting with desperate enemy forces.

U.N. troops that had fought in the Busan Perimeter routed the enemy ahead of them and connected up with U.S. X Corps. Together, they defeated the last fighting North Korean soldiers in South Korea. ■

Maj. Gen. Oliver P. Smith, Coast Guard, 1st Marine Division (left), receives a friendly gesture from General MacArthur (right), who has just presented General Smith with the Silver Star (September 21, 1950). *NARA photo.*

General MacArthur

Born and raised in a military family (his father, Arthur MacArthur, Jr., was the highest-ranking Army officer at one time), Gen. Douglas MacArthur was destined to serve in the military. MacArthur became one of only a handful of men to earn the rank of a five-star general, and is the only man to have served as a field marshal in the Philippine Army. He played a prominent role in the Pacific Theater during World War II, and led the United Nations Command during the Korean War until President Truman relieved him of duty.

Born on January 26, 1880, at the Little Rock Barracks in Arkansas, MacArthur's early childhood was spent on western frontier outposts where his father was stationed. "It was here I learned to ride and shoot even before I could read or write," he noted.

MacArthur graduated as valedictorian of the West Point Class of 1903 before serving as a junior officer in the years leading up to World War I. During that time, he was stationed in the Philippines, served as an aide to his father in the Far East, and participated in the American occupation of Veracruz, Mexico. In World War I, he formed the remarkable Rainbow Division by combining troops from many National Guard units. He rose in rank to become division chief of staff, brigadier general, and divisional commander. Following the war, he led significant reforms while superintendent at West Point, held two commands in the Philippines, and led the 1928 American Olympic Committee. His service during World War II established him as the ideal officer to head the military efforts in the Korean War.

In April 1951, after he was relieved of duty, MacArthur returned to the United States, where he was welcomed as a hero, although he continued to be a critic of President Truman's policy in Korea.

General MacArthur lived the remainder of his years quietly, serving as chairman of Remington Rand, a maker of electrical equipment and business machines, and spending time with his family. He died at age 84 on April 5, 1964, at Walter Reed Army Hospital in Washington, D.C., and was buried at the MacArthur Memorial in Norfolk, Virginia.

Four LSTs unload on the beach at Incheon as U.S. Marines gather equipment to move rapidly inland on September 15, 1950. Landing ships were stuck in the deep mud flats between one high tide and the next (September 15, 1950). *Photo by C. K. Rose, U.S. Navy.*

South Korean troops raise their national flag in front of the Capitol after retaking Seoul from the North Koreans (September 27, 1950).
Photo from Yonhap News.

A Navy AD-3 divebomber pulls out of a dive after dropping a 2,000-pound bomb on the North Korean side of a bridge over the Yalu River at Sinuiju, into Manchuria (November 15, 1950). *U.S. Navy photo.*

CHAPTER 10

North to the Yalu

The Korean War was fought, in large part, on the ground by infantry soldiers. While air and water resources were critical to the successful outcome of the war, much of the action took place in the trenches. This was nowhere more evident than in the push northward following the U.N. victories in the Busan Perimeter, the landing at Incheon, and the recapture of Seoul.

After these successes, President Truman sent General MacArthur a top-secret National Security memorandum, authorizing him to unite all of Korea under Syngman Rhee, if possible. The orders to march, however, came with one strict limitation: the northward offensive should only continue if China and the Soviet Union remained out of the war.

By October 1, the U.N. Command repelled the Korean People's Army northwards, past the 38th parallel; the Republic of Korea's forces crossed after them into North Korea, followed a few days later by the U.N. Command forces. North Korea is divided down its center by the rugged Taebaeksan Mountains, making it necessary for the U.S. 8th Army, with its U.N. units attached, to drive northward on the west side of the range, while U.S. X Corps landed on the east coast and advanced northward on a separate front to the east side of the range.

The ground troops that drove up western Korea captured a string of cities, including Pyongyang, the North Korean capital, on October 19. Their destination was north to the Yalu River, the boundary between China and North Korea—despite warnings by China that they would attack if U.S. troops crossed the 38th parallel.

At this point, General MacArthur assured President Truman and others that China had no real intention of intervening and was only making empty threats. Even if the country did decide to get involved, MacArthur insisted, their forces would be spotted and destroyed by air power.

In truth, however, although MacArthur didn't realize it, the People's Republic of China had already entered the war. Chinese reinforcements had begun marching toward the U.N. forces' location and, under cover of night, were positioning themselves for their first offensive move, which would once again turn the tide of the war.

The first fighting between the U.N. and Chinese troops took place at the Battle of Unsan on November 1, when thousands of Chinese began a surprise attack. Unprepared, U.N. forces retreated. However, this initial victory caused Soviet Premier Joseph Stalin to change his mind, and the Soviets also became more involved in the war, providing crucial air cover, equipment, and other supplies to the reinvigorated North Korean military. ■

Marines searching a shattered building in a methodical quest for North Korean stragglers and suicide snipers. *NARA photo.*

Dropping Down a Message

Solomon Jamerson, who was awarded a Silver Star for his service in the Army, recalls how it felt after the success at the Busan Perimeter and Incheon landing: "We had been talking about having to be evacuated from the peninsula, and with the Incheon invasion coming in the middle of September, that took away all the possibility of them pushing us off .... We started moving forward, and morale was very high at that point."

Jamerson served as an aerial observer and recalls flying over enemy territory one day, noticing someone who looked like a farmer walking along a road. Something didn't seem right, however, and Jamerson sensed an ambush targeting advancing ground troops. Sure enough, a shot burst out of a nearby house. Jamerson knew he had to let the troops below know. "We had a little message pad in the aircraft, and you wrote your little message out and put it into a bag with a heavy metal weight on it, and you go and drop it off," he said. "That was our only communication with the infantry .... After we dropped this message down to the commander, we went back up and continued directing fire on all the various locations."

It was getting close to nightfall, and there were no landing lights at the base, so Jamerson and his pilot were told to return. "[But] the pilot said, 'I'll stay with you as long as you think you can do some good up here.' So we continued firing and then finally had to take off to the base."

Initially, the pilot was threatened with a court martial because of his refusal to return to the base. "[But] the commander down on the ground was so pleased with our actions, he put us both up for the Silver Star," Jamerson noted. "I've never had the opportunity to find out who that commander was, but I would have loved to have heard what he thought about the activity we had that afternoon."

Men of the 1st Cavalry Division fighting in a train station in Pyongyang, Korea (October 19, 1950). *NARA photo.*

It All Changed When the Chinese Came

Army Pvt. Donald Byers arrived in Korea as a replacement soldier for the Incheon landing. With the success there, and the rapid retreat of the North Korean troops, many soldiers thought the war was over. "I was just infantry," he notes, "an ammo-bearer to the machine gun squad. Everything was great; the war was all over."

"That all changed when the Chinese came in," Byers recalled. "It was pretty horrific. You wake up in the middle of the night, and all hell was breaking loose. There were bombs going off and artillery, and bullets going off right in front of our noses. We set up our machine guns and were firing across the river and into the mountains—that's where the flashes of gunfire were coming from. It was bitter cold. Thirty-eight degrees below zero, and no place to go to get out of it."

Byers and his buddies fought the Chinese bitterly for weeks in seesaw battles back and forth. "This was war," he says, "not much but cleaning weapons and shooting what you could." Typically, the shooting took place at night, and during the day, the soldiers would pull back and rest. Near the end, that changed. "[The Chinese] just kept on charging, during the daytime and nighttime too. We were firing our machine guns, using up all the ammo we could, and killing many of them."

"We were totally surrounded," Byers said, "and we didn't think we were getting out of there. We just thought, 'Kill as many of them as we can because we're going to die anyway.' Being a PFC, I didn't get to talk to commanders; we didn't know anything about the strategy of the war. All I saw was my platoon sergeant, and he just said, 'Keep firing.'

"On the third day, when the task force came in with the tanks and broke us out of the encirclement, the Chinese just melted away into the mountains from there, so we knew that we were safe, that we were going to get out."

The railway station and plaza at Daejon, Korea, are scenes of great activity as refugees flee south from the Communist invaders and U.S. and Korean troops move north to the battle front (July 6, 1950). *NARA photo.*

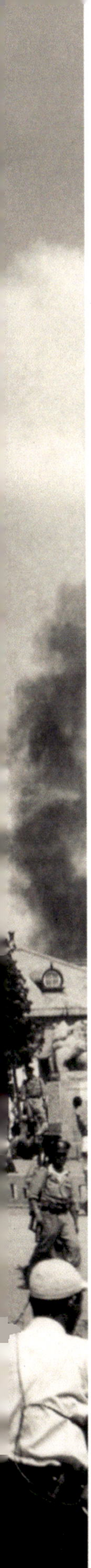

Buddies aid wounded man of 24th Infantry Regiment, after a battle 10 miles south of Cheorwon, Korea (April 22, 1951). *Photo by Cpl. Tom Nebbia, U.S. Army.*

China Joins the War

After their successive losses and frantic retreat in September, the North Koreans knew they could not continue the war without help. North Korean President Kim Il-Sung had been in constant contact with both Chinese and Soviet leaders, pleading for essential equipment and especially more soldiers. Although Stalin said the Soviets would not directly intervene, China reluctantly responded to the request, feeling obligated because tens of thousands of North Koreans had fought in China's recent civil war.

Although General MacArthur felt certain any movement by the Chinese would be spotted by U.N. aerial reconnaissance efforts, Chinese People's Volunteer Army began their involvement in the war undetected. They accomplished this by only moving at night and hiding under camouflage by sunrise. During daylight or while marching, soldiers remained motionless if an aircraft appeared; violators who exposed themselves to possible enemy observation were shot. Under these conditions, a three-division army marched 286 miles to the combat zone in 19 days, resulting in a surprise attack against the U.N. Corps.

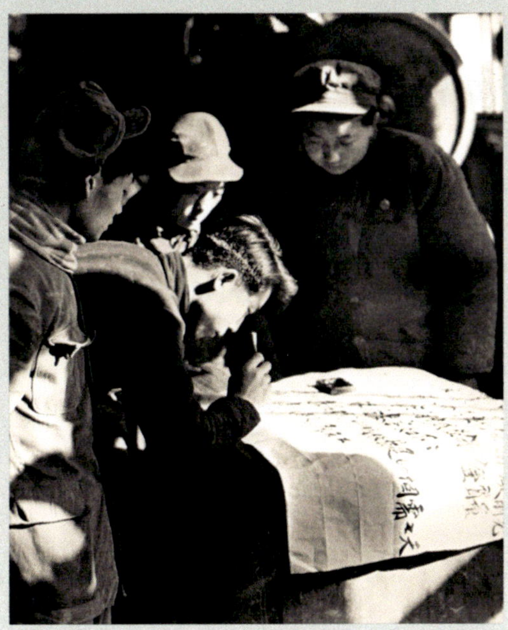

Volunteers from a North China machine factory sign up for military service in North Korea (early 1950s). *NARA photo.*

B-29s of the U.S. Air Force drop their 500-pound bombs on a strategic target in North Korea. These planes devastated enemy North Korea supply lines, industrial areas, and troop concentrations with their precision bombing. *Photo courtesy of Air and Space Museum.*

CHAPTER 11

MiG Alley and Air Power

The Korean War marked several firsts for the U.S. Air Force. It was the first war that extensively used jets and helicopters, the first major war against an agricultural nation, and the first war during the nuclear era. It also marked the last war where propeller aircraft was predominantly used.

Initially, the war didn't start out with significant air presence. The North Korean forces depended on a small force of aging, propeller-driven, Soviet aircraft left over from World War II, and President Truman wanted the U.S. Air Force strength focused in Europe, to serve as a strong warning against the Soviet Union to avoid any action.

Although the Air Force, much like the other branches of the military, was not expecting war in Korea, it responded quickly. The older B-29 bombers did their job well, wreaking havoc on North Korean communication centers, military installations, and transportation networks, as well as slowing down the advance of the enemy. In addition, the Air Force transported much-needed troops and equipment from Japan to Korea, evacuated American citizens, and provided important intelligence through aerial reconnaissance.

During the war, the northwest portion of North Korea, where the Yalu River empties into the Yellow Sea, became a key location for the Air Force. Dubbed "MiG Alley" because the Soviet MiGs made their first appearance there, it was the site of numerous dogfights, and is considered the birthplace of jet-to-jet combat.

Primarily an agricultural nation, Korea offered few industrial or military targets, so the Air Force's traditional strategic bombing was pointless. Instead, the Air Force focused on raids on supply routes, bombing tanks, moving troops, and flying missions that required close coordination with land or sea forces.

Airlifts also played a key role in the war, especially during the first year when ground troops were often separated during rapid advances or retreats and had to be rescued. In addition, air services were essential for delivering food, ammunition, medical supplies, and mail. Cargo planes made much larger deliveries, including jeeps, big guns, and even a bridge; they also evacuated wounded soldiers to Japan.

With assistance from the U.S. Navy and Marines, the U.S. Air Force maintained air superiority throughout the war and played a significant role in ending the war.

Air Rescue helicopter about to land at an advanced air station in Korea. During one operation, 12 Sikorsky S-55 helicopters moved a battalion of 1,000 Marines more than 16 miles in four hours. *NARA photo.*

View of F-86 airplanes on the flight line getting ready for combat (June 1951). *NARA photo.*

F4Us (Corsairs) returning from a combat mission over North Korea circle USS Boxer as they wait for planes in the next strike to be launched from her flight deck—a helicopter hovers above the ship (September 4, 1951). *U.S. Navy photo.*

Tons from the Air

On August 12, 1950, the USAF dropped 625 tons of bombs on North Korea; two weeks later, the daily tonnage increased to some 800 tons. U.S. warplanes dropped more napalm and bombs on North Korea than they did during the whole Pacific campaign of World War II. As a result, 18 North Korean cities were more than 50 percent destroyed. The war's highest-ranking American POW, U.S. Maj. Gen. William F. Dean, reported that most of the North Korean cities and villages he saw were either ruins or snow-covered wastelands.

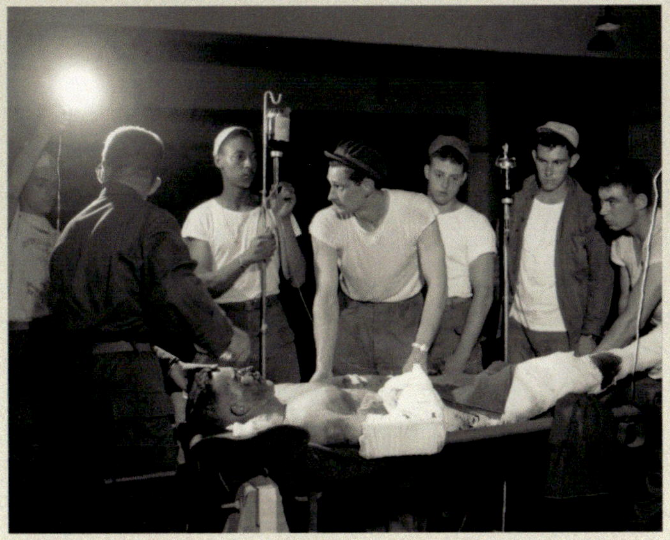

A seriously wounded soldier of the 116th Engineers, prior to his operation at the 121st Evacuation Hospital, in Yeongdeung-po (August 17, 1951). *Photo by G. Dimitri Boria, U.S. Army.*

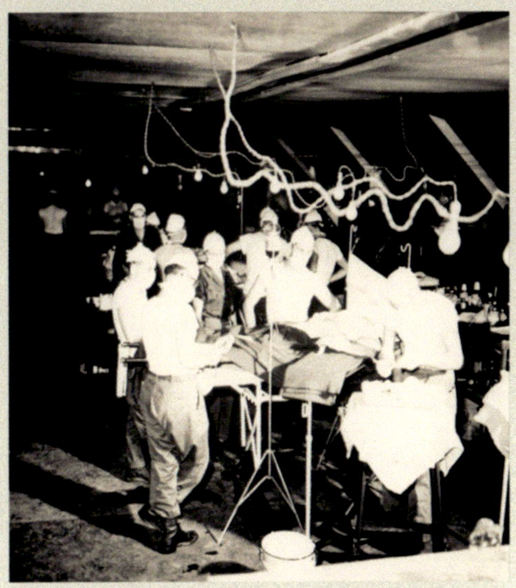

Surgery is performed on a wounded soldier at the 8209th Mobile Army Surgical Hospital, 20 miles from the front lines. *U.S. Army photo.*

MASH Units

Helicopters made their first wartime appearances during the Korean War, specializing in transporting soldiers in trouble. They were especially effective in evacuating wounded men from the front lines and flying them to nearby Mobile Army Surgical Hospitals, or "MASH" units, which also made their first wartime appearances during the Korean War.

The purpose of MASH units was to place experienced medical personnel closer to the front so that they could treat the wounded sooner and more successfully. Casualties were first evaluated and treated at the front line, then moved to a battalion aid station, and finally transferred to a MASH. During the Korean War, a seriously wounded soldier who made it to a MASH unit alive had a greater than 97 percent chance of survival once he received treatment.

"The creation of MASH units was a really fine move on the part of the military," observes Dr. Dale Drake, an anesthesiologist who spent 16 months serving in a MASH. "It was a place where more definitive surgery could be performed with qualified workers, certified surgeons, and anesthesiologists and so on, and yet it was only a few miles from the action of war. At night, at least from the tent I was in, you could see the flash of artillery, and it seemed like it was not very far away, perhaps seven or eight miles."

Drake and his wife, Cathy, met while they were both serving in a MASH unit during the war; Cathy was a nurse. They both worked with Dr. H. Richard Hornberger, who wrote several books after he returned from the Korean War under the pseudonym of Richard Hooker. He collaborated with W. C. Heinz on one of those books—*MASH: A Novel about Three Army Doctors*—which inspired the well-known movie and TV series of the same name.

After the war, the Drakes visited Hornberger one night, and they sat up well past midnight, reminiscing about their MASH days. "Dr. Hornberger had a man there who was a writer, and we didn't know that," Cathy recalls. "He was just visiting. So we told all these kinds of stories, and laughing and everything. I guess maybe a year later or six months later, we get the first book of his, and it said, 'Born the night you blew in.'"

Although the book was written based, at least in part, on some of the memories the Drakes shared that night, life in a MASH unit was definitely different from the one shown in the movies. "I think that's all for consumption by the TV public," Drake observes. "The real thing, it should have been serious, and it was serious. As far as social life at the MASH, I'm not saying it was nonexistent, but there wasn't much to offer, really."

Marines of the 5th and 7th Regiments, who stood up to a surprise onslaught by three Chinese divisions, withstand a winter storm.
Photo by Sgt. Frank C. Kerr, U.S. Marine Corps.

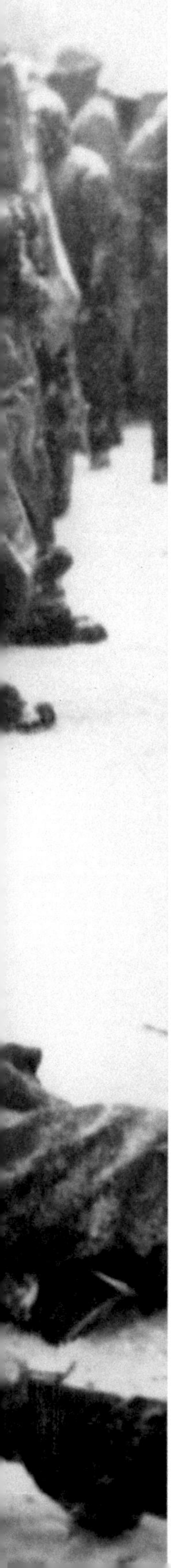

CHAPTER 12

A Brutal Winter

Winter began warmly enough, with the U.S. 7th Division feasting on hot turkey dinners upon reaching the south bank of the Yalu River on the east side of North Korea only three days before Thanksgiving. The campaign to win the war by Christmas seemed imminent. Little did the 7th Division know they were in for the most brutal winter they could imagine. The massive influx of Chinese forces over the North Korean border surprised U.N. forces, shattering any ideas of Christmas at home. Instead, U.N. troops were ordered to fall back on all fronts. Troops had to give up ground they had gained valiantly, as the biggest evacuation in U.S. military history began.

While the U.N. worked to arrange a cease-fire, U.N. forces fought hard to maintain critical positions as troops north of them retreated. Bridge sections were dropped by parachute to rebuild critical bridges needed for escape. Marines carved an airstrip in the ice so that wounded, too critical to move by land or sea, could be airlifted out. They held crucial mountain passes for days at a time in detestable conditions, they battled in weather 50 degrees below zero, and food and supplies were air-dropped to help them make their way.

Perhaps the most brutal battle of the winter was at the Changjin Reservoir (Chosin). The 1st Marine, 3rd Infantry, 7th Infantry Divisions, and the 41 Commando of the Royal Marines (UK) were trapped by the Chinese when the evacuation was ordered. General Oliver P. Smith exclaimed, "Retreat, hell! We're not retreating, we're just advancing in a different direction!" Retreat or advance, the soldiers went nowhere. Faced without an escape route, the divisions fought hard and managed to maintain their position against the onslaught of Chinese soldiers. When the road to escape finally opened, their retreat was slowed by continued battle.

Regimental Combat Team 31 of the 7th Infantry Division, later known as Task Force Faith, guarded the right flank of the Marine advance toward Mupyong-ni. Chinese forces east of the reservoir nearly destroyed the task force team, and many of those who did manage to withdraw had to cross the frozen ice.

In all, the soldiers who managed to survive the battle at Changjin marched over 60 miles from the Changjin Reservoir to Hagaru-ri, through Hell Fire Valley to Koto-ri and then Hamhung before finally reaching Hungnam.

At Hungnam, the Navy Fleet commanded by Rear Admiral Doyle waited to finalize the evacuation. The 3rd Division continued to hold Chinese troops while U.N. forces boarded the Navy fleet. The evacuation totaled over 100,000 soldiers, 17,500 vehicles, 350,000 tons of equipment, and 91,000 Korean civilians.

Pfc. Preston McKnight, 19th Infantry Regiment, uses his poncho to get protection from the biting wind and cold, in the Yeoju area, during a break in action against the Chinese forces (January 10, 1951). *Photo by Cpl. E. Watson, U.S. Army.*

Leathernecks of the First Marine Division fan out to guard flanks of main column marching on road between Koto-ri and Hagaru-ri during the First Marine Division's heroic breakout from the Changjin Reservoir. *NARA photo.*

The road back: Astonished Marines of the 5th and 7th Regiments, who stood up to a surprise onslaught by three Chinese divisions, hear that they are to withdraw. In five days, from November 28 to December 3, they fought back 15 miles through Chinese forces to Hagaru-ri on the southern tip of the Changjin Reservoir, where they reorganized for the epic 40-mile fight down mountain trails to the sea. *NARA photo.*

U.S. Marines fighting in the streets of Yeongdeungpo, south of Seoul (September 20, 1950). *Photo by Lt. Robert L. Strickland and Cpl. John Romanowski, U.S. Army.*

CHAPTER 13

Battles over Seoul

As the new year dawned, the enemy struck southward in massive offensives, particularly across the Imjin River north of Seoul, as well as to the east along the west central front where they drove down onto Gapyeong and Chuncheon.

ROK units, taken by surprise, withdrew in great numbers. Gen. Matthew B. Ridgway, who had taken command of U.S. Eighth Army following the death of Gen. Walton Walker in a driving accident in December, believed the Chinese might encircle the bulk of his army.

After conferring with his corps commanders, General Ridgway decided to strategically evacuate Seoul on January 3. Chinese commanders were astounded, but entered the capital the following day. From Seoul, the Chinese forces proceeded southward 30 miles to Osan on January 7, where American units held their advance in check. However, savage fighting went on in the mountains east of Seoul, where the Chinese offensive seemed unstoppable. Against recommendations of some of his senior staff, Ridgway ordered U.N. commanders to cease rolling back and take to the offensive. The Chinese reacted with yet another offensive on February 11. U.N. Command forces on the west central front, east of Seoul, were driven down to the Wonju area.

One epic action of this era took place at Jipyeong-ni on February 13–15. The U.S. 23rd RCT commanded by Col. Paul L. Freeman, Jr., with the First Ranger Company and an attached French Battalion, had been left in a salient position by the withdrawing U.N. forces. The Chinese moved on the 23rd RCT with 25,000 troops. After two days and nights, the enemy had suffered more than 5,000 casualties. Freeman's troops had held fast, having suffered 51 soldiers killed, 250 wounded, and 42 missing.

General Ridgway launched the U.N. offensive Operation Killer on February 22, closely followed by Operation Ripper (March 7–April 4), with the objective of driving the enemy back beyond the 38th parallel. Facing intense bombing and possible encirclement from the east, Chinese forces withdrew from Seoul. The U.S. Third ID and the ROK First ID liberated the capital city on March 14.

In April, President Truman relieved General MacArthur as supreme commander of the U.N. forces and General Ridgway took over. The enemy launched another massive offensive in late April, but U.N. Command forces drove them back decisively.

By June 1951, both sides were forced to consider that a military victory might be too costly. Chinese and North Korean officials agreed to hold ceasefire discussions at the ancient capital of Kaesong on the north side of the Imjin River. An armistice to end the war seemed to be in the making. ■

U.N. troops continue advance: elements of the 27th Infantry Regiment, 25th Infantry Division pass by a burning house, as U.N. forces launch Task Force PUNCH against the Chinese forces eight miles southwest of Seoul (February 7, 1951). *NARA photo.*

A barricade held by men of the 1st Marine Division during the street fighting in Seoul. *NARA photo.*

Pfc. Albert Lumanais, 1st Battalion, 1st Regiment, 1st Marine Division, searches out remaining snipers as U.N. forces saturate Seoul. *NARA photo.*

With a life-and-death fight for Seoul, a U.S. Marine spots a sniper and gets ready to return fire. *NARA photo.*

U.N. Command troops fighting in the streets of Seoul. *NARA photo.*

U.S. Maj. General Matthew B. Ridgway (left), appointed Supreme Allied Commander in 1951, with U.S. Gen. Mark W. Clark, Commander in Chief of the United Nations Command in Korea. *NARA photo.*

Truman Replaces MacArthur

On April 11, 1951, President Truman relieved General MacArthur of his command at the helm of the United Nations Command Forces. MacArthur had gained quite a bit of popularity in the United States, and even globally, for his leadership of the Allied Forces during World War II, and his dismissal during the Korean War remains controversial even today.

After World War II, MacArthur had been assigned to oversee the occupation of Japan, and was stationed in Asia when North Korea invaded South Korea. He seemed the natural choice to become the leader of the U.N. forces in the fight for freedom there. The highly successful Incheon landing had been his brainchild, a military move that many called genius. However, it was also the MacArthur-directed full-scale invasion of North Korea that followed that led to China joining the North Koreans.

Although the U.N. troops had been forced to withdraw from North Korea, they had made progress under General Ridgway during the early months of 1951, and President Truman saw an opportunity to suggest a negotiated peace. MacArthur knew the president's intention, but he publicly called for China to surrender instead and wrote a letter which was read on the floor of the U.S. House of Representatives on April 5, a letter critical of Truman's Europe-first policy and limited-war strategy in Korea. The letter ended with, "We must win. There is no substitute for victory."

The letter was the last straw. After months of private and public bickering, President Truman called MacArthur home. In May and June of 1951, the Senate Armed Services Committee and the Senate Foreign Relations Committee held a joint inquiry into the circumstances surrounding MacArthur's relief, concluding that "the removal of General MacArthur was within the constitutional powers of the President, but the circumstances were a shock to national pride."

Infantrymen of the 27th Infantry Regiment, near Heartbreak Ridge, take advantage of cover and concealment in tunnel positions, 40 yards from the enemy (August 10, 1952). *Photo by Feldman, U.S. Army.*

CHAPTER 14

Battles of the Punchbowl

Despite the Chinese agreement to discuss an armistice, Mao Zedong didn't want to end the war in defeat, and approved a plan to win limited victories through violent night attacks and infantry infiltration. So while officials worked to agree on peace, U.N. troops were forced to continue to fight.

Much of the fighting took place in the Punchbowl, a natural geologic bowl several miles across and encircled by steep mountains, creating a terrain that made planning and maneuvering particularly challenging. The Punchbowl battles were bitter and bloody, with thousands of lives lost.

One of those battles was Bloody Ridge. Beginning in mid-August, U.N. troops began moving to seize a series of hills where they believed enemy troops were hiding, and after a week of fierce fighting, succeeded in capturing most of the area.

The win was short-lived, however; North Korea counterattacked and the battle raged for 10 days. Ultimately the North Koreans abandoned the ridge, establishing position only 1,500 yards away on a seven-mile ridge that would soon earn the name Heartbreak Ridge.

This ridge was also dotted with hills, and a pattern of attack quickly emerged: U.N. troops began bombarding a hill with aircraft, tanks, and artillery fire before infantry soldiers would clamber up the rocky slopes, taking each enemy bunker by hand-to-hand combat. The victors, however, were exhausted, short on supplies, and ill-equipped for the inevitable counterattack launched by fresh North Korean troops.

This pattern continued for two weeks, before a new strategy was planned to cut off reinforcements. This plan required tanks, so U.N. forces were deployed to build a road for the tanks. These soldiers worked under enemy fire much of the time but accomplished the task, and tanks began rolling in.

Coincidentally, the U.N. attack started just as a Chinese division was moving toward Heartbreak to relieve the North Koreans. They got a glimpse of the strategy, and when fighting started, anti-tank trenches and guns were in place. The enemy killed soldiers and destroyed tanks, before U.N. Command forces cut off supply roads and won the hills along Heartbreak Ridge. After 30 days of costly battle, U.N. forces stood victorious.

These were just two of the many Punchbowl battles, each one important in its own way as U.N. officials negotiated an end to a war that had gone on far too long with no substantial gains for either side. ■

Pfc. Roman Prauty, a gunner with 31st RCT (crouching foreground), with the assistance of his gun crew, fires a 75mm recoilless rifle near Oetlook-tong, Korea, in support of infantry units directly across the valley (June 9, 1951). *Photo by Peterson, U.S. Army.*

CHAPTER 15

The Iron Triangle

Despite heavy losses in the Punchbowl, Chinese leaders felt their "active defense" had worked. U.N. forces had given up major offensive operations and, in fact, would spend the rest of the war concentrating on defensive strategies. However, this change had more to do with the U.S. public's growing protest against limited-objective battles than with intimidation by Chinese manpower.

The armistice talks moved to Panmunjeom in October 1951, and both sides agreed on most issues, including the creation of a demilitarized zone and enforcement of the armistice after the shooting stopped.

What neither side could agree on, however, was the handling of prisoners of war. For almost two years, officials would try to reach a consensus on what to do with the tens of thousands of Communist Chinese and North Koreans who, the American officials correctly supposed, would rather not return to their homelands.

And during those two years, despite the fact that both sides knew peace was in sight, the fighting continued to rage on. In one of the few U.N. offensives during this time, several attacks were made in the Iron Triangle, a key transportation and communication area approximately 60 miles north of Seoul, and the most direct route to the Republic of Korea capital.

Key battles for ownership in the area included the Battles of White Horse, Triangle Hill, and Pork Chop Hill. During 10 days of fighting at the Battle of White Horse Hill, the hill changed hands 24 times before the U.N. finally conquered it. The resulting destruction was so complete that the hill looked like a threadbare white horse, hence its name. Apart from American tank, artillery, and air support, the battle was fought completely between ROK and Chinese troops.

The battle of Triangle Hill followed close behind; this conflict was bitter and bloody but not nearly as successful. After more than a month of repeated attempts to capture the area, including nearby Sniper Ridge, escalating numbers of casualties forced U.N. leaders to call off attacks, and the Chinese regained original ownership.

The Battle of Pork Chop Hill was a two-part battle; U.N. troops won the first battle in April when the Chinese withdrew after only two days of fighting. A second battle in July, however, involving many more soldiers on both sides, resulted in a five-day battle that ultimately ended with a U.N. withdrawal. ■

Wounded soldier helped to safety during the battle for Pork Chop Hill. *NARA photo.*

Holding Outpost Harry

A pivotal battle in the Iron Triangle took place at Outpost Harry, with more than 88,000 rounds of artillery fired by the Chinese alone. A strategic location dearly desired by the Chinese, Outpost Harry blocked the Chinese view down the valley and shielded a portion of the area from direct enemy fire. Even more importantly, U.N. officials felt that losing that outpost may cause the Chinese to continue fighting instead of reaching an armistice agreement, which they felt was fairly close. U.N. troops were told to "hold Outpost Harry at all costs."

The outpost was only guarded by a single company of either American or Greek soldiers, so the Communist enemy expected an easy victory. Over the period of eight days, some 13,000 Chinese soldiers flooded the area, while five companies (four American and one Greek) took turns defending the outpost. Most of the fighting took place during the dark of night, with daylight hours interrupted sporadically by enemy gunfire but spent primarily removing the dead, treating the wounded, and repairing and fortifying the area.

Ultimately, the U.N. troops did hold on, although the cost in lives was high. The five rifle companies received the distinctive Distinguished Unit Citation for their heroic efforts during this battle, the first time in history that five companies shared that honor.

Supply warehouses and dock facilities at an east coast port feel the destruction of para-demolition bombs dropped by the Fifth Air Force's B-26 Invader light bombers. *USIA photo.*

The USS *Missouri* fires 16-inch shell into enemy lines. *NARA Photo.*

The Battlefront Is a Terrible Place

Kenneth F. Gibson, a sergeant in the Marines, recalls the last few weeks of the war: "We were confined to South Korea. I got there after they had already crossed the 38th parallel and went up to the Manchurian border, and that's when the Chinese came into the war. And we withdrew all the way down into Busan before we were reorganized and fought our way back to the 38th parallel, where the war came to a final conclusion. It was a devastated place, and Korean civilians who had gone as far south as they could to escape the battle were living in a mess, just like any other war-torn country. We fought in combat; my particular unit was a small artillery platoon, and I had 29 men in the platoon. We had so many Chinese and North Korean soldiers against us that we were almost wiped out. We did not retreat. We stayed. And we were replaced at one time with another Marine company, and we went back and rebuilt, got more men, and went at it again. The battlefront is a terrible place . . . sometimes it's hard to talk about those experiences."

Scrimmage Line

Lou Sardina was a private working on a tank who fought in the last battles of the war. "It was rough going," he says, "because it was nothing but taking hills and killing. That was all we did. That first morning I can still remember just as vividly as it if happened yesterday . . . . The Chinese were shooting at us so the bullets were going above our heads; you could hear them."

"The machine gunners go over your head," Sardina continued, "but as soon as you get too close, the machine gunners have to stop or they'll shoot you, so now it's between you and the enemy. And that's called a scrimmage line . . . . We were the first ones up, and it was tough going. Guys got killed. What you're doing is you're going uphill and they're shooting and throwing grenades down at you, but they can't shoot down straight if the hill is up straight, but once you get to that point . . . you're not more than fifty, twenty yards. And now you're just going after them. This is it; this is combat. That's what it is. And up you go. And they're all shooting and you're going up just like it was the Civil War, like taking charge . . . . You're in another zone. The blood and adrenaline is ripe, and you don't even know... Climbing up those hills, if you did it on your own you'd be tired, but you're not. But . . . after you take the hill, that's when you shake. The adrenaline starts, and you just shake. It was 10 days that we did that. One day just ran into the next. You didn't know if it was Sunday or Monday or Tuesday or Wednesday. It was just up and down one hill and the others, and the whole division was pushing . . . and that's where the line was stagnant until the armistice."

The families of the returning POWs waving and greeting USNS *General Nelson M. Walker* as it docks at Fort Mason, California (August 23, 1953). *Photo by Pfc. Brink, U.S. Army.*

CHAPTER 16

The Fighting Ends

Armistice negotiations had barely progressed for months, but in March 1953, Joseph Stalin died. Support for the war quickly eroded in the Soviet Union, with the Soviets voting to end the war.

Chairman Mao knew he could not continue the war without Soviet assistance, and negotiations began to move much faster, with the Chinese ultimately agreeing to voluntary repatriation. That meant that POWs who wanted to return to their homelands would be released immediately, while those wanting to stay would be transferred to the care of a neutral nation for screening. The Chinese and North Koreans also agreed to the exchange of sick and disabled POWs.

Republic of Korea leader Syngman Rhee became the obstacle now. He had never publicly given up the charge to march north and unify, and in private he had alluded to the fact that he would only agree to an armistice if the United States agreed to a mutual security alliance and pledged $1 billion in economic aid.

Ultimately, however, Rhee was persuaded to accept the outlined stipulations, although he never signed it. On July 27, 1953, the armistice agreement was officially signed by representatives from the United Nations, China, and North Korea. Interestingly, although the agreement called for continued peace talks, no peace treaty was ever signed.

The border between the Republic of Korea and North Korea returned to roughly where it had been before war broke out—near the 38th parallel, dipping slightly below the parallel in the west but extending far beyond the parallel in the east. The two Koreas were separated by the Demilitarized Zone (DMZ), a 2.5 mile–wide buffer zone that extends for about 160 miles across Korea.

Adherence to the armistice agreement is monitored by members of the Neutral Nations Supervisory Commission. In addition, large numbers of troops from the two Koreas are stationed on both sides of the line and along the coastline and on outlying islands, making it the most heavily militarized border in the world.

The armistice agreement outlines exactly how many military personnel and what kind of weapons are allowed in the DMZ, as well as the patrolling action allowed by soldiers from both sides. Since the signing of the agreement, sporadic outbreaks of violence and North Korean hostilities have resulted in the deaths of more than 500 Republic of Korea soldiers and 50 U.S. soldiers along the DMZ. ■

Men of the 24th Infantry Regiment move up to the firing line in Korea (July 18, 1950). *Photo by the U.S. Army.*

Pfc. Edward Wilson, 24th Infantry Regiment, wounded in the leg while engaged in action against the enemy forces near the front lines in Korea, waits to be evacuated to an aid station (February 16, 1951). *Photo by Pfc. Charles Fabiszak, U.S. Army.*

Korean War Marks the End of Segregation for U.S. Troops

With Executive Order 9981 on July 26, 1948, President Truman ordered the desegregation of the military with Executive Order 9981. When the United States entered the Korean War in 1950, military units were still segregated, but as the military struggled with heavy losses, desegregation became necessary to maintain fully manned units. Three years after President Truman had signed the executive order, the U.S. Army formally announced its plans to desegregate. The results were noticeably favorable and caught the attention of many in command. General Ridgway had personally observed the 24th Infantry's problems with segregation and felt strongly that desegregation was more efficient and more proper.

The desegregation of the military during the Korean War was a catalyst for desegregation efforts back home.

Many African-American soldiers were heroes during the Korean War, earning numerous medals and commendations. Roscoe Robinson, Jr., served as a platoon leader and rifle company commander in Korea, earning a Bronze Star and later becoming the first African-American to hold the rank of general. Ens. Jesse L. Brown was the first African-American aviator in the history of the U.S. Navy and was posthumously awarded the Distinguished Flying Cross. Second Lt. Frank E. Petersen, Jr., became the Marine Corps' first African-American pilot and first flag officer. Capt. Daniel "Chappie" James, Jr., received the Distinguished Flying Cross for his actions in Korea, and later became the first African-American to reach four-star rank in the military.

Segregation officially ended in the military in 1954, when the last segregated unit was disbanded. It had been nearly six years since President Truman's executive order, and in that time nearly a quarter of a million black service members had been integrated into the U.S. Armed Forces. But the fight for equality back home would take several more years. As soldiers returned from Korea, they often found their hometowns still completely segregated.

A Korean girl places a wreath of flowers on the grave of an American soldier at the U.S. Military Cemetery at Danggok. *U.S. Army Photo.*

A Country and People Worth Fighting For

Located on a strategic peninsula, Korea is bordered by two powerful countries: China on the northwest and Russia on the northeast. Japan is just east. Because of its geographic location, Korea has conducted brisk cultural exchanges with its larger neighbors. It has also frequently been the target of aggression.

After occupation by Japan in 1910, the Korean people's dogged determination to persevere and fight for what was right continued after the Japanese relinquished control of the country at the end of World War II. This determination became an essential aspect of the Republic of Korea's astounding ability to rebuild after the devastating effects of the Korean War. Strong traditions of hard work, pride, and refusal to give up served South Koreans well as they moved past the war and forward into the next century, clearly showing why they were a country and people worth fighting for.

Bodily remains of U.S. service members returned from North Korea to Osan Air Base, Republic of Korea. *U.S. Air Force photo by Tech. Sgt. Ashley Tyler.*

A Father Finally Returns

The family of Major Storms. *Photo courtesy of Sam Storms.*

Army Maj. Harvey Storms served in Italy and North Africa under General Patton in Word War II. He later re-enlisted and served in Japan with his wife and young family before volunteering to serve in Korea when the fighting broke out. Sam, his oldest son, was just nine years old when he said goodbye to this father at the Tokyo train station. He vividly remembers his dad walking away on the platform, then looking back at him. It would be the last time Sam would see his father.

Major Storm and the soldiers of the 7th Infantry Division, along with ROK soldiers who Storm had trained in Japan, successfully landed at Incheon and would make their way to the Chosin Reservoir in North Korea. At Chosin, the U.S. Army and Marine Corps would be surrounded and overwhelmed by Chinese forces. Fighting against below-zero temperatures, Major Storm commanded the 3rd Battalion and would lead the attack up Hill 1221 to take out a machine gun nest. He was last seen by fellow solders continuing to direct on the battlefield after sliding down an icy hill and having sustained over ten bullet wounds in his chest and arms. He was posthumously awarded several medals for his valor, including the Silver Star and the Purple Heart.

When Major Storms was killed and became missing in North Korea, he left behind his young wife, three young sons, and another baby boy about to be born. Sadly, his wife, Helen, would pass away just ten years later, leaving the four boys to be raised by family friends and neighbors in La Feria, Texas. The boys continued the search for their father's remains and even visited South Korea to see his name there on memorials.

After the June 12, 2018, meeting between President Trump and North Korea's Kim Jong Un, 55 caskets of American remains were returned from North Korea to the United States that August. Major Storms's remains were identified on July 29, 2019. Sam Storms, the oldest son of Maj. Harvey Storms, received a phone call informing him that his father had been identified. He says, "I was driving down the road when I received the call. I had to pull off the road and started bawling. We thought they would never recover his remains. But we were hoping it would happen someday and it did. He's been lost and now he's found." He encourages other families still waiting for their loved ones to be found to never give up hope.

With his platoon engaged with an immediate enemy breach, 1st Lt. Baldomero Lopez left the safety of his bunker in order to throw a grenade into a nearby enemy pillbox. This act of bravery exposed him to hostile fire, and his right throwing shoulder was hit by automatic gunfire. Lopez then stumbled backward into his own bunker and accidentally dropped the grenade. With his throwing shoulder injured, 1st Lt. Lopez could not recover and throw the grenade in time to save his fellow Marines. Instead, he dragged his body over the grenade and sacrificed his life by absorbing the full impact of the explosion. For his exceptional courage, fortitude, and devotion to his duty and fellow Marines, 1st Lt. Baldomero Lopez was posthumously awarded the Medal of Honor. Lopez is pictured in this famous iconic photo (shown above) of Marines climbing the seawall at the Incheon Landing on September 15, 1950.

My dad, Tae, at 11 years old, standing free in Incheon with the eldest of the two brothers who crossed with him. This uncle was accidentally killed by American bombs on a return trip to rescue his mother from North Korea. *All images provided by Tina Chong.*

Duty, Honor, Country

by Tina Chong

Many people don't know this, but my dad escaped North Korea when he was 11 years old.

I grew up knowing this about him, but as most Asian-American, parent-child relationships go, I never delved into the details of his personal life. I attended West Point for college and spent the majority of my cadet years in a third-floor corner room in MacArthur barracks. The view out my window overlooked the back of MacArthur's statue and into the superintendent's home where MacArthur used to reside with his mother during his tenure at West Point. The significance of me, a Korean-American and direct benefactor of his actions in the Korean War, living in his barracks, overlooking his statue, and living next to his former home was lost on me until my parents visited the campus and genuflected in silent admiration at his statue.

As I learned more about my dad's past, it would impart a sort of density and hue on the trajectory of my own life as an American and an Army combat veteran, and a deep sense of gratitude for the generation of soldiers who've laid the foundation of freedom for Korea.

My dad crossed the 38th parallel with two of his older brothers on their first attempt. To elude roving guards yet maintain the integrity of the group, my dad's eldest brother slung a white towel over his shoulder for his younger brothers to follow in the middle of the night. Hours later, they made it to South Korea and established themselves in the city of Incheon, a city my dad now considers his South Korean hometown.

Several years later, the Korean War broke out and the Chinese Army's advances south forced my father to relocate to a refugee camp in Pusan. His extended family joined him there, concocting a mishmash of relatives festering together in a cramped shack, including his five adolescent cousins. Whenever I connect with family members about this time, they always mention how hungry they were. To this day, my uncle eats dinner as slowly as possible—never taking a meal for granted, savoring every chew.

Tae circa 1960 in South Korea.

The success of General MacArthur's amphibious assault into Incheon pushed the Chinese Army to the Yellow River, simmering the Korean War down to an armistice and formalizing Korea into the two countries we see today. Dad finished his military compulsory service, graduated college, and was in one of the first classes to matriculate into the Korean Institute of Science and Technology (KIST).

Emboldened by MacArthur and the vision of American prosperity, my dad, like so many parents of my generation, bought a one-way ticket to America with $300 in his pocket.

By today's standards, $300 does not seem like much, but compared to my dad's paltry upbringing in Korean winters, it was plenty for the perennial 70-degree weather of California. Dad slept on the couches of family until he settled into a kitchen-less studio in Hollywood. With his degree from KIST, Dad quickly snagged a job with industry stalwart Ducommun Metals, and began his next pursuit of finding a life partner. For most immigrants, marriage is mainly a means to provide stability, and in the off chance, depth and beauty in the long term. My parents married with this understanding, and my sister and I were born shortly after.

Southern Californian suburban life was the dawn of quotidian comfort and the end of my parent's struggles. Peace and the convenience of manicured, bedroom communities were the hallmarks of their new beginnings—their American dreams. When I reflect upon those days, I find my upbringing to be indistinguishable from most middle-class American families—*Home Alone 2* and swim lessons at our local pool—with nothing that indicated the styles of a North Korean defector.

Within this banal backdrop, my dad's estranged past revisited him on a quiet afternoon. While drinking coffee and listening to Korean radio, Dad heard a pithy advertisement from a pastor offering to reconnect families in North Korea. It had been nearly 50 years since Dad left his North Korean home, so with his curiosity piqued and nothing to lose, he called the number in the advertisement.

A year passed with no signs of success. Then one day, with no notice or fanfare, he received an envelope with a North Korean flag and a letter from his two youngest sisters with pictures from a wedding and a family portrait.

(Note: A family portrait and redacted translation of the letter is on the right.)

My dad continued to correspond with them for over ten years, with letters, pictures, and of course, whenever possible, American dollars. With each exchange, excitement built around the prospect of seeing one another.

Eventually, a window of opportunity opened up: the North Korean border relaxed its requirements and the political climate felt safe enough to make a visit. Excited by this once-in-a-lifetime opportunity, Dad discussed a trip to North Korea with my mom.

However, she said "absolutely not." My mom wasn't antagonizing my dad. When the opportunity to visit his sisters came up, I was several years into studying at West Point and decided I wanted to pursue a career as an Army officer. September 11 was in America's rearview mirror, and the Army had launched itself into heavy deployment cycles to Iraq or Afghanistan, guaranteeing that all soldiers would see combat in the near future. My mom was concerned that Dad's visit to North Korea would create suspicions around our family's allegiance to the United States and upend my military career.

Knowing the trip was a major risk to my future, Dad passed on seeing his sisters with little further contemplation. He decided not to share this with me at the time, out of concern for the guilt I'd feel on top of the stresses of cadet life. Over time, the North Korean border closed and the country's increased scrutiny made the trip unrealistic in my dad's old age. I wish he had just gone. I would later find out that that opportunity was Dad's last chance to see his sisters.

I'm often thanked for my service and the "sacrifice" I've made serving in the military. But frankly, the price of freedom is paid in different ways by different people. For me, it was a young adulthood of challenging but salient life experiences overseas. For other service members, such as our Korean War veterans, it is the loss of limbs, mental health, or life itself. My dad's price of admission, which he also paid for my sister and me, was to leave his family and then forego ever seeing them again. In light of what people like my dad and our Korean War veterans have done, the uniform term "sacrifice" doesn't capture the deeply significant and varied contributions given by others for the ideals of this country. "Sacrifice," within that backdrop, is an inequitable term for my military tenure.

In 1962, General MacArthur addressed West Point's student body with a famous speech, a portion of which became mandatory for all members of the Long Gray Line to memorize verbatim.

"Duty, Honor, Country—those three hallowed words reverently dictate what you ought to be, what you can be, what you will be. They are your rallying points: to build courage when courage seems to fail, to regain faith when there seems to be little cause for faith, to create hope when hope becomes forlorn. Unhappily, I possess neither that eloquence of diction, that poetry of imagination, nor that brilliance of metaphor to tell you all that they mean."

This, all of this above, is my dad, the portrait of my father—an understated man, the King of Kindness, and a silent dam of patience and sacrifice. I also don't possess the eloquence, poetry, or brilliance to tell you what "Duty, Honor, Country" means, but I do find a beautiful and understated reflection of that mantra, ironically, in one of those people MacArthur saved from the refugee camps of Pusan.

And to our Korean War veterans, on behalf of the generations of Koreans who've prospered both in America and Korea, we thank you for your sacrifice.

Our North Korean family members, including Tae's youngest sister (bottom right), with whom he was finally able to correspond through letters after more than 50 years of no contact.

To my dearest sister and brother whom I miss so much.

To receive letters and photos from my brother and sister whom I had not heard from for over 50 years feels like a dream. It's impossible to write all the happiness I feel in this letter. I had never known the faces of my father, brother, or sister, and never had the chance to call for them. I am Jiyoung. I have not been able to sleep since hearing from you and I've been looking at your photos several times each day.

As I pick up a pen to write this letter, the terrible images of the war that occurred in Korea come to mind. I know that you (brother) miss the scenes of our old home in [redacted], but even in our beautiful and peaceful hometown many people died as a result of bombing and fights. Uncle [redacted] and his family, as well as our cousins also passed before the war ended. I was also injured in my left leg. Such bad fortune and sadness were felt by many people from the war.

Mother never forgot about the separated family. She always hoped for the unification of our countries before eventually passing in 1975. There is no one left in [redacted]. I hope that all us separated siblings can meet in the future. I wish that our countries will unite as soon as possible. I can't wait for the day when we're reunited.

I wish everyone in your family good health. Goodbye.

June 27, 1991

U.S. Army veteran Tina Chong as a West Point cadet with parents, Tae and Min, attending her 2LT bar pinning ceremony and being commissioned as an Army aviation officer.

Soldiers and KATUSA from 123rd Brigade Support Battalion, 3rd Armored Brigade Combat Team, 1st Armored Division, zero their weapons in preparation for the upcoming qualification range. *Photo courtes of NARA.*

CHAPTER 17

KATUSA

The Korean Augmentation to the United States Army (KATUSA) program was established during the early days of the Korean War, and provides an opportunity for qualified Korean draftees who are fluent in English to apply for full-time duty in a U.S. Army unit. Those who apply for the program are randomly chosen by lottery.

KATUSA is a branch of the Republic of Korea Army consisting of Korean drafted personnel who are augmented to the Eighth United States Army (EUSA). The branch does not form an individual military unit; instead, small numbers of KATUSA members are dispatched to fill a variety of positions within the EUSA. While KATUSA members are managed by the ROK Army on a personnel level, they live and work with the U.S. enlisted soldiers and junior NCOs. This type of augmentation is unique throughout the United States Army worldwide.

The KATUSA program remains essential to the safety of the Republic of Korea. The program also greatly benefits America by providing the U.S. military with Korean-speaking soldiers and allowing greater military functionality and maneuverability throughout the Korean peninsula. KATUSA soldiers serve as translators between the local populace and help U.S. soldiers who are new to the peninsula understand Korean customs and language. Both countries learn from each other and assist one another, especially with the threat of North Korea looming over South Korea. This symbiotic relationship saves the United States money and manpower and provides the ROK with additional security while standing as a powerful symbol of the two nations' friendship and mutual support.

U.S. Army Gen. James D. Thurman notes that the program personifies the teamwork that keeps the Korean–American alliance strong. "Working together as a team has helped build mutual trust, common understanding, and cooperation between our countries, which is an inseparable bond we share today," he said. "Today we have more than 3,300 KATUSAs who continue to stand side by side with their U.S. partners as we deter aggression and preserve peace and stability on the peninsula."

A grief-stricken American infantryman whose buddy has been killed in action is comforted by another soldier. In the background, a corpsman methodically fills out casualty tags (Hakdong-ni area, Korea, August 28, 1950). *Photo by Sgt. 1st Class Al Chang, U.S. Army.*

CHAPTER 18

STATISTICS OF THE KOREAN WAR

The Korean War Veterans Memorial on the National Mall will have a new focal point in 2022: a Wall of Remembrance featuring the names of more than 36,000 American Armed Forces who died and over 7,100 Korean Augmentation to the U.S. Army (KATUSA) who died in the Korean War. Their names will be organized by rank and respective branch of service, demonstrating how the war's burden fell unevenly across the military.

The Fallen:

United States Army	29,857
United States Marine Corps	4,522
United States Navy	688
United States Air Force	1,587
ROK KATUSAs	7,174
Total Fallen	36,634

Total American service members: 36,634

Total KATUSA service members: 7,174

The war cost the United States approximately $100 billion (over $1 trillion in 2022 dollars).

During the course of the war, the United States provided some 50 percent of total ground forces, the ROK 40 percent, and the remaining U.N. nations 10 percent.

CHAPTER 19

A GRATEFUL NATION HONORS THE MEMBERS OF THE ARMED FORCES OF THE UNITED STATES AND THE KOREAN AUGMENTATION TO THE UNITED STATES ARMY WHO GAVE THE LAST FULL MEASURE OF DEVOTION IN DEFENSE OF FREEDOM

UNITED STATES ARMY

PRIVATE

JOHN AARON JR
VINCENT G ABBATE
LEROY ABBOTT
JAMES ABDON
CHARLES L ABEL JR
GEORGE E ABELES
CHARLIE ABERCROMBIE
BILLY R ABLES
ROBERTO ABREU-GARCIA
BILL J ACINELLI
DELANO H ACKER
JACK M ACKERMAN
WILLIAM C ACKERMANN
LUIZ A ACOSTA-MARTINEZ
CLYDE E ADAM
CLAYTON D ADAMS
ELBERN T ADAMS
JAMES C ADAMS
JOHN Q ADAMS
LEWIS E ADAMS
LOYD E ADAMS
OLIVER ADAMS
RICHARD L ADAMS
RUFUS ADAMS
HARRY G ADAMSON JR
HAROLD L ADDINGTON
ALPHONSO ADDISON
ROBERT A ADELMAN
SYLVAN W ADELSGRUBER
VIRGIL B ADKINS
FREDERICK J AESCHLIMAN
RALPH J AGOSTINI
JOSE M AGUAYO-PEREZ
ENRIQUE AGUIAR-MARQUEZ
GILBERTO AGUILAR
PEDRO L AGUON
EDWARD J AIKEN
JOHN A AIMER
VIRGIL F AITKENS
LE ROY J AITKIN
KAZUSKI AKAZAWA
FREDERICK K AKINA
PAUL ALBAUGH
DURHAM O ALBERT
JOSEPH R ALBERT
VERLE S ALBERTSON
ESTELL C ALBERTY
CARLO L ALBI
FRANK ALCARAZ
ALEJANDRO A ALCENCIO
JOHN T ALCOCK
PHILLIP F ALCORN
LLOYD H ALDERFER
ELLSWORTH L ALDERMAN
JOSEPH A ALDO
ALPHONSE ALDRIDGE
HARRY H ALDRIDGE
CHARLES B ALEXANDER
JOSEPH S ALEXANDER
LEROY B ALEXANDER
LARRY E ALFORD
FRANCISCO ALGARIN-RODRIGUEZ
TEODORO ALICEA
RAMON ALICEA-REYES
JAMES ALLBRITTON
LARRY C ALLEMAN
CHARLES ALLEN
ERIC G ALLEN
GORDON R ALLEN
JAMES R ALLEN
JEAN R ALLEN
JOHN A ALLEN JR
JOSEPH N ALLEN
MARCELLOUS ALLEN
MAX ALLEN
CHARLES J ALLEND
GREGORIO ALLENDE-CEPEDA
WILMER L ALLEY
GEORGE A ALSTON
JAMES M ALSTON
WILLIAM E ALTOMARE
JAMES E ALTUM
ADALBERTO N ALVAREZ
JOHN J ALYANAKIAN
WILLIAM D AMBERGER
HERTZEL J AMDUR
WAYNE R AMELUNG
ANDREW J AMENDOLA
ROGER D AMES
JOHN C AMMONS
THURMAN R AMMONS JR
NORMAN E AMSDEN
RAY M AMURO
BO-GUK AN
BONG-HAK AN
BONG-SANG AN
BONG-YANG AN
BYEONG-CHEOL AN
BYEONG-HUI AN
BYEONG-OK AN
BYEONG-SIK AN
BYEONG-SU AN
BYEONG-SU AN
BYEONG-TAEK AN
DAE-JAE AN
DEOK-SU AN
DOL-I AN
DOL-RYUL AN
DONG-MU AN
DONG-SIK AN
GAP-YONG AN
GI-CHEON AN
GI-HWAN AN
GIL-CHUL AN
GI-SU AN
GO-GEUN AN
GWON-HEUNG AN
GYO-YUN AN
GYU-YEOL AN
HUI-BONG AN
HUI-YEOL AN
HWA-JUNG AN
HYO-SEOK AN
HYO-YEONG AN
IL-HWA AN
IM-SAENG AN
I-MUN AN
IN-SU AN
JAE-HO AN
JAE-MUK AN
JAE-RYUL AN
JAE-UK AN
JEUNG-SU AN
JIN-GI AN
JONG-JIN AN
JONG-O AN
JONG-SEON AN
JU-BONG AN
JU-BONG AN
JUNG-HWA AN
JU-YEONG AN
MYEONG-YONG AN
SANG-BONG AN
SANG-CHEOL AN
SANG-GU AN
SANG-MAN AN
SANG-PYO AN
SANG-SAM AN
SANG-WON AN
SEOK-JUN AN
SEOK-MUN AN
SEON-EUNG AN
SEONG-RYONG AN
SEON-YEONG AN
SUN-GEUN AN
TAE-GAP AN
TAE-GWON AN
TAEK-HYEON AN
TAE-SU AN
YANG-IL AN
YEONG-BOK AN
YEONG-CHEOL AN
YUN-HO AN
FRED ANDERS
HARRY D ANDERSEN
ALLEN G ANDERSON
BILLY G ANDERSON
CARL E ANDERSON JR
CLINTON L ANDERSON
JAMES T ANDERSON
JOHN H ANDERSON
KENDALL G ANDERSON
NALTON J ANDERSON
RAYMOND W ANDERSON
RICHARD P ANDERSON
ROBERT E ANDERSON
ROBERT H ANDERSON
THOMAS E ANDERSON
TOMMY J ANDERSON
WILLIAM ANDERSON
WILLIAM G ANDERSON
WILLIAM H ANDERSON
WILLIAM P ANDERSON JR
WILLIE L ANDERSON
ALBERT S ANDREWS
HOWARD D ANDREWS
KENYON E ANDREWS
LUTHER M ANGE
VICTORIO E ANGELINE
GEORGE ANGELUS
ERNEST L ANTHONY
LINDY R ANTONIO
GEORGE APAO
AUGUST L APO
HECTOR L APONTE
HERBERT G APPEL
FRANCIS E APPIS
DAVID G APT
ARTHUR L ARAGON
SEICHI ARAKAKI
WILFRED H ARAKAWA
ALEXANDER G ARCHER
ALBERTO ARCHILLA-VALLELLANES
PANGRA ARCIDIACONO
THEODORE M ARD JR
JOSEPH R AREL
ANTHONY E AREZZO JR
LUIS F ARMADA-JUARBE
JOE T ARMAS
ROBERT W ARMSTRONG
WILSON C ARMSTRONG
JOHN G ARNETT
BILLY A ARNOLD
ERVIN L ARNOLD
GEORGE C ARNOLD
JAMES J ARNOLD
MIGUEL A ARROYO
RUBEN ARROYO-ABREU
MELVIN ARTHUR
KEITH L ARVIDSON
ROBERT W ASHBAUGH
THOMAS R ASHLEY
KENNETH W ASQUITH
LEONARD H ATKINS
GEORGE J ATKINSON
MONROE J AUBAIN
IRA A AUGENBLICK
EDDIE D AUMAN
JOHN A AUMON
EDWARD C AUST
DON L AUSTIN
RAYMOND S AUSTIN JR
CLARENCE K G AUYONG
ALLEN O AVARA
CLARENCE R AVENT
CLARENCE T AVILA
STANLEY L AVILA
BILLY W AWTREY
JAMES M BABER
FRANK S BACA
ERNEST H BACHMANN
RICHARD L BACON
WILLIAM F BADEN
BOK-I BAE
BONG-SIL BAE
BYEONG-SU BAE
CHANG-DAE BAE
CHANG-HO BAE
CHANG-HYEON BAE
CHANG-JO BAE
CHAN-SIK BAE
DAE-GEUN BAE
DEOK-GYU BAE
DOL-I BAE
DONG-BAE BAE
DONG-RYEON BAE
GANG-HWA BAE
GI-CHEOL BAE
GI-RO BAE
GI-YONG BAE
GYEONG-DO BAE
HWA-JUN BAE
HYEONG-GI BAE
HYO-CHEOL BAE
HYO-MUN BAE
IN-CHIL BAE
JEONG-GEON BAE
JEONG-HAK BAE
JEONG-PAN BAE
JONG-DEOK BAE
JONG-GUK BAE
JONG-HYEON BAE
JONG-TAE BAE
JONG-YUN BAE
JUNG-GWON BAE
JUN-HO BAE
MU-GU BAE
MU-GYU BAE
SANG-GI BAE
SANG-I BAE
SEOK-GO BAE
SEOK-GU BAE
SEOK-GWON BAE
SE-YUL BAE
SU-BAEK BAE
SU-HWAN BAE
SU-JO BAE
TAE-GEUN BAE
TAE-GU BAE
TAE-GYU BAE
TAE-YONG BAE
U-SEONG BAE
WI-SIK BAE
WON-SEOK BAE
YEONG-BOK BAE
BAEK-SU BAEK
BONG-GI BAEK
CHA-GI BAEK
CHAN-SU BAEK
CHIL-JONG BAEK
DEOK-GI BAEK
DONG-SIK BAEK
DU-CHEON BAEK
DU-MAN BAEK
EUN-SU BAEK
GAP-JU BAEK
GI-HO BAEK
GI-HYEON BAEK
GI-MUN BAEK
GYEONG-DON BAEK
GYU-HWA BAEK
GYU-HYEON BAEK
HAK-SU BAEK
HEUM-PAN BAEK
HO-BIN BAEK
HWI-SEON BAEK
IL-GI BAEK
IM-GI BAEK
IN-JUN BAEK
JIN-GYEONG BAEK
JONG-GYU BAEK
JUN BAEK
JUN-IN BAEK
MAL-SUL BAEK
MAN-SU BAEK
MYEONG-SEON BAEK
NAK-HYO BAEK
NAK-HYO BAEK
NAM-DOL BAEK
OK-SEOK BAEK
SAM-HO BAEK
SE-GWAN BAEK
SEONG-RYEOL BAEK
SEUNG-TAE BAEK
SEUNG-TAE BAEK
SU-BOK BAEK
SU-MAN BAEK
YUN-HYEON BAEK
RONALD C BAER
PEDRO BAEZ-DE JESUS
JOSEPH E BAHLEDA
BERT G BAILEY
CHARLES BAILEY
ROSS BAILEY
SESCO L BAILEY

1 ARMY

WILLIAM C BAILEY
VERNON BAIRD
BURTON E BAKER
DONNIE E BAKER
ERNIE L BAKER
GANES L R BAKER
JIMMY A BAKER
JUNE M BAKER
K W BAKER
KENNETH C BAKER
LEONARD A BAKER
PAUL E BAKER
ROBERT L BAKER
ROBERT W BAKER
SAMUEL D BAKER
STANLEY L BAKER
VICTOR BAKER
WILLIAM M BAKER
HAROLD M BALDWIN
ROBERT BALLARD JR
WILLIAM J BALLARD
HOWARD E BALLENTINE
HOMER R BALLOU
DURRELL M BALTHAZOR
BONG-YEONG BAN
DONG-CHAN BAN
GEUN-SIK BAN
HAENG-GWAN BAN
JONG-OK BAN
SUN-HWAN BAN
YEONG-HWAN BAN
YUN-WON BAN
CHANG-SU BANG
DU-HYEON BANG
GEUK-JU BANG
GYEONG-AN BANG
GYEONG-SIK BANG
GYEONG-WON BANG
HYE-WON BANG
SANG-JIN BANG
SEONG-BONG BANG
SIK-WON BANG
SUN-YONG BANG
YEONG-SEONG BANG
YONG-GEUN BANG
FRANK W BANKSTON
RUBIN G BARA
ANDREW BARAKOSKIE
CLIFFORD A BARBER
ELMER G BAREFOOT
CALVIN K BARGER
JESSE J BARKER
LEONARD H BARKLAGE
ELMER L BARKLEY
FRANCIS B BARKS
GEORGE T BARLOW
ERNEST W BARNES
ROBERT A BARNES
JERRY W BARNETT
JOSEPH L BARNETT
RICHARD C BARNETT
ROBERT N BARNETT
JOSEPH J BARNEY
KENNETH R BARNHILL
CHARLES J BARON JR
JAIME BARRETO
JOHN J BARRETT JR
JAMES F BARRIER
RICHARD J BARRY
EDWARD J BARSKITAS
JOHN L BARTBERGER
GEORGE H BARTHOLOMEW
LAWRENCE H BARTLEY
WAYNE J BARTLEY
ELDON L BARTON
FRANKLIN D BARTON
JAMES M BARTON
HIRAM L BASCO
DONALD B BASHAW
LESTER W BASON
PHILIP J BASS
ROBERT L BASS
HOWARD H BAUERNFIEND
PHILLIP J BAUGHANS
ALLEN E BAUGHER
GERALD L BAUMAN
WILLIAM M BAUMGARDNER
GERALD F BAUMGARTNER
HAROLD J BAUS

PHILIP C BAUS
BUDDY H BAXTER
DOUGLAS BAXTER
WALTER J BAXTER JR
JESUS C BAZAN
CHARLES BEACH JR
FLOYD T BEACH
JOHN S BEACHER
BILLY BEAR
CARRIE L BEASLEY
HENRY E BEASLEY
WILBUR E BEASLEY
GERALD G BEASON
ROBERT A BEAUDETTE
BANDY BEAVERS JR
JOSEPH S BECK
ROBERT C BECK
WILLIAM G BECK
RUSSELL R BECKER
RAYMOND J BEDORE
JOSEPH L BEEL
CHARLES P BEELER
FRANK N BEERWA
GERALD L BEGGS
RAYMOND J BEHRINGER
ARTHUR J BELIVEAU
AUGUSTINE A BELKO
BEAUMONT B BELL JR
DONALD I BELL
ALFRED M BELLAVIGNA
ROBERT P BELLE
ELZA L BELLEW
CHARLES O BELLON JR
JOSE E BELLON-RODRIGUEZ
GLEN E BELLOW
VINCENT P BELSTLE
MILFORD C BELT
LLOYD E BELTZ
HAROLD V BENDER
WILLIAM BENDER JR
JOHN D BENDIX
LANDON E BENEDICT
TORNEY R BENEFIEL
DENSON H BENEFIELD
MARTIN BENGE
JAMES A BENGER
RICHARD C BENITEZ
CALVIN BENNETT
CLYDE W BENNETT
EARL BENNETT
HENRY A BENNETT
KENNETH L BENNETT
SNOWDEN BENNETT JR
KENNETH L BENSON
LEO M BENTKOWSKI
FRANCIS H BENTLEY
JERRY D BENTLEY
JOHN E BENTON
WILLIAM BENTON JR
HENRY BERENDOWSKI
WALTER E BERG
STANLEY E BERGERON
WALTER P BERHING
BROMLEY E BERKELEY
SULLY I BERMAN JR
LEO J BERNAL
NATIBIDAD BERNAL
JORGE BERNAL-MEDINA
GERALD N BERNHART
ROBERT W BERNIER
ROBERT L BERNLOEHR
VICTOR M BERRIOS-DIAZ
LUIS BERRIOS-VELAZQUEZ
LEONARD BERRY
JERALD J BERRYESSA
GERALD J BERTRAND
JOSEPH P BERUBE
HERBERT BESCH JR
ARNOLD L BEST
BAXTER H BETTS JR
HENRY J J BETZ JR
ARTHUR G BEZART
CARL J BICHLER
PAUL H BIENVENU
CHARLES L BIGGER
GUY K BIGGERSTAFF
EDGAR D BIGGS
JOSEPH E BILBY
HUBERT L BILL
RICHARD J BILLINGER

BILLY C BILLINGTON
JOSEPH B BILOHLAVEK
JAMES C BILTY
CLARENCE E BINDT
GEORGE L BING
JAMES F BINKLEY
JAMES E BIONAZ
CHARLES F BIRD
PAUL F BIRMINGHAM
FRANK BISELIS
EULIS E BISHOP
JAMES E BISHOP
JOSEPH H BISHOP
ROBERT A BISHOP
GORDON R BITTELL
BENNIE M BIVENS
LLOYD J BIXBY
HUEY G BLACK
JAMES W BLACK
JOHN L BLACK
JUNIOR BLACK
HAROLD E BLACKBURN
VINNER E BLACKLEY
BENJAMIN R BLACKWELL
THOMAS L BLACKWELL
WILLIAM C BLAIN
JAMES R BLAIR
RAYMOND J BLAIR
ROY T BLAIR JR
THEODORE W BLAISDELL
CHARLES C BLANCHETTE JR
W C BLAND
CHARLES D BLANKENSHIP
STANLEY P BLASE
HUBERT F BLASHILL
JERRY C BLEEN
GEORGE H BLEICHER
CURTIS J BLEVINS
CHARLES BLOOM
GUY BLOSSER JR
EVANS G BLOUNT
REX P BLOW
ADOLPH D BLUEDOG
LEE BLUIT
HOYT B BOATWRIGHT
JOHN A BODEWIG
PETER B BODNARIK
LESTER W BOERNER
DONALD E BOGAN
GLEN D BOGARD
HOWARD J BOGENSCHILD
CHARLES W BOGGS
RAYMOND N BOHELER
JOSEPH R BOITANO
FREDERICK BOLAND
ROBERT J BOLAND
WILLIAM H BOLANDER
CHARLES E BOLDEN
ROBERT J BOLEN
DARWIN E BOLER
BILLY R BOLIN
GEORGE D BOLTON
MARSHALL D BOLTON
ANGEL BONANO-DE JESUS
FRANK L BONAR
MALCOLM D BOND
ZACK A BONE
MARCUS H BONGARD
ROBERT L BONNER
EDWIN A BONNETTE
BOBBY R BOOHER
WALTER M BOOKER
CHARLES X BOONE
HARRY W BOORD
TRUMAN L BOOTH
GLEN E BOOTHE
FRANK J BOPP
EMANUEL BORG
WILLIAM C BORGMAN
WILLIAM R BORING
MAXMILLIAN J BORKOWSKI
ARTHUR W BORST
LOREN C BORTZ
GEORGE E BORUS
MERLIN W BORWICK JR
FREDRICK W BOSSERT
JOHN BOSTICK
FRED J BOTT JR
JAMES M BOUGHTER
CHRISTOS S BOUKEDES

HARRY J BOURDEAU
JOSEPH R BOURGEOIS
WILLIAM C BOURKE
ELZIE R BOWEN
HORACE N BOWERS JR
PAUL B BOWERS
LARRY A BOWLES
ARCHIE J BOWLING
MORRIS A BOWLING
CURTIS L BOWMAN
JACK T BOWSER
ROLAND L BOWSER
STANLEY B BOWSHER
BOBBY S BOX
JAMES A BOYCE
JOHN G BOYD
JOSEPH E BOYD
SIMON BOYD
GLENNON J BOYER
WILLIAM H BOYER
DOUGLAS R BOYLE
EARL B BOYLE
ALFREDO BRACAMONTE
BILLIE E BRACKENBURY
FLOYD BRADLEY JR
KENNETH E BRADLEY
LEWIS BRADLEY JR
NAPOLEON BRADLEY
PETER J BRADLEY
VERLAN R BRADSHAW
ROBERT E BRAILEY
PHILIP F BRAITHWAITE
JAMES S BRAMBLETT JR
ELMER J BRANCH
SAMUEL A BRANCH JR
STERLING BRANDON JR
JACK BRANHAN
PAUL A BRANNOCK
JAMES E BRANNON JR
FLOYD P BRANT
THOMAS E BRATCHER
JULIAN N BRATHWAITE
WAYNE F BRAUN
GEORGE BRAZELL JR
PAUL R BRAZELL
JAMES BRAZIL
WILLIS M BREDE
VIRGIL L BREEDLOVE
WILLIAM M BREEDLOVE
MAURICE N BRENGARD
DANIEL A BRENNIE
IRVIN L BRENT
LYLE A BREST
JAMES R BRETT
CARL D BREWER
HUGH H BREWER
EDWARD F BRIDENHAGEN
MILTON H BRIDWELL
NORMAN E BRIGGS
J W BRIGHT
WILLIAM F BRIGMAN
JACOB S BRINDLE
EPHRIAM L BRINSON
GROVER BRINSON JR
HARVEY B BRISSON
THOMAS J BRITT
STEVE N BRKLICH
CHARLES H BROADNAX
RICHARD R BRODHEAD
LEROY J BROEDERS
DOMINIC A BRONELE
ROBERT J BRONSON
DALE H BROOKS
DAVID C BROOKS
EDWARD W BROOKS
LAWRENCE C BROOKS
ROY E BROOKS
BUFORD E BROUGHTON
REED O BROUSSARD
ALVIN H BROWN
CHARLES E BROWN
CHARLES J BROWN
CHARLES L BROWN
CURTIS W BROWN
DUANE D BROWN
EARL J BROWN
EARL W BROWN
EUGENE F BROWN
FRANKLIN D BROWN
GEORGE BROWN

GLENN C BROWN
HERBERT F BROWN
JAMES D BROWN
JAMES F BROWN
JAMES W BROWN
JIMMIE L BROWN
MICHAEL J BROWN
PAUL E BROWN
RALPH J BROWN
ROBERT N BROWN
SAMUEL D BROWN
SHELBY B BROWN JR
THOMAS BROWN
WALLACE BROWN
WALTER B BROWN JR
WALTER E BROWN
WILLIAM R BROWN
J W BROWNING
PERRY H BROWNING
BRUCE M BROYLES
KENNETH C BRUBAKER
RALPH T BRUCE
WILLARD J BRUETTE
RUSSELL BRUIN
HOMER BRUINGTON
WESLEY BRUMBLES
GEORGE B BRUNNHUBER
PEDRO BRUNO-VIDAL
LOUIS B BRUSSE
JOHN L BRUSTER
WILLIAM J BRYAN
CECIL BRYANT JR
DON W BRYANT
GILBERT BRYANT JR
KINNEY BRYANT
WILLIAM F BRYANT
JIN-HWAN BU
JOEL H BUCHANAN
HAROLD C BUCHHOLZ
GLENFORD BUCKALEW
LAWRENCE K BUCKHORN
ELDON O BUDKE
LEROY M BUECHEL
ROY E BUELL
FRANK S BUENO
JOHN R BUGG
EDWIN L BUHLER
BASIL B BULLARD
BENJAMIN F BULLARD
FLOYD D BULLER
WILLIAM A BULLINGER
WAYNE F BULLIS
ELMO BULLOCK
FRED C BUMGARDNER
DONALD A BUNTENBACH
HANSEL BUNTON JR
GERARD R BURBACH
HERSHEL B BURCH
JOSEPH D BURCH
CHARLIE BURDEN JR
STEWART C BURDICK
WILLIAM BURFORD
JOSEPH BURGIN JR
ANTHONY R BURGIO
JOHN K BURGIO
MIGUEL BURGOS-VELAZQUEZ
BILLY R BURKE
WILLIAM J BURKE JR
MERRITT R BURKETT
LOUIS V BURKHALTER
GLENN E BURKHART
HOWARD BURKHART
JACK D BURKS
FOUNT V BURNETT
ROBERT M BURNETTE
RAYMOND E BURNHEIMER
JULIAN W BURNS
RAYMOND BURNS
GERALD R BURRIS
WILLIAM BURROUGHS
KEMPER H BURT
EDDIE BURTON
LEONARD L BURTON
RAY BURTON
CLARENCE M BUSH
HAROLD C BUSH

LEON R BUSH
LESTER BUSH
WARREN M BUSHMAN
CHARLES D BUSIC
JOSEPH W BUTLER
PAUL L BUTLER
LANDIS L BUTTON
RAYMOND W BUTYNSKY
CHAN-IK BYEON
DONG-SIK BYEON
GU-SEON BYEON
GYEONG-YEONG BYEON
GYU-SU BYEON
JAE-HWAN BYEON
JAE-HWAN BYEON
JONG-HUI BYEON
JONG-MUN BYEON
JONG-MUN BYEON
JONG-SEOP BYEON
JONG-SU BYEON
JONG-WON BYEON
SANG-CHEOL BYEON
SU-AM BYEON
SU-GYU BYEON
STANLEY F BYKOWSKI
JOSEPH BYNUM
CARL BYRD
JACK BYRD
MILTON C BYRD
ORVIL W BYRD
RICHARD E BYRD
WILLIAM H BYRD
EDWARD L BYTNAR
JOSE A CABALLERO-ROSARIO
DONALD O CABLE
JOHN J CABRAL
JOHNNIE R CABRERA
DONALD CADDELL
CHARLIE F CAGLE
MILTON L CAGLE
FRANK P CAIN
JOHN M CAIN
JACINTO CALCANO-ORTIZ
FRANKLIN D CALCUTT
DANIEL CALDEIRA
THEARTIS CALDWELL
LEE R CALHOUN
SAMMIE D CALHOUN
JAMES D CALLAHAN
VERNON A CALLAWAY
GEORGE E CALVERT
JAMES O CALVERT
GEORGE G CAMERON
PORTER S CAMERON
FELIPE F CAMPA
DUNCAN A CAMPBELL JR
JOSEPH F CAMPBELL
JOSEPH L CAMPBELL
LLOYD C CAMPBELL
WARREN R CAMPBELL
FRANCISCO L CANDIA
GORDON A CANFIELD
CLYDE E CANNON
DORAN L CANTER
ROY W CANTERBURY
EARL E CANTRELL
ERWIN A CAPEN
SAMIE CAPERS
SALVATORE L CAPITELLI
VINCENT CARAMADRE
JESSE CARBAJAL
ROBERT N CARBRAY
CLYDE D CARDER
LORIMER P CARDIEL
EDWARD J CARDIN
ANGEL M CARDONA-MARRERO
JOSEPH M CARDONE
JOSEPH CARDOZA
JOHN M CARDWELL
MATTHEW CAREY
MAURICE F CAREY
JOSEPH C CARFIELD
SANTO A CARGOLA
ARTHUR P CARLSEN
HENRY B CARLSON
JOHN A CARLSON JR
ROBERT E CARLSON
HAROLD L CARNAHAN
JOHN W CAROL
ROBERT W CARPENTER
BERNARD E CARR
DUANE E CARR
HAROLD CARR JR
LUTHER E CARR
THOMAS F CARR
JOSE U CARRASCO
LEANDRO C CARRASCO
LAWRENCE E CARRIER
JORGE L CARRION
MARCIAL CARRION-CONTRERAS
LUIS CARRION-MARTINO
JOHN J CARROLL
PETER J CARROLL
ROLAND S CARROLL
MIGUEL R CARTAGENA-COLON
EDWARD A CARTER
JAMES CARTER JR
JOHN W CARTER
JOSEPH R CARTER
LEO CARTER
RAY CARTER
SIDNEY C CARTER JR
THOMAS F CARTER
CHARLES C CARY
DANIEL A CARY
FERNANDO CASAS JR
CHARLES L CASEY
FLOYD CASH
JOE CASHWELL
BILLY G CASKER
HARRY L CASSELL
PETE CASTANA
WILLIAM J CASTLEMAN JR
CHARLES CASTORENA
LOUIS CASTRATARO
HECTOR L CASTRO
IGNACIO C CASTRO
RUBEN CASTRO
CHARLES V CATHEY
ROBERT E CATLOW
CHARLIE L CATO
BILLY J CAUSEY
LEWIS P CAUSEY
MARION F CAUTHEN
WINIFRED CAUTHEN JR
NICK J CAVALIERO
JAMES H CAVANAUGH
WILLARD S CAVE
NORMAN G CAWTHORN
DONALD C CAZEL
RAYMOND CECIL
RICHARD J CECULSKI
HOWARD F CEDARS
ISRAEL CENTENO
BONG-DAL CHA
BON-HWAN CHA
BYEONG-SE CHA
DEOK-O CHA
DONG-CHEOL CHA
DONG-CHEOL CHA
DONG-JIN CHA
DONG-OK CHA
GU-DONG CHA
GYEONG-SAM CHA
HU-JAE CHA
HYEONG-JUN CHA
HYEON-U CHA
JAE-HAN CHA
JIN-HAN CHA
JIN-WON CHA
JIN-WON CHA
JUN-HWAN CHA
JU-PIL CHA
SAM-JO CHA
SAM-JO CHA
SANG-BOK CHA
SANG-DAE CHA
SANG-IL CHA
SANG-SU CHA
SANG-YEONG CHA
WAN-HUI CHA
YONG-TAEK CHA
JOHN G CHADEK
KENNETH L CHADWICK
CHEOL-HUI CHAE
DONG-RYEOL CHAE
HYEONG-O CHAE
JUNG-GI CHAE
SEOK-GON CHAE
SEOK-YEOL CHAE
SEONG-YEOL CHAE
SEONG-YONG CHAE
ROBERT E CHAFFIN
EDWARD G CHAIRESS
ALFRED M CHALFIN
ANDREW CHAMBERS
CLARENCE CHAMBERS
HUGH S CHAMBERS
LESLIE D CHAMBERS
DONALD W CHAN
DAVID CHANCE
CARL H CHANDLER
HERBERT W CHANDLER
KENNETH H CHANDLER
PRENTICE S CHANDLER
CHARLES R CHANEY
DONALD L CHANEY
JUOQUIN M CHAPA
R B CHAPLIN
ROBERT J CHARETTE
WILLIAM H CHARLES
LEO E CHARLEY
PAUL J CHARLIER
GERALD L CHARTRAND
GEORGE I CHASE
JOHN L CHASE
CHARLES CHAVEZ JR
EDWARD J CHAVEZ
GILBERT E CHAVEZ
RUBEN CHAVEZ
NARCISCO CHAVIS JR
DANIEL E CHECOLA
ROBERT V CHEEK
JAMES L CHEERS
BU-JUN CHEON
HUI-BEOM CHEON
JANG-HWAN CHEON
JANG-SU CHEON
JEONG-GI CHEON
JEONG-GI CHEON
PAN-GYEONG CHEON
PUNG-GI CHEON
SAM-GYEONG CHEON
SANG-SUK CHEON
SO-TAEK CHEON
YEONG-SEOK CHEON
YONG-HAK CHEON
HAROLD D CHESBRO JR
GEORGE R CHESNEY
GEORGE R CHESSER
ANTONINO CHIARELLO
JOSEPH F CHIAVETTA
JAMES N CHILDRESS
RAYMOND A CHILDS
JAMES L CHITTY
AM-SONG CHOI
BANG-U CHOI
BOK-GI CHOI
BOK-SU CHOI
BONG-HO CHOI
BONG-HYEONG CHOI
BONG-SEOP CHOI
BONG-SIK CHOI
BO-PIL CHOI
BU-DOL CHOI
BYEONG-GAP CHOI
BYEONG-GEUN CHOI
BYEONG-GYU CHOI
BYEONG-GYU CHOI
BYEONG-HWA CHOI
BYEONG-RYONG CHOI
BYEONG-SIK CHOI
BYEONG-UK CHOI
CHA-GYU CHOI
CHANG-DEOK CHOI
CHANG-GYUN CHOI
CHEOL-MU CHOI
DAE-SUN CHOI
DAE-U CHOI
DAE-YONG CHOI
DAE-YUN CHOI
DEOK-CHA CHOI
DEOK-GIL CHOI
DEOK-SAENG CHOI
DEOK-SEONG CHOI
DEOK-YUN CHOI
DONG-CHAN CHOI
DO-YA CHOI
DU-HAE CHOI
DU-MAN CHOI
DU-YEONG CHOI
EUNG-SIK CHOI
EUN-RYUL CHOI
GANG-HWAN CHOI
GAP-SEOK CHOI
GAP-WON CHOI
GEON-GIL CHOI
GEUM-BAE CHOI
GEUN-HYEONG CHOI
GEUN-MAN CHOI
GEUN-SU CHOI
GIL-SU CHOI
GI-SU CHOI
GI-WON CHOI
GI-WON CHOI
GWANG-YEONG CHOI
GWAN-HONG CHOI
GYEONG-HO CHOI
GYEONG-SEON CHOI
GYU-HAK CHOI
GYU-HO CHOI
GYU-SUL CHOI
HAE-CHIL CHOI
HAE-DON CHOI
HAE-GAP CHOI
HAE-GON CHOI
HAE-GON CHOI
HAE-MUN CHOI
HAE-SEOK CHOI
HAE-SEONG CHOI
HAE-SU CHOI
HAN-EON CHOI
HANG-BIN CHOI
HAN-SAENG CHOI
HEUNG-SEON CHOI
HOE-JO CHOI
HONG-TAEK CHOI
HWA-SEON CHOI
HYEON-BAEK CHOI
HYEON-CHAN CHOI
HYEON-GU CHOI
HYEON-JIN CHOI
HYEON-JIN CHOI
HYEON-MU CHOI
HYEON-O CHOI
HYEON-SIK CHOI
HYO-YEOL CHOI
HYO-YONG CHOI
I-DAE CHOI
I-JU CHOI
IK-GEUN CHOI
IK-SU CHOI
IL-SEOP CHOI
IL-SEOP CHOI
IM-HO CHOI
IM-SIK CHOI
IN-BAEK CHOI
IN-GYU CHOI
IN-JAE CHOI
IN-SEOK CHOI
JAE-CHUN CHOI
JAE-DAL CHOI
JAE-GEUN CHOI
JAE-HUI CHOI
JAE-IK CHOI
JAE-SU CHOI
JAE-SUK CHOI
JEOM-BONG CHOI
JEONG-BONG CHOI
JEONG-GU CHOI
JEONG-GU CHOI
JEONG-HO CHOI
JEONG-OK CHOI
JEONG-SU CHOI
JEONG-SUK CHOI
JEONG-SUL CHOI
JEUNG-SU CHOI
JIN-U CHOI
JIN-YEOL CHOI
JONG-BYEONG CHOI
JONG-HO CHOI
JONG-OK CHOI
JONG-RYEOL CHOI
JU-BEOM CHOI
JU-BONG CHOI
JU-HAE CHOI
JU-HO CHOI
JUNG-HWAN CHOI
JUN-SEOK CHOI
JUN-SIK CHOI
JU-RAK CHOI
MAN-CHUL CHOI
MAN-JO CHOI
MAN-YONG CHOI
MI-HYEON CHOI
MUN-GYU CHOI
MUN-UNG CHOI
MYEONG-GYU CHOI
MYEONG-JIN CHOI
MYEONG-JUN CHOI
MYEONG-SONG CHOI
MYEONG-U CHOI
MYEONG-U CHOI
MYEONG-YEON CHOI
NAM-HA CHOI
OE-CHEOL CHOI
PAN-GYU CHOI
PAN-YONG CHOI
SAM-RYONG CHOI
SAM-YONG CHOI
SANG-GON CHOI
SANG-JIN CHOI
SANG-MAN CHOI
SANG-MAN CHOI
SANG-MYEONG CHOI
SANG-RANG CHOI
SANG-SU CHOI
SANG-TAE CHOI
SANG-TAEK CHOI
SANG-U CHOI
SANG-YEOL CHOI
SEOK-GYU CHOI
SEOK-HONG CHOI
SEOK-YONG CHOI
SEONG-GWAN CHOI
SEONG-HAE CHOI
SEONG-HO CHOI
SEONG-JO CHOI
SEONG-OK CHOI
SEONG-SU CHOI
SEUNG-YEOL CHOI
SE-WON CHOI
SO-AM CHOI
SU-AM CHOI
SU-CHEON CHOI
SU-JEOM CHOI
SUN-EOK CHOI
SUN-JO CHOI
SUN-TAE CHOI
SU-YEOL CHOI
SU-YONG CHOI
TAE-GEUK CHOI
TAE-GEUN CHOI
TAE-HWAN CHOI
TAE-JU CHOI
TAE-SU CHOI
U-JONG CHOI
UN-HAK CHOI
WON-BONG CHOI
WON-BONG CHOI
WON-SEOP CHOI
YANG-GYU CHOI
YEONG-BEOM CHOI
YEONG-DEUK CHOI
YEONG-GEUN CHOI
YEONG-HO CHOI
YEONG-HWAN CHOI
YEONG-JIN CHOI
YEONG-MAN CHOI
YEONG-SU CHOI
YONG-BOK CHOI
YONG-GU CHOI
YONG-GU CHOI
YONG-HO CHOI
YONG-HO CHOI
YONG-SIK CHOI
YONG-SUL CHOI
YONG-UN CHOI
HAVY O CHORN
EDWARD G CHOTKEY
LEO J CHOUINARD
EARL E CHRISTIAN
WILLIAM F CHRISTIAN
JOHN P CHRISTIANSON
JOHN R CHRISTLE

3 ARMY

MICHAEL CHRISTODULOU
PHILIP J CHRISTOPHER
ALVIN J CHRISTY
WILBUR R CHRISTY
BONG-SIK CHU
BONG-SIK CHU
BYEONG-YUN CHU
GYEONG-HWAN CHU
GYU-AN CHU
IN-SIK CHU
JEONG-GWAN CHU
JEONG-WAN CHU
JUN-HO CHU
SEOK-YEOP CHU
WON-YONG CHU
YONG-HWA CHU
VINCENT P CIARAMITARO
GEORGE CIPRIANO
ROBERT A CISLER
RUDOLPH CISNEROS
CHARLES V CLAEYS
EDWIN L CLANCY
RICHARD E CLAPP
ALEXANDER CLARK SR
CLAUDE E CLARK
FREDERICK T CLARK
LEONARD W CLARK
RAYMOND L CLARK
WARREN M CLARK
WILLIAM D CLARK
MARION L CLARY
WALTER E CLASS JR
ROBERT G CLATWORTHY JR
FLOYD M CLAYPOOL
EARL F CLAYTON
EDWARD O CLEABORN
LOUIS C CLEMENTS
ROBERT N CLENDENIN
FRANK J CLEVELAND
WAYNE K CLICK
SAMMIE L CLIFTON
HAROLD H CLINE
BOB G CLINTON
JAMES V CLODFELTER
EVANS CLOUD JR
CHARLES W CLOUGH
JIMMY R CLOUGHLY
JAMES COACHMAN JR
FREDERICK D COATES JR
ROBERT COATES
ROBERT L COBB
DONALD R COCHRAN
JOHN W COCHRAN
JOE P COELHO
JOHN E COFFIE
RONAL W COFFMAN
WILLIE F COFIELD
DAVID J COHEN
NORMAN COHEN
RICHARD W COHENOUR
JAMES R COINTMENT
RICHARD A COLALUCA
GEORGE T COLANGELO
SALVATORE COLAO
JOHNNY B COLE
PHILLIP M COLE
ELMER L COLEMAN
GLYNN A COLEMAN
JOHN C COLEMAN
WILFRED E COLEMAN JR
BUFORD COLESON
LEE E COLEY
RICHARD D COLLAGE
CHARLES H COLLINS
CLAIRENCE H COLLINS
CLAUDE E COLLINS
EDWARD E COLLINS
ESTLE L COLLINS
FRANK COLLINS
GALVIS COLLINS
JOHN W COLLINS
OLIVER COLLINS JR
SCOOP O COLLINS
WILLIAM E COLLINS JR
WILLIAM L COLLINS
WILLIAM R COLLINS
WOODROW COLLINS
JOAQUIN COLON-ALICEA
PEDRO COLON-BURGOS
ISRAEL COLON-FANTAUZZI
WILFRIDO COLON-RAMOS
FELIX COLON-REYES
FILOMENO COLON-VELAZQUEZ
RAYFORD J COMEAUX
JOE C COMIER
LOUIS COMIS
CHARLES R COMPTON
CHARLES W CONARROE
HERIBERTO CONCEPCION-DIAS
HENRY E CONGLETON
MARVIN G CONICA
CHARLES K CONNELLY
RONALD T CONNELLY
RAYMOND E CONNER
ANDREW E CONNOR JR
CHRISTIAN L CONOVER
JACK D CONRAD
THOMAS E CONROY JR
EDWARD L CONSYLMAN
JOSEPH P CONTI
JAMES A CONWAY
EDWARD L CONYERS
CHARLES A COOK
CHARLES J COOK
CHARLES R COOK
EMIL E COOK JR
HOWARD D COOK
LEWIS D COOK
PAUL K COOK
RICHARD K COOK
ROY R COOK
JACKSON COOKE
DENIS V COOPER
JAMES W COOPER
RICHARD R COOPER
UTAH N COOPER
ROBERT H COPE
EVERETT L COPELAND
ROBERT C COPPAGE
HILIARY E CORBETT
DONALD R CORBY
WILLIAM E CORCORAN
SIMON CORDERO-BARRETO
ANIBAL CORDERO-DE LA ROSA
MARVIN R CORKLE
RALPH B CORLEY
MARTIN V CORN
ROY G CORNELL
HENRY CORNIES JR
DAN CORRALEZ
JOE L CORREIA
DANIEL A CORRELL
DONALD F CORRIVEAU
ROBERT W CORSETTI
JUAN F CORTES
JOSE CORTES-CONCEPCION
RUDOLPH CORTEZ
RODOLFO COSME-ALMEZTICA
JOHN COSTON JR
CLARENCE S COTA JR
ALBERT H COTTER
FRANCISCO COTTO-SIERRA
ARTHUR R COTTRILL
WILLIAM W COUNCIL
MICHAEL T COUNIHAN
SIMILIAN COURVILLE
JAMES J COUVILLIER
BOBBY G COVER
CLAYBORN L COX
DONALD G COX
DONALD W COX
EUGENE M COX
JOSEPH E COX
WESLEY G COX
WILLIAM A COX
ADRIAN G COYLE
ROGER T COYLE
RONALD B COYNE
DAVID E CRABTREE
HENRY CRAFT JR
LUTHER O CRAIG
EARL H CRAM
RICHARD E CRAMER
DON E CRAMMER
JOHN W CRANFIELD
RICHARD CRATIC
JOHN H CRAWBUCK
LINDEN G CRAWFOOT
CLAUDE I CRAWFORD
JAMES T CRAWFORD
JOHN E CRAWFORD
JOSEPH CRAWFORD
KENNETH E CRAWFORD
MCKINLEY CRAWFORD
RALPH W CRAWFORD
RAYMOND A CRAWFORD
THOMAS A CREAMER JR
FRANK J CRESHINE
ALLEN R CRESSEY
ALPHONSO CREW
MANCIE L CREWS
GEORGE A CRIBBIE
ARNOLD L CRIDLAND
RAYMOND J CRIMMINS
PETER P CRISONA
JERONE C CROCKER
JOHNNY CROCKETT SR
JOHNNY CROFT JR
WILLIAM V CROKE
RICHARD R CROOK
CHARLES M CROPSEY
CECIL CROSBY
LYNNWARD T CROSBY
THOMAS E CROSS
JACK R CROSTA
ROBERT E CROTEAU
DALE D CROW
DAVID F CROW
WILTON P CROW JR
WILLIAM N CROWELL
FRANK T CROWLEY
EWELL D CROZIER
CHARLES M CRUM
CHARLES R CRUM
CLENTON D CRUMLEY
ERNESTO CRUZ-ALICEA
JUAN CRUZ-ALICEA
FELIX CRUZ-GUZMAN
RAFAEL CRUZ-MARRERO
JUAN A CRUZ-MARTINEZ
TOMAS E CRUZ-SANTOS
ERNEST P CUDDEFORD
EUGENE CULLER JR
TURNER F CULPEPPER JR
KENNIE CUMMINGS
ROBERT L CUMMINGS
RICHARD F CUMMINS
ROBERT L CUMMINS
DANIEL D CUNNINGHAM
DANIEL E CUNNINGHAM
EUGENE M CUNNINGHAM
ODELL CUNNINGHAM
ROBERT A CUNNINGHAM
WILLIAM T CUNNINGHAM
WILLIAM H CUPPLES
DOMINIK CUPRYNIAK
PAUL F CURRY
JEROME E CUSIMANO
GEORGE E CUTHBERT
WILLIAM DACEK
YEONG-HONG DAE
CALVIN A DAGGETT
ROY E DAHLKA
EARL W DAHNKE JR
RICHARD C DAIGLE
JAMES F DAIRDA
RUSSELL E DAKE
CURTIS L DALE
HAROLD E DALE
ROBERT L DALEN
ARTHUR DALLISON
EMANUEL L DALTON
CHARLES S DALY
JAMES H DAME
CHARLES DAMIANO
JOHN C DAMICO
AARON W DAMRON
WILLIAM S DAMRON
CONRAD R DANIELS
GEORGE T DANIELS
JOSEPH P DANIELS
JUDGE DANIELS
WILLIAM J DANIELS
KENNETH L DANKS
LUTHER B DANNEL
ROSCOE E DANNER
ARTHUR M DARLING
NORMAN E DAUB
ALLEN J DAUGHERTY
ROOSEVELT M DAUGHTRY
WALTER H DAUGHTRY
DANIEL DAVALOS
KENNETH E DAVENPORT
VANDERBILT DAVES
EDWARD DAVID
ROBERT L DAVID
EDWARD E DAVIDSON
LEWIS J DAVIES
NED E DAVIES
ANGEL R DAVILA
ALFRED D DAVIS
BOBBY DAVIS
CHARLES F DAVIS
CLARK M DAVIS
EDWARD DAVIS
FRANKIE L DAVIS
HAROLD W DAVIS
HERBERT H DAVIS JR
HERBERT L DAVIS
JACK E DAVIS
JACK R DAVIS
JAMES B DAVIS
KENNETH R DAVIS
LESLIE DAVIS
RICHARD E DAVIS
ROBERT DAVIS
ROBERT A DAVIS
ROBERT L DAVIS
WILLIAM DAVIS
WILLIAM E DAVIS
WILLIAM T DAVIS JR
WILLIE D DAVIS
BOBBIE DAWSON
LAVERNE DAWSON
THOMAS E DAWSON
EARLIE DAY
GLEN R DAY
MAYNARD N DAY
FREDRICO F DEALBA
BOBBY L DEAN
EARL DEAN
MARTIN R DEAN JR
GENNARO S DE ANGELIS
HOMER G DE ANGELIS
ALEXANDER DEANS
REGINALD M DEAS
WILLIS R DEBERRY
CHARLES A DE BLASI
HENRY C DE BOER
PAUL E DE CEUKELEIRE
DELMAS G DECKER
ERNEST F DECKER
ERNEST E DEERING
JOHN R DEFOREST
LLOYD D DEGLER
BILLY D DEHART
RAFAEL R DE JESUS-FIGUEROA
CHARLES L DELAFIELD
RUFUS DELANCY
LAWRENCE H DELANY
DANIEL DE LA ROCHA
DAMASO DE LEON-PHILLIPS
PABLO E DELGADO
RUDOLFO DELGADO JR
MIGUEL A DELGADO-COLON
FRANCISCO DELGADO-DIAZ
PEDRO DELGADO-NIEVES
LEONIDES DELGADO-PACHECO
PATSY M DELLACCIO
CHARLIE E DELONEY
JOSEPH A DEL PIZZO
FERDINAND DEL VALLE-CANCEL
PAUL L DEMOREST
WILLIE L DENARD
JIMMY R DENMON
FREDERICK W DENNE
CLIFFORD R DENNEY
JERRY L DENNIS
JOHNNY C DENNIS
DANIEL W DENT
WILLIAM A DENT JR
GEORGE DE NYSE
ERNEST DEOCHOA
ROBERT P DEPETRO
JOSEPH DE PIETRO
ANGELO DEPOLITO JR
HOWARD L DEPUE
BENEDIK M DEREK
CARLO F DERIVI
ADAM J DEROUEN
ROBERT F DE ROUSSE
ROBERT E DERR
EARNEST E DERRINGER
ARMAND R DESCHENES
GEORGE T DESHIELDS
RICHARD L DESMOND
GERALD G DESMUL
DONALD J DETTLING
ROBERT W DEUTSCH
THOMAS H DEVAULT
ROBERT M DEVINE
MICHAEL L DE VITA
ANTHONY R DE VITO
JOHN F DEVLIN
STUART A DEWALT JR
CHARLES E DEWEES
JOHN F DEWEY
ASBERT L DIAZ
BLAS DIAZ
PHILLIP R DIAZ
VICTORIANO DIAZ
ADOLFO DIAZ-CHARBONIER
JOSE F DIAZ-JIMENEZ
ALFONSO DIAZ-LEBRON
RICARDO DIAZ-MARTINEZ
CLEMENTE I DIAZ-NIEVES
FRANCISCO DIAZ-RODRIQUES
DALE L DIBBLE
ANTHONY J DICARLO
LOUIS R DICK
CALVIN S DICKERSON
JACK L DICKMAN
PAUL H DICKSON
ROBERT J DIDIER
PAUL A DIETERLE
KENNETH W DIETZ
FREDERICK DIGILIO
DONALD W DILLARD
JOHN F DILLON
WINFRED DILLON
JAMES A DILVER
WALLACE J DILWOOD
GLENN F DINGER
WILLIAM J DINSDALE JR
DANIEL DI PASQUO
TONY DIRK
MARIO A DISENSO
WILLIAM J DISKIN
DARL D DIXON
JAMES E DIXON
ROBERT E DIXON
WILLIAM M DIXON
BEOM-HWAN DO
EUL-GU DO
GYEONG-CHUL DO
HUI-JUN DO
SAM-BONG DO
SANG-PIL DO
SU-GWAN DO
YEONG-JUN DO
JOHN A DOBY
JOSEPH V DOCCHIO
LAWRENCE D DOCKERTY
MYEONG-DU DOKGO
DONALD J DOLEZAL
WILLIAM A H DOLLAR
HENRY R DOMINGUEZ
FLOYD W DONAHOO

CHRISTOPHER P DONALL
DENIS J DONOGHUE
SAMUEL J DONOHOE JR
ALFRED W DONOHUE
JOHN F DONOVAN
MAURICE P S DONOVAN
JAMES A DOOLEY JR
JOHNNIE K DOOLEY
WILLIAM N DOOLEY
THOMAS A DORRELL
WILLIAM H DOTSON
PRESTON G DOUCET
JOHN B DOUGAN
DONALD P DOUGHERTY
EDWARD M DOUGHERTY
ALLEN D DOUGLAS
CHARLES G DOUGLAS
ROBERT DOUGLAS
WILLIAM DOUGLAS
THAD DOUGLASS
ERNEST J DOVER
GLYNN A DOWDY
JAMES H DOWDY
ALVIN DOWLEYNE
MATTHEW R DOWNS
ROBERT I DOWNS JR
CHARLES C DOYLE
ANDREW G DRABANT
ALLEN E DRALLMEIER
GEORGE W DREISBACH
CHARLES DRENGBERG
CLEVE DRIVER
ARTHUR E DROUIN
BYEONG-SU DU
PHILLIP M DUARTE
JOHNNIE R DUCK
JAMES H DUCKWORTH
WILLIAM T DUFFY
GERALD L DUFRANE
ALVIN L DUHON
KIBBIE DUHON
JAMES R DULIN
STANLEY DUMPMAN
E W DUNCAN
HERMAN C DUNCAN
PHILLIP DUNCAN
RICHARD E DUNCAN
WILLIAM J DUNCAN
RONALD B DUNHAM JR
BENJAMIN F DUNKLE JR
HAROLD L DUNKLE
EVERETT D DUNN JR
GEORGE W DUNN JR
JAMES J DUNN
PAUL L DUNN
RALPH R DUNN
RICHARD T DUNN
SYLVESTER DUNN
DONALD L DUNNAWAY
JOHN A DUNNING
ALFRED A DUPLISSIS
JOHN L DUPRE JR
WAYNE L DUPUIS
JUNIUS DUPUY
ERNEST DURAN
TONY G DURAN
RUDY F DURAZO
CHARLES H DURHAM
JAMES R DURHAM
JOHN DUSCHANE
WALTER D DUSOBLOM
EDWARD W DUSTON
EUGENE J DUTRA
MICHAEL A DWORSHAK
RICHARD T DWYER
DOYLE J DYE
ROBERT L DYE
DONALD C DYER
MARLAN A DYMENT
PAUL EARHART
JOHN J EARLEY
JOSEPH P EARLS JR
WILLIAM B EARLS
CONLEY C EARWOOD
CHARLES J EASTMAN
ARCHIE L EATON
DONALD W EBERSOLE
DONALD F EBERT
MELVIN H EBERT
JOHN O EBERWEIN

KEITH W ECHELBERGER
THEODORE ECKHARDT
KENNETH R EDGAR
ERNEST E EDGE
PERCY W EDGE
JAMES S EDMONDS JR
JESSE W EDMONSON
CARL W EDWARDS
CECIL C EDWARDS
JAMES J EDWARDS
JAMES S EDWARDS
JOHN L EDWARDS
ROBERT E EDWARDS
RAUL G EGAN
THOMAS E EGAN
CARL EGGERS JR
ARNOLD E EGGLESTON
MARVIN L EGGLESTON
MYRLE W EHLE
VINCENT J EICHOLTZ
DARYL K EISENMAN
EYVIND A EKSET
GLEN R ELDER
FRITZ P ELIASSEN
CLYDE W ELKINS
PAUL E ELKINS
EUGENE M ELLINGSON
RICHARD S ELLIOT
JUNNIE L ELLIOTT
CHESTER L ELLIS
DELTON ELLIS
DONALD R ELLIS
JAMES R ELLIS
BOBBY L ELLISON
VIRGIL J ELLISON
HOWARD C ELMES
LINCOLN ELMORE
EARL P ELSWICK
GEORGE I ELSWORTH
BORIS A ELY
LOWELL E ELY
BOB J EMERSON
ROBERT L EMERY
ROY W EMHOFF
FIDEL EMMANUELLI
ALBERT H ENGER
ALVIN ENGLISH
JAMES P ENRIGHT JR
SU-BONG EO
CHEON-YEONG EOM
DEOK-SU EOM
GYU-SEOP EOM
IK-U EOM
IL-CHEON EOM
JAE-CHANG EOM
JAE-HWAN EOM
JU-BOK EOM
SANG-GON EOM
UN-SEOP EOM
HOMER A ERB
HAROLD E ERHARDT
DONALD M ERICKSON
RICHARD D ERICKSON
ROBERT L ERICKSON
WESLEY E EROLA
CHARLES G ERVIN
GRANVILLE C ERVING
JOSEPH L ERWIN
JOSEPH ESCOURIDO
JOHN S ESHIMA
JOSEPH ESPINOZA
FRANK J ESPOSITO JR
JOHN A ESPOSITO
GABRIEL V ESQUEDA
JOHNNIE P ESTRADA
DONALD H ESWAY
RAY W ETTER
ROBERT R EUBANKS
MUN-BAL EUN
SEONG-SU EUN
STOWELL EUSTIS
CHARLES H EVANS
CLIFFORD G EVANS
GEORGE C EVANS
GEORGE J EVANS
JAMES H EVANS
JAMES R EVANS
JOHNNY B EVANS
WARD EVANS JR
WILLIE G EVANS

WILLIAM L EVERETT
DONALD E EVERLY
THOMAS D EVESLAGE
WILLIAM G EWING
BILLIE J EXLINE
CLARENCE E EZELL
GERALD A FABER
DONALD A FABRIZE
LEWIS FABRIZIO
LAWRENCE FAHEY
JOHN B FAHL
KENNETH R FAIRCHILD
ALFRED L FAIRFIELD
JOSEPH J FAIRO
ROBERT G FAITH
WALTER J FALLESCHING
GLENN W FANNIN
JACK R FANNON
WILLIAM L FARABEE
JACK FARLEY JR
GEORGE R FARMER
NORMAN L FARMER
JOSEPH E FARRELL
FRANK FARUZZI
ROBERT C FAULKNER
DONALD F FEIST
JUAN C FEJERANG
WILLIE J FELDER
WARREN J FELDGES
SEGUNDO FELICIANO-
QUINONES
GEORGE L FELKON
WILLIE FELLOWS JR
OSCAR M FELTS
LUTHER FENDLEY JR
GORDON O FENGSTAD
JAMES H FENNER
MARVIN J FENSKE
HENRY A FERAZZOLI
GEORGE D FERGUSON
OTTIE K FERGUSON
EMIL F FERNANDEZ
CALVIN D FERNAU
ALBERT S FERRARA
ALBERT J FERRARI
DAVID J FERRARI
FRED D FETTER
EUGENE L FEY
MAYER D FIANCE
WILLIAM C FICOR
ROBERT L FIELD
DONALD L FIELDER
SAINT E FIELDS
STANLEY A FIELDS
SALVADOR FIGUEROA-
MASSAS
LUIS FIGUEROA-MEDINA
ANGEL L FIGUEROA-
OTERO
EDWARD A FINCH
DONALD E FINGERS
HOWARD W FINN
RICHARD T FINNIGAN
WARREN A FISH
DAVID L FISHER
JOHN A FISHER
PERVIS FISHER
RICHARD L FISHER
RONALD J FISHER
WILLIAM M FISHER
FREEMAN O FITZ
LAWRENCE E FITZGERALD
THOMAS A FITZPATRICK
JAMES M FLANIGAN
RICHARD A FLECK
RICHARD E FLEISCHER
GEORGE J FLERX
CHARLES F FLETCHER
FRED C FLETCHER
TERRENCE W FLETCHER
WILLIAM L FLETCHER
KENNETH C FLETKE
CORNELIUS H FLINT
ANDRES FLORES
FRANK R FLORES
POLITO FLORES
JUAN R FLORES-
NAVARRO
JOE FLOWERS
ALBERT S FLOYD

ERNEST L FLOYD
JAMES E FLOYD
NEWT H FLOYD
JAMES D FLUD
CLIFFORD A FLY
LEONARD A FOGLE
DUANE L FOLEY
BURKEMAN FONTENOT
RAFAEL A FONT-GUZMAN
JOHN FOOT
JAMES W FORAN
WESLEY O FORBORD
DOUGLAS FORD
JAMES L FORD
PATRICK H FORD JR
RALPH W FORDYCE
DOYLE FOREMAN
JAMES L FORENZA
JUAN C FORTIS
FRANCIS W FORTNEY
GARFIELD FOSTER
HAROLD E FOSTER
JAMES H FOSTER
LARRY F FOSTER
MILTON FOSTER
ROBERT A FOSTER
WILSON P FOSTER
ROBERT E FOSTIE
SANFORD W FOUTY
ALVIE L FOWLER JR
CHARLIE H FOWLER
GEORGE F FOWLER
WALTER W FOWLER
WILLIAM C FOWLER
ALFRED W FOX
JOHN E FOX
RICHARD A FOX
ROBERT J FOX
ROBERT L FOX
TOPEL C FOX
PETER K FRAENKEL
EARNEST FRANCE
GILBERT D FRANCIS
ELIAZAR FRANCO
ROBERT F FRANK
JAMES L FRANKLIN
JAMES L FRANKLIN
JOHN FRANKLIN JR
EDWIN F FRANZ
ORVILL E FRANZEN
DONALD M FRASHER
JACK L FRATER
ALFRED L FRATTO
DAVID W FRAZIER
ELAM L FRAZIER
JOE P FRAZIER
NICHOLAS J FREDERICK
WILLIAM H FREDERICK JR
RALPH T FREDERIKSEN
WILLIAM T
FREDRICKSON JR
STACY H FREEMAN
RUDOLPH C FREGOSO
JOE L FREITAS
CHARLIE FRENCH
EARL R FRENCH JR
JOHN W FREYMILLER
DEWEY M FRIDAY
ERNEST D FRIEL
JAMES B FRIEL
CHARLES P FRITZ JR
JOSEPH B FROMHOLD
WILLIAM B FROST
HAROLD E FRYAR
ARBY A FRYER JR
KYRLE S FRYLING JR
JOHN J FUCITO
DONALD E FUEGLEIN
RICHARD FUGATE
SAMUEL A FUJII
VERNON E FULKERSON
DONALD A FULLER
KEMPER FULLER
NOAH D FULLER
JAMES G FUNDERBURK
EUGENE L FUNKHOUSER
CECIL A FURMAN
JAMES T FUTCH
SHERWOOD D FYLER
MURPHY J GABRIEL

CARL L GABRIELSON
LOUIS R GACCIONE
DANIEL F GAGLIARDI
FLETCHER GAINES
ANGEL GALAN-ALICEA
MANUEL J GALINDO JR
ROBERTO R GALINDO
PATRICK J GALLAGHER
GUADALUPE GALLART
JOHN A GALLIGAN
PAUL E GALLOWAY
CANDELARIO GALLOZA-
MENDOZA
RICHARD GALPIN
SANG-GI GAM
ROY F GAMACHE
ELDRIDGE M GAMBLE
GILBERT GAMBLE
WILLIAM GAMBRELL
GORDON C GAMMON
ALFREDO M GAMPON
PEDRO A GANAL
IKE GANDY
SEIKEN GANEKU
BANG-JUNG GANG
BONG-HEON GANG
BONG-HYEON GANG
BYEONG-SAM GANG
BYEONG-UK GANG
CHA-DOL GANG
CHA-GEUN GANG
CHA-MAN GANG
CHANG-HO GANG
CHANG-JUNG GANG
CHANG-SEON GANG
CHIL-SEONG GANG
DAE-BAEK GANG
DAE-EUNG GANG
DAE-GYUN GANG
DEOK-EON GANG
DEOK-SU GANG
DONG-SU GANG
DU-MAN GANG
DU-SON GANG
EUL-SEOK GANG
EUNG-DO GANG
GAP-I GANG
GAP-SU GANG
GEUM-OK GANG
GYEONG-DAE GANG
GYEONG-RAE GANG
GYEONG-TAEK GANG
GYU-SEOK GANG
GYU-SEOP GANG
HAE-YONG GANG
HAK-BONG GANG
HAK-GU GANG
HUI-GON GANG
HUI-SEONG GANG
HYEON-SEOK GANG
IL-BONG GANG
IL-GYU GANG
IM-JIN GANG
IN-HWAN GANG
IN-SU GANG
IN-SU GANG
IN-SUN GANG
JAE-SI GANG
JAE-SU GANG
JA-JEONG GANG
JANG-HO GANG
JEOM-AM GANG
JEOM-SIK GANG
JEONG-OK GANG
JEONG-SEOK GANG
JEONG-SU GANG
JIN-SIK GANG
JONG-DAE GANG
JONG-TAE GANG
JUN-PAL GANG
MAN-GYU GANG
MI-SIK GANG
MU-HWAN GANG
MUN-HO GANG
MUN-JO GANG
NAM-HAE GANG
PAL-YUN GANG
RAK-SUN GANG
SA-CHAN GANG
SAM-GYU GANG

5 ARMY

SAM-SU GANG
SANG-U GANG
SANG-YONG GANG
SEOK-JIN GANG
SEOK-YEON GANG
SEONG-GWAN GANG
SEON-GIL GANG
SEON-SU GANG
SEON-YONG GANG
SEUNG-JUNG GANG
SE-YONG GANG
SI-JEONG GANG
SIN-JONG GANG
SIN-JUN GANG
SO-BONG GANG
SUN-GU GANG
SUN-GU GANG
SU-WON GANG
TAE-BONG GANG
TAE-BONG GANG
U-JUNG GANG
U-YONG GANG
U-YONG GANG
WON-YANG GANG
YEONG-SIK GANG
YONG-BEOM GANG
YONG-GI GANG
YONG-MAN GANG
YUN-HYEON GANG
ALBERT E GANN
VALENTINE R GANNON
RUFINO GARALDE
DALE T GARBER
ARTHUR D GARCIA
ARTHUR S GARCIA
DOMINGO GARCIA
EDDIE M GARCIA
EMILIO GARCIA
JOHN R GARCIA
JOSE E GARCIA
MANUEL L GARCIA
ORLANDO GARCIA
PAUL GARCIA
RAYNALDO C GARCIA
REGINALD J GARCIA
IRENE GARCIA-AYALA
RAFAEL GARCIA-OJEDA
ISABEL GARCIA-OQUENDO
CARLOS GARCIA-RIVERA
DEMETRIN GARCIA-RODRIGUEZ
FELIX GARCIA-RODRIGUEZ
LADON A GARDNER
ALBERT W GARLAND
ARVIL R GARNER
LESTER R GARNER
MAX F GARNER
STANLEY C GARNETT
ROGER W GARREPY
BOBBY R GARRETT
HARRY A GARRETT
BILLY E GARTIN
HUMBERTO GARZA
CHARLIE P GASKINS
ROLAND L GATES
THOMAS V GATES
WALLACE GAUDINIER
ARTHUR G GAULT
JAMES C GAUN
GERALD P GAUTHIER
CHARLES L GAY
JAMES H GAY
MICHAEL A GBUR
WILLIAM L GEARY
MARVIN C GEIGER
WILLARD F GEIVETT
PAUL E GENINO
CHARLES M GENTLE JR
WILLIAM D GENUNG
HOGAL M GEORGE
THOMAS C GEORGE
JAMES J GERAGHTY
JOSEPH GERCHMAN
KENNETH G GERHARD
ROBERT A GERLACH
HARLEY G GERTH
ROBERT H GERTSEN
CHARLES E GETTINGS
ERNEST E GETTS
YONG-HAE GEUM
ROBERT F GEYER
JOSEPH GIACOPELLI
FRANK J GIANITELLI
CARL W GIBBONS
CLIFFORD L GIBBS
CHARLES L GIBSON
DENNY J GIBSON
DON E GIBSON
DONALD D GIBSON
FRANK W GIBSON
GARRETT F GIBSON
HOWARD J GIBSON
LONNIE E GIBSON
ZOLLIE GIBSON
WILLIAM E GIFFEN
ALBERT P GIGUERE
GAP-SEON GIL
MAL-DONG GIL
SANG-CHUN GIL
BILLY M GILBERT
GARLAND GILBERT
JAMES H GILBERT
SYLVESTER E GILBERT
WILLIAM E GILBERT
BOBBY D GILL
JOHN H GILL
LOUIS M GILL
J W GILLAND
EVAN L GILLESPIE
WILLIAM M GILLIAND JR
EDWARD E GILLILAND
KNOTS GILMORE
WAYNE E GING
ROBERT L GINGER
ANDREW GIRARD
JAMES W GITTINGS JR
SALVATORE GIUSTO
WILBUR E GLACE
PETER GLADWELL JR
MICHAEL W GLASER
AUGUST J GLASMEIER
JOSEPH M GLAVINA
KENNETH H GLAWF
JACK D GLENN
LEONARD G GLICA
VERNON H GLIDDEN
ALPHONSO L GLOVER
DEOK-HONG GO
DO-HWAN GO
DONG-SUN GO
GAP-CHUL GO
GEUM-SEOK GO
GONG-I GO
GWANG-GEUN GO
HAE-JAE GO
HAN-CHEOL GO
HUI-YUN GO
HWA-SEOK GO
HYEONG-SU GO
HYE-SEOK GO
IN-YONG GO
I-YONG GO
JAE-BONG GO
JAE-JUNG GO
JANG-HWANG GO
JIN-IL GO
JONG-BEOM GO
JONG-SIL GO
JU-SIK GO
MAN-GYU GO
MAN-GYU GO
MI-MAN GO
MUN-GUK GO
SANG-BAEK GO
SANG-SIK GO
SEUNG-BOK GO
SI-CHAN GO
TAEK-GYU GO
YEONG-CHAE GO
YEONG-DAE GO
YEONG-HWA GO
YEONG-HWAN GO
YONG-SU GO
YONG-SU GO
JOHN M GODWIN
EDWIN GOEDE JR
RICHARD H GOERLICH
WILLIAM C GOETZ
WILLIAM O GOETZ
DONALD A GOGGINS
DONALD C GOKEL
WALTER T GOLDEN
MISTER GOLDMAN
LAWRENCE GOLDSTEIN
LEROY GOLDSTEIN
CHARLES P GOLISANO
BENJAMIN GOMEZ
DONG-GWANG GONG
DU-SEOK GONG
IL-SIK GONG
IN-PAL GONG
MAN-GAP GONG
OE-TAEK GONG
UI-HUI GONG
ALEX L GONZALES
DOMINGO J GONZALES
GEORGE C GONZALES
ROOSEVELT GONZALES
TORIBIO M GONZALES
ANASTACIO GONZALEZ
ARNOLD GONZALEZ
MANUEL Y GONZALEZ
ESTEBAN GONZALEZ-ABREU
JULIO J GONZALEZ-CALZADA
DEMETRIO GONZALEZ-CARDONA
RAMON A GONZALEZ-CRUZ
PABLO GONZALEZ-ENCARNACION
PEDRO G GONZALEZ-GARCIA
LEONIDES GONZALEZ-MARTINEZ
ISMAEL GONZALEZ-PIZARRO
JUAN A GONZALEZ-RAMIREZ
JUAN GONZALEZ-RIVERA
AMELIO GONZALEZ-SANTIAGO
DAVID GOOCH
THOMAS E GOOD
WILLIAM H GOOD
JOHN W GOODHEART
JOHN S GOODLIVE JR
THOMAS GOODLOE
GERALD W GOODNER
ANDREW J GOODWIN
BERT L GOODWIN
ROBERT J GOODWIN
ROBERT L GOODWIN
LEROY GOOSEN
ROBERT J GORA
EDWIN S GORAJ
CLYDE O GORDON
DAVID M GORDON
HOMER G GORDON
RAYMOND D GORMAN
WILLIAM C GORMLEY
EARL D GOSHORN
EDWARD J GOURINSKI
WILLIAM S GRABLE
ROBERT B GRACE III
REGINALD F GRADIAS
ALTON E GRAF
RENE GRAFALS-RIVERA
RODNEY F GRAFF
BILLY J GRAHAM
JAMES W GRAHAM
ROBERT L GRAHAM
LAWRENCE D GRANTHAM
JAMES GRAVELY
JACK N GRAVES
PAUL A GRAVES
JACK W GRAVLEY
ALFRED W B GRAY
BILLIE J GRAY
RICHARD E GRAY
DAVID A GRAYBEAL
DONALD R GRAYBEAL
ANTHONY P GRECCO
AL GREEN JR
BENNY L GREEN
BILLY F GREEN
DEMON C GREEN
GEORGE W GREEN
GROVER G GREEN
HERSCHEL D GREEN
HUESTON M GREEN
JOE C GREEN
LOWELL GREEN JR
RASTUS E GREEN
ROBERT G GREEN
ROBERT K GREEN
ROBERT R GREEN
TOM W GREEN
TOMAS A GREEN
WILLIAM E GREEN
WILLIE J GREEN
JEROME E GREENBERG
JAMES H GREENE
JOHN T GREENE
RICHARD D GREENE
JOSE GREEN-RODRIGUEZ
FRANCIS C GREENWOOD
FREDERIC W GREER
LESTER R GREER
PRESSGROVE GREER
WILLIAM J GREER
ROBERT L GREGGS
DONALD V GREGORY
FRED A GREGORY
JOE B GREGORY JR
RICHARD J GREGORY
ARTHUR O GRICE
WILLIAM H F GRIECHEN
EDWARD GRIEFENSTINE
CHARLIE L GRIFFETH
BRADLEY J GRIFFEY
HORACE A GRIFFIN
JAMES E GRIFFIN
VERBEL J GRIFFIN
WILLIE D GRIFFIS
WILLIAM S GRIFFITH
CLIFFORD J GRIGNON
BOYD F GRIM
CARL D GRIMES
JOSEPH E GRIMES JR
ROBERT H GRINSTEAD
LEONARD J GRISCONES
ROBERT W GRISSOM
WILLIAM J GROGAN
ROBERT B GROHMANN
ARTHUR GROOMS
WILLIE L GROOMS
JOHN J GROOT
NELSON T A GROULX
JAMES R GROVE
EUGENE M GRUBBS
ANTHONY C GRUZINSKI
AM-I GU
BON-HA GU
BON-WON GU
CHA-NANG GU
GANG-SU GU
GANG-SU GU
GYEONG-IL GU
HAE-YUN GU
JAE-DO GU
JAE-HOE GU
JAE-HYEON GU
JA-EUN GU
JA-IL GU
JA-IL GU
JA-SU GU
JA-YO GU
JEOM-YEONG GU
JU-SU GU
MYEONG-HOE GU
SIK-I GU
WON-HUI GU
WON-HUI GU
WON-JO GU
YEONG-HONG GU
YEON-SU GU
JOHN E GUERUE
HOWARTH I GUILFORD
PAUL E GUILL
MAN-SEOK GUK
TAE-YEOL GUK
BENJAMIN GULIZIA
WILLIAM K GUM
LEON GURFEIN
WALTER H GURLEY
ORVILLE E GUSTAFSON
PATRICK W GUTHRIE
FIDENCIO GUTIERREZ
GILBERT GUTIERREZ
LUCIO R GUTIERREZ
ANGEL GUTIERREZ-JIMENEZ
ANGEL GUTIERREZ-SUAREZ
WILLIAM L GUYTON
SALVADOR M GUZMAN
LEOVIGILDO GUZMAN-ROSARIO
JAMES S GUZZI JR
BOK-GEUN GWAK
BYEONG-GON GWAK
DONG-YEONG GWAK
DO-YEONG GWAK
GI-SU GWAK
JONG-GU GWAK
JONG-I GWAK
JONG-YONG GWAK
MAN-GON GWAK
RAK-GYU GWAK
RYUL-CHAN GWAK
SAM-WON GWAK
SANG-PIL GWAK
SEONG-GEUN GWAK
SEONG-SU GWAK
SU-MAN GWAK
TA-GWAN GWAK
YEONG-DO GWAK
YONG-AM GWAK
YUN-SEOP GWAK
BYEONG-YEONG GWON
DAL-MAN GWON
EON-JUNG GWON
GAP-SUL GWON
GEON-SANG GWON
HAN-SAENG GWON
HO-MUN GWON
HYEOK-DONG GWON
I-DONG GWON
IN-BEOM GWON
JAE-YUN GWON
JIN-JU GWON
JONG-HEON GWON
JONG-HO GWON
JUNG-HAN GWON
MAL-YONG GWON
MAN-SU GWON
MIN-NO GWON
MOK-SUL GWON
O-CHEONG GWON
O-GIL GWON
O-SEOK GWON
O-SUL GWON
SANG-BEOM GWON
SANG-HO GWON
SANG-OK GWON
SEOK-SIK GWON
SEONG-HAK GWON
SEONG-U GWON
SUN-GI GWON
SUN-GUK GWON
TAE-HO GWON
TAE-SEONG GWON
YANG-GWAN GWON
YEONG-BOK GWON
YEONG-DEOK GWON
YEONG-GIL GWON
YEONG-IK GWON
YEONG-TAEK GWON
YEONG-WON GWON
YU-DAE GWON
YU-HYEON GWON
CHANG-SUN GYE
WAN-JUN GYE
BOK-MAN HA
BONG-GEUN HA
BYEONG-NAM HA
CHA-SU HA
CHI-MUN HA
CHUN-HWA HA
DEOK-YONG HA
GI-SU HA
GWAN-IL HA
GWI-SEOK HA
GYU-TAEK HA
IN-DAE HA
JAE-SAM HA
JI-DAL HA
JIN-DO HA

JIN-HO HA
MAN-JONG HA
MYEONG-GU HA
O-GWON HA
SANG-TAE HA
SANG-UK HA
SEOK-GYU HA
TAE-BONG HA
YONG-CHAE HA
YONG-DEOK HA
ROBERT E HAACK
RAY A HABOURNE
DONALD E HABUL
BILLY A HADLEY
GEORGE J HADLEY
STEVEN P HAEG
HARRY N HAGADORN
DARWYN L HAGEN
WILLIAM A HAGER JR
CHARLES HAGERICH
YOSHIO HAGIWARA
BERNIE F HAGLER JR
ALLAN E HAGLUND
EDDIE HAGOOD JR
ALBERT W HAJDUK
HERMAN F HALE
ISAAC K HALE
PAUL HALE
CHARLES A HALEY
DONALD L HALFERTY
ABNER C HALL
ADAM H HALL
DWAINE HALL
GARLAND R HALL
HARRY R HALL
JERRY HALL JR
JOSEPH H HALL JR
LENDELL HALL
LEROY HALL
RAYMOND D HALL
VINCENT R HALL
WILLIAM E HALL
WALTER HALLAM
DARROW T HALLIGAN
ROBERT E HALLORAN
HERBERT J HALM
SEOK-HWAN HAM
TAE-HYEON HAM
YONG-HO HAM
DAVID V HAMAN
S R HAMBRICK
HERMAN HAMES
EDWARD T HAMILL
DONALD E HAMILTON
THOMAS A HAMILTON
FRED HAMLIN
SAMUEL C HAMLIN
ROBERT H HAMM
TOMMIE HAMMOCK
CLIFFORD HAMMOND
ROGER W HAMMOND JR
EMILE HAMPTON JR
LEROY HAMPTON JR
BOK-SEOK HAN
BOK-SU HAN
BONG-GI HAN
BYEONG-YUN HAN
CHA-BONG HAN
CHANG-DEOK HAN
CHAN-GI HAN
CHANG-SU HAN
CHA-SIK HAN
CHUNG-GEUN HAN
DAE-MIN HAN
DEOK-JEON HAN
DEOK-SEONG HAN
DEOK-SUN HAN
DONG-HWAN HAN
DONG-OK HAN
DO-SU HAN
GI-BONG HAN
GWANG-HUI HAN
GYO-YEONG HAN
HONG-DO HAN
HONG-JEON HAN
HYEONG-MO HAN
HYEONG-U HAN
HYEON-IL HAN
HYO-WON HAN
JEONG-HYEON HAN

JEONG-SEOK HAN
JEONG-SEOP HAN
JEONG-SEOP HAN
JEONG-SU HAN
JONG-SU HAN
JONG-TAEK HAN
NAM-DO HAN
O-GWON HAN
OK-DEUK HAN
ON-YONG HAN
SAM-GYU HAN
SANG-JE HAN
SANG-JU HAN
SEOK-RYONG HAN
SEONG-CHEON HAN
SEONG-GYU HAN
SO-SUL HAN
SU-BOK HAN
SU-CHEOL HAN
SU-NAM HAN
TAE-GEUN HAN
TAE-GIL HAN
TAE-SANG HAN
TAE-SEOK HAN
UI-DONG HAN
UI-SU HAN
WON-JUN HAN
WON-SUK HAN
YEONG-CHEOL HAN
YEONG-DONG HAN
YEONG-GYO HAN
YEONG-GYU HAN
YEONG-JIN HAN
YEONG-JO HAN
YEONG-SANG HAN
YEONG-SEOK HAN
YEONG-SEONG HAN
YEONG-SU HAN
YEONG-SUL HAN
YEONG-YEOM HAN
YONG-GWON HAN
YONG-SU HAN
CARLOS L HANCHETT
MILTON HANCOCK JR
WILLIAM J HANCOCK
BOBBY L HANDLIN
WALTER J HANES
JOHN T HANNA
JERRY B HANNAH
CLARENCE E HANNEN
ROBERT W HANNIGAN
JOHN W HANSARD
EDWARD C HANSON
LYLE E HANSON
MILNOR J HANSON
DANIEL W HANUS
GENE O HANZER
HOWARD M HARBIN
GORDON W HARCOURT
JOHN A HARDEN JR
VERNON C HARDIN
THURMOND C HARDISON
KENNETH L HARDWICK
JAMES W HARDY
LEON HARDY JR
RAY L HARDY
WILLIAM R HARDY
TOMMIE HARGES JR
ALAN HARGRAVE
OBIE E HARGROVE
RICHARD C HARGUS
WILSON B HARJO
GARY L HARLAN
HAROLD E HARLEY
CHARLIE HARMON
PAUL H HARMON
ROY B HARMON
ARTHUR L HARPEL
BILL F HARPER
CLAUDE L HARPER JR
EVERETTE C HARPER
JOSEPH T HARPER
ROBERT M HARPER
THOMAS M HARPER
DONALD F HARR
DANIEL C HARRINGTON
GEORGE W HARRINGTON
HENRY J HARRINGTON

ARVID J HARRIS
BOBBY R HARRIS
CLARENCE HARRIS JR
DONALD W HARRIS
HAROLD W HARRIS
JACK D HARRIS
JACK E HARRIS
JAMES A HARRIS
JAMES C HARRIS
JAMES G HARRIS
LEWIS A HARRIS
PARRION R HARRIS
RASTINE HARRIS
ROOSEVELT HARRIS
WILKIE HARRIS JR
WILLIAM D HARRIS
WILLIAM L HARRIS
WILLIAM L HARRIS
WILLIE L HARRIS
CHARLES HARRISON
HUBERT C HARRISON
OREN B HARRISON JR
ROBERT L HARRISON
DALE L HARSHBARGER
LAWRENCE J HARTLIEB
EDWARD J HARTZOLD
CHARLES G HARVEY
EARL D HARVEY
JOHN C HARVEY
LAWRENCE T HARVEY
DONALD F HASH
WARREN F HASKINS
GEORGE R HASLETT
JOHN T HASSELL
CHARLES HASTINGS
WILBUR D HASTINGS
ROY HATAWAY
EMBREE H HATCHER
LEROY G HAUGER
JUNIOR L HAVENS
CHARLES R HAWES
JAMES L HAWKINS
ROBERT C HAWKINS
WILSON HAWKINS JR
ROSCOE L HAWN
HOWARD V HAWSE
CLARENCE E HAWTHORNE
VERNON A HAWTHORNE
RYLAND E HAYDEN
ALBERT R HAYDOCK
ALFRED G HAYES
CECIL W HAYES
DOVER D HAYES
PETER S HAYES
FREDDYE L HAYGOOD
ELWOOD W HAYNES
PAUL HAYNES
WILLIAM C HAYNES
ROBERT A HAYS
JAMES B HAYSLETT
CARMON C HAYWOOD
HARKNESS W HAZELWOOD
OWEN F HEALEY
THOMAS J HEALY
CRAIG H HEARN
ROBERT L HEARN
EDSEL HEATHCOCK
WILLIE S HEATHERLY
KENNETH R HECK
LESTER A HECKER
HOWARD D HECTOR
BENJAMIN L HEDDEN
LOUIS M HEDIN
HERMAN HEDRICK
HOWARD E HEDRICK
ROY W HEDRICK
EARL W HEDRINGTON JR
DONALD O HEESEN
BOBBIE D HEFFNER
ARNOLD M HEGG
JAMES R HEILIGH
JOSEPH H HEINBACH
HENRY T HEINS
ORLINE W HELING
EURIAH HELMS
WARREN B HEMSTROUGHT
ROLAND A HENDERSHOT
ALBERT W HENDERSON

ARTHUR R HENDERSON
JAMES A HENDERSON
MORRIS HENDERSON
LOUIS B HENDREN
JAMES H HENDRICKS
OWEN W HENDRICKS
WILLIAM H HENDRICKS
BERTRAM B HENDRICKSON
HARVEY V HENDRICKSON
CHARLES R HENDRIX
RAYMOND L HENDRIX
JULIUS HENLEY JR
VERNON R HENNIGAN
LUVERN O HENNING
GERARD M HENRICH
CLIFTON D L HENRY
JERALD W HENRY
MICHAEL P HENRY
OTIS HENRY JR
ROBERT L HENRY
C B HENSLEY
COLLIE HENSON
ERNEST H HENSON
GLENN E HENSON
ROBERT E HENSON
WALTER L HENTZ
BOK HEO
BONG-CHUL HEO
CHEOL-GAP HEO
DEOK-GEUN HEO
GAP-CHEON HEO
GI-MAN HEO
GWAN HEO
GWANG-YEONG HEO
GYEONG-CHEOL HEO
GYEONG-DU HEO
HEON HEO
HO HEO
HUI HEO
I HEO
JEONG-SIL HEO
JEON-SEOK HEO
JONG-GAP HEO
JONG-SIK HEO
JUN HEO
MAN-SIK HEO
MO-JEONG HEO
MUN-BEOM HEO
MYEONG-RYUL HEO
SAM-BONG HEO
SANG-GWANG HEO
SEOK-GEUN HEO
SEOK-YONG HEO
SEONG-BIN HEO
SU-HWAN HEO
SU-JANG HEO
SU-YONG HEO
TAE-WON HEO
U-BONG HEO
YEONG-GWI HEO
YEONG-JUN HEO
YEON-SU HEO
YONG-SIK HEO
CLAYTON F HEPHNER
JESSIE E HERMOSILLO
NEAL R HERN
PAULINO E HERNAEZ
ANDRES HERNANDEZ
ANTHONY HERNANDEZ
CARLOS M HERNANDEZ
GUSTAVO HERNANDEZ
JOSE HERNANDEZ
JUAN G HERNANDEZ
ROBERT P HERNANDEZ
RUBEN HERNANDEZ
TRINIDAD HERNANDEZ
EDUVIGIS HERNANDEZ-GONZALEZ
JOSEPH M HERNDON
JULIAN HERRERA
BASIL H HERRHOLZ
JOHN P HERRMANN
PAUL E HERRON
ROXY A HERRON
LAVERNE M HETTENBACH
EUGENE J HEUMILLER
RICHARD D HICKEY
STERLING C HICKEY JR
ARVIL HICKS
CHARLES HICKS

ELLIS HICKS
HENRY L HICKS
JOHN E HICKS
NEWGAMES HICKS
EDWARD J HIGGINS
PAUL D HIGGINS
ALLEN HIGGS JR
KENNETH W HIGGS
GEORGE D HIGHBERGER
GILBERT R HIGUERA
HARRY S HILBURGER
HAROLD S HILDEBRAND
WILLIAM H HILDEBRAND
JOHN J HILGERSON JR
GEORGE E HILL
HERMAN E HILL
JAMES HILL JR
ROBERT HILL JR
ROBERT E HILL
ROBERT J HILL
ROBERT L HILL
JAMES D HILLE
VIRGIL C HILLIARD
GEORGE W HILTON
SELVEN HILTON
HENRY HIMMEL JR
DAVID C HINDMAN
SAM HINES
LEE R HINTON
LEE P HINTZ
HENRY G HIOTT
EDWARD K HIRAKAWA
DONALD C HIRN
GERALD M HIRONIMUS
EDMOND HITZIGER
WOODROW W HIXON
SHIGEO HIYANE
MOSES K HOAPILI JR
HOWARD R HOCE
LONNIE HOCKADAY
LESTER L HODGE
TOMMIE L HODGE
WILLIAM M HODGE
THEODORE R HODGES
WILLIAM E HODGES
HERBERT G HOEHN
DONALD L HOFFENKAMP
MARTIN J HOFFMAN
WILLIAM B HOFFMAN
WILLIAM R HOFFMAN
JAMES A HOFIUS
GERALD D HOFMEYER
RALPH L HOFSTETTER
BILLY R HOGAN
JOHN R HOGAN
ROBERT W HOGAN
FREDERICK W HOGERT
JAMES D HOGGATT
JAMES W HOGUE
HENRY E HOHNE
FREDDIE G HOIT
WALTER M HOJARA
BOBBY B HOLBROOK
GLENN P HOLENBECK
JOHN D HOLLAND
WAYNE R HOLLAND
JACK A HOLLARS
RICHARD R HOLLEY
DELBERT J HOLLIDAY
GLENN E HOLLINGSHEAD
ARTHUR W HOLLOWAY
JAMES A HOLLOWAY
PAUL G HOLLOWAY
SHERLYN HOLLOWAY
WILLIAM G HOLLOWAY
ALFRED L HOLM
JOHN W HOLMAN
GILBERT E HOLMES
JOHN E HOLMES
WILLARD B HOLMES
NATHAN HOLMON JR
RAYMOND H HOLSCH
HENRY E HOLT
CARL H HOLTHAM
TOMIO HONDA
AM-MUN HONG
BONG-SUN HONG
BYEONG-TAE HONG

7 ARMY

CHANG-SEOP HONG
DU-SEON HONG
GI-BONG HONG
GI-TAE HONG
GYEONG-HO HONG
HAN-MO HONG
IL-CHUL HONG
IN-HWAN HONG
JAE-BONG HONG
JAE-CHEOL HONG
JAE-JIN HONG
JIN-GYEOK HONG
JONG-HA HONG
JONG-MYEONG HONG
JONG-SIN HONG
JONG-SIN HONG
NAM-SEON HONG
OK-BONG HONG
PYEONG-HYEON HONG
SA-HYEON HONG
SEONG-BO HONG
SEONG-DO HONG
SEONG-GU HONG
SEONG-HAN HONG
SEONG-JIN HONG
SEONG-JUN HONG
SEONG-U HONG
SUN-GU HONG
SUN-HYEON HONG
TAE-HYEONG HONG
TAE-SUN HONG
UI-U HONG
U-SEONG HONG
YEONG-DAE HONG
YEONG-SEON HONG
YEONG-UI HONG
YONG-YEOP HONG
JAMES J HOOD
WILBERFORCE HOOD
ALFONSO E HOOKS
WILLIAM J HOOLIHAN
NILS V HOOTMAN
ELBERT L HOPES
JAMES R HOPKINS
BILLY E HOPPER
WILLIAM P HOPPER
MERWIN K HORN
ROBERT J HORNE
WILLIAM D HORNER
GLEN W HORNSBY
BILL HORTON
LOVIE L HORTON
HENRY G HORWATH
BILLY E HOUGH
ADELBERT R HOUSE
WINFIELD S HOUSE
WAYNE E HOUSER
ELDON E HOUSH
JAMES M HOUSTON
LONZO HOUSTON
KENNETH B HOVIS JR
CHARLES H HOWARD
EDDIE HOWARD JR
FRANK R HOWARD
JAMES A HOWARD JR
JAMES W HOWARD
WILLIAM T HOWARD
ZEBULON HOWARD
HAROLD HOWELL
LLOYD B HOWELL
LUTHER R HOWELL
GARY B HOWSE
EDWARD D HOWSER
ORVILLE C HOWZE
LESTER G HOYT
LELAND C HUCKS
JAMES L HUDDLESTON
WINSTON H
HUDGINS JR
CON D HUDNALL
LAMAR G HUDSON
GLENN E HUFFMAN
RUFUS G HUFFSTICKLER
BOBBY F HUGHES
CLAUDE E HUGHES
ELZIE F HUGHES
FLOYD W HUGHES
FRANKIE B HUGHES
JACK W HUGHES
JAMES L HUGHES

LEROY HUGHES
PHILIP T HUGHES
PHILLIP C HUGHES
ROY T HUGHES
WALTER L HUGHES
GARY F HULBURT
CHARLES O HULL
MAX R HUMBARGER
MELVIN J HUMES
BARNUM R HUMISTON
DOUGLAS E HUMPHREY
ELRIN M HUNDLEY
BYRON J HUNT
CHARLES E HUNT JR
DAVID J HUNT
LAWRENCE E HUNT
RICHARD HUNT
WILLIAM C HUNT
CHARLES O HUNTER
GERALD J HUNTER
HENRY H HUNTER
JAMES L HUNTER
JOE HUNTER
JAMES B HUNTLEY
ROBERT G HURLEY
DAVID A HURR
DONALD L HURST
HAROLD E HUTCHENS
DONALD L
HUTCHINSON
BARNEY E HUTCHISON
JACK W HUTCHISON
WILLIAM HUTNICK JR
ROBERT D HUTSON
JAMES A HUTTON
WILLIAM L HUYETTE
BO-GYEONG HWANG
BOK-GEUN HWANG
BOK-SU HWANG
BONG-JAE HWANG
BYEONG-HAN HWANG
BYEONG-RYEOL HWANG
BYEONG-SU HWANG
CHANG-GEUN HWANG
CHANG-HYEON HWANG
CHANG-HYEON HWANG
CHA-OK HWANG
CHA-SIK HWANG
CHEONG-SU HWANG
CHI-O HWANG
CHI-WON HWANG
CHUN-YEOP HWANG
DEOK-GYO HWANG
DO-SEOK HWANG
DU-HO HWANG
DU-HO HWANG
DU-IK HWANG
DU-YONG HWANG
GEUM-DEUK HWANG
GEUM-DONG HWANG
GIL-SU HWANG
GWANG-SAENG HWANG
GWAN-HYEON HWANG
GWAN-JO HWANG
GWAN-JO HWANG
GYU-BOK HWANG
GYU-HYEON HWANG
GYU-SEONG HWANG
HAK-YUN HWANG
HA-SU HWANG
HA-YEON HWANG
HEUNG-JU HWANG
IL-GYU HWANG
IN-HO HWANG
IN-HWAN HWANG
IN-RYONG HWANG
JAE-GUK HWANG
JAE-MUN HWANG
JEONG-SU HWANG
JIN-SEOK HWANG
JONG-PIL HWANG
JONG-SEOK HWANG
JU-WON HWANG
MI-JI HWANG
MYEONG-HO HWANG
PAN-SEOK HWANG
PIL-TAEK HWANG
RI-DONG HWANG
SAM-DOL HWANG
SANG-JU HWANG

SANG-MUN HWANG
SEOK-JO HWANG
SEONG-BOK HWANG
SEONG-HO HWANG
SEONG-YEOL HWANG
SEON-PIL HWANG
SEON-SU HWANG
SU-JIN HWANG
TAE-GEUN HWANG
TAE-GYU HWANG
TAE-O HWANG
UI-CHUL HWANG
UN-I HWANG
YEONG-DAE HWANG
YEONG-JU HWANG
YEONG-JU HWANG
YEONG-SIK HWANG
YONG-GAP HWANG
YONG-YEON HWANG
RAYMOND G HYATT
ROBERT J HYDE
CHUN-SIK HYEON
DEOK-I HYEON
GWON-MAN HYEON
GYEONG-UK HYEON
HONG-GWI HYEON
HUI-SEOK HYEON
JONG-GEUN HYEON
SANG-MAN HYEON
SUN-JE HYEON
WON-GEON HYEON
BRENDAN P HYLAND
ROBERT E HYNES
JOE W IBAY
DAVID W ICHO
MIGUEL IGARTUA JR
BOK-SUN IM
BOK-SUN IM
BYEONG-CHUN IM
BYEONG-CHUN IM
BYEONG-GEUN IM
BYEONG-PO IM
CHAE-HYEON IM
CHA-JONG IM
CHANG-GEUN IM
CHANG-HO IM
CHANG-SU IM
CHEOL-GYU IM
CHUN-SEOK IM
CHUN-WON IM
DAE-GYU IM
DAE-HYEON IM
DAE-SEONG IM
DAE-YONG IM
DONG-GEUN IM
GEUN-TAE IM
GIL-BONG IM
GIL-SU IM
GWANG-RYUL IM
GWANG-SEOK IM
GYEONG-HAK IM
GYU-HYEOK IM
HAK-BIN IM
HONG-GEUN IM
HUN-PYEONG IM
HYEONG-TAEK IM
HYEON-JUN IM
HYO-CHUL IM
HYO-SEUNG IM
IL-SIK IM
IN-CHEOL IM
IN-GYU IM
IN-GYU IM
IN-SU IM
JAE-MAN IM
JAE-SU IM
JA-GYEONG IM
JANG-GON IM
JEOM-AM IM
JEOM-BONG IM
JEOM-SU IM
JEONG-CHUN IM
JEONG-HO IM
JIN-BAE IM
JONG-CHAN IM
JONG-CHAN IM
JONG-GU IM
JONG-HWA IM
JONG-MU IM
JONG-UN IM

NO-SU IM
SA-BIN IM
SAM-TAEK IM
SANG-GAK IM
SANG-HO IM
SANG-O IM
SANG-TAE IM
SANG-UK IM
SEOK-JO IM
SUN-OK IM
SUN-SIK IM
SU-RYONG IM
TAE-GEUN IM
TAEK-SU IM
UI-GUN IM
UNG-BIN IM
U-SIK IM
YEONG-CHUNG IM
YEONG-HO IM
YEONG-SIK IM
YONG-HA IM
YONG-TAE IM
YUN-GI IM
YUN-JONG IM
UN-BOK IN
EDWARD INGRAM
GENE M INGRAM
GEORGE INGRAM
ANDERSON F INMAN
BILLY M IRBY
MALCOLM D IRELAND
CIPRIAN IRIZARRY-
RODRIQUEZ
DENNIS IRVING
BERNARD A ISAACS
ANTHONY T ISKIERKA
DAYTON F ISLEY
GUISEPPE ISOLANO
JOSEPH M ISOM
PAUL E ISRAEL
LESTER G IVANCICH
LACY C IVEY
DAVID JACKMON
BAILEY JACKSON JR
BOBBY J JACKSON
CALVIN JACKSON
DONALD L JACKSON
DOUGLAS G JACKSON
EARL K JACKSON
EUGENE L JACKSON
GENERAL E JACKSON
IRBY L JACKSON
JEFF D JACKSON
JOHN E JACKSON
JOHN T JACKSON
LAMAR J JACKSON JR
LAWRENCE JACKSON
LEROY A JACKSON
MILTON K JACKSON
ROBERT E JACKSON
RONALD M JACKSON
WILBURN JACKSON
WILLIAM JACKSON JR
WILLIAM T JACKSON
WILLIAM T JACKSON
GEORGE L JACOBS
HERBERT J JACOBS JR
ROBERT T JACOBS
RONALD D JACOBS
LEO W JACQUES
FELTON L JAMERSON
FRANK O JAMERSON
ALBERT JAMES JR
JOHNNIE L JAMES
WILLIAM R JAMES
WILLIAM R JAMES
HOWARD W JANES
BONG-GI JANG
BU-SEON JANG
BYEONG-GWON JANG
BYEONG-IL JANG
BYEONG-UI JANG
CHANG-GYU JANG
DAE-YEOL JANG
DAN-OK JANG
DEOK-SEONG JANG
DO-HYEON JANG
DONG-SIK JANG
DO-SEONG JANG
DO-YEOL JANG

DU-CHAN JANG
DU-HWAN JANG
DU-HWAN JANG
DU-SANG JANG
EUL-SUL JANG
EUL-SUL JANG
GANG-SU JANG
GI-BOK JANG
GI-DONG JANG
GI-HYEON JANG
GI-JUN JANG
GI-YEONG JANG
GI-YEONG JANG
GWANG-GYUN JANG
GYEONG-SIK JANG
GYEONG-SU JANG
GYEONG-SU JANG
GYEONG-WON JANG
HAK-SUK JANG
HA-SANG JANG
HO-CHUL JANG
HO-GEON JANG
HONG-SIK JANG
HONG-SIK JANG
HO-SEON JANG
HO-YEOL JANG
I-DEOK JANG
IK-CHUN JANG
IN-SIK JANG
IN-SU JANG
JAE-HAN JANG
JAE-HYEON JANG
JAE-SIK JANG
JAE-SIK JANG
JAE-YEO JANG
JANG-GIL JANG
JEONG-HU JANG
JEONG-SIK JANG
JI-BONG JANG
JI-BONG JANG
JI-HWA JANG
JIN-CHUL JANG
JIN-SANG JANG
JONG-HWAN JANG
JONG-SEOP JANG
JUNG-HO JANG
MAN-HWA JANG
MU-HYEON JANG
MYEONG-HWAN JANG
MYEONG-SU JANG
MYEONG-SU JANG
NAK-BONG JANG
RAK-SANG JANG
SAM-JUNG JANG
SANG-DEOK JANG
SANG-GYU JANG
SE-BONG JANG
SE-HWAN JANG
SEOK JANG
SEOK-YONG JANG
SEONG-GYU JANG
SIN-SEON JANG
SO-YONG JANG
SU-BONG JANG
SUN-JO JANG
TAE-HO JANG
TAEK-BONG JANG
TAE-OK JANG
TAE-OK JANG
TAE-SU JANG
YEONG-DEOK JANG
YEONG-DEOK JANG
YEONG-GIL JANG
YEONG-MYEONG JANG
YONG-DAE JANG
YONG-SEOK JANG
YONG-SU JANG
YUN-HWI JANG
YUN-HYEOK JANG
RICHARD T
JANKOWSKI
RUDY JANN
JOHN A JANSKY
HENRY JANSMA
JAMES JANUARY
THOMAS R JARRARD
CALVIN C JARRELL JR
MONT JARRELL
DONALD R JARVIS
RAYMOND F JARVIS

8 ARMY

CARTER W JAUDON JR
EDWARD R JAYNES
CHEOL-YONG JE
HYEON-GYU JE
HYEON-SU JE
IL-SU JE
JIN-GYEONG JE
MYEONG-GUK JE
PAN-CHUL JE
SEOK-I JE
SIN-GEUN JE
SUN-GYU JE
YEONG-YEOP JE
HARRY F JEFFERSON
JOHN D JEFFERSON
LOYD JEFFERSON
ROBERT L JEFFREY
JOSE D JEMENTE
CHARLES JEMISON
ALBIN R JENKINS
CARL C JENKINS
GEORGE W JENKINS
HOWARD L JENKINS
KERMIT E JENKINS
WILLIAM L JENKINS
DELBERT G JENNETTE
ELIJAH L JENNINGS
RALPH JENNINGS JR
KENNETH L JENSEN
RICHARD A JENSEN
DONALD P JENTZSCH
BONG-MUN JEON
BYEONG-YEON JEON
DAL-MUN JEON
DEOK-GEUN JEON
DO-GAP JEON
EO-SIK JEON
EUNG-CHUL JEON
GEON-I JEON
GWON-MUN JEON
GYEONG-ROE JEON
HYANG-SIK JEON
HYEON-SIK JEON
I-SU JEON
JAE-HO JEON
JAE-SUL JEON
JONG-MIN JEON
MAN-SUL JEON
PYEONG-SIK JEON
SAM-MAN JEON
SEOK-GWI JEON
SU-SEOK JEON
TAE-WON JEON
UK-CHAN JEON
WON-YEONG JEON
YEONG-JONG JEON
YONG-DAL JEON
YONG-DONG JEON
YONG-EON JEON
YONG-GON JEON
YONG-SU JEON
YUN-PIL JEON
BAEK-HAK JEONG
BOK-JUN JEONG
BOK-JUNG JEONG
BOK-MUK JEONG
BONG-HWAN JEONG
BONG-SAM JEONG
BONG-SIK JEONG
BO-YEONG JEONG
BYEONG-GYUN JEONG
CHA-MO JEONG
CHANG-GAP JEONG
CHANG-JO JEONG
CHANG-RAK JEONG
CHANG-SEON JEONG
CHANG-YONG JEONG
CHEOL-SU JEONG
CHEOL-YEONG JEONG
CHEON-DEOK JEONG
CHEON-DEUK JEONG
CHI-DU JEONG
CHUN-MO JEONG
DAE-HAN JEONG
DAL-YEONG JEONG
DEOK-HYEON JEONG
DEOK-MAN JEONG
DEOK-SANG JEONG
DEOK-SU JEONG
DO-JAE JEONG
DONG-GI JEONG
DONG-GYU JEONG
DONG-GYU JEONG
DONG-JUN JEONG
DONG-WON JEONG
DONG-YUN JEONG
DU-SAENG JEONG
DU-SEOK JEONG
DU-SIK JEONG
EOK-MAN JEONG
EUL-SAENG JEONG
GAE-CHUL JEONG
GAE-I JEONG
GAP-DEOK JEONG
GAP-SEOK JEONG
GEUM-SU JEONG
GEUM-SU JEONG
GI-BAEK JEONG
GI-BONG JEONG
GI-CHEON JEONG
GI-HO JEONG
GIL-BONG JEONG
GIL-SU JEONG
GIL-YONG JEONG
GI-RYONG JEONG
GI-SU JEONG
GI-TAE JEONG
GI-WAN JEONG
GI-YEONG JEONG
GI-YONG JEONG
GO-CHEON JEONG
GU-CHEOL JEONG
GUK-SEOK JEONG
GU-MIN JEONG
GWI-HWAN JEONG
GYEONG-CHUL JEONG
GYU-BOK JEONG
GYU-BONG JEONG
GYU-CHEOL JEONG
GYU-HWA JEONG
GYU-JU JEONG
HAE-GEUN JEONG
HAE-SANG JEONG
HAE-SU JEONG
HAE-UN JEONG
HA-GYO JEONG
HAK-SEONG JEONG
HAK-SU JEONG
HAK-U JEONG
HAK-YONG JEONG
HAN-GWON JEONG
HAN-JIN JEONG
HA-UK JEONG
HO-DEOK JEONG
HO-GI JEONG
HONG-RYUL JEONG
HONG-TAEK JEONG
HONG-U JEONG
HWA-SIK JEONG
HYEON-DAE JEONG
HYEONG-SUN JEONG
HYEON-GUK JEONG
HYEON-JO JEONG
HYEON-JO JEONG
HYEON-SEOK JEONG
HYO-GEUN JEONG
IL-JEON JEONG
IL-RANG JEONG
IL-SAENG JEONG
IN-HO JEONG
IN-HO JEONG
IN-HONG JEONG
IN-JO JEONG
IN-SU JEONG
IN-SUL JEONG
IN-SUL JEONG
IN-TAE JEONG
JAE-CHEOL JEONG
JAE-CHEON JEONG
JAE-HWA JEONG
JAE-HYEON JEONG
JAE-MAN JEONG
JAE-SEOK JEONG
JAE-SIK JEONG
JAE-SU JEONG
JAE-SUL JEONG
JAE-SUL JEONG
JAE-TAE JEONG
JAE-YEOL JEONG
JAE-YONG JEONG
JANG-PYO JEONG
JEONG-GEUN JEONG
JEONG-GEUN JEONG
JEONG-HO JEONG
JEONG-SEOK JEONG
JEONG-SU JEONG
JEON-SIK JEONG
JIN-AN JEONG
JIN-BONG JEONG
JIN-BU JEONG
JIN-DEOK JEONG
JIN-EUNG JEONG
JIN-GIL JEONG
JIN-GU JEONG
JIN-HO JEONG
JIN-HWAN JEONG
JIN-HYEONG JEONG
JIN-SEON JEONG
JI-TAEK JEONG
JO-MUK JEONG
JU-NAM JEONG
JUNG-GEUN JEONG
JUN-MIN JEONG
JUN-WON JEONG
JU-SEONG JEONG
MAN-CHAE JEONG
MAN-CHANG JEONG
MAN-DEUK JEONG
MUN-CHEOL JEONG
MUN-JO JEONG
MYEONG-AM JEONG
MYEONG-SEOK JEONG
NAM-JUN JEONG
NO-SANG JEONG
PAN-JU JEONG
PAN-SIK JEONG
PYEONG-NAN JEONG
SAM-DO JEONG
SAM-RYONG JEONG
SAM-SIK JEONG
SAM-SIK JEONG
SAN-AM JEONG
SANG-DEOK JEONG
SANG-GYU JEONG
SANG-JO JEONG
SANG-RAK JEONG
SANG-RYE JEONG
SANG-SU JEONG
SANG-TAE JEONG
SANG-TAE JEONG
SEOK-GU JEONG
SEOK-JO JEONG
SEOK-SU JEONG
SEONG-DO JEONG
SEONG-GYU JEONG
SEONG-GYU JEONG
SEONG-GYU JEONG
SEONG-HWA JEONG
SEONG-MUN JEONG
SI-HO JEONG
SI-HO JEONG
SI-YONG JEONG
SO-SEOK JEONG
SU-BOK JEONG
SU-DO JEONG
SUN-GEON JEONG
SUN-GIL JEONG
SU-YEONG JEONG
TAE-BEOM JEONG
TAE-DONG JEONG
TAE-GYU JEONG
TAE-GYU JEONG
TAE-HO JEONG
TAE-HO JEONG
TAE-HONG JEONG
TAE-HUN JEONG
TAE-HWAN JEONG
TAEK-I JEONG
TAEK-SU JEONG
TAE-SU JEONG
TAE-SU JEONG
TAE-YEONG JEONG
UI-JO JEONG
UI-TAEK JEONG
U-JU JEONG
UN-IL JEONG
UN-JANG JEONG
U-SU JEONG
U-SU JEONG
WON-CHEOL JEONG
WON-CHEOL JEONG
WON-GI JEONG
WON-JO JEONG
WON-MU JEONG
WON-PYO JEONG
WON-SEONG JEONG
WON-SIK JEONG
YANG-GI JEONG
YEONG-BOK JEONG
YEONG-BOK JEONG
YEONG-GI JEONG
YEONG-GYU JEONG
YEON-GI JEONG
YEONG-SEOK JEONG
YEONG-SEOP JEONG
YEONG-SU JEONG
YEONG-SU JEONG
YEONG-SUL JEONG
YEONG-TAEK JEONG
YEON-SEOK JEONG
YONG-GI JEONG
YONG-GU JEONG
YONG-HA JEONG
YONG-JO JEONG
YONG-SEOK JEONG
YU-GU JEONG
YUN-BONG JEONG
YUN-JO JEONG
HARLAN R JEPPSON
DONALD W JERMAN
JAMES L C JETER
KARL R JETTER
BONG-HO JI
BYEONG-TAE JI
GWAN-SU JI
HYEONG-GU JI
JEONG-CHUN JI
JONG-BAE JI
NIN-HO JI
TAEK-YEONG JI
YEONG-DU JI
YEON-GIL JI
YEONG-SU JI
YUN-SIK JI
ISMAEL JIMENEZ-NIEVES
BONG-SU JIN
CHEON-GIL JIN
DU-SAM JIN
GIL-SANG JIN
GWANG-UN JIN
GYEONG-CHANG JIN
GYEONG-DO JIN
HWA-JUN JIN
I-JUN JIN
JEONG-BOK JIN
JEONG-HYEON JIN
JEONG-MO JIN
JEONG-SEOK JIN
JIN-DEUK JIN
MUN-SANG JIN
NAM-IL JIN
SAM-MUN JIN
SEOK-BOK JIN
SEOK-JU JIN
SEONG-GIL JIN
SEON-GYU JIN
SUN-HO JIN
YONG-GEUN JIN
BOK-DONG JO
BOK-MAN JO
BONG-HYEON JO
BONG-MUN JO
BONG-SEOK JO
BYEONG-GEUN JO
BYEONG-GYUN JO
BYEONG-JE JO
BYEONG-SEON JO
BYEONG-WAN JO
BYEONG-YEOL JO
CHANG-GU JO
CHANG-JE JO
CHEOL-HYEONG JO
CHEOL-JU JO
DAL-YEONG JO
DONG-CHEOL JO
DONG-HWAN JO
EUNG-SU JO
EUNG-SU JO
GANG SIK JO
GEUM-ROE JO
GI-HU JO
GI-SANG JO
GWANG-HWAN JO
GWAN-GU JO
GWI-SEOK JO
GYEONG-GU JO
GYEONG-JE JO
GYU-CHAN JO
GYU-DONG JO
GYU-HWAN JO
GYU-HYEON JO
GYU-JEONG JO
GYU-MUN JO
GYU-SANG JO
HANG-DONG JO
HAN-JE JO
HEUNG-GEUN JO
HEUNG-SIK JO
HO-JE JO
HONG-CHEOL JO
HONG-SEON JO
HUI-HAN JO
HWA-CHUN JO
HWA-SEOK JO
HYEONG-SU JO
IL-BONG JO
IL-DO JO
IL-JE JO
JEONG-GAE JO
JEONG-JE JO
JEONG-JE JO
JEONG-JO JO
JEONG-YEOL JO
JIN-GU JO
JONG-GIL JO
JONG-SIK JO
JUNG-JAE JO
JUNG-JIN JO
MAN-GYU JO
MI-GAP JO
MYEONG-GI JO
MYEONG-HWAN JO
MYEONG-RYONG JO
MYEONG-YONG JO
MYEON-HAENG JO
OE-SEOP JO
OK-GYU JO
OK-HAENG JO
OK-RYONG JO
PAL-BONG JO
PIL-JONG JO
PIL-YEONG JO
SAM-BONG JO
SAM-JAE JO
SAM-TAEK JO
SANG-DAE JO
SANG-RAE JO
SANG-YUN JO
SEOK-BOK JO
SEOK-YEONG JO
SEON-DONG JO
SEONG-BAE JO
SEONG-HAK JO
SEONG-HWAN JO
SEONG-JAE JO
SEONG-JIN JO
SEONG-RIM JO
SEONG-WON JO
SEONG-YONG JO
SEON-JE JO
SI-SEOK JO
SSANG-YONG JO
SU-JE JO
SU-MAN JO
SUN-GIL JO
SUN-HO JO
SUN-HWA JO
SUN-JE JO
TAEK-YUN JO
TO-YONG JO
WON-GYU JO
WON-GYUN JO
YANG-HYEONG JO
YEONG-BONG JO
YEONG-CHUL JO
YEONG-GI JO
YEONG-HO JO
YEONG-HO JO
YEONG-HWAN JO
YEONG-HYEON JO

9 ARMY

YEONG-JIN JO
YEONG-SIK JO
YEONG-SIK JO
YONG-BAEK JO
YONG-DAE JO
YONG-DEOK JO
YONG-DEOK JO
YONG-GIL JO
YONG-GU JO
YONG-GWON JO
YONG-JU JO
YONG-MUN JO
YONG-O JO
YONG-SANG JO
YONG-SEOK JO
YONG-SEON JO
YONG-SEOP JO
YONG-TAEK JO
YONG-WAN JO
YU-BONG JO
YUN-TAEK JO
JAMES L JOE
CALEB JOHNKINS JR
FRANK R JOHNS
MORRIS W JOHNS
ALFRED L JOHNSON
ANDREW JOHNSON JR
ARTHUR O JOHNSON
ARTHUR W JOHNSON
BEN JOHNSON
BOBBY L JOHNSON
CARL W JOHNSON
CECIL E JOHNSON
DONALD M JOHNSON
EARL N JOHNSON
EUGENE JOHNSON
EUGENE V JOHNSON
FRED A JOHNSON
FRED S JOHNSON
FREDERICK JOHNSON
GRANVILLE K JOHNSON
HARRY W JOHNSON JR
HENRY JOHNSON
JAY D JOHNSON
JOHN E JOHNSON
JOHN H JOHNSON
JOSEPH JOHNSON
LEE G JOHNSON
MACK D N JOHNSON
MERTON R JOHNSON
MILTON E JOHNSON
NATHANIEL B JOHNSON
NORMAN C JOHNSON
OLIN L JOHNSON
ROBERT JOHNSON JR
ROBERT D JOHNSON
ROBERT F JOHNSON
SELDON T JOHNSON
SIDNEY L JOHNSON
THEODORE R JOHNSON
THOMAS M JOHNSON
TRUMAN E JOHNSON
VERNON V JOHNSON
WALLACE L JOHNSON
WARREN E JOHNSON
GEORGE E JOHNSTON
GERALD W JOHNSTON
WILLIAM R JOHNSTON
ROY T JOHR
JOSEPH E JOLLEY
ALBERT T JONES
ANDREW W JONES
ANTHONY J JONES
BASKIL JONES
CHARLIE JONES
DELMAN J JONES
EUGENE JONES
GEORGE K JONES
GLEN D JONES
JAMES D JONES
JAMES E JONES
JAMES L JONES
JESSE JONES JR
JESSE D JONES
JESSIE L JONES
JOSEPH JONES
JOSEPH JONES
LESLIE M JONES
LEWIS J JONES
MERRILL A JONES

MILARD F JONES
MOSES JONES JR
OSBORN JONES
RAY M JONES
ROBERT J JONES
RONNIEMORE A JONES
RUSSELL A JONES
THOMAS E JONES
WILLIAM C JONES JR
WILLIAM D JONES
WILLIAM J JONES
NEIL E JOPPIE
ARCHIE A JORDAN
EUGENE JORDAN
JAMES JORDAN
LEWIS P JORDAN
EDWARD V JORGENSEN
JODIE A JORGENSON
FRANCIS R JOSEPH
WILLIAM JOSEPH
JAMES O JOYCE JR
BARNABAS JOYNER
EDWIN A JOYNER
BONG-HO JU
BONG-SIK JU
BYEONG-MAN JU
CHANG-DON JU
CHANG-SUL JU
CHI-GU JU
DEOK-YONG JU
GI-HUI JU
GIL-SIN JU
GWANG-DEUK JU
GYEONG-HOE JU
GYU-SEON JU
JAE-YUN JU
JEONG-SU JU
JIN-SU JU
JUN-DEUK JU
MAENG-DEOK JU
MAN-JIN JU
MUN-SIK JU
SANG-RAK JU
SEOK-NO JU
SEONG-HO JU
YUN-JONG JU
ESTEBAN JUAREZ
DANIEL S JUDGE
DENZIL L JUDY
WILSON L JUNEAU
CARL F JUNKER
SYLVESTER J JUREK
BOHDAN JURKIW
JOHN J JURMU
LAWRENCE A JUSTI
ALVIS JUSTICE
ROLLIN J KAAT
DENVER A KAIN
HASKELL KAIZERMAN
EUGENE M KALIN
HERBERT K KALINO
NORMAN L KAMINGA
ALBERT KAMINSKY
BENJAMIN S KAMOKU
FRED T KANEKURA
BILLIE G KANELL
CHARLES G KANIATOBE
JOSEPH M KANNEY
RICHARD S KANOSKI
ANTHONY KAPFENSTEINER
MANFRED KAPP
ERNEST H KAPPELMANN JR
ROBERT L KAPPENMAN
ROBERT C KARPINEN
JAMES H KASINGER
LEO L KASSELMAN
JOHN L KATERMAN
FRANK KATO
SAMUEL K KAUHANE JR
WILLIAM M KAWASHIMA
JAMES A KEARNEY
KENNETH L KEELING
JUNIOR D KEEN
FREDERICK KEENE JR
GEORGE P KEENEY
ELMER W KEESEE JR
CARL KEETH JR

THOMAS F KEHOE
FRANCIS M KEIFER JR
HAROLD A KEIRAN
CHARLES C KEISER
EUEL J KEITH
LESTER R KEITH
SEEBE J KEITH
GUS KEKIS
BASIL KEKLAK
DAVID K KELIIKULI
JOHN D KELLEHER
JOHN F KELLEHER
EDWARD B KELLER
JOHN F KELLER JR
RICHARD D KELLER
ROBERT W KELLER
BILLIE F KELLEY
CHARLES KELLEY JR
GEORGE A KELLEY
MARVIN O KELLEY
ROBERT E KELLEY
ROBERT G KELLEY
TOMMY R KELLEY
WESLEY R KELLEY
BURLIN V KELLIS
LEO H KELLNER
BERNARD L KELLOGG
AUBREY H KELLY
CHARLES KELLY JR
JOHN H KELLY
THOMAS KELLY
THOMAS J KELLY
WILLIAM F KELLY
WILLIAM W KELLY
ROBERT J KELP
RAYMOND L KEMP JR
ELVIS M KEMPER
RICHARD KENDALL
KELLY K KENDRICK
CARLON F KENNEDY
DONALD P KENNEDY
ROBERT L KENNEDY
WILLIAM C KENNEDY
LLEWELLYN E KENNESON
KENNETH W KENSLOW
BILLIE F KENT
PAUL B KENTON
WAYNE KENTON
DANNY J KEOGH
CHARLES F KERBER
MAXIMO KERCADO-FEBRES
DONALD A KERN
JAMES P KERNEY
THOMAS F KERNS
LESTER P KERR
WILLIAM R KERR
LAWRENCE H KESSICK
ELVIN L KETCHUM
PINKNEY R KETCHUM
SAMUEL L KETCHUM
ORBIN KEYS
CARL R KEYSER
JAMES M KIDWELL
DANIEL J KIERNAN
RICHARD A KILE
CLARENCE A KILLIAN
LEO E KILLINGSWORTH
FRANK R KILROY
BAEK-SEOK KIM
BAE-SEOK KIM
BAE-SEON KIM
BANG-U KIM
BAN-SEOK KIM
BOK-DONG KIM
BOK-GU KIM
BOK-GYU KIM
BOK-GYUN KIM
BOK-I KIM
BOK-MAN KIM
BOK-RYEON KIM
BOK-SIK KIM
BOK-SIK KIM
BOK-SU KIM
BOK-YONG KIM
BONG-CHUL KIM
BONG-DU KIM
BONG-GON KIM
BONG-GYU KIM
BONG-HWAN KIM

BONG-JO KIM
BONG-JO KIM
BONG-MUN KIM
BONG-RYUL KIM
BONG-RYUL KIM
BONG-SEON KIM
BONG-SIK KIM
BONG-SU KIM
BONG-YUL KIM
BU-AN KIM
BYEONG-CHAE KIM
BYEONG-DU KIM
BYEONG-GEUN KIM
BYEONG-GIL KIM
BYEONG-GON KIM
BYEONG-HO KIM
BYEONG-HWAN KIM
BYEONG-MUN KIM
BYEONG-SU KIM
BYEONG-SU KIM
BYEONG-U KIM
CHA-BOK KIM
CHA-BONG KIM
CHA-GU KIM
CHA-MAN KIM
CHAN-BAE KIM
CHAN-CHUN KIM
CHANG-BAN KIM
CHANG-CHEOL KIM
CHANG-DONG KIM
CHANG-GEUN KIM
CHANG-GYU KIM
CHANG-GYU KIM
CHANG-GYU KIM
CHANG-GYU KIM
CHANG-HO KIM
CHANG-MYEONG KIM
CHAN-GON KIM
CHANG-SEOK KIM
CHANG-SIK KIM
CHANG-SUL KIM
CHANG-UK KIM
CHANG-UN KIM
CHANG-WON KIM
CHAN-GWON KIM
CHANG-YEOL KIM
CHANG-YUL KIM
CHAN-I KIM
CHAN-JUNG KIM
CHAN-SEOK KIM
CHAN-SEON KIM
CHAN-SIK KIM
CHAN-SU KIM
CHAN-SU KIM
CHA-SUK KIM
CHEOL KIM
CHEOL-GEUN KIM
CHEOL-GON KIM
CHEOL-GON KIM
CHEOL-RYONG KIM
CHEOL-SU KIM
CHEOL-SU KIM
CHEON-BAE KIM
CHEON-I KIM
CHEON-IL KIM
CHEON-MAN KIM
CHEON-MAN KIM
CHEON-SEOK KIM
CHEON-SIK KIM
CHEON-U KIM
CHI-JO KIM
CHIL-SU KIM
CHIL-YONG KIM
CHIL-YONG KIM
CHI-MIN KIM
CHI-SAN KIM
CHO-YEON KIM
CHUN-DEOK KIM
CHUNG-HO KIM
CHUNG-JANG KIM
CHUNG-RYANG KIM
CHUN-PYO KIM
CHUN-SIK KIM
CHUN-SIK KIM
DAE-BOK KIM
DAE-GEUN KIM
DAE-HOE KIM
DAE-HUI KIM
DAE-IL KIM
DAE-JUN KIM

DAE-JUN KIM
DAE-RO KIM
DAE-SEON KIM
DAE-SIK KIM
DAE-SU KIM
DAE-SUK KIM
DAL-GEUN KIM
DAL-JU KIM
DAL-SU KIM
DAL-YONG KIM
DEOK-CHUL KIM
DEOK-HO KIM
DEOK-IL KIM
DEOK-JIN KIM
DEOK-JO KIM
DEOK-MAN KIM
DEOK-MAN KIM
DEOK-SANG KIM
DEOK-SEONG KIM
DEOK-SEOP KIM
DEOK-SU KIM
DEOK-SU KIM
DEOK-SUL KIM
DEOK-WON KIM
DEOK-YEON KIM
DEUK-CHEON KIM
DEUK-GIL KIM
DEUK-SIL KIM
DO-HWAN KIM
DONG-AM KIM
DONG-CHEOL KIM
DONG-CHUL KIM
DONG-DEOK KIM
DONG-DEOK KIM
DONG-DEUK KIM
DONG-GEUN KIM
DONG-GON KIM
DONG-GU KIM
DONG-GU KIM
DONG-GYU KIM
DONG-GYU KIM
DONG-GYU KIM
DONG-HA KIM
DONG-HO KIM
DONG-HWA KIM
DONG-I KIM
DONG-IN KIM
DONG-JE KIM
DONG-JIN KIM
DONG-JUN KIM
DONG-MIN KIM
DONG-O KIM
DONG-SEON KIM
DONG-SEON KIM
DONG-SEONG KIM
DONG-SEOP KIM
DONG-SU KIM
DONG-SU KIM
DONG-SUL KIM
DONG-SUL KIM
DONG-SUN KIM
DO-SAENG KIM
DO-SEON KIM
DO-WON KIM
DO-YA KIM
DO-YEONG KIM
DO-YEONG KIM
DO-YUL KIM
DU-AM KIM
DU-BAEK KIM
DU-CHEOL KIM
DU-JEON KIM
DU-MAN KIM
DU-MAN KIM
DU-SEON KIM
DU-SIK KIM
DU-SU KIM
DU-SU KIM
DU-WON KIM
DU-YEON KIM
EUL-GU KIM
EUL-JUN KIM
EUL-JUN KIM
EUL-YONG KIM
EUN-CHUN KIM
EUN-DAE KIM
EUNG-CHEOL KIM
EUNG-CHUL KIM
EUNG-DAE KIM
EUNG-DU KIM

10 ARMY

EUN-GI KIM
EUNG-JIN KIM
EUNG-JIN KIM
EUNG-YONG KIM
GAP-CHUL KIM
GAP-CHUN KIM
GAP-DEOK KIM
GAP-MYEONG KIM
GAP-OK KIM
GAP-SAENG KIM
GAP-SEON KIM
GAP-SU KIM
GAP-SU KIM
GAP-UN KIM
GAP-YEON KIM
GEOL-RYONG KIM
GEUM-SEOK KIM
GEUN-JU KIM
GEUN-OK KIM
GEUN-TAE KIM
GI-BOK KIM
GI-BONG KIM
GI-BONG KIM
GI-DEUK KIM
GI-DONG KIM
GI-HAK KIM
GI-HO KIM
GI-HWAN KIM
GI-HWAN KIM
GI-IN KIM
GI-JUN KIM
GIL-CHO KIM
GIL-HYEONG KIM
GIL-JO KIM
GIL-MAN KIM
GIL-SANG KIM
GIL-SUN KIM
GIL-YONG KIM
GI-RYONG KIM
GI-SAENG KIM
GI-SAENG KIM
GI-SANG KIM
GI-SIK KIM
GI-SU KIM
GI-SU KIM
GI-SU KIM
GI-TAE KIM
GI-TAEK KIM
GI-YEOL KIM
GI-YONG KIM
GI-YONG KIM
GI-YONG KIM
GO-BONG KIM
GONG-SU KIM
GU-HO KIM
GU-HONG KIM
GUK-JU KIM
GU-MAN KIM
GUN-MO KIM
GWANG-CHEON KIM
GWANG-CHUL KIM
GWANG-GON KIM
GWANG-HAN KIM
GWANG-HWAN KIM
GWANG-I KIM
GWANG-JIN KIM
GWANG-O KIM
GWANG-SU KIM
GWANG-SU KIM
GWANG-SU KIM
GWANG-SUL KIM
GWANG-YEOL KIM
GWAN-HA KIM
GWAN-SU KIM
GWI-BOK KIM
GWI-BONG KIM
GWI-HWAN KIM
GWI-SU KIM
GYEONG-BOK KIM
GYEONG-DAL KIM
GYEONG-DEOK KIM
GYEONG-DEOK KIM
GYEONG-DEUK KIM
GYEONG-DO KIM
GYEONG-HO KIM
GYEONG-HONG KIM
GYEONG-HUI KIM
GYEONG-HUN KIM
GYEONG-HWA KIM
GYEONG-IL KIM

GYEONG-JO KIM
GYEONG-JONG KIM
GYEONG-MAN KIM
GYEONG-RYUL KIM
GYEONG-SEOP KIM
GYEONG-SU KIM
GYEONG-TAE KIM
GYEONG-YEON KIM
GYEONG-YONG KIM
GYO-BAEK KIM
GYO-DEOK KIM
GYO-DO KIM
GYO-SUN KIM
GYU-BOK KIM
GYU-GYUN KIM
GYU-JUN KIM
GYUN-HUI KIM
HA-DAN KIM
HAE-DO KIM
HAE-DU KIM
HAE-GU KIM
HAENG-YONG KIM
HAE-SAN KIM
HAE-SIK KIM
HAE-UN KIM
HAE-YONG KIM
HAE-YONG KIM
HA-HWAN KIM
HA-HYEON KIM
HAK-GI KIM
HAK-GON KIM
HAK-JE KIM
HAK-RYUL KIM
HAK-SEON KIM
HAK-SU KIM
HAK-SUL KIM
HAK-SUN KIM
HAN-BYEONG KIM
HAN-CHUL KIM
HAN-GI KIM
HAN-GI KIM
HAN-GON KIM
HAN-RYUL KIM
HAN-SANG KIM
HAN-SEON KIM
HAN-SIK KIM
HAN-SU KIM
HAN-TAEK KIM
HA-WON KIM
HEUNG-CHAN KIM
HEUNG-GU KIM
HEUNG-MAN KIM
HEUNG-NAK KIM
HEUNG-SIK KIM
HEUNG-SUL KIM
HEUNG-SUL KIM
HEUNG-TAEK KIM
HO-CHAN KIM
HOE-GEUN KIM
HO-GI KIM
HO-JEONG KIM
HO-JIN KIM
HO-JUNG KIM
HONG-BAE KIM
HONG-BEOM KIM
HONG-BIN KIM
HONG-EUN KIM
HONG-GEUN KIM
HONG-GWAN KIM
HONG-GYU KIM
HONG-JIP KIM
HONG-JIP KIM
HONG-SEOK KIM
HONG-YEONG KIM
HONG-YONG KIM
HONG-YONG KIM
HO-YONG KIM
HUI-GYEONG KIM
HUI-JIN KIM
HUI-UK KIM
HUI-UK KIM
HWANG-DAE KIM
HWAN-GI KIM
HYEONG-CHEOL KIM
HYEONG-DO KIM
HYEONG-GON KIM
HYEONG-GON KIM
HYEONG-JAK KIM
HYEONG-SANG KIM
HYEONG-SEON KIM

HYEONG-SEOP KIM
HYEON-JO KIM
HYEON-JUNG KIM
HYEON-SIK KIM
HYEON-SONG KIM
HYEON-YUL KIM
HYO-BEOM KIM
I-BAEK KIM
I-BONG KIM
I-CHEON KIM
I-DEOK KIM
I-GYU KIM
IK-DU KIM
IK-HWAN KIM
IK-HYEONG KIM
IK-JONG KIM
IL-AN KIM
IL-BAEK KIM
IL-BOK KIM
IL-BOK KIM
IL-BOK KIM
IL-GWANG KIM
IL-HAN KIM
IL-HO KIM
IL-MAN KIM
IL-YONG KIM
IL-YONG KIM
IL-YONG KIM
IM-CHUL KIM
IM-DEOK KIM
IM-DOL KIM
I-NAM KIM
IN-BAEK KIM
IN-CHAN KIM
IN-CHAN KIM
IN-GAP KIM
IN-GI KIM
IN-HAK KIM
IN-HWAN KIM
IN-HWAN KIM
IN-JO KIM
IN-JU KIM
IN-OK KIM
IN-SAENG KIM
IN-SANG KIM
IN-SEOK KIM
IN-SEONG KIM
IN-SU KIM
IN-SU KIM
IN-SU KIM
IN-SU KIM
IN-SU KIM
IN-TAE KIM
I-SU KIM
I-SU KIM
I-YONG KIM
JAE-BIN KIM
JAE-BIN KIM
JAE-DEOK KIM
JAE-GEUM KIM
JAE-GEUN KIM
JAE-GI KIM
JAE-GIL KIM
JAE-GWAN KIM
JAE-GYEONG KIM
JAE-GYUN KIM
JAE-HAN KIM
JAE-HO KIM
JAE-HO KIM
JAE-HO KIM
JAE-HONG KIM
JAE-HONG KIM
JAE-HUI KIM
JAE-HYEON KIM
JAE-HYEON KIM
JAE-I KIM
JAE-IL KIM
JAE-JEONG KIM
JAE-JUN KIM
JAE-O KIM
JAE-SEOK KIM
JAE-SEONG KIM
JAE-SIK KIM
JAE-SIK KIM
JAE-SU KIM
JAE-SU KIM
JAE-SU KIM
JAM-AK KIM
JANG-GAE KIM
JANG-GEUN KIM

JANG-GYUN KIM
JANG-HWAN KIM
JANG-HWAN KIM
JANG-OK KIM
JA-SIK KIM
JE-EOK KIM
JE-EON KIM
JEOM-AM KIM
JEOM-BONG KIM
JEON-DO KIM
JEONG-AM KIM
JEONG-AP KIM
JEONG-BOK KIM
JEONG-CHAE KIM
JEONG-DAE KIM
JEONG-DO KIM
JEONG-EUP KIM
JEONG-GEUN KIM
JEONG-GON KIM
JEONG-GWON KIM
JEONG-HO KIM
JEONG-HO KIM
JEONG-HO KIM
JEONG-HO KIM
JEONG-HUN KIM
JEONG-HWA KIM
JEONG-HWAN KIM
JEONG-HWAN KIM
JEONG-HWAN KIM
JEONG-IL KIM
JEONG-MAN KIM
JEONG-MI KIM
JEONG-MUK KIM
JEONG-MUN KIM
JEONG-NAM KIM
JEONG-NAM KIM
JEONG-NO KIM
JEONG-OK KIM
JEONG-RAE KIM
JEONG-RAK KIM
JEONG-RYONG KIM
JEONG-SIK KIM
JEONG-SU KIM
JEONG-SU KIM
JEONG-SU KIM
JEONG-SU KIM
JEONG-SU KIM
JEONG-TAE KIM
JEONG-TAE KIM
JEONG-TAEK KIM
JEONG-U KIM
JEONG-U KIM
JEONG-UK KIM
JEONG-UN KIM
JEONG-YEON KIM
JEONG-YONG KIM
JEONG-YONG KIM
JEONG-YUN KIM
JEUNG-SEOP KIM
JI-BAE KIM
JI-BAEK KIM
JI-GWAN KIM
JI-HWAN KIM
JI-HYEON KIM
JIN-BOK KIM
JIN-CHEOL KIM
JIN-CHEOL KIM
JIN-CHEON KIM
JIN-DONG KIM
JIN-GI KIM
JIN-GON KIM
JIN-GYU KIM
JIN-HWAK KIM
JIN-HWAN KIM
JIN-HWAN KIM
JIN-HYEOK KIM
JIN-JU KIM
JIN-OK KIM
JIN-RYONG KIM
JIN-SEOP KIM
JIN-SEUNG KIM
JIN-TAEK KIM
JIN-WON KIM
JIN-YEOP KIM
JIN-YEOP KIM
JI-UNG KIM
JI-WAN KIM
JO-HAK KIM
JONG-AK KIM
JONG-AN KIM

JONG-BEOM KIM
JONG-BOK KIM
JONG-CHEOL KIM
JONG-CHEOL KIM
JONG-CHEOL KIM
JONG-CHEOL KIM
JONG-CHEOL KIM
JONG-CHEOL KIM
JONG-DAE KIM
JONG-DAE KIM
JONG-DEOK KIM
JONG-DEOK KIM
JONG-DEUK KIM
JONG-GEUN KIM
JONG-GI KIM
JONG-GI KIM
JONG-GIL KIM
JONG-HAE KIM
JONG-HAE KIM
JONG-HAN KIM
JONG-HAN KIM
JONG-HO KIM
JONG-HO KIM
JONG-HO KIM
JONG-HWAN KIM
JONG-HWAN KIM
JONG-HWAN KIM
JONG-HYEON KIM
JONG-JUN KIM
JONG-MAN KIM
JONG-MAN KIM
JONG-MOK KIM
JONG-MU KIM
JONG-MYEONG KIM
JONG-PIL KIM
JONG-RAK KIM
JONG-RYEOL KIM
JONG-RYEOL KIM
JONG-SEOK KIM
JONG-SEONG KIM
JONG-SEONG KIM
JONG-SEONG KIM
JONG-SEOP KIM
JONG-SIK KIM
JONG-SU KIM
JONG-SU KIM
JONG-SU KIM
JONG-SU KIM
JONG-SUL KIM
JONG-TAE KIM
JONG-U KIM
JONG-UK KIM
JONG-UNG KIM
JU-BU KIM
JU-GIL KIM
JU-HWAN KIM
JU-JUN KIM
JUNG-CHAN KIM
JUNG-DAE KIM
JUNG-GO KIM
JUNG-GYEONG KIM
JUN-SAM KIM
JUN-SIK KIM
JUN-SU KIM
JU-RI KIM
JU-SANG KIM
JU-SIK KIM
JU-SU KIM
KWAE-CHEOL KIM
MAENG-AM KIM
MAENG-JO KIM
MAL-TAEK KIM
MAN-BAEK KIM
MAN-DO KIM
MAN-DU KIM
MAN-JE KIM
MAN-JIN KIM
MAN-SE KIM
MAN-SEOK KIM
MAN-SEOK KIM
MAN-SIK KIM
MAN-SU KIM
MAN-SU KIM
MAN-SU KIM
MAN-YEONG KIM
MAN-YONG KIM
MI-JE KIM
MI-JUN KIM
MI-JUN KIM
MIL-SEONG KIM

11 ARMY

MIN-HWAN KIM
MIN-JAE KIM
MIN-TAE KIM
MI-SEON KIM
MO-SEOK KIM
MU-IL KIM
MU-IL KIM
MU-JIN KIM
MUN-CHEOL KIM
MUN-GI KIM
MUN-GYO KIM
MUN-HUI KIM
MUN-HUI KIM
MUN-JUN KIM
MUN-SEOK KIM
MUN-SEOK KIM
MUN-SEONG KIM
MUN-SEONG KIM
MUN-SEONG KIM
MUN-SU KIM
MU-SEONG KIM
MU-SU KIM
MU-YEONG KIM
MU-YEONG KIM
MYEONG-BOK KIM
MYEONG-CHAN KIM
MYEONG-CHAN KIM
MYEONG-DEOK KIM
MYEONG-DEUK KIM
MYEONG-DO KIM
MYEONG-DONG KIM
MYEONG-DU KIM
MYEONG-GYU KIM
MYEONG-HWAN KIM
MYEONG-HWAN KIM
MYEONG-JO KIM
MYEONG-MAN KIM
MYEONG-O KIM
MYEONG-SAN KIM
MYEONG-SU KIM
MYEONG-SU KIM
MYEONG-YONG KIM
NAK-GEON KIM
NAK-HWAN KIM
NAK-HYEON KIM
NAM-DAE KIM
NAM-GYU KIM
NAM-JAE KIM
NAM-JO KIM
NAM-JU KIM
NAM-RYONG KIM
NAM-SIK KIM
NAM-SIK KIM
NAM-YEOL KIM
NO-YEOL KIM
NO-YONG KIM
O-BONG KIM
O-DEUK KIM
OK-BAE KIM
OK-DONG KIM
OK-GYUN KIM
OK-HYEON KIM
OK-JUN KIM
OK-SU KIM
O-TAE KIM
PAN-GIL KIM
PAN-GWON KIM
PAN-SIK KIM
PAN-SU KIM
PIL-GAP KIM
ROK-I KIM
RO-SEOK KIM
RYEON KIM
SAM-CHEOL KIM
SAM-DO KIM
SAM-DOL KIM
SAM-DONG KIM
SAM-GU KIM
SAM-GWAK KIM
SAM-JO KIM
SAM-JU KIM
SAM-JUN KIM
SAM-JUNG KIM
SAM-MAN KIM
SAM-OK KIM
SAM-RYONG KIM
SAM-SEON KIM
SAM-YUL KIM
SANG-BAE KIM
SANG-CHEOL KIM

SANG-CHEOL KIM
SANG-DO KIM
SANG-DON KIM
SANG-EON KIM
SANG-GAK KIM
SANG-GAP KIM
SANG-GAP KIM
SANG-GI KIM
SANG-GI KIM
SANG-GYU KIM
SANG-HO KIM
SANG-IL KIM
SANG-JIN KIM
SANG-JIN KIM
SANG-JIN KIM
SANG-MAN KIM
SANG-MIN KIM
SANG-O KIM
SANG-RYEOL KIM
SANG-SIK KIM
SANG-SU KIM
SANG-SU KIM
SANG-SU KIM
SANG-SU KIM
SANG-YEOL KIM
SANG-YEOL KIM
SANG-YEON KIM
SANG-YONG KIM
SANG-YONG KIM
SANG-YUL KIM
SE-GEUN KIM
SE-GU KIM
SE-HUN KIM
SE-JAE KIM
SE-JUN KIM
SEOK-CHAN KIM
SEOK-CHAN KIM
SEOK-CHUL KIM
SEOK-DONG KIM
SEOK-DONG KIM
SEOK-GU KIM
SEOK-GWON KIM
SEOK-GYU KIM
SEOK-HYEON KIM
SEOK-HYEON KIM
SEOK-JIN KIM
SEOK-JO KIM
SEOK-JU KIM
SEOK-JUN KIM
SEOK-MUK KIM
SEOK-MUN KIM
SEOK-SANG KIM
SEOK-SU KIM
SEOK-SU KIM
SEOK-TAE KIM
SEOK-WON KIM
SEOK-YONG KIM
SEOK-YUN KIM
SEOL-GYU KIM
SEONG-BEOM KIM
SEONG-BEOM KIM
SEONG-BEOM KIM
SEONG-BOK KIM
SEONG-CHAN KIM
SEONG-CHEON KIM
SEONG-DAE KIM
SEONG-DAE KIM
SEONG-DAL KIM
SEONG-GON KIM
SEONG-GU KIM
SEONG-GYUN KIM
SEONG-GYUN KIM
SEONG-HAK KIM
SEONG-HEON KIM
SEONG-HO KIM
SEONG-HO KIM
SEONG-HUI KIM
SEONG-JU KIM
SEONG-OK KIM
SEONG-RYUL KIM
SEONG-SU KIM
SEONG-YEOL KIM
SEONG-YEOL KIM
SEONG-YUL KIM
SEON-HA KIM
SEON-HO KIM
SEON-IL KIM
SEON-MAN KIM
SEON-TAE KIM
SEUNG-CHEOL KIM

SEUNG-HYEON KIM
SEUNG-OK KIM
SI-DAE KIM
SI-JIN KIM
SI-JUNG KIM
SI-TAE KIM
SI-YEONG KIM
SO-AM KIM
SO-DO KIM
SO-GAE KIM
SO-JO KIM
SO-RYONG KIM
SO-SUL KIM
SO-YEONG KIM
SU KIM
SU-BOK KIM
SU-BOK KIM
SU-CHAN KIM
SU-DO KIM
SU-GWANG KIM
SU-HWAN KIM
SU-HYEOK KIM
SU-IL KIM
SUL-HWAN KIM
SUL-YONG KIM
SU-MAN KIM
SU-MUN KIM
SU-NAM KIM
SUN-BOK KIM
SUN-GUK KIM
SUN-HWA KIM
SUN-JEONG KIM
SUN-JO KIM
SUN-SEOK KIM
SUN-SIK KIM
SU-O KIM
SU-UK KIM
SU-YEOL KIM
TAE-BOK KIM
TAE-BOK KIM
TAE-BONG KIM
TAE-CHUL KIM
TAE-GYUN KIM
TAE-HEON KIM
TAE-HEUNG KIM
TAE-HO KIM
TAE-HWAN KIM
TAE-HWAN KIM
TAE-HYEON KIM
TAE-JIN KIM
TAE-JO KIM
TAE-JUN KIM
TAEK-RYUL KIM
TAE-MU KIM
TAE-RYUL KIM
TAE-SEOK KIM
TAE-SEOK KIM
TAE-SIK KIM
TAE-SIK KIM
TAE-SUN KIM
TAE-YEON KIM
TAE-YONG KIM
TAE-YU KIM
TA-GWAN KIM
U-BEOM KIM
U-BOK KIM
U-BONG KIM
U-CHEON KIM
U-DONG KIM
U-DONG KIM
U-GON KIM
U-GON KIM
U-GWAN KIM
U-HO KIM
U-HO KIM
UI-GWAN KIM
UI-GYEONG KIM
UI-JUN KIM
UI-TAE KIM
UN-GI KIM
UN-SU KIM
UN-YONG KIM
UN-YU KIM
U-RYUL KIM
U-TAEK KIM
WAN-GYU KIM
WAN-SU KIM
WAN-WON KIM
WI-GYEONG KIM
WOL-CHUL KIM

WON-BAE KIM
WON-CHIL KIM
WON-DO KIM
WON-DOL KIM
WON-GEUN KIM
WON-GUK KIM
WON-GUK KIM
WON-HYEON KIM
WON-HYEON KIM
WON-SEOK KIM
WON-SIK KIM
WON-TAE KIM
YANG-DO KIM
YANG-GU KIM
YE-HO KIM
YEONG-BAE KIM
YEONG-BOK KIM
YEONG-BOK KIM
YEONG-BOK KIM
YEONG-BOK KIM
YEONG-BOK KIM
YEONG-BONG KIM
YEONG-CHEOL KIM
YEONG-CHEOL KIM
YEONG-CHUN KIM
YEONG-DAE KIM
YEONG-DAE KIM
YEONG-DO KIM
YEONG-DON KIM
YEONG-GEUN KIM
YEONG-GEUN KIM
YEONG-GEUN KIM
YEONG-GWAN KIM
YEONG-GWON KIM
YEONG-GYU KIM
YEONG-GYU KIM
YEONG-GYU KIM
YEONG-HAK KIM
YEONG-HEON KIM
YEONG-HO KIM
YEONG-HO KIM
YEONG-HUI KIM
YEONG-HUN KIM
YEONG-HWA KIM
YEONG-HWI KIM
YEONG-HYEON KIM
YEONG-JAE KIM
YEONG-JAE KIM
YEONG-JI KIM
YEONG-JIN KIM
YEONG-JO KIM
YEONG-JO KIM
YEONG-JO KIM
YEONG-MAN KIM
YEONG-MOK KIM
YEONG-MUN KIM
YEONG-NAM KIM
YEONG-O KIM
YEONG-SAENG KIM
YEONG-SEOK KIM
YEONG-SEON KIM
YEONG-SIK KIM
YEONG-SIK KIM
YEONG-SIK KIM
YEONG-SIL KIM
YEONG-SIL KIM
YEONG-SONG KIM
YEONG-SU KIM
YEONG-SU KIM
YEONG-SU KIM
YEONG-TAE KIM
YEONG-TAEK KIM
YEONG-U KIM
YEONG-WON KIM
YONG-BEOM KIM
YONG-BOK KIM
YONG-CHEOL KIM
YONG-CHEOL KIM
YONG-CHEOL KIM
YONG-CHUL KIM
YONG-CHUL KIM
YONG-DAE KIM
YONG-DAL KIM
YONG-DAM KIM
YONG-DEOK KIM
YONG-DO KIM
YONG-DO KIM
YONG-DO KIM
YONG-GEUN KIM
YONG-GI KIM

YONG-GI KIM
YONG-GI KIM
YONG-GI KIM
YONG-GUK KIM
YONG-GUK KIM
YONG-GWAN KIM
YONG-GWON KIM
YONG-GYU KIM
YONG-GYU KIM
YONG-HA KIM
YONG-HAK KIM
YONG-HAK KIM
YONG-HO KIM
YONG-I KIM
YONG-JAE KIM
YONG-JO KIM
YONG-JUN KIM
YONG-MUK KIM
YONG-MUN KIM
YONG-O KIM
YONG-PYO KIM
YONG-SAENG KIM
YONG-SEOK KIM
YONG-SIK KIM
YONG-SU KIM
YONG-SU KIM
YONG-SU KIM
YONG-SU KIM
YONG-TAE KIM
YONG-TAEK KIM
YONG-UK KIM
YONG-WON KIM
YU-AN KIM
YU-DO KIM
YU-DO KIM
YU-GEUN KIM
YU-GI KIM
YU-GON KIM
YU-GWON KIM
YU-GYEONG KIM
YU-HWAN KIM
YU-JEONG KIM
YU-JU KIM
YUN-EON KIM
YUN-GYU KIM
YUN-HAN KIM
YUN-HWAN KIM
YUN-IL KIM
YUN-MAN KIM
YUN-OK KIM
YUN-SAM KIM
YUN-SEOK KIM
YUN-SIK KIM
YUN-SU KIM
YUN-TAE KIM
YUN-YEONG KIM
YU-PUNG KIM
YU-SEOK KIM
YU-SEOP KIM
YU-SU KIM
ERNEST W KIMBLE
ARTHUR W KIMMEL
GAYLE C KINCADE
RONALD E KINCH
WILLIAM L KINDER
CLARENCE B KING
DARRELL L KING
DOREL E KING
DUNBAR A KING
EDDIE KING
JAMES E KING
JOHN N KING JR
LONNIE KING
WILBUR A KING
WILLIS G KING
LARRY P KINLER
RICHARD L KINLOCH
BERNARD A KINNALLY
FRANCIS L KINNEY
FRANK E KINNEY
RICHARD S KINOSHITA
PAUL KIRBY
STERLING R KIRBY
GERALD F KIRCHNER
LEO J KIRCHNER
HIROSHI KIRIU
CHARLES B KIRK
WILLIAM KIRK JR
HUBERT A KIRKCONNELL

12 ARMY

DANIEL W KIRKLAND
JAMES KIRKLAND
LAWRENCE E KIRKLEY
ROBERT R KIRKLIN
JOHN E KIRKSEY
REIN KIRSIMAGI
JOHN W KIRWIN
BILL KISER JR
RUBEN W KITCHENS
ANTHONY L KITTELL
WILLIAM KITTLE
HERBERT R KLAEREN
RICHARD H KLASE
JULIUS R KLEBBE
JOHN A KLEIN
ROY D KLEIN
JOHN W KLEIST
STANISLAUS KLIMOWICZ
JOHN F KLINE
LEROY F KLING
GEORGE P KLINKHAMMER
RONALD J KLOECKNER
CARL F KLUTTS
DONALD W KNAPP
HAROLD K KNIGHT
ROY E KNOPP
RUDOLPH S KNOTTS
GERALD T KNOWLES
RALPH E KNUTH
FLOYD V KNUTSON
ARTHUR R KOBIE
PAUL E KOCHANSKI
VICTOR M KOCHER
LEONARD C KOEHLER
FREDERICK C KOENIG
GLENN E KOHN
SATORU KOJIRI
WILLIAM J KOK
RICHARD A KOLAR
GARY B KOLB
HARVEY A KOLBERG
ROBERT E KOLLING
CHARLES KOLODY
RAYMOND H KOLTHOFF
KEN K KONDO
ANDREW KONTRIK
CHARLES E KOONCE
LEROY D KOOPER
FRANK J KOPERDAK JR
JAMES J KOPF
ROBERT E KOPP
JAMES L KORNEGAY
GEORGE J KOSCIK
GEORGE T KOSKINAS
STANLEY F KOUNTNEY
ALOYSIUS W KOZLOWSKI
ROBERT E KRAFT
JOSEPH P KRAHEL
BERNARD C KRAUS
DON G KRAUSE
LESTER K KREIBICH
ZDZISLAW KRELOWSKI
MASON H KRENZEL
JOE C KRESNO JR
EUGENE KRESSIN
HENRY A KREY
RICHARD KRIEG
JOHN A KRIPOTON
STEVE J KROLL
WILLIAM C KROLL
EUGENE A KROPP
JAMES V KRUGER
WALLACE M KRUSZEWSKI
CHARLES W KUBICSKO
EDWARD L KUHAR
DONALD W KUHN
RAYMOND J KUHN
VITO P KUIZINAS
GEORGE M KUMAKURA
JAMES W KUMPULA
ADEN H KUNTZ
BILLIE KURGAN
MARVIN W KURTZ
WALTER E KURTZ
GEORGE A N KWOCK
WILLIAM S KYLES
ROBERT L KYSER
RAFAEL LABOY-MARTINEZ
CHARLIE M LACAZE

FREDERICK C LACKEY
GEORGE L LACKEY
VINCENT F LACKMAN
ROBERT F LACOUT
PETER J LADA JR
EDWARD LADAO
WILLIAM H LADD
ARTHUR J LAFEVERS
LEROY LA FONTAINE
WILLIAM J LAFRANCE
ROBERT LAGUARDIA
WILLIAM F LAHRNER
DAN B LAIL
WALTER L LAJEUNESSE
JESSE F LAKE
PAUL LALATOVICH
RAFAEL LAMAR-GUERRA
CHARLES R LAMBERT
OTIS H LAMBETH
VERNON A LAMORE
DONALD P LAMPENFELD
MAURICE E LAND
ROBERT E LANDRETH JR
JOHN M LANDRY
ROBERT LANDRY
ROBERT V LANE
ROBIN L LANE
THOMAS M LANE JR
HOMER V LANEHART
ROBERT T LANEY
ROOSEVELT LANFAIR
EDWARD A LANG
ROBERT A LANG
FRANCIS G LANGENFELD
JOSEPH D LANGFORD
ROY E LANGRELL
JACK D LANIER
JERRY D LANSFORD
JOHN H LANTRY
JOSEPH E LAPINSKI
WILBROD L LAPLANTE
LEO H LAPOINTE
CLAYTON J LAROSE
WILLIAM B LARRY
EDGAR J LARSON
STANLEY S LARSON
DAVID R LASKY
DEAN W LASS
ANTONIO V LASTELLA
WILL C LASUER
LUTHER L LASWELL
BOBBIE J LATHAM
CLIMON N LATHAN JR
EDWARD H LATOURNEAU
JOSEPH R LAUZON
HAROLD LAVALA
RAYMOND LA VALLEY
JOHN G LAVELLE JR
PATRICK J LAVIN
FRANK C LAVORA
GEORGE H LAWALL
ROBERT LAWRENCE
WILLIAM B LAWRENCE
WILLIAM C LAWRENCE
WILLIAM L LAWRENCE
BOBBY E LAWSON
ELMER L LAWSON
RICHARD A LAWSON
ROBERT C LAWSON
ELLISON J LAWTON
THOMAS A LAXTON
JOHN C LAYFIELD
GENE R LAYTON
WILLIAM C LAZENBY
RALPH E LEAF
KENNETH C LEASE JR
REGINALD L LEBLANC
MEUS LE BLEU
NELSON G LEBRON
JOSE E LEBRON-MENDEZ
BILLY LE COMPTE JR
ALBERTO LEDESMA
GILBERT LEDESMA
WILTON C LEDOUX
ABRAHAM LEE
ARNOLD T LEE
BAE-ROK LEE
BOK-DONG LEE
BOK-GYUN LEE

BOK-HUI LEE
BOK-NAM LEE
BOK-OK LEE
BOK-RYONG LEE
BOK-U LEE
BONG-DONG LEE
BONG-GEUN LEE
BONG-HWAN LEE
BONG-JAE LEE
BONG-JEOM LEE
BONG-ROK LEE
BONG-SE LEE
BONG-YEONG LEE
BO-U LEE
BU-GI LEE
BYEOK-HWAN LEE
BYEONG-CHEOL LEE
BYEONG-CHEON LEE
BYEONG-CHUN LEE
BYEONG-DU LEE
BYEONG-GAP LEE
BYEONG-GUK LEE
BYEONG-HA LEE
BYEONG-HO LEE
BYEONG-HO LEE
BYEONG-IL LEE
BYEONG-JU LEE
BYEONG-MAN LEE
BYEONG-RYANG LEE
BYEONG-SE LEE
BYEONG-SIK LEE
BYEONG-TAE LEE
BYEONG-YONG LEE
CHA-EON LEE
CHA-GEUN LEE
CHA-JO LEE
CHANG-GON LEE
CHANG-HWA LEE
CHANG-HYEON LEE
CHANG-NAM LEE
CHANG-NO LEE
CHANG-SEOK LEE
CHANG-SIN LEE
CHANG-SU LEE
CHANG-SU LEE
CHANG-U LEE
CHANG-YEOL LEE
CHANG-YONG LEE
CHANG-YONG LEE
CHAN-U LEE
CHA-SEOK LEE
CHA-SEONG LEE
CHA-SIL LEE
CHA-SIL LEE
CHA-SU LEE
CHEOL-GEUN LEE
CHEOL-HO LEE
CHEOL-U LEE
CHEON-IL LEE
CHEON-SEOK LEE
CHEON-SU LEE
CHEON-U LEE
CHOE-YEONG LEE
CHUN-HEUNG LEE
CHUN-OK LEE
CHUN-SAM LEE
CHUN-SEON LEE
CHUN-SIK LEE
CHUN-SIK LEE
CHUN-SIL LEE
DAE-BONG LEE
DAE-SEON LEE
DAE-U LEE
DAL-CHANG LEE
DAL-O LEE
DAL-SU LEE
DAL-YEONG LEE
DEOK-GYU LEE
DEOK-MAN LEE
DEOK-YEONG LEE
DEUNG-U LEE
DO-GYU LEE
DO-HYEON LEE
DO-IL LEE
DO-IL LEE
DOL-SU LEE
DONALD LEE
DONG-CHIL LEE
DONG-GYU LEE
DONG-GYUN LEE

DONG-HWA LEE
DONG-HWAN LEE
DONG-HWAN LEE
DONG-HYEOK LEE
DONG-JIN LEE
DONG-MU LEE
DONG-OK LEE
DONG-SU LEE
DONG-SU LEE
DO-SANG LEE
DU-MAN LEE
DU-SEONG LEE
DU-SEONG LEE
DU-WON LEE
ERNEST A LEE
EUL-MAN LEE
EUL-TAE LEE
EUN-SEUNG LEE
EUN-U LEE
GANG-DEOK LEE
GANG-HWI LEE
GANG-HYEON LEE
GANG-HYEON LEE
GANG-JU LEE
GANG-MUN LEE
GANG-YEOP LEE
GANG-YONG LEE
GAP-JIN LEE
GAP-SU LEE
GAP-SU LEE
GAP-YONG LEE
GEON-HO LEE
GEUM-BOK LEE
GEUM-BONG LEE
GEUM-CHEOL LEE
GEUN-SIK LEE
GEUN-U LEE
GEUN-YEONG LEE
GEUN-YEONG LEE
GI-BONG LEE
GI-BONG LEE
GI-CHEOL LEE
GI-CHUL LEE
GI-HA LEE
GI-HAN LEE
GI-HO LEE
GI-HONG LEE
GI-HONG LEE
GI-HYEON LEE
GI-HYEON LEE
GI-I LEE
GI-JONG LEE
GIL-GAP LEE
GIL-MAN LEE
GIL-SIN LEE
GIL-UNG LEE
GI-SAM LEE
GI-SEOK LEE
GI-SEOK LEE
GI-SIK LEE
GI-TAEK LEE
GI-YEONG LEE
GI-YONG LEE
GU-HONG LEE
GU-HWAN LEE
GUK-SIK LEE
GUK-YEONG LEE
GUN-UN LEE
GWANG-GEUN LEE
GWANG-HO LEE
GWANG-HUI LEE
GWANG-HUI LEE
GWANG-JIN LEE
GWANG-JIN LEE
GWANG-SEOP LEE
GWAN-JUN LEE
GWAN-SU LEE
GWAN-U LEE
GYE-HO LEE
GYEONG-BAE LEE
GYEONG-JUN LEE
GYEONG-RAK LEE
GYEONG-SANG LEE
GYEONG-SEOK LEE
GYEONG-SEOK LEE
GYEONG-YEOL LEE
GYEONG-YEOP LEE
GYEONG-YONG LEE
GYEONG-YONG LEE
GYO-SEONG LEE

GYU-AM LEE
GYU-BOK LEE
GYU-CHEOL LEE
GYU-GYEONG LEE
GYU-HA LEE
GYU-HO LEE
GYU-HO LEE
GYU-HWAN LEE
GYU-JEONG LEE
GYU-JEONG LEE
GYU-JIN LEE
GYU-JONG LEE
GYU-SAENG LEE
GYU-SEOK LEE
GYU-SEOK LEE
GYU-SEONG LEE
GYU-SU LEE
GYU-SU LEE
GYU-TAE LEE
GYU-TAEK LEE
HAE-IK LEE
HAENG-SIK LEE
HAK-DONG LEE
HAK-JUN LEE
HAK-SUN LEE
HAK-U LEE
HAK-YONG LEE
HAN-BOK LEE
HAN-GI LEE
HAN-HUI LEE
HAN-JIN LEE
HAN-JO LEE
HAN-MYEONG LEE
HAN-U LEE
HAYWARD R LEE
HEON-CHANG LEE
HEON-GYU LEE
HEUNG-BYEONG LEE
HEUNG-DAE LEE
HEUNG-YONG LEE
HO-AN LEE
HO-DONG LEE
HO-JIK LEE
HONG-BEOM LEE
HONG-GYU LEE
HONG-JAE LEE
HONG-U LEE
HONG-UN LEE
HONG-YEONG LEE
HONG-YUN LEE
HO-SE LEE
HO-SEOK LEE
HO-SUN LEE
HO-YEON LEE
HO-YEONG LEE
HUI-CHEOL LEE
HWANG-SU LEE
HWAN-SEONG LEE
HWA-RYONG LEE
HWA-YEOL LEE
HWA-YEONG LEE
HYEOK-GI LEE
HYEOK-RAE LEE
HYEOK-SANG LEE
HYEON-GEUK LEE
HYEONG-GEUN LEE
HYEONG-SEOK LEE
HYEONG-SU LEE
HYEON-MO LEE
HYEON-MOK LEE
HYEON-MOK LEE
HYEON-O LEE
HYEON-U LEE
HYE-SU LEE
I-HO LEE
IK-SEOP LEE
IL-GEUN LEE
IL-GYU LEE
IL-SEOP LEE
IL-YEONG LEE
IM-CHUL LEE
IM-HWAN LEE
IN-CHAE LEE
IN-DEUK LEE
IN-GYU LEE
IN-RAN LEE
IN-SAENG LEE
IN-SANG LEE
IN-SU LEE
IN-TAEK LEE

13

ARMY

IN-UK LEE
IN-WAN LEE
IN-YEONG LEE
I-YONG LEE
JAE-DEOK LEE
JAE-DONG LEE
JAE-GAP LEE
JAE-GEUM LEE
JAE-GEUN LEE
JAE-GEUN LEE
JAE-GON LEE
JAE-GYU LEE
JAE-HO LEE
JAE-HONG LEE
JAE-HWAN LEE
JAE-IK LEE
JAE-JIN LEE
JAE-JO LEE
JAE-SEON LEE
JAE-SUN LEE
JAE-U LEE
JAE-U LEE
JAE-WON LEE
JAE-YEONG LEE
JAE-YUN LEE
JANG-CHUN LEE
JANG-HO LEE
JANG-HUI LEE
JANG-HUN LEE
JANG-HWAN LEE
JANG-ROK LEE
JANG-SEOK LEE
JANG-U LEE
JANG-WON LEE
JEOM-SIK LEE
JEOM-SU LEE
JEOM-SU LEE
JEONG-BIN LEE
JEONG-CHANG LEE
JEONG-CHUN LEE
JEONG-DEOK LEE
JEONG-DU LEE
JEONG-EUNG LEE
JEONG-GYU LEE
JEONG-HUN LEE
JEONG-HWAN LEE
JEONG-MAN LEE
JEONG-SEOK LEE
JEONG-SEUNG LEE
JEONG-SIK LEE
JEONG-SIK LEE
JEONG-SU LEE
JEONG-SU LEE
JEONG-U LEE
JEONG-U LEE
JEONG-U LEE
JEONG-U LEE
JEONG-WOL LEE
JEONG-YUN LEE
JEUNG-SU LEE
JIN-GYU LEE
JIN-HO LEE
JIN-HWAN LEE
JIN-SANG LEE
JIN-SANG LEE
JIN-SEOP LEE
JIN-SU LEE
JIN-TAEK LEE
JIN-U LEE
JIN-YEONG LEE
JONG-BAE LEE
JONG-CHAE LEE
JONG-CHEOL LEE
JONG-CHEOL LEE
JONG-GAE LEE
JONG-GEUN LEE
JONG-GEUN LEE
JONG-GEUN LEE
JONG-GIL LEE
JONG-GU LEE
JONG-GU LEE
JONG-GWON LEE
JONG-HAK LEE
JONG-HO LEE
JONG-HO LEE
JONG-HO LEE
JONG-HO LEE
JONG-HWAN LEE
JONG-HWAN LEE
JONG-HWAN LEE
JONG-HWAN LEE
JONG-IN LEE
JONG-JAE LEE
JONG-JIN LEE
JONG-MAN LEE
JONG-MUN LEE
JONG-MUN LEE
JONG-MUN LEE
JONG-NAK LEE
JONG-OK LEE
JONG-PAN LEE
JONG-RIP LEE
JONG-SEONG LEE
JONG-SEONG LEE
JONG-SEONG LEE
JONG-SIK LEE
JONG-SONG LEE
JONG-SU LEE
JONG-SU LEE
JONG-SUN LEE
JONG-TAE LEE
JONG-TAK LEE
JONG-WAN LEE
JONG-YONG LEE
JONG-YUN LEE
JUNG-GI LEE
JUNG-HUI LEE
JUNG-U LEE
JUN-HUI LEE
JUN-HUI LEE
JUN-PIL LEE
JUN-SIK LEE
JUN-U LEE
KWAE-MAN LEE
MAK-SIN LEE
MAL-JU LEE
MAN-BAL LEE
MAN-BOK LEE
MAN-HOE LEE
MAN-HONG LEE
MAN-SEOK LEE
MAN-SUL LEE
MAN-U LEE
MAN-YONG LEE
MIN-CHEOL LEE
MO-YEOL LEE
MU-CHUN LEE
MUL-SU LEE
MUN-GI LEE
MUN-HAK LEE
MUN-HUI LEE
MUN-SEON LEE
MUN-SIK LEE
MU-SEON LEE
MU-SIK LEE
MU-YONG LEE
MU-YONG LEE
MYEONG-AM LEE
MYEONG-GU LEE
MYEONG-JUN LEE
MYEONG-RYUL LEE
MYEONG-WI LEE
MYEONG-YONG LEE
NAK-JO LEE
O-DONG LEE
OE-GEUN LEE
OK-PIL LEE
O-RYONG LEE
PAL-BEOM LEE
PAL-SU LEE
PAN-SIK LEE
PAN-SIK LEE
PAN-SU LEE
PAN-SU LEE
PIL-DU LEE
PIL-SEONG LEE
PIL-U LEE
PYEONG-SU LEE
RAYBURN D LEE
ROBERT M LEE
RYEON LEE
RYUK-DONG LEE
SA-BEOM LEE
SAM-CHEOL LEE
SAM-GU LEE
SAM-GU LEE
SAM-JUN LEE
SAM-SAENG LEE
SAM-SAENG LEE
SAM-SU LEE
SAM-YEON LEE
SAM-YONG LEE
SANG-BAEK LEE
SANG-BEOM LEE
SANG-BOK LEE
SANG-BOK LEE
SANG-BONG LEE
SANG-BONG LEE
SANG-CHEOL LEE
SANG-CHEOL LEE
SANG-CHIL LEE
SANG-DEUK LEE
SANG-DON LEE
SANG-GON LEE
SANG-GU LEE
SANG-GU LEE
SANG-GUN LEE
SANG-GWON LEE
SANG-GWON LEE
SANG-GYU LEE
SANG-HAE LEE
SANG-HAK LEE
SANG-HAN LEE
SANG-HO LEE
SANG-HO LEE
SANG-HUN LEE
SANG-JAE LEE
SANG-JO LEE
SANG-JUN LEE
SANG-JUN LEE
SANG-MAN LEE
SANG-MAN LEE
SANG-MUN LEE
SANG-MYEONG LEE
SANG-NAK LEE
SANG-NO LEE
SANG-O LEE
SANG-OK LEE
SANG-OK LEE
SANG-OK LEE
SANG-ROK LEE
SANG-RYONG LEE
SANG-SEON LEE
SANG-SEON LEE
SANG-SIK LEE
SANG-SIK LEE
SANG-SU LEE
SANG-SU LEE
SANG-SU LEE
SANG-SU LEE
SANG-SUL LEE
SANG-SUN LEE
SANG-TAE LEE
SANG-TAEK LEE
SANG-U LEE
SANG-UK LEE
SANG-UN LEE
SANG-UN LEE
SANG-YEOL LEE
SE-OK LEE
SEOK-BONG LEE
SEOK-BONG LEE
SEOK-DO LEE
SEOK-GEUN LEE
SEOK-GEUN LEE
SEOK-GI LEE
SEOK-GU LEE
SEOK-HWA LEE
SEOK-HYEON LEE
SEOK-JIN LEE
SEOK-SUN LEE
SEOK-UN LEE
SEOK-YEONG LEE
SEON-BONG LEE
SEONG-CHAN LEE
SEONG-DEOK LEE
SEONG-DU LEE
SEONG-DU LEE
SEONG-GEOL LEE
SEONG-GEUN LEE
SEONG-GIL LEE
SEONG-GUK LEE
SEONG-HAN LEE
SEONG-HO LEE
SEONG-HO LEE
SEONG-HWAN LEE
SEONG-HWAN LEE
SEONG-IL LEE
SEONG-JIN LEE
SEONG-JU LEE
SEONG-SIK LEE
SEONG-SU LEE
SEONG-U LEE
SEONG-U LEE
SEONG-YEONG LEE
SEON-JEOM LEE
SE-U LEE
SE-U LEE
SEUNG-CHEOL LEE
SEUNG-DEOK LEE
SEUNG-DEOK LEE
SEUNG-HO LEE
SEUNG-MAN LEE
SEUNG-MUN LEE
SEUNG-RYEOL LEE
SEUNG-SON LEE
SEUNG-U LEE
SEUNG-UN LEE
SI-DONG LEE
SI-IK LEE
SIK LEE
SIL-GYEONG LEE
SI-YEONG LEE
SO-CHUL LEE
SONG-DAE LEE
SONG-PYEONG LEE
SO-YONG LEE
SU-AM LEE
SU-BEOM LEE
SU-DEOK LEE
SU-DON LEE
SU-EUL LEE
SU-GYU LEE
SU-HYEONG LEE
SU-IN LEE
SU-IN LEE
SU-MAN LEE
SU-MAN LEE
SU-MAN LEE
SU-MUN LEE
SUN-BONG LEE
SUN-EUNG LEE
SUN-GEUM LEE
SUN-HAENG LEE
SUN-HWAN LEE
SU-SEOL LEE
SU-TAE LEE
SU-UK LEE
SU-YEONG LEE
SU-YEONG LEE
TA-AM LEE
TAE-BONG LEE
TAE-GEUN LEE
TAE-GYU LEE
TAE-HO LEE
TAE-HO LEE
TAEK-SEOP LEE
TAE-MUK LEE
TAE-SEOK LEE
TAE-SEONG LEE
TAE-SU LEE
TAE-YEONG LEE
TAE-YONG LEE
TAE-YONG LEE
TAE-YONG LEE
U-CHAN LEE
U-CHANG LEE
U-DEOK LEE
U-GAP LEE
U-HYEON LEE
UI-BOK LEE
UI-CHUL LEE
UI-DONG LEE
UI-JUNG LEE
UI-YEON LEE
U-JEONG LEE
UN-DO LEE
UN-GEUN LEE
UN-HYEON LEE
UN-O LEE
UN-U LEE
U-RIM LEE
U-SEOK LEE
U-SIK LEE
U-YEONG LEE
WAN-GI LEE
WAN-SIK LEE
WAN-SU LEE
WILLIAM C LEE
WILLIE LEE
WON-AM LEE
WON-BO LEE
WON-DAE LEE
WON-DONG LEE
WON-DONG LEE
WON-GAP LEE
WON-GUK LEE
WON-HA LEE
WON-HEUNG LEE
WON-HUI LEE
WON-HYEONG LEE
WON-JO LEE
WON-JU LEE
WON-JU LEE
WON-SEONG LEE
WON-SIK LEE
WON-TAE LEE
WON-U LEE
WON-UK LEE
YANG-U LEE
YEO-CHUL LEE
YEOM-MIN LEE
YEONG-DO LEE
YEONG-GEUN LEE
YEONG-GI LEE
YEONG-GI LEE
YEONG-GU LEE
YEONG-HAN LEE
YEONG-HEUNG LEE
YEONG-HO LEE
YEONG-HO LEE
YEONG-HUI LEE
YEONG-HWAN LEE
YEONG-JAE LEE
YEONG-JO LEE
YEONG-JO LEE
YEONG-MAN LEE
YEONG-MAN LEE
YEONG-MU LEE
YEONG-MU LEE
YEONG-MUN LEE
YEONG-SU LEE
YEONG-SUK LEE
YEONG-TAEK LEE
YEONG-UN LEE
YEON-JU LEE
YEON-RO LEE
YONG-BOK LEE
YONG-EOP LEE
YONG-GEUN LEE
YONG-GI LEE
YONG-GIL LEE
YONG-HA LEE
YONG-HAN LEE
YONG-HAN LEE
YONG-HWAN LEE
YONG-JIN LEE
YONG-JUN LEE
YONG-MAN LEE
YONG-MUN LEE
YONG-PAN LEE
YONG-PO LEE
YONG-SIK LEE
YONG-SU LEE
YONG-SUL LEE
YONG-TAE LEE
YU-HYEONG LEE
YUN-JIP LEE
YUN-MAN LEE
YUN-SANG LEE
YUN-SEOK LEE
YUN-SIK LEE
YU-SEON LEE
YU-WON LEE
WILLIAM LEEMANS
JACK D LEFEVER
WILLIAM J LEFEVERS
ROBERT G LEFFLER
CHARLES R LE FORCE
LAURENCE A LEFRANCOIS
MARION LEGARE
JOHN H LEGETTE
BENJAMIN S LEGGETTE JR
THOMAS LEGGS
ADAM A LELL
LOYD O LEMARR
JOHN J LEMES
GEORGE L LEMONS

14 ARMY

STANLEY L LENCICKI
LEONARD E LENSKE
EUGENE C LENTZ
ARDEN J LENZ
CLARENCE B LEON
GARY M LEONARD
OWEN L LEONARD JR
JACOB P LEONELLO
HARLAN A LEOS
CLARENCE A LESTER
JOHN LESZCZYNSKI
JAMES LEVI JR
CHARLES T LEWIS
GEORGE W LEWIS
ISAAC LEWIS JR
JAMES E LEWIS
JAMES W LEWIS
ROBERT N LEWIS
STEWART C LEWIS JR
WALTER B LEWIS JR
WILLIAM LEWIS
RICHARD J LEYDEN
SAMUEL A LIBERTZ
SAMUEL S LIBRAN-GARCIA
VIRL M LIEBRENZ
DONALD J LILEK
HAROLD R LILES
ROBERT W LILIENTHAL
EVANS LILLY
JOHN G LIND
WILLARD T LINDBORG
WILLIAM C LINDER JR
R L LINDSAY
JAMES A LINDSEY
WALTER G LINDSEY
PHILIP G LINDWURM
WILLIAM LINGERMAN
GOLDEN W LINKOUS
GILES C LINTHICUM
WILLIAM B LINTHICUM
ROBERT S LINTON
BILLY LIOLIN
HENRY L LIPES
HERBERT C LIPPERT
EUGENE B LIPPS
LAWRENCE LISCANO
JAMES R LISTER
JOHN Q LITTLE
ARCHIE J LIVINGSTON
FIDEL LLANOT-CORA
CLIFFORD A LLEWELLYN
JAMES J LLOYD
MILES D LLOYD
JOHN A LOCKHART
JUNIOR LOCKLEAR
FRANK LODOLCE
PRESTON LOFTIN
DAVID LOGA
CARL D LOGAN
HERBERT H LOGAN
HENRY E J LOHMER
LINN F LOIDA
ALFRED A LOKEN
CECIL LONCASESION
CECIL C LONG
CLINTON LONG
EDWARD LONG
FRED H LONG
JAMES E LONG
TYSON R LONG
VINCENT T LONG
CHARLES W LOOMIS
ARNOLDO V LOPEZ
FRANK LOPEZ JR
LARRY C LOPEZ
MIKE R LOPEZ
RAYMOND LOPEZ
JOSE A LOPEZ-BATIZ
ORLANDO LOPEZ-OQUENDO
FRANCIS J LOPRETA
ELMER M LORENZO
MANNIE L LOSHAW
ARTHUR E LOSURE
CLARENCE LOUDEN JR
ERNEST H LOUDEN
EDWARD D LOUIS
CHARLES A LOVE
EDWIN N LOVE
EMMETT L LOVE
ROOSEVELT LOVE
VAUN A LOVEDAY
ROBERT W LOVELL
EDWARD LOVINS
BERT C LOWE
BILLY J LOWE
GERALD A LOWE
PHILIP LOWE
STANLEY R LOWE
JAMES E LOWERY
JAMES H LOWRANCE
WALLACE B LOYD
DAVID L LUCAS
GEORGE LUCAS
ROY LUCAS JR
RUSSELL K LUCAS
JOSE LUCCA-TORRES
MANUEL LUCERO
SEFERINO C LUCERO
GERALD P LUCHT
WILLIAM F LUDWIG
DANIEL E LUEBBERS
ROBERT C LUEDTKE
RUBEN LUGO-CABRERA
WILLIAM LUGO-SANTIAGO
CARLO A LUHTA
LOUIE M LUISI
CHEW W LUM
NORMAN J LUMB
ELBERT R LUNCE
JAMES W LUND
CLIFTON D LUNDY JR
FRANK A LUNEDI
JAMES E LUNSFORD JR
RAYMOND E LUTES
WILLIAM A LYLE
PAUL E LYLES
HAROLD M LYNCH
JAMES J LYNCH
JOHN F LYNCH
EVERETT D LYNN
GALEN L LYON
GORDON E LYONS
JAMES H LYONS
JAMES R LYONS
VERNON LYONS
JEONG-OK MA
SANG-EON MA
ISSAC S MABE
GEORGE J MABIN
HIRAM T MABRY
BUHL J MACE
ROLETTE MACE
ARTHUR S MACEDO JR
WILLIAM P MACFARLANE
LEROY F MACK
ERNEST MACKEY
RICHMOND E MACKEY
JOSEPH E MACKLIN
KENNETH N MACLEAN
LLOYD S MACLEOD
JAMES L MACLIN
JAMES A MACMILLAN
EDWARD W MACNEILL JR
LEO J MACZUGA
OSCAR B MADDEN
WALTER J MADDEN
ROBERT L MADDOX
FRANK T MADRIGAL
HARUO MAEDA
ROBERT F C MAENHOUT
WILLIAM T MAGEE
MARVIN V MAGGETT
ANTHONY J MAGGI
LAWRENCE W MAGOUIRK
FRANCIS P MAGUIRE
JOSEPH E MAGUIRE
WILLIAM R MAGYAR
JOHN F MAHAR
NORMAN J MAHLER
DUANE E MAHNESMITH
EDDIE R MAHONE
THOMAS J MAIDENS
BILLY MAINOUS
ERASMO MAISONET-SANTIAGO
ALBERT A MAJOMUT
JOSEPH J MAKARA
ANTONIO M MALACARA
LALO S MALDANADO
JOSE M MALDONADO-AYALA
ANGEL M MALDONADO-TORRES
ROBERT L MALE
ROBERT J MALONE
SHERMAN W MALONE
RUBIN R MALTBIE
JAMES A MALY
THOMAS V MANAHAN
TONY L MANCUSO
ALBERT J MANGINI
SELMAN D MANGRUM
MARIO J MANISCALCO
HAROLD R MANN
JACKIE N MANN
OTTO MANN
ROBERT M MANN
WALTER E MANNINEN
IRA MANNING
PETER MANSUETO
RICHARD J MANZEL
LAVERN E MAPLE
FRANK M MARASSA
MELVIN G MARCHBANKS
MIKE MARCIN JR
HENRY L MARCINKOWSKI
ADRIAN T MARCUS
JOHN MARIANO
SALVATORE A MARIANO
JOE W MARIGNA
IGNATIUS MARINELLO
FRANK MARINO
ROY L MARJAMA
LOUIS MARKITELLO
WILBUR L MARKOS
KENT M MARKS
TOM J MARPLE
MARTIN MARQUEZ
EFIGENIO MARQUEZ-HERNANDEZ
ALEXANDER P MARRA
ISMAEL MARRERO-NEGRON
JOSE MARRERO-RIVERA
JOHN I MARRUSO
ALBERT MARSHALL JR
MELVIN E MARSHALL
RICHARD L MARSHALL
WENDELL W MARSHALL
CECIL G MARTIN
CLAIRE MARTIN
DICKIE C MARTIN
DONALD W MARTIN
EDWARD F MARTIN
EUGENE W MARTIN
GEORGE MARTIN JR
JAMES F MARTIN
JAMES W MARTIN
LEON E MARTIN
ORLEY C MARTIN
REX C MARTIN
ROBERT L MARTIN
ROBERT L MARTIN
ROBERT V MARTIN
SYLVESTER H MARTIN
BASILIO MARTINEZ
CARLOS A MARTINEZ
EFREN G MARTINEZ
ERNEST R MARTINEZ
GUALBERTO MARTINEZ
JESUS C MARTINEZ
JOSE E MARTINEZ
JOSEPH A MARTINEZ
MANUEL MARTINEZ
MANUEL MARTINEZ JR
NICOLAS MARTINEZ
TOMAS MARTINEZ-CANDELARIO
JUAN MARTINEZ-ROSADO
RAYMOND R MARTY
DAVID F MARYE
RALPH S MASATUSUGU
JASON MASCHIST
DOMENICK J MASH
MANUEL R MAS-MUNIZ
EARON L MASON
EDWARD M MASON
ROBERT G MASON
LUIS A MASSANET-ALMODOVAR
HERIBERTO MASSAS-ROBLES
BOBBY J MASSEY
OSCAR T MASSIE
ALVA R MASTERS
ROBERT O MASTERSON
DANIEL D MATHENA
JAMES P MATHERS
CHARLES MATHEWS JR
MELVIN G MATHIS
MELVIN G MATLOCK
RUFUS W MATLOCK
GABRIEL MATRISCIANO JR
LEROY MATSEN
CHARLES R MATSON
GARY E MATSON
HOWARD L MATSON
GLENN MATTHEWS
IRVING P MATTHEWS
LEXIE D MATTHEWS
JOHN B MATTHYS
CLARENCE B MAUER
EARL L MAULDIN JR
ROBERT C MAUPIN
OVIDE L MAURICE
JAMES P MAURICIO
GLENN E MAXWELL
HENRY C MAXWELL
DONALD A MAY
HENRY E MAY
RAYMOND F MAY
WILBUR MAYCOX
LARRY J MAYEAUX
ROY E MAYER
THOMAS C MAYER
EUGENE M MAYES
HERSHEL B MAYES
WELDON E MAYFIELD
DONALD R MAYNARD
NORMAN J MAYNARD
BENIGNO MAYOL-FIGUEROA
GEORGE A MAZALAN
JOSEPH A MAZURKIEWICZ
FRANK J MAZZARELLA
BILLY L MCABEE
ERNEST G MCADAMS
RONALD L MCADAMS
GEORGE U MCADEN
ALVIE W MCALEXANDER
BILLY R MCALLISTER
JACK E MCALLISTER
MADISON B MCATEE
AARON H MCBRIDE
JAMES F MCBRIDE
DAVID L MCBURNEY
JOESPH E MCCABE
SHERMAN W MCCAFFERY JR
ERNEST J MCCAMPBELL
CECIL D MCCAN
JOHN J MCCANN
JOHN J MCCANN
CHARLES E MCCARNEY JR
EDWARD F MCCARTHY
HOMER C MCCARTHY JR
ERNEST G MCCAULEY
EARL E MCCLEARY
HERBERT MCCLENDON
HORACE I MCCLENNON
JAMES C MCCOMIC
STANLEY R MCCONNELL
JAMES A MCCOOL
IRVIN M MCCORD
EDWARD J A MCCORMACK
BILLY G MCCORMICK
JOHN J MCCORMICK
SHERMAN T MCCORMICK
JOHN B MCCOWEN
GLEN B MCCOY
LLOYD MCCOY
ROBERT H MCCOY
WILLIAM T MCCRACKEN
CLINTON H MCCRAY
WADE A MCCRAY
CECIL J MCCREARY
JAMES MCCULLOUGH
JOSEPH D MCCULLOUGH
WILLIE J MCCULLOUGH
ROBERT W MCCULOUGH
GILBERT L MCCURRY JR
HENRY MCCUTCHEN JR
JAMES E MCCUTCHEON
DELMAR T MCDANIEL
HENRY MCDANIELS JR
PATRICK E MCDEARMON
BILLY D MCDONALD
GEORGE J MCDONALD
JACK E MCDONALD
JOHN D MCDONALD
PAUL J MCDONOUGH
ALBERT R MCDOWELL
PAT A MCELMURRY
AUGUSTUS O MCELROY
ELMER C MCELVAIN
CLIFFORD W MCFADDEN
CURTIS R MCFADDEN
WALTER F MCFARLAND
JAMES F MCGARITY
FREDERICK T MCGAUGH
HENRY R MCGAULEY
DAVE MCGEE
MAURICE MCGHEE
WILLIAM T MCGHEE
LADELL MCGILL
LEONARD S MCGINNIS
FRANK J MCGLINCHEY
DONALD C MCGOWAN
PHILIP T MCGOWAN
EDMUND J MCGRATH
DANIEL E MCGRAW
PAUL A MCHALE
RICHARD J MCHARGUE
NORMAN MCINNIS
HARRY H MCINTIRE
RICHARD H MCINTIRE
KENNETH L MCINTYRE
MAX E MCKANEY
JAMES H MCKECHNIE
JOHN J MCKENNA
HERBERT R MCKENZIE
JAMES E MCKENZIE
WILLIAM M MCKEY JR
LANCE L MCKINNEY
PAUL L MCKITTRICK
FRANCES E MCLAIN
JAMES T MCLAREN
ANDREW R MCLAUGHLIN
EDWARD J MCLAUGHLIN
LORAN L MCLAUGHLIN
ROBERT D MCLAUGHLIN
ARTIS MCLEAN
GERALD W MCLEAN
ALEXANDER MCLELLAN
FRANK H MCLEOD
WYNARD C MCMAHAN
ROBERT A MCMANUS
REVEREND J MCMILLIAN
JERRY H MCMILLION
ROBERT R MCMILLON
VICTOR E MCMINN
JOSEPH B MCMULLEN JR
JOHN H MCNEILL
RICHARD O MCNITT
RUSSELL H MCQUAIN
GILBERT D MCQUEEN
JAMES R MCVEE
MARVIN D MEADE
ANDREW J MEADOWS JR
CLEVELAND F MEADOWS
VERNON MEADOWS
JEROME D MECHLER
FRANK MEDEIROS
JOSEPH MEDEIROS
JAMES T MEDFORD
EDWARD MEDINA

15 ARMY

EFRAIN MEDINA-GUZMAN
HARRY H MEDINA-PADILLA
FRED MEDLEY JR
ALFRED C MEEK
RAYMOND D MEEKS
RICHARD E MEGIN
PAUL J MEHLE
JOHN D MEIKLE
JOHN H MEINERS
ERVIN S MELCHER JR
JOHN J MELCHIOR
EDWARD MELDONIAN
ANGEL MELECIO-HERNANDEZ
LEOPOLDO MELECIO-LOPEZ
KENNETH L MELLENTHIEN
FRANCIS J MELLO
RUSSELL D MELSER
LEAMON S MELTON
ALFRED W MELVIN JR
JESUS MENDIOLA
VINCENTE M MENDOZA
ELLSWORTH B MENEELEY
JUAN B MENENDEZ
WILLIAM H MENKE JR
JUAN MERCADO-GONZALEZ
SAMUEL MERCADO-TORRES
PAULINO MERCED-MARTYS
FRANK MERCURIO
HUBERT A MEREDIETH
EMANUEL R MERIDA
NATHAN MERLING
JAY J MERMILLIOD
RALPH C MERRILL JR
DAVID A MERRITT
WILLIAM MERRITT
WILLIAM J MERRITT
CHARLES R MERROW
CHARLES W MERTZ
RUDY V MESA
FELIX A MESIAVECH
JOHN H MESSER
CHARLES G MESSICK
JAMES H METCALF JR
THOMAS C METZ
CLARENCE T MEUSE
RAYMOND J MEYER
J B MEYERS
HENRY MEZZATESTA JR
ARMAND MEZZPOERA
DONALD L MICHOFF
GEORGE W MIDDLEBROOK JR
JOSEPH V MIELE
ROGER E MIELS
THOMAS J MIGLIACCIO
LEONARD MIGUEL
FLOYD M MIKELL
ARTHUR K MIKULIK
LLOYD O MILENDER
JAMES W MILES
THEODORE MILES
GEORGE R MILEY
ROBERT T MILEY
ALFRED L MILLER
ARTHUR L MILLER
ARTHUR R MILLER
AUGUSTUS MILLER
CECIL MILLER
CHARLES D MILLER
CHARLES H MILLER
DONALD R MILLER
DUANE A MILLER
EARL K MILLER
EDDIE M MILLER JR
GENE P MILLER
GERALD E MILLER
IRA L MILLER JR
JAMES N MILLER
JOHN L MILLER
KENNETH R MILLER
KENNETH S MILLER
LINUIS D MILLER
LLOYD J MILLER JR
MARVIN L MILLER
RICHARD P MILLER

ROBERT A MILLER
ROBERT F MILLER
THOMAS M MILLER
PERRY H MILLIKEN
CRAWFORD MILLS
FREDERICK E MILLS
JERRY E MILLS
LASTER MILLS
BAK-SIK MIN
BYEONG-DAE MIN
BYEONG-HEON MIN
BYEONG-JU MIN
BYEONG-JUN MIN
BYEONG-SUK MIN
CHUN-GI MIN
EUL-DEUK MIN
GAP-SIK MIN
GYEONG-CHEON MIN
HEUNG-BOK MIN
JAE-SIK MIN
JONG-SIK MIN
SANG-EON MIN
SEON-SIK MIN
YEONG-SUK MIN
JOHN F MINER
JAMES W MINERD
JOSEPH MINJACK
GILBERT J MINNING
RICHARD M MINTON
JAMES R MINYARD
ALEXANDER O MIRANDA
HECTOR L MIRANDA-GONZALEZ
CRESCENCIO MIRELEZ
DONALD D MISEMER
CONRAD P MISTLE
LINDBERGH MITCHAM
ROBERT F MITCHAM
CARLTON E MITCHELL
COY F MITCHELL
FINNIE C MITCHELL JR
JOHN G MITCHELL
MICHAEL V MITCHELL
WILLARD G MITCHELL
WILLIAM C MITCHELL JR
WILLIAM L MITCHELL
WILLIAM M MITCHELL
JAMES MIUCCIO
ALAN T MIYAHIRA
ROBERT K MIYAMOTO
ICHIRO R MIYASAKI
MILTON J MLASKAC
ALEXANDER MOBLEY JR
EMERY L MODOS
ARNE O MOE
RICHARD L MOESCH
LEROY J MOFFETT
GENE A MOHNEY
BRUCE O MOILANEN
RALPH MOISA
VICTOR MOLINA-RIVERA
ANTHONY J MOLINARO
WILLIAM J MONAHAN
JOHN MONDELLO
ANGEL L MONGE-RODRIGUEZ
BILLY J MONKS
FORREST A MONROE
PAUL MONROE
RONDO J MONROE
DONALD L MONSON
MANUEL V MONTANA JR
ERASMO MONTANEZ-RIOS
AMADO MONTANO
ADOLFO MONTEBERDE
HOUSTON E MONTFORT
EMERY MONTGOMERY
GIFFORD E MONTGOMERY
JAMES E MONTGOMERY
PERCY L MONTGOMERY
RAYMOND MONTGOMERY
SHERLIN D MONTGOMERY
WILLIE L MONTGOMERY
EDDIE J MONTIEL
RENE R MONTIGNY
GILBERTO MONTOYA
STEPHEN MONTOYA

EDWARD MOODY
MARTIN F MOONEY
BRADDY MOORE III
CHARLES S MOORE
CLAUDE F MOORE JR
CLELL MOORE
EDWARD J MOORE JR
ERNEST L MOORE
FRANK MOORE JR
GENE S MOORE
HOWARD E MOORE
ISADORE O MOORE
JACK D MOORE
JAMES E MOORE
JAMES E MOORE
JOHN W MOORE
MERLE M MOORE
NORMAN E MOORE
PAUL J MOORE
REX D MOORE
RICHARD L MOORE
JACK J MORACK
CARMELO O MORALES
DAVID O MORALES
JOHN A MORALES
OSCAR M MORALES
WILLIAM MORALES
VICTOR M MORALES-ALAMO
DIONISIO MORALES-RIVERA
VAL MORALES-TIRDO
JACK H MORAN
WILLIAM G MORAN
BARBATIM MORANTE
MELVIN W MORDEN
RUSSELL A MORECRAFT
WELDON J MORELAND
ALBERT G MORENO
BENIGNO MORENO
AUSTIN MORGAN
CHARLES F MORGAN
CLARENCE J MORGAN
DANNIE C MORGAN
DAVID L MORGAN
DENNIS R MORGAN
PAUL E MORGAN
DONALD F MORIARTY
RICHARD MORING
TETSUE MORIUCHI
PEARL H MORMAN
JOHN E MORONE
JOHN M MORONSKI
JULIUS L MOROZ
ROLAND W MORRIS
RICHARD W MORRISEY
EDWARD M MORRISON
JAMES K MORRISON
JAMES L MORRISON
JOHN MORRISON
NORMAN W MORRISON
JOHN A MORRISSEY
PETER P MORRONE
HENRY MORROW
ROBERT A MORSE
DONALD R MORTON
JAMES W MORTON
ARCHIE J MOSCHELLA JR
DANIEL W MOSS
HENRY MOSS JR
FLOYD R MOTT
COLLINS MOULDEN JR
JACKIE L MOWERY
WALTER L MOWRER
DONALD L MOYER
JAMES A MOYER
THOMAS J MOYNIHAN JR
WILLIAM P MULLARKEY
JOHN J MULLEN
ROBERT A MULLIGAN
PRESTON MULLINS JR
EDWARD L MULROONEY
IRISH W MUMPOWER
BONG-JO MUN
BONG-JUN MUN
BONG-SU MUN
BYEONG-DONG MUN
BYEONG-DU MUN
BYEONG-GEUN MUN
BYEONG-HWAN MUN

BYEONG-YONG MUN
CHANG-GON MUN
CHANG-JIN MUN
DAL-HO MUN
EUNG-RYEO MUN
GEUN-SU MUN
GWANG-JUN MUN
GWANG-JUN MUN
GWANG-SIK MUN
HEON-HO MUN
HONG-UI MUN
IL-GAP MUN
IN-HO MUN
JAE-GEOL MUN
JANG-CHUN MUN
JANG-GEUN MUN
JANG-MAN MUN
JONG-DEOK MUN
JONG-DU MUN
JONG-SU MUN
JUN-HYEON MUN
JU-SEONG MUN
MAN-O MUN
MYEONG-GIL MUN
OK-OK MUN
SAM-JIN MUN
SANG-BOK MUN
SANG-RYONG MUN
SEOK-YONG MUN
SEONG-DAE MUN
SEON-JU MUN
SEO-YEONG MUN
SE-WON MUN
UI-HO MUN
YEONG-CHEOL MUN
YEONG-MAN MUN
JAMES D MUNDAY
VALENTE V MUNOZ
THOMAS J MURCHISON
LONNIE MURDOCK
GEORGE J MURILLO
CHRISTOPHER M MURPHY JR
EUGENE O MURPHY JR
JAMES P MURPHY
JOHN D MURPHY
MONROE P MURPHY
ROBERT M MURPHY
ROBERT W MURPHY
WILLIAM H MURPHY
WILLIAM H MURPHY
CARL D MURRAY
JAMES H MURRAY
NORVAL L MURRAY
ROBERT L MURRAY
TOBIAS MURRAY JR
LAWRENCE G MUSARRA
JE-HWAN MYEONG
CHARLES A MYERS
DONALD E MYERS
ELLIS E MYERS
HARRY F MYERS
JAMES W MYERS
JOHN R MYERS
ROBERT W MYERS
SAMUEL J MYERS JR
HARVEY A MYKRANTZ
DEUK-CHIL NA
DO-HYEONG NA
HEUNG-SEOK NA
HYEON-CHEOL NA
JIN-YUN NA
JONG-SEOK NA
TAE-GYU NA
VINCENT L NABHOLZ
ERNEST A NAGAI
WILLIAM E NAGAL
YEICHI NAKASATO
WILLIE C NALL
BYEONG-UK NAM
DU-GONG NAM
DU-HONG NAM
GI-HYEON NAM
GYEONG-HUI NAM
HONG-SIK NAM
JAE-HYEON NAM
JAE-SEON NAM
JEOM-DO NAM
JIN-HUI NAM
KWAE-HUI NAM

MYEONG-SU NAM
SANG-UN NAM
SEOK-WON NAM
SEONG-HO NAM
SEONG-YEOL NAM
SI-HWAN NAM
UN-SEOK NAM
WON-DO NAM
YONG-CHAN NAM
JOHN E NAPIER
FRANK J NAPOLITANO
RAYMOND NARANJO
JOSEPH O NASH
HAROLD C NASS
VINCENT C NAVARRA
RALPH O NAVARRO
JORGE NAVARRO-BERNARD
HERLEY E NAVE JR
CHARLIE NEACE JR
EMMETT NEAL
HOUSTON A NEAL
ODELL W NEALY
JOHN J NEAREY
JAMES J NEATON
EUGENE A NEEB
DOUGLAS M NEEL
LOYD R NEELY
MANUEL H NEFF
GILBERTO NEGRON-VEGA
PERCY W NEIGHBORS
RICHARD L NEIGHBORS
WILLIAM L NEIL
PAUL H NEILSON
ANTONE NELSON
DAVID J NELSON
JEROME S NELSON
LAURIN R NELSON
OSCAR R NELSON
WILLIAM E NELSON
DION L NEMAN
ALVIN M NEMITZ
THOMAS J NESIS
JOHN W NETKA JR
MAJOR J NETTLES
EUGENE Q NEUBAUER
SAM E NEVAREZ
LAWRENCE W NEVILLE
ROBERT B NEVILLE
JAMES E NEWCOMB
BOBBY R NEWLAND
JOHN E NEWLAND JR
HAROLD D NEWMAN
KENNETH O NEWSOM
ROBERT H NEWSOM
GILMER G NEWTON
ROBERT L NICKSON
WILLIAM C NIDIFFER
CLARENCE R NIEBOER
HENRY F NIEDERRITER JR
CYRUS L NIELSEN
HARRY S NIELSEN JR
JOHN E NIELSEN
CHESTER NIEMIC
DAVID NIEVES-MORALES
GERARD M NISCIA
CHARLES L NIX
VICTOR H NIX JR
CALVIN K NIXON
BOK-SUL NO
BYEONG-SIK NO
CHANG-U NO
CHA-SIL NO
CHEON-SEOP NO
CHIL-GEUK NO
DAL-GU NO
EUNG-DU NO
EUNG-GYU NO
GEUM-CHIL NO
GEUM-SIK NO
GYEONG-HYEON NO
GYEONG-O NO
HAE-JEONG NO
HYEONG-GEOL NO
HYEONG-SEOP NO
IN-SU NO
IN-TAEK NO

16 ARMY

IN-WON NO
JAE-JEON NO
JEONG-SIK NO
JONG-HYEON NO
JUNG-SIK NO
SANG-GYEONG NO
SEONG-GYU NO
SEONG-SU NO
SEONG-U NO
SU-MUN NO
TAE-JONG NO
YONG-MAN NO
JAY T NOBLES
ALFRED E NOLAN
DONALD F NOLAN
WILLIAM E NOLL
VERN H NORDQUIST
ROBERT C NOREAU
JAMES W NORMAN
RICHARD P NORMAN
CLIFFORD E NORRIS
GEORGE D NORRIS
EMERY B NORTHCUTT
ELMER E NORVELL
WILLARD V NORWICK
EARL R NOTBOHM
REINO NOUSIAINEN
PAUL J NOVICK
BERT L NOWAK
LEE R NOWLIN
FRANCIS J NUCE
JOHN R NULF
LESTER J NUNLEY
WALTER R NYE
DENNIS J NYHAN
WILLIAM N NYKYTUK
BYEONG-HWAN O
BYEONG-JU O
CHA-YEOL O
CHEOL-HO O
CHUN-SEONG O
DU-SIK O
GEUN-HAK O
GI-SEOK O
GUK-JUN O
GWANG-JI O
GYEONG-YONG O
GYU-MYEONG O
HAK-BONG O
HAK-YEON O
HAN-JUN O
HEUNG-SU O
IL-GEUN O
JAE-BONG O
JAE-HUI O
JAE-YUN O
JEOM-SUL O
JI-HWAN O
JIN-SIK O
JONG-CHAN O
JU-HWAN O
JUN-BONG O
MUN-SU O
MUN-SUL O
MYEONG-SU O
PAE-SEONG O
SANG-CHEOL O
SANG-HWAN O
SE-DON O
SE-GYEONG O
SE-JUN O
SEOK-GEUN O
SEOK-U O
SEONG-GEUN O
SEONG-JONG O
SE-YEON O
SO-GU O
SU-HWAN O
SUN-BONG O
SUN-DAE O
TAE-HO O
TAE-MAN O
TAE-YEON O
WON-JIN O
YEONG-CHEOL O
YEONG-DEOK O
YEONG-SEOP O
YONG-DEOK O
YONG-JEON O
YUN-CHEOL O

ELMER OBERLANDER
IRWIN J OBORN
CHARLES R OBRIEN
JAMES D OBRIEN
LARRIE D OBRIEN
ROBERT J OBRIEN
ROBERT W OBRIEN
ALBERTO OCHOA
RAYMOND R OCONNOR
ERNEST R ODELL
JIMMIE L ODEN
ELIJAH ODOM
EDWARD F ODONNELL
EDWARD G OFFERDAHL
NEIL N OGASAWARA
HENRY OGDEN JR
JAMES A OGLESBEE
JACK J OGLESBY
JAMES A OGLETHORPE
CORDELL OHARA
CHEOL-U OK
CHI-BU OK
CHI-JU OK
CHI-SEOP OK
CHI-SUK OK
GI-DONG OK
GI-EOP OK
JANG-HWAN OK
NOE-SEOK OK
SEOK-JU OK
SEONG-DO OK
TAE-GEUN OK
TAE-YUN OK
YEONG-CHEOL OK
YEONG-JONG OK
YEONG-JUN OK
TOGO OKAMURA
JOHN R OKEEFE
RICHARD N OLAGUE
ROBERT E OLDENBURG
EDWARD M OLDFIELD
JOE A OLINGER
ALBERT S OLIVAS
LORENZO OLIVAS
JACK A OLIVER
JOE B OLIVER JR
RUDOLPH W OLIVER JR
WALTER H OLIVER
VICTOR OLIVERAS-
LLANTIN
EDWARD C OLMAN
DONALD L OLSON
JEONG-HO ON
JONG-WON ON
GEORGE E ONEAL
EUGENE F ONEILL
LUTHER D ONEILL
VINCENT W ONEILL
JOHN S ONISZCZAK
LEONARD S ONORATO
ROLAND C OPEL
GEORGE OQUENDO
ANTONIO ORAMAS-
MORENO
STEVE ORESON JR
HENRY R ORETTA
BRUNO R ORIG
FRANCISCO ORLANDI-
VILLAFANE
ROBERT L ORMAN
PEDRO ORNELAS
RUDOLPH R OROZCO
JACK F ORR
JOHN E ORTEGA
JUAN P ORTEGAS
EARL ORTIZ
MANUEL A ORTIZ
RUBEN M ORTIZ
JUAN ORTIZ-FRANCO
JOSE R ORTIZ-GOMEZ
MIGUEL A ORTIZ-
HERNANDEZ
MARCELINO ORTIZ-
MORENO
RAFAEL ORTIZ-ORTEGA
OSCAR ORTIZ-ORTIZ
JOSE ORTIZ-RODRIGUEZ
CLAUDE W ORTMAN
CHARLES E OSBORNE
JOHN H OSBORNE

GUILLERMO OSORIO-
GUZMAN
ALBERT OSTROWSKI
ROBERT C OTTERBEIN
GEORGE R OTTO
HOWARD OUTLEY
HARVIN J OVERBEEK
GEORGE E OWENBY
FRANK OWENS JR
JOSEPH F OWENS
RAYMOND E OWENS
ROBERT J OWENS
HARVEY OXNER
ROBERT J OZELAS
GONZALO M PABLO
VINCENT D PACELLI
EDWARD P PACEWICZ
PASCUAL PACHECO-
ROMAN
JUAN L PACHECO-TAPIA
MARCELINO PADILLA JR
LUPE R PADRON
JOHN PADUA
ANTHONY E PAGANO
HENRY PAGE
ROBERT E PAGE
WILLIAM E PAGE
HERMAN T PAIGE
MURAL R PAINTER JR
PAUL E PAKIDIS JR
GINO PALAMARA
DOUGLAS K PALEN
ROBERT W PALITTI
ALLEN L PALMER
DONALD W PALMER
HAROLD E PALMER
JAMES O PALMER
MILBURN H PALMER
WARREN E PALMER
AMADO PALOMARES JR
ANGELO A PANARO
FRANCIS PANNO
SAVERIO PANZITTA
MILTON M PAPENFUSS
WILLIAM P PAPPAPETRU
JAMES T PAPPAS
JAMES PARHAM
JAMES PARISH
ROBERT A PARISH
BOK-AM PARK
BOK-DO PARK
BOK-GEUN PARK
BOK-SU PARK
BO-NAM PARK
BONG-AN PARK
BONG-DO PARK
BONG-GU PARK
BONG-GUN PARK
BONG-HWAN PARK
BONG-JAE PARK
BU-MAN PARK
BYEONG-CHEOL PARK
BYEONG-GIL PARK
BYEONG-GU PARK
BYEONG-HEUM PARK
BYEONG-HUI PARK
BYEONG-I PARK
BYEONG-SEON PARK
BYEONG-SIK PARK
BYEONG-SU PARK
CHAE-MIN PARK
CHANG-GON PARK
CHANG-HUN PARK
CHANG-MAN PARK
CHANG-MU PARK
CHANG-SEOP PARK
CHANG-SIK PARK
CHANG-SUN PARK
CHANG-YEON PARK
CHAN-OK PARK
CHA-SU PARK
CHEOL-GYU PARK
CHEOL-NYEON PARK
CHEOL-YEONG PARK
CHEON-SU PARK
CHIL-BONG PARK
CHIN-IN PARK
CHI-SANG PARK
CHU-I PARK
CHUN-GEUN PARK

CHUN-HO PARK
CHUN-SEOK PARK
CHUN-SU PARK
CHUN-TAE PARK
DAE-BYEOK PARK
DAE-GEUN PARK
DAE-GYU PARK
DAE-HO PARK
DAE-JIN PARK
DAE-SIK PARK
DAE-TAE PARK
DAE-YONG PARK
DAL-JU PARK
DAL-SEONG PARK
DAL-SIK PARK
DAL-SU PARK
DAL-SU PARK
DAL-SU PARK
DEOK-AM PARK
DEOK-CHUL PARK
DEOK-JAE PARK
DEOK-SU PARK
DEOK-SU PARK
DEOK-TAE PARK
DO-GIL PARK
DONG-GAP PARK
DONG-GAP PARK
DONG-GEUK PARK
DONG-HWAN PARK
DONG-IL PARK
DONG-JIN PARK
DONG-RAE PARK
DONG-SEOK PARK
DONG-SIK PARK
DONG-SU PARK
DO-YONG PARK
DU-GAP PARK
DU-HUI PARK
DU-HYEON PARK
DU-MAN PARK
EON-GYU PARK
EUL-DO PARK
EUNG-CHEON PARK
EUN-SIK PARK
EUN-YEOL PARK
GAP-DO PARK
GAP-YEOL PARK
GEON-DONG PARK
GEUM-JO PARK
GEUM-OK PARK
GEUN-DOL PARK
GEUN-JO PARK
GEUN-SEOK PARK
GI-CHUN PARK
GI-DAE PARK
GI-GYEONG PARK
GI-HA PARK
GI-HO PARK
GI-HO PARK
GI-HWAN PARK
GI-HYEON PARK
GI-JEONG PARK
GI-JIN PARK
GIL-GYU PARK
GIL-HUI PARK
GIL-SEON PARK
GIL-TAE PARK
GI-OK PARK
GI-SEON PARK
GI-SEOP PARK
GI-SIK PARK
GI-SU PARK
GI-SU PARK
GI-TAE PARK
GI-TAE PARK
GI-U PARK
GI-WON PARK
GI-WON PARK
GI-YEONG PARK
GONG-HYEON PARK
GONG-SU PARK
GON-YUN PARK
GWANG-BOK PARK
GWANG-GYU PARK
GWANG-MUN PARK
GWANG-SEOK PARK
GWANG-SU PARK
GWANG-YONG PARK
GWAN-GYU PARK
GWAN-YEOL PARK

GWI-OK PARK
GYEONG PARK
GYEONG-CHEON PARK
GYEONG-GYU PARK
GYEONG-HUI PARK
GYEONG-SI PARK
GYEONG-SIK PARK
GYEONG-SU PARK
GYEONG-YUN PARK
GYE-WON PARK
GYU-GEOL PARK
GYU-HAK PARK
GYU-HYEON PARK
GYU-SU PARK
HAE-DONG PARK
HAE-HAK PARK
HAE-HONG PARK
HAE-RYONG PARK
HAE-SUL PARK
HAE-WON PARK
HA-GYEONG PARK
HAK-BONG PARK
HAK-HUI PARK
HAK-MYEONG PARK
HAN-GYU PARK
HAN-I PARK
HAN-O PARK
HAN-O PARK
HAN-SANG PARK
HAN-SANG PARK
HA-WON PARK
HEUNG PARK
HEUNG-SU PARK
HO-CHUL PARK
HO-DONG PARK
HO-GEUN PARK
HONG-CHAN PARK
HONG-SIK PARK
HO-SIK PARK
HUI-IL PARK
HUI-SU PARK
HYEONG-GI PARK
HYEON-U PARK
HYO-GEUN PARK
I-GAP PARK
IK-SU PARK
IK-SU PARK
IL-DONG PARK
IL-HUN PARK
IL-JUN PARK
IL-SU PARK
IL-YONG PARK
IM-CHUL PARK
IM-CHUL PARK
IM-SAENG PARK
IM-YUN PARK
IN-GU PARK
IN-GYU PARK
IN-GYU PARK
IN-GYU PARK
IN-HAE PARK
IN-HAN PARK
IN-HO PARK
IN-HO PARK
JAE-GU PARK
JAE-GYU PARK
JAE-GYU PARK
JAE-HO PARK
JAE-HO PARK
JAE-HWA PARK
JAE-HWAN PARK
JAE-JIN PARK
JAE-MAN PARK
JAE-MUN PARK
JAE-SIK PARK
JAE-SU PARK
JANG-SU PARK
JANG-SUN PARK
JEONG-BOK PARK
JEONG-DAE PARK
JEONG-GUK PARK
JEONG-GWON PARK
JEONG-HO PARK
JEONG-HO PARK
JEONG-RAE PARK
JEONG-SANG PARK
JEONG-SU PARK
JEONG-SUN PARK
JEONG-SUN PARK
JEONG-TAE PARK

17 ARMY

JEONG-UI PARK
JI-CHAN PARK
JI-GAP PARK
JI-HO PARK
JIN-EOP PARK
JIN-HWAN PARK
JIN-SUN PARK
JIN-U PARK
JOHN D PARK
JONG-BONG PARK
JONG-CHEOL PARK
JONG-GEUN PARK
JONG-GI PARK
JONG-GIL PARK
JONG-HYEON PARK
JONG-JIN PARK
JONG-RYEOL PARK
JONG-SEOK PARK
JONG-SIK PARK
JONG-SUL PARK
JONG-TAE PARK
JONG-TAE PARK
JONG-WON PARK
JU-BOK PARK
JU-MAN PARK
JUNG-GEUN PARK
JUNG-GI PARK
JUNG-IN PARK
JUNG-SEON PARK
JUN-TAE PARK
JU-RAE PARK
JU-SIK PARK
KWAE-CHEOL PARK
MAN-BOK PARK
MAN-DAL PARK
MAN-GYU PARK
MAN-JO PARK
MAN-SEOK PARK
MAN-SEUNG PARK
MAN-SIK PARK
MAN-SIK PARK
MAN-YEONG PARK
MIN-HO PARK
MU-DONG PARK
MUN-CHIL PARK
MUN-GYU PARK
MUN-I PARK
MUN-MAN PARK
MU-SIK PARK
MYEONG-GYU PARK
MYEONG-HO PARK
MYEONG-HWAN PARK
MYEONG-HWAN PARK
MYEONG-JAE PARK
MYEONG-JO PARK
MYEONG-JU PARK
MYEONG-JUN PARK
MYEONG-SEOK PARK
MYEONG-SIK PARK
MYEONG-SU PARK
MYEONG-SU PARK
NAM-HYEON PARK
NAM-RYUL PARK
NAM-SEON PARK
NEUNG-HYEON PARK
NO-CHEOL PARK
NO-HWAN PARK
NO-TAEK PARK
OE-SUL PARK
OE-WON PARK
OK-MAN PARK
PAN-CHUL PARK
PAN-IK PARK
PAN-IL PARK
PAN-SIK PARK
PAN-SU PARK
PAN-SUK PARK
PIL-DONG PARK
PIL-GYU PARK
PIL-JU PARK
PIL-SU PARK
PIL-SU PARK
SA-DONG PARK
SAM-CHAN PARK
SAM-DAL PARK
SAM-HO PARK
SAM-RANG PARK
SAM-RYUL PARK
SAM-SIK PARK
SANG-CHEOL PARK

SANG-CHEON PARK
SANG-CHUN PARK
SANG-GEUN PARK
SANG-GI PARK
SANG-GI PARK
SANG-GYU PARK
SANG-JIP PARK
SANG-JO PARK
SANG-MOK PARK
SANG-NYEON PARK
SANG-OK PARK
SANG-SU PARK
SANG-UN PARK
SANG-YONG PARK
SE-CHAN PARK
SEO-GU PARK
SEOK-DO PARK
SEOK-GEUN PARK
SEOK-HUI PARK
SEOK-JUN PARK
SEOK-SAN PARK
SEOK-SU PARK
SEON-DAL PARK
SEON-GAP PARK
SEONG-CHEON PARK
SEONG-DEOK PARK
SEONG-GEUN PARK
SEONG-GI PARK
SEONG-GWAN PARK
SEONG-GWON PARK
SEONG-GYEONG PARK
SEONG-HO PARK
SEONG-HO PARK
SEONG-HWA PARK
SEONG-HWA PARK
SEONG-IL PARK
SEONG-IP PARK
SEONG-JAE PARK
SEONG-MIN PARK
SEONG-SU PARK
SEONG-SUL PARK
SEONG-YONG PARK
SEONG-YONG PARK
SEONG-YONG PARK
SEON-HYEON PARK
SEUNG-HAK PARK
SEUNG-HANG PARK
SEUNG-HYEON PARK
SEUNG-IL PARK
SEUNG-JO PARK
SEUNG-JUN PARK
SEUNG-MAN PARK
SIN-HO PARK
SO-AM PARK
SONG-HAK PARK
SO-YONG PARK
SU-DEOK PARK
SU-DONG PARK
SU-GEUN PARK
SU-GWON PARK
SU-HONG PARK
SU-HYEON PARK
SU-HWAN PARK
SUL-I PARK
SU-MAN PARK
SUN-DEOK PARK
SUN-GEUN PARK
SUN-GYU PARK
SUN-JEONG PARK
SUN-NEUNG PARK
SU-SEONG PARK
SU-SEUNG PARK
SU-YEONG PARK
SU-YONG PARK
SU-YONG PARK
TAE-JE PARK
TAE-JUNG PARK
TAE-MUN PARK
TAE-SAN PARK
TAE-SEOP PARK
TAE-SU PARK
TAE-UN PARK
TAE-YONG PARK
TA-GWAN PARK
U-AM PARK
U-AM PARK
U-GON PARK
U-IL PARK
U-IL PARK
UI-SU PARK

UI-YEONG PARK
UN-RAE PARK
WANG-SU PARK
WAN-RYEOL PARK
WON-CHUL PARK
WON-CHUN PARK
WON-CHUN PARK
WON-DEOK PARK
WON-DO PARK
WON-JUN PARK
YANG-NAM PARK
YEONG-BOK PARK
YEONG-BONG PARK
YEONG-DAE PARK
YEONG-DO PARK
YEONG-DONG PARK
YEONG-GEUN PARK
YEONG-GI PARK
YEONG-GUK PARK
YEONG-GWAN PARK
YEONG-GYU PARK
YEONG-HAN PARK
YEONG-HO PARK
YEONG-HO PARK
YEONG-HWAN PARK
YEONG-JAE PARK
YEONG-NAM PARK
YEONG-NAM PARK
YEONG-SA PARK
YEONG-SE PARK
YEONG-SEOK PARK
YEONG-SU PARK
YEONG-TAE PARK
YEONG-TAE PARK
YEONG-U PARK
YONG-CHUL PARK
YONG-DAL PARK
YONG-DON PARK
YONG-GEUN PARK
YONG-GU PARK
YONG-JIN PARK
YONG-JO PARK
YONG-SU PARK
YONG-SU PARK
YONG-SUL PARK
YONG-SUL PARK
YU-BOK PARK
YU-BYEONG PARK
YUN-DAL PARK
YUN-GYEONG PARK
YUN-GYU PARK
YUN-HWAN PARK
YUN-JANG PARK
YUN-JE PARK
YUN-NAM PARK
YUN-OK PARK
YUN-SU PARK
F D PARKER
HARRY J PARKER
JAMES E PARKER
LEROY PARKER SR
RICHARD T PARKER
RONALD E PARKER
VINCENT PARKER
DAVID O PARKHURST
CHARLES W PARKS
DONALD L PARKS
LAUREL E PARKS
ARTHUR J PARMENTER
THOMAS E PARRISH
WILLIE P PARRISH
WILLIAM D PARTIN
EDDY G PARTRIDGE
RICHARD B PASCHALL
THOMAS L PASTORIUS
LELAND M PATE
FELIX P PATOVSKI
PRESTON C PATRICK JR
BENNIE W PATTERSON
BOBBIE J PATTERSON
CLARENCE E PATTERSON
GEORGE PATTERSON
ITHAL T PATTERSON
JEROME E PATTERSON
OLIVER J PATTERSON
RICHARD W PATTERSON
ORLANDO R PATTISON
DELMAR PATTON
TEDDY L PAUL
CHARLES R PAULSEN

HERMAN E PAULY
LEO S PAVILCEK
CHARLES D PAYNE
EDDIE L PAYNE
J F PAYNE
WILBERT PAYNE
ALVARO PAZ-LANSOT
JOHN T PEACE
BROUGHTON PEACOCK
WILLIE L PEAK
ANDREW D PEARISH
RAYMOND T PEARSON
DARRELL D PEASLEY
WILLIAM E PEAVERS
WILLIAM H PECKHAM
DOMENICK PECORARO
RALPH A PECOT JR
KENNETH R PEDERSEN
JAMES E PEEK
EUGENE P PEERY
RUDOLPH PELLEGRINI
ALVAH J PENNOCK
NORTON C PEPPMULLER
AARON PEREZ
ALEJANDRO G PEREZ
JOSE S PEREZ
ISIDRO PEREZ-CRUZ
MIGUEL A PEREZ-LOUBRIEL
ISMAEL PEREZ-ROMAN
DANIEL B PERIO
JAMES C PERKINS
JESSE B PERKINS
WILLIAM G PERKINS
ELMER J PERRY
WILLIAM C PERSINGER
CLIFFORD A PERSONS
HARVEY E PERUSSE
PAUL PETERMAN
GERALD T PETERS
RICHARD E PETERS
ARMAND A PETERSEN
CHARLES E PETERSON
DEAN V PETERSON
JACK D PETERSON
JACOB J PETERSON
PLINIO PETERSON-
PARODIS
NEIL P PETRAGLIA
RALPH J PETRELL
VERNON E PETRI
JOHN W PETWAY
GEORGE A PFUSCH
BOBBY J PHARR
WILLIAM A PHARRIS JR
WILLIAM T PHELAN
BAYARD G PHELPS
BOBBIE D PHELPS
JOHN M PHELPS
LOWELL E PHELPS
GEORGE W PHILLIPPE
ALVIN L PHILLIPS
CHARLES F PHILLIPS
CHARLES L PHILLIPS
HUGH B PHILLIPS
JACKIE L PHILLIPS
JAMES K PHILLIPS
JOSEPH F PHILLIPS
RICHARD E PHILLIPS
RICHARD L PHILLIPS
ALVIN PHIPPS
WILLIAM A PICARD
ERNEST M PICKENS
GEORGE PICKETT JR
JAMES E PICKETT
JAMES L PICKETT
WILLIAM R PICTUN
DONALD L PIERCE
FLENOIL PIERCE
GEORGE PIERCE JR
JOSEPH P PIERCE
ROBERT E PIERCE
ROBERT F PIERCE
WALTER J PIERCE
EARL R PIERCY
RODERICK A PIERCY
EVERETT F PIERON
TAYLOR O PIERSON
RAYMOND E PIETRZAK
MARLIN L PIGOTT
DONALD L PIKE

MANLEY R PILGRIM
FRANK J PILLON
OTIS E PINGLETON
JOSEPH J PINNA
EDMUNDO PINTOR
WALLACE R PIPER
THOMAS PIPIC
PARIS J PIPKIN
CLIFFORD A PIRTLE
CLYDE B PITTILLO
RAY J PITTMAN
CLEO PITTS
SAMUEL P PIZZO
BENJAMIN S PLATER
NORMAN C PLINSKE
EDWARD V PLISKA
ALBERT W PLUMB
HAROLD R PLUMLEY
JAMES R PLUMMER
KENNETH D POCKEY
GERARD J POIRIER
CHARLES L POKOJSKI
GILBERT K POLAND
ANGELO G POLETIS
BENJAMIN POOLE
HAROLD J POOLE
JACK E POOLE
JOHN E POOLMAN
CRISANTO N POPA
LEONARD T POPHAM
JUAN PORTELA-SIERRA
CARTER S PORTER
CHARLES A PORTER
JACK D PORTER
JOHN K PORTER
ROBERT M PORTER
THOMAS A POSEY
DAVID E POST
CLIFFORD E POSTON
CHARLES POTTER
MYRON L POTTER
ASHFORD E POTTS
CHARLIE M POTTS
LAWRENCE W POTTS
LESTER M POUNDS JR
RICHARD C POUPARD
CLAYTON L POUST
JAMES L POWELL
JAMES R POWELL
ROBERT L POWELL
WILLIAM S POWELL JR
JERRY B POWERS
KENNETH W POWERS
RICHARD C POWLEY
ALVIN J PRADAT
CHARLES H PRATT
ELMER PRATT
ROBERT D PRATT
JAMES L PRESSEY
WILLIAM R PRESSLEY
DAVID R PRESTON
RONALD L PRESTON
VICTOR M PRESTWOOD
LOUIS PREVOST
CHARLES H PRICE JR
HUGHEY D PRICE
JERRY L PRICE
JOHN F PRICE
MINER W
PRIDEMORE JR
WESLEY PRINCE JR
ARNIE R PRITCHETT
DIXIE C PRITCHETT
FRANK PROVENZANO
THADDEUS PRZESLICA
ALFRED A PUCCI
CLYDE PUGH
DAVID L PUGH
DONALD O PUGH
JOE L PUGH
JOHN PUGH
CHARLES E PULIDO
LOUIS D PULLANO
MELVIN J PUMPER
EDWARD J PUNCH
CHARLES PURDON JR
JEROME A PURNELL JR
LINZY L PUTMAN
GENE A PUTZIER
WALTER PUZACH

18 ARMY

SEOK-RYEOL PYEON
JAMES H PYKE
SANG-GEUN PYO
SUN-BONG PYO
WON-JO PYO
WILLIAM H QUALE
CURTIS W QUALLS
RUFF G QUEEN
WINSTON R QUEEN
DONALD W QUELL
JOHN E QUICK
RICHARD B QUIGLEY
THOMAS J QUIGLEY
CHARLES P QUINN
WILLIAM J QUINN
MANUEL M QUINTANA
AUGUSTIN QUINTERO
FREDERICK J QUINTON
SANTIAGO QUIROZ
GYEONG-DEOK RA
YEONG-SUN RA
GREEN RABON JR
PHILIP T RADECKER
KENNETH C RADEKE
LAZEL RADEN
LYLE L RADER
JAMES C RAGER
JOHN RAGLAND JR
FRANK P RAGONE
CLAUDE R RAINER JR
SEBASTIAN J RAINERI
CHARLES A RAINES
JAMES D RAMEL
LLOYD C RAMEY
CARLOS B RAMIREZ
ERNEST E RAMIREZ
JOSE M RAMIREZ JR
LUPE H RAMIREZ
ISAIAH RAMOS
LUIS M RAMOS-CRUZ
PEDRO RAMOS-DIAZ
PEDRO A RAMOS-
ECHEVARRIA
NARCISO RAMOS-ORTIZ
JESUS RAMOS-ROMAN
ORLANDO L RAMOS-
TORRES
BILLY G RAMSEY
CARRELL O RAMSEY
DONALD E RAMSEY
IRVANULE RAMSEY
ROBERT E RAMSEY
RICHARD C RAMSIER
DANIEL C RANDALL
EARLAN V RANDALL
LESTER N RANDALL
WILLIAM P RANEY
CHARLES D RANKIN JR
GEORGE C RANKINS
DAVID C RAPER
LUIGI J RAPONE JR
NORMAN L RASK
JOHN E RASMUSSEN
WALTER J RASSAT
JOSEPH J RATAY
ARTHUR RATCLIFF JR
RALPH G RATHBURN
HAROLD G RATLIEFF
ORA W RATLIFF
CHARLES W RAWLS
ALBERT RAWSON
DEMPSEY E RAY
JAMES RAY
NAPOLEON RAY
ROY RAY JR
EDWARD J RAYLES
ALPHONSE H
RAYMOND JR
ROBERT V READ
WILLIAM T READ JR
DONALD L READE
BILLY E REAGAN
JOSEPH P REAGAN
WALTON R REAGAN
JOHN B REAHL
JOHN N REAM JR
CHESTER F REAS JR
JOHN J REBER JR
RAYMOND RECCHIA
DONALD R REDD

GEORGE H REDDING
JAMES B REDIKER
CHARLES E REED
FRANKLIN J REED
HARRY R REED
NATHANIEL REED
PAUL R REED
WILLIAM H B REED
WILLIAM A REEDY
GEORGE REESE JR
WILLIAM N REESE JR
DARYL D REEVES
THOMAS J REGAN
EDWARD L REICK
HENRY S REID
JOHN REINHARDT JR
JOHN P REINHARDT JR
ELTON W REINISCH
ROBERT N REITMEYER
RICHARD G RELVA
HERMAN L REMBERT
NORMAN E RENFROW
JOSE G RENNER
JOHN RENTERIA
ARCHIE J REON
JUNIOR W REPP
QUENTIN L REQUA
HUGO E RESS JR
MORRIS L RETHMEIER
WILLARD J REY
HUMBERTO L REYES
MANUEL G REYES
ADELA REYES-FALCON
ANTONIO REYES-MEDINA
LUIS E REYES-RIVERA
HERBERT W REYNOLDS JR
LINDBERG REYNOLDS
WILLIAM H REYNOLDS
WINFRED L REYNOLDS
ROBERT E RHOADS
JAMES A RHODES
JOHNNIE B RHODES
CARLTON J RICE
CURTIS R RICE
TEDDY W RICH
HUNTER J RICHARDS
JOSEPH T RICHARDS
LOWELL E RICHARDS
DELTON M RICHARDSON
EARL R RICHARDSON
GEORGE W RICHARDSON
LESLIE O RICHARDSON
ONEIL B RICHARDSON
ROBERT B RICHARDSON
RUFUS S RICHARDSON
WAYNE L RICHARDSON
AFTON L RICHISON
CLYDE J RICKARDS
EUGENE H RICKS
RAYMOND RIDEAU
JOHN H RIDER
LAWRENCE J RIEDMANN
EDWARD R RIEDY
EDWIN A RIETZ
MERYL G RIGGENBACH
EARL L RIGGINS JR
BOBBY L RIGGS
RAY L RIGGS
JOHN P RIGNEY
CHESTER E RIGSBY
ALFRED RILEY
GEORGE RILEY
JAMES H RILEY
CHARLES A RING
CONYARD L RING
RALPH E RING
VICTOR J RIOLI
MANUEL RIOS-ORTIZ
LEROY A R RITENOUR
GEORGE RITTEREISER
JESUS RIVAS
FLOYD RIVERA
JOSE T RIVERA
PEDRO A RIVERA
JOSE R RIVERA-COLON
ISMAEL RIVERA-CRESPO
JUAN RIVERA-GONZALEZ
MIGUEL RIVERA-
MERCADO
LUIS M RIVERA-RIVERA

ELIAS RIVERA-SERRANO
ARMANDO F RIVERO
GUIDO RIZZO
ERIC ROACH
GLENN V ROACH
WENDELL E ROACH
GEORGE R ROARK
JOHN B ROBART
JAMES S ROBASON
CHARLES E ROBB
LEONARD C ROBBINS
ALLEN M ROBERSON
HARRY P ROBERSON
OTTO S ROBERSON JR
TEDDY E ROBERSON
WAYNE ROBERSON
JOSEPH M ROBERTI
ALBERT S ROBERTS
ARLYS I ROBERTS
AUBRIE ROBERTS
CARL W ROBERTS
CLARENCE C ROBERTS
CLAYTON L ROBERTS
EARL E ROBERTS
EUGENE I ROBERTS
GEORGE B ROBERTS
HERBERT L ROBERTS
HOWARD M ROBERTS
JACK ROBERTS
JACK W ROBERTS
JAMES B ROBERTS
JEFF ROBERTS JR
RICHARD F ROBERTS
ROY L ROBERTS
STEPHEN G ROBERTS
WILLIAM J ROBERTS
WILLIAM M ROBERTS
JAMES P ROBERTSON
JOSEPH K ROBERTSON
SAMUEL ROBERTSON
ROBERT F ROBINETTE
CLAVIN T ROBINSON
DONALD W ROBINSON
EDDIE ROBINSON
FOY S ROBINSON
GEORGE A ROBINSON
HOMER ROBINSON JR
JOE ROBINSON
JOHN ROBINSON JR
LEE O ROBINSON
LOUIS ROBINSON
MARVIN L ROBINSON
RALPH G ROBINSON
ROY ROBINSON
WILDA E ROBINSON
WILLIAM A ROBINSON
WILLIAM J ROBINSON
PAUL L ROBISON
ROBERT W ROBISON
ROBERT C
ROCKENBAUCH
PAUL E ROCUS
CHARLES E RODGERS
JAMES T RODGERS
JEROME H RODGERS
ROBERT R RODGERS
ABELARDO RODRIGUEZ
ALEJANDRO RODRIGUEZ
EARL G RODRIGUEZ
JOSE M RODRIGUEZ
NARCISO RODRIGUEZ
ROLANDO R RODRIGUEZ
CARLOS RODRIGUEZ-
ALFONSO
NICHOLAS RODRIGUEZ-
ALICEA
OVIDIO RODRIGUEZ-
BATTISTINI
ROBERTO RODRIGUEZ-
BURGOS
RAFAEL RODRIGUEZ-
DEL TORO
PEDRO J RODRIGUEZ-
OQUENDO
ALCIDES RODRIGUEZ-
OTERO
RAFAEL RODRIGUEZ-
RIVERA
JOAQUIN RODRIGUEZ-
RUIZ

HERIBERTO RODRIGUEZ-
SANTIAGO
JULIO RODRIGUEZ-
SANTIAGO
HECTOR R RODRIQUEZ
EMORY L ROE
EDDIE L ROEBUCK
RICHARD L ROEMER
NORMAN E ROESBERRY
PAUL R ROESE
DAVID S ROESSLER
CARL R ROGERS
CLINTON R ROGERS
EUGENE ROGERS
FLOYD A T ROGERS
FREDERICK G ROGERS
KENNETH E ROGERS
RALPH D ROGERS
RANDOLPH R ROGERS
RICHARD M ROGERS
ROBERT L ROGERS JR
RUBE ROGERS
WILLIAM E ROGERS
WILLIE L ROGERS
JOHNSON T ROLLES
JOSEPH A ROLLICK
HENRY L ROLLING
CHARLES W ROLLINS
CLAUD ROLLINS
GRADY L ROLLINS
JUAN ROLON-HERNANDEZ
LARRY A ROMANELLI
ANGEL L ROMAN-
MORALES
AIME ROMANO
CHARLES B ROMERO
HUMBERTO ROMERO
HAROLD J RONAN
ERNEST E ROOKER
JOHN H ROOKS
ROBERT L ROOKS
HECTOR P ROSA
FRANK L ROSALES
ELIU ROSARIO
HUMBERTO ROSARIO-
SANTOS
DOMINGO R ROSAS
EMILIO ROSAS-MUNIZ
EDWARD D ROSCOE
NOKOMIS J ROSE
NORMAN E ROSECRANTS
MARTIN B ROSEN
KARL R ROSENBACH
SOL ROSENBERG
FRED D ROSENTHAL
GEORGE A ROSENTHAL
WILLIAM E ROSHIA JR
CAROL B ROSS
ENOCH ROSS
JOHN E ROSS
RICHARD C ROSS
JOSEPH N ROSSANO
JOSEPH W ROSZAK
JOHN E ROTARIUS
OSCAR F ROTH
RICHARD ROTH
CHARLES R ROTHER
JOSEPH R ROUSSIN
JOSEPH T ROWAN
PHILLIP L ROWE
WILLIAM E ROWE
HAROLD M ROWELL
MILFORD N ROWLAND
RAYMOND F ROWLAND
HINTON C ROYCE
ERNEST R ROYE
ROBERT D ROYSTER
JOHNNY L ROYSTON
OSCAR RUBART JR
LUIS E RUBIO-ARROYO
HURLEY B RUCKER
WILLIAM F RUDDER
JACK E RUDDICK
ROBERT F RUDER
JAMES J RUDICK
DELMAR W RUEDIGER
VERN O RUGH
DONALD E RUITER
JOSEPH T RULE
GEORGE D RUSS

ROBERT C RUSS
HOYT O RUSSELL
LEONARD E RUSSELL
JOSE O RUSSI-RAMOS
LOUIS S RUTH
HILLARD V
RUTHERFORD
CARROLL O
RUTHSTROM
JAMES RUTLEDGE
JESSIE W RUTLIFF
JIM J RYAN
RICHARD W RYSAVY
FRANK C RYSIAWA
BYEONG-GYUN RYU
BYEONG-HUI RYU
BYEONG-SEON RYU
CHEOL-U RYU
CHUN-SANG RYU
DAL-O RYU
GI-GAP RYU
GI-MUK RYU
GWANG-DO RYU
HAE-GWANG RYU
HWANG-CHEOL RYU
HYANG-GEUN RYU
I-CHEON RYU
IN-GON RYU
JAE-GYU RYU
JAE-JO RYU
JAE-SU RYU
JEONG-GAP RYU
JEONG-HO RYU
JEONG-YEOL RYU
JONG-TAE RYU
JU-RYEOL RYU
MI-CHEOL RYU
MYEONG-HWAN RYU
PAN-SU RYU
SAENG-YEONG RYU
SEONG-DO RYU
SEONG-JIN RYU
SEUNG-DEOK RYU
SU-RYEOL RYU
TAE-SIK RYU
U-YONG RYU
YUN-HYEONG RYU
BYEONG-GWAN SA
GONG-TAK SA
SEONG-HWAN SA
YU-SU SA
IGNACIO A SAAVEDRA
MICHAEL E SABEL
ROBERT C SABINE
GEORGE A SABOURIN
ALBERT V SACCA
SALVADORE F SACCO
EUGENE SADDLER
FAUSTO SAGADRACA
JOSEPH J SAHTILA
MASAYA SAITO
KENNETH M
SAKAMOTO
HECTOR SALAMAN-
ARROYO
GREGORIO B SALAS
ESTEVAN SALAZAR
JOE SALAZAR JR
PIO M SALAZAR
AIVARS K SALENIEKS
ANGEL SALGADO-
TORRES
OWEN E SALISBURY
ALFRED L SALTER
RICHARD D SALVATORE
JOHN S SAMSON
JOHN L SANBORN
JORGE G SANCHEZ
JUAN SANCHEZ-
MENDEZ
JESUS SANCHEZ-
RODRIGUEZ
EARL SANDERS JR
FREDERICK W SANDERS
GENE A SANDERS
JAMES SANDERS
JOSEPH M SANDERS
RICHARD G SANDERS
WADE C SANDERS
ROBERT J SANDERSON

19 ARMY

FLOYD A SANDLIN
ALBERTO SANDOVAL
ANTONIO SANDOVAL
PHIL SANDOVAL
RALPH E SANDS
ALFRED T SANFORD
ISADORE SANFORD
LUIS G SANTANA-MARTINEZ
MIGUEL SANTANA-MARTINEZ
JOSEPH P SANTARSIERO
ANTHONY C SANTELLA
CANDIDO SANTIAGO-ALVARADO
JUAN F SANTIAGO-NAVARRO
CARMELO SANTIAGO-RUIZ
JOSEPH F SANTILLO
HERMAN E SANTISTEVAN
RICHARD J SANTISTVAN
LOUIS N SANTOPIETRO
DOMINGO SANTOS-CRUZ
MANUEL SANTOS-RIVERA
CHARLES R SAPP
MANUEL SARATE
HAROLD J SARGEANT
RICHARD H SARPOLA
ROBERT W SARVER
THADDEUS R SARWINSKI
LEORIS SASSER
GONZALO SATOR
LEVINE H SAUERWINE JR
ANDREW A SAUNDERS
JOHN E SAUNDERS
JOSEPH E SAUVE
JAMES T SAVAGE
LEO P T SAVARD
EDWARD J SAVKO
DOIL B SAWYER
GILBERT D SAXTON
HAROLD M SAYLOR
PETER J SCACCIA
ANTHONY N SCALZO
LAURENCE O SCARBERRY
JACK K SCARBOROUGH
RUDOLPH M SCATENI
HOWARD C SCHAAP
CHARLES H SCHAEFER
DONALD L SCHAEFER
GEORGE J SCHAEFER
HENRY C SCHARLOTT JR
ROBERT R SCHATZ
FREDRICK I SCHAUER
DOUGLAS F SCHAUF
ALBERT E SCHAWLEM JR
JAMES C SCHECK
ELMER H SCHEFFLER
FRANK J SCHELTENS
ROBERT R SCHIRMER
RUSSELL SCHLABAUGH
DELMOND W SCHLEGEL
ROY V SCHLENKER
WALTER J SCHLOMER JR
KENNETH SCHLOTFELDT
RAYMOND J SCHMELZER
JENS S SCHMIDT
VERNON E SCHMIEDL
ALPHONSE R SCHMITT
RAYMOND SCHMOLDT
WILLIAM J SCHNEIDER
BLAIR D SCHOFFSTOLL
WILLIAM G SCHOLZE
CURTIS B SCHOOLEY
RICHARD L SCHOTT
DONALD R SCHRAMM
ALLEN W SCHREINER
HENRY D SCHRIEFER
ELMER H SCHRIEVER
MAYNARD R SCHROEDER
ROBERT I SCHROEDER
MERL A SCHROY
ROBERT L SCHUBBE
ALFORD E SCHUFT
WILLARD F SCHULDT
JOHN T SCHULTE JR
FLOYD SCHULTZ
JOHN A SCHULTZ
RAYMOND J SCHUMER
GERALD O SCHUNKE
RAYMOND R SCHWARTZ
ROBERT C SCHWARTZ
BRANDT E SCHWARZ
CLIFFORD W SCHWEGLER
ARTHUR A SCHWIND
HENRY A SCIPIONI
BOBBY G SCOGGINS
JAMES W SCOLF
PILTON SCOON
FELIX SCOTT
FRANK J SCOTT
JOE B SCOTT
JOHN SCOTT
LESTER W SCOTT
RICHARD W SCOTT
ROBERT L SCOTT
JAMES M SCRIBER
FRANCIS J SCULLY
EDGAR M SEABORN
ALBERT SEABROOK
ISRAEL SEABROOKE
EARL F SEALE JR
WARREN SEARS
DONALD L SEBASTIAN
GEORGE SEBEST
GENE SECHMAN
REYNALDO SEDILLOS
JACK C SEELINGER
WILLIAM L SEERY
GEORGE P SEGURA
LLOYD J SEGURA
JAMES A SEIBOLD
ROBERT L SELDON
CHARLES L R SELF
STANLEY S SELINGER
LESTER C SELKE
WILLIAM J SELLERS
LEONARD R SELLICKSON
ROALD E SELLIE
FLOYD S SELVIDGE
GEORGE SEMOSKY JR
MARTIN SENKOWSKI
BOK-GEON SEO
BONG-HWA SEO
BONG-UN SEO
BO-SUL SEO
BYEONG-DU SEO
BYEONG-GUK SEO
BYEONG-GUK SEO
BYEONG-JIN SEO
CHANG-GEUN SEO
CHANG-SEOK SEO
CHAN-SU SEO
DAE-YUN SEO
DEOK-SEON SEO
DU-WON SEO
EOK-CHU SEO
EUL-GYU SEO
EUL-JO SEO
EUL-MAN SEO
EUNG-SU SEO
EUN-SU SEO
GANG-SEOK SEO
GAP-I SEO
GAP-SEOK SEO
GI-JUN SEO
GI-JUN SEO
GI-TAEK SEO
GWANG-CHUN SEO
GWANG-EOK SEO
GWON-JO SEO
GYU-TAE SEO
GYU-TAE SEO
HAK-I SEO
HAN-GYU SEO
HO-HO SEO
HO-SEOK SEO
HO-SEOK SEO
HUI-GYUN SEO
HUI-MYEONG SEO
HYEONG-BEOM SEO
HYEONG-OK SEO
HYEON-TAEK SEO
HYEON-TAEK SEO
JAE-YUN SEO
JEOL-GON SEO
JEONG-BEOM SEO
JEONG-DON SEO
JEONG-OK SEO
JIN-U SEO
JONG-HUN SEO
JONG-SEONG SEO
JONG-TAEK SEO
JU-SEOK SEO
MAN-GAP SEO
MUN-SU SEO
MYEONG-O SEO
MYEONG-O SEO
MYEONG-SU SEO
RYU-DEUK SEO
SAM-DO SEO
SAM-SIK SEO
SANG-DON SEO
SANG-DU SEO
SANG-EON SEO
SANG-GYO SEO
SANG-GYU SEO
SANG-GYU SEO
SANG-YEONG SEO
SEOK-GAP SEO
SEOK-GYU SEO
SEOK-JEOM SEO
SEOK-MUN SEO
SEOK-SU SEO
SEOK-SUN SEO
SEOK-TAEK SEO
SEONG-GYU SEO
SEONG-GYU SEO
SEONG-HAK SEO
SEONG-O SEO
SEONG-O SEO
SEUNG-YONG SEO
SO-HUI SEO
TAE-HAN SEO
TAEK-GU SEO
TAE-YONG SEO
U-DEOK SEO
U-DEOK SEO
WAN-MIN SEO
WON-HEUM SEO
WON-TAEK SEO
YANG-SU SEO
YEONG-HO SEO
YEONG-SU SEO
YONG-AM SEO
YONG-CHEOL SEO
YONG-HAK SEO
YONG-HAK SEO
YONG-JU SEO
DONG-CHEON SEOK
HUI-IK SEOK
JEONG-GYUN SEOK
JIN-O SEOK
JIN-O SEOK
JONG-BAEK SEOK
MYEONG-CHEOL SEOK
SANG-GI SEOK
SEOK-YONG SEOK
UNG-NANG SEOK
BOK-YUL SEOL
JEONG-HO SEOL
JIN-CHUL SEOL
JIN-GEON SEOL
UN-GIL SEOL
YEONG-GEUN SEOL
YEONG-SIK SEOL
YEON-JU SEOL
BYEONG-JIN SEON
BAEK-I SEONG
BO-HEON SEONG
BOK-HWAN SEONG
BOK-YONG SEONG
CHAN-JO SEONG
DO-YEONG SEONG
DU-YEONG SEONG
GANG-YEONG SEONG
GEUN-SU SEONG
GIL-YONG SEONG
HYEON-GAP SEONG
I-SU SEONG
JAE-GEUN SEONG
JAE-GYEONG SEONG
MAEK-DO SEONG
MUN-SEONG SEONG
NAK-JUN SEONG
RAK-HONG SEONG
SANG-HO SEONG
SU-YEONG SEONG
YEOL-GYEONG SEONG
YONG-UN SEONG
GOK-SU SEONU
TONY SERCEL JR
HENRY SERGENT
ANTHONY D SERNA
FRANK G SERNA
ANSELMO SERRANO-SERRANO
JORGE R SERRA-ORSINI
NICOLAS L SERRATO
JOSE M SERRATTO
ARTHUR SETARO JR
NORMAN C SETZER
CHARLES E SETZLER
BYEONG-HUI SEUNG
GWANG-HYEON SEUNG
MARVIN D SEVERE
LEONARD T SEWELL
PAUL J SEWELL
WILLIAM G SEWELL JR
VIGGO E SEWER
MARTIN F SEYMOUR
EDGAR L SHADRICK
KENNETH R SHADRICK
HAROLD R SHAFFER
ROBERT R SHAFFER
WILLIAM A SHAFFER
PAUL SHAFFRON
STANFORD G SHAHAN
EARL H SHANAVER
JOSEPH M SHANNON
LARRY SHANNON
CHARLES R SHARP
DONALD W SHARP
FRANKLIN D SHARP
GERALD C SHAVER
IRVIN E SHAVER
ROBERT L SHAVERS
ALBERT L SHAW
BILLY D SHAW
JAMES F SHAW
JAMES P SHAW
KENNETH R SHAW
LIONEL SHAW
WILLIAM R SHAW
ROY C SHAWVER
WARREN D SHEAFOR
ALAN D SHEARER JR
WILLIAM F SHEEHAN
WILBUR K SHEEHY JR
JOHN E SHEETS
CHARLES SHEHORN JR
GEORGE W SHELBY
HARRY D SHELTON
ROY SHELTON
ROBERT SHENAULT
HAROLD R SHEPARD
HOWARD SHEPHERD
TONEY J SHERARD
ALBERT SHERMAN
ANDREW E SHERMAN
FRANCIS E SHERWOOD
HOWARD T SHERWOOD
SHELDON A SHERWOOD
WILLIAM H SHERWOOD
MATHEW SHEVROVICH JR
WAYNE N SHIELDS
WILLIAM F SHIFFLET
DONALD A SHINABERY
BERT SHINAULT
NOBUO SHISHIDO
TOMMY E SHIVERS
JACK M SHOCKLEY
CHARLES H SHOE
FARRIS D SHOEMAKER
CLARENCE J SHOOK
CLIFFORD T SHORT
JACK A SHORTER
EDGAR R SHOULTS
ERWIN T SHOWALTER
J M SHOWS
DELBERT SHREVE
RICHARD E SHREWSBERRY
ANDREW C SHUCK
CARL SHUFORD
BILLY SHULER
IRVING SHULMAN
PHILIP SHUTMAN
WILLARD J SIBLEY
EDMUNDAS G SICAS
LESLIE A SICILIANO
WALTER J SIECZKA
MERLE W SIEGERSMA
CLARENCE A SIEMERS
THOMAS J SIGLEY
EDMUND G SIGMUND
DAVID T SIIRA
DANIEL K SIKES
JOSEPH M SILVIA
CHUN-TAEK SIM
DEOK-TAEK SIM
GWANG-SIK SIM
GYEONG-UK SIM
GYO-SEON SIM
GYO-TAK SIM
IK-HWAN SIM
IN-SEOP SIM
JAE-MUN SIM
JONG-CHEOL SIM
MAN-SIK SIM
MUN-BO SIM
SANG-BAE SIM
SANG-DON SIM
SANG-JIN SIM
SEON-GU SIM
SEON-SEOK SIM
WI-SAENG SIM
JOSEPH A F SIMARD
LELAND K SIME
RUDOLPH C SIMEONE
CALVIN C SIMMONS
EARL S SIMMONS
EDWARD L SIMMONS
GEORGE E SIMMONS
IRVIN O SIMMONS JR
JOHN W SIMMONS
JOSEPH D SIMMONS
MILLARD E SIMMONS
WALTER L SIMMONS
WILLIAM D SIMMONS
MATTHEW A SIMPSON
ALFRED SIMS
DAVID SIMS
GEORGE M SIMS
JIMMIE B L SIMS
RAY SIMS
AN-SIK SIN
BI-HO SIN
BO-CHEOL SIN
BOK-MAN SIN
BOK-SU SIN
BONG-SUN SIN
CHANG-SEON SIN
CHANG-SUN SIN
CHA-SIK SIN
CHEOL-SE SIN
CHEOL-U SIN
CHEOL-U SIN
CHUN-SIK SIN
CHUN-SIK SIN
DANG-GWON SIN
DEOK-SIK SIN
DEOK-YUN SIN
DU-SAM SIN
EOK-HO SIN
EUNG-YEOL SIN
GAP-DONG SIN
GI-HWAN SIN
GIL-HO SIN
GWANG-HO SIN
GWANG-SU SIN
HAE-SUL SIN
HEUNG-SIK SIN
HONG-SIK SIN
HYEON-DEOK SIN
HYEON-GI SIN
HYEONG-SIK SIN
HYEON-GUK SIN
HYEON-JUNG SIN
HYEON-MUN SIN
HYEON-MYEONG SIN
HYEON-SU SIN
HYEON-UK SIN
HYO-U SIN
IL-HO SIN
IM-SIK SIN
IM-SIK SIN

20 ARMY

IN-GYUN SIN
JAE-CHUN SIN
JAE-HAK SIN
JANG-GON SIN
JANG-HYEON SIN
JANG-SU SIN
JEONG-DAE SIN
JEONG-HYEON SIN
JEONG-TAE SIN
JEONG-YUN SIN
JIN-HO SIN
JONG-IN SIN
JONG-SU SIN
JONG-TAE SIN
JUNG-HAK SIN
JUNG-HO SIN
JUN-SIN SIN
MAN-HO SIN
MYEONG-CHEOL SIN
NAM-CHEOL SIN
OK-SIK SIN
PAL-JONG SIN
SA-DEOK SIN
SAM-DEOK SIN
SAM-DEUK SIN
SANG-CHEOL SIN
SANG-DAE SIN
SANG-JO SIN
SANG-SEOP SIN
SEOK-GYU SIN
SEONG-HAK SIN
SEONG-MI SIN
SEONG-SIK SIN
SU-IL SIN
SUN-WANG SIN
TAE-GEUN SIN
TAEK-SA SIN
UI-SIK SIN
YANG-SIK SIN
YEONG-DO SIN
YONG-I SIN
YONG-MUN SIN
YONG-TAEK SIN
YONG-TAEK SIN
YU-GWON SIN
YUN-MAN SIN
CLIFFORD L SINCLAIR
CHARLES L SINGLETON
JESSE C SINGLETON
MARION L SINGLETON
ROBERT SINGLETON
WALTER SINIAWSKI
BRUMITT G SINOR
GERALD T SINZ
ROBERT J SIPES JR
SAMUEL SISCO
JOE C SISK
CHARLES T SISSON
ROBERT L SIVAGE
CLIFFORD SIZEMORE
HOWARD R SKAALERUD
DONALD N SKEAN
ROBERT E SKEEN
IRVIN K SKEENS
ROBERT S SKEES
CHESTER A SKIBICKI
ROBERT K SKINNER
GEORGE M SKOGSTAD
JAMES M SKUPNIEWICZ
JAMES J SLANE
RICHARD J SLATER
HARRY L SLATES
JAMES A SLAUGHTER
CHARLES W SLAVEN
WILLIAM A SLAYBACK
ALBERT L SLEET
GERALD G SLEMMER
EDWARD SLIVA JR
CARL T SLOAN
DONALD E SLOAN
ALVIN E SLOSS
HOWARD L SLOSSON
ANTHONY F SLYSZ
ROBERT SMALLS
HOWARD I SMALLWOOD
BILLY R SMEDLEY
RICHARD E SMELCER
HENRY J SMIETANA
ALBERT SMITH
ALFRED E SMITH

ALFRED J SMITH
AMON K SMITH
ANTHONY M SMITH
AUGUST O SMITH
BEN T SMITH JR
BERNARD SMITH
BERNARD L SMITH
CHARLES D SMITH
CLARENCE W SMITH
CLYDE D SMITH
CURTIS N SMITH
DAVID R SMITH
DON SMITH
EARL SMITH
EMMITTE SMITH
ERNEST M SMITH
FORREST F SMITH
FRANK J SMITH
FREDERICK O SMITH
GEORGE E SMITH
GORDON R SMITH
HARRY B SMITH
HENRY E SMITH
HOWARD E SMITH
ISAAC SMITH
JAMES C SMITH
JAMES L SMITH
JAMES N SMITH
JAMES W SMITH
JOE P SMITH
JOHN C SMITH
JOHN E SMITH
JOHN E SMITH
JOHN H SMITH
JOHN L SMITH
JOHN S SMITH
JOHN W SMITH
KENNETH B SMITH
KENNETH L SMITH
LAURENCE M SMITH
LAVERNE N SMITH
LELAND R SMITH
LEONARD G SMITH
LEONARD H SMITH
LEVERE E SMITH
LOWELL E SMITH
MARCUS H SMITH
MOSES SMITH
PAUL R SMITH
PERON SMITH
PHILIP C SMITH
RICHARD E SMITH
ROBERT E SMITH
ROBERT L SMITH
ROY SMITH
ROY L SMITH
ROY L SMITH
THOMAS J SMITH
VIRGIL J SMITH
WALTER M SMITH
WENDELL E SMITH
WILFORD B SMITH
WILLIAM D SMITH
WILLIAM H SMITH
ERNEST L SMITHER
EDWARD I SMITHLEY
JAMES F SMUTEK
JAMES W SNELL
PHILIP SNETHEN
EDWARD M SNIFFEN
RUSSELL L SNOOK
CHARLES H SNYDER JR
CHARLES L SNYDER
JACKSON E SNYDER
RAYMOND A SNYDER
WALTER A SNYDER
IN-CHEOL SO
ERNEST A SOBECK JR
ALBERT T SOBIERAJ
EUGENE R SOBREK
RALPH SODERSTROM
ARNOLD D SOLOMON
JAMES E SOMERS
HUGH N SOMMER JR
JERRY W SOMMERS
CECIL E SOMMERVILLE
CHANG-UI SON
CHAN-I SON
CHEOL-HEON SON
CHEON-SU SON

DAE-IL SON
DAE-YEON SON
DAL-BONG SON
EUN-GEUN SON
GAP-YONG SON
GEUN-SEON SON
GI-BO SON
GI-CHEON SON
GI-HO SON
GI-HONG SON
GI-HONG SON
GI-MUN SON
GI-SANG SON
GI-SIN SON
GWAN-MAN SON
GWI-YEOL SON
GYEONG-MAN SON
GYEONG-SU SON
GYU-SU SON
HAN-JU SON
HWA-MO SON
IM-JO SON
I-SU SON
JAE-DON SON
JAE-GEUN SON
JAE-WON SON
JEONG-DOL SON
JEONG-HEON SON
JIN-BAEK SON
JIN-CHI SON
JIN-EOK SON
JIN-GI SON
JIN-GI SON
JUNG-HYEON SON
SAM-RYONG SON
SANG-JUN SON
SANG-RYEOL SON
SANG-SEOK SON
SEOK-CHEOL SON
SEOK-JU SON
SEOK-JU SON
SEONG-HUI SON
SEONG-JAE SON
SE-SUN SON
SU-MYEONG SON
SUN-MYEONG SON
U-HYEON SON
UN-BOK SON
WON-DAE SON
YEONG-DEOK SON
YEONG-GWON SON
YEONG-HO SON
YEONG-MUN SON
YEONG-SU SON
YEONG-WON SON
YONG-DAE SON
YONG-DEUK SON
YONG-SU SON
YUN-CHEOL SON
BOK-MAN SONG
BOK-SUL SONG
BONG-RO SONG
BYEONG-MUN SONG
BYEONG-U SONG
CHANG-HO SONG
CHEOL-JUNG SONG
DEOK-SEONG SONG
DEOK-SUN SONG
DONG-JUN SONG
DU-HO SONG
EUL-SIK SONG
GAP-BOK SONG
GAP-JO SONG
GEUM-SEOK SONG
GEUN-HWA SONG
GI-HO SONG
GI-HONG SONG
GIL-SIN SONG
GYEONG-SEOP SONG
GYEONG-TAEK SONG
HAK-SEON SONG
HAN-BOK SONG
HAN-GIL SONG
HUI-GYU SONG
HWA-SEOK SONG
HYEON-HO SONG
HYEON-JIK SONG
I-BOK SONG
IL-DONG SONG
JAE-GWAN SONG

JAE-HONG SONG
JAE-HUI SONG
JAE-WAN SONG
JANG-HWAN SONG
JONG-BOK SONG
JU-SEONG SONG
MIN-YEOP SONG
MYEONG-GI SONG
MYEONG-GIL SONG
MYEONG-HEON SONG
MYEONG-HWA SONG
MYEONG-MO SONG
RAE-DEUK SONG
SE-CHAN SONG
SE-JIN SONG
SEOK-BOK SONG
SEOK-DO SONG
SEOK-DU SONG
SEONG-EON SONG
SEONG-HAK SONG
SE-YUN SONG
SUL-I SONG
SUN-SEOK SONG
SU-YONG SONG
TAE-HO SONG
TAE-ON SONG
WON-BONG SONG
WON-SIK SONG
YEONG-BONG SONG
YEONG-DAE SONG
YEONG-JIN SONG
YEONG-JUN SONG
YEONG-SIK SONG
YEONG-SIK SONG
YEON-JIN SONG
YU-BANG SONG
FRANK H SONOSKI
WALTER R SOOTS
DAVID B SOTO
SANTOS SOTO
TONY SOTO
GORDAN D SOUDERS
ALFRED J SOUTHORN
RICHARD W
SOUTHWORTH
LAWRENCE SOUZA
DOUGLAS H SOWERS
KENNETH C SOWERS
MICHAEL SPAGNOLA
JOHN B SPAIN
ROBERT A SPARKMAN
JAMES T SPARKS
CLOID V SPEAKMAN
PAUL R SPEAR
SPERO G SPEAR
RICHARD SPEECH JR
IGENE SPEIGHT
MICKEY R SPENCER
OLAF SPENCER JR
THOMAS W SPENCER
ROBERT W SPERBECK
DONALD G SPERL
ELLIOTT E SPERRY
PAUL F SPICE
RICHARD SPINGARN
LEE F SPOFFARD
MARVIN R SPRINGER
ELVERN SPRINGFIELD
ALLEN A SPRINGSTEEN
CLYDE A SPRINGSTON
WARREN H SPRINKLE
CLARENCE E SPROUSE
ROBERT L SPURLOCK
GEORGE F SQUIGGINS
CHARLES L SQUIRES
ANTHONY D SROK
MERRIL L SRONCE
JAMES W STABLES
GENE E STACY
JAMES I STACY JR
PHILIP B STAHLEY
VERNON D STALLINGS
PAUL STAMPER
CLYDE J STANBACK
JESSIE M STANFORD
CLANCY D STANLEY
JESSIE R STANTON
OLLIE V STARCHER
OLEN C STARK
HERMAN F STARKEY

DELBERT L STARNES
RAYMOND E STASH
ROBERT W STAUB
GEORGE F STEBBINS
NELSON STEEDLEY
ROBERT D STEEL
AURTHOR G STEELE
DARRELL R STEELE
ROBERT R STEELE
WILLIAM STEELE JR
IVAN M STEENBERGH
DANIEL F STEFFEN
DONALD E STEFFEN
ROGER A STEIN
HAROLD J STEINHILBER
ITALO L STELLA
JOHN A STELLINE
ROBERT J STELTER
LAWRENCE F STENZEL
ARNOLD E STEPHENS
BENJAMIN STEPHENS
DALE L STEPHENS
DANIEL T STEPHENS
ELMORE J STEPHENS
JAMES F STEPHENS
WILLIAM E STEPHENS
MERLE M STEPHENSON
JOHN M L STERN JR
CROCKET B STEVENS
EDWARD R STEVENS
J T STEVENS JR
JAMES P STEVENS
RICHARD C STEVENS
ROBERT B STEVENS
THADDEUS F STEVENS
MAX B STEVENSON
DAVID D STEWARD
BILL J STEWART
EARL B STEWART
GERALD W STEWART
HENRY C STEWART
HOWARD J STEWART
HUELL J STEWART JR
JOHN W STEWART JR
LAWRENCE STEWART
STANLEY STEWART
WELDON F STEWART
BILLY J STICE
GARY S STICKLES
JERRY D STILES
KENT W STINGER
WILLIAM R STINNETT
ELMORE STINSON
PAUL STIPANDIC JR
RICHARD N STIRR
JESSE H STOCKWELL
EARLE V STOKES
JOHN R STOKES
ARTHUR STOLAR
DALE R STOLLBERG
HAROLD J STONE
HARRY W STONE JR
JOHN G STONE
KELLY L STONE
LAFE E STONE
LAWRENCE M STONE
OLIVER STONE JR
DONALD M
STONESTREET
JOHN D ST ONGE
JOHN J STOPPIELLO
RUSSELL B STOUT
ANTHONY C STRACUZZI
RALPH B STRATTON
JOHN C STREET
ROYCE U STRICKLAND
PAUL C STRICKLER
GENE STRINGER
WILLIAM E STROBEL
MARK A STROHL JR
CARL A STROM
CHARLES M STRYKER
DONALD C STUART
FREDERICK STUCKEY
OSCAR N STUCKI
ADDIS STURDIVANT
EDGAR W SUCKOW
ROBERT T SUITOR
CLINTON V SULLIVAN
FRANCIS R SULLIVAN

21

ARMY

JAMES D SULLIVAN
JOHN L SULLIVAN
LEONARD J SULLIVAN
RALPH F SULLIVAN JR
ROBERT E SULLIVAN
CHARLES F SUMMERTON
ROBERT D SUMTER
ALLEN L SUTTON
FREDERICK G SUTTON
JOHNIE SUTTON
RAYMOND D SUTTON
HERBERT H SUZUKI
RICHARD L SVITEK
FRANCIS R SWAINSON
PHILIP O SWANK
ERNEST A SWANSON
RUSSELL E SWANSON
FRED D SWART
EDWARD L SWEARINGER
EDWARD E SWEENEY
KIETH A SWEET
CARL L SWEIGART
WILBUR W SWENEY
THEODORE SWICZKOWSKI
JACK SWIFT JR
DAVID L SWIHART
JAMES SWINIARSKI
CARL E SWINT
GAYLE L SWOPE
GEORGE A SWOPE
DELBERT V SWYGART
ERNEST J SYZEMORE
ROBERT J SZAYWAY
THADDEUS S SZUKALA
STANLEY J SZYMANSKI
VICTOR TABARRINI
DONALD F TACKETT
JU-HO TAE
SANG-CHEOL TAE
ELIAS B TAFOYA
JOHN M TAFOYA
PAUL B TAFT
MANT M TAIT
IK-SU TAK
SUN-YEOP TAK
YONG-GUK TAK
HERBERT T TAKAMATSU
BOBBIE L TALLEY
DENNIS R TALLEY
JAMES W TALLEY
KANAME R TAMASHIRO
OSAMU TAMURA
CLARENCE A TANGNEY
CECIL R TANKERSLEY
JAMES N TANKSLEY
YUKIWO TANOUYE
ROGER M TANSEY
ISSIAH TANSIL
HENRY L TANSLEY
JOSEPH TAORMINO
THOMAS L TAPLEY
JOE H TARPLEY
RAYMOND M TARTT
LESLIE W TARVER
THEODORE M TASKER JR
JOHN R TASSET JR
DICK G TATE
THOMAS E TATE
RICHARD D TATRO
JAMES TATUM
FERNANDES S TAVARES
ALLEN R TAYLOR
CLIFFORD A TAYLOR
DELBERT L TAYLOR
DONALD H TAYLOR
DONALD M TAYLOR
DUNBAR TAYLOR
GLENN H TAYLOR
HOYTE R TAYLOR
JOE D TAYLOR
JOHN C TAYLOR JR
JOSEPHUS W TAYLOR
OSCAR L TAYLOR
RAYMOND TAYLOR JR
RICHARD B TAYLOR
ROBERT L TAYLOR
RONALD G TAYLOR
THOMAS A TAYLOR
WAYNE D TAYLOR
WILLIAM E TAYLOR

WILLIAM E TAYLOR
WILLIAM G TAYLOR
WILLIAM R TAYLOR
WORTH W TAYLOR
THOMAS C TEMPLE
YOSHIKIO TENGAN
CLAUDE E TENNANT
JULIUS S TEPAKEYAH
WILLIAM TERAKEDIS
JAMES TERRELL JR
JOSEPH T TERRITO
PAUL J TERRY
ROGER E TERRY
THURMAN TERRY
ROY A THACKER
FLOYD E THATCHER
MAURICE E THAXTON
NORBERT J THEISEN
HUBERT J THERIOT
ARNOLD L THOMAS
CHRISTIAN A THOMAS
DONALD J THOMAS
EDDIE J THOMAS
FRANK THOMAS
GARLAND C THOMAS
GEORGE H THOMAS
HENRY THOMAS
JACK H THOMAS
JAMES THOMAS JR
JAMES H THOMAS
JERRY D THOMAS
JERRY R THOMAS
JOHN A THOMAS
JOHNNY W THOMAS
LEONARD THOMAS
MERLE G THOMAS
RICHARD E THOMAS
ROBERT H THOMAS
SAMUEL THOMAS JR
SAMUEL THOMAS
TROY L THOMAS
WILLIAM A THOME
CLARENCE H THOMPSON
DONALD O THOMPSON
ERNEST E THOMPSON
FRANK H THOMPSON
HAROLD S THOMPSON
JOHNNIE THOMPSON
LORENZO D THOMPSON
PERCY L THOMPSON
RODNEY D THOMPSON
ROLAND D THOMPSON
WARREN E THOMPSON
CHARLES D THOMSON
DONALD J THOMSON
GORDON W THOMSON
JOHN C R THOMSON
HAROLD H THORNE
JACK S THORNTON
DUNCAN L THORSTEINSON
WOODIE B THREAT
ALVIN D THURMAN
RICHARD F THURSIE
RUSSELL E THURSTON
DARRELL J TIBBEN
CHARLES O TIBBETTS
CONNIE L TIBBS
JESSIE T TIBBS
CHARLES L TICE
JOHN J TIERNAN
MICHAEL J TIERNEY
MAX G TIGER
HAROLD B TILGHMAN
BERNARD J TILLMAN
HERBERT E TILLMAN
WALLACE L TIMM
HARRY L TINDAL
BOBBY A TINGLE
ALBERT D TITMAN
DAVID O TITUS
JOSEPH A TOCCO
JOSEPH T TOCCO
SILVIO N TOCCO
FREDERICK E TODD
LEON D TODD
JOSEPH H TOECUS
HOWARD M TOHILL
ALTON L TOLER
MARION E TOLLESON

GLENN E TOMES
CLARENCE TONEY
DONALD R TONEY
RONALD H TOOKER
FRED TOOMEY
GEORGE W T TORBETT
ROBERT J TORESS
RICHARD TORKELSON
RAMON P TORO
JOSE A TORO-HERNANDEZ
ANGEL M TORRES
PETE TORRES
FRANCISCO TORRES-BELLO
MANUEL TORRES-LUGO
JOAQUIN TORRES-ORELLANA
ANTONIO TORRES-ORTIZ
NEMESIO TORRES-OTERO
GILBERTO TORRES-RODRIGUEZ
WILSON TORRES-SEGARRA
JOSEPH A TORREZ
CHARLES P TORTORICI
JESUS I TOVES
FRANK TOW
ROOSEVELT TOWNS
CLIFFORD D TOWNSEND
GROVER C TOWRY
ROBERT W TRACY
GEORGE B TRAMMELL
WILLIAM D TRAMMELL
LAWRENCE TRAPANOTTO
GILBERT M TRAVIS
PETER TREADWAY
GEORGE F TREDER
THOMAS E TREDWAY
CLAYTON A TRELOAR
RICHARD R TRENHOLM
DON L W TRENT
IRA V TRENT
JAMES H TRICE
ROBERT J TRICOMI
WILLIAM L TRIETSCH
JOHN A TRIGG JR
WILLIAM J TRIMBLE JR
JOSEPH F TRINKAUS
JOHN H TRINKLE
LOWELL C TRIPLETT
MANNING TROTTER
JOSEPH W TROY
ANTHONY J TRUISI
BIVIANO TRUJILLO
THOMAS E TRUMAN
KENNETH T TRUTNA
WALTER M TUCK
CLIFFORD O TUCKER
FRANCIS J TUCKER
ADOLPH TUNSTALL JR
EDMUND J TURCOTTE
LAWRENCE G TURCZYN
JEFF TURMAN
JOHN H TURMAN
ROBERT J TURNBULL
ALLEN D TURNER
ALLEN T TURNER
BERRY W TURNER
DAVID C TURNER
RICHARD C TURNER
ROBERT G TURNER
WELDON G TURNER
DAVID A TUROVH
KENNETH E TUTTLE
VITO C TUZZOLINO
GENE A TWITCHELL
EMILE TYLER
RODNEY TYLER
JAMES B TYNES
PAUL E TYRRELL
BOK-DO U
BOK-DONG U
BONG-OK U
BONG-TAE U
BU-GI U
BYEONG-HO U
BYEONG-MAN U
DO-HYEON U
GI-DEOK U

GWANG-YONG U
GYE-SU U
HAK-BONG U
HONG-GI U
HUI-MYEON U
HYO-SEOK U
IN-GI U
JAE-DEOK U
JEONG-GI U
JI-SANG U
SANG-SU U
SUN-SAENG U
SUN-SAENG U
TA-RYONG U
WON-SEOP U
NOBORU UEHARA
LAVERN C ULLMER
HERMAN A ULRICH
HAROLD L UNDERWOOD
HERBERT UNDERWOOD
RALPH F UNDERWOOD
JAMES B UPCHURCH
CHARLES E UPSHAW
MANUEL S URANGA
HERMAN E URCH
EDWARD E URIA
LEROY C URQUHART
CURTIS USHER
CLIFFORD L UTTER
ROBERT T UYEDA
TAKEO UYEHARA
FRANK E VAAGE
ANDREW VAGANKA
ROBERT J VAHLSING
EUGNE VALENTINE
FREDDIE H VALENTINE
ROBERT F VALENTINE
EDWARD S VALENZUELA
FRANK J VALENZUELA
DOMINICK V VALLE
EMIL J VALLECORSE
JUAN B VALLESTEROS
NELLO VALOROSI
EDWARD C VAN ARSDALE
WILLIAM R VAN BROOK
CHARLES E VANCE
LINDE J VANDER
WILLIAM VANDERVOORT
JOSEPH R VANDEVENTER JR
BRYANT VAN DYKE
GEORGE VAN DYKE
CHARLES C VAN ELSBERG
HENRY W VAN HARN
HOWARD G VAN HORN JR
RALPH VANLEAR JR
ANDREW VANNESS
KENNETH T VANNETT
JAMES VANNOY
LESLIE A VAN POUCKE
CHARLES R VAN WEY
FRED J VANWHY
JOSEPH B VARCELLI
AVELARDO VARELA
RENE VARGAS-GRAFALS
RICHARD J VARGO
GENE C VARNER
PATRICK J VARVEL
DONALD VASHON
ARTURO VASQUEZ
WILLIAM R VAUGHN
HILARIO C VAZQUEZ
FLOR VAZQUEZ-RODRIGUEZ
RONALD J VECCHIE
ENRIQUE VEGA JR
EPIFANIO VEGA
JUAN VEGA-PERDOMO
FRANCISCO VEGA-RODRIGUEZ
ISMAEL VELAZQUEZ-LOPEZ
ARMANDO VELEZ-AUGUSTO
MIGUEL A VERA

IRA H VERILL
WILLIAM M VERMILLION JR
GEORGE E VERNON
HOWARD P VERRET
JOSEPH S VEVERKA
DONALD G VICK
CHARLES VICKERS
CHARLES J VICKERY
FILBERT J VIGIL
JOSE G VIGIL
ORACE M VIGIL
RAYMOND A VILAGE
LUIS A VILLAFANE
ROBERT C VILLALVA
ANGEL VILLEGAS
PEDRO G VILLEREAL
RAYMOND M VINCENT
CECIL VINES
ROBERTO VIRELLA-MIRANDA
ARTHUR J VOGEL
LEO S VOGEN JR
JAMES VOID
JOHN H VOIGHT
ROBERT J VOLACK
RICHARD H VOLZ
TONY VOREH
CHARLES A VOREL JR
WILLIAM H VORPAGEL
PRESTON W VORTISH
FRED G VOSS
ROBERT A VRADENBURGH
GEORGE A WADE
LEONARD L WADE
SAMUEL H WADE
WILLIE R WADE
DONALD E WADSWORTH
FREEMAN M WADSWORTH
DONALD L WAGNER
GEORGE J WAGNER JR
JAMES R WAGNER
RALPH P WAGNER
ROBERT G WAGONER
MARTIN J WAHL
JOHN W WAJDA
JOSEPH W WAKEFIELD
NEAL V WAKELY
JOHN G WALCZAK
HARRY L WALEGA
ROMAN F WALETZKE
CHARLES E WALKER
DAVID S WALKER
HAROLD R WALKER
ISHMAEL W WALKER
JAMES E WALKER
JAMES I WALKER
JAMES P WALKER
JAMES S WALKER
JOE C WALKER
LAWRENCE R WALKER
MATTHEW WALKER
NOAH WALKER
RICHARD D WALKER
ROBERT WALKER
WALTER L WALKER
WILLIAM E WALKER SR
WILLIAM J WALKER
BILL S WALLACE
CARLSON E WALLACE
EMIL E WALLACE
FLOYD WALLACE
HOWARD E WALLACE
JAMES A WALLACE
JOHN W WALLACE
CHARLES H WALLER
JAMES L WALLIS
JAMES L WALLS
JESSE J WALLS
MARLIN N WALRAVEN
JOHN P WALSH
SHULLER WANAMAKER
JUN-GI WANG
WAN-JIP WANG
DONALD E WARD
EDWARD W WARD
JOHN H WARD

22 ARMY

LESTER J WARD
WILLIAM J WARD
WILLIE E WARD JR
RAYMOND E WARDELL
JACK W WARDLAW
FRED R WARDZINSKI
JAMES WARE
STANFORD WARE
JESSIE P WARLICK
DAVID F WARMOTH
MARVIN L WARNER
NORMAN C WARNER
WALTER T WARSHAL
JAMES F WASHBURN
MELVIN G WASHBURN
JOHN H WASHINGTON
LOTT H WASHINGTON
PERRY L WASHINGTON
PETER E WASHINGTON
RAYMOND WASHINGTON
RUFUS WASHINGTON
ALBERT H WATERHOUSE JR
ALBERT WATKINS
EDDIE M WATKINS
MILTON K WATKINS
WILLIAM R WATKINS
CHARLES WATSON
CLIFTON H WATSON
GLENN E WATSON
HENRY L WATSON
HOWARD R WATSON
JOHN W WATSON
ROBERT B WATSON
STEPHEN A WATSON
WILLARD K WATSON
WILLIAM E WATSON
WILLIAM H WATSON
SPENCER R WATT
ARNOLD WATTS
ENOCH WATTS
JAMES W WATTS
HERBERT H WAYMER
ELDON D WAYMIRE
WILLIAM H WAYNICK
WINTON L WAYTS
CARLOS D WEAVER
CHARLES E WEAVER
CLYDE W WEAVER
CURTIS P WEAVER JR
EDWARD T WEAVER
LARRY A WEAVER
KENNETH O WEBB
DONALD E WEBBE
GRANT WEBER
DONALD L WEBSTER
HERBERT E WEBSTER
RICHARD A WEEKS
VESTER W WEEKS
AMOS D WEESE
FREDERICK C WEICHLER JR
RAYMOND H WEILAND
JAMES P WEIR
CHARLES J WEISER
CARL P WEISS
SHERWIN B WEISS
DOUGLAS L WELCH
WILLIAM C WELCH JR
RAYMOND E WELLEY
JOSEPH R WELLMAN
ARTHUR L WELLS JR
DENVER L WELLS
GEORGE W WELLS
HARVEY L WELLS
JAMES E WELLS
WILLIE WELLS
EDWARD H WELSCH
DONALD L WELSH
DONALD G WEMPLE
GLENN D WENCK
MARVIN R WENGER
ROMAN L WENINGER
LEIGH M WENTWORTH
MARK A WENTWORTH
WALTER L WENTZ
RODNEY D WENZEL
ALVIN F WERBE
DONALD A WERKHEISER
CLEMENT L WERY
BENNY L WEST
CHARLES E WEST

KENNETH R WEST
RANDELL WEST
JAMES C WETHERELT
ELWOOD E WEYANDT
DAVID G WHEAT
RAY R WHEATON
DAVID F WHEELER
FLOYD L WHEELER JR
JAMES D WHEELER
LOWELL T WHEELER
WILLIAM A WHEELER
FRANCIS J WHIPPLE
ALBERT W WHITE
DAVID R WHITE
DWIGHT C WHITE
EDGAR T WHITE
EUGENE WHITE
HARRY E WHITE JR
HOWARD E WHITE
HUGHIE A WHITE
J W WHITE
JACKIE J WHITE
JAMES E WHITE
JAMES H WHITE
JAMES W WHITE
JOHN WHITE JR
LEROY J WHITE
LLEWELLYN WHITE
NOEL E WHITE
PAUL F WHITE
PRECHEA C WHITE
RUTHERS WHITE
WILLIAM WHITE JR
WILLIAM G WHITE
WILLIAM J WHITE JR
WILLIE E WHITE JR
ROBERT L WHITEHEAD
PETER WHITELIGHTNING
WILLIAM S WHITEMAN
JAMES WHITENER
GERALD B WHITEROCK
JOSEPH C WHITESELL
BILLY E WHITESIDE
HOWARD WHITFIELD
JESSE E WHITFORD
WILLIAM R WHITLOCK
ANDREW A WHITMORE
JOHN T WHITT
EVERETT R WHITWORTH
VERNON I WHORLEY
SEONG-GI WI
JOSEPH R WIATRAK
GILBERT A WIBBENMEYER
MARVIN E WIEBELHAUS
CARL F WIEGAND
H P WIGGINS
JOHN G WIGGINS
MARVIN L WIGGINS
ROBERT G WIGHT
CARLIE A WIKE
CHARLES B WILCOX
JOE D WILCOX
KENNETH E WILCOX
LYMAN L WILCOX
HAROLD G WILDER
JOHNNY R WILDS
FARREL K WILEY
CHARLES C WILHELM
JACK T WILKE
R C WILKERSON
FRANKLIN H WILKEY
VAN L WILKS
JOSEPH W WILLARDO JR
EDDIE M WILLETTE
ALEXANDER WILLIAMS
ALLEN V WILLIAMS
AMOS WILLIAMS
ARTHUR L WILLIAMS
ARTHUR L WILLIAMS
AUGUSTUS A WILLIAMS
AVERILL WILLIAMS
CHARLES WILLIAMS
DAN R WILLIAMS
DARWIN M WILLIAMS
DOUGLAS B
WILLIAMS
EARL J WILLIAMS
FRED WILLIAMS
GERALD E WILLIAMS
GERALD M WILLIAMS

HARRY E WILLIAMS
JACK K WILLIAMS
JAMES M WILLIAMS
JAMES W WILLIAMS
JASPER D WILLIAMS
JOHN WILLIAMS JR
JOHN M WILLIAMS
JOHNNIE WILLIAMS JR
JOHNNY B WILLIAMS
JOSEPH WILLIAMS
KENNETH G WILLIAMS
LAWRENCE J WILLIAMS
LEONARD WILLIAMS
LEONARD J WILLIAMS
LEWIS WILLIAMS
MAURICE WILLIAMS
PAUL E WILLIAMS
RAY G WILLIAMS
RICHARD D WILLIAMS
RICHARD M WILLIAMS
ROBERT A WILLIAMS
ROBERT E WILLIAMS
RONALD R WILLIAMS
ROOSEVELT WILLIAMS
ROOSEVELT WILLIAMS
THOMAS WILLIAMS
TONY N WILLIAMS
TRUMAN H WILLIAMS
WILLIE S WILLIAMS
BOB WILLIAMSON
CECIL L WILLIAMSON
CHARLES WILLIAMSON
EUGENE E WILLIAMSON
GEORGE H WILLIAMSON
MELVILLE WILLIAMSON
JOHN WILLIFORD
THOMAS B WILLINGHAM
CARLOS E WILLIS
CORNELL F WILLIS
DOYLE D WILLIS
MONROE B WILLOUGHBY
CARLTON R WILLS
JOSEPH D WILLS JR
ARTHUR C WILSON JR
CHARLES G WILSON
CHARLES H WILSON
DUANE E WILSON
EDWARD J WILSON
ERNEST E WILSON
FRANCIS E WILSON
FREDERICK D WILSON
GERALD H WILSON JR
ISAAC WILSON
JAMES E WILSON
JAMES R WILSON
JESSIE WILSON
JONN B WILSON
LEON K WILSON
MERBLE E WILSON
PAUL A WILSON
RICHARD E WILSON
ROBERT D WILSON
RUDOLPH WILSON
SYLVESTER WILSON
WALTER WILSON JR
WARREN W WILSON
WILLIE J WILSON
JAMES A WINBORN
BEN L WINCE
OTTO B WINCHELL
JOHN L WINCHESTER
ROBERT L WINE
BENJAMIN WINIKOFF
MARVIN J WINKLER
DONALD E WINTERS
NORMAN P WINTERS
ROBERT J WINTERS
MERL D WIRT
HAROLD D WIRTZ
WILLIAM J WIRTZ JR
ALBERT V WISWELL
J D WITCHER
JOHN T WITKOWSKI
JAMES H WOEST
THOMAS R WOLF
WENDELL D WOLF
SAMUEL N WOLFSDORF
RAYMOND P
WOMAN DRESS
CHIL-GYU WON

GEUN-SANG WON
HEUNG-HO WON
HYEONG-YUL WON
IN-TAE WON
SANG-CHIM WON
SEON-YU WON
SU-JAE WON
KAN W WONG
GENE A WOOD
GEORGE C WOOD
HAROLD T WOOD
RAYMOND G WOOD
THOMAS O WOOD
WILLIAM L WOOD
WILLIAM F WOODALL
WESLEY R WOODBURY
DARWIN E WOODCOCK
CHARLES L WOODRUFF
DELBERT D WOODRUFF
EARL E WOODS
FREDERICK E WOODS
JACOB WOODS
JAMES W WOODS
WILLIAM E WOODS
JOSEPH E WOODWARD
ROBERT A WOODWARD
CLAUDE WOOLDRIDGE
CLARENCE W WOOLFOLK
JACK L WOOLLEY
ERNEST F WOOLUM
THOMAS B WOOTTEON
LYMAN W WORKMAN
HENRY G WORMAN
JOHN M WORTMAN JR
CLYDE M WRIGHT
FLOYD WRIGHT
GEORGE H WRIGHT
JAMES L WRIGHT
JAMES M WRIGHT
JAY E WRIGHT
JOHN F WRIGHT
JOSEPH WRIGHT
JOSEPH R WRIGHT
MACK WRIGHT III
ONZIE L WRIGHT
RICHARD K WRIGHT
ROBERT A WRIGHT
SIDNEY S WRIGHT
STINER WRIGHT
SYLVESTER WRIGHT
WILLIE K WRIGHT
WILLIAM L WRIGHTSEL
FRED N WUJCIK
WALTER A WUOTILA
WOLFGANG W WURZER
BILLY D WYATT
ERNEST W WYCKOFF
RONALD WYN
YEONG-GI YA
LAWRENCE M YAEGER
JUAN YANAS
CLELLAN YANCEY
NORMAN J YANCEY
FELIX M YANEZ
JOE G YANEZ
BOK-MAN YANG
BONG-MUN YANG
BYEONG-SIK YANG
DEOK-GI YANG
DONG-JUN YANG
GEUM-BONG YANG
GI-HO YANG
GYEONG-SIK YANG
HO-YONG YANG
HUI-UN YANG
HWAN-SEONG YANG
I-DEUK YANG
JAE-WAN YANG
JAE-WON YANG
JEONG-HYEON YANG
JUNG-SIK YANG
OK YANG
SANG-GON YANG
SANG-GWON YANG
SEOK-MAN YANG
SEONG-MAN YANG
SEONG-MO YANG
SEONG-YEOL YANG
SU-HYEON YANG
SU-MYEONG YANG

SU-SIK YANG
UI-BAE YANG
YONG-GWAN YANG
DENNIS W YANKEE
JEROME O YANKOWITZ
VALENTINE J YANTA
DONALD A YAP
BOBBY K YATES
JOHN C YATES
MELVIN O YATES
JONG-DAE YE
JONG-GEUN YE
THOMAS W YELTON
EDDIE E YENGICH
BONG-GU YEO
DONG-SU YEO
HONG-JEONG YEO
MAN-SUL YEO
PYO-SANG YEO
SANG-CHUN YEO
SANG-PIL YEO
SEONG-DONG YEO
SEON-HO YEO
UN-JANG YEO
UN-JANG YEO
YEONG-TAE YEO
CHI-MAN YEOM
CHUN-SIK YEOM
DO-CHI YEOM
DONG-GIL YEOM
HAE-DONG YEOM
HAN-HO YEOM
JEONG-SIK YEOM
NAM-YONG YEOM
OK-JIN YEOM
SO-GON YEOM
YONG-JO YEOM
YONG-JU YEOM
CHARLES R YETSKO
WALTER E YOCKEY
TETSUMI YOKOOJI
JO-HUI YONG
JAMES D YORK
WILLIE M YORK
FRANK A YOUNG
JOHN M YOUNG
JOSEPH P YOUNG JR
KENNETH E YOUNG
PAUL A YOUNG
RALPH C YOUNG
RALPH G YOUNG
ROBERT L YOUNG
WILLIAM H YOUNG
BILLY E YOUNGBLOOD
FERMIN YPARRAGUIRRE
BONG-AM YU
BONG-GI YU
BONG-SIK YU
BYEONG-HUI YU
CHAN-JONG YU
CHEOL-BOK YU
CHEOL-SU YU
DAE-AM YU
DAL-GI YU
DAL-SANG YU
DAL-YEON YU
DEOK-HO YU
DONG-GEUN YU
DONG-SIK YU
GI-DO YU
GI-JUN YU
GI-YUN YU
GWANG-YEOL YU
GWI-DOL YU
GYE-SU YU
HAK-PIL YU
HEUNG-GIL YU
HWA-YUL YU
HYEONG-GEUN YU
HYEON-SIL YU
IL-JUN YU
IN-SIK YU
IN-SU YU
JAE-CHEOL YU
JAE-SIK YU
JEOM-DAE YU
JIN-DEUK YU
JONG-HAK YU
JONG-YEOL YU
MUN-SIK YU

23 ARMY

O-AM YU
SANG-SUN YU
SEOK-DO YU
SEOK-JIN YU
SEONG-JU YU
SEONG-O YU
TAEK-BOK YU
U-JIN YU
WON-GI YU
WON-JONG YU
YEONG-GEUN YU
YEONG-YEON YU
YONG-AM YU
AN-HAK YUN
AP-SEOP YUN
BAN-GIL YUN
BONG-CHEON YUN
BONG-GU YUN
BONG-HA YUN
BYEONG-DAE YUN
BYEONG-GYU YUN
BYEONG-HO YUN
BYEONG-HWA YUN
BYEONG-JEONG YUN
BYEONG-SEON YUN
BYEONG-YONG YUN
CHANG-HAN YUN
CHANG-SIK YUN
CHEON-SU YUN
CHIL-GEUN YUN
CHUNG-UI YUN
DEOK-GAP YUN
DEOK-YEOL YUN
DO-WON YUN
DU-MAN YUN
GANG-JO YUN
GI-HWA YUN
GI-HWAN YUN
GI-JIN YUN
GI-JUNG YUN
GIL-SAENG YUN
GI-NAM YUN
GI-O YUN
GI-SEONG YUN
GU-CHEOL YUN
GUK-HYEONG YUN
GWANG-SU YUN
GWAN-SEOP YUN
GYEONG-BAE YUN
GYEONG-DO YUN
GYEONG-HO YUN
GYEONG-HYEOK YUN
GYEONG-MAN YUN
GYEONG-TAE YUN
HAE-YEONG YUN
HAE-YONG YUN
HAK-MYEONG YUN
HAN-JEOM YUN
HO-GEUN YUN
HONG-GEUN YUN
HO-RYEOL YUN
HYE-GYUN YUN
HYEONG-SIK YUN
HYO-YEOP YUN
I-CHEOL YUN
I-JO YUN
IL-GU YUN
I-MAN YUN
JAE-BOK YUN
JAE-BONG YUN
JAE-SAM YUN
JAE-YEONG YUN
JANG-HUI YUN
JEONG-HYEOK YUN
JEONG-O YUN
JEONG-RAE YUN
JI-GWAN YUN
JIN-NO YUN
JIN-SEOK YUN
JONG-DO YUN
JONG-MUN YUN
JONG-WON YUN
JU-DEOK YUN
JUNG-GEUN YUN
JUNG-GWAN YUN
MAENG-WON YUN
MAN-GEUN YUN
MAN-YONG YUN
MONG-SU YUN
MYEONG-CHEOL YUN
MYEONG-HA YUN
MYEONG-SE YUN
MYEONG-WON YUN
NEUNG-HYEON YUN
OK-GEUN YUN
OK-SUL YUN
O-YEONG YUN
PYEONG-MUN YUN
SAENG-HYO YUN
SAM-BONG YUN
SANG-AM YUN
SANG-GI YUN
SANG-GYEONG YUN
SANG-MYEONG YUN
SANG-SU YUN
SANG-UK YUN
SEOK-BONG YUN
SEOK-DONG YUN
SEOK-GYEONG YUN
SEONG-GWON YUN
SEONG-MAN YUN
SE-WON YUN
SIN-IL YUN
SO-DONG YUN
SU-BONG YUN
SU-CHEON YUN
TAE-DONG YUN
TAE-GEUN YUN
TAE-IL YUN
TAE-SU YUN
U-BONG YUN
U-HYEON YUN
UI-SIK YUN
YANG-GI YUN
YANG-HYEON YUN
YEONG-BONG YUN
YEONG-HA YUN
YEONG-U YUN
YONG-HYEON YUN
YONG-PIL YUN
YUN-DAL YUN
YUN-HAN YUN
STEVE A ZAGURSKIE
EUGENE C ZAHM
ARTHUR J ZAKALYK
ARTHUR ZAMARRIPA
ALEXANDER J ZAREMBA
ALBERT V ZARZETSKI
RALPH E ZECCHINI
JOHN H ZECH
GLENN J ZEILINGER
TOM ZELELES
MARVIN H ZEMPEL
JOSEPH C ZERBO
GEORGE F ZIESCH
LAWRENCE J ZIGERELLI
JACK E ZIPFEL
DAVID E ZOLLMAN
RICHARD C ZSELTVAY
CHARLES ZUMAR
ROLAND H ZURFLUH
RAYMOND A ZURLA
ROBERT L ZUVER
MELVIN T ZYCHOWICZ

PRIVATE FIRST CLASS

MARION V AARON
MYLO S AASER
RICHARD E ABBEY JR
CHARLES L ABBOTT
FRANCIS R ABBOTT
DONALD R ABEL
JAMES A ABEL
WILLIAM B ABERNETHY JR
NORBERT J ABRAHAM
HARALD ABRAHAMSEN
RONALD C ABRAHAMSON
MANUEL ABREU JR
EDWARD F ACCARIZZI
LOUIS V ACEVEDO
NICOLAS ACEVEDO-CRUZ
JUAN A ACEVEDO-TIRADO
MARION A ACITELLI
EDWIN F ACKLEY
PHILIP W ACKLEY
DAVID ACOSTA
LUPE P ACOSTA
JOSE ACOSTA-MARTINEZ
HENRY ACUNA
BILLIE J ADAIR
WALTER J ADAMOWICZ
AMBROS R ADAMS
ARTHUR L ADAMS
AUBREY G ADAMS
BERNARD B ADAMS
CALVIN P ADAMS
DARYL T ADAMS
DENNIS L ADAMS JR
GEORGE R ADAMS
HAROLD L ADAMS
ISAAC F ADAMS
J D ADAMS
JACKIE L ADAMS
JAMES H ADAMS
JOHN H ADAMS
LEWIS C ADAMS JR
LLOYD C ADAMS
LOREN V ADAMS
MARVIN E ADAMS
MELVIN R ADAMS
ROBERT E ADAMS
THESSALONIANS ADAMS
WILLIAM H ADAMS
SAMUEL ADDISON
CLIFFORD ADKINS
FLETCHER ADKINS
WILLARD J ADKISSON
GEORGE H ADLAM
MAXWELL ADLER
JOSEPH L ADLESIC
SEYMOUR R ADSEM
JUNIUS B AGNELLI JR
HENRY P AGNEW
JORGE L AGOSTINI
ANTONIO AGOSTO-BERRIOS
RICARDO A AGRAIT
MANUEL N AGUAYO
JAMES G AGUDA
JESUS T AGUIGUI
FLORENCIO C AGUILERA
LUCIANO AGUILERA
JOSE M AGUIRRE
HOWARD J AHLES
ERIC L AHLSTROM JR
JOHN P AIKSNORAS
ALBERT AINSWORTH JR
DONNIE J AIRINGTON
HOWARD D AKARD
WILLIAM R AKERS
JOHN E AKEY
WILLIS L AKINS
WILLIS T AKINS
CHARLES AKSAMIT
DANIEL ALARCON
DAVID ALBANESE
BILLIE D ALBERS
DONALD O ALBERT
JAMES D ALBEY
CHARLES R ALBRIGHT
ELZIA R ALBRIGHT
RICHARD V ALBRIGHT
ANTONIO ALCAZAR-LUGO
JAMES R ALDRIDGE JR
LEONEL ALEMAN
EARL ALEXANDER
GEORGE R ALEXANDER
HOWARD E ALEXANDER
JAMES T ALEXANDER
JOHNNIE C ALEXANDER JR
LAWRENCE W ALEXANDER JR
MARVIN I ALEXANDER
SUMMEY R ALEXANDER
THOMAS R ALEXANDER
HECTOR ALFARO-ALFARO
CLIFFORD W ALFORD
RAYMOND K ALFORD
LUIS ALICEA-COTO
CHARLIE R ALITZ
DONALD P ALLAN
JACK ALLBRITTON
RAYMOND L ALLBRITTON
ANGELO S ALLEGRETTO
ARTHUR B ALLEN
CHARLES W ALLEN
CHARLIE E ALLEN
CLYDE ALLEN JR
COMMER E ALLEN
DAVE ALLEN JR
DONALD E ALLEN
ELLERY D ALLEN
ELMER G ALLEN
HERBERT L ALLEN
JACKIE D ALLEN
JAMES E ALLEN
JAMES R ALLEN
JIMMIE ALLEN
KENNETH N ALLEN
PAUL A ALLEN
PAUL T ALLEN
ROBERT F ALLEN
ROBERT N ALLEN
ROY L ALLEN
VAN ALLEN
WARREN R ALLEN
RAY C ALLEY
JULIUS E ALLGOOD JR
JAMES E ALLISON
RICHARD J ALLISON
WINFRED L M ALLISON
JOHN W ALLMOND
BERNARD ALMEIDA
JOSEPH ALMEIDA
SIXTO ALMODOVAR-SEGARRA
DONALD ALPERS
FOSTER L ALSTON
DWAIN K ALT
FRANCIS R ALTAVILLA
ROBERT J ALTEMUS
MACARIL Q ALVA
HECTOR L ALVARADO
JOHN ALVARADO
SANTOS V ALVARADO JR
WILLIAM I ALVARADO
ERNEST ALVAREZ
HIGINIO ALVAREZ
ANTHONY P ALVIS
DENNIS W ALWARD
RICHARD G AMADON
WILLIAM P AMAKER
DONALD F AMBEAU
RALPH E AMEND
JOSEPH J AMENDOLA
LORENZA AMERSON
ROBERT B AMEZCUA
ROBERT L AMICK
ALFREDO AMIS
BOB T AMIS
JAMES D AMMONS
OTTO AMMONS
CHARLES G AMOS
GENERAL P AMOS
FERDINAND V AMTHOR
JOSE A AMY-SANTIAGO
BYEONG-HO AN
BYEONG-YEOP AN
DAE-SEONG AN
DONG-JU AN
DU-CHANG AN
DU-SEONG AN
GI-OK AN
GYEONG-GYE AN
GYEONG-SUN AN
HAK-JUNG AN
JAE-UK AN
JIN-HO AN
JONG-RIM AN
JONG-ROK AN
JONG-SEONG AN
JONG-SU AN
JU-YONG AN
SANG-CHANG AN
SANG-YEO AN
SEOK-I AN
SEONG-DO AN
TAE-GYEONG AN
TAE-GYU AN
UN-GYEONG AN
YONG-HO AN
ROBERT M ANCEL
CHARLES A ANDERSEN
A C ANDERSON
ALFRED ANDERSON JR
ALFRED J ANDERSON
BILLY G ANDERSON
CLARENCE D ANDERSON
CLYDE T ANDERSON
DONALD T ANDERSON
DUANE W ANDERSON
GALE C ANDERSON
GLENN M ANDERSON
GORDON E ANDERSON
HAROLD E ANDERSON
HARRY W ANDERSON
HERMAN E ANDERSON JR
JAMES E ANDERSON
JAMES F ANDERSON
JAMES V ANDERSON
JESSE K ANDERSON
JOHN W ANDERSON
JOHN W ANDERSON
KEITH ANDERSON
LARRY J ANDERSON
LLOYD G ANDERSON JR
LLOYD P ANDERSON
LORIS W ANDERSON
MERWYN D ANDERSON
PERRY A ANDERSON
PLEZE ANDERSON
PORT A ANDERSON JR
RAYMOND O ANDERSON
RICHARD E ANDERSON
ROBERT A ANDERSON
WARREN L ANDERSON
WILLIAM C ANDERSON
LOPE A ANDINO-FONSECA
EMILIANO ANDINO-PEREZ
JOHN P ANDONIAN
EDWARD C ANDRES
JAMES R ANDRESEN
JOSEPH J ANDREW
GEORGE A ANDREWS
HAROLD Q ANDREWS
HOWARD ANDREWS
JOSEPH ANDREWS
ROBERT ANDREWS
SHIRLEY B ANDREWS JR
WILLIAM D ANEY
JACK E ANGEL
JOSEPH ANGELI JR
MAURICE ANGLAND
DONALD E ANGLE
ARTEMUS F ANGLES
VITO L ANGONA
ERNEST M ANGUS
RUSSELL ANNIS
JOSEPH W ANTHONY
STANLEY H ANTHONY
VITTORIO M ANTONIO
HAROLD B ANTRIM
SAMUEL ANZELLOTTI JR
ABIE L APODACA
FRANCISCO J APONTE
JUAN P APONTE
HERBERT L APPLE
ROBERT L APPLIN
MICHAEL J AQUILINO
GREGORIO N ARAGONES
FRANK ARAUJO
JULIAN S ARBONIES
EUGENE J ARCAND
JOHN ARCH
GILBERT A ARCHAMBEAULT
WALTER G ARCHAMBO
B R ARCHER
GEORGE W ARCHER JR
JOHN D ARCHER
JOSE A ARCHULETA
JOSE L ARCHULETA
JUAN ARCHULETA
JUAN B ARCHULETA
HERBERT ARDIS
NICHOLAS G AREMIA
HUGH R ARENDALE
ALFRED A ARENOBINE

24 ARMY

JOSEPH S ARGENZIANO JR
FLORENCIO ARIAS
WALTER J ARKENBERG
HENRY ARMADA
HERBERT ARMBRUSTER
RICHARD E ARMENTROUT
JAMES R ARMER
JOHN H ARMOUR
THOMAS J ARMOUR
ERNEST H ARMS JR
CLARENCE D ARMSTRONG
DENNIS R ARMSTRONG
JAMES H ARMSTRONG
JOHN D ARMSTRONG
RAYMOND F ARMSTRONG
THURMAN N ARMSTRONG
WALTER G ARMSTRONG
WAYNE F ARMSTRONG
WILLIAM N ARMSTRONG
ELMER L ARNDT
HARRY ARNOLD JR
JAMES A ARNOLD
WALLACE M ARNOLD
WALTER T AROSE JR
STANLEY C ARREDONDO
JOHN ARREOLA JR
RAYMOND C ARRIAGA
EULISES ARRIGOITIA-GOMEZ
ANDREW B ARRINGTON
FERNANDO L ARRIOLA
CLAYTON ARROWWOOD
WILLIAM R ARTHUR
WILLIAM O ARTRIP
ALBERT H ASAU
HENRY H ASCENCIO
CARMELO ASENCIO-GUZMAN
DEAN M ASH
AUGUSTUS ASHE
HENRY L ASHENFELTER
BOBBY L ASHER
RALPH S ASHER
FRANCIS A ASHEY
PAUL ASHFORD JR
BILLY J ASHLEY
CHARLES ASHLEY
DONALD J ASHLEY
PHILLIP J ASPINWALL
MANFORD W ASTILL
WILFORD ASTOR
JULIAN ASUNCION
JOHN R ATENCIO
ALBERT E ATKINS
CARSON J ATKINSON
ENRIQUE M ATKINSON
HOWARD C ATKINSON JR
STANLEY J ATKINSON
ALEXANDER AUBREY
ALFRED E AUBUCHON
MONTE M AUEN
CHESTER R AUGUST
THOMAS W AUGUST
ROBERT J AUKERMAN
ARTOMIO AULET-MERCADO
COSMO F AURIGEMMA
EARL E AUSTIN
SAMSON AUTHEMENT JR
BOB D AUTREY
LAVERLE AVANT
HERBERT AVERY
WILLIAM D AVILES
BURTON C AWTREY
HAROLD R AXELSON
THOMAS E AXTELL
ANGEL AYALA-ESQUILIN
ENRIQUE AYALA-FERRER
GEORGE F AYERS
ALBERT J AYO
EARL C AYOTTE
RONALD W AYOTTE
ALFRED R BABICZ
ROBERT A BABIN
PHILIP A BABINE
EDWARD J BAC
ABEL BACA
FLORENTINO C BACARRO
THOMAS M BACHOP
CLAUDE E BACHTELL

RAYMOND W BACKHAUS
KENNETH R BACON
ROGER A BACON
JAMES B BADON JR
DANIEL BADURIA JR
BONG-JO BAE
CHANG-MOK BAE
DONG-DAE BAE
GI-JUN BAE
IL-YONG BAE
JAE-WAN BAE
JONG-GAP BAE
JONG-HAK BAE
JONG-HYO BAE
JONG-TAE BAE
JU-MO BAE
TAEK-DOL BAE
YEONG-CHUN BAE
CHANG-HO BAEK
CHUNG-GEUN BAEK
DEOK-AM BAEK
DEOK-BU BAEK
GAK-HO BAEK
I-HYEON BAEK
JANG-SEON BAEK
JANG-YONG BAEK
JEONG-GI BAEK
JEONG-HEUM BAEK
JUNG-GI BAEK
MAN-HEUM BAEK
NAM-GU BAEK
NAM-HYEON BAEK
PAN-GEUN BAEK
RAE-JEOM BAEK
SEOK-JO BAEK
YANG-SEON BAEK
YEONG-DONG BAEK
YEONG-GI BAEK
YONG-DEUK BAEK
HARRY W BAER
JACK W BAER
NEFTALI BAEZ-CANINO
FELIX P BAGINSKI
RALPH L BAILETS
ARTHUR G BAILEY
CLAIR E BAILEY
GLEN A BAILEY
HENRY M BAILEY
JAMES J BAILEY
PAUL R BAILEY
RALPH E BAILEY
TROY W BAILEY
WALTER J BAILEY
WILLARD E BAILEY
ALLAN R BAIN
CHARLES W BAIRD
ANTHONY BAJKOWSKI
ALBERT M BAKER
CHARLES A BAKER
CHARLES B BAKER
DAVID BAKER
EDDIE C BAKER
FRANCIS L BAKER
FRED BAKER
GEORGE A BAKER
GEORGE R BAKER
HERBERT E BAKER
JAMES L BAKER
JOHN D BAKER
LEE D BAKER
MELVIN E BAKER
NATHANIEL BAKER
PAUL E BAKER
RALPH V BAKER
RICHARD M BAKER
ROLAND BAKER
SIDNEY BAKER
WADE BAKER
WEBSTER R BAKER
WILLIAM D BAKER
WILLIAM R BAKER
ELROY H BAKKER
THEODORE W BAKKER
JOSEPH V BAKSA
PASTOR BALANON JR
STANLEY J BALASA
JOSEPH W BALBONI
WILLIAM H BALDREE
WATSON A BALDWIN
DONALD J BALES

CECIL R BALL
CLARENCE H BALL
JAMES H BALL
JOHN W BALL
MATHIS O BALL JR
OLIVER BALL JR
WALTER J BALL
DALE R BALLARD
GEORGE F BALLARD
GUY A BALLARD
HARLAN G BALLARD
ROGER BALLARD
JAY T BALLENGER
RICARDO BALLESTERO
FREDERICK L BALLING
KEITH D BALLWAHN
HENRY R BALMER
JOHN BALOG
RICHARD J BALOG
FRANCIS M BAMBINO
JONG-WON BAN
MYEONG-HO BAN
STANLEY A BANACH
JAMES J BANCZAK
WILLIAM E BANE
BYEONG-GYU BANG
GIL-DONG BANG
MIN-YEOL BANG
SANG-DO BANG
GERALD O BANGERT
CALVIN E BANKS
JOSEPH BANKS
RAY L BANKS
THOMAS J BANKS
WILBUR S BANKS
COY E BANNER
GEORGE C BANNING
SALVATORE BARBAGALLO JR
FRANKLIN D BARBE
JOHN P BARBEE
LEROY R BARBER
LODEAN A BARBER JR
LOYD E BARBER
CEFERINO I BARBOSA-MARRERO
ROBERT L BARBOUR
JIMMIE E BARCOM
JUAN M BARELA
ALEX BARESKI
DAVID D BARFIELD
WILLIAM B BARGER
FRED BARGO JR
CHARLES H BARKER
EDGAR N BARKER
JOHN G BARKER
MALEN W BARKER
WILLIAM G BARKER
THOMAS E BARKSDALE
ROY A BARLETTANI
JOSEPH M BARNA
GILBERT E BARNARD
WILLIAM M BARNARD
DONALD E BARNES
ELLIS BARNES
GEORGE BARNES JR
KENNETH W BARNES
LEE R BARNES
RAYMOND C BARNES
SAMUEL BARNES
WILLIAM O BARNES
EARL J BARNETT
FRANKIE L BARNETT
IVEY G BARNETT
JAMES J BARNETT JR
JOHN R BARNETT
LEWIS A BARNETT JR
MELVIN H BARNETT
ROBERT A BARNETT
WILBURN H BARNETT
HOMER E BARNETTE
WILLIAM BARNEY JR
CARL L BARNHART
DALE G BARNHART
RONALD P BARON
CHARLES E BARR
WALLACE E BARR
MANUEL A BARRAZA
GEORGE BARRELL
ARLIE P BARRETT

DAVID M BARRETT
J B BARRETT
JESSE BARRETT
SILAS F BARRETT
EUGENE A BARRICA
BENNIE T BARRON
EDWARD M BARRON
GEORGE L BARRON
RUBEN BARRON
EDWIN S BARROW
EUGENE C BARRY
JOSEPH E BARTLE
LYNN E BARTLEY
RAYMOND J BARTLEY
MATTHEW P BARTNICK
THEODORE J BARTOL
MICHAEL F BARTOLA
BRUCE O BARTON
DONALD J BARTON
GENE E BARTON
JOHN E BARTON
EARL D BASCO
FREDDIE BASHA
EDWIN R BASHAM
JOHN H BASHAM
MARLIN F BASINA
KENNETH F BASKERVILLE
CURTIS D BASKIN
GERALD D BASQUIN
CHARLIE O BASS
LONZA Z BASS
NOVA L BASS
ROY C BASS
WILLIAM T BASS JR
HENRY D BASSETT
WILLIAM S BASSETT
DWINO J BASSIGNANI
WILLIAM R BASTIE JR
MARION F BATCHELOR
LAWRENCE H BATER
FRANCIS N BATES
RONALD D BATESON
LUTHER R BATEY JR
JOSEPH BATISTE
HAROLD L BATREZ
JAMES M BATSON
LLOYD BATTEN
CHARLES R BATTERSHELL
AMOS BATTLE
MIKE BATTLE JR
PORTER W BATTS
GERALD A BAUER
GERALD W BAUER
WILLIE BAUER
RICHARD R BAUGHAN
DONALD E BAUGHMAN
RICHARD E BAULK
EDGAR D BAUMAN
GEORGE A BAUMER
RAYMOND BAUMGARDNER
RALPH J BAX
GEORGE V BAXLEY
JACK E BAXTER
LAWRENCE BAXTER
MARK E BAYLARK
WILLARD E BAYLES
CHARLIE F BAYLOR
JIMMIE D BAYS
ARCHIE C BEACH JR
REX J BEACH
ROBERT J BEACHY
THOMAS J BEAHM
ROBERT L BEALE
JUDSON H BEALL
GORDON R BEAM
BONNIE D BEARD
DAVID L BEARD
ROBERT D BEARD
ROBERT N BEARD
CLYDE BEARSTAIL
JOHN A BEASLEY
MORRIS F BEASLEY
WILLARD G BEASLEY
GLEN I BEATTY
VICTOR P BEAUCHAMP JR
WILLIAM G BEAUDOIN
JAMES W BEAUMONT
GERARD E BEAUPRE
THOMAS L BEAVERS

EVERT H BEBEE
DONALD K BECHTEL
JOHN H BECHTEL
RICHARD L BECHTEL
LEO D BECK
LEWIS O BECK
WILLIAM E BECK
FERRILL A BECKER
GROVER BECKER
MELVIN H BECKER
WILLIAM F BECKER
ROBERT H BECKETT
HENRY L BECKHAM
WILLIE BECKLEY
CARL F BECKLIN
CHARLES W BECKLIN
DARWIN P BECKWITH
J D BECKWITH
FRED BEDDINGFIELD
JASPER W BEDDINGFIELD
NORMAN C BEDELL
WILBERT C BEECHER
ROBERT E BEEDE
BERNARD A BEEMON
FRANK W BEGASSE
JOHN E BEGGS
CHRISTIAN A BEHR JR
FLOYD J BEICHNER
JOSIAH S BEILER JR
DALE L BEISHIR
WILLIAM E BEITEL
ARTHUR N BELANGER
DONALD N BELCHER
JOSEPH A BELFIORE
EARL L BELK
ALTON R BELL
ALVIN D BELL
CHARLIE D BELL
DONNIE E BELL
EDMOND V BELL
GARY A BELL
JAMES D BELL
JOHNNIE C BELL
LAWRENCE BELL
THOMAS F BELL
VESTEEN BELL JR
WARDELL A BELL
WILLIAM D BELL
WILLIAM G BELL
ROY K BELLAMY JR
JAMES BELLAN
LOWELL W BELLAR
SALVATORE T BELLAVIA
JAMES E BELLER
ROSARIO J BELLIO
RICHARD R BELLON JR
ALBERT BELLUCCI
ROBERT BELLUS
GEORGE A BELMAR
FRANKEY D BELTZ
WILLIAM B BELTZ
JUAN D BENAVENTE
DONALD J BENDER
EARL E BENDER
ROBERT L BENDER
FRED W BENEDICT
JOSEPH A BENEDINO
JAMES W BENEFIEL
ROBERT F BENEKE
JAMES H BENFIELD
CLAUDE F BENGTSON
OTIS P BENJAMIN
WILLIAM M BENN
JOSEPH A BENNER
WARREN W BENNER
BERT A BENNETT
BILLY G BENNETT
EMORY L BENNETT
GRANVIL L BENNETT
HARRY M BENNETT
HOYT J BENNETT
HUGHES BENNETT
RICHARD W BENNETT
RUSSELL M BENNETT JR
VANDERBILT H BENNETT
WILLIAM D BENNETT
WILLIAM M BENNETT
ROBERT W BENNINGTON
MARCEL P BENOIT

25 ARMY

DAVID BENSON
LAVERNE G BENSON
MAURICE BENSON JR
WILLIAM BENSON
BILLY J BENTLEY
CORYDON W BENTON
PAUL A BENTON
XAVIER J BENZIGER JR
KARL BERA
THOMAS H BERARDI
IGNACIO M BERASIS
JENNINGS H BERDINE
ALFRED M BERES
CHARLES W BERG
STANLEY M BERG
WILLIAM BERG JR
RALPH O BERGE
LLOYD M BERGER
STANLEY L BERGER
DWIGHT M BERGERON
PAUL BERGERON
LEON J BERGHOUSE
RICHARD D BERGLAND
HAROLD E BERGQUIST
ROBERT H BERLEMANN
JOE M BERNAL
MAURICE J BERNING
JAMES A BERNINGER
CLARENCE R BERRETH
HENRY L BERRIEN
JACKIE G BERRIER
GILBERTO A BERRIOS
PEDRO M BERRIOS
CANDIDO BERRIOS-ORTIZ
JORGE BERRIOS-SANTIAGO
ANTONIO BERRIOS-SUAREZ
ARTHUR BERRY JR
BENNY BERRY
BILLY BERRY
JAMES BERRY
L J BERRY
RICHARD W BERRY
JOSEPH P BERTANI
ROBERT L BERTOLIO
CHARLES E BERTRAM
THOMAS E BERTRAM JR
JOHN BESKON
WILLIAM H BESS
CARL H BEST
JAMES L BEST
HORACE BETHEA
GEORGE L BETTS
CLIFFORD A BETZ
ARTHUR Q BEVERLY
OTIS E BEVERLY
DEAN H BEYER
EMETERIO BEZARES-ROMERO
DANIEL C BIANCO
VITO J BIANCO
KENNITH L BIARD
OVAL O BICKEL
ROBERT T BICKEL
LEROY BICKERS
NELSON A BIDDLE
CARLOS R BIDOPIA
WILLIAM R BIEDENKAPP
THOMAS BIENASZEWSKI
JAMES C BIERER
JIMMIE B BIERNER
LEON D BIESHEUVEL
RICHARD E BIGELOW
LESTER W BIGGS
EUGENE J BIGNESS
FAREL R BILLS
MICHAEL G BILYEU
HOLMAN B BINGHAM
JIMMIE D BINGHAM
JOHN R BINNICKER
SILAS BIRCHMORE JR
GALEN S BIRKELAND
GARY A BIRKHIMER
MELVIN A BIRKHOLZ
DONALD L BISHOP
JAMES D BISHOP
PINK K BISHOP
ROBERT G BISHOP
WESLEY W BISHOP JR
ORVILLE C BJERKEBEK

ROBERT BJORGE
ADRIAN BLACK
CLEMENT L BLACK
FRITZ F BLACK
JAMES E BLACK
ROBERT A BLACK
ROBERT H BLACK
ROBERT J BLACK
STEPHEN BLACK
WILLIAM H BLACK
MACK J BLACKMON
REMUS M BLACKWOOD
RUSSELL E BLADE
KENNETH E BLADES
WENDELL E BLAGG
BOBBY R BLAIR
ELZIE L BLAIR
GEORGE W BLAIR
LARRY L BLAIR
ROBERT R BLAIR
SAMUEL B BLAIR
WARREN D BLAIR
REYNOLDS G BLAKE
MAX H BLALOCK
EDWARD B BLANCHARD
HARLAN D BLANCHARD
DAVID P BLAND
DON G BLANDFORD
CHARLES L BLANKENSHIP
RANDOLPH M BLANKENSHIP
ROY B BLANKENSHIP
WILLIE F BLANKS
EMORY M BLANTON
PAUL J BLASCZYK
JOSEPH BLASIOLE
THOMAS J BLATARIC JR
EDWARD F BLAZEJEWSKI
BRUCE A BLEGEN
HERENE K BLEVINS
LONIE K BLEVINS
WILLIAM H BLEVINS
ERICH W BLEY
ROBERT S BLOCK
HAROLD G BLODGETT
RUSSELL E BLODGETT
DELOY BLOOD
FREDERICK J BLOOM
ROBERT F BLOOM
JOHN C BLOUNT JR
BILLIE S BLUE
EMERSON R BLUE
WILLIE E BLUE
NELSON F BLUM
JOHN T BLUME
ANDREW G BLUMHOEFER
HOWARD BLUTTMAN
ROY S BOACH
CLARENCE E BOATWRIGHT
SWANSON L BOBBITT
HOWARD T BOBO
EUGENE BOCKHORN
HENRY W BODE JR
KENNETH A BODEKER
ERNEST L BODISON
WILLIAM V BOEHLER JR
HENRY C BOEHLING
JOHN A BOEHM
RICHARD F BOEHME
HENRY F BOETTICHER
CLIFFORD R BOGARD
CLAYTON L BOGART JR
WILLIAM T BOGART
ROBERT A BOGERT
ELMO D BOGGS
HOWARD L BOHNER
ELMER M BOISSEAU JR
JACQUES A BOISSONNEAULT
EUGENE R BOISVERT
CHARLIE BOITNOTT JR
GI-HANG BOK
ARTHUR A BOLAND
FRANCIS J BOLDEN
GEORGE E BOLDEN
FREDDIE R BOLDS
VLADIMIR BOLDYREV
GERMAN O BOLEN

RICHARD G BOLES
ALVIN J BOLF
PHILIP L BOLIN
ROY L BOLING
LLOYD J BOLLES
JOSEPH M BOLOGNA
JOHN L BOLSTER
FRANK J BOLT
ELMER BOLUS
JOHN D BOMER
WETZEL Z BONAR
LEONARD BONCZKOWSKI
CHARLES E BOND
LEE W BOND
RALPH A BOND
ROBERT D BOND
HARVE BONDS JR
LEROY BONE
FRANK J BONFIGLIO
DOMINGO BONILLA-ALMEDINA
JULIO BONILLA-VEGA
RICHARD J BONKOWSKI
FRANK V BONOMO
JOHN F BONSER
JOHN R BONZO
GEORGE G BOOKER
OSCAR L BOOKER
WALTER G BOOKER
JAMES L BOONE
WILLIE BOONE
GILBERT H BOOTH
HERBERT H BOOTH
IZEA BOOTH
DENMAN G BOOTON
JOHN M BORAH
ALFRED C BORDEAU
DONALD L BORDEN
EDWARD F BORELL
CLIFFORD J BORING
DONALD M BORN
MARVIN L BORROR
CHARLES L BORTNER JR
CARLOS P BORUNDA
LLOYD J BOSBEN
ALBERT C BOSFORD
MARVIN L BOSHER
NICK E BOSKO
FRANK BOSTIC
CHARLES L BOSTICK
HARRY F BOSTROM
WILLIAM G BOTTORFF
LAWRENCE J BOUCHARD
LEONARD R BOUGHAN
JAMES H BOUGHTON
EARL C BOULDIN
JOSEPH W BOULWARE
ROBERT L BOURDEAU
GEORGE D BOURDIEU
G W BOURRAGE
RICHARD R BOVE
EDWIN A BOWDEN
GLENN L BOWEN
RICHARD BOWEN
JEFFERSON A BOWERS
JOHN R BOWERS
LESTER J BOWERS
RUSSELL H BOWERS JR
FRANK BOWIE
RICHARD A BOWLER
MILAS E BOWLIN
CHARLES F BOWLING
DARRELL R BOWLING
JERRY C BOWLING
KARL F BOWLING
JAMES C BOWMAN
GEORGE W BOYCE
RONALD L BOYCE
ALTON C BOYD
BARNEY J BOYD
CHARLES E BOYD
JAMES E BOYD
JOHN D BOYD
MOSE BOYD JR
RICHARD A BOYD
ROBERT J BOYD
WILLIAM O BOYD
WILLIAM T BOYD
ALFRED N BOYER JR
GERALD F BOYER

SILAS W BOYIDDLE
EDWARD P BOYKIN
FREEMAN E BOYKIN
HUGH J BOYLAN
ALBERT BOYLE
RALPH L BOYLES
JOSEPH BOZZA JR
WILLIAM T BRACEWELL
JIMMIE G BRACKEN
NORMAN C BRACKETT
HAROLD F BRADDOCK
JAMES BRADDOCK
ROBERT D BRADEN
CLARK M BRADFORD
EDWARD F BRADFORD JR
HERBERT L BRADFORD
PAUL G BRADFORD
WALTER J BRADICICH
DONALD R BRADISH
ALFORD L BRADLEY
BOBBY L BRADLEY
CHARLES W BRADLEY
EARL L BRADLEY
PAUL R BRADLEY
RAYMOND G BRADLEY
WILLIAM J BRADLEY
WALLACE B BRADLY
DAVID F BRADSHAW
GEORGE E BRADWAY
JOHN T BRADY
CHARLES T BRAGG
CHARLES W BRAGG
NICHOLAS M BRAGG
ORVAL R BRAGG
RAYMOND F BRAGG
WILLIAM P BRAGG JR
EDWARD F BRAKES
JAMES L BRAMBO
RAY G BRAMHILL
JAMES T BRAMMER
BOBBY P BRANCH
JOHN E BRANCH
MANUEL BRANCO
CHARLES A BRANDENBURG
RALPH D BRANDENBURG
DELBERT BRANDON
THEODORE A BRANDOW
EDWARD D BRANDT
ALBERT C BRANDVOLD
CLYDE BRANHAM
EARL F BRANHAM
HAROLD D BRANHAM
OLIVER BRANHAM
DONALD J BRANNON
GEORGE J BRANT
JAMES E BRANT
MARVIN E BRANTING
MARSHALL K BRANTLEY
MELVIN A BRASHEARS
VERNON L BRASWELL
CHARLES E BRATTON
VICTOR BRAUD
ROBERT F BRAUNS
HENRY J BRAUTIGAM
HAROLD R BRAVARD
CHARLES W BRAXTON
EDMOND R BRAXTON JR
GERALD BRAY
GLENN L BRAY SR
ERVIN E BRECKENRIDGE
JAMES E BRECKENRIDGE
HARRY B BREEDEN
JOSEPH N BREEDEN
ROY G BREEDLOVE
MORRIS W BREEZEE
RALPH F BREITFELD
MURRAY J BRENNAN
FRED A BRENNER
ROGER E BRENT
STERLING M BRENT
CHARLES F BRESSLER
JESSIE J BRETZ
ANTON E BREWER
CLYDE I BREWER
PINCKNEY A BREWER
WILLIAM E BREWER
THOMAS BREWSTER
JOSEPH W BRIAND
JOE F BRICKER

BERLEY C BRICKLEY
CHARLES E BRIDGE
JAMES R BRIDGER
KENNETH L BRIDGER
LINDY L BRIDGES
M J BRIDGES
DONALD L BRIDGEWATER
CHARLIE BRIERS
ALLAN F BRIGGS
JAMES H BRIGGS
ROBERT L BRIGGS
LESLIE BRIGHAM
JAMES L BRIGHT
ROBERT BRIGHT
MAC BRILLANTES
NEWTON W BRINGLE
EARL T BRINSON
CHARLES E BRINTLE
JAMES V BRIODY
LEO P BRIONES
HENRY BRISCO JR
KENNETH J BRISCOE
BENJAMIN F BRISTOW
JAMES L BRITTON
GEORGE R BROADHURST
THOMAS G BROADWATER
HUBERT J BROCK
WILBORN W BROCK
HARVEY L BROCKER
EDWARD G BROCKWAY
LOUIS BRODUR
ARNEL J BROOKS
CARL P BROOKS
CHARLES E BROOKS
CLARENCE M BROOKS
CLIFTON E BROOKS
EARL G BROOKS
HERMAN BROOKS
JACK E BROOKS
JEROME J BROOKS
JOHN W BROOKS JR
JULIAN T BROOKS
LEOTIS BROOKS
LLOYD K BROOKS
WILLIAM P BROOKS
WILLIAM T BROOKS
CHARLES L BROOME
RICHARD D BROTHERS
WOODROW BROUGHMAN
VICTOR E BROUSEK
EDWARD BROUSSARD JR
EDWARD J BROUWER
SAMUEL E BROWER
WILLIAM J BROWER
ALBERT L BROWN
ALLEN R BROWN
ALONZO W BROWN
ALVIN L BROWN
ARTHUR L BROWN
BENNER B BROWN
BILLY C BROWN
BUFORD M BROWN
CHARLES J A BROWN
CHARLES W BROWN
DAMON K BROWN
DAVID L BROWN
DONALD W BROWN
DOYL G BROWN
EARL BROWN
EMORY L BROWN
FERRIS BROWN
FRANKLIN W BROWN
GEORGE A BROWN
GILBERT H BROWN
HAROLD B BROWN
HERBERT W BROWN
HUGH M BROWN
INDA BROWN
JACOB BROWN JR
JAMES BROWN JR
JAMES A BROWN
JAMES G BROWN
JOE L BROWN

JOHN BROWN
JOHN E BROWN
JOHN H BROWN JR
JOHN L BROWN
JOSHUA E BROWN
JUELYNN O BROWN
KEITH E BROWN
KENNETH BROWN
LESLIE BROWN JR
MARVIN G BROWN
MCKINLEY BROWN
MELVIN L BROWN
PALMER H BROWN JR
PAUL M BROWN
PHILLIP E BROWN
RAYMOND R BROWN
RICHARD A BROWN
RICHARD H BROWN
ROBERT E BROWN
ROBERT E BROWN
RUFUS BROWN JR
SAMUEL BROWN JR
SAMUEL BROWN JR
SAMUEL C BROWN
SOLOMON M BROWN
STANLEY BROWN
VERNON L BROWN
WALTER BROWN JR
WILLIAM A BROWN
WILLIAM F BROWN
WILLIE BROWN
DONALD L BROWNAWELL
WILLIAM W BROWNBACK JR
EARL A BROWNE
KENNETH A BROWNE
BILLY J BROWNING
JAMES E BROWNING
JOSEPH D BROWNING
ROBERT L BROWNING JR
SEVERY B BROXHOLME
CARROL BROYLES JR
DONALD D BRUCE
JACKSON BRUCE
RUDOLPH L BRUCKNER JR
DAVID C BRUIN
ARTHUR BRUINSMA
CLIFFORD J BRUINSMA
DANIEL T BRUMAGEN
JAMES D BRUMLEY
PAUL W BRUMLEY
DALLAS R BRUMMETT
WALTER L BRUMMETT
WALTER T BRUNER
LEROY C BRUNNER
EDWARD J BRUNO
GIOVANNI M BRUNO
JOHN F BRUNO
CLETUS F BRUNSWICK
JAMES R BRUNT
THAD BRUTON JR
ROBERT W BRUVELEIT
BOBBIE L BRYAN
BOOKER T BRYANT JR
CHARLES J BRYANT
EMMITT R BRYANT
FREDERICK F BRYANT
JUNIOR R BRYANT
LEROY W BRYANT
ROY L BRYANT
WILLIAM J BRYANT
ROGER C BRYCE
EDWARD R BUCHAN
ERNEST L BUCHANAN
JOHN E BUCHANAN
ROBERT L BUCHER
BILL E BUCK
RICHARD I BUCKINGHAM
JERRY G BUCKMAN
JOSEPH G BUCKNAVAGE
ROBERT M BUCKNER
ROBERT E BUDD
IRVING C BUDNICK
JOHN T BUDNY
JOSEPH R BUENO
PETER BUFFA JR
GREGORY E BUFORD

ALFRED R BUIE
HERBERT E BUIK
MELVIN G BUIST
AMBROSE BULLERMAN
JOHNNIE R BULLOCK
MARK B BULLUCK
EARL G BUMPAS
ALVIN G BUNCH
ARTHUR BUNCH
CURTIS E BUNCH
EDGAR A BUNKER
RICHARD E BUNN
CARROL E BUNYARD
WILLIAM BURACZEWSKI
GEORGE E BURCH
NAMAN BURCH
ROBERT G BURCH
WILLIAM J BURCH
JESSE L BURCHAM
WATER C BURCHELL
JOHN G BURCHETT
JOSEPH C BURD
RICHARD G BURDETTE
HERBERT H BURDICK
EARL J BURGESS
JOHN A BURGESS
JOHN P BURGESS
WILLIAM A BURK
ARLYNN C BURKE
CRAWFORD W BURKE JR
DAVID S BURKE
DOUGLAS A BURKE
LAWRENCE E BURKE
ROBERT L BURKE
WILLIAM J BURKE
BILLIE R BURKEEN
EDWARD M BURKHEAD
DONALD M BURKHOLDER
DONALD W BURKS
SILAS BURKS
LAWRENCE L BURLEIGH
CHARLES E BURLEY
ERNEST BURNET
ANTHONY L BURNETT
GIBSON BURNETTE
RALSTON L BURNEY JR
BERNARD J BURNOTT
BENJAMIN BURNS JR
CHARLES P BURNS
DONALD P BURNS
FRED BURNS JR
JAMES A BURNS
JERE E BURNS
ROBERT D BURNS
VERNON BURNS
WALTER G BURNS
WILLIE H BURNSIDE JR
J C BURR
JAMES BURR
MELVIN J BURRELL
BUDDY B BURRIS
RUDY L BURROLA
BOBBY B BURROUGHS
BUFORD BURROW JR
ERNEST E BURRUEL
LEVI BURS
JOSE F BURSET-MELENDEZ
HOMER L BURT
LLOYD L BURTON
SAMUEL L BURTON
WILLIE G BURTON
CHARLES R BUSCH
HERMAN BUSCHSCHULTE
REUBEN H BUSH
WILLIAM C BUSHROD
WILLIAM J BUSHWAY
ERNEST BUSICO
GEORGE E BUSKIRK
ODELL BUSLER
WILLIAM H BUSSEY
ERVIN J BUSSIAN
PAUL J F BUSSIERE
FRANK J BUSTAMANTE
JAMES T BUTCHER
LEWIS A BUTERAKOS
ELDON D BUTLER
GENE P BUTLER
KENNETH E BUTLER
PAUL M BUTLER
ROBERT C BUTLER

WILLIAM E BUTLER
RONALD E BUTTERY
ANTHONY F BUTTINSKY
WILLIAM R BUTZ
EDWIN R BUXTON
BILLIE J BYARD
BOBBY L BYARS
GYU-SEOP BYEON
JAE-HAN BYEON
JEOM-YEONG BYEON
JONG-GU BYEON
SU-HAK BYEON
TAE-YEOP BYEON
WON-SEOP BYEON
CHARLES E BYERS
HAROLD E BYERS
JACKIE B BYNUM
CLAYTON J W BYRD
ERVIN A BYRD
THOMAS J BYRNE
WILLIAM P BYRNE
ELMER E BYRUM JR
JAMES D CABALLERO
JIMMIE CABE
SIDNEY G CABELL
ISAAC S CABRERA
ARTURO CADENA
ROY J CADY
NICOLA CAFARO
GEORGE W CAGLE
SAMUEL C CAHOW
JIM C CAIN
ROBERT R CALAHAN
JENARO R CALDERON
ODELL CALDWELL
SHERMAN H CALDWELL
VEODIS E CALDWELL
OTTO B CALEGARI
FRANK M CALI
MODESTO CALIMANO-TEXIDOR
JAMES L CALKINS
JAMES R CALLAGHAN
THOMAS J CALVELAGE
SUPREMO CALVES
HARVEY E CALVIN
LOUIS C CAMACHO JR
MIGUEL A CAMACHO-ROMAN
DAVID CAMERON JR
JAMES H CAMERON
JOSEPH A CAMERON
ONESIMUS J CAMISCIOLI
THOMAS A CAMMARANO
PHILIP D CAMMAROTA
ALEXANDER CAMPBELL
ALTON R CAMPBELL
ALVIN B CAMPBELL
EARL A CAMPBELL
GEORGE G CAMPBELL
JOHN B CAMPBELL
LAVERNE H CAMPBELL
OMAR P CAMPBELL
RAZOR J CAMPBELL
RICHARD F CAMPBELL
WILLIAM J CAMPION
ARTHUR E CAMPOMIZZI
GILBERT CAMPOS
CECIL H CANADY
ROBERT C CANALES
RUDOLPH M CANALES
JOHN P CANAVAN
DONALD L CANFIELD
CHIL-YONG CANG
LEWIS E CANIE
DONALD R CANNON
HUGH L CANNON
JACK E CANNON
SALVATORE CANTARELLA
ROBERT CANTELMO
FREDERICK CANTERBURY
LUTHER E CANTLEY
MILTON CANTOR
GLENN W CANTRALL
JOHN CANTY
MAX L CAPERTON
DAYTON L CAPLINGER
BENIGNO R CARABALLO
JUAN CARAMBOT-ORTIZ
CODY E CARAWAY

WILLIAM J CARBAUGH
OSWALD E CARBONNEAU
DAVID W CARD
MARCEL M CARDENAS
WILLIE R CARDENAS
EDWARD A CARDINAL
ORLANDO CARDONA
HUGH T CARDWELL
JOE L CARDWELL
GERALD D CAREY
STANLEY G CAREY JR
BRICE G CARGIN
ROCCO CARIDI
JAMES A CARL
JOHN J CARLISLE
JAMES L CARLOCK
HAROLD D CARLSEN
CHARLES E CARLSON
HAROLD J CARLSON
SIGURD L CARLSON
DONALD M CARMICHAEL
ARCHIE L CARMON JR
GERALD D CARNES
JAMES N CARON JR
CARMEN A CAROSELLA
DOUGLAS R CARPENTER
GERALD W CARPENTER
HAROLD L CARPENTER
OTIS C CARPENTER
AORISE W CARR
CLIFFORD L CARR
GEORGE G D CARR
HOWARD L CARR
JAMES T CARR
PATRICK F CARR
PAUL E CARR
WILLIAM H CARR
RICARDO CARRASCO
MARION CARREATHERS
RICHARD J CARRELL
CURTIS E CARRERE
OSCAR G CARRIERE
ALEJANDRO CARRILLO
ALEXANDER A CARRILLO
RAUL CARRILLO
ROBERT R CARRINGTON
BILLY W CARROLL
CORNIE E CARROLL
EDWIN E CARROLL
GARLAND R CARROLL
GEORGE CARROLL
JAMES CARROLL
JOHN E CARROLL
ROBERT L CARROLL
WILLIAM G CARROLL
MURRAY B CARROW
VERNON C CARSON
WILLIAM O CARSTARPHEN
ROBERT L CARSTENSEN
ANDREW CARTER
BRYANT W CARTER
CLARENCE O CARTER
CLYDE M CARTER
CORNELIUS CARTER JR
DONOVAN E CARTER
EDWARD R CARTER
GEORGE E CARTER
HAROLD B CARTER
HENRY L CARTER
JAMES M CARTER
JOSEPH C CARTER
RAYMOND CARTER
SAMUEL R CARTER
THOMAS CARTER
WILLIAM H CARTER
WILLIAM L CARTER
WILLIE E CARTER
FRANK P CARUSO JR
FRANK B CARVER
JOHN E CARVER
WILLIE L CARVER
HERBERT V CASANOVA JR
CHARLES E CASE
FRANK L CASEY
JOHN J CASEY JR
JOSEPH F CASEY
KENNETH C CASEY
RUSSELL M CASEY
MCWILLIAM J CASH
BOBBY R CASHION

DANIEL CASILLAS
ROBERTO L CASILLAS
CLYDE H CASPER
RICHARD CASPER
PATRICK T CASSATT
ARTHUR C CASTANEDA
DONALD E CASTEEL
JOHN A CASTEEL
EDMUND L CASTELLO
ANTHONY J CASTIGLIA
AUGUSTINE CASTILLO
PABLO A CASTILLO
RAFAEL CASTILLO-QUINONES
CLIFFORD C CASTLE
WILLIAM R CASTLEBERRY
RICARDO CASTOR JR
JESUS B CASTRO
LUIS G CASTRO-CORDERO
JUAN CASTRO-HENRIQUEZ
MONROE CATER JR
ROBERT S CATHCART
EDWARD W CATLOS
WILLIAM J CAUGHEY
WILBUR O CAUL
PAUL O CAUSEY
CHARLES L CAVE
MACK D CAVENDER
JAMES R CAWTHON
ROBERT J CAYE
ARMANDO CEDENO-RAMOS
LINDEN CENTERS
AMERICO D CERASUOLO
WAYNE L CERVENKA
CHI-SU CHA
JEOM-GAE CHA
JUNG-GEUN CHA
PIL-MYEON CHA
SAM-JO CHA
YANG-HO CHA
YONG-GAP CHA
SELBY F CHABOT
NILTON CHACON-SOTO
EARBIE CHADDRICK
GEORGE R CHADWELL
JAMES R CHADWICK
HWA-BYEONG CHAE
YEONG-JO CHAE
ALDEN R CHAFFIN
ROY O CHAFFIN JR
LEO CHAFFINS
HENRY CHAISSON
DALE E CHALFANT
GEORGE J CHALLENDER
FRANCIS E CHAMBERLAIN
ALVERNON A CHAMBERS
BENNIE E CHAMBERS
GRADY L CHAMBERS
HORACE CHAMBERS
OSRIC E CHAMBERS
RICHARD J CHAMBERS
WILLIAM J CHAMBERS
WILLIAM J CHAMBERS
WILLIS M CHAMBERS
HARVEY L CHAMBLES
SAMUEL A CHAMI
JOHN T CHAMPAGNE
MORRIS J CHAMPAGNE
AUBRY W CHAMPION
FELIPE A CHAMPION
JOHN CHAMPION
MERRILL A CHAMPION
JOSEPH D CHANCERY
JAMES O CHANDLER
JOHN W CHANDLER JR
ROBERT C CHANDLER
TEDDY R CHANDLER
JACK A CHANEY
JAMES G CHANEY
WILSON CHANEY JR
ROBERT E CHANNON
ROSS H CHAPIN
CHARLES W CHAPMAN

27 ARMY

KENNETH E CHAPP
BILLIE F CHAPPELL
JAMES R CHAPPELLE
FRANK C CHARCAS
FRANK J CHARIDO
ANTHONY J CHARLES
MARVIN R CHARLES
RAYMOND M CHARLES
ARTHUR CHARLESTON
ANDREW CHARNICHKO
GEORGE P CHARNOCK
FRED CHARNOW
DUPREE CHARVIS
RENE P CHASEZ
JOHN H CHASTAIN
JOHN W CHASTAIN
VASKEL T CHASTEEN
THOMAS J CHATIGNY
LOUIS CHATMAN
ARNOLD F CHAVEZ
BENNY R CHAVEZ
BERNARD R CHAVEZ
DANIEL V CHAVEZ
DON CHAVEZ
JOSE M CHAVEZ
MIGUEL S CHAVEZ
RALPH G CHAVEZ
SILAS E CHAVEZ
VINCENT J CHAVEZ
BURNICE CHAVIS
ROBERT E CHEATUM
ROBERT H CHEEKS III
LOUIS CHEFF
BYEONG-HUI CHEON
GYEONG-UK CHEON
HYEONG-GI CHEON
JEONG-HEON CHEON
JI-BOK CHEON
SEONG-MUN CHEON
YEONG-MUN CHEON
LAWRENCE A CHERAMIE
RICHARD F CHERRY
DARROL C CHESLEY
GUY O CHESLEY
DONALD H CHESTNUT
ROLAND B CHESTNUT
JOSEPH L CHETTLE
GUMERSINDO CHEVRE
ROY CHICHENOFF
GILBERT L CHIDESTER
BONNIE CHILCUTT
RUSSELL H CHILDS
DENNIS J CHISM
CAIN CHISOLM
ALBAN CHMIELEWSKI
LOYD L CHOAT
BOK-GYU CHOI
BOK-MAN CHOI
BONG-YONG CHOI
BYEONG-HA CHOI
BYEONG-JO CHOI
BYEONG-UK CHOI
CHANG-O CHOI
CHANG-SIK CHOI
CHEOL-HO CHOI
CHEOL-YONG CHOI
CHI-WON CHOI
DAE-SEOK CHOI
DEOK-SANG CHOI
DEUK-RYUL CHOI
DONG-BONG CHOI
DONG-GEUN CHOI
DONG-IN CHOI
DONG-JUN CHOI
DONG-SEON CHOI
EUNG-SIK CHOI
GAM-ROK CHOI
GI-CHEOL CHOI
GI-DAL CHOI
GI-RIP CHOI
HAE-CHEOL CHOI
HAE-GI CHOI
HAE-GYEONG CHOI
HAE-JO CHOI
HWA-PUNG CHOI
HYO-YONG CHOI
IN-GEOL CHOI
IN-HAK CHOI
IN-HWAN CHOI
JEONG-YONG CHOI

JONG-RYUL CHOI
JUN-CHEOL CHOI
JUN-SIK CHOI
MAN-DONG CHOI
MAN-HUI CHOI
MAN-SU CHOI
MIN-HO CHOI
SANG-HO CHOI
SANG-SIK CHOI
SEONG-GIL CHOI
SEONG-GYU CHOI
SEON-GI CHOI
SEONG-OK CHOI
SEONG-SUK CHOI
SEON-GU CHOI
SEON-JO CHOI
SE-RIM CHOI
SIN-CHEOL CHOI
SUK-RO CHOI
TAEK-JIN CHOI
TAE-SEOK CHOI
TAE-SIK CHOI
TA-GWAN CHOI
YEONG-GON CHOI
YEONG-OK CHOI
YEONG-SIK CHOI
YEONG-SU CHOI
YEONG-TAK CHOI
YONG-CHEOL CHOI
YONG-TAE CHOI
YONG-YUN CHOI
YU-SEOP CHOI
FRANK CHOJNOWSKI JR
ELLIS A CHOMA
MARCHMONT T F CHONG
MARTIN CHOVANEC JR
CYRIL M CHRISJOHN
GEORGE K CHRISTENSEN
JACK W CHRISTENSEN
LOYAL E CHRISTENSON
RICHARD J CHRISTENSON
CLAIBORN CHRISTIAN
ROLAND E CHRISTIAN
STUART B CHRISTIAN
HARRY A CHRISTMAN
WALTER R
CHRISTOFFERSEN
JOHN F CHRISTY
JOHN C CHRONISTER
DEUK-YEOP CHU
SU-IL CHU
YEONG-JI CHU
STANLEY J CHUDOBSKI
DAN D CHULIBRK
WILFRED Y W CHUN
FREDDIE E CHURCH
HAROLD C CHURCH
MACK CHURCH
MERLE E CHURCH
ANTHONY J CICALESE
JOHN CICCARELLI
MICHAEL V CICCHELLA
WILLIAM E CICON
EDWIN W CIESIELSKI
BERT F CINKOVICH
MODESTO CINTRON-
PAGAN
ARTHUR D CIRINO-RIVERA
SAMUEL J CIRULLI
ARTHUR CISNEROS
JAMES O CLAMP
EVERELL V CLANIN
FRANCIS I CLAPPER
EUGENE E CLARDY
JAMES R CLARIN
ANDREW CLARK
BARTHOLOMEN N CLARK
BOBBY J CLARK
CHARLES L CLARK
CLIFFORD E CLARK
CURTIS W CLARK
DONALD J CLARK
DONALD J CLARK
GLENN M CLARK
HAROLD R CLARK
HENRY D CLARK
HOWARD L CLARK
JAMES CLARK JR
JEWEL CLARK
JOSEPH E CLARK

KEITH K CLARK
MEACHEM W CLARK
O C CLARK JR
RICHARD N CLARK
ROOSEVELT CLARK
STUART G CLARK
VERN R CLARK
WALTER H CLARK
WILLIAM J CLARK
WILLIE CLARK
ROBERT J CLARKE
WILSON D CLARKE
RUSSELL W CLARKSON JR
EDWARD W CLARNO
ROBERT O CLATTER
WALTER R CLAUSSEN
ALEX C CLAY
ARTHUR CLAY
ROBERT E CLAY
WILLIE L CLAY
DENVER R CLAYTON
HOWARD E CLAYTON
JAMES W CLAYTON JR
RAYMOND H CLAYTON
ROBERT J CLAYTON
DELMON CLEAVER
CHARLES M CLEM
ANTHONY J CLEMENS JR
JOHN J CLEMENS
ELZIE G CLEMENTS
TERRELL C CLEMENTS
FRED C CLEMONS
DOMINICK CLESCERI
CLIFTON CLEVELAND
PAUL A CLEVELAND
STANLEY K CLEVELAND
BRUCE W CLEVENGER
ARTHUR A CLIFTON
MILO F CLIFTON
RALPH D CLIFTON
WILLIAM J CLINE
HAROLD CLINKSCALE
JACK B CLOIN
JAMES F CLOPTON
ARCHIE J CLOSSON
ROBERT E CLOUSER
ALFRED W CLOWERS
ROBERT J CLUKEY
LESLEY W CLYBURN
CHARLES A COBB
JAMES O COBB
FRANKLIN E COBLE
FRANK A COBURN
HOWARD COBURN
ANTHONY L COCCHI
COONFIELD COCHRAN
HUBERT F COCHRAN
JACK D COCHRAN
JAMES L COCHRAN
L G COCHRAN
LAWRENCE R COCHRAN JR
ELMER M COCKRELL
WILLIAM F CODY
JAMES F COE
ALLAN A COELHO
WALTER L COEN
CHARLES L COFFEE
WILLIAM W COFFEE
CLIFFORD V COFFEY
GORDON R COFFEY
J C COFFEY
JACK D COFFEY
JAMES W COFFIN
MELVIN S COFFMAN
CHARLES D COGAR
EARL COGGIN
ROBERT H COGHLAN
CECIL K COGLAN
CARMELO A COGNATA
FRANK COHAN
BERNARD COHEN
MAX H COHOE
JONAS COIT JR
CLYDE COKER
FLOYD T COKER
LOUIS A COLAGEO
DOMENIC COLAMETA
JAMES L COLARUSSO JR
MUSSENDEN S COLBERG
JAMES C COLBERT

ALBERT C COLBY
DAVID L COLBY
CHARLES M COLE
DAVID L COLE
DONALD P COLE
EDWARD L COLE JR
FRANK N COLE
HENLY P COLE JR
MERLE L COLE JR
RANDOLPH J COLE
SHIRLEY W COLE
WILLIAM H COLE
OLIVER COLEGROVE
DANIEL COLELLO
ALFRED L COLEMAN
BLAINE M COLEMAN
CHARLES COLEMAN
DENNIS W COLEMAN JR
FRANCIS W COLEMAN
WILBUR B COLFORD
EITHER M COLLAZO
JOSEPH P COLLETTE
WILLIAM COLLETTI
CHARLES E COLLIER
JOHN A COLLIER
TOLAND J COLLIER
WILLIE L COLLIER
CHARLES L COLLINGS
CHARLES E COLLINS
GERALD J COLLINS
GLENN E COLLINS
HENRY COLLINS JR
JAMES R COLLINS
JEWEL W COLLINS
JOHN E COLLINS
JOHN W COLLINS
JOSEPH COLLINS
MARVIN R COLLINS
PAUL M COLLINS
ROBERT E COLLINS
ROY J COLLINS
SIDNEY L COLLINS
WILLIAM COLLINS
WILLIAM K COLLINS
MARION L
COLLINSWORTH
CONCEPCION COLON
EURIPIDES A COLON
ANTONIO COLON-FLORES
MARIANO COLON-
MARTINEZ
GAETANO A COLONNA
LUIS COLON-NEGRON
ARQUELIO COLON-
RODRIGUEZ
FRANCISCO A COLON-
RODRIGUEZ
CLYDE R COLVIN
THOMAS L COLVIN
ANTHONY COMBS
CARL B COMBS
FORREST G COMBS
HORACE G COMBS JR
ROBERT L COMBS
JOSEPH W COMEAU
EUGENE C COMER
CHARLIE L COMOLLI
RUDY COMPARIN
JOHNNY H COMPTON
FRANK W CONARRO
PERRY J CONAWAY
CASIMIRO CONCEPCION-
ESQUILIN
RAMON CONCEPCION-
PABON
ROBERT CONDER
ELISHIE M CONDICT
ELBERT A CONDLEY
RICHARD G CONDON
VICTOR J CONDROSKI
ROBERT E CONDY
JOHN L CONFER
RICHARD A CONFER
GEORGE T CONGLETON JR
JOHN D CONKERTON JR
GEORGE W CONKLIN JR
JOHN E CONKLIN JR
CLIFTON W CONLEY
JAMES T CONLEY
JAMES W CONLEY

DELMAR E CONNER
ROBERT J CONNER JR
DONALD C CONNETT
MARK CONNOLLY
ROBERT C CONNOLLY
ADELBERT CONOVER
MERRILL S CONRAD
RICHARD L CONRAD
WILBUR L CONRAD
JOHN K CONROY
MICHAEL F CONROY
PATRICK J CONROY
ROBERT F CONSIDINE
HENRY CONSIGLI JR
JAMES L CONSTANT
GERLANDO P
CONSTANTINO
MARIO CONTILIANO
ESPETACION
CONTRERAS JR
LIANDRO
CONTRERAS JR
RUDOLPH R
CONTRERAS
BROOKS E CONWAY
CHARLES F COOK
EDWARD H COOK
ELI W COOK
HAROLD D COOK
HENRY W COOK JR
IRVIN H COOK JR
J C COOK
JOHN E COOK
KERMIT E COOK
LAMONTE B COOK
MAURICE E COOK
ROSCOE COOK JR
WILLIAM R COOK
ALBERT B COOKE
JOHN P COOKE
LEON O COOKE
LEROY D COOKE
LESLIE L COOLEY
PAUL R COOLEY
JOHN J COONEY
EARL R COONROD
ARTHUR COOPER
CHARLES R COOPER
DAVID Q COOPER
DAVID R COOPER
DONALD D COOPER
GEORGE COOPER
JACK R COOPER
JIMMIE R COOPER
JOHN J COOPER
NORWOOD C COOPER
PAUL R COOPER JR
RALPH L COOPER
RICHARD J COOPER
ROBERT L COPE
ELLIS H COPELAND JR
JAMES H COPELAND
MELVIN C COPELAND
WILLIAM B COPELAND
KEARNEY C COPLEY
VINCENT A COPPOLA
THOMAS J CORACI
EARNEST J CORBETT
KENNETH L CORBETT
GEORGE A CORBIN
MCCRARY CORBIN
FREDERICK A CORBINE
CLARENCE CORBY JR
JOHN CORCORAN
CHARLES CORDER JR
DOYLE E CORDER
ZENON CORDERO-
CAJIGAS
CHARLES O CORDLE
CARMELO CORDONE
JOE D CORDOVA
RICHARD E COREY
THOMAS R CORK
ROBERTO CORKILL
JOHNNY M CORLEY
LAMOINE V CORMICAN
ARNOLD CORNELIUS
EDWARD S CORNELL JR
PAUL D CORNELL
ROBERT L CORNIBE

28 ARMY

JAIME CORONA
BENJAMIN M CORREA
JESUS D CORREA
DANIEL CORREIA
FRANCIS D CORRETTE JR
FRANK CORRIGAN
HAROLD G CORSON
RODRIGUEZ F CORTES
JOSUE CORTES-BOISJOLI
ANGEL L CORTES-
OSTOLAZA
FELIPE CORUJO
RICHARD COSH
DONALD C COSS
L T COSSEY
TED W COSSIN
JOHN L COSTA
CHARLES A COSTELLO
JOHN T COSTELLO
JOSEPH P COSTELLO
MARVIN COSTNER
JOSEPH J COSTROFF
FRANCIS H COTE
ROGER B COTE
COMER C COTNEY
ANGEL COTTO-
HERNANDEZ
ELIJAH COTTON
DONALD COTTRELL
ROBERT A COUEY
DELBERT COULAM
DOUGLAS B COULTER
JULIUS C COULTER
PHILLIP W COULTER
JOHN A COULTON
ERNEST COUNTS
JOHN H COURCHAINE
CALVIN C COUSINS
CHARLES M COUSINS
JOSE R COUVERTIER
ELVIN R COVLIN
JOHN E COWAN
MOSES COWAN JR
VESTAL R COWAN
WILLIAM W COWAN
LOYD COWDEN JR
RAY P COWDIN
CLARE E COWEE
ROY A COWLES
ERNEST W COX
EVERLE COX
GLENN L COX
HAROLD E COX
JAMES A COX
JAMES G COX
KENNETH R COX
MARSHALL L COX
NORMAN D COX
PAUL D COX
ROBERT F COX
ROBERT L COX
ULYSSES M COX JR
WILLIAM C COX
ALLEN B COYNER
DONALD E COZAD
PAUL C CRABTREE
LONNIE E CRADDOCK
WILLIAM G CRADDOCK
WILLIAM E CRAGO
ARMAND CRAIG JR
HARRY E CRAIG
JERRY P CRAIG
WILLIAM E CRAIG
WILLIE CRAIG
RUFUS P CRAIGHEAD
BILLY CRAIL
DAVID R CRAIN
HARRY F CRAMER
WINFORD R CRAMER
JACK A CRANDELL
ROBERT L CRANE
MATTHEW CRANKOVICH
GEORGE E CRANOR
FRANCIS CRATER JR
CHESTER CRAVEN
BOBBY G CRAWFORD
CHARLES F CRAWFORD
DAVID A CRAWFORD JR
ELMER E CRAWFORD
GEORGE C CRAWFORD JR

SAMUEL L CRAWFORD
STANLEY C CRAWFORD
THOMAS CRAWFORD
THOMAS A CRAWFORD
WILLIAM F CRAWFORD
WILLIAM L CRAWFORD
WALLACE CREAMER
HOLLIS M CREASY
JAMES A CREAZZO
CIRIACU CREDO
CLAYTON F CREECH
LLOYD R CRELLER
ROY N CRENSHAW
EUGENE R CREUZIGER
BRYANT CREWS
JAMES CREWS
JAMES R CRIDER
CHARLES R CRIGER
ARTHUR E CRIM
THEODORE D CRISS
ALBERT L CROFT JR
VARNOLD G CROGHAN
FRED W CROMER
CLARENCE CROMIER
EUGENE CRON
STANLEY W CROOK
FLOYD D CROOKS
DONALD W CROPPER
FRANK M CROPPER
ROBERT D CROPPER
JAMES Z CROSBY
LOUIS N CROSBY
JAMES H CROSS
JIMMIE C CROSSLAND
FRANKLIN W CROSSMAN
MILTON V CROUCH
JOHN B CROUSE
PAUL CROUSE
SANFORD D CROWE
ALLEN B CROWELL
NEIL J CROWLEY
WILLIE B CROWLEY
RAYMOND F CROWN
MARVIN V CRUCE
Y J CRUM
CHESTER A CRUSE
HERBERT H CRUSE
SHERMAN P CRUTS JR
AMADEO A CRUZ
FREDDY CRUZ
LEONAL M CRUZ
MARTIN CRUZ JR
RAMON CRUZ
ROBERTO CRUZ-ESPINOSA
PEDRO A CRUZ-OTERO
JESUS CRUZ-RAMOS
PABLO CRUZ-ROSA
TOMAS E CRUZ-SANTOS
ISMAEL CRUZ-VELEZ
ANTONIO CUADRADO-
RIVERA
DAVID E CUBBY
DAVID L CUDGER JR
JOHNNY H CUELLAR
ALFREDO CUEVAS
CECIL W CULDICE
JOHN A CULHANE
DONALD F CULLEN
ROLAND W CULLINS
FREDDIE L CULMER
ARNOLD D CULP
ROY K CULPEPPER
CHARLES L CULVER
JOHN P CUMBELICH
CHARLIE W CUMMINGS
JACOB C CUMMINGS
JOHN P CUMMINGS
PAUL D CUMMINGS
CARL E CUMMINS
ELZA M CUMMINS
AUGUSTUS V
CUNNINGHAM
CHARLES B CUNNINGHAM
FRANK CUNNINGHAM JR
JAMES L CUNNINGHAM
JIMMIE D CUNNINGHAM
KENNETH CUNNINGHAM
KENNETH E CUNNINGHAM
RAYMOND L
CUNNINGHAM

THOMAS W CUPRAK
GEORGE A CURLEY JR
DONALD J CURRAN
PATRICK J CURRAN
RICHARD P CURRAN
NORMAN R CURRIE
OWEN J CURRIE JR
EDWARD R CURRY
ERNEST L D CURRY
GLENN D CURRY
MAURICE L CURRY
EDWARD L CURTIN
JOHN C CURTIS
LLOYD N CURTIS
ROBERT L CURTIS
VIRGIL M CURTIS
WILLIAM R CURTIS
JESS M CUSHING
ROBERT M CUSTER
VERNON C CUSTER
DONALD J CUTLER
HUGHIE CUTSHALL
FRED CUTTER
CHARLES W CUTTS
THOMAS A CUVA
EDWARD C CWIKLA
JOSEPH E CYBULSKI
JOSEPH E CYR
MICHAEL CZARNIEWSKY
LEO P CZUBAK
DANIEL J DABKIEWICZ
CHESTER L DABROWSKI
FREDERICK H DAEHNKE
HARLAN R DAGGETT
THOMAS J DAGON
ARLEN C DAHL
DENNIS DAHL
WILBERT P DAIGLE
PHILLIPPE DAIGNEAULT
JOHN D DAIL
ALLEN R DALE
EDWARD B DALE
OLIVER DALE
DANIEL E DALEY
JAMES M DALEY
JACK E DALLAS
CARMEN J DALLESANDRO
BENITO DALLEVA
JOSEPH A DALSZYS
EDMUND F DALTON
GENE D DALY
BERNARD A DAMATO
GEORGE G DAMICO
DONALD W DANA
JOHN DANCIK
CHARLES DANDREA
PASQUALE C DANDREA
JAMES E DANIEL
MELVIN B DANIEL
RICHARD A DANIEL
BOBBIE R DANIELS
CHARLES C DANIELS
CURTIS L DANIELS
GUS J DANIELS JR
ISOM J DANIELS
JAMES R DANIELS
JOHN DANIELS JR
PAUL E DANIELS
THEOTIS DANIELS
OTIS DANIELY
RALPH E DANILSON
JOHN DANNUNZIO
RICHARD DANSBERRY
WILLIAM E DARBY
RAY J DARCY
THOMAS P DARCY
ALVIN DARDAR
NORMAN O DARLING
ROY E DARRELL
ALLEN D DASHIELL
ROBERT DASHKOVITZ
LITTLE N DATES
WAYNE R DAUBERT
HENRY F DAUGHERTY
JAMES F DAUGHERTY
LLOYD W DAUGHERTY
WILLIAM G DAULTON
HAYDEN H DAVENPORT
HENRY DAVENPORT
JIMMY J DAVENPORT

WILLIAM E DAVENPORT
EDWARD S DAVEY JR
WILLIAM S DAVEY
EMENELIO DAVID-
PEDROGO
GERALD E DAVIDSON
JAMES G DAVIDSON
ROBERT J DAVIDSON
RALPH H DAVIDTER
CLAIR L DAVIE
HERBERT E DAVIE
EVERETT E DAVIES
ROBERT L DAVIES
CARLOS DAVILA-RIVERA
BELLINGER DAVIS JR
BILLIE D DAVIS
BYRON S DAVIS
CURTIS DAVIS
DONALD H DAVIS
DONALD L DAVIS
DONALD L DAVIS
EARL G DAVIS
EDDIE DAVIS JR
EZEKIEL A DAVIS
GEORGE H DAVIS JR
GEORGE J DAVIS
HAYWARD DAVIS
HENRY L DAVIS
HERSCHEL D DAVIS
IVERSON DAVIS
J D DAVIS JR
JACK A DAVIS
JAMES J DAVIS
JERRY DAVIS
JOHN L DAVIS
LEO C DAVIS
MAX O DAVIS
MORTON C DAVIS
RICHARD E DAVIS
ROSCOE M DAVIS
RUSSELL G DAVIS
SAMUEL L DAVIS
SANFORD J B DAVIS
THOMAS L DAVIS
TROY C DAVIS
WALTER E DAVIS
WELDON A DAVIS
WILLIE DAVIS
WILLIE D DAW
MELNIE H DAWES
JUREL O DAWSON
NORMAN F DAWSON
BILLIE W DAY
CHARLES N DAY
CLARON O DAY
DAVE H DAY JR
DONALD DAY
ROBERT J DAY
ROBERT W DAY
WAYNE H DAY
WILLIAM A DAY
ROBERT M DAYTON
ROLLAND G DEACON
BOYDEN M DEAN
JOHN R DEAN
LEWIS D DEAN
MARION V DEAN
ROBERT E DEAN
ROBERT E DEAN
MARCELO C DEANDA
ARTHUR B DEARING
GEORGE B DEASE
CHARLES L DEASON
ROBERT M DEAVOR
MICHAEL DE BENEDICTUS
BILLY A DEBORD
WILLIAM L DEBRUYN
WILBUR H DE BUSK
WALTER DEC
RICHARD J DECANDIO
FRANCIS R DECAPOT
LEO N DE CICCO
HOBART DECKER
LEE D DECKER
ROBERT W DECKER
RONALD R DECKER JR
ELBERT C DE COOK
WILLIAM P DECOTO
DANIEL D DECREASE
ROBERT C DEEL

WILLIAM P
DEER WITH HORNS
ALEX DEESE
GERALD J DE FLORA
BENJAMIN C DEFOREST
CHARLES M DEFRANCE
SAMUEL W DEFREESE
RICHARD J DE FREITAS
GILBERT L DEGRANT
JEROME S DE GROOT
WILLIE B DE HERRERA
THOMAS E DEHM
JUAN DE HOYOS-LOPEZ
THOMAS L DEIGNAN JR
ANDREW F DEISENROTH
TOMAS DE JESUS-
ADORNO
PABLO A DE JESUS-
FELICIANO
RAMON R DE JESUS-
MEDINA
EFRAIN A DE JESUS-
NIEVES
LORENZO DE LA CRUZ
JAMES D DELANEY
JAMES G DELANEY
FRANCIS N DELANO
LLOYD M DE LEON
CALIXTE J DELESHA
ALFRED DELGADO
GILBERT J DELGADO
PEDRO A DELGADO
RENE DELGADO-
ACOSTA
RAMON DELGADO-
GONZALEZ
SABINO DELGADO-
RESTO
MANUEL DELGADO-
RODRIQUEZ
WENCESLAO DELGADO-
UBILES
JOSEPH W DELLER
RICHARD P DELLIGATTI
HOWARD E DELON
HAROLD T DELONG
ELLIE E DELOZIER
HUBERT A DELPH
CLIFFORD A DELPHIN
ANGELO J DEL POZZO
FREDERICK D
DEL PRIORE
RAYMOND DEL TORO
RALPH J DEMAIO
ANTHONY P DEMANNO
WILFRED K DE MEULE
KENNETH E DEMIERE
JAMES J DE MIERI
CHARLES R DE MILTE
ROLLAND W DEMO
GENERAL DEMONBREUN
FREDERIC C DENBIGH
ANTONIO V DE NIGRIS
PEDRO A DENIZA
J B DENKINS
JAMES R DENNEHY JR
NORMAN W DENNEY
THOMAS A DENNEY JR
HENRY P DENNING
CHARLES M DENNIS
FRANK S DENNIS
HENRY W DENNIS
WILLIAM H DENNIS
RALPH E DENNISON
RUSSELL L DENNISON
PAUL E DENNY
WILLIAM M DENSON
CLARENCE E DEON
FERDINAND N
DEPAPPA JR
ROGER E DE PATIE
DAVID E DEPEW
GERALD A
DEPPERSCHMIDT
PHILIP V DERAGON
EDGAR R DERN JR
EUGENE C DE ROSE
WESLEY G DERRICK
LAWRENCE K DESAU
VERNON L DESHIELDS

29 ARMY

GROVER W DESHOTEL
HARRY B DETTMERING
FRANK S DEVERS JR
LEROY L DEVILBISS
WESLEY E DE VRIES
DONALD L DEWEES
JOHN W DEWERFF
LEE A DEWEY
RODGER B DEWEY
DONALD B DEWITT
JOHN D DEYOE
REGINALD B DE YOUNG
MANUEL DIAZ JR
LUIS DIAZ-ACEVEDO
DEMETRIO DIAZ-ALGARIN
FERNANDO L DIAZ-COLON
RAFAEL DIAZ-COTO
FERNANDO DIAZ-RAMOS
CLARENCE M DIBBLE JR
LOUIS R DICAMILLO
LOUIS A DI CARLO
HOBERT C DICK
WILLIAM L DICK JR
LYNDWBURG DICKENS
BRISTER DICKERSON
DALLAS W DICKERSON
GROVER T DICKERSON
PAUL L DICKERSON
ROGER W DICKERSON
EPHRAM L DICKEY
DONALD R DICKINSON
MATTHEW L DICKINSON
CHARLES A DICKMAN
RONALD J DICKS
FRANKLIN P DICKSON
RICHARD B DICKSON
SERAFINO S DI CRISPINO
MARK R DI DOMENICO
ROBERT DIEDRICH
ROBERT J DIEGEL
JEROLD W DIEMER
GORDON A DIETRICH
FIORE J DI GIORGIO
LOUIS J DI GREGORIO
NICHOLAS P DI LEO
ARVLE DILL
CARL DILL
RAY G DILLARD
ROBERT E DILLARD
GERALD D DILLER
CARLTON E DILLON
EARL E DILLON
GEORGE A DILLON
JOHN J DILLON
JOHN L DILLON
JOHN T DILWORTH
RAYMOND L DI MALEO
CHARLES W DINAN
MILTON J DINERBOILER
BERNIE DINGESS
FRANK D DINWIDDIE
HENRY J DIONNE
RALPH DI PALMA
FRANK E DI PASQUALE JR
JOSEPH F DI PIETRO
JOSEPH V DI PIETRO
DALE D DIRKS
PETER A DISABELLA
LEONARD J DISHMAN
DANIEL J DISYLVESTER
CLYDE M DITTENHAFER
GEORGE E DITTMER
CHARLES R DI ULIO
WINFIELD DIVINE
FRANK J DIVIS JR
MARVIN DIX
DONALD C DIXON
JOHNNIE E DIXON
WAYNE E DIXON
WILLIE H DIXON
JONG-HAK DO
YONG-HO DO
ALBERT D DOBBINS
ROBERT J DOBBINS
JAMES A DOBBS
RICHARD D DOBIE
WARD A DOBSON
DONALD E DOCKSTADER
DENNIS R DODD
HOWARD H DODD

PETER J DODD
RICHARD F DODMEAD
KENNETH DODSON
FRANK R DOERR
JOHN H DOHERTY
ERNEST L DOLEZAL
ALBERT J DOLGE
ROBERT A DOLL
JACK DOLLAHAN
ROBERT P DOMAN
JOSEPH DOMETROVICH JR
DAVID DOMINGEZ
BUDDY DOMINGUEZ
LUIS R DOMINGUEZ
RICHARD DOMINGUEZ
MORTIMER DOMROE
VINCENZO G DONAGLIA
DANIEL D DONAHUE
JOSEPH P DONAHUE
DANIEL DONALDSON
REMO DONINI
RAY S DONOHEW
DERRICK F DONOVAN
FRANCIS C DOOGAN
EDWARD J DORAN
ROBERT G DORAN
WILLIAM F DORAND
FRED A DORRIS
LEONARD H DORSCH
HAROLD R DORSEY
CHARLES J DOSTART
CECIL F DOTSON
GLENN F DOTY
MARION R DOTY
JOSEPH DOUCET
MARVIN N DOUD JR
AMOS DOUGLAS JR
CARL E DOUGLAS
DEWAIN DOUGLAS
DONALD A DOUGLAS
LEO DOUGLAS
ROBERT DOUGLAS
WILLIAM S DOUGLAS
HORACE M DOVE
LEROY J DOVE
PAUL W DOVERSPIKE
EARL G DOW
CHARLES D DOWELL
CLARENCE M DOWELL
EDWARD G DOWELL
GUY DOWELL
DON D DOWLER JR
JAMES R DOWLING
LACY DOWLING
CHARLES E DOWNEY
JAMES T DOWNS
WALTER J DOYLE
GLENN D DOZIER
MICHAEL J DRAHOS
CHARLES E DRAKE
DARREL E DRAKE
LEROY M DRAPER
ROBERT J DRAUGELIS
ANDREW F DRESKE
ALBERT S DRESS
HOWARD L DREYER
WILLIAM B DRIESBAUGH
JAMES DRIGGERS JR
CHARLES D DRISCOLL
JAMES DRIVER
CHANCEY E DRONEY
JOHN J DROZDOWICZ
HENLEY D DRUMMOND
KENNETH E DRYDEN
BERNARDINO O DUARTE
DONACIANO DUARTE
MIGUEL T DUARTE
RODOLFO V DUARTE
ADELARD D DUBE
ROBERT H DU CHEMIN
CHOY J DUCK
DAVID H DUDLEY
NORMAN P DUFRESNE
DAVID J DUGGAN
FRED DUGGER
LINDY M DUGGER
JOHN DUKARM
EARL C DUKE
ROY E DUKE
FRANK DUKES

ROBERT L DUKES JR
DONALD J DULAC
HAROLD B DULYEA
GILBERT D DUMAIS
RALPH W DUNBAR
CHARLES J DUNCAN
CHARLES W DUNCAN
RAYMOND E DUNCAN
JAMES W DUNHAM
GEORGE W DUNLAP
JOHNNY E DUNLAP
JAMES W DUNN
LARRY M DUNN
SAMUEL V DUNN
KENNETH L DUNNAWAY
ALVA L DUNSWORTH
ARTHUR W DUNTON JR
RAYMOND J DUPUIS
GLEN M DUPUY
LEO J DUQUETTE
STANLEY G DURACHTA
HAROLD D DURAN
HORACE DURAN
JOSHUA R DURAN
JOSEPH R DURANT
LEON DUREIKO
DONALD C DURFEE
ALFONZO A DURNELL
JOSEPH A DUROVEC
RONALD D DUSEK
MIKE W DUTCHAK
FAY J DUTSON
BILLIE J DUTTON
CRAIG S DWINNELL
KARL L DYE
ROBERT L DYE
HORACE G DYER
THOMAS G DYER
MICHAEL DYONDYA
MICHAEL L DZIELSKI
EDWARD M DZIURA
ANDREW E EADS
LLOYD M EADS JR
ROBERT J EARL JR
GEORGE R EARLY
LAURENCE P EARLY
RUTHERFORD EARLY
JOSEPH F EARTBAWEY
WENDELL EASLEY
ROSCOE W EASTERLING
ROBERT EASTLACK
DONALD V EASTMAN
ARTHUR T EASTWOOD
GLENNON W EATON
WILLIAM N EATON
JOSEPH D EBARB
LEWIS W EBERNIKLE JR
WAYNE E EBRIGHT
TOMMIE L ECHOLS
CHARLES K ECKARD
HERRON M ECKELS JR
ALBERT ECKERDT
JOHN F EDDY
CHARLES EDEN
FRANCIS M EDGEMON JR
JAMES L EDMONDS
HENRY F EDMONSON
LEROY EDWARD
CLARENCE EDWARDS
CLEVELAND EDWARDS
ELIJAH EDWARDS
ELZIA M EDWARDS
HAROLD R EDWARDS
HERBERT R EDWARDS
KENNETH J EDWARDS
ODIS W EDWARDS
WILLARD H EDWARDS
WILLIAM H EDWARDS
WILLIAM T EDWARDS
WILLIE J EDWARDS
WILLIS L EDWARDS
GERALD H EFFA
KENNETH A EFFENBECK
ROBERT C EGELKRAUT
HERBERT P EGGERS
IRWIN L EGGERT
LOWELL J EGGERT
ROBERT D EGLEY
BEN J EHLE
RUDOLPH EHLERS JR

HAROLD H EIDEMILLER
JAMES W EILERS
JOHN F EILERS
KENNETH R EISENHARDT
IVAN O ELAM
DAVID N ELANDER
DONALD E ELDRIDGE
MELBURN H ELDRIDGE
RAYMOND W ELGLAND
DANIEL A ELIAS
VERNON C ELIASON
DICK J ELIOT
GEORGE D ELKINS
TELLUS H ELKINS
WILLIAM G ELLERINGTON
CHEVLYN M ELLINGSON
LOUIS T ELLIOTT
SHELBY F ELLIOTT
WAYNE F ELLIOTT
CHARLES R ELLIS
FRED M ELLIS
GRADY W ELLIS
RICHARD D ELLIS
WALTER L ELLIS
EMMETT P ELLISON
JAMES H ELLISON
CHARLES V ELLSWORTH
JOE S ELMORE
WALTER ELSE
EDWARD H ELTZROTH
GLEN G ELUS
SOLOMON EMANUEL
DELBERT D EMEHISER
DONALD L EMERY
JAMES R EMERY
PAUL EMORY JR
HOWARD W EMRICK
BENJAMIN R ENCINAS
EDWARD R ENDERS
RAYMOND A ENDERSON
HACHIRO B ENDO
JAMES W ENGDAHL
STANLEY ENGEHOLM
JAMES N ENGELHARDT
LEO F ENGELHART
DAVID E ENGLAND JR
EMERY J ENGLAND
KENNETH R ENGLEMAN
ROBERT B ENGLISH
TED ENGLISH
PAUL A ENO
HENRY P ENOKA
GEORGE W ENOS
JOSEPH E ENRICO
MARVIN C ENRIGHT
WILLIAM ENRIQUEZ
MUN-SEON EO
JU-TAEK EOM
YONG-HAK EOM
GLEN E EPPERSON
MARTIN EPPINGER
RUSSELL C EPPINGER
LOUIS W EPSTEIN
NOEL EPSTEIN
EDWIN O ERICKSON JR
EUGENE L ERICKSON
HAROLD L ERICKSON
WALTER H ERICKSON
RAYMOND C ERICSON
DANIEL G ERSTE
CHARLES D ERTLE
WILLIAM C ESCALANTE
TEOFILO ESCALERA
LYLE E ESCHENBRENNER
GEORGE J ESCOBAR
PABLO A ESCOBAR JR
MARTIN S ESKIN
BENNY L ESPARZA
ROBERT G ESPEY
JOSE E ESPINOZA
RICHARD D ESPINOZA
VICTOR ESPOSITO
CRUZ G ESQUIBEL
JESUS ESQUIBEL
CARL K ESTELL
EUGENE ESTEP
WAYNE ESTEP
RAYMOND E ESTES
RICHARD L ESTES
THOMAS C ESTES

WILLIAM T ESTES
ANGEL J ESTEVES-RIVERA
MILTON L ESTILL
ALFONSO A ESTRADA
CECIL ESTRADA
CLIFFORD ETHERIDGE
HERBERT G ETTEL
RANDOLPH EUBANKS
JOHN V EUDY JR
RAYMOND R EUFIMIA
JAMES A EUMAN
HUI-SUN EUN
GEORGE E EUSTIS
CHARLES O EVANS
CORBIT EVANS
CURTIS D EVANS
DONALD E EVANS
DONALD L EVANS
EDWIN L EVANS
HERBERT W EVANS
J C EVANS
JAMES L EVANS
JOSEPH W EVANS
JUNIOR C EVANS
OWEN M EVANS
ROY B EVANS
THOMAS L EVANS
VERNON L EVANS
WALLIS J EVANS
WILLIAM E EVANS
WILLIAM L EVANS
CHARLES W EVERATT
USREY H EVERHART
WALTER F EVERSON
ALBERT T EVONSKA
JACK F EWART
HARRY W EWING
JOHN D EWING
GORDON L EYER
DANIEL J EYLER
ERNEST FABBI
ALFRED J FABER
WILLARD F FADDIS
WILLIE J FAGAIN
FREDERICK R FAGAN JR
CHARLES W FAIDLEY
JAMES E FAIN
WILLIE FAIR
RICHARD M FAIRBANKS
JESSE H FAIRLESS
CLARENCE E FAIRROW
ROBERT F FALCO
DONALD P FALDET
MICHAEL J FALESHOCK
JOHN E FALIN
HENRY J FALK
HARRY J FALKENBURG
ALEXANDER C FALKOWSKI
FORTUNATO C FALLANCA
DANIEL FALLIND JR
RICHARD L FALLON
GEORGE N FALVEY
LEO F FALVEY
CHARLES L FALWELL
MAXIE FANCHER
WILLIAM J FANTOZZI
JOSEPH G FARIA JR
HAROLD FARIAS
LINO FARIAS
MARION D FARIES
NICOLO D FARINA
PAUL L FARINACCI
ROBERT W FARIS
ISAAC FARISS
EARL J FARLEY
HOMER C FARLEY
RONALD J FARLEY
HARVEY L FARMER
MELVIN E FARMER
GEORGE J FARRELL JR
JAMES F FARRELL
WILLIAM T FARRELL
JOHN A FARREN III
ERNEST FARROW
RAYMOND A FASHONE
FRANK R FAULHABER
LYNN R FAULKNER

30 ARMY

PRINCE E FAULKNER
ROBERT A FAULKNER
ALBERT H FAUST
HAROLD O FAY
DOMINICK J FAZIO
MILTON FEDCHISIN
WALTER C FEDER
STEPHEN FEDERINIEC
MICHAEL FEDIKOVICH JR
DENVER FEE
JOSEPH L FEENEY JR
PATRICK J FEENEY
EDMOND G FEENY
MYRON H FEINSTEIN
RAUL R FELICIAN
CARLOS D FELICIANO
JOSE A FELICIANO
JULIO FELICIANO-NIEVES
BIENVENIDO FELICIANO-OTERO
MIGUEL A FELIX V
PABLO FELIX-RODRIGUEZ
STERLING F FELIZ
EARL W FELKER
MARSHALL G FELLOWS
HARLON C FELTNER
THOMAS E FELTON
RAYMOND R FELTS
RICHARD F FENNESSEY
ROBERT G FENSTERMAKER
JOHN R FENTON
ANDREW C FERGUSON JR
DAVID L FERGUSON
JOSEPH R FERGUSON
VINCENT A FERGUSON
JOSE A FERIA-VILANOVA
ANTHONY K FERNANDES
JOE D FERNANDEZ
AUGUST R FERRACANE
VINCENZO FERRANTE-ALERS
ALBERT A FERRARIS
ALFRED G FERRARO
JAMES L FERRELL
JOHN W FERRELL
GEORGE FERRI
VERNON G FERRIS
NICHOLAS FERZETTI JR
RAYMOND A FESSLER
SALVATORE FICHERA
JOSEPH F FIELD
PAUL E FIELD
BERT L FIELDS
CURTIS L FIELDS
GERALD J FIELDS
RODGER E FIELDS
LUIS A FIGUEROA
LUIS FIGUEROA-BARBOSA
FRANCISCO FIGUEROA-MUNIZ
LUIS R FIGUEROA-OTERO
JOSE FIGUEROA-RODRIGUEZ
JOHN A FILENER
WALTER F FILKINS
CLEMOND W FILLER
DONALD L FILLER
PHILLIP J FILLION
FRANK O FINCH
ROY L FINCHER
HARRY J FINDLEY
ROBERT E FINK
WILLIAM P FINLAN
LEONARD E FINLAY
GREEN FINLEY JR
JERRY L FINLEY
CLIFFORD C FINN JR
JOHN B FINN
PAUL E FINN
THOMAS J FINNEGAN JR
LAWRENCE FINNERAN
GLEN D FINNEY
COY F FIRESTONE
LEWIS M FIREY JR
GEORGE J FISCHER
JAMES F FISCHER
JUNE H FISCUS
ALVA R FISHER
DONALD E FISHER
JAMES E FISHER

JEWELL R FISHER
JOE H FISHER
KENNETH C FISHER
LEVIN F FISHER
NORMAN R FISHER
ROBERT W FISHER JR
THOMAS F FISHER
DONALD D FISLAR
FRANCIS L FITCH
MAJOR W FITZGERALD
HARRY B FITZGIBBONS
THOMAS J FITZGIBBONS
HOWARD FITZHUGH
MICHAEL FITZPATRICK
CARL J FITZWATER
BILLY J FIXICO
FRANCIS L FLAGG
EDMUND R FLAHERTY
THOMAS L FLAHERTY
PETER F FLAIME
RAYMOND R FLAIR
ROY FLAMING
JIMMY G FLANAGAN
SAMUEL H FLANARY
DOUGLAS L FLANNERY
RICHARD FLEISCHMANN
CHARLES J FLEMING
JOHN FLEMING
RONALD R FLEMING
THOMAS H FLEMING
WILLIAM J FLEMMING
OSCAR FLENORY
MARSHALL E FLETCHER
JESSE L FLICKINGER
JAMES H FLING JR
MERTON V FLOE
JOHN C FLORA
EDWARD S FLORCZYK
JOHN A FLOREK
ERNESTO M FLORES
MANUEL FLORES
WILL F FLORES
JULIO FLORES-BAEZ
EDWARD G FLORESKUL
GERMAN FLORES-MALDONADO
RAYMOND E FLORTARD
WAYNE K FLOTO
KENNETH R FLOWERS
OBERT B FLOWERS
ODIS B FLOWERS
CECIL R FLOYD
JACK FLOYD
JAMES E FLOYD
JERRY FLUG
ROBERT N FLUNO
NORMAN E FLYNN
PHILIP D FLYNN
ROY S FLYNN JR
ROBERT D FOGLE
LLOYD O FOGT
JAMES J FOLEY
MICHAEL E FOLEY
ROBERT J FOLEY
CHARLES C FOLLESE
ERWIN J FOLMAR
JAMES H FOMOND
WALTER A FONDER
OLIVER FONG
MIGUEL A FONSECA
MANUEL E FONSECA-ACEVEDO
BENJAMIN FONTAINE
JOSEPH C FONTENOT
SAMUEL FONVILLE
FRANK E FOOTE JR
DEWEY A FORBES
JOHN J FORBES JR
ALVIS L FORD
CHARLES W FORD
ERNEST C FORD
EUGENE W FORD
FRANKIE J FORD
HENRY L FORD
HERSHEL FORD
PAUL R FORD
ROBERT M FORD
LEROY S FORDAHL
NORMAN H FORDER
JACK C FOREMAN

WILLIAM J FOREMAN
NORMAN D FORGET
JOHN C FORKEL
KENNETH B FORRESTER
THOMAS L FORSHAY
ROBERT W FORSYTHE
DONALD FORTNER
GILBERT H FORTNER
KENNETH C FOSS
BENNY G FOSTER
CEARVEST FOSTER
CHARLES E FOSTER
CLYDE N FOSTER
HARRY S FOSTER
LEWIS C FOSTER
ROBERT J FOSTER
SPURGE FOSTER
THOMAS E FOSTER JR
BURL FOSTON
CHRIS FOTINOS
BERNARD E FOUCHEY
EDWARD J FOUNTAIN
CLARENCE D FOUST JR
NOEL L FOUTS
DORSEY R FOWLER
HARRY T FOWLER
COLBY G FOX
JAMES L FOX
JARED W FOX
JOHN F FOX
RICHARD FOX
RICHARD A FOX
ROBERT F FOX
ROBERT L FOX
WILLIAM C FOX
SAM FOY
JOSEPH P FRAGOSA
MELVIN P FRAHM
ROBERT J FRALICH
EDDIE L FRANCIS
KAYE D FRANCIS
RICHARD E FRANCIS
WILLIAM R FRANCIS
GEORGE FRANCISCHELLI
JULIO E FRANCO
BENOIT R FRANCOEUR
JOSEPH F FRANCZAK
LARRY A FRANK
WILLIAM A FRANK
CARL T FRANKE JR
FRANCIS FRANKEY
ALLEN FRANKLIN
BENJAMIN A FRANKLIN
HAROLD FRANKLIN
JAMES B FRANKLIN
JAMES L FRANKLIN
JOHN D FRANKLIN JR
WINBURN B FRANKLIN
ALFONSO FRANKS
HENRY A FRANKS
GEORGE A FRANTZ
ADAM D FRASURE
C L FRAZE
CARLTON FRAZIER
DONNIE L FRAZIER
JAMES C FRAZIER
JOHN W FRAZIER
REGINALD E FRAZIER
ROBERT FRAZIER
DONALD L FREDENBURG
RALPH L FREDRICKSON
MARVIN E FREED
CHARLES F FREEMAN
DARIEL J FREEMAN
HAROLD W FREEMAN
JAMES W FREEMAN
JAMES W FREEMAN
NIEL M FREEMAN
ROBERT A FREEMAN
ARTHUR R FRENCH
ELVIN E FRENCH
JENNINGS FRENCH
CECIL T FRETWELL
HARVEY L FREY
HUGH G FREY
STANLEY W FREY
BILLIE J FRICKER
ROBERT E FRIDAY
DONALD A FRIEDLY
FREDERICK A FRIEDMAN

WILLIAM B FRIEND JR
RALPH G FRINGELI
HERMAN R FRISKE
CHARLES D FRISZ
CLARENCE H FRITSCHE
JOSEPH E FRITZ
ERNEST A FROEB
JERROLD FRONZOWIAK
CARL D FROST
DONALD W FROST
JOHN S FROST
LEWIS B FROST
PAUL A FROST
JAMES H FRYE
SAMUEL O FRYE
VERNON F FRYE
THOMAS J FRYER JR
MARVIN C FRYSINGER
CLARENCE FUDGE JR
DALE L FUGATE
JOSEPH J FUGATE
LEONARD FUGATE
JAMES B FUGETT
DONALD A FUHRMAN
FREDERICK E FUHRMAN
JUNICHI FUJIMOTO
TAKESHI FUJITA
RALPH T FUKUMOTO
YOSHIMI FUKUMOTO
ORLAN J FULKS
FRANCIS J FULLAM
HENRY A FULLER
ROBERT L FULLER
WILLIAM E FULLER
WILLIE C FULLER
WIRT C FULLER JR
DONALD V FULLERTON
HAROLD O FULLERTON
MARVIN C FULTON
WAYNE L FUNKHOUSER
ERNEST V FUQUA JR
LEONARD L FURBEE
FRANCIS N FUREY
WALTER F FURMAN
ROBERT E FURR
LESTER J FURSETH
PALMER G FUSON
NORMAN FUSSELL
HAROLD E FYE
JOHN W GABLE
JAMES S GABLEHOUSE
CHARLES R GABRIEL
JAMES M GABY
RUDOLPH V GACOBELLI
WILLIAM R GAEUMAN
MARTIN H GAGE
GORDON W GAGER
SYDNEY A GAGER
ANTONIO T J GAGNON
JESSE E GAGNON
MELVIN A GAINES
VAN E GAINES
GARY P GAINEY
JIMMIE J GAITAN
WILLIE GAITHER JR
ALFREDO GAJETON
SUN-HAENG GAL
THOMAS P GALBERTH JR
PRESILIANO GALBON
ORVILLE J GALE
STEWART J GALE
GEORGE M GALES
MICHAEL GALETIE
RAFAEL GALINDO-CAPIEL
DONALD W GALLAGHER
PATRICK J GALLAGHER
HERMAN D GALLANT
MARCEL A GALLANT
CHARLES P GALLARDO
GILBERT G GALLEGO
POLITO G GALLEGOS
HAROLD J GALLOWAY
IRVEN GALLOWAY
JOSE M GALNARES JR
MANUEL G GALVAN
OSVALDO R GALVAN
PETER GALVIN
AMES J GAMACHE
LEO A GAMACHE

RAYMOND A GAMBA
JAMES D GAMBILL
CALVIN D GAMBLE
DAVID T GAMBLE
HENCE GAMBLE
LAWRENCE C GAMBLE
HARRY P H GAMBREL
JAMES R GAMWELLS
ALBERT GANCHUK
BONG-HWAN GANG
BYEONG-RYEOL GANG
CHANG-GIL GANG
CHAN-SUN GANG
CHUN-BAEK GANG
DAE-BAEK GANG
DAE-GEOL GANG
DAE-U GANG
DAE-YONG GANG
DEOK-JIN GANG
GEUM-SEOK GANG
HAE-JIN GANG
HAK-SU GANG
HO-JUNG GANG
HO-MYEONG GANG
HUI-JUNG GANG
HWAN-SIK GANG
HYO-BONG GANG
IN-JUN GANG
JAE-EUN GANG
JAE-GYU GANG
JEOM-JU GANG
JIN-HO GANG
JU-CHEOL GANG
MIN-GU GANG
MUN-DOL GANG
NAM-HYEONG GANG
SANG-BOK GANG
SEOK-JO GANG
SEONG-IL GANG
SEONG-JIN GANG
SIN-BONG GANG
TAE-U GANG
YONG-DOL GANG
YONG-UN GANG
EDWARD J GANIS
CLAY W GANN
ROBERT R GANN
WALTER J GANT
BILLIE S GANTT
LAWRENCE J GAPINSKI
RICHARD C GARABEDIAN
ABEL GARCIA
BARTOLOME GARCIA
CARLOS GARCIA
DOMINGO GARCIA
EDWARD L GARCIA
ERNESTO GARCIA JR
FRED N GARCIA
JACK GARCIA
JOSE A P GARCIA
JOSE M GARCIA JR
PERFECTO GARCIA
PORFIRIO H GARCIA
RAUL G GARCIA
SERAFIN R GARCIA
STEVEN M GARCIA
TONY GARCIA
ISMAEL GARCIA-CLARA
JOSE M GARCIA-CRUZ
CANDIDO GARCIA-ROSADO
GEORGE B GARDEN JR
MONTON L GARDER
DONALD F GARDINER
MURVEE D GARDINER
BEVERLY A GARDNER
CHARLES T GARDNER
FREDERICK G GARDNER
JAMES D GARDNER
JAMES D GARDNER
LAWRENCE B GARDNER
JOSEPH J GARGIULO
FELIX GARLAND
RUDOLPH C GARLAND
PAUL P GARMAN
WILTON E GARMON
JAMES W GARNER
PATRICK J GARNER
THEO L GARNER JR

31 ARMY

GREGORIO GARNICA
BEN GARRETT
HERBERT J GARRETT
JAMES P GARRETT
RALPH E GARRETT
WILLIAM F GARRETT
GERALD D GARRIS
MURREL GARVIN
THEODORE E GARVIN
GEORGE GARVIS
GEORGE E GARY
LOUIS A GARY
ARMANDO M GARZA
MIKE M GARZA
NICOLAS C GARZA
RICARDO GARZA
BILLIE L GASKINS
CLARENCE L GASKINS
LEROY P GASPARD
CHARLES GASS
JAMES E GATCHEL
DOYT K GATES
HAVERT L GATES
HUSTON E GATES
EDWARD E GATH
EUGENE GATHERS
DALE GATTEN JR
WILLIAM R GAUL
BROOKHART E GAVE
EUGENE A GAWLIK
ULYSSES GAYLE JR
WILLIAM A GAYLORD
JOSEPH G P GAZAILLE JR
JAMES H GEARHART
WILLIAM R GEARHART
BILLY L GEARY
STERLING GEARY JR
EDGAR N GEATER
ERVIN A GEBHARDT
ROBERT E GEDNEY
CLARENCE W GEE
JAMES D GEESLIN
ROBERT F GEIGER
JACK H GEIS
RONALD J GEIS
ROBERT L GEISE
CHRISTOPHER R GEISZLER
ARMAND J GENDREAU
FRANK J GENDUSA
HAROLD A GENGLER
THOMAS J GENIS
CHARLES C GENTRY
TROY L GENTRY
HAROLD W GEOIT
BURTON J GEORGE
CHARLES GEORGE
CHRISS GEORGE JR
EDWARD GEORGE
LARSON GEORGE
RALPH F A GEORGE
WILBUR G GEORGE
HAROLD O GEORGESON
WILLIAM R GERAGHTY
DONALD C GERBER
EDWARD J GERBER
ROSARIO GERENA
JOHN L GERIG JR
DONALD L GERRITS
DANIEL W GERRITY
ROBERT M GERRON
JOHN P GERSHEWSKI JR
RICHARD F GERSTNER
ROBERT GERSTNER
ALBERT R GERTH
ROBERT J GERVAIS
SEOK-MU GEUM
GEORGE R GFELLER
GEORGE GHERGHESCU JR
GEORGE GIA
DOMINIC GIANCHETTA JR
FRED J GIANGRASSO
CARL R GIBBONS
JAMES GIBBONS
RICHARD P GIBBONS
BILLY H GIBBS
JOE P GIBBS
WALTER H GIBBS
GEORGE W GIBEAUT JR
GEORGE G G GIBLIN
CHARLES E GIBSON

CLIFTON E GIBSON
DALLAS W GIBSON
ELBRIDGE C GIBSON
GEORGE O GIBSON
GUY T GIBSON
HAYWARD L GIBSON
HENRY E GIBSON
JOHN R GIBSON
LEWIS C GIBSON
LUTHER E GIBSON
ROYCE C GIBSON
WILLIAM A GIBSON
KIMBOUGH GIDDENS
HERBERT L GIDEON
RICHARD F GIESE
TROY H GIFFORD
DAE-WAN GIL
U-JAE GIL
CLARENCE J GILBERT
DANIEL N GILBERT
DAVID O GILBERT
FOSTER GILBERT JR
MARVIN L GILBERT
ROBERT G GILBERT
RUSSELL J GILBERT
GEORGE E GILCHRIST
RICHARD C GILKEY
ROBERT L GILKISON
GERALD S GILL
HOWARD L GILL
IRVING L GILL
SAMUEL F GILL JR
PAUL J GILLASPY
RAY GILLETT
ROBERT L GILLETTE
BILLY J GILLEY
EDWARD L GILLEY
CLAUDE GILLIAM
CHARLES L GILLILAND
WILLIAM L GILLILAND
RICHARD A GILLIS
DONALD L GILMORE
LAWRENCE J GILMORE
HIRAM E GILROY
CLIFFORD T GILSTAD
MARVIN C GILVIN
EDMUND G GINCLEY
WILBUR G GINCLEY
ALVER H GINN
WILLIAM V GIOVANNIELLO
DALLAS L GIPSON
GLENN H GIPSON
OSCAR P GIRANY
VERNON E GIRDLEY JR
EDWIN GIRON
HARRY C GITTELSON
CHARLES J GITZLAFF
VINCENZO GIUFFRIDA
THOMAS F GIVENS
ELMER T GLADDEN
JAMES W GLADDEN
BENJAMIN F GLADNEY
LEROY GLADNEY
LOUIS A GLADNEY
CHARLES R GLADSTONE
HAROLD B GLANCY
FRANK E GLASGOW
RALPH N GLASGOW
MORRIS GLASPER
ARTHUR W GLASS
CECIL R GLASS
HERMAN GLASS
JOHN R GLASS
RAYMOND GLASS
MARTIN J GLASSER
CLAUDE GLAZE
ROBERT L GLAZE
BILLY F GLESSNER
WILLIAM A GLICK
VERNON R GLIDDEN
MORGAN G GLINKERMAN
CARNESE GLOVER
DOYLE E GLOVER
JOSEPH R GLOVER
ROBERT T GLOVER
ALPHONSE A GLOWACZEWSKI
LEROY M GLUCKMAN
JOHN G GNALL

BONG-CHEOL GO
JEONG-HAK GO
JEONG-IK GO
JEONG-JU GO
JIN-SEOK GO
JONG-CHEOL GO
PIL-AM GO
SEONG-GEUN GO
EUAL GOAD
HOMER J GOAD
WILLIAM E GOAN
ARVLE G GOBER
BERNARD J GOBLE
JACK M GODDARD
EARL J GODFREY
WILFORD G GODFREY
ELI GODWIN
DUANE E GOEBEL
THEODORE J GOERGE
RUEBEN J GOERL
CHARLES C GOETSCHIUS
HARRY GOETTING
WILLIE K GOFF
JOSEPH N GOGGLEYE
STANLEY A GOGOJ
LAVERN P GOHL
WILLIAM R GOINS
ALFRED GOLD
LAWRENCE M GOLD
MATHEW J GOLDA JR
LEONARD S GOLDBERG
BILLY R GOLDEN
DONALD E GOLDEN
HERBERT GOLDEN
ROBERT L GOLDEN
BERNARD GOLDING
ELMER E GOLDMAN
JOHNNY W GOLDMAN
THOMAS O GOLDSBERRY
HAROLD B GOLDSMITH
RAYMOND J GOLDSMITH
JACK L GOLDSTON
JAMES E GOLDSWORTHY
BENJAMIN J GOLSTON
ANTONE GOMES
JOHN H GOMES JR
ROBERT GOMES
GUSTAVO K GOMEZ
JOSEPH GOMEZ
LUIS GOMEZ
PETE GOMEZ JR
RICHARD Z GOMEZ
VINCENTE G GOMEZ
WILLIAM C GOMEZ
MAN-YEONG GONG
SEOK-GEUN GONG
HARRY J GONIA
HAROLD L GONSALVES
RICHARD GONSIOROWSKI
ALFONSO GONZALES
CONRAD GONZALES
GILBERTO GONZALES
JOE GONZALES
JOE F GONZALES
SERVANDO GONZALES
GEORGE L GONZALEZ
JUAN E GONZALEZ
LUIS GONZALEZ
ROBERTO G GONZALEZ
SANTOS GONZALEZ
VICTOR GONZALEZ
MANUEL GONZALEZ-BERNARD
CARMELO GONZALEZ-CORDERO
ISRAEL GONZALEZ-NAZARIO
JUAN E GONZALEZ-ORTIZ
JUSTO GONZALEZ-ORTIZ
EUSEBIO GONZALEZ-OSORIO
VICTOR R GONZALEZ-PEREZ
WILLIAM GONZALEZ-PIERLUISSI
PORFIRIO GONZALEZ-RENTA
ANGEL GONZALEZ-ROSARIO

ISRAEL GONZALEZ-SAEZ
WILLIAM GONZALEZ-SOTO
DINSMORE T GOOCH JR
JOHN A GOOCH
JOHN E GOODALL
ROBERT GOODALL
MOWREY GOODBREAD
ALLEN R GOODE
JOHN GOODE
LUTHER O GOODING JR
DONALD R GOODMAN
GROVER D GOODMAN
WENDELL R GOODMAN
DONALD J GOODRIDGE
CARL B GOODSELL
FRANK GOODWIN JR
MARTIN H GOODWIN
WILLIAM D GOODWIN
WILLIAM P GOODYEAR
DELBERT B GORBY
JAMES E GORDLEY
CHARLES J GORDON
ERNEST J GORDON
GEORGE L GORDON
RICHARD J GORDON
WILLIAM L GORDON
HAROLD L GORMAN
NORBERT J GORMAN
WESLEY H GORTON
RAY V GOSE
ALBERT A GOSNELL
EUGENE E GOSNEY
DWIGHT M GOSS
PATRICK J GOSS
WILLIAM H GOSS JR
EDWARD GOSSAR
FRANK J GOSSMANN
AUBREY P GOSVENER
MARCELO GOTAY-MALDONADO
MITSURO GOTO
SATOSHI GOTO
NELSON S GOULD
WILLIAM T GOULD
WILFRED J L GOULET
MARION E GOWER
GEORGE E GOWIN
FREDERICK GRACZYK
WILLIAM J GRADDY
ROBERT E GRAF
ROBERT L GRAFF
PHILIP G GRAFFEO
RILEY J GRAGG
BILLY J GRAHAM
GLENN W GRAHAM
ISADORE R GRAHAM JR
JAMES J GRAHAM
JARRELL D GRAHAM
JOHN H GRAHAM
JOSEPH GRAHAM JR
LEONARD F GRAHAM
ORVILLE E GRAHAM
ROBERT L GRAHAM
WILEY GRAHAM JR
WILLIAM M GRAHAM
PEDRO R GRAJALES-NIEVES
JAMES W GRAM
RONALD R GRAMS
CARL J GRANBERRY
CALVIN C GRANT
CHARLES GRANT
JOHNNY W GRANT
PAUL GRANT
WILBUR L GRASS
RONALD J GRASSOLD
JOSEPH W GRAUSE JR
CHARLES L GRAVEL
JOSEPH C M GRAVEL
MARION GRAVES
NELSON L GRAVES
PAUL E GRAVES
RILEY W GRAVES
ALBERT N GRAY
CEIRCELL GRAY
EMORY B GRAY
ERNEST GRAY
HOWARD G GRAY
IRA A GRAY
LEO H GRAY

ROBERT H GRAY
ROBERT L GRAY
ROY R GRAY JR
WILLIAM C GRAY
CLYDE B GRAYSON
DAVID J GRAYSON
ROSARIO GRECO
ALBERT B GREEN
ALLEN R GREEN
ARTHUR W GREEN
DAVID E GREEN
EDGAR L GREEN
EDWIN L GREEN
ELMER D GREEN
FRED W GREEN
GILBERT A GREEN
JIM GREEN
JOHNNIE GREEN
RICHARD B GREEN
ROBERT E GREEN
ROBERT L GREEN
WALTER W GREEN
PAUL GREENBERG
A C GREENE
CLAUD GREENE JR
EARL GREENE
EDWARD H GREENE
JOSEPH P GREENE
WILLIAM E GREENE
LELAND L GREENHAGEN
JAMES E GREENLEAF
ROBERT L GREENUP
RUDOLPH V GREENWAY
MELVIN T GREENWOOD
ANDREW L GREER
JOHN A GREER
ROBY H GREER
EARL L GREGORY
OTIS C GREGORY
RAYMOND GREGORY
EUGENE W GRENDELL
DONALD T GRENIER
JAMES A GRESHAM
FRANK S GRESS
ARNOLD G GRESSER
ROBERT E GREY
HENRY GRICE
MILTON R GRIEFF
JUAN A GRIEGO
ROBERT R GRIESE
ALFRED A GRIESS
LEE L GRIFE
FRANCIS J GRIFFIN JR
FRANK M GRIFFIN
GLEN W GRIFFIN
LOY GRIFFIN
SILAS E GRIFFIN
WALTER C GRIFFIN JR
WILLIAM J GRIFFIN
ROBERT S GRIFFITH
SAMUEL C GRIFFITH
WALTER L GRIFFITH
BENJAMIN W GRIGGS JR
EUGENE C GRIGSBY
FINLEY GRILLS
RAYMOND GRIMES
WILLIAM D GRIMM
OLIVER E GRIMMETT
WILLIAM O GRIMMIG
CHARLES E GRIMPE
LAWRENCE D GRINE
THEODORE GROENEVELD
CLARENCE R GROGAN
GEORGE R GROLL
BILLY S GROOMS
ROLLIE D GROOMS
ENO J GROS JR
WILLIAM E GROSE
GEORGE P GROSS
JAMES T GROSS
JOHN E GROSS
KENNETH B GROSS
MYRON E GROSS
WALTER F GROSS
RICHARD F GROTH
BERNARD GROTKOWSKI
MELVIN R GROUNDS

32 ARMY

GEORGE R GROVE
JAMES A GROVE JR
JOHN S GROVER
WILLIAM H GROVER
ROBERT GROVES JR
JOHN F GROVIER
JOHN E GROW
KENNETH H GROW
STANLEY A GRUDZINSKI
ANGEL GRUTTADAURIA
BON-WAN GU
DEOK-HWAN GU
JA-HAN GU
JONG-GAP GU
MAN-BON GU
SEON-DO GU
SEONG-DEOK GU
SEONG-RYEONG GU
YEONG-BOK GU
JESUS GUAJARDO
JOE R GUAJARDO
DANIEL P GUALTIERE
ANASTACIO GUARDIAN
GEORGE H GUENTHER
JOSE A GUERRA
HECTOR GUERRERO
MOSES G GUERRERO
GEORGE E GUEST
FRED E GUFFEY
HENRY GUGLICIELLO
SERGIO P GUIANG
THOMAS R GUIHEEN
RICARDO GUILLET-
LORENZO
CHARLES C GUINN
ANTHONY GUINTA
STANLEY J GUNDLACH
WILLARD H GUPTON
EDWIN M GURECKY
ALEJANDRO GURULE JR
GILBERT M GUSHIKEN
HAROLD W GUSTAFSON
HENRY L GUSTAFSON
YOSHINOBU GUSUKUMA
JOSE R GUTIERREZ
JESSE V GUYER
JOHN M GUYER JR
SALBADOR GUZMAN
BONG-TAE GWAK
BYEONG-HWAN GWAK
JONG-HO GWAK
JUN-YEONG GWAK
SANG-YEONG GWAK
FRANCIS J GWALTNEY
JULIUS J GWAZDACZ
CHA-YONG GWON
GAP-HO GWON
GI-SANG GWON
GYEONG-SIK GWON
HAK-YONG GWON
IK-HO GWON
IL-GON GWON
JAE-BOK GWON
JAE-SIK GWON
JUNG-HAN GWON
JU-SEONG GWON
MYEONG-GAP GWON
SANG-JUN GWON
SEOK-SU GWON
SI-DU GWON
TAE-SEONG GWON
TAE-SUL GWON
YEONG-HWAN GWON
YEONG-JIN GWON
YEONG-RAE GWON
YONG-SEONG GWON
DERRY GYDEN JR
CHANG-SUL HA
DAE-HO HA
DO-JIN HA
HAE-YONG HA
HUN-MO HA
PAN-GU HA
SAM-JU HA
WALTER C HAAG
WILLIAM C HABBARD
ROBERT E HABERERN
WALTER C HACKENBERG
JAMES E HACKENBURG
THOMAS J HACKETT

ADRIAN A HACKNEY
JOHN T HADDING JR
ERNEST H HADDOCK
MILTON D HADGES
W B HADLEY
CHARLES D HADNOT
RUDY H HAFERKAMP
NEAL W HAFERMAN
CLAUDIUS F HAGAN
JOHN HAGAR
CHARLES H HAGEMIER
DAVID R HAGEN
RONALD W HAGEN
RAYMOND W
HAGERTY JR
WAYNE G HAGY
EDWIN E HAHN
HARRY E HAHN
RAYMOND A HAILI
OVA L HAIRE
WILBUR C HAIRSTON
CHARLES G HAITZ
DOUGLAS I HALCOMB
THOMAS R HALDEMAN
ERNEST HALE
JAMES T HALE
JAY L HALE
SHIRLEY D HALE
LOUIS R HALEY JR
ANDREW HALL
CARLTON E HALL
CHARLES H HALL JR
CLINTON J HALL
DARRELL G HALL
GALE HALL
GENE T HALL
GEORGE W HALL
HARRISON E HALL
HEDREY D HALL
JULIUS E HALL
LEROY S HALL
MARVIN HALL
ROBERT K HALL
RONALD L HALL
RUSSELL L HALL
SAMUEL A HALL
SAMUEL S HALL III
THEODORE K HALL
TOMMIE L HALL
WALLACE L HALL
WILLIAM HALL JR
WILLIE HALL
FREDERICK W HALLETT
CLARENCE T HALLIDAY JR
RONALD E HALLIMAN
ROBERT D HALLMARK
ROBERT E HALLOWELL
LEONARD D HALLUM
KENNETH L HALM
KENNETH N HALSOR
BOBBY J HALSTEAD
VERLYN S HALVERSON
LEROY K HALVORSON
MITSUO HAMADA
PATRICK K HAMADA JR
KENICHI HAMAGUCHI
RODNEY N HAMAGUCHI
FRANCIS D HAMBLIN JR
SHELLY D HAMBRICK
CHARLES E HAMERQUIST
CLYDE HAMILTON
EUGENE E HAMILTON
FREDDIE L HAMILTON
GLENN E HAMILTON
JOSEPH W HAMILTON
LEON D HAMILTON
PERCY D HAMILTON
RAYMOND W
HAMILTON
ROBERT HAMILTON
ROBERT E HAMILTON
WILLIAM J HAMILTON
BILLY R HAMLIN
ELMER R HAMLIN
ALBERT E HAMM
JAMES F HAMM
GERALD E HAMMER
AMBROSE B HAMMEREL
DONALD J HAMMOND
FRANK E HAMMOND

GEORGE W HAMMOND
LYMAN HAMMOND
JAMES L HAMMONDS
FRED F HAMMONTREE
CHARLIE D HAMPTON
DAVID L HAMPTON
KENDRICK HAMPTON
AUREL G HAMPU
DAE-OK HAN
GAP-CHUL HAN
GYEONG-HYEON HAN
HO-SEOK HAN
IN-JE HAN
IN-SEOK HAN
JIN-GU HAN
NAM-GYEONG HAN
NEUNG-SEOK HAN
SAM-GU HAN
SAM-YEONG HAN
SANG-GIL HAN
SANG-SUN HAN
SEOK-MYEON HAN
YEONG-JO HAN
YUN-JO HAN
YUN-SU HAN
YUN-SU HAN
ROME H HANCE
RUSSELL HANCHARYK
DANNY J HANDLEY
MAC A HANDLEY
KENNETH N HANDY
RAYMOND T HANDY
MARVIN L HANEY
IRVIN E HANK
ROBERT H HANKE
THOMAS E HANKS
ROBERT HANLEY
ERNEST M HANLIN
ROBERT D HANNA
WILLIAM T HANNAN
BILLY D HANNIG
GILBERT P HANNWEEKEA
ARTHUR HANSEN JR
BERNARD N HANSEN
DAN H HANSEN
MARTIN A HANSEN
WAYNE C HANSEN
HAROLD C HANSHAW
WILLIAM H HANSHAW
NICHOLAS J HANSINGER
HARLAN B HANSON
HARLAN T HANSON
JACK G HANSON
LUTHER D HANSON
FREDERICK J HAPGOOD
EDWARD E HARBER
RONALD E HARBOUR
NORWOOD H HARDER
HOWELL W HARDGRAVE
MICHAEL P HARDIMAN
GEORGE E HARDIN
UNCAS B HARDIN
HORACE C HARDING
RICHARD L HARDWICK
ISAC HARDY
LESTER R HARDY
ROBERT J HARDY
WILLIAM H HARE
RICHARD F HARLA
HAROLD W HARLAND
WILLIAM A HARLESS
JESSE HARLOW JR
RICHARD C HARMAN
AVERY E HARMON
DONALD R HARMON
JAMES HARMON
JOHN A HARMON
GARRIET A HARMS JR
CHARLES K HARNED
DONALD G HAROLD
MEARL L HARP
RALPH A HARP
JAMES L HARPE
HOWARD T HARPER
JOSEPH M HARPER
MERLIN L HARPER
MITCHELL HARPER JR
ROBERT R HARPER
WILBERT R HARPER
FRED W HARPSTER

JEFFERY W HARRELL
JOHN P HARRICH
JAMES A HARRINGTON
ROBERT F HARRINGTON
FORREST D HARRIOTT
ALBERT N HARRIS
ARNOLD HARRIS
AUSTIN L HARRIS
BUSTER HARRIS
CHARLES E HARRIS
DUGAN HARRIS
EDWARD P HARRIS
ELLIS HARRIS
GEORGE HARRIS
HERMAN G HARRIS
ISADORE HARRIS
JAMES HARRIS
JAMES C HARRIS
JASPER L HARRIS
LAWRENCE HARRIS JR
LENVIL D HARRIS
MANUEL HARRIS
MONTGOMERY HARRIS
RICHARD J HARRIS
ROBERT HARRIS JR
THOMAS W HARRIS
WALTER L C HARRIS
ELBERT D HARRISON
FRANCIS E HARRISON
HENRY G HARRISON
JAMES HARRISON JR
JAMES M HARRISON
LOUIS HARRISON
LOWELL G HARRISON
RALPH L HARRISON
RICHARD E HARRISON
SHIRLIE D HARRISON
EDWARD S HARRY JR
LEWIS S HARSHER
KENNETH S HART
RICHARD H HART
WILLIAM HART
ROBERT E HARTHUN
ARTHUR G HARTLEY JR
CLARENCE G HARTLEY
JAMES E HARTLEY
CHARLES W HARTMAN
DAVID R HARTMAN
GEORGE E HARTMAN
MYRON A HARTMAN
WOODROW P
HARTMAN
HARRY J HARTMANN
ROBERT E HARTSOCK
HAROLD L HARTSON
GERALD L HARTWICK
VERNON G HARTWIG
BAXTER R HARVEL JR
ARTHUR E HARVEY
ARTIE A HARVEY
CARTHEL E HARVEY
JOE W HARVEY
WILSON H HARVEY
JOE H HARVISON
CHARLES T HASLET
ISIAH HASSEL
CHARLES A HASTE
DONALD W HASTINGS
ROSS E HASTINGS
THOMAS J HASTINGS
KENNETH G HATCH
LOUIS J HATCHER
CECIL HATFIELD
ANDREW E HATHAWAY
GORDON E HATHAWAY
HAROLD W HATLEY
ROBERT C HATLEY
WILLIAM H HATLEY JR
SYDNEY HATTON
WILLIAM B HATTON JR
FRED L HATZOLD
CARL F HAUER JR
ROBERT O HAUGEN
OTHO L HAUGHN
HAAKON M HAUGLAND
ORVIS A HAUGTVEDT
RAYMOND HAUN
CHRISTIAN W HAUSER
ARNOLD HAVELKA
TATE M HAVNAER

HENRY M HAWKINS
WILLIAM M HAWKINS
VERPO L HAWKS
ROBERT S HAWN
CHARLES R HAWSEY
RICHARD Y HAYAKAWA
CHARLES B HAYDEN
BILLY A HAYES
GEORGE W HAYES
JACK B HAYES
JAMES O HAYES
JAMES P HAYES
JOHN E HAYES
RALPH H HAYES
RICHARD W HAYES
SYLVESTER R HAYES
DONALD A HAYNES
ETHYL B HAYNES
JAMES L HAYNES
RICHARD C HAYNES
HAROLD
HAYNESWORTH
ROBERT E HAYNIE
DOYLE E HAYWARD
CERL V HEAD
RICHARD G HEAD
CHARLES T HEADLEY
HOWARD F HEALD
DANIEL M HEALY
ELBERT E HEARD
SAM HEARD
OLLIE L HEARELL
GEORGE E
HEARNSBERGER
RICHARD M HEASER
ROBERT S HEATER
ROBERT E HEATH
VINCENT F HEATH
CLARENCE M HEATON
HERMAN F HEATON
JAMES L HEATON
JOHN A HEAVENER
LEONARD HEBB
SYLVIO L HEBERT
ROBERT A HECHT
ROBERT W HECKMAN
JAMES R HEDGCOTH
CLIFTON E HEDGESPETH
EDGAR S HEFFLEY
ROBERT M HEFFNER
EVERETTE R HEFNER
HERBERT HEGGAR
GEORGE D HEICHEL
HOMER A HEICHEL
ARTHUR V HEIDE
WILBERT M HEIDER
WARREN E HEIM
FREDERICK HEINLEIN
RICHARD H HEINS
DALE A HEISE
ADOLF F HEISSLER
HENRY W HEIT JR
DONALD R HEITKAMP
CLARENCE M HEITMAN
DELMER F HELD
ARTHUR W HELDERMAN
CHARLES R HELGERSON
DONALD R HELGESON
RUSSELL L HELIE
JOSEPH HELKE
GLENWOOD C HELMAN
THEODORE H HELMICH
JAMES E
HELMONDOLLAR
WALLACE W HELMS
WLADYSLAW L
HELNARSKI
CHESTER R HELSEL
JOSEPH E HELSEL
DONALD C HELT
ORVIL HELTON
FRANK R HEMBREE
JOHN J HEMENWAY
MILTON F
HEMMINGSEN
WILLIAM C HEMSHER
HAROLD R
HENDERSHAW
ALEXANDER
HENDERSON

33 ARMY

CHARLES L HENDERSON
ERNEST W HENDERSON
HOWARD HENDERSON
JAMES E HENDERSON
MARTIN HENDERSON
NORMAN R HENDERSON
RALPH HENDERSON
ROY A HENDERSON
CHARLES H HENDRICKS
JOHN T HENDRICKS
JOSEPH L HENDRICKS JR
ALBERT G HENDRICKSON
ROBERT C HENDRY
JIMMY E HENNESS
KENNETH S HENNING
DONALD N HENNRICKS
AGUSTUS HENRY
DONALD E HENRY
ERNEST A HENRY
KENNETH HENRY JR
MAURICE I HENRY
PAUL J HENRY
ROBERT L HENRY
WILBERT R HENRY
ROBERT M HENSLER
DAROLD D HENSLEY
CHARLES R HENSON
BYEONG-MUN HEO
CHEOL-SOE HEO
EOK-JO HEO
GONG-DAL HEO
HYEOK HEO
JAE-GYU HEO
JEONG-DAE HEO
JEONG-JUN HEO
NAM-PYO HEO
YEONG-GYU HEO
HERBERT G HER
PAUL G HERALD
PETER M HERARDO
JAMES D HERB
HARLEY K HERBSTER
MICHAEL HERLIHY
THEODORE J HERMAN
CHARLES R HERMES
ANTONIO P HERNANDEZ
DOMINGO HERNANDEZ
ERNESTO G HERNANDEZ
FRANCISCO A
HERNANDEZ
GEORGE HERNANDEZ
GUILLERMO HERNANDEZ
JESUS S HERNANDEZ
JUAN C HERNANDEZ
MAX F HERNANDEZ
ARMANDO HERNANDEZ-
CONCEPCION
PEDRO A HERNANDEZ-
HERNANDEZ
EDUARDO HERNANDEZ-
JIMENEZ
HERBERT HERNANDEZ-
RODRIGUEZ
LUIS HERNANDEZ-
RODRIGUEZ
ALBERT E HEROLD
JESSE E HERPECHE
EDWARD L HERRERA
ELOY HERRERA
GUILBERTO HERRERA
LORENZO HERRERA
LYLE E HERRICK
DARWIN E HERRIN
EUGENE HERRING
GRANT J HERRING
RALPH D HERRING
EUGENE H HERRMANN
JESSIE E HERRON
THOMAS A HERTZLER
JACK A HERZET
EDWARD J HESS
EDWARD J HESS JR
KENNETH L HESS
ROBERT E HESSENFLOW
JOSEPH F HESSION JR
JOHN F HESSLER
WILL H HESTER
THURMAN B HETZLER
WILLIAM M HEU
WILLIAM F HEUER

CLYDE L HEWITT
DWIGHT M HEWITT
ROBERT A HEWITT
ROBERT L HEWITT
RICHARD D HEWLEN
JAMES C HIBBEN
DONALD R HIBBS
DAMON W HICKERSON
ORMAN L HICKERSON
JOHN M HICKEY
ERNEST F HICKLING
EVANS HICKMAN
HOMER HICKMAN
ROBERT R HICKMAN
WILLIAM G HICKMAN
WILLIAM H HICKMAN JR
ARB HICKS JR
AREWOOD W HICKS
JAMES E HICKS
MARTIN L HICKS
THOMAS HICKS
BERNARD P HIEGERT
SADAYASU HIGA
WALTER W HIGASHIDA
CHARLES H HIGDON
ELIJAH J HIGGINS
JAMES E HIGGINS
WILLIAM K HIGGINS
GARLAND R HIGGS
WILLIAM O HIGGS JR
BENJAMIN F HIGH
CHARLES HIGH
URAL W HIGHTOWER
RONALD J HIGUERA
RAY W HILDEMAN
JOHN HILEMON
A V HILL
CHARLIE H HILL
DANIEL G HILL
DONALD G HILL
EDWIN E HILL
JOHN A C HILL
LEROY A HILL
MELVIN J HILL
NORMAN F HILL
RICHARD D HILL
ROBERT L HILL
ROBERT L HILL
ROBERT L HILL
SAMUEL B HILL
SHERMONT M HILL
THOMAS W HILL
WAYNE W HILL
WILLIAM A HILL
JAMES W HILLEN
DELBERT J HILLMAN
CHESTER E HILLS
HUNTER HILLS
FRANK D HINES
MILTON HINES JR
ROLLIE W HINES
ROBERT F HINEY
WESTON HINKLEY
WILLIAM H HINKSON
NED HINNANT JR
HENRY E HINSON
BOBBIE J HINTON
ARANARI HIRAGA
GEORGE O HISER
PAUL L R HITCH
VELMON HITCHCOCK
THOMAS L HITT
WILLIAM H HITT
EDWARD V HLADIK JR
BILL F HOBBS
CAROL H HOBBS
HOY E HOBBS
KENNETH W HOBBS
ROBERT L HOBBS
ROBERT W HOBSON
BRUCE A HOCHSTETLER
ARTHUR L A HODAPP
CHARLES J HODGE
ODELL A HODGE
WILBUR L HODGE
WILLARD P HODGE
ARTHUR A HODGES JR
CHARLES E HODGES
OTMER F HODGES JR
RALPH L HODSON

VERNE E HODSON
IRVIN D HOEFLICH
RICHARD E HOEHN
RAYMOND T HOEPPNER
GABRIEL R HOERNER
FRANK K HOESCH
JOHN L HOEY
STANFORD I HOFF
FRANK V HOFFMAN
FRANKLIN R HOFFMAN
JEROLD C HOFFMAN
JO HOFFMAN
MARVIN R HOFFMAN
RALPH R HOFFMAN JR
RONALD A HOFFMAN
WARREN J HOFMAN
JAMES F HOGAN
KENNETH A HOGAN
MARK L HOGAN
SYLVESTER J HOGAN
PEARLIE HOGANS
KARL HOHER JR
GEORGE H HOLBROOK
WILLIAM HOLBROOK JR
JOHN J HOLDEN
J P HOLDER
FRANKLIN J
HOLDRIDGE JR
EBNER C HOLKE
WILLIAM A HOLLADAY
ARLIE HOLLAND
EARL L HOLLAND
LELAND L HOLLAND
WILLIE L HOLLAND
ROY W HOLLENBAUGH
JAMES M HOLLEY
RAYMOND F HOLLIDAY
ROY L HOLLIFIELD
JAMES N HOLLIMON
CURTIS HOLLINGER
WILLIAM H
HOLLINGSWORTH
EDWIN HOLLIS
PAUL H HOLLMAN
ARTHUR HOLLOWAY
HERSCHEL E HOLLOWAY
CLIFFORD A HOLLY
RICHARD G HOLLYOAK
EARL HOLMES
JAMES R HOLMES
JOHN H HOLMES
L C HOLMES JR
LAWSON HOLMES
OLIVER W HOLMES
RICHARD D HOLMES
RICHARD L HOLMES
RONALD W HOLMES
PENTTI J HOLMROOS
NORMAN R HOLSINGER
MAX S HOLT
PAUL S HOLTZCLAW
WILFRED J HOLZMAN
LAWRENCE HOMEN
CLYDE E HOMESLEY
EDWARD A HOMSEY
EUGENE R HONEL
DALLAS HONEYCUTT
J W HONEYCUTT
LOUIS C HONEYMAN JR
DU-SEON HONG
HAK-BO HONG
JAE-MAN HONG
NAM-GI HONG
SUN-CHEONG HONG
SUN-MO HONG
SUN-TAE HONG
UI-YONG HONG
JACK HONIXFELT
HASKEL H HOOD
LAWRENCE C HOOD
PHILIP T HOOGACKER
RUSSELL E HOOK
VERNARD K HOOKANO
CHARLES H HOOKER
JOE E HOOKER
LEO H HOOKS
ALONZA L HOOPER
ROBERT M HOOPER JR
WILLIAM L HOOPER
MARION D HOOVER

O B HOPE JR
ARTHUR HOPFENSPERGER
DONALD L HOPKE
FRANK S HOPKINS
GENE L HOPKINS
HOWARD A HOPKINS
JIMMIE L HOPKINS
RUSSELL C HOPKINS
GEORGE HOPPER JR
WILLIAM C HORENSKY
HUBERT F HORN
SAMUEL J HORN
BILLIE D HORNE
WALTER C HORNER
FLOYD J HORNING
ROBERT A HOROWITZ
DOYLE C HORST
DUANE F HORTON
HAROLD E HORTON
HUBERT HORTON JR
ISAAC HORTON
ROOSEVELT HORTON
CLARENCE G HOSCH
CLARENCE E HOSKINS JR
CLYDE R HOSKINS
DALE O HOSKINS
ROBERT E HOSLER
EDWARD HOSTLER JR
THOMAS A L HOTTE
FREDERICK HOTTIN
JOSEPH A HOUCHENS
ARNOLD J HOUDEK
RONALD L HOUDEK
RODNEY H HOUGHTON
EUGENE O HOULE
EUGENE T HOUSE
HARVEY J HOUSE
MARLYN F HOUSER
ROBERT D HOUSER
BERNARD HOUSTON
BOBBY L HOUSTON
DANIEL B HOWARD
HENRY C HOWARD
JOHN C HOWARD
BERNARD L HOWE
GILBERT L HOWELL
HARLEY D HOWELL
HAROLD J HOWELL
VIRGIL L HOWELL
WILLIAM HOWELL JR
WILLIAM L HOWELL
BENJAMIN B HOWER
WAYNE E HOWERTON
DONALD C HOYSTRADT
DONALD L HOYT
EMIL J HRISKO
CLAYTON HRISTOPULOS
MILAN HRNCIAR
JOHN F HRONEK
LESTER HUBBARD
RAYMOND E HUBBARD
WILLIAM HUBBARD JR
RALPH O HUBBELL
ROBERT D HUBBS
GENE HUBER
WILLIAM J HUBER JR
MARION E HUDECEK
CARL H HUDSON
CARROLL W HUDSON
HAROLD L HUDSON
JAMES HUDSON JR
RAYMOND F HUDSON
WILLIAM J HUDSON
RONALD D HUEBNER
CARL HUEY JR
EMERSON P HUFF JR
GRANGE W HUFF
KENNETH L HUFF
RONALD C HUFFMAN
ROY L HUFFMAN
LELAND V HUGGINS
ALBERT J HUGHES
BRUCE J HUGHES
FRED L HUGHES
GERARD HUGHES
JOHN A HUGHES JR
MORRIS E HUGHES
RAY T HUGHES
ROBERT E HUGHES
WAYNE G HUGHES

DALTON R HUGHEY
KENNETH P HUHN
PAUL F HUKILL
JOHN HULA
HAROLD L HULETT
ARLTON C HULL
WILLIAM H HULSKA
MILES N HULTBERG
RALPH M HUMMEL JR
WILLIAM E HUMMEL
JOSEPH HUMPHERY
JAMES O HUMPHREY
THOMAS H HUMPHREY
WILFRED H HUMPHREY
JAMES W HUMPHRIES
MATTHEW HUNNICUTT
ROBERT K HUNSINGER
ARNOLD M HUNT
CHARLIE J HUNT
DANIEL HUNT
DUANE M HUNT
FREDERIC L HUNT JR
GWYN R HUNT
RAY D HUNT
ROBERT D HUNT
WILLIAM J HUNT
DAVID F HUNTER
DONALD E HUNTER
EDWARD D HUNTER
FORREST L HUNTER
JAMES W HUNTER
MACKABEE HUNTER JR
WILLIAM C HUNTER
JAMES E HUNTLEY
ROBERT L HUPEL
WARREN O HURDLE
WILLIAM HURLEY
ELIJAH P HURSEY
BILLIE J HURST
CHARLES W HURST
CHARLEY L HURST
ELMER B HURST
FRANKLIN D HURST
HENRY D HURST
JAMES HURST
ALBERT F HURTT
DONALD J HUSHELPECK
PHARES I HUTCHERSON
THOMAS E
HUTCHERSON
GERALD W
HUTCHINSON
RICHARD D
HUTCHINSON
DAVID C HUTCHISON
ROBERT W HUTCHISON
CLYDE C HUTSON
GEORGE H HUTTO
HERBERT H HUTTON
CHARLIE E HUX
BOK-SEONG HWANG
BOK-SEUNG HWANG
BONG-YEON HWANG
BONG-YONG HWANG
DU-YEONG HWANG
I-GI HWANG
IK-SEONG HWANG
IK-YEON HWANG
JAE-GYU HWANG
JEONG-GYU HWANG
JIN-HWAN HWANG
MYEONG-DEOK
HWANG
SEON-HYEON HWANG
SEON-JUN HWANG
SU-BONG HWANG
SUN-CHANG HWANG
SUN-GI HWANG
TAE-DO HWANG
YONG-JUN HWANG
S A HYATT JR
RICHARD K HYBARGER
YONG-JIN HYEON
EMORY E HYLTON
MARTIN A HYNEK
THEODORE A HYSON
ELIA J IANNELLI
PAUL J IDDINGS JR
WILLIAM C IGO
TAMIYA IKEDA

34 ARMY

CHAE-YEOL IM
CHUNG-SIL IM
CHUNG-SIL IM
DAE-O IM
DEOK-SU IM
DEOK-SUN IM
GI-SANG IM
GI-U IM
GWANG-SUN IM
GYEONG-HO IM
GYEONG-SUN IM
JA-YUN IM
JONG-HWAN IM
NAM-GI IM
SUN-TAEK IM
TAE-JUNG IM
YEONG-JO IM
YEONG-SIK IM
YONG-DEOK IM
YONG-OK IM
WALTER S INGALLS
ROLLAND J INGERSOLL
CLARENCE B INGLE
BURNETT H INGRAM
JOHN E INGRAM
WILLIAM S INLOES
MARK INOKUCHI
FRANCISCO IRIZARRY
OBDULIO IRIZARRY-GERENA
GERALD IRWIN
WILLIAM J IRWIN
THOMAS ISAAC JR
RAYMOND E ISERMAN JR
WALLACE K ISHIKAWA
KIYOSHI ISHIMIZU
ROBERT S ISHIMOTO
RICHARD ISOVITSCH
YUKINOBU ITO
RALPH M IULIANO
JOHN E IVINS
ROBERT D IVISON
OSAMU IWAMI
SHOGO IWATSURU
PAUL IZOR
FRANCISCO A IZQUIERDO
AMEL C JACKL
ARCHIE C JACKSON
BILLY J JACKSON
CAROL J JACKSON
DAVID JACKSON JR
GEORGE JACKSON
GEORGE W JACKSON JR
HAROLD S JACKSON
HAROLD S JACKSON
HERBERT JACKSON
IRVIN L JACKSON
J C JACKSON
JAMES A JACKSON
JAMES L JACKSON
JESSE C JACKSON
JOHN W JACKSON
KNAUSBERRY JACKSON
OLIVER JACKSON
ROBERT H JACKSON
RONALD C JACKSON
RONALD C JACKSON
ROY R JACKSON
WALTER JACKSON
WILLIAM JACKSON
WILLIAM D JACKSON
WILLIAM R JACKSON
WILLIAM R JACKSON JR
WALTER G JACOB
FLEMING B JACOBS JR
HERMAN L JACOBS
LLOYD W JACOBS
ROBERT H JACOBS
NORMAN W JACOBSON
VERNELLE JACOBSON
RONALD R JACQUES
ERICH W JAHN
RICHARD JAHNKE
FRANK J JAKABOSKY
EUGENE JAKIELEK
JOHN R JALAS
CHARLES E JAMES
JOHN W JAMES
JOSEPH H JAMES
LARRY P JAMES
ROBERT H JAMES
PAUL JANCO
AN-SAENG HWAN JANG
BONG-JO JANG
CHANG-HWAN JANG
DONG-I JANG
EOK-JO JANG
GAP-CHEON JANG
GUK-HWAN JANG
GYEONG-GON JANG
GYEONG-HO JANG
GYO-SANG JANG
HAE-SU JANG
HEUNG-SIK JANG
HONG-GU JANG
IK-HWA JANG
JAE-HO JANG
JAE-YEON JANG
JE-BONG JANG
JIN-HWAN JANG
JONG-SAM JANG
JUN-MUK JANG
MUN-SU JANG
OK-MAN JANG
PAL-BONG JANG
PAL-SU JANG
SAM-DONG JANG
SAM-SI JANG
SE-OK JANG
SEOK-BONG JANG
SEONG-BAE JANG
SEONG-GWI JANG
SEONG-YEOL JANG
SON-RYONG JANG
SU-BONG JANG
TAE-JIN JANG
TAE-SU JANG
WON-TAE JANG
YEONG-EUN JANG
YEON-GUK JANG
YONG-HA JANG
FRANK P JANOWITZ
EDWARD W JANSEN
MARVIN T JANSSEN
RICHARD J JAQUES
ROSELIO JARAMILLO
J D JARNAGIN
WALTER S JAROSIK
CLEVELAND JARRELL
BEN R JARRETT
JESSE L JARRETT SR
JOHN JARRETT
DONALD C JASKULSKE
EARL JASPER
CHARLES L JASPERSON
JOSEPH JASZEMSKI
JACK L JAYNE
JOHN S JEFFCOAT
DONALD J JEFFERS
EDWARD V JEFFERSON
JAMES JEFFERSON
JAMES H JEFFERSON
SAM H JEFFERSON JR
THOMAS E JEFFERSON
JAMES H JEFFERYS
WAYNE O JEFFORDS
ALFORD JEFFREY
PAUL E JEFFRIES
VICTOR L JEFFRIES
GERALD J JENDRASZEK
BENJAMIN W JENKINS
CALVIN JENKINS
EDWARD JENKINS
FLOYD B JENKINS JR
HARLAND D JENKINS
JOHNNIE A JENKINS
RICHARD E JENKINS
RAYMOND P JENNER
FRANK P JENNINGS
HASKELL G JENNINGS
GEORGE R JENSEN
ROY L JENSEN
SYLVESTER L JENSEN
AE-CHUL JEON
BOK-HEUNG JEON
BYEONG-SUK JEON
CHI-BOK JEON
DAE-BONG JEON
HAE-SEOK JEON
HAN-I JEON
JAE-GANG JEON
JAE-WON JEON
SANG-HWAN JEON
SEOK-BONG JEON
SO-DEUK JEON
SO-SUL JEON
SU-JIN JEON
TAE-WON JEON
YEOL-SANG JEON
YONG-MAN JEON
AM JEONG
BONG-GIL JEONG
BONG-MUN JEONG
CHA-JO JEONG
CHANG-SUN JEONG
CHAN-HUI JEONG
CHEOL-HO JEONG
CHUN-GAP JEONG
DAE-SU JEONG
DAL-HAN JEONG
DAL-SU JEONG
DEOK-KWAE JEONG
DEOK-SU JEONG
DONG-MAN JEONG
DONG-U JEONG
DONG-WON JEONG
DU-HONG JEONG
EOK-JO JEONG
GEUM-RYONG JEONG
GEUM-SU JEONG
GI-HYEON JEONG
GIL-HO JEONG
GU-JONG JEONG
GYEONG-HO JEONG
GYEONG-SEOK JEONG
GYU-SEOK JEONG
HAE-DONG JEONG
HAENG-YEON JEONG
HAE-SEONG JEONG
HAN-JIN JEONG
HO-YEONG JEONG
HWAN-GI JEONG
HYO-JEOM JEONG
IN-GEUN JEONG
JAE-HWAN JEONG
JEONG-CHUL JEONG
JEONG-GIL JEONG
JEONG-HO JEONG
JIN-BOK JEONG
JIN-HA JEONG
JIN-HO JEONG
JIN-OK JEONG
JONG-GYU JEONG
JONG-RIM JEONG
JU-SEOK JEONG
MAE-SUL JEONG
MA-SEONG JEONG
MIN-SEONG JEONG
NAM-GU JEONG
NAM-SU JEONG
OK-JUN JEONG
PAN-DEOK JEONG
PAN-JO JEONG
SANG-CHUN JEONG
SANG-YONG JEONG
SEOK-DAE JEONG
SEOK-JO JEONG
SO-SIK JEONG
SO-TAEK JEONG
SU-BONG JEONG
SUN-BONG JEONG
TAE-HONG JEONG
TAE-HYEON JEONG
TAE-HYEON JEONG
TAE-YONG JEONG
U-JIN JEONG
U-SANG JEONG
U-SU JEONG
WAN-SEOP JEONG
WON-JAE JEONG
WON-SIK JEONG
WON-SIK JEONG
YEONG-GYO JEONG
YEONG-HO JEONG
YEONG-SIK JEONG
YUN-SEOP JEONG
RICHARD JEROME
PAUL S JERZAK
MARVIN D JESSEN
JAMES JESSIE
ZEE A JETER JR
DANIEL B JEWELL
JAE-CHEON JI
JEONG-YEONG JI
JONG-DEUK JI
ELVIS J JIMES
GYU-HYEON JIN
JONG-HO JIN
MYEON-SUL JIN
SANG-RYUL JIN
SEUNG-UN JIN
MARVIN H JINES
BONG-GU JO
BONG-JIN JO
BONG-RYUL JO
BONG-SEOK JO
BYEONG-JE JO
BYEONG-SUL JO
BYEONG-WAN JO
DONG-GEUN JO
GI-UNG JO
GYEONG-BONG JO
GYEONG-MUK JO
GYEONG-NAE JO
GYU-JEONG JO
HAK-JONG JO
HEON-JE JO
HO-JE JO
HO-SU JO
HYO-GU JO
I-JE JO
IL-HEUNG JO
JEOM-YONG JO
JEONG-DONG JO
JEONG-SU JO
JONG-SAENG JO
MIN-HAENG JO
MU-GYU JO
NAM-HUN JO
NAM-JAE JO
SANG-GYU JO
SEONG-BAEK JO
SEONG-JAE JO
TAE-SEOP JO
TAE-WON JO
YEONG-HWA JO
YONG-BOK JO
YONG-HWA JO
YONG-SEONG JO
YONG-SU JO
YONG-WON JO
YUN-HO JO
YUN-SEOK JO
KENNETH J JOBIN
JOSEPH B JOE
MARTIN P JOHMANN
LEROY JOHN
ROBERT L JOHN
PHILIP E JOHNS
RONALD L JOHNS
ALEX JOHNSON
ALFRED JOHNSON
ALTON T JOHNSON
ARTHUR JOHNSON
BENJAMIN JOHNSON JR
BOBBIE J JOHNSON
BOBBY JOHNSON
CASSIUS E JOHNSON
CHARLES L JOHNSON
CHARLES R JOHNSON
CHARLES R JOHNSON
CLIFFORD R JOHNSON
DARREL V JOHNSON
DAVID A JOHNSON
DAVID H JOHNSON
DEAN B JOHNSON
DONALD H JOHNSON
DONALD J JOHNSON
DONALD R JOHNSON
EDGAR JOHNSON
EDGAR E JOHNSON
EDMUND R JOHNSON
EVERETT E JOHNSON
FRANCIS M JOHNSON
FRED R JOHNSON
GEORGE J JOHNSON
GORDON R JOHNSON
HERBERT JOHNSON
HERBERT C JOHNSON
HERBERT C JOHNSON JR
IRL O JOHNSON JR
IRVING D JOHNSON
JACK W JOHNSON
JAMES JOHNSON
JAMES JOHNSON
JAMES A JOHNSON
JAMES A JOHNSON
JAMES N JOHNSON
JAMES W JOHNSON
JESSIE JOHNSON
JOHN B JOHNSON
JOHN H JOHNSON
JOHN H JOHNSON
JOHN M JOHNSON
JOHN P JOHNSON
JOSE JOHNSON
JOSEPH E JOHNSON
KENNETH J JOHNSON
KENNETH M JOHNSON
KENNETH M JOHNSON
LEON JOHNSON
LEROY JOHNSON
LYLE E JOHNSON
MELVIN J JOHNSON
MERLYN P JOHNSON
MYRON JOHNSON
NATHANIEL JOHNSON
PAUL L JOHNSON
ROBERT JOHNSON
ROBERT L JOHNSON
ROBERT M JOHNSON
ROGER JOHNSON
RONALD J JOHNSON
ROOSEVELT JOHNSON
ROSAMOND JOHNSON
SAMUEL W JOHNSON
TOMMY JOHNSON
TOMMY J JOHNSON
TRAVIS M JOHNSON
VICTOR E JOHNSON
WALTER C JOHNSON
WALTER F JOHNSON
WESLEY JOHNSON
WILFORD JOHNSON
WILLIAM JOHNSON
WILLIAM C JOHNSON
WILLIAM D JOHNSON
WILLIAM D JOHNSON
WILLIAM H JOHNSON
WILLIAM H JOHNSON
WILLIAM J JOHNSON
WILLIAM Z JOHNSON
WILLIE P JOHNSON
GEORGE JOHNSTON
HAROLD D JOHNSTON JR
JOSEPH E JOHNSTON
RICHARD E JOHNSTON
ROBERT F JOHNSTON
ROBERT L JOHNSTON
WALDO J JOHNSTON
PAUL J JOINER
ROBERT R JOLY
ASTON JONES
BOBBY J JONES
CHARLES C JONES
CLARENCE E JONES
CLARENCE G JONES
CLARENCE J JONES
CLIFFORD L JONES
DAVID R JONES
DAVIS W JONES
DONALD L JONES
EDGAR D JONES
ENSLEY JONES
EUGENE N JONES
EVERETT M JONES
FLOYD JONES JR
FLOYD L JONES
FRANK L JONES
FRANKLIN L JONES
GEORGE JONES
GEORGE L JONES
GILBERT V JONES
HENRY JONES
HERBERT E JONES
JACK O JONES
JOE JONES JR
JOE D JONES

35 ARMY

JOHN E JONES
JOHN P JONES
JOHN W JONES
JOHNNY C JONES
JOSEPH JONES
KENNETH R JONES
LAWRENCE JONES
LEROY JONES
LISBURN H JONES
LORENZO JONES
LOTCHIE J R JONES
MILLARD JONES
MILTON M JONES
OLIVER R JONES
RAYMOND L JONES
REEVES S JONES
RICHARD K JONES
ROBERT C JONES
ROBERT L JONES
RUFUS J JONES
TIMOTHY JONES
WILLIAM H JONES
WILLIAM H JONES
WILLIAM N O JONES
WILLIAM T JONES
WILLIAM T JONES
NICHOLAS W JONQUIL
BENJAMIN F JORDAN
CHARLES T JORDAN JR
GEORGE A JORDAN JR
HAROLD R JORDAN
LESTER L JORDAN
MACK A JORDAN
RICHARD W JORDAN
ROBIE L JORDAN
THOMAS M JORDAN
DALE E JORGENSEN
GEORGE A JORGENSEN
THOMAS J JORGENSON
RAYMOND E JOSE
DAVID J JOSEPH
GERARD JOSEPH
JOHNNIE JOSEPH JR
MORRIS E JOSEPH
JAMES L JOSHUA
BOYD L JOTHEN
RICHARD M JOURNEY
WILLIAM G JOY
DAVID A JOYCE
GEORGE F JOYCE
LLOYD V JOYNER
BYEONG-TAE JU
HYEON-SANG JU
JAE-JUN JU
JAE-WAN JU
JEONG-TAE JU
JIN-O JU
MYEONG-SU JU
SANG-TAE JU
SANG-WON JU
SU-BOK JU
YEONG-SU JU
YEONG-SU JU
PORFIRIO JUAREZ JR
VICTORIANO JUAREZ
RAY A JUDAY
MORRIS R JUDD
JOSEPH JUMPER
BRONISLAW M JURAS
EDWARD P JURISTY
FRANCIS R JURKOVIC
JAMES W JUSTICE
KELLY JUSTICE
MARION W JUSTICE
WALLACE JUSTICE
HILARY W JUSTMAN
STANLEY J KACAR
CHARLES J KACHELE
ROBERT J KACZMAREK
RICHARD A KADLEC
ROBERT C KADLEC
EDWARD D KAFARA
LEONARD J KAHL
FREDERICK C KAHNT
ANTHONY KAHOOHANOHANO
LELAND R KAHRMANN
CLARENCE L KALAMA
ALBERT KALAWE
ARTHUR W KALDAHL

CARL A KALKER
HERMAN B KAMAI
WILLIAM M KAMAKAOKALANI JR
HAROLD D KAMHOLZ
ERNEST KAMINSKI
HENRY KAMOWSKI
DAVID B KAMPA
JOHN W KAMPSCHNEIDER
JOHN J KANE
JOHN R KANE
KENNETH KANE
HARRY Y KANESHIRO
JACK S KANESHIRO
RICHARD A KANSKI
GERALD D KAPPLER
RAYMOND J KARAISEKY
PAUL E KARCH
WILLIAM C KARIN
WILLIAM G KARINEN
ROBERT D KARKALIK
ROBERT R KARR
ADOLPH R KARTES
AMEL O KASINGER
JAMES K KASPRZAK
WILLIAM A KAST
STANLEY J KASZA
JOHN H KATILIUS
ROBERT N KATLAREK
ROSS W KATZMAN
ALEXANDER K KAUAHI
EDGAR H KAUFFMAN
FRANK E KAUFMAN
LUTHER W KAUFMAN
MASAYOSHI KAWAHARA
SUYEO KAWAHARA
MASAMI KAWAMURA
HAROLD L KAY
MINORU KAYA
BILLY J KAYS
CLYDE D KEAR
DONALD J KEARNEY
HARRY L KEARNEY
CARL L KEARNS
ROBERT G KEARNS
CHARLES H KEATING
CHARLES J KEEL
CHARLES E KEELEY
FURMAN KEELEY
BOBBY W KEEN
WILLIAM R KEENAN
LEON L KEENE
FLETCHER M KEENER
JIMMIE KEESE
WALTER L KEETON
ROBERT D KEIM
ROBERT L KEISH
DANIEL J KEISTER
CURTIS A KEITH
DANNY R KEITH
DONALD G KEITH
ISAIAH H KEITH
JOSEPH K KEKOA
PATRICK M KELIHER
FAY N KELL
RICHARD D KELLAM
JACK E KELLAMS
ALBERT KELLER
ERNEST R KELLER
RODNEY V KELLER
RUSSELL R KELLER
GEORGE S KELLETT
HAROLD D KELLETT
CHARLES A KELLEY
FRANK H KELLEY
LESLIE L KELLEY
RAYMOND E KELLEY
VERNON L KELLEY
EDWARD J KELLY JR
GEORGE A KELLY
HERBERT KELLY
JOHN L KELLY JR
LOUIS C KELLY
ROBERT T KELLY
WARREN F KELLY
WILLIS E KELLY
JOSEPH KELSEY
GENE B KELSO
GLEN G KEMERY
DAVID R KEMPER

JOHN W KENAWELL
RANDOLPH L KENDALL
RONALD E KENDALL
LINDSEY KENDELL
GEORGE J KENDLE
JAMES R KENEALY
EDWARD D KENNEALLY
CHARLES K KENNEDY
DONALD J KENNEDY
GEORGE B KENNEDY
JAMES E KENNEDY
MICHAEL L KENNEDY
THEODORE KENNEDY
KENNETH E KENNY
KENNETH I KENNY
ARTHUR KENOLIO
ERNEST R KENT
MORRIS H KENT
ROBERT W KENZEL
BILLY J KEOUGH
JOHN W KEPHART
ROBERT L KEPLEY
WALTER H KERCE
JOHN T KERCHINSKY
CHARLES K KERR
JACK KERR
JOHN KERWIN
JAMES L KESSLER
ROBERT W KETCHINGMAN
LAWRENCE R KETELHOHN
ANDREW R KETTERMAN
ARTHUR V KEY
ROBERT E KEY
PAUL D KHULA
LINN E KIBLER
RUSSELL C KIBLINGER
MILES H KIDD
JESSE L KIDDY
VIRGIL J KIGAR
AMOS L KIGHT
MASAYUKI KIHARA
PAUL M KILLAR
CHARLES O KILLIAN
EDWARD M KILLIAN
WILLIAM L KILLINGSWORTH
ALBERT W KIM
BANG-U KIM
BEOM-HO KIM
BI-GYUN KIM
BOK-GIL KIM
BOK-GYU KIM
BOK-SUL KIM
BOK-YUN KIM
BONG-GI KIM
BONG-GYU KIM
BONG-OK KIM
BONG-SU KIM
BONG-SU KIM
BONG-SU KIM
BONG-U KIM
BYEONG-DAE KIM
BYEONG-GI KIM
BYEONG-GWON KIM
BYEONG-JU KIM
BYEONG-JU KIM
BYEONG-SEOK KIM
BYEONG-SU KIM
BYEONG-TAE KIM
BYEONG-TAEK KIM
BYEONG-TAK KIM
CHAN J P KIM JR
CHANG-DONG KIM
CHANG-GI KIM
CHANG-GWI KIM
CHANG-HUN KIM
CHANG-SEOK KIM
CHANG-SU KIM
CHANG-UK KIM
CHAN-JE KIM
CHAN-SIK KIM
CHAN-YEONG KIM
CHARLES C S KIM
CHA-YEONG KIM
CHEOL-HWAN KIM
CHEOL-SU KIM
CHEOL-UNG KIM
CHEOL-WON KIM

CHI-GON KIM
CHIL-GWON KIM
CHUN-GWON KIM
DAE-BOK KIM
DAE-HWAN KIM
DAE-YEON KIM
DEOK-GYU KIM
DEOK-HWAN KIM
DEOK-SU KIM
DEOK-TAE KIM
DONG-GI KIM
DONG-SEOP KIM
DONG-SIK KIM
DONG-UN KIM
DONG-YEOL KIM
DO-SEOK KIM
DO-SIK KIM
DO-SU KIM
DU-CHEON KIM
DU-SIK KIM
DU-SIK KIM
EOK-HWAN KIM
EUNG-CHAN KIM
EUNG-GUK KIM
EUNG-YONG KIM
EUN-GYU KIM
GAP-JU KIM
GEUM-JO KIM
GEUN-TAE KIM
GI-AN KIM
GI-CHUL KIM
GI-DONG KIM
GI-HAE KIM
GI-HYEON KIM
GI-JUN KIM
GI-JUN KIM
GI-SEON KIM
GI-TAE KIM
GI-YEONG KIM
GU-SIK KIM
GU-YEONG KIM
GWANG-SU KIM
GWANG-SU KIM
GWAN-SIK KIM
GWAN-YONG KIM
GYEONG-DAL KIM
GYEONG-DONG KIM
GYEONG-HUI KIM
GYEONG-HWAN KIM
GYEONG-HWAN KIM
GYEONG-RYONG KIM
GYEONG-SU KIM
GYEONG-SU KIM
GYEONG-YONG KIM
GYU-TAE KIM
GYU-YONG KIM
HAE-DU KIM
HAE-SIL KIM
HAE-YONG KIM
HA-JUNG KIM
HAK-CHEON KIM
HAK-GWON KIM
HAK-JEOM KIM
HAK-MAN KIM
HAK-SIK KIM
HAK-SU KIM
HAK-SU KIM
HAK-TAE KIM
HA-SEOK KIM
HEUNG-JE KIM
HEUNG-JUN KIM
HONG-DAE KIM
HONG-PIL KIM
HONG-SIK KIM
HU-GON KIM
HUI-JU KIM
HWA-JU KIM
HWAN-JUN KIM
HWA-SIK KIM
HYEON KIM
HYEON-DO KIM
HYEONG-SAM KIM
HYEONG-TAE KIM
HYEONG-UK KIM
HYEON-SU KIM
HYO-WON KIM
I-GU KIM
IM-DAL KIM
IN-RYUN KIM
IN-SIK KIM

IN-SU KIM
IN-SUN KIM
JAE-CHANG KIM
JAE-CHEOL KIM
JAE-GIL KIM
JAE-HWA KIM
JAE-JUN KIM
JAE-MYEONG KIM
JAE-SEOK KIM
JAE-SIK KIM
JAE-SU KIM
JAE-YONG KIM
JANG-DAE KIM
JEOM-BAE KIM
JEOM-DAL KIM
JEOM-DEUK KIM
JEOM-JUN KIM
JEOM-SUL KIM
JEONG-BEOM KIM
JEONG-DO KIM
JEONG-HWAN KIM
JEONG-HWAN KIM
JEONG-JO KIM
JEONG-SU KIM
JI-HAN KIM
JIN-CHAN KIM
JIN-GON KIM
JIN-HO KIM
JIN-HWAN KIM
JIN-MAN KIM
JIN-O KIM
JIN-SU KIM
JIN-WON KIM
JONG-DAE KIM
JONG-DAE KIM
JONG-EOP KIM
JONG-GEUK KIM
JONG-GU KIM
JONG-HO KIM
JONG-IK KIM
JONG-MAN KIM
JONG-SEONG KIM
JONG-SEONG KIM
JONG-SIK KIM
JONG-SIK KIM
JONG-TAEK KIM
JONG-WON KIM
JONG-WON KIM
JUK-IL KIM
JUNG-HWA KIM
JUN-GI KIM
JU-SEOK KIM
JU-YEON KIM
MAN-SEOK KIM
MAN-SIK KIM
MAN-SU KIM
MI-SU KIM
MUN-HAN KIM
MUN-TAEK KIM
MUN-UNG KIM
MYEONG-DO KIM
MYEONG-GAE KIM
MYEONG-GIL KIM
MYEONG-GON KIM
MYEONG-HAK KIM
MYEONG-JO KIM
MYEONG-SIK KIM
MYEONG-SIL KIM
NAM-JIN KIM
NAM-MUN KIM
NAM-SUL KIM
OK-CHEON KIM
PAL-YONG KIM
PAN-GIL KIM
PAN-MUN KIM
SAENG-GI KIM
SA-JIN KIM
SA-JO KIM
SAM-JA KIM
SAM-JUN KIM
SAM-RYONG KIM
SANG-CHAN KIM
SANG-DEOK KIM
SANG-DOL KIM
SANG-DON KIM
SANG-EON KIM
SANG-EOP KIM
SANG-GEUN KIM
SANG-GI KIM
SANG-HO KIM

36 ARMY

SANG-HYEOK KIM
SANG-MYEONG KIM
SANG-RYEOL KIM
SANG-SEON KIM
SANG-YONG KIM
SA-YEON KIM
SEOK-GON KIM
SEOK-MAN KIM
SEONG-BAE KIM
SEONG-BOK KIM
SEONG-BONG KIM
SEONG-HAK KIM
SEONG-HO KIM
SEONG-JONG KIM
SEONG-YEON KIM
SEONG-YEONG KIM
SEON-GYEONG KIM
SEONG-YONG KIM
SI-MOK KIM
SO-MAN KIM
SU-BAEK KIM
SU-BEOM KIM
SU-CHAN KIM
SU-GYEOM KIM
SU-HYEON KIM
SUL-GEUN KIM
SU-NAM KIM
SUN-JO KIM
SU-TAEK KIM
SU-YEONG KIM
TAE-BOK KIM
TAE-GYU KIM
TAE-RYONG KIM
TAE-SIK KIM
U-AM KIM
UK-GI KIM
UN-GI KIM
UN-SEOP KIM
WAN-SIK KIM
WON-CHIL KIM
WON-GYEONG KIM
WON-JIN KIM
WON-JIN KIM
WON-SU KIM
YANG-GEUN KIM
YEONG-BAEK KIM
YEONG-CHANG KIM
YEONG-CHUL KIM
YEONG-CHUN KIM
YEONG-DU KIM
YEONG-GI KIM
YEONG-GON KIM
YEONG-GON KIM
YEONG-GYU KIM
YEONG-HWAN KIM
YEONG-JIN KIM
YEONG-JO KIM
YEONG-JU KIM
YEONG-MIN KIM
YEONG-SIK KIM
YEONG-SUL KIM
YEONG-SUL KIM
YEONG-SUN KIM
YEONG-TAK KIM
YEONG-U KIM
YEON-SU KIM
YONG-BEOM KIM
YONG-BOK KIM
YONG-CHAN KIM
YONG-GI KIM
YONG-HAK KIM
YONG-RAE KIM
YONG-SU KIM
YONG-TAE KIM
YU-BOK KIM
YUN-DO KIM
YUN-GIL KIM
YUN-SU KIM
FRED V KIMBRELL JR
HERBERT L KIMBRO
WILLARD A KIMLE
SEIKI KIMURA
CHARLES B KINCAID
ROBERT KINCAID JR
ANTHONY A KINCEL
TOMMY KINDER JR
DONALD A KINDSETH
ARMSTEAD KING
CHARLES J KING JR
CHARLEY L KING
DONALD R KING
HERBERT KING
HOMER G KING
JACK E KING
JACK R KING
JOHN E KING JR
LOYD KING JR
MICHAEL T KING
MORRIS O KING
RALPH KING
RALPH K KING
RAY R KING
RICHARD W KING
ROBERT C KING
ROBERT V KING
ROBERT W KING
THOMAS R KING
VERNON R KING
WELTON B KING
WILLARD G KING
WILLIAM A KING
GROVER D KINNEY
HOWARD C KINNEY JR
JOHN A KINNEY
JOHN S KINNEY
RALPH L KINNEY
RAYMOND D KINNUNEN
HAROLD A KINZER
JEROME J KIPPLEY
CHARLES E KIRBY JR
JACK D KIRBY
JESSE L KIRBY
LAMAR KIRBY
ROBERT D KIRBY
ALBERT KIRK JR
HAROLD E KIRK
WILLIAM G
KIRKENDALL JR
CHARLES KIRKPATRICK
JUNIOR R KIRKPATRICK
ROY L KIRKPATRICK
JONATHAN KIRKSEY
PAUL W KIRSCHMANN
ROBERT S KIRSCHNER
DARELL D KIRSTINE
EDWARD KIRTZ
GLENN A KISE
ROY G KISER
GEZA KISH
RICHARD E KISSICK
GEORGE T KITCHENS
TRACEY KITCHINGS JR
DAVID R KITTLESON
JAMES L KITTRELL
CARL D KITZMILLER
NORMAN L KLARIS
FRED P KLASSEN
CHARLES R KLATT
GEORGE C KLAUSSNER
GERALD J KLEIMEYER
GEORGE D KLEIN
GEORGE R KLEIN
MELVIN R KLEIN
SIDNEY R KLEIN
GLEN W KLEINSCHMIDT
JOHN KLEMIATOF
RICHARD KLENZ
HOWARD V KLEOPFER
EDWARD A KLEPAJDA
BURTON F KLEPPINGER
LAVERNE R KLEVGARD
WILLIAM P KLIMITCHEK
JOSEPH W KLIMSEY JR
EDGAR H KLINDWORTH
CHARLES W KLINE
EARL E KLINE
JAMES F KLINGLER
ROBERT T KLOGY
RAYMOND L KLOPP
GENE F KLOS
WALTER B KLOSE
ROGER E KLOUSER
KENNETH W KLUG
WARREN E KLUG
EDWARD G KNAPP
OTHELLO C KNAPPER
RUSSELL L KNEISLEY
HARRY F KNEPP
JOHN H KNIGGE JR
DONALD E KNIGHT
EARLE O KNIGHT
FRANKLIN J KNIGHT
HAROLD KNIGHT
JAKE KNIGHT JR
JAMES H KNIGHT
JOHN F KNIGHT
L C KNIGHT
NOAH O KNIGHT
ROBERT L KNIGHT
ROSCOE KNIGHT
WALTER E KNIGHT
ROY J KNIPE
OLEY B KNIPP
HARRY A KNOKE
ERWIN H KNOPE
LEO KNOTT JR
HERBERT KNOWLTON
ANDREW KNOX
JAMES E KNOX
WILLIAM R KNOX
JACK L KNUDSON
FELIX H KOCH
JACK H KOCH
KERMIT K KOCH
THOMAS KOCH
TAKASHI KOCHI
ROBERT E KOEHLER
ROBERT H KOEHLER
WALTER T KOEHLER
BOB J KOEHN
HARRY W KOELMEL
SAMMY G KOENIG
EDWARD C KOENKE JR
GEORGE E KOESTLER
BERNARD R KOGER
JOSHUA K KOHN
EDWARD L KOHOUT
JOHN L KOHUT
ROBERT A KOLASINSKI
DELOS G KOLBE
WILLIAM S KOLLER
LORENZO KOLLOCK
GEORGE A KOLP
JOSEPH KOMENDEK
DONALD M KONRAD
JIM KONTOS
YOUNG C KOO
EUGENE KOONTZ
GEORGE KOPTA
ARTHUR E
KORBMACHER
CHARLES E KORCZ
GEORGE R KOREM
JOHN KORTYNA JR
MUNEO KOSHIMIZU
EDWARD S KOSIENIAK
DONALD KOSMECKI
NICHOLAS L KOSTOFF
BRANKO KOTUR
ROBERT M KOUNS
FRED R KOVALYAK
LEO F KOVAR
EDWARD M KOWALKO
SUEO KOYANAGI
THADEUS S KOZLOWSKI
RALPH E KRALICEK
CORNELIUS W KRAMER
JAMES H KRATZ
VEER M KRAUSE
LEONARD M KRAVITZ
RAYMOND A KRAWCZYK
DAVID W KREBS
GEORGE J KREBS
DANIEL L KREMER
GEORGE KRESSICH
HARRY J KREY
GUNTHER H KRIEGER
JOSEPH KRIWCHUK
ALEX E KROLL
DAVID T KROUSE
ERNEST R KROUT
EDWARD A KRUCEK
DONALD D KRUEGER
PAUL J KRUK
JANIS KRUMINS
MARTIN M KRUMP
MICHAEL KRUTTY
PETER KUBIC
NICKOLAS A KUBOVICH
HENRY J KUCHARCZYK
DOUGLAS S KUECHLER
MELVIN L KUEHL
ADRIAN A KUENLE
WILLIAM F KUHLMAN
BERNARD W KUHN
CHARLES E KUHNS
HOMER K KUHNS
RAYMOND E KUHR
STEPHAN F KULDANEK
WALTER J KULIK
DAN C KUNA
GEORGE H KUNC
HARLAN E KUNDE
JOHN KUNDRATIK
MOSES E KUNI
NICKOLAUS KUNTZ
WILLIAM F KUNZ
LEONARD KUPAU
RICHARD KUPAU
OLIVER B KUPFERLE
CLARENCE P KUPP
SUSUMU KUROSAWA
WALTER H KURPYTA
ARTHUR R KURTS
SAMUEL L KURTZ
JOSEPH P KUSHNIR
ADRIAN J KUSIOLEK
JACK H KUTCHEY
KIYOMITSU KUTSUNAI
VERLYN E KUTZ
SHOSO KUWAHARA
RICHARD T KUZNIAR
HAROLD KVAM
KENNETH W KYLE
ROBERT W LA BAR
PAUL LA BARR
AMERICO M LA BELLA
EDWARD W LABOSSIERE
ROBERT C LABREE
HADEN R LACEY
ARNOLD B LACKIE
BOOKER T LACKLAND
GERARD F LACOURSE
GEORGE LACRO
JAMES R LACY
ROBERT C LACY
SIMON LADELL
EUGENE J LADSON
KENNETH F LAESSIG
ROBERT L LAFAVE
MERTON V LA FAVOR
DALE M LAFFERRE
CHARLES S LAFLEUR
REGINALD P LAFLEUR
PAUL E LA FOND
SALVATORE LA FRANCA
TEOFILO LAGANSUA
ROBERT E LAGESS
JOHN A LAGHNER
JAMES J LA GRANGE
LEONARD E LAHM
WILLIAM A LAHTI
CARROLL F LAING
DONALD E LAIRD
JOHN LAJEUNESSE
FRANK N LAKE
DAVID W LAM
KENNETH L LAM
WILLIAM W LAM
MICHAEL LAMAGNA
RAYMOND C LAMANCE
ROBERT N LAMASTUS
CHARLES M LAMB
WILLIAM E LAMB
DANIEL R LAMBERT
DELBERT M LAMBERT
GERALD G LAMBERT
JOSEPH A LAMBERT
RICHARD L LAMBERT
CHAUNCEY V LAMBETH
LEROY A LAMONT
ALICIDE H LAMOUREUX
ABRAHAM E LAMOUTTE
DOUGLAS H W LAMP
EDWARD J LANAUSKAS
ROY A LANCASTER
THOMAS W LANCASTER
HERMAN LANCE
JEAN A LANCTOT
WILLIAM G LAND
JERRY T LANDERS
ROBERT B LANDERS
EDMUND LANDRY
JAMES E LANDRY
BRINK E LANE
CLARENCE E LANE
JAMES K LANE
JAMES P LANE
LEROY LANE
MELVIN H LANE
MORRIS H LANE
ROBERT C LANE
IRVIN E LANEHART
CHARLES R LANFORD
ARTHUR G LANG
LLOYD L LANG
MILTON F LANG
RAYMOND J LANG
ELMER R LANGE
JOHNNY D LANGE
EUGENE LANGENFELD
WALLACE J LANGLITZ
RICHARD F LANGOWSKI
ORLIN N LANIER
FREDERICK W
LANKFORD
JOHN J LANNON
CHARLES L LANSDELL
CLIFFORD R
LANSDELL JR
THEODORE R LANSKY
ROY D LAPHAM
HARRY F LAPICH JR
JOHN F LAPINSKI
GEORGE R LAPLANTE
JEAN P LAPLANTE
NORMAND L LAPLANTE
WALTER B LA POINTE
WILLIAM J LAPRADE
LUIS P LARA
FRANK F LARDINO
JOSE F M LARGE
BONIFACIO T LARGUSA
LORIN H LARKIN
AUGUSTINE LARKINS
ANTHONY R LA ROSSA
DAVID A LARRABEE
EMIL A LARSEN JR
JAMES T LARSEN
LAWRENCE E LARSEN
GERALD R LARSON
ORVALL P LARSON
RICHARD E LARSON
ALVIN A LARTIGUE
PAUL M LARUE
EARL M LASALLE
JOHN C LASATER
MARVIN J LASHLEY
EDWARD R LASHOK
JOHN LASIUK JR
ISMAEL LASSALLE-VELEZ
PAUL A LASSAN
DONALD T LASSITER
JOHN H LASSITER
WILLIAM H LASSITER JR
WINIFRED LASSITER
GLENN D LATHAM
LESLIE B LATHAM
SHELDON W LATHAM
BEONDRED K LATHAN
GEORGE G LATTIN
CHARLES W
LAUDERDALE
JOHN W LAUF
ROBERT LAUFER
DONALD E LAUGHLIN
GEORGE E LAURENCE
DOUGLAS J LAURENT
ROY C LAVIA
RICHARD LAW
THEODORE LAW JR
MARTIN A LAWING
LEON B LAWLESS
CHARLES LAWRENCE
DERENFRU W
LAWRENCE
DONALD E LAWRENCE
IRVIN G LAWRENCE
JAMES W LAWRENCE
JOHN R LAWRENCE

37 ARMY

THEODORE W LAWRENCE
WILLIAM W LAWRENCE
JOHN E LAWSON
WILLIAM S LAWSON
CARL S LAY
ELMER L LAYMON
JAMES T LAYNE
ADOLPHUS M LEACH
CHARLES L LEACH
CARLTON H LEADBETTER
CHARLES LEAK
WILLIAM M LEAKE JR
ANTONIO A LEAL
VICTOR C LEAL
ROBERT W LEAMAN
JOE Z LEAMON
EDWIN J LEARY
THOMAS J LEAVEY
WILLIS C LE BARRON
ORESTE I LE BLANC
ROLAND L LE BLANC
DAVID LEBRON-LEBRON
BRUCE P LECLAIR
JOHN B LEDBETTER
HOWARD R LEDFORD
J T LEDFORD
BAEK-WON LEE
BOK-MAN LEE
BO-WAN LEE
BO-YEOL LEE
BU-SU LEE
BU-YEONG LEE
BYEONG-SAM LEE
BYEONG-TAE LEE
BYEONG-WON LEE
CHA-BEOM LEE
CHA-HWAN LEE
CHANG-GEUN LEE
CHANG-HO LEE
CHANG-U LEE
CHAN-U LEE
CHARLES S A LEE
CHUN-BONG LEE
CHUN-DO LEE
CHUN-U LEE
CORDELL LEE JR
DAE-HYEON LEE
DAE-SEOK LEE
DAE-YONG LEE
DAL-YEONG LEE
DEOK-RYONG LEE
DONALD D LEE
DONG-SEOK LEE
DONG-SIK LEE
DONG-SONG LEE
DO-SEOK LEE
DU-GYEONG LEE
DU-WON LEE
DU-YEOL LEE
GANG-HEON LEE
GANG-OK LEE
GAP-TAE LEE
GIL-JONG LEE
GIL-NAM LEE
GI-SU LEE
GI-TAE LEE
GWAN-MUK LEE
GWAN-U LEE
GWON-HAENG LEE
GYE-CHEOL LEE
GYEONG-SIK LEE
GYE-WON LEE
GYO-UNG LEE
GYU-HYEON LEE
GYU-JUN LEE
GYU-YEONG LEE
HAK-YONG LEE
HAN-OK LEE
HERBERT Y LEE
HO-JONG LEE
HUI-JEONG LEE
HWA-SEOP LEE
HWA-SIK LEE
HYEON-DEOK LEE
HYEON-HO LEE
HYEON-MO LEE
HYEON-SIK LEE
HYEON-TAEK LEE
HYEOP-JONG LEE
HYO-SEON LEE

HYO-SUN LEE
IL-DO LEE
IL-HYEONG LEE
IL-U LEE
IM-DEUK LEE
ISAAC LEE JR
JAE-CHEOL LEE
JAE-DEUK LEE
JAE-GU LEE
JAE-GYUN LEE
JAE-HA LEE
JAE-I LEE
JAE-NAM LEE
JAE-SANG LEE
JAE-SANG LEE
JAE-YEONG LEE
JAMES C LEE
JANG-CHUN LEE
JANG-U LEE
JEONG-BOK LEE
JEONG-GI LEE
JEONG-IL LEE
JEONG-O LEE
JEONG-OK LEE
JEONG-SEOK LEE
JEONG-SEOK LEE
JIN-TAE LEE
JONG-AN LEE
JONG-BEOM LEE
JONG-BOK LEE
JONG-BYEONG LEE
JONG-DAE LEE
JONG-DAE LEE
JONG-DAL LEE
JONG-GU LEE
JONG-GUK LEE
JONG-HAK LEE
JONG-HO LEE
JONG-HO LEE
JONG-SEOK LEE
JONG-SEOK LEE
JONG-SEOK LEE
JONG-SIK LEE
JONG-TAE LEE
JONG-TAEK LEE
JONG-YEOL LEE
JONG-YEOL LEE
JONG-YONG LEE
JU-BONG LEE
JUNG-HO LEE
JUN-YEONG LEE
JU-SEOK LEE
JU-SIK LEE
MAN-CHO LEE
MAN-JU LEE
MAN-SU LEE
MIN-JAE LEE
MO-YEOL LEE
MUN-I LEE
MUN-I LEE
MU-SAM LEE
MYEONG-NAK LEE
NAM-JAE LEE
OK-CHUL LEE
PAN-SU LEE
PYEONG-SUN LEE
RAYMOND E LEE
ROBERT E LEE
SANG-DO LEE
SANG-GEON LEE
SANG-HO LEE
SANG-JEOM LEE
SANG-MAN LEE
SANG-SU LEE
SANG-TAE LEE
SANG-UK LEE
SANG-WON LEE
SANG-YEON LEE
SE-DO LEE
SEOK-GYU LEE
SEOK-U LEE
SEOK-YONG LEE
SEON-DONG LEE
SEONG-GEON LEE
SEONG-GYU LEE
SEONG-HA LEE
SEON-GI LEE
SEONG-YU LEE
SEONG-YUN LEE
SE-SIK LEE

SEUNG-BAEK LEE
SI-JUN LEE
SI-U LEE
SU-BAEK LEE
SU-GIL LEE
SUN-CHAN LEE
SUN-HUI LEE
SUN-IK LEE
SUN-MO LEE
SUN-SIK LEE
TAE-GEON LEE
TAE-GYEONG LEE
TAE-GYEONG LEE
TAE-HYEOK LEE
U-BONG LEE
U-CHUN LEE
U-DEOK LEE
U-DEOK LEE
UI-JUNG LEE
UN-YONG LEE
U-RYONG LEE
U-SUN LEE
WON-CHUL LEE
WON-MO LEE
WON-TAE LEE
WON-TAE LEE
YEONG-GEUN LEE
YEONG-GEUN LEE
YEONG-GI LEE
YEONG-GU LEE
YEONG-HAK LEE
YEONG-HO LEE
YEONG-HWA LEE
YEONG-MAN LEE
YEONG-RAE LEE
YEONG-SIK LEE
YEONG-SUL LEE
YEONG-TAE LEE
YEON-HO LEE
YONG-AM LEE
YONG-GU LEE
YONG-JIN LEE
YONG-JIN LEE
YONG-JIN LEE
YONG-JO LEE
YONG-SU LEE
YONG-TAE LEE
YU-MAN LEE
YUN-GI LEE
YUN-HWAN LEE
YUN-SAN LEE
YUN-SIK LEE
DAVID H LEEDY
DELMAN E LEEDY
GENE N LEEPER
WILLIAM R LEES
TONY R LEET
RICHARD C LEFFLER
ALBERT LEFTWICH
JORGE LEGARRETA
JOSEPH H LEGEE
ALFRED J LEGER JR
MANCEL N LEGG
RAYMOND LEGGET
DONALD H LEHTO
DEWEY LEIBY JR
WILLIS E LEICHLITER
EUGENE G LEIDER
ROY S LEIDY
ROBERT W LEIGHTON
MATT P LEINEN
VANCE R LEINEN
WARREN H LEINING
JOHN E LEIST
ARNOLD C LEISTIKOW
EUGENE L LEITCH
PHILLIP L LEITCH
RALPH L LEITNER
ARTHUR W LEIVISKA
JOSEPH A LEMME
JOHN R LEMMEN
ANTHONY R LEMOINE
EARL J LEMOINE
SHERWIN A LEMON
ARVIL LEMONS
WILLIAM E LENDER
JOHN J LENO
FRANK J LENTE
ANGEL LEON
GUERRERO J LEON

CHARLES W LEONARD
DWIGHT F LEONARD JR
EARNEST W LEONARD
EDWARD J LEONARD
EDWIN R LEONARD
HERBERT A LEONARD
JAMES J LEONARD JR
DONALD M LEONHARD
JAMES R LESLEY
ALBERT F LESLIE
ARMANDO D LESPRON
WILLIAM A LESTER
ROGER N LETENDRE
EWALD A LETINICH
LEON LETTS JR
EDMOND D LEVASSEUR
WELCOME LEVERETT
JOSEPH A LEVESQUE
JOSEPH H LEVESQUE
MARION LEVINE
RUBIN LEVINE
WALTER J LEVITSKI
LEO LEVY
EDWARD J LEWANDOWSKI
ERNEST S LEWANDOWSKI
ROBERT J LEWELLING
ELMER E LEWELLYN
ABE LEWIS
ALBERT E LEWIS
CHARLES A LEWIS
CHARLIE L LEWIS
DANIEL H LEWIS
DUANT E LEWIS
EARL LEWIS
EMMETT E LEWIS
HARRY A LEWIS
HERMAN O LEWIS
JACK T LEWIS
JAMES A LEWIS
JAMES J LEWIS JR
LLOYD B LEWIS
LUCIUS LEWIS
O C LEWIS
PHILLIP G LEWIS
ROBERT O LEWIS
WILLIE LEWIS
CONRAD J LEXVOLD
LORAN K LIBBERT
SALVATORE V LIBRETTI
ELROY C LICHEY
MURRAY LICHTMAN
HARRY H LIDDLE JR
EARL F LIEBAL
RALPH O LIEN
WALTER D LIEN
RUDOLFS LIEPA
JOHN P LIEUWEN
CHARLES E LIFORD
ALVIN R LIGGINS JR
JAMES E LIGHT
JOHNNY D LIGHT
RICHARD T LIGHTLE
ROGER W LIGHTNER
GERALD G LILE
HERBERT LILIENTHAL
MAX W LILLER
DONALD E LILLEY
JACK E LILLEY
EDMUND B LILLY
JOHN J LINDAHL
RUNE LINDAHL
CHARLES A LINDBERG
LINDOR H LINDBLADE
ERWIN A LINDEMANS
PRESTON J LINDEN
MAX A LINDSAY
RAYMOND L LINDSAY
JOHN R LINDSEY
CARLO A LINDSTROM
FLOYD A LINDSTROM
CHARLES T LINDWALL
EDGAR L LINE
GEORGE L LINE
ORVILL F LINEBAUGH
WILLIAM R LINER
CHARLES P LINK
HAVILAND J LINK
ROY W LINNE
MELVIN E LIPSCOMB

WILLIAM T LIPSCOMB
FRANK I LIPSCOMBE
JOHN H LISENBY
JOHN P LISKOWSKI JR
JOHN W LISTON JR
JOHN K LITCH JR
HENRY LITMANOWITZ
BLAINE L LITTLE
KEITH J LITTLE
WALLACE R LITTLE
MELVIN J LITTLE BEAR
JOHN LITTLEHAWK JR
FRANKLIN LITTLEJOHN
HAROLD L LITTLEJOHN
RALPH LITTLER JR
EDMUND J LITWINOWICZ
WALTER S LIVERMORE
JAMES O LIVESAY
CLIFFORD L LIVINGSTON
LAWRENCE LIVINGSTON
RAYMOND S LIVINGSTON
DONALD D LIZOTTE
ALVIN S LLOYD JR
ARNOLD F LOBO
THOMAS J LOCHRANE
DONALD E LOCKARD
HOLICE LOCKARD
WILLIAM C LOCKARD
EDDIE LOCKETT JR
JOHNNY B LOCKETT
SPENCER L LOCKHART
JAMES P LOCKMAN
JOHN B LOCKWOOD
WILLIAM A LOCKWOOD
JAMES N LOCUS
JOSEPH B LODDER
SAL LODOLCE
ROBERT D LOEH
VERNON R LOESHER
LAVERNE J LOETHER
JULIUS H LOFGREN
ARTHUR F LOFTUS
CHARLES E LOGAN
CLARENCE LOGAN JR
JOHN LOGAN
JOHN J LOGAN
ROBERT C LOGAN
WILLIAM F LOGAN
MILDON H LOGE
FLOYD B LOGGINS
EARL R LOGSTON
JOHN A LOMBARDI
JOSEPH J LOMBARDI JR
CHARLES H LONG
JAC E LONG
JACOB W LONG
JUNIOR LONG
JUNIOR E LONG
KENNETH J LONG
OWEN C LONG
WILLIAM M LONG
PAUL F LONGALE
STEPHEN H LONGAMORE
JOSEPH LONGO
RALPH A LONGO
VINCENT LONGO
LEOPOLDO LONGORIA
HORACE J LONGSHORE
WILLIAM O LONGWAY
CHARLES LOOKINGBILL
THOMAS H LOOMIS
HAROLD W LOONEY
ANTHONY J LOPA
JOSEPH W LOPES JR
ANGEL L LOPEZ
CRISTOBAL LOPEZ
EDWARD E LOPEZ
ELOY E LOPEZ
ESMAEL LOPEZ
FELICIANO F LOPEZ
FERNADO L LOPEZ
JOHN A LOPEZ
JOHN L LOPEZ
JOSE M LOPEZ

38 ARMY

JOSEPH B LOPEZ
RAUL T LOPEZ
TONY LOPEZ
VICTOR M LOPEZ
PABLO LOPEZ-ALMODOVAR
ROBERT LOPEZ-JIMENEZ
LUIS LOPEZ-ORONOZ
FELIX LOPEZ-SANCHEZ
CHARLES A LORD
EDWARD L LORD
ERIC R LORD
ROBERT E LORENZ
WAYNE E LORENZEN
JOSEPH LORIO
JOHN L LOSH
KENNETH H LOTT
HARLEY J LOTTMAN
ARNOLD E LOUDERMILK
JAMES H LOURY
ARTHUR LOVE JR
HERBERT G LOVE
MATTHEW LOVE
ROBERT J LOVE
ROBERT V LOVEDAY
LARRY LOVELESS
DONALD W LOVERN
JAMES T LOVETT
ANTHONY J LOVOLO
CHARLES R LOW
JAMES F LOWE
JAMES G LOWE
JOHNSON LOWE JR
RAY J LOWE
ROY LOWE
THOMAS LOWE
THURMAN J LOWE
WILLIAM R LOWE
JAMES E LOWERY
THOMAS E LOWERY
LYLE L LOWMAN
ROY G LOWMAN
ELLSWORTH J LOWRY
HARVEY E LUBY
IRVIN M LUBY
EARL B LUCAS
MARSHALL R LUCAS
RICHARD A LUCAS
ALFRED G LUCERO
ELIAS W LUCERO
LOUIS LUCERO
HERMINIO LUCIANO-RODRIGUEZ
EDWARD LUCID
PAUL LUCIK
JOSE B LUCIO
PABLO LUCIO
WARREN A LUCIO
HENRY LUCKE
JAMES E LUDWIG
SCHRADER E LUDWIG
SANTIAGO B LUERA
HAROLD E LUGENBEEL
HERMAN J LUJAN
ORVILLE D LUKE
HORACE LUKER
KING A LUM
CHARLES E LUNBECK JR
EDWARD A LUND
JOHN LUNDELIUS
WINSTON K LUNDERVOLD
JOHN F LUNDUSKI
RICHARD M LUNN
LLOYD B LUNSFORD
ARTHUR E LUSIGNAN
BILLY J LUSK
EUGENE V LUSZEWICZ
ANTHONY LUTI
BILLY J LUTZ
ROBERT G LUTZ
WILLIAM P LUYENDYK
ROBERT M LYDOLPH
BYRON K LYKINS
CLARENCE B LYKINS
WILLIE L LYLES
HAROLD P LYNCH
WILLIAM C LYNCH
WILLIAM T LYNCH
JAMES L LYNN
JESSE D LYONS

WAYNE B MAAS
FREDERICK D MAASBERG
PACIFICO MABANAG
ARNETT C MABRY
RICHARD W MACADAM
JAMES R MACDONALD
WILLIAM R MACDONALD
BERNARD A MACDOUGALL
JACKIE M MACE
WILLIAM B MACE
GILBERT V MACHADO
EDWARD P MACHALA
DANIEL J MACHCINSKI
MICHELO A MACINO
ARTEMUS A MACK
HERBERT U MACK
PAUL MACK JR
JOHN R MACKEY
WILLIAM L MACKEY
RICHARD B MACKIN
GLENN R MACKLEY
BILLY M MACLEOD
MALCOLM D MACLEOD
HAROLD P MACMUNN
ROBERT J MACON
WILLIAM H MADDEN
WILLIAM T MADDIX
PLEASANT M MADDOX
WILLIAM E MADDOX
ALPHONSO MADISON
HUBERT A MADOSH
LEONARD I MADRID
EUGENE MADRILEJO
EUGENE A MAECKEL
HANFORD K MAEDA
HILARIO A MAES
EDWARDO MAGANA
ALBERT J MAGERS
DALE L MAGERS
CECIL J MAGNER
LAWRENCE G MAGNUS
JAMES L MAGUIRE
LEO W MAGUIRE
JOHN B MAHER
MICHAEL F MAHER
KENNETH R MAHONEY
WALTER A MAHONEY
RICHARD W MAHR
DONALD A MAIER
GEORGE A MAITLAND
ARTHUR MAJESKE JR
LAWRENCE S L MAKI
MEREL R MALAK
DANIEL MALDONADO
LUCIANO M MALDONADO
PEDRO MALDONADO
RUDOLPH T MALDONADO
VICTOR S MALDONADO
RAFAEL MALDONADO-JIMENEZ
JAIME MALDONADO-MORALES
DANIEL D MALETTA
JERRY L MALEY
GENO J MALISE
HARRY E MALLERY
WILLIAM MALLICK JR
FRANCIS P MALONE JR
FRANCIS M MALONEY
GEORGE J MALOOL
OLIN B MALOTT
CHARLES P MALOY
ARTHUR W MALTAIS
DONALD F MALTESEN
GEORGE H MAMMES
GUY G MANCHESTER
RONALD J MANCINI
EUGENE T MANDICK
DONALD A MANDRIER
PATRICK J MANGAN
RICHARD A MANGAN
ROBY L MANGUM
CHARLES M MANHOLLAN
JAMES E MANN
BILL D MANNING
JAMES E MANNING
NORMAN S MANNING

JAMES S MANNINO
BILLY E MANRING
JAMES E MANSELL
BEVERLY S MANTON
FRANKLIN MANUEL
WILLIAM D MANUEL
BENNY MARAGIOGLIO
MYRON P MARBLE
ANTHONY J MARCHINO
ARMANDO R MARCIAS
O C MARCUS JR
SALVATORE A MARCUZZO
BENNIE Z MARES
PAUL F MARET
WALLACE K MARKLAND
JOHN M MARKO
DON D MARKS
EUGENE L MARKS
HARRY T MARKS
JAMES I MARKS JR
ROBERT A MARKS
JAMES E MARLER
FRED J MARLEY
FRANKIE D MARLOW
CHARLES S MARLOWE
GILBERT MARQUEZ
JASPER V MARQUEZ
JOHN T MARR
JOHN A MARREN
DARIUS M MARRERO
OTTO E MARSCHKE
FRENCH E MARSH
GEORGE W MARSH
TEDDY C MARSH
CALVIN C MARSHALL
CLARENCE E MARSHALL
ELLIS MARSHALL
FORREST M MARSHALL
GEORGE G MARSHALL
MERLIN E MARSHALL
PAUL J MARSHALL
RALPH E MARSHALL
RALPH I MARSHALL
BOBBY R MARSTON
DARELL L MARSTON
RONALD W MARTENS
WAYNE N MARTENS
ALBERT J MARTIN
BOYD M MARTIN
CHARLES L MARTIN
CLAUDE E MARTIN
CLYDE B MARTIN
CLYDE H MARTIN JR
EARL MARTIN
EDWARD L MARTIN
EDWARD R MARTIN
ELMER E MARTIN
EUGENE R MARTIN
GILBERT L MARTIN
GLEN R MARTIN
HARVEY J MARTIN
HERBERT O MARTIN
J D MARTIN
JAMES MARTIN
JAMES A MARTIN
JAMES F MARTIN
JAMES W MARTIN
JIMMIE G MARTIN
JOHN W MARTIN
JOHNNIE W MARTIN
JOSEPH J MARTIN
KENNETH E MARTIN
LADSON K MARTIN
NICHOLAS MARTIN
NICHOLAS P MARTIN
ROBERT C MARTIN
WILLIAM B MARTIN
WILLIAM H MARTIN JR
WILLIAM M MARTIN
WILLIAM R MARTIN
ALFREDO L MARTINEZ
ERNEST L MARTINEZ
JESUS P MARTINEZ
JOHN A MARTINEZ
JOSEPH A MARTINEZ
LEE R MARTINEZ
LUIS MARTINEZ
LUIS B MARTINEZ
LUIS P MARTINEZ JR
ROMEO M MARTINEZ

TRINIDAD MARTINEZ
WENCESLAO MARTINEZ
XAVIER P MARTINEZ
CRISTINO MARTINEZ-COLON
ISRAEL MARTINEZ-GONZALEZ
JUAN MARTINEZ-HERNANDEZ
LUIS MARTINEZ-HERNANDEZ
RAMON MARTINEZ-LANDRON
LUIS MARTINEZ-PASTRANA
RAFAEL MARTINEZ-ROSARIO
JOHN MARTINKO
EDWARD G MARTONE
ALBERT E MARTY
DONALD M MARX
JOHN M MASCH
JOHN L MASNARI
BILLIE F MASON
CHARLES D MASON
JAMES L MASON
KENNETH J MASON
LOWELL D MASON
PAUL MASON
RAY S MASON
RICHARD L MASON
THOMAS E MASON
THOMAS J MASON
WALTER J MASON
RAYMOND P MASPERI
ANTHONY MASSEY JR
EDWARD D MASSEY
ELMORE MASSIE
IVAN MAS-SILVA
MARCOS A MASSINI-TORRES
JORGE MASSO-FIGUEROA
DANIEL D MAST
STEVE A MASTABAYVO
EMMET P MASTERS
LOUIS R MASTERS
TOMMY E MASTERSON
ROBERT L MASTIN
BRONSON J MASTNE
WILLIAM A MASTROIANNI
GIOVANNI B MASTROINNI
DANIEL N MATA JR
FRANK C MATA
RANDOLPH E MATHER
GEORGE A MATHEWS
RICHARD J MATHEWS
HOWARD J MATHIS JR
JACK E MATHIS
JOHNNIE J MATHIS
MARIO MATIAS-REMIGIO
MICHAEL J MATONIS JR
PETER T MATSIKAS
EDWARD MATSON
HEISHIN MATSUDA
KUMAJI MATSUDA
RICHARD R MATTHESS
ARNOLD B MATTHEWS
GEORGE H MATTHEWS
ROBERT MATTHEWS
ROY W MATTHEWS
GERALD J MATTINGLY
HARRY E MATTIS JR
HERBERT H MATTOCKS
HENRY E MATTON JR
JAMES H MATTOON
WILLIE E MATTOX
HENRY J MATTSON
ANTHONY M MATTUCCI
MARIAN J MATUSZEWSKI
GREGORIA E MATUTINO
MELVIN R MATZEN
CHARLES R MAULDIN
SYDNEY R MAULDIN
CLIFTON W MAUPIN
DONALD V MAUS
HERBERT R MAX
IRA A MAXAM
FRANKIE L MAXEY

JOSEPH S MAXSON
HERBERT R MAXWELL
JOSEPH T MAXWELL
ALFRED MAY
DONALD R MAY
ELTON L MAY
GUS MAY
MELVIN C MAY
ROBERT N MAY
GEORGE M MAYBERRY
JOHNNY H MAYBERRY
CLINTON G MAYE
DONALD F MAYERLE
CHARLES F MAYES
JAMES D MAYES
ROBERT A MAYES
ROBERT C MAYES
LANNIS J MAYEUX
CHARLIE MAYFIELD JR
WILLIAM K MAYHUGH
JERRY K MAYNARD
RAY L MAYNARD
WILLIAM D MAYNARD
JOHN M MAYO
PAUL W MAZE
RALPH J MAZZAUFO
THOMAS F MAZZULLA
WILLIAM F MCADOO
DAVID E MCAFEE
EMMETT J MCALISTER
MICHAEL J MCALPIN
CHARLES H MCATEE
JAMES A MCATEER
DONALD J MCAVOY
ROBERT MCBRIDE
ROBERT L MCBRIDE
JACKIE L MCBROOM
HUGH G MCBRYDE
DONALD J MCCABE
JOHN E MCCABE
JOHN W MCCABE
ROBERT L MCCAIN
CLARENCE A MCCALL
MARVIN E MCCALL
HOLLIS R MCCALLISTER
WILLIAM F MCCALLISTER
KENNETH MCCARTAN
EDWARD J MCCARTHY
HAROLD P MCCARTNEY
WILLIAM J MCCARTNEY
TROY D MCCARTY
FRANK C MCCAULEY
CORNELIUS P MCCLAFFERTY
GAYLON L MCCLAINE
HERMAN L MCCLATCHEY
LEROY MCCLEAIN
ALFRED J MCCLINTOCK
WILLIAM MCCLUGGAGE
CHARLES E MCCLURE
CLARENCE MCCLURE JR
FERDINAND J MCCLURE
FRED H MCCLURE
GILBERT N MCCLURE
HERMAN C MCCLURE
JESSIE D MCCLURE
KENNETH C MCCLURE
LEROY S MCCLURE
SAM MCCLURE
RONALD P MCCLUSKEY
LUTHER E MCCLUSKY
LEE F MCCOATS
HERMAN L MCCOLLUM JR
LEON B MCCOLLUM
BEUFORD MCCOMAS
RONALD J MCCOMB
CLOYD M MCCOMBIE
ROBERT H MCCOMMONS
GERALD J MCCONKEY
PAUL MCCONNELL
RONNIE A MCCONNELL
MARSHALL MCCOOK
MICHAEL A MCCORMACK
CHARLES D MCCORMICK

39 ARMY

FRED G MCCORMICK
JAMES J MCCORMICK
ORAN MCCORMICK
ROBERT L MCCORMICK
WADE L MCCORMICK
RICHARD C MCCOWAN
CARL R MCCOY
CHARLES E MCCOY
DONALD MCCOY
GERALD V MCCOY
GRADY L MCCOY
JOE MCCOY
JOHN J MCCOY JR
SHAFTER MCCOY JR
BUFFORD E MCCRAW
LOUIS A MCCULLAR
JOHN G MCCULLIN
JOSEPH E MCCULLOUGH
ROBERT E MCCULLOUGH
ROBERT R MCCUNE
RICHARD E MCCURLEY
FREDDIE P MCDANIEL
HOWARD H MCDANIEL
HUGHLON MCDANIEL
JAY D MCDANIEL
JOHN H MCDANIEL
RAY E MCDANIEL
RAYMOND D MCDANIEL
WENDELL E MCDANIEL
EMMETT MCDAVID JR
EUGENE J MCDERMOTT
JOSEPH T MCDERMOTT JR
THOMAS E MCDERMOTT
BOBBY W MCDONALD
DONALD D MCDONALD
JACK MCDONALD
JAMES A MCDONALD
NORBERT A MCDONALD
RALPH G MCDONALD
ROGER G MCDONALD
JOHN J MCDONNELL
FESTUS J MCDONOUGH
JOHN C MCDONOUGH
PHILLIP J MCDONOUGH
ROBERT E MCDONOUGH
CHARLES W MCDOWELL JR
CLYDE R MCDOWELL
GEORGE C MCDOWELL
REED C MCDOWELL
CLEM D MCDUFFIE
BOB D MCELHANEY
PATRICK J MCELHOLM
CHARLES D MCENERNY
PATRICK MCENERY
LARRY C MCEWEN
KENDRICK A MCFADDEN
WILLIAM MCFADDEN
BILLIE E MCFALL
DAVID L MCFARLAND
DONN A MCFARLANE
EDWARD Q MCFARREN
JAMES J MCGARTH
DAVID F MCGEE
FLOYD D MCGEE
WALTER C MCGETTIGAN
WILLIE F MCGHEE JR
WILLIAM R MCGILL
CHARLES R MCGINNIS
JOHN J MCGINTY
OTHER G MCGINTY
HAROLD W MCGLOTHIN
CHARLES R MCGLYNN
JOHN P MCGONIGLE
JOHN P MCGOVERN
CLIFTON J MCGOWAN
DONALD MCGOWAN JR
EDWARD R MCGRATH
ORVILLE B MCGRATH
ROSS R MCGRATH
RICHARD P MCGRAW
JAMES L MCGUFFIN
BOBBY A MCGUIRE
EDWARD J MCGUIRE JR
PATRICK W MCGUIRE
STANLEY R MCGUIRE
WILLIE J MCGUIRE
EVERETT E MCHENRY
BROWNLOW
MCINTOSH JR
CURLIE MCINTOSH

CHARLES T MCINTYRE
DEAN I MCINTYRE
MARSHALL F MCKAIN
DONALD R MCKAY
HENRY L MCKEE
LOUIS F MCKEE
PAUL L MCKEE
HERBERT V MCKEEHAN
JOE P MCKEEHAN
KENNETH M MCKEEN
RICHARD A MCKELVEY
DANIEL MCKENNA
EDWARD J MCKENNA
RICHARD J MCKENNA
HUBERT MCKENZIE
JOHN L MCKENZIE
RONALD W MCKENZIE
DONALD L MCKEON
ROBERT E MCKEON
JOSEPH T A MCKEOWN
JOHN F MCKIBBIN
ROBERT J MCKIE
ROBERT B MCKIM
GORDON L MCKINLEY
JOHN MCKINLEY JR
KONRAD J MCKINLEY
RALPH H MCKINLEY
CHARLES T MCKINNEY
PRESTON L MCKNIGHT
BILLY J MCLAIN
MCDOYLE MCLANE
CLINTON G MCLAUGHLIN
JACK E MCLAUGHLIN
JOHN J MCLAUGHLIN
JOSEPH E MCLAUGHLIN
PAUL J MCLAUGHLIN
RAYMOND
MCLAUGHLIN
ANDREW G MCLEOD
WALTER L MCLEOD JR
WILLIAM MCLEOD
PETER J MCLINKO
DWIGHT D MCMAHON
JAMES P MCMAHON
BILLY E MCMANUS
GEORGE H MCMANUS
PAUL D MCMANUS
KENNETH E MCMEEKIN
MICHAEL S MCMENAMIN
JAMES L MCMILLAN
HAROLD D MCMILLON
HARRY E MCMULLEN
DONALD E MCMURRAY
WILLIAM E MCMURTRIE
GEORGE W MCNAMARA
RAYMOND J
MCNAMARA
ROBERT E MCNAMARA
CLARENCE E MCNAMES
WALTER D MCNARY
DONALD MCNAUGHTON
O M MCNEAL
ROBERT D MCNEAL
CHARLES M MCNEIL
FRANCIS L MCNEIL
RICHARD G MCNEIL JR
ROBERT W MCNEIL
CURTIS MCNEILL
PATRICK J MCNULTY
WILLIAM H MCNUTT
WILLIAM N MCPHERSON
CLINTON MCRAE
EDWARD P MCSHANE
ROBERT L MCSHAW
THOMAS MCVICKER
MARION G MEACHAM JR
WILLIAM C MEAD
FREEMAN R MEADE
CHARLES R MEADOWS
ERNEST C MEADOWS
JESSE C MEADOWS
KENNETH W MEADOWS
MERLE L MEADOWS
HOMER G MEARS
ROY C MEATHENIA
DOUGLAS F MEBANE
EDMUND B MEDEIROS
RAMON MEDERO
LOY L MEDINA
LARRY O MEEKS

RAYMOND L MEGERLE
JAMES J MEGLAN
EARL R MEHAFFEY
JOSEPH L MEHER JR
LEO M MEHLER
FREDRICK MEHLHORN
GEORGE H MEIER JR
OTTO A MEIER
RICHARD W MEIGGS
HOMER L MEINEN
AUGUST W MEINHARDT JR
KENNETH W MEINTS
CHARLES F MEISNER
DAVID T MEJIA
EDWARD MEKILO
JOHN H MELDRUM JR
GILBERT MELENDEZ
JOSE M MELENDEZ
EUGENIO MELENDEZ-
CINTRON
ROBERTO MELENDEZ-
SANCHEZ
BILLIE G MELTON
CHARLES W MELTON
J P MELTON
JAMES A MELTON
WILLIAM S MELTON
CHARLES MELVIN
CLIFFORD E MELVIN
RALPH L MELVIN
RICHARD C MELVIN
GAYLARD D MELVOLD
EDWARD MENARD
WALTER C MENARD
JOE G MENCHACA
CLARENCE R MENCLEWICZ
JOHN C MENDEL
ROBERT E MENDENHALL
JOSEPH R MENDONCA
JAMES J MENDOZA
JERRY J MENDOZA
JOSEPH MENDOZA
JOSEPH R MENDOZA
MANUEL MENDOZA
ROBERT R MENSCH
CLOYD L MENSER
HUGH MENZIES JR
ELIAS MERCADO
HUMBERTO MERCADO JR
LOUIE MERCADO
RAFAEL MERCADO-
ANDINO
JOSE MERCADO-GOMBOA
JOSEPH H R MERCIER
VINCENT J MEROLA JR
ANTHONY G MERRIETT
KENNETH W MERRILL
ROY T MERRIMAN
DONALD R MERRITHEW
JAMES MERRITT
DAVID F MERSHON
ALLEN C MERTES
EDGAR MERZ JR
HAROLD R MESSER
DONALD D METCALF
EDWARD M METCALF
GENE A METZ
GILBERT METZGER
JOSEPH D METZO
NORMAN O MEUNIER
HARRY MEYER JR
JAMES E MEYER
JOSEPH K MEYER
RODNEY K MEYER
WAYNE O MEYER
WILLIAM MEYER
CHARLES E MEYERS
WAYNE A MEYERS
RENE MEZA
JOSEPH MICEL JR
RAYMOND A MICELE
JAMES P MICELI
EDWARD E
MICENHAMMER
JUNIOR E MICHAEL
WILLIAM F MICHAEL
MELVIN J MICHAELS
LELAND P MICHALAK
JOSEPH E G MICHAUD
ALVIN J MICHEL

MAX R MICHIEL
LEWIS V MICK
JAKE E MICKAEL
LEON E MICKELSON
ROBERT MICKELSON
ROBERT D MICKLE
DONALD MIDDENDORF
RALPH MIDDLETON
ALEXANDER J MIDGETT
ROBERT C MIELKE
ERNEST MIER
JOSEPH R MIEZEJEWSKI
HARRY MIGUEL
LLOYD L MIGUEL
CARNELL J MIKELL
HAROLD E MIKESELL
CHARLES N MILAM
LIN MILAM
GILBERT D MILBURN
CHARLES A MILES
CLAUD MILES
CLIFTON F MILES
CLYDE C MILES
HERBERT A MILES
VERNON J MILGATE
GEORGE H MILK
GUSTAVO A MILLAN
BILLY F MILLER
BOBBY MILLER
CHARLES D MILLER
CHARLES E MILLER
CHARLES E MILLER JR
DONALD G MILLER
EDISON W MILLER
EDMUND H MILLER JR
ELBERT MILLER
ERLING P MILLER
ERVIN A MILLER
EUGENE E MILLER
EUGENE R MILLER
GUS E MILLER
HARLAN H MILLER
HARRY L MILLER
HERMAN W MILLER
JACK H MILLER
JACKIE E MILLER
JAMES L MILLER
JOHN G MILLER
JOHN T MILLER
JOHNNIE E MILLER
JOSEPH C MILLER
KENNETH R MILLER
L C MILLER
LLOYD E MILLER
LLOYD K MILLER
MERLE W MILLER
MIKE A MILLER JR
PAUL E MILLER
RAYMOND E MILLER
RAYMOND L MILLER
RICHARD E MILLER
ROBERT C MILLER
ROBERT D MILLER
ROBERT G MILLER
ROBERT G MILLER
ROBERT L MILLER
ROBERT S MILLER
RUBY L MILLER
THOMAS W MILLER
TRENTON S MILLER
VERDIS L MILLER
VERNON R MILLER
WALTER C MILLER
WILLIAM F MILLER
WILMAR R MILLER
ROBERT M MILLNER
ALVIN F MILLS
BRUCE R MILLS
DONALD F MILLS
DOYLE MILLS
EDDIE L MILLS
EUGENE O MILLS
HILERY W MILLS
LAIRD C MILLS
MARVIN L MILLS
THERLOUS MILLS
WALTER T MILLS JR
WILLIAM E MILLS
WILLIAM J MILLS
EUGENE G MILLSAPS

JUDSON A
MILLSPAUGH JR
WALLACE D MILNER
WILLARD H MILNER
CHARLES W MILTON
VINCENT A MIMM
WILLIAM W MIMS
TAE-SIK MIN
GEORGE Y MINAKATA
LEONARD E MINEER
ANDREW J MINER
DONALD W MINER
RONALD S MINIARD
MATTHEW A
MINICHILLO
ROBERT W MINKLER
EARL G MINNICK
CHARLES M MINOR
JOHN MINOR
T L MINOR JR
TRAVIS E MINOR
HAROLD C MINYARD
ERASTO MIRANDA
VICTOR M MIRANDA
JAMES E MISHLER
GERALD L MISNER
EUGENE R MISNIK
ALFRED D MITCHELL JR
BENNIE H MITCHELL
BOBBY A MITCHELL
DELFORD MITCHELL
EVERETT L MITCHELL
FRANCIS L MITCHELL
JOHN MITCHELL JR
JOHN MITCHELL JR
JOHN W MITCHELL
RICHARD W MITCHELL
ROBERT MITCHELL
ROBERT E MITCHELL
ROBERT E MITCHELL
WILLIAM B MITCHELL JR
WILLIAM D MITCHELL
DONALD S MIYAJIMA
DANIEL T MIYASHIRO
TAMOTSU MIYASHIRO
TSUNEMATSU
MIZUSAWA
EUGENE MOATS
HERBERT A MOATS
MELVIN L MOATS
PEPPINO N MOBILIO
RUFUS D MOBLEY
WILLIS W MOBLEY
RAYMOND D MOCCIO
ALBERT D MOEN
FRANK R MOEN
HOWARD M MOEN
CLARENCE R
MOENING JR
FLOYD W MOFFITT
SAMUEL D MOGG
WILLIAM A MOHLMAN
RICHARD E
MOHOWITSCH
HARRY A MOHR
RICHARD D MOHR
AUGUST A MOLINA
BENJAMIN MOLINA
EPIPHANIO G MOLINA
JUAN MOLINA-GUZMAN
ANTHONY MOLINARO
ADOLFO MOLINARY-
DE SANCHEZ
SANTOS MOLINA-
SERRANO
LOUIS N MOLINO
JAMES A MOLNAR
LOUIS MOLNAR
MARVIN L MOLTER
DAVID P MOMPHER
EUGENE J MONAGHAN
JESSIE MONDAY
JEREMIAH F
MONGAN JR
WALTER J MONGEON
STANLEY T MONKUT
JACK D MONNOT
NAPOLEON MONROE
FRED W MONSON JR
ALFRED J MONTAGNA

40 ARMY

GUY E MONTAGUE JR
JOHN W MONTAGUE JR
PAT MONTANA
JOHN MONTANO JR
TONY A MONTANO
DONALD D MONTELEONE
ANDREW J MONTELLO
C W MONTGOMERY
FLOYD W MONTGOMERY
JAMES C MONTGOMERY
FELES MONTOYA
JOE E MONTOYA
JOSE P MONTOYA
RONALD E MONTROSS
BOBBY E MOODY
HORACE A MOODY
JOEY MOODY
ROBERT J MOODY
KENNETH L MOOMEY
FRANCIS J MOONEY
JOHN MOONEY
ARTHUR A MOONEYHAM
CALVIN L MOONEYHAM
ALFRED H MOORE JR
BENNY A MOORE
CHARLES I MOORE
CLARENCE N MOORE
CURTIS MOORE
DAVID L MOORE
DORSE MOORE
EARL J MOORE
FLOYD E MOORE
GEORGE J MOORE
HERCULES MOORE
JACK MOORE
JAMES R MOORE
JOHN D MOORE
JOHN H MOORE
JOHN L MOORE
JOHN M MOORE
JOHN W MOORE
JOHNNIE E MOORE
JOSEPH F MOORE
LENZEY MOORE
LOUIS A MOORE
LUCIEN S MOORE
MILFORD J MOORE
MORRIS G MOORE
MYRAL N MOORE
ROY E MOORE
THOMAS E MOORE
THOMAS F MOORE JR
THOMAS O MOORE JR
THOMAS P MOORE
THOMAS R MOORE
W C MOORE
WILLIAM C MOORE
PAUL MOOSE
CARLOS Y MORALES
JOSEPH S MORALES
TONY MORALES
CRISTOBAL MORALES-LOZADA
HOWARD E MORAN
JAMES E MORANY
ANDREW J MOREN
JOE G MORENO
RAMON R MORENO
ADOLFO MORENO-TIRADO
RAYMOND E MORFORD
HOWARD A MORGAN
HOWARD J MORGAN
JACK W MORGAN
JAMES A MORGAN
JOHN A MORGAN
LAWRENCE D MORGAN
RALPH C MORGAN
VERN A MORGAN
PAUL E MORGENSTERN
HENRY I MORIARTY
JENRO MORILLO
JAMES M MORISAKO
DONALD E MORISSETT
KIOCHI MORIWAKI
FUMIO MORIYAMA
DAVID A MORNINGSTAR
JAMES E MORPHEW
ALBERT H MORRIS
BURTIS L MORRIS JR

CHARLES G MORRIS
FORREST P MORRIS
GEORGE J MORRIS
HARRY R MORRIS
HUGH J MORRIS
JAMES R MORRIS
JOHN P MORRIS
MARION E MORRIS
MILTON MORRIS JR
RONALD G MORRIS
RONALD R MORRIS
RUFUS R MORRIS
WILLIAM A MORRIS
WILMER W MORRIS
THOMAS O MORRISH
CLARENCE T MORRISON
JAMES F MORRISON
LANE MORRISON
RAYMOND H MORRISON
WILLIAM F MORRISON
CHARLES L MORRISS
EDMUND V MORRISSEY
JOYCE R MORROW
ROBERT S MORROW
CHALMIS L MORRRIS
DALE B MORSE
DURLIN J MORSE
ROBERT C MORSE
WILBUR G MORSE
WILLIAM C MORTESEN
FLOYD MORTON
JOHN A MOSELEY
EARNEST MOSER
MAX H MOSER
WALTER MOSES JR
CHARLES R MOSLANDER
JAMES MOSLEY
WILLARD L MOSLEY
HESSEY C MOSS
THOMAS A MOSSO
SENATOR MOTEN JR
CLAUDE B MOTLEY JR
JOHN D MOTLEY
MADISON MOTON
SHIZUO MOTOYAMA
MUREL R MOTT
GORDON C MOTZ
FOREST E MOUGEY
FRANCIS C MOULTANE
CHARLES H MOUNCE
CARL E MOURER
ROBERT W MOUSER
HARVE C MOWRY
LEWIS G MOXLEY
ISIDORE A MOY
HOBERT C MOYE
MANUEL R MOYEDA
KENNETH D MOYNITHAN
RALPH C MOZEE
LEONARD F MRAZEK
DONALD E MROTEK
FRANK L MUDRYK
ALVIN F MUECK
EDWARD C MUELLER
EDWIN H MUELLER
HERMAN B MUELLER
LAWRENCE C MUELLER
MORTON D MUELLER
NORBERT J MULGREW
JACK R MULHOLLEN
GEORGE MULIK
DELBERT E MULINEX
BILL T MULKEY
THOMAS L MULL
DONALD MULLANE
JAMES E MULLARKEY
JIM G MULLEN
ROLAND B MULLEN
PAUL F MULLICANE
VERNON G MULLIGAN
CARL H MULLIN JR
STACY A MULLINAX JR
JAMES C MULLINS
JOE S MULLINS
PATRICK A MULLINS
JOHN W MULVENNA
BANG-U MUN
DAE-HO MUN
DEOK-SANG MUN
DU-SIK MUN

EUNG-BOK MUN
JAE-HONG MUN
JAE-YEOL MUN
JANG-JU MUN
JEONG-HWAN MUN
JONG-SUN MUN
SANG-HO MUN
YEONG-HWAN MUN
WILLIAM A MUNCY
ALBERT O MUNIZ-TORRES
PETER MUNJIAN
OLIVER B MUNN
JOHN S MUNOS
JOSE E MUNOZ
DAVIS S MUNS
MELVIN O MUNSON
DONALD L MUNSTER
TSUKASA MURAOKA
YUKIO MURATA
JOHN J MURDICH
DALE MURDOCK
JACKIE L MURDOCK
HARRY E MURNIGHAN
CALVIN B MURPHREE
GLEN W MURPHY
JOHN F MURPHY
KENNETH H MURPHY
RICHARD J MURPHY
ROBERT M MURPHY
THOMAS C MURPHY JR
THOMAS E MURPHY
THOMAS J MURPHY
WILLIAM F MURPHY
WILLIAM J MURPHY
WINFERD R MURPHY
ARNOLD L MURRAY
DUANE L MURRAY
FREDERICK MURRAY
HAROLD B MURRAY
IZEI MURRAY
LUTHER E MURRAY
RAYMOND M MURRAY
ROBERT J MURRAY
VICTOR R MURRAY
WILLIAM L MURRAY
MIKE MURRIETA
EUGENE E MURTAUGH
JOSEPH MUSHKO
EDWARD D MUSHRUSH
EDWARD M MUSICH
VIRGIL D MUSSELMAN
FRANK A MUTH
RAPHERD C MUXLOW
CALVIN A MYATT
GYU-GEUN MYEONG
BOBBY G MYER
GEORGE D MYER
ALLIE E MYERS
BRYAN MYERS JR
CAROL R MYERS
FRED K MYERS
GEORGE W MYERS
GUY K MYERS
LEON C MYERS
ROBERT J MYERS
THOMAS MYLES
EDGAR L MYNATT
HORACE E MYRICK
EDWIN J MYSLINSKI
VERNON MZHICKTENO
JAE-HUI NA
JU-WON NA
JOHN H NABORS
JOHN E NAETZKER
FERRIS J NAHAS
SEISO NAKAMA
NOBORU NAKAMURA
WATARU NAKAMURA
SATOSHI NAKASATO
SHINICHI NAKATA
JOSEPH J NALEPKA
CHAN-U NAM
EOK-I NAM
GI-CHANG NAM
GI-HO NAM
GI-SEOP NAM
HYEONG-NAM NAM
HYO-GUK NAM
JEOM-BONG NAM
JIN-HUI NAM

MAN-SIK NAM
SEOK-GYU NAM
SEOK-WON NAM
RAYMOND J NAMBA
CHARLES F NANCE
JOHN J NANNERY JR
ALFRED W NAPIER
JOSE A NAPOLEON-ESCUDERO
AGAPITO D NARANJO
MARTIN R NAREY
REINALDO NARVAEZ
MARINE NARVAEZ-MONTALVO
CHARLES NASH
JOSEPH NASIELSKI
REX E NASON
LOUIS F NATALE
AUREO NAVARRO-MATOS
JOSE E NAVARRO-RODRIGUEZ
CLIFFORD M NAYLOR
JOHN E NAYLOR
JOHN L NAYLOR
EARL C NAZELROD
ALFRED L NEAL
CLARENCE J NEAL
DUANE B NEAL
FRANK A NEAL
JESSIE P NEAL
ROBERT B NEAL
SILAS NEAL JR
HARRY NEANOVER
SANFORD C NEARHOOF JR
CLYDE L NEARPASS
CHARLES F NEARY
PHILIP E NEAVIL
GEORGE R NEDLEY JR
AL G NEEDHAM
ROBERT NEELY JR
RICHARD H NEER
R BENTLEY NEESE
RICHARD E NEFF
ROBERT E NEFF
TED C NEFF
CARLOS M NEGRON
JAMES H NEIGHBORS
NORMAN L NEIHEISEL
JOSEPH J NEITZER
ALVIN H NELSON
BENJAMIN F NELSON JR
CARL T NELSON
CHARLES L NELSON
CLAYBURN E NELSON
ELI M NELSON
ERNEST E NELSON
HERBERT S NELSON
JAMES A NELSON
JAMES E NELSON
JAMES H NELSON
JAMES L NELSON
JOHN NELSON JR
LAURENCE H NELSON
PAUL R NELSON
SAM NELSON JR
THOMAS E NELSON
THURMAN E NELSON
WILLIAM A NELSON
WILLIAM B NELSON JR
WILMONT A NELSON
ALEX L NEMETH
CECIL E NESBIT
DUNNICK N NESS
JOHN H NESS
DAVID L NESTOR
OSCAR H NETTLES
CURTIS T NEUE
DONALD M NEUFELD
GARY J NEUMANN
CANDIDO NEVAREZ-DIAZ
FRED G NEVILLE
WILLIE I NEW JR
JAMES L NEWBAUER
JAMES R NEWBERRY
CHARLES E NEWCOMB
CHARLES E NEWEL
CALVIN C NEWELL
JEROME E NEWELL
TOMMY NEWELL

BILLY G NEWMAN
GEORGE R NEWMAN
GERALD L NEWMAN
JACK D NEWMAN
LAMAR E NEWMAN
LEONARD H NEWMAN
MARVIN L NEWMAN
SYLVESTER NEWMAN
THOMAS H NEWMAN
JOHNIE R NEWSOME
CHARLES L NEWTON
RICHARD C NEWTON
CHARLES H NEY
FELIX R NEZ
GEORGE K S NG
LOUIS B NICHOL
ROBERT L NICHOLAS
BERNARD N NICHOLS
HERMAN R NICHOLS
JOE H NICHOLS
SYLVESTER NICHOLS JR
MEMMINGER A NICHOLSON
WILLARD E NICKENS
LONNIE NICKLES
AUGUST M NICOLAI
HERBERT A NICOLAUS JR
ROBERT A NICOLL
HAROLD B NIDIFFER JR
KENNETH W NIEB
JOSEPH G NIEBERLEIN
HOWARD C NIELSEN
HOWARD W NIEMEYER
ROY M NIER
JUAN E NIEVES-CASTRO
CARLOS M NIEVES-LOPEZ
DANIEL NIEVES-MORALES
ARNOLD E NIEWALD
RICHARD K NIREI
RICHARD K NISHIDA
ERNEST B NITSCHE JR
DANIEL J NIWA
DANIEL W NIXDORF
BYEONG-GIL NO
GYU-HWAN NO
JAE-UK NO
SANG-OK NO
YUN-GON NO
WILLIAM NOBLE JR
WAYNE O NOBLES
ROY V NOCETI
ERNEST W NOCKEMAN
JAMES L NOE
ROBERTO V NOGALES JR
THOMAS J NOLAN
WILLIAM D NOLAN
WILBUR W NOLDA
ARTHUR P NOLEN
ROBERT A NOLEN
WILLIE E NOLEN
JAKE R NOLL
WILLIAM W NOLZE
GERALD M NOONE
JOHN G NORDSTROM
HAROLD K NORFLEET
CLARENCE NORICE JR
JOHN A NORLANDER
RALEIGH T NORLIEN
VINCENT P NORLING
JOHN F NORMAN
BILLY B NORRIS
HOWARD G NORRIS
JOHN A NORRIS
LLEWELLYN F NORRIS
MERLE E NORRIS
THURKESE NORRIS
PHILIP W NORSEWORTHY
VIRGIL L NORTHCUTT
LEON NORTON
ROBERT D NORTON
TOMMIE L NORWOOD
HENRY C NOTBUSCH
WILLIAM J NOTTER
DONALD W NOVACEK
JERRY O NOVAK
MIKE R NOVAK
NORBERT A NOVOTNY

41 ARMY

EDWARD D NOWACZYK
BERT J NOWAKOWSKI JR
DONALD R NULLMEYER
RAYMOND NUNEZ JR
LOUIS G NUXOLL
AARON NYDICK
CHANG-HWAN O
CHUN-SIK O
GEUN-SU O
GI-TAE O
IN-GWAN O
JEOM-SU O
JONG-HWAN O
MUN-JU O
SEONG-YEOL O
SUN-GYUN O
YONG-EOP O
YONG-GIL O
YUN-PIL O
WALTER R OAK
JOSEPH S OAKS
PAUL N OAKS
DOUGLAS A OATES
NELSON I G OATSVALL
TADASHI OBANA
WILLIAM OBERRY
DONALD P OBRIEN
PAUL T OBRIEN
ARNOLD OCHOA
HERADIO OCHOA
MARCOS M OCHOA
BERNARD R OCONNELL
EDMUND D OCONNELL
JAMES E OCONNELL
DONALD G OCONNOR
WILLIAM J OCONNOR
RUSSELL M ODBERG
GORDON L ODELL
ROBERT L ODELL
THOMAS C ODENBAUGH
CARL ODIERNO
BILLY J ODOM
JESSIE ODOM
DANIEL T ODONNELL
EDWARD F ODONNELL
OREN M ODUM
LEONARD M OFFICER
SUETOSHI OGATA
JOE H OGBURN
RICHARD OGIER
MICHAEL J OGINSKI
LEROY OGLE
JAMES E OGRADY
TAKEO OGUSUKU
THOMAS R OHANLON
CHARLES A OHEARN
ROBERT G OHLER
CHI-HYEON OK
MAURICE F OKAIN
ARTHUR I OKAMURA
EUGENE W OKEEFE
JOHN F OKEEFE
HISAO OKIMOTO
CLIFFORD H OKINAGA
HIROSHI OKU
ANTONIO M OLACHEA
EDWARD J OLDENBURG JR
VINCENT M OLDING
PETER OLEARCHIK
PETER OLES
ALFREDO B OLGUIN
LOUIS D OLGUIN
VICTOR OLISH
ALBERT R OLIVAS
HAROLD E OLIVER
KENNETH E OLIVER
MACK C OLIVER
WILLIAM J OLIVER
ALBERT OLLIE JR
CHARLES L OLLOM
HUGH A OLSEN
LUDVIG E OLSEN
ALBERT S OLSON
GEORGE H OLSON
JOHN E OLSON
LELON A OLSON
RICHARD L OLSON
SIGURD C OLSON
STANLEY R OLSON
VERNON D OLSON
DONALD W OLSZEWSKI
LEONARD OLSZEWSKI
ROBERT L OLT
CHARLES R L OLTMAN
LOUIS OLUICH
ROBERT OLVERA
JAMES E OMALLEY
ROBERT ONDISH
CLAYTON L ONEIL
EDWARD ONEILL
FRED C ONEILL
JOHN H ONEILL
MORRIS A ONEILL
MILTON T ONOMURA
GEORGE F OQUINN
ARTHUR P OREAR
RICHARD B OREILLY
EDWARD D ORNDORFF
RICHARD L OROARK
DONALD A ORR
MILTON L ORR
RICHARD T ORR
JOE H ORREN
ROBERT C ORRIS
EPPIE J ORTEGA
JOSE H ORTEGA
VICERO ORTEGA-NIEVES
MANUEL ORTEGA-PEREZ
FRED G ORTIZ
LUIS A ORTIZ
RAFAEL ORTIZ-CAMACHO
DANIEL ORTIZ-CLAUDIO
JUAN ORTIZ-COSME
RAMON ORTIZ-DURAN
CIRILO ORTIZ-NEGRON
ESTEBAN ORTIZ-RODRIQUEZ
ANDREW J ORZEHOWSKI
DONALD G OSBORN
JAMES P OSBORN
WILLIAM T OSBORN
CHARLES F OSBORNE
JOHN H OSBORNE
RICHARD A OSBORNE
ROBERT W OSBORNE
ROBERT OSBY
ALFRED J OSHEA
KENNETH A OSHINSKI
FELIX OSORIO-MARTINEZ
JOSEPH F OSOVICK JR
ARNOLD J OSTENDORF
ROBERT H OSTENDORF
ROBERT H OSTERBERG
ROBERT D OSTLER
CHESTER OSTROWSKI
THEODORE OSTROWSKI
GAYLON C OSWALT JR
LOUIS OTERO
ALEJANDRO OTERO-COLON
CLIFFORD L OTIS
JOHN E OTT
KENNETH J OTT
GEROME E OTTERSON
CHARLES F OTTO
WILLIAM E OTTO
GEORGE W OUELLET
JOSEPH R OUELLETTE
JACOB K OVERBAY
CLAYTON OVERBEE
CLAUD OWEN
GLEN R OWEN
HERBERT R OWEN
PAUL C OWEN
REUBEN D OWEN
BERNARD A OWENS
BILLY E OWENS
EDISON F OWENS
ERWIN P OWENS
JESSIE OWENS JR
JOHN R OWENS
NORRIS OWENS
VOLA J OWENS
BILL F OWSLEY
RALPH M OZBUN
WALTER E OZIAS
EDSEL PAAVOLA
CHARLIE J PACE
CASIMIRO PACHECO
YILUARDE PACHECO-BARTOLOMEI
LUIS PACHECO-LESPIER
THOMAS R PACINI
LEO M PACKER
PANTOLION M PACLEB
RICHARD M PADEN
WILLIAM J PADGETT
GILBERTO J PADILLA
RAUL PADILLA
CARMELO PADIN-RUIZ
ALBERT W PAEPKE JR
HARRY E PAETZ
CECIL E PAGE
JAMES W PAGE
JERRY J PAGE
LOVELL PAGE
RUFFUS D PAGE
CHARLES T PAGEL
JACK G PAINE
KENNETH E PAINTER JR
JAMES PALENAPA
AUGUST P PALLASIA
ROBERT G PALLESEN
BUD T PALMATIER
BOB R PALMER
JOHN W PALMER
STEPHEN G PALMER
THOMAS L PALMER
CLARENCE W PALSGROVE
JOE M PANARO
PETER J PANETSKI
ANTHONY F PANETTA
HOOVER T H PANG
JIMMY PANTOZOPULOS
JOHN C PAPADEMETRIOU
RAPHAEL J PAPARILLO JR
JOHN M PAPICH
SAM W PAPPAS
CHARLES N PARADEIS
JOHN R PARADISE
CHARLES G PARISH
JOHN F PARISH JR
BAE-GEUN PARK
BAE-GYU PARK
BEOM-EUN PARK
BONG-GWAN PARK
BONG-JO PARK
BONG-YUN PARK
BYEONG-GWON PARK
BYEONG-HYEON PARK
BYEONG-YUN PARK
CHANG-JU PARK
CHANG-RYEON PARK
CHEOL-GYU PARK
CHEOL-JUN PARK
CHEON-SUL PARK
CHI-SU PARK
CHUN-SIK PARK
DAE-DEUK PARK
DEOK-DONG PARK
DEOK-GON PARK
DEOK-I PARK
DEOK-MAN PARK
DEOK-YUN PARK
DONG-GEUN PARK
DONG-MUN PARK
DONG-MUN PARK
DONG-SEOK PARK
DO-SAENG PARK
DU-HA PARK
DU-HUI PARK
DU-SAM PARK
EOK-JI PARK
EON-HWAN PARK
GIL-BONG PARK
GI-MOK PARK
GI-NAM PARK
GI-RYONG PARK
GI-SE PARK
GU-RYONG PARK
HAE-CHEOL PARK
HAN-HO PARK
HAN-HYO PARK
HAN-SIK PARK
HO-IM PARK
HONG-I PARK
HOWARD G PARK
HUI-JO PARK
HUI-MUN PARK
HUI-SU PARK
HUI-SU PARK
HYEONG-GEUN PARK
IL-DO PARK
IN-GYU PARK
IN-GYU PARK
I-YONG PARK
JAE-BU PARK
JAE-GEUN PARK
JAE-MYEONG PARK
JAE-SIK PARK
JAE-SIK PARK
JAE-WAN PARK
JAE-WAN PARK
JAE-YUN PARK
JANG-GYU PARK
JEOM-BONG PARK
JEOM-SIK PARK
JEONG-DU PARK
JEONG-MU PARK
JEON-HYEON PARK
JI-HAN PARK
JIN-HWAN PARK
JO-JE PARK
JONG-CHUN PARK
JONG-HYEOK PARK
JONG-JIN PARK
JUN-YEOL PARK
MAL-YONG PARK
MIN-GYU PARK
NAM-SIK PARK
NAM-SU PARK
NO-CHUN PARK
PIL-SU PARK
SA-HO PARK
SAM-SEOK PARK
SANG-CHEOL PARK
SANG-RAE PARK
SANG-WON PARK
SA-OK PARK
SEON-GEUN PARK
SEONG-GYO PARK
SEONG-GYU PARK
SU-CHEON PARK
SU-HYEON PARK
SUN-MUN PARK
SU-YONG PARK
TAE-GYU PARK
TAE-IK PARK
TAE-JIN PARK
TAE-YUN PARK
UN-HAK PARK
WILSON PARK
WON-HO PARK
WON-JO PARK
WON-SUL PARK
YEONG-GU PARK
YEONG-HO PARK
YEONG-HO PARK
YEONG-HWAN PARK
YEONG-JO PARK
YEONG-RAE PARK
YEONG-SEON PARK
YEONG-SIK PARK
YEONG-SUL PARK
YONG-RAE PARK
YONG-SEON PARK
YONG-SEOP PARK
YONG-SU PARK
YONG-SUN PARK
YU-HWAN PARK
YUN-GEUN PARK
YUN-GYU PARK
ALFRED P PARKER
BILLY L PARKER
CHARLES D PARKER
CHARLES R PARKER
CLINTON W PARKER
EDWARD S PARKER
FLOYD B PARKER
JACK D PARKER
JAMES E PARKER
MEDFORD O PARKER
OSCAR B PARKER
PATSEY C PARKER
ROBERT H PARKER
STANLEY PARKER
THOMAS L PARKER
ALFRED PARKS
DOUGLAS A PARKS
EDWARD C PARKS
HAROLD P PARKS
JACK F PARKS
JAMES H PARKS
JOHN L PARKS
RALPH L PARKS
HAROLD J PARKSION
MARTIN H PARLET
WILLIAM E PARMER
JESUS C PARRA
WILLIAM E PARRA
LEROY PARRISH
RAY PARROTT
MAX B PARSON
CHARLES W PARSONS
DARRELL J PARSONS
EARL J PARSONS
HARRY F PARSONS
JULIAN K PARSONS
GENERAL H PARTIN
JAMES V PARZIALE
ALFRED R PASCHELKE
EDWARD A PASCOE
JAMES F PASELL
JAMES S PASHNEE
WAYNE F PASS
ROSARIO J PASSARELLI
WALTER J PASTUSZEK
BILLY C PATE
JACK K PATE
ARMAND A PATENAUDE
ELMIRO PATITUCCI
GEORGE J PATRICK
HOMER T PATRICK
JAMES PATRICK
EDWIN E PATTEN
JAMES PATTEN JR
ROY M PATTEN
BILLY J PATTERSON
CLARENCE F PATTERSON
CLAUZELL PATTERSON
HAROLD F PATTERSON
JAMES S PATTERSON
JAMES W PATTERSON
REGINALD W PATTERSON
JACK D PATTON
JAMES A PATTON
JOHNNY L PATTON
ROBERT E PATTON
WALLACE D PATTON
KENNETH D PAUL
ROBERT L PAUL
RALPH PAULEY
LUTHER R PAULING
JESUS PAULOMA
WAYNE H PAULSEN
ROBERT J PAUN
JOSEPH PAVLAK
DALKO D PAVLETICH
ROBERT S PAVLICK
ANTONI M PAWLIK
CALVIN F L PAYNE
CHARLES E PAYNE
ERNEST E PAYNE
EUGENE E PAYNE
FRANK D PAYNE
HAROLD B PAYNE
JAKE PAYNE
JOHN A PAYNE
ROBERT L PAYNE
THOMAS L PAYNE
WILLIAM G PAYTON JR
AARON PEARCE
CARL W PEARL
LOUIS G PEARL
HENRY C PEARSON
JAMES R PEARSON
JIMMY F PEARSON
RICHARD E PEASE
BILLY R PEAVEY
ALBERT PECHA
RICHARD L PEDERSEN
DELBERT J PEDERSON
LEROY O PEDERSON
MARVIN W PEDERSON
ANGEL O PEDROZA
MARCEL C PEETERS
JOHN H PEKKALA
CLAUDE PELLETIER

MAYNARD M PELLINEN
WILLIAM H PELTON
THOMAS R PEMBLE
LOUIE PENA
URBANO PENA
RAFAEL PENA-RODRIQUEZ
VANCE L PENDARVIS
SYLVESTER PENDER
WILLIS W PENDERGRAF
MICHAEL PENGRIN
ARNOLD PENN
ROBERT J PENN
NICHOLAS PENNA
JAMES H PENNINGTON
LOUIS A PENNINGTON
ROBERT A PENNY
PAUL P PENSAK
HENRY T PEOPLES
EDWARD J PEPIN
ALOYSIUS PEPION JR
FIDEL PERALTA
GEORGE A PERDRIZET JR
ROLAND M PERELL
ERNEST H PERES
ALFRED PEREZ
ALONZO PEREZ
ARTHUR J PEREZ
JESSE G PEREZ
MANUEL G PEREZ
MARCOS H PEREZ SR
RENE PEREZ
SERAFIN PEREZ-BAEZ
ARCADIO PEREZ-TORRES
LUIS PEREZ-VILLEGAS
CHARLES R PERKEY
ALGIE PERKINS
ALVA J PERKINS
CHESTER PERKINS
LLOYD R PERKINS
MALCOLM D PERKINS
ROBERT E PERKINS
RONALD J PERNACK
MARVIN PERPER
HENRY J PERREAULT
SILVIO T PERRELLA
WILLIAM F PERRELLA
RALPH L PERRIN
FREDERICK PERROTTA
EDWARD E PERROTTI
ALFRED P PERRY
CLARENCE A PERRY
CLYDE A PERRY
DONALD E PERRY
FRANK W PERRY
GERALD L PERRY
HAROLD PERRY
MONROE PERRY JR
NORMAN C PERRY
THOMAS O PERRY JR
WILLIAM R PERRY
JAMES PERSIANNI
ZELMAR PERSON
WILLIAM PERSONETT
JAMES L PERTS
EDWARD PESKA
NICKOLAS PETCOSKY
ALBERT W PETERS
DANIEL G PETERS
DELBERT O PETERS
FRANK W PETERS
LEONARD L PETERS
RALPH E PETERS
RAYMOND D PETERS
ROBERT K PETERS
TRAVIS L PETERS
DEAN H PETERSEN
FRED A PETERSEN JR
GERALD B PETERSON
JERRY H PETERSON
LYLE E PETERSON
ORVILLE P PETERSON
PHILIP O PETERSON
RONALD D PETERSON
ANDREW F PETHO
WHEELER E PETHTEL JR
EDMUND F PETRIE
ADELCHI A PETRILLO
DELMAR L PETROWSKE
HAROLD J PETTICORD
DAVID E PETTIS

RAYMOND C PETTIT
GEORGE PETTY JR
WELFORD B PEYTON
RALPH R PFEIFFER
HARRY E PHELPS
RICHARD PHELPS
ROBERT J PHILIPPEN
DON L PHILIPPS
BILLY A PHILLIPS
CARSON PHILLIPS
CHARLIE A PHILLIPS
GERALD J PHILLIPS
JAMES D PHILLIPS
JAMES W PHILLIPS
JOHN A PHILLIPS
JOHN E PHILLIPS
JOHN E PHILLIPS
JEIRL B PHIPPS
JOE D PIASSE
ALTON H PICKARD
CLARENCE D PICKENS
ROBERT P PICKERING
CARLTON F PICKETT
JAMES E PIER
EDWARD E PIERCE JR
LEONARD L PIERCE JR
ROBERT D PIERCE
THOMAS C PIERCE JR
WILLIAM M PIERCE
SAMUEL PIERRE JR
CLEMENT PIETRASIEWICZ
EMERALD W PIKE
RAYMOND S PIKE
ROBERT E PILCH
HERBERT K PILILAAU
CONROY T PINA
DAVID F PINA
FERNANDO F PINA-CALIZ
BOBBIE N PINCKNEY
JAMES W PINEDA
CARTER N PING
JOSEPH L PINKHAM
CLYDE M PINKSTON
VIRGIL F PINKSTON
ARLIN J PINNEO
JAMES PINTO
FOLEY D PIPER
WALTER F PIPER
JOHN P PISANI
JOSEPH PISTONETTI
LEONARD E PISULA
CHARLES D PITRE JR
BYRON H PITTMAN
CHARLES PITTMAN JR
GERALD E PITTMAN
NORMAN E PITTMAN
RUSSELL G PITTMAN
ROBERT L PITZINGER
GILBERTO PIZANA
DUANE K PLACE
DANIEL W PLANK
CHARLES R PLANTZ
JOSEPH G PLEASANTS
ROGER W PLESHEK
ALPHONSO H PLONK
ALEXANDER M PLOTKIN
GERALD R PLOTNER
RAPHAEL PLOTZKI
MAX L PLUMMER
HARRY E PLUNKETT
ROBERT F PLZAK
EDWARD P
PODMAJERSKY
CHESTER POE JR
REGINALD R POE
ROBERT H POE
ANTHONY J POFFAHL
JAMES F POGUE
MARION B POGUE
OTIS H POGUE
DONALD J POHLMAN
WILLIAM R POHLMAN
JOHN POINTECK JR
BERNARD A POIRIER
RENE G POITRAS
EDWARD POJATINA
HOWARD L POLARIE
GEORGE J POLCER JR
DAVID E POLING
FORREST C POLING

ROBERT P POLK
AUBREY W POLLARD
CLYDE D POLLARD
GLEN D POLLARD
PERTIE A POLLARD
JAMES A POLLOCK
ANTHONY POLOTTO JR
PEDRO POMALES-
POMALES
RALPH E POMEROY
BURNELL C POND
STANL PONIEWIERSKI
ELVIS J POORE
JOHN H POORE
ROBERT L POPPE
HOMER L PORT
ALEC W PORTER
BILL J PORTER
CECIL L PORTER JR
GEORGE A PORTER
JIMMY T PORTER
MOSE PORTER
PERCY B PORTER JR
FRANK PORTUGAL
RICHARD PORTWOOD
KARNIG A PORYAZIAN
JOHN J POSCH
HAROLD T POSEY
ARTHUR H POST
RONALD A POSTANCE
ANDREW G POSTMA
DONALD B POTRATZ
CALVIN R POTTER
LEROY W POTTER
ROBERT POTTER
JAMES W POTTS JR
ROY H POTTS
ALVIN E POTZ
THOMAS J POULIN
GEORGE A POULSON
GERALD J POULSON
BRUCE A POURCIAU
JAMES D POW
BROOK T POWELL
HAROLD L POWELL
JOSEPH C POWELL
RICHARD M POWELL
SAMUEL B POWELL
SIDNEY POWELL
W D POWELL
WALDO A POWELL
WILLIAM POWELL
EARL L POWERS
FRANK L POWERS
JOHN K POWERS
MIGUEL POZOS
PEDRO T PRADO-
PACHECO
CARL G PRANGE
EUGENE J PRASKA
LOVELL E PRATER
VERNON E PRATER
ROBERT L PRATHER
CLIFFORD F PRATT
JOHN E PREE
LESLIE E PREECE
ROBERT H PRENTICE
CHARLES PRENTISS
DELBERT F PRESCOTT
SIDNEY T PRESCOTT
NOAH PRESLEY JR
IRVING A PRESS
CHESTER PRESTON
JESSE L PRESTON
VIRGIL W PRESTWOOD
CLOYSE A PRIBLE
CHARLES F PRICE
COY W PRICE
JAMES E PRICE
TALMADGE PRICE JR
THOMAS R PRICE
WILLIAM D PRICE
DALE P PRICKETT
HERBERT R PRIDE
EARNEST L PRIDEMORE
EDWARD N PRIEST
JAMES W PRIEST
CHARLES W M PRINCE
MARVIN E PRINCE
WADE PRINCE JR

OWEN PRIOR
DONALD E PRITCHARD
AUGUST PRITCHETT
CHESTER PRITCHETT
EUGENE PRITCHETT
HOMER C PRITCHETT
RONALD D PRITCHETT
THOMAS E PRIVETT
GENE F PROCTOR
DONALD J PROFFITT
HOMER PROFFITT
LEONARD E PROVOST
HENRY C PRUITT
HARVEY E PRYNE
GEORGE T PRYOR
NICHOLAS S PUCCI
VIRGIL L PUCK
CHARLES C PUCKETT JR
CLINTON S PUCKETT
CARL R PUETZ
JAMES J PUGEL
RUDOLF PUGEL
JACK PUGH JR
JOSEPH F PUGLIESE
VITO R PUGLIESE
RICHARD G PUHL
ROBERT E PUHL
JOSEPH P PULAK
THOMAS M PULLEY
BEN O PULLIAM
OLAF P PULVER
THOMAS L PULVER
BENNY L PUMMELL
CHARLES W PURCELL
FRANCIS S PURCELL
LOYD E PURCELL
JOHN E PURPLE JR
ROBERT PURSIFULL
MARIANI PURUGGANAN
JOHN H PURVEY
FRED R PUTMAN
RICHARD E PUZIO
HEUNG-SU PYEON
GAP-MAN PYO
WALTER P PYTAK
LEON J PYTEL
DONALD J
QUACKENBUSH
ROBERT D QUATIER
MANUEL QUATROCHE
LOUIS G QUEARY
BOBBY L QUEEN
EDWARD A QUEJA
BILLY QUESENBERRY
ROBERT H QUILLMAN
CLAUDE J QUINN
THOMAS S QUINN
WILLIAM A QUINN
WILLIAM L QUINN JR
ANTONIO QUINONES-
NATAL
WILLIAM H QUINT
HILBERTO S QUINTANA
JUAN QUINTANA
MANUEL S QUINTANILLA
ALBERT E QUINTERO
MARINO QUIRINDONGO
ROBERT QUIROZ
GEUM-HAK RA
OK-GYUN RA
ROBERT L RABB
RUDOLPH RABER
RONALD RABOYE
IRVIN A RACKLEY
MYRON F E RADANK
WAYNE S RADEBAUGH
JAMES W RAFFERTY
LLOYD I RAGAR
CARL W RAGIN
LESLIE D RAGLAND
VIRGIL F RAGLAND
JAMES V RAGUSA
RUSSELL L RAHN
HERBERT RAINEY
WILLIAM L RAINEY
STERLING RAISBECK
HOMER F RAMEY
FRANK R RAMIREZ
IGNACIO RAMIREZ
JESUS J RAMIREZ

REYNALDO S RAMIREZ
URBAN M RAMIREZ
JORGE RAMIREZ-AYALA
ANTULIO RAMIREZ-
BAERGA
ISMAEL RAMIREZ-JUSINO
RAMIRO RAMIREZ-
LOPEZ
BURGESS RAMOS JR
JESSE S RAMOS
JUAN RAMOS
LAWRENCE RAMOS
MARTIN M RAMOS
PABLO RAMOS
ANDRES RAMOS-AYALA
JOSE RAMOS-
RODRIGUEZ
HOWARD W RAMSER JR
JAMES N RAMSEY JR
LEE R RAMSEY
BENJAMIN RAND
ROBERT C RAND
BOBBY RANDALL
FRED RANDALL
HAROLD RANDLE
EVANS RANDOLPH JR
ALGRIT H RANEY
DONALD D RANEY
FREDERICK W RANGER
RAYMOND L RANGER
PAUL J RANIERI
MILLAGE RANKIN
ROBERT RANKIN
THOMAS D RANKIN
HENRY RANSOM JR
CURTIS C RAPER
DAVID J RAPP
JACK W RAPPS
MILON E RARDON
ROBERT T RARICK
WILLIE RASHA
DONALD E RASKE
JOHN N RASMUSSEN
KENNETH A RASMUSSEN
RAY L RASMUSSEN
ROBERT RASOR
ISHMEAL RATLIFF
LEONARD RATTER
KARL L RATTLER
ROBERT M RAUEN
EUGENE R RAUSCH
DANIEL J RAVEN
DAVID L RAVENELL
KENNETH E RAVITZ
PATRICK J RAWLINGS
ROBERT E RAWLINS
CHESTER
RAWRYNKIEWICZ
GERALD L RAY
LEWIS C RAY
DANIEL J RAYBUCK
JERRY J RAYBURN
ERNEST RAYMOND JR
GERARD J RAYMOND
GEORGE RAYMORE
RALPH O RAYNES
RICHARD B READY
ERNEST J REALE
BRUCE A REAM
BRUCE L REAMES
HERMAN REASBY
WALTER R
REASONOVER
WILLIAM I REBUCK
JOHN W RECTOR
HORN W RED
JAMES V REDDEN
LEROY H REDDICK
JOHN R REDDIN
RICHARD F REDDING
CHESTER W REDFORD
AUGUST J REDMAN JR
AMZIE O REED
BAZILE REED JR
CHARLES E REED
CHARLES R REED
FREDDY T REED
GERRE N REED
HOWARD R REED
JUNIOR E REED

43 ARMY

KENNETH E REED
LINWOOD REED
MELVIN REED
PAUL D REED
RAY W REED
SAMUEL REED
THOMAS C REED
THOMAS C REED
WILLIE REED
HOWARD R REEDER
JACK N REEDER
GEORGE REESE
GRADY D REESE
JODIE S REESE JR
JOHN REESE JR
JOHN E REESE
WILLIE REESE
OTTO REEVES
PAUL I REEVES
RICHARD W REEVES
HERBERT J REEVIS
THOMAS J REGAN JR
ROBERT J REHM
KENNETH W REICH
NORM T REICHENBERGER
ARONES V REID
HAROLD REID JR
HUGH C REID
LLOYD W REID
LYLE E REID
QUIN P REIDY
MARCUS G REINHARD
ROBERT B REINHARD
VERNON C REINHARDT
DUANE C REINHART
NOEL F REINHART
WILLIAM W REISER
RALPH W REISINGER
WALTER L REISINGER
FRANCIS R REISWITZ
EDWARD J REITER
CLARENCE REMER
LLOYD D RENANDER
JERRY H RENEW
JAMES M RENNE
ANTHONY W RENNEBERG
MEINHARDT RENNICH
JAMES D RENTSCHLER
BARNEY C RENTZ
MICHAEL D RESTAINO
ROBERT H REXIUS
JUVENTINO G REYES
WILLIAM REYES
ERCIDES REYES-DE JESUS
MARCOS REYES-RODRIGUEZ
ARMANDO REYES-VELEZ
ARCHIE L REYNOLDS
ARTHUR D REYNOLDS
EDWARD R REYNOLDS
ELWOOD D REYNOLDS
HENRY REYNOLDS
MELVIN E REYNOLDS
RUSSELL F REYNOLDS
WILLIAM H REYNOLDS
ADOLPH C REYNOSO
BILLY J RHEA
ISAAC B RHEUARK
ECKARD A RHOADES
EDWARD W RHOADS
EUGENE D RHOADS
ROBERT L RHOADS
RALPH RHODEHAMEL
DONIS E RHODEN
BILLY J RHODES
CLYDE RHODES JR
ELDEN P RHODES
JAMES D RHODES
JAMES E RHODES
STANLEY Q RHODES
MARK L RHOTEN
EUGENE E RHYNER
CARL RIBOT-SALGADO
GEORGE S RICCARDO
ALBERT M RICCI
CURTIS R RICE
DONALD RICE
HERBERT RICE JR
HOWARD RICE
JAMES RICE

THEODORE L RICH
ELMER G RICHARD
ERNEST B RICHARD
ROLAND R RICHARD
ARTHUR D RICHARDS
ARTHUR L RICHARDS
DONALD R RICHARDS
LEONARD L RICHARDS
LOUIS J RICHARDS
ARTHUR RICHARDSON
CLARK B RICHARDSON
DAVID G RICHARDSON
DEAN E RICHARDSON
DONALD RICHARDSON
DWIGHT E RICHARDSON
EDWARD H RICHARDSON
HAROLD RICHARDSON
JAMES H RICHARDSON
MARTIN J RICHARDSON
ORVIL C RICHARDSON
OTHA RICHARDSON
PAUL E RICHARDSON
PRATER H RICHARDSON JR
ROBERT B RICHARDSON
WALTER J RICHARDSON
WILBERT G RICHARDSON
WILLIAM M RICHARDSON
AGGIE L RICHEY
CHARLES R RICHMOND
CLYDE E RICHMOND
JAMES R RICHMOND
ROBERT E RICHMOND
JOHNNIE D RICHTERS
EUGENE T RICKE
ERNEST L RICKERT
THOMAS L RICKETT
KENNETH J RICKRODE
FRANK RICO
FREDERICK C RIDDAGH
BILLY J RIDGE
CECIL D RIFFLE
EDWARD W RIGDON
GENE F RIGGLE
KARL L RIGGLE
HERSCHEL M RIGGS
GEORGE L RIGHTS
ALVIN S RIGSBY
JAMES D RIGSBY
CHARLES L RILEY
GEORGE P RILEY
LAWRENCE T RILEY
REGINALD A RILEY
ERNEST L RINEHART
RAYMOND S RINES
EMMETT W RING
CHARLES E RINGER
RICHARD RIORDAN
FELIX RIOS
FLORENCIO RIOS
WILLIAM RIOS-BARBOSA
GASPER RIOS-MORALES
ROBERT W RITCHEY
JOHN G RITTER
RONALD RITTER
STANLEY C RITTER
THEODORE E RITTKO
JOHN S RIVAS
ANDY M RIVERA
ANGEL A RIVERA
FERNANDO RIVERA JR
JOSE H RIVERA
JUAN RIVERA
JUAN F RIVERA
LEONCIO P RIVERA
MIGUEL RIVERA
RUBEN RIVERA
RAFAEL RIVERA-ARUZ
ANGEL RIVERA-BENITEZ
HORACE RIVERA-CANCEL
FRANCISCO RIVERA-CARRION
ROBERTO RIVERA-CLAUDIO
PEDRO RIVERA-CRUZ
DOMINGO RIVERA-ESPINEL
REYES RIVERA-GONZALES
ANTONIO RIVERA-ILDEFONSO
JUAN RIVERA-VAZQUEZ
RICHARD E RIVERS
MICHAEL RIZDY

JOSEPH A RIZZI
EDWARD J RIZZO
CLIFFORD E ROALF
HAROLD E ROARK
CHARLES F ROBBINS JR
RAY N ROBBINS
WILLIAM B ROBBINS
DONALD A ROBERGE
LLOYD E ROBERSON
WILL ROBERSON JR
WILLIE J ROBERSON
CHARLES C ROBERTS
CURTIS E ROBERTS
DONALD R ROBERTS
EVERETT R ROBERTS
FINIS W ROBERTS
FREDDIE J ROBERTS
GERALD R ROBERTS
HENRY D ROBERTS
HUDSON ROBERTS JR
IVAN ROBERTS
JAMES J ROBERTS
JOHN W ROBERTS
KENNETH J ROBERTS
KENNETH N ROBERTS
MELFRED K ROBERTS
RAYMOND L ROBERTS
ROBERT I ROBERTS
ROBERT L ROBERTS
CLONNIE R ROBERTSON
ERNEST C ROBERTSON
HOWARD L ROBERTSON
JAMES L ROBERTSON
PAUL E ROBERTSON
SAMUEL A ROBERTSON
SYDNOR F ROBERTSON
THOMAS R ROBERTSON
WILFRED C ROBIDOUX
JOSEPH A ROBILLARD JR
GORDON L ROBINS
ALVIN ROBINSON
CECIL ROBINSON
CHARLES S ROBINSON
FRANK ROBINSON
GEORGE ROBINSON
GLEN A ROBINSON
JAMES N ROBINSON
JOE M ROBINSON
JOHN L P ROBINSON
LELAND S ROBINSON
LEON ROBINSON
LLOYD R ROBINSON
MAX D ROBINSON
OLIN D ROBINSON
ROBERT H ROBINSON
WILBUR J ROBINSON
WILLIAM L ROBINSON
LELAND W ROBISON
FRANK P ROBLES
ISMAEL ROBLES-DE JESUS
RAYMOND C ROBSON
DONNIE F ROBY
HUBERT ROCHESTER
JASPER ROCK JR
JACKIE H ROCKWELL
RICHARD ROCLAWSKI
MANUEL R RODARTE
ARTHUR D RODDY
BILLIE J RODEISCHAK
RALPH A RODEMER
FRANKLIN E RODGERS
LAWRENCE C RODGERS
ROBERT S RODGERS
THEODORE E RODNEY
CALVIN L RODRIGUE
ALFREDO RODRIGUEZ
BONIFACIO RODRIGUEZ
ENRIQUE RODRIGUEZ
ENRIQUE G RODRIGUEZ
HENRY RODRIGUEZ
JULIO R RODRIGUEZ
MARIO J RODRIGUEZ
OMAR L RODRIGUEZ
PEDRO RODRIGUEZ
ROBERT D RODRIGUEZ
RODDY E RODRIGUEZ
SAMUEL RODRIGUEZ
THEODORE RODRIGUEZ
JOSE RODRIGUEZ-BERMUDEZ

LUIS RODRIGUEZ-BORRERO
ANDRES RODRIGUEZ-LOPEZ
FLORENCIO RODRIGUEZ-LOPEZ
RAFAEL RODRIGUEZ-LOPEZ
ALFONSO RODRIGUEZ-MONTANEZ
ANGEL RODRIGUEZ-OLIVERAS
JUAN A RODRIGUEZ-PEREZ
JUAN RODRIGUEZ-SANTIAGO
JOSE S RODRIGUEZ-VARGAS
DONALD E RODSTROM
RICHARD L ROESKE
COSTANZO ROGATO
CHARLES F ROGERS
DANIEL B ROGERS JR
DONALD W ROGERS
HAROLD F ROGERS
HARRY L ROGERS
JAMES D ROGERS
JOE ROGERS JR
LLOYD G ROGERS
SYLVESTER ROGERS
THEODORE A ROGERS
TOMMIE E ROGERS
WILLIAM H ROGERS
JOSEPH R ROGINSKIE
RAY A ROGNAS
WILLIAM ROHR
JIM L ROHRBAUGH
NILS M ROJAS
HAROLD J ROLFE JR
GEORGE ROLLER
SAMUEL S ROLLINS JR
JUAN A ROLON
ERNESTO T ROMAN
FRANK M ROMAN
PAUL A ROMAN
FRANK P ROMANDETTI
MICHAEL M ROMANELLI
PABLO ROMAN-MARRERO
RICHARD J ROMANUS
REGINALD E ROMEO
ARISTEO ROMERO
EDDIE J ROMERO
JOE C ROMERO
MANUEL T ROMERO
NELSON R ROMERO
ROSENDO G ROMERO
CELIO ROMERO-CALES
JOHN D ROMINE
CARMEN A ROMITO
ANGEL P ROMO
KENNETH L ROMPALSKI
CLARENCE M RONAN
DONALD H ROOP
GEORGE F ROOS
FRANKLIN T ROOSEVELT
BILLY J ROPER
EARL G ROPER
JOSE J ROQUE-LEON
JUAN A ROSA
CARLOS ROSA-CASTRO
PEDRO ROSADO-ROSADO
ADOLFO G ROSALES
RAUL ROSALES
REHENO G ROSALEZ
ALEJANDRINO ROSARIO-DE JESUS
GUILLERMO ROSA-RIVERA
FRANK R ROSAS
ANTHONY ROSATI
RAYMOND J ROSBECK
ARTHUR J ROSE
DARROW A ROSE
DOUGLAS W ROSE
EDWARD R ROSE
FRED ROSE JR
GLENN A ROSE
HARVEY L ROSE
HERMAN ROSE
LEONARD E ROSE
ROBERT L ROSEMA
VALDEAN G ROSENBOOM
DICK ROSENGRANT
ALFRED M ROSENTHAL
FLOYD R ROSETTE
DONALD L ROSEVINK

ROBERT W ROSHON
ANDREW C ROSS
CALVIN L ROSS
DELMER W ROSS
HALDEAN ROSS
JOSEPH B ROSS
KENNETH W ROSS
MCELREE A ROSS
RAYMOND E ROSS
RAYMOND T ROSS
RICHARD ROSS JR
ROBERT A ROSS
DEWEY ROSSEL
JACK S ROSSELL
RICHARD D ROSSER
WILLIAM T ROSSER
KENNETH A ROSSIN
GERALD V ROSSITER
JAMES A ROSTOLLAN
ROBERT E ROTH
DONALD K ROTHERMEL
JAMES F ROUDEBUSH
ERNEST R ROULEAU
JAMES A ROUND
JIMY R ROUNDTREE
WILLIE ROUNDTREE
ROY E ROUSE
ULYSEE ROUSE
EDWARD U ROUTH
HOWARD D ROUTT
SALVADOR J ROVELLO
WALTER D ROWATT
JOHNNY ROWE
MORRILTON C ROWE
VILES C ROWE
WILLIAM E ROWE
WILLIAM F ROWE
ERNEST J ROWLAND
JIMMY ROWLAND
DAVID A ROWLEY
HAROLD C ROWLEY
FRANCIS ROY
HAYWARD J ROY
PAUL J ROY
WILLIAM F ROY
SOLOMON R ROYAL
CASMERE J ROZANSKI
LEOPOLDO RUBERT
ROBERT G RUCINSKI
EDWARD K RUCKS
FRANCIS J RUDDEN
FREDERICK A RUDGE
WILLIAM H RUEGER
ROY L RUFUS
HERBERT E RUGAR
HAROLD T RUGGLES
ALBERT A RUIU
ABRAHAM RUIZ
JOHN G RUIZ
NORBERTO RUIZ
VICTOR M RUIZ
FRANCISCO RUIZ DE PORRAS-SARMIENTO
JOHN E RUMMEL
CLARENCE C RUNDLE
CECIL A RUNK
LEROY J RUNNER
EDWARD J RUNT JR
MARION A RUSH
LARRY W RUSHING
DONALD J RUSHMORE
JAMES B RUSHTON
EARL RUSS
JOHN M RUSS
CHARLES A RUSSELL
CHARLES P RUSSELL
EUGENE E RUSSELL
FRANK S RUSSELL
HERMAN M RUSSELL JR
JACK P RUSSELL
JOHN H RUSSELL
JOHN T RUSSELL
FRED RUSSENBERGER
VINCENT J RUSSO
DONALD W RUST
JOHNIE B RUTHEFORD
KENNETH S RUTHERFORD
SALVATO RUTIGLIANO
ALBERT J RUTKOWSKI

ANTHONY RUTKOWSKI
ELVIN A RUTLAND
CHARLES J RUTLEDGE
WADE E RUTLEDGE
WILLIE M RUTLEDGE
ROBERT L RUTT
LUTHER E RUTTER
FRANK RUZON
EDWIN C RYALS
JAMES F RYAN
JOHN J RYAN
JOHN O RYAN
ROBERT A RYAN
DONALD C RYBICKI
PHILLIP W RYDBERG
DANIEL F RYDER
LOREN RYLANCE
BAE-HEON RYU
CHANG-YEONG RYU
DAL-HYEONG RYU
GAK-YEOL RYU
HAE-GONG RYU
JANG-SU RYU
JI-SEONG RYU
JU-HUI RYU
SA-CHAE RYU
SEONG-BAEK RYU
SEUNG-YEOL RYU
SIN-HWA RYU
SUN-SEOK RYU
PAUL T RZECZOWSKI
KERRY C SABANTY
FRED P SABARINE
GUISSEPPE SABELLA
BERNARD J SABIN
JERRY SABINO
JOSE P SABLAN
JOHN SABLYAR
EMERY J SABO
PASCAL SACCO
JOSEPH D SACCULLO
HOWARD S SACHS
GLENN O SACHTELEBEN
RICHARD E SAD
EUGENE J SADEK
ALLEN T SAKAMOTO
JAMES N SAKAMOTO
DOSS L SALADIN
DONACIANO SALAZAR
JOHN J SALAZER
JUAN SALDANA
ROBERTO SALDANA
JOHN W SALERNO
JOSEPH SALERNO JR
JAMES SALISBURY
RAYMOND SALLEE
DONALD W SALMON
DAVID W SALSBERY
EARL C SALTZ
RALPH J SALVATI
BILLY J SALYER
AMBERS B SAMMONS
VAN B SAMMONS
STANLEY SAMOLINSKI
HAROLD N SAMPLE
WILLIAM B SAMPLE
FRANK J SAMSA
WICKCLIFF J SAMUEL
ANTOINE T SAMUELS
ENRIQUE SANABRIA
ARCADIO SANABRIA-ALGARIN
LINWOOD B SANBORN
GREGORIO G SANCHEZ
JAMES R SANCHEZ
JESSE B SANCHEZ
JOSE SANCHEZ
KENNETH L SANCHEZ
WILLIAM SANCHEZ
WILLIAM SANCHEZ
WILLIAM Q SANCHEZ
VIRGIL SANCHEZ-COLON
JESUS SANCHEZ-RODRIGUEZ
PABLO SANCHEZ-TORRES
JAMES F SAND
JAMES B SANDEFUR
GEORGE W SANDERBECK
DONALD C SANDERS
EDDIE SANDERS
J D SANDERS
JAMES B SANDERS
JAMES W SANDERS
JOHN W SANDERS
MCDONALD SANDERS
TONY M SANDERS
WILLIE L SANDERS
PAUL E SANDERSON
ROBERT S SANDRETZKY
ANTHONY G SANDWELL
CHARLES D SANFORD
ROYAL W SANFORD
SANTO SANKITTS
JOSEPH J SANSALONE
RUDY J SANTACRUZ
ERNEST S SANTESSE
FRANK SANTI
ANGEL SANTIAGO
ANGEL L SANTIAGO
LUIS SANTIAGO
DOMINGO SANTIAGO-APONTE
EMILIO SANTIAGO-BONILLA
FARIS SANTIAGO-CRESPO
ANDREW SANTIBANEZ
GEORGE J SANTORE
JOAQUIN S SANTOS
MANUEL SANTOS
JESUS SANTOS-CRUZ
MARIANO SANTOS-DAVILA
ERNESTO SANTOS-JIMENEZ
GILBERTO SANTOS-ROSA
AGAPITO SANTOS-SANTIAGO
CLIFFORD N SAPP
PHILIP SARABIA
MICHAEL J SARACO
SALVADOR J SARATE
ARNOLD L SARDESON
EARL SARGENT
HARRY L SARGENT JR
DAVID SARINE
MIKE SAROIAN
TAKESHI SASAKI
RALPH SASSER
ROBERT M SATCHELL
THOMAS J SATCHELL
LEO C SATTER
GLENN R SATTERFIELD
ROGER SATTERFIELD
CHARLES F SAUER
JON E SAUER
WARREN E SAUER
FREDERICK A SAUNDERS JR
HARRY L SAUNDERS
JAMES B SAUNDERS JR
JAMES M SAUNDERS
RICHARD A SAUNDERS
MERLE L Z SAVAGE
DWIGHT E SAVILLE
LEO R SAVOIE
EUCLIDE J SAVOY JR
EARL H SAWYER JR
GEORGE J SAWYER
LEVI L SAWYER
GERALD H SAXTON
FRED B SAYRE
TONY SCAFFIDI
GARLAND R SCALF
JAMES C SCANLON
JAMES H SCARBOR
GEORGE SCARBOROUGH
FRANCIS SCARLETT
ROBERT E SCHAEFER
WALTER J SCHAEKEL
CLARK D SCHAFFER
MELVIN R SCHAMBER
RONALD B SCHAMBERGER
RICHARD E SCHARMACK
GEORGE W SCHEETZ JR
JOHN J SCHELLHAMMER
HUBERT C SCHERDIN
JOHN F SCHERER
PAUL W SCHILDT
WILLIAM G SCHILLER
FERDINAND C SCHILLINGER
JACK W SCHINDLER
JOHN SCHINE JR
RAYMOND G SCHLECHT
EARL E SCHLEGEL
CHRISTOPHER SCHLITZ
WARREN M SCHLOSSER
MELVIN A SCHMATZ
ARTHUR E SCHMIDT
CARROLL E SCHMIDT
FRANK X SCHMIDT
ROBERT C SCHMIDT
FRANCIS G SCHMITT
VILAS R SCHMOECKEL
ERVILLE W SCHNEIDER JR
JOSEPH W SCHNEIDER
ROGER F SCHNEIDER
ROLLIN E SCHNEIDER
GILBERT E SCHNURR
CHRISTIAN R SCHOELLER JR
GLENN S SCHOENMANN
RUBEN SCHOENWALD
MARION K SCHOFFNER
JULIUS J SCHOLTZ
WILLIAM D SCHONDER JR
SAINT E SCHOOLFIELD
WILLIAM A SCHOTT
GEORGE SCHOULTHIES
RUEBEN SCHRAEDER
PAUL M SCHRECENGOST
JOHN C SCHROBILGEN JR
GORDON T SCHROEDER
PETER J SCHUIL
CLAIR C SCHUKNECHT
ROY A SCHULTE JR
BERTRAM E SCHULTZ
WALTER M SCHULZ
HENRY J SCHUMACHER
WALTER SCHUMAN
JOHN C SCHUMANN
RALPH E SCHUMITSH
HORACE I SCHUMPERT JR
EUGENE A SCHUSTER
MERLIN N SCHUSTER
JOHN SCHWED JR
BOBBY R SCHWEINGRUBER
RAYMOND K SCHWEITZ
EUGENE C SCHWEND
PAUL R SCHWOEGL
EUGENE SCIPIO
JOSEPH G SCLAFANI
JAMES L SCOGGINS
WALTER P SCOTON
AMOS L SCOTT
BENNIE L SCOTT
CHARLES D SCOTT
CHARLES W SCOTT
CLETIS E SCOTT
EDWARD H SCOTT
FLOYD E SCOTT
FLOYD E SCOTT
FRANK B SCOTT JR
FRED E SCOTT
GEORGE R SCOTT
GRATTIN SCOTT
HENRY SCOTT
JESSIE L SCOTT
KENNETH W SCOTT
LENWARD SCOTT JR
LOWELL L SCOTT
MARLE D SCOTT
NEIL R SCOTT
ROBERT F SCOTT
ROBERT L SCOTT
ROBERT T SCOTT
SAMMIE R SCOTT
THOMAS E SCOTT
WILLIAM E SCOTT
WILLIAM J SCOTT
WILMER O SCOTT
HENRY SCOTTI
EDMUND G SCOULLAR
JOHN R SCROGEY
ROBERT D SCRUGGS
WILLIAM SCULLY
LARRY L SEABORN
WILLIAM O SEAL
EARL E SEALS
LEONARD H SEALS
LEROY D SEAMAN
ROBERT L SEAMAN
ALBERT G SEAMON
JAMES D SEAMSTER
DALTON J SEARCY
DONALD F SEARS JR
ALFONSO N SEBIA JR
FOREST B SECKMAN
ELMER W SECORE
CHESTER T SECREASE JR
FELIPE T SEDILLO
CLELL O SEE
WILLIAM R SEGGIE
ALBERT J SEGHETTI
ALVIN A SEIFERT
CHESTER J SEIFERT
CHARLES R SELBY
DONALD H SELBY
LLOYD F SELBY
ARTHUR W SELDON JR
RICHARD A SELF
SAMUEL D SELF
ISREAL SELLA-RAMOS
A L SELLERS
DALLAS SELLERS
DANIEL W SELLERS
DONALD E SELLERS
HAROLD G SELLERS
J L SELLERS
LEROY O SELLERS
LONNIE J SELLERS
ROGER E SELLERS
VERNON L SELVESTER
DELOY G SEMINGSON
JOHN SEMULKA JR
HENRY T SENAHA
FLOYD L SENTER JR
BONG-SU SEO
CHANG-GYO SEO
CHANG-SU SEO
GWI-DEOK SEO
GYEONG-DEUK SEO
GYEONG-GU SEO
HO-WON SEO
JAE-SEON SEO
JEONG-DAL SEO
JEONG-HYO SEO
JEONG-MUN SEO
JIN-EUN SEO
JIN-GEUN SEO
MI-BONG SEO
SAM-RYONG SEO
SANG-CHEOL SEO
SANG-UK SEO
SEOK-MAN SEO
TAEK-GU SEO
UI-SU SEO
WON-DO SEO
YEONG-GI SEO
YEONG-GIL SEO
YEONG-HUI SEO
YONG-SEOK SEO
GYEONG-GYUN SEOK
JAE-JO SEOL
SUN-GWAN SEOL
GI-DEOK SEONG
NAK-JUN SEONG
YEONG-PYO SEONG
ANGEL L SEPULVEDA-TORRES
ANTONIO SEQUEIRA
SAMUEL SERPE
EUGENE R SERRA
DANIEL V SERRANO
VALENTIN I SERRANO
EUGENE A SERRE
CHESTER P SESCILLA
ROBERT SESTITO
HARRY E SETHMAN
RAYMOND J SETTLE
GERALD A SETTLES
THOMAS E SEWARD
BOBBY L SEXTON
BOYD S SEXTON
RALPH J SEYLER
LAWRENCE D SEYMORE
PAUL R SEYMOUR
ALLEN H SHACKELFORD
FREDERICK D SHADDEN
JOHN F SHADEL
WILLARD J SHAFER
GEORGE L SHAFFER
JACK W SHAFFER
RAYMOND C SHAFFER
WILLIAM E SHAFFER
WILLIAM H SHAFFER
GEORGE SHAMOON
LARRY R SHANE
JOEL SHANKLIN
CARL G SHANNON
JOHN D SHANNON
WILMA SHANNON
HAROLD S SHARER
JOHN F SHARON
BRAXTON W SHARP
FELIX G SHARP
JOHN T SHARP
ORAL R SHARP
WILLIAM J SHARP
WILLIAM W SHARP JR
HARRY SHARPE
HAROLD SHAULL JR
DAVID W SHAW
DONALD D SHAW
EULAS M SHAW
LEE SHAW JR
MARVIN K SHAW
WILLIAM SHAW
WILLIE C SHAW
JAMES A SHAWVER
JACKIE L SHAY
JOHN J SHAY JR
JAMES W SHEA JR
JEREMIAH J SHEA
VELMER SHEARER
ERWIN W SHEEHAN
FRANCIS L SHEEHAN
ABRAHAM SHEFTEL
JAMES A SHELBY
JOHN A SHELEMBA
FRED P SHELGREN
RALPH J SHELLHAAS
LAWRENCE E SHELORK
CHARLIE SHELTON
CHESTER W SHELTON
EDDIE L SHELTON
GEORGE SHELTON JR
JIM SHELTON JR
LYLE R SHELTON
REYNARD E SHENTON
FLOYD SHEPARD
LEON M SHEPARD
CLAUDE L SHEPPARD
LOWELL B SHEPPARD
FRANK W SHERIDAN
WILLIAM L SHERIDAN
LOUIS F SHERIFF
JOHN B SHERLOCK
ALLEN SHERRY JR
VERNON W SHERRY
LOUIS H SHERWOOD
FRANKLIN D R SHETTERS
RICHARD J SHETTLER
ALVIN R SHIELDS
MARK SHIELDS
HERBERT R SHIFFLETT
LAWRENCE Y SHIMA
SHINGO E SHIMABUKURO
CALVIN T SHIMATA
TOSHIO SHIMONOYA
EDWARD A SHINE
ALBERT J SHINKUS
CHARLES T SHIPLEY
GENE E SHIPLEY
CLYDE W SHIPMAN
HOWARD I SHIPMAN
LOWELL D SHIPMAN
JACK E SHIPP
LEONARD W SHIPP
JOHN G SHIPTON
FRED D SHIRLEY
TAKASHI SHISHIDO
WILLIAM L SHOEMAKER
CHARLES H SHOFFIT
LONNIE R SHOOK
ROBERT A SHOOT
WILLIAM G SHOPE
GEORGE S SHORT
HERSCHEL G SHORT
JAMES M SHORT
MARVIN E SHORT
RICHARD L SHORT
THOMAS L SHORT
ROBERT G SHOULDERS

45 ARMY

LOUIS C SHRADER
JIM C SHREVES
FREELAN SHREWSBURY
CHARLES T SHROYER
REMBERT D SHULTS
BENDUM D SHUMATE
ELMER L SHUMATE
GLEN L SHUPE
GENE E SHUPP
LEE SHUR JR
LESLIE A SHY
RALPH W SIDEBOTTOM
WILLIAM SIDES JR
PETER M SIDORKA
ANTHONY R SIDOTI
RALPH E SIEFRING
WILLIAM J SIEH
DONALD H SIELAFF
WALTER E SIEMON
PAUL M SIERS
DANIEL T SIFUENTES
JOHN V SIGALA
HAROLD G SIGMON
JESUS C SIGUENZA
WILLIAM R SIGWART
WILLIE J SILER
ESTIL SILKWOOD
MAURICE R SILLS
ALBERTO I SILVA
DAVID SILVA
EUGENE W SILVA
CESAR SILVA-MADURO
RAUL SILVA-SANTIAGO
ALFRED SILVER
ROGER M SILVERNAIL
J S SILVERS
BAL-TAE SIM
JAE-BONG SIM
JAE-IK SIM
JAE-YUN SIM
SEON-DONG SIM
EUGENE N SIMIELE
ALLEN E SIMMONS
ARTHUR SIMMONS
GLEN D SIMMONS
JAMES R SIMMONS
JESSE E SIMMONS
JOHNNIE L SIMMONS
ROBERT J SIMMONS JR
ROBERT W SIMMONS
RONALD P SIMMONS
ROSS D SIMMONS
VERNIE D SIMMONS
WILLIAM R SIMMONS
WILLIAMS L SIMMONS
WILLIE C SIMMONS
WILLIE C SIMMONS
PRINCE A SIMMS
JOSEPH C SIMON
JOSEPH H SIMONEAU
CALVIN H SIMONS
ROBERT L SIMONS
ERNEST V SIMONSON
JAMES D SIMPSON
JOHN M SIMPSON
LEE A SIMPSON
ORVILLE L SIMPSON
SAMUEL T SIMPSON
ALFRED R SIMS
CLAUDE T SIMS
ERNEST E SIMS
HOLLY B SIMS
SHELBY T SIMS
TRUMAN D SIMS
DAE-YONG SIN
DONG-YEOP SIN
GANG-PIL SIN
GAP-SEON SIN
GEUN-HO SIN
GIL-DONG SIN
GWANG-SEOK SIN
GWAN-SUN SIN
GYEONG-HYU SIN
GYEONG-SEOP SIN
HWAN-IL SIN
HYEON-DAL SIN
HYEON-GIL SIN
HYEON-SE SIN
JAE-GEUN SIN
JEONG-YEOP SIN
JONG-BONG SIN
JONG-SEOK SIN
MONG-SIK SIN
PAN-DEUK SIN
SANG-GEUN SIN
SEOK-GYUN SIN
TAE-SUL SIN
UN-HAK SIN
YEOL-U SIN
YEONG-JO SIN
YEON-TAE SIN
YONG-BONG SIN
YONG-TAE SIN
FAIRRIS F SINCLAIR
FREDERICK L SINCLAIR
KARL G SINGER
GERALD C SINGLETARY
WILLIAM SINGLETON
WILLIAM E SINGLETON
HARVEY E SINGLEY
NICHOL L SINISCALCHI
EDWARD B SINKLER
ANGELO SIRAGUSA
RENO G SIROIS
BENNY SIRSKI
ALBERT J SIS
CLYDE E SISSOM
ALLEN P R SISSON
THOMAS L SISSON
ROBERT E SJOLANDER
EDWIN SKAGGS
PERRY A SKAGGS
RICHARD M SKAPYAK
JOHN O SKAUG
CALVIN L SKEEN
CHARLES M SKERO
PETER B SKIBA
WALTER L SKIBA
PHILLIP C SKILES
ROGER B SKILLINGS
KENNETH L SKINNER
RUSSELL J SKINNER
JAMES E SKIPPER
GARDIE M SKIVINGTON
CHARLES H SKROBANEK
EUGENE SLACK
CARL C SLADE
KENNETH E SLAGLE
DONALD G SLANEY
CHRISTOPHER SLATER
DONALD K SLATER
THOMAS A SLATER
RAYMOND E SLATTERY
HAYDEN W SLATTON
ANDREW J SLAUGHTER
WILLIAM SLEDGE
DONALD C SLEMP
FREDRICK J SLIPKA
CHARLES SLOAN
JAMES SLOAN
LAURENCE E SLOAN
LAWRENCE H SLOAN
WESLEY D SLOAN
JOHN A SLOAT
RICHARD F SLOAT
RAYMOND A SLOOP
FRED G SMACK
JAMES W SMAGLIK
ROBERT E SMALLEY
DAVID M SMALLS
CHARLES F SMARR
GEORGE A SMART
GERALD R SMART
JAMES SMART
NORMAN SMART
ROBERT E SMELTZER JR
KENNETH H SMILEY
JAMES J SMILIE
ALLEN L SMITH
ARNOLD G SMITH
BILLY E SMITH
BILLY J SMITH
CARL D SMITH
CARL E SMITH
CARL S SMITH
CARLTON J SMITH
CECIL E SMITH
CECIL E SMITH
CHARLES E SMITH
CHARLES M SMITH
CHARLES R SMITH
CHARLIE L SMITH
CLAUDE R SMITH
CLIFFORD H SMITH
CLIFTON E SMITH
CLYDE J SMITH
DAVID M SMITH
DEAN C SMITH
DONALD G SMITH
DONALD M SMITH
DOYLE E SMITH
DUANE W SMITH
EDGAR F SMITH
EDWARD F SMITH
EDWARD M SMITH
EDWIN G SMITH
ELIJAH SMITH JR
ELMER D SMITH
EUGENE SMITH
EUGENE E SMITH
FLOYD A SMITH
FRED SMITH
FRED H SMITH JR
FRED L SMITH
FREDERICK T SMITH
GABRIEL J SMITH
GENE J SMITH
GENEJO SMITH
GEORGE A SMITH
GEORGE C SMITH
GEORGE E SMITH
GEORGE J SMITH
GERALD SMITH
GILBERT R SMITH
GLENN F SMITH
GOVAN R SMITH
GROVER C SMITH
HAROLD L SMITH
HARPER H SMITH
HARRISON SMITH JR
HARRY W SMITH
HARVEY E SMITH
IVORY V SMITH
J D SMITH
JACK A SMITH
JACK R SMITH
JAMES E SMITH
JAMES E SMITH
JAMES F SMITH
JAMES H SMITH
JAMES H SMITH
JAMES K SMITH
JAMES K SMITH
JAMES M SMITH
JAMES R SMITH
JAMES R SMITH
JAMES W SMITH
JIMMY D SMITH
JOE W SMITH
JOHN A SMITH
JOHN C SMITH
JOHN L SMITH
JOHN W SMITH
JOHN W SMITH
JOSEPH C SMITH
KIMBALL E SMITH
LAWRENCE A SMITH
LOUIS K SMITH
LYMAN J SMITH
MANUEL Y SMITH
MARION L SMITH
MARVIN W SMITH
MAURICE K SMITH
PAUL A SMITH
PAUL T SMITH
RAY W SMITH
RAYMON L SMITH
RAYMOND A SMITH
REGINALD D SMITH
ROBERT A SMITH
ROBERT F SMITH
ROBERT J SMITH
ROBERT J SMITH
ROBERT L SMITH
RODERICK C SMITH
ROGER B SMITH
ROGER W SMITH
RONALD M SMITH
ROY H SMITH
SAM H SMITH
SAMUEL SMITH
SHERRY J SMITH
SHERWIN V SMITH
THERLO G L SMITH
THOMAS A SMITH
THOMAS C SMITH
THOMAS F SMITH
THOMAS J SMITH
TOMMY H SMITH
TROY N SMITH
WALTER L SMITH JR
WESLEY F SMITH
WILBUR L SMITH
WILLIAM E SMITH
WILLIAM E SMITH
WILLIAM G SMITH JR
WILLIAM H SMITH
WILLIAM J SMITH
RAYMOND J SMOLINSKI
CHAFFINE SMOTHERS
RICHARD T SMOTTS
GEORGE B SMUDSKI
WILLIAM H SMUGI
JAMES G SMYROS
DALE V SNARE
ELMER L SNAY
ALBERT SNEED
EOTHER L SNEED
WILLIAM C SNEED
DELBERT R SNELL
JAMES W SNELL
CHARLES H SNELLING
ADELBERT SNICKLES
NORMAN B SNIDENBACH
ALFRED E SNIDER
ARLON P SNIDER
DELMAR R SNIDER
RAYMOND J SNIEZYK
ALAN S SNOUFFER
BILLY J SNOW
EARL M SNOW
THOMAS G SNOWDEN
DONALD C SNYDER
ELWOOD M SNYDER
FRED M SNYDER
GEORGE T SNYDER
IVAN J SNYDER
LEO M SNYDER
DEOK-MIN SO
EDWIN A SOARES
ARGENE J SOBEHART
HERBERT N SODEN
MARVIN W SODERSTROM
RAYMOND J SOISTMAN
JOHN A SOKOL
ADELAIDO M SOLIS
RICARDO F SOLIS
JOE A SOLIZ JR
MATILDE SOLIZ
DONALD R SOLLARS
JOHN SOMAN
EDWARD H SOMMERFELD
EMMETT R SOMMERVILLE
BOK-MAN SON
BYEONG-HWAN SON
BYEONG-MUN SON
CHANG-UK SON
CHEOL-SUN SON
CHI-HEON SON
DAE-GI SON
DEOK-HYEON SON
DEOK-JO SON
GWANG-MAN SON
GYEONG-DEUK SON
HEUNG-JU SON
HYEONG-SU SON
I-SIK SON
JEOM-SEOK SON
JONG-GAP SON
MU-SIK SON
SE-HWAN SON
SEOK-CHUN SON
WON-SU SON
YONG-HAK SON
AE-TAEK SONG
BONG-HUI SONG
CHANG-SUN SONG
CHEOL-SU SONG
DAE-BONG SONG
GI-JU SONG
GI-YUN SONG
HAK-GYU SONG
HEON-GU SONG
IM-HAK SONG
JANG-HO SONG
JANG-I SONG
JEONG-HO SONG
JEONG-YEOL SONG
JEUNG-HO SONG
JONG-GIL SONG
MU-O SONG
NAM-GUK SONG
SEOK-GEUN SONG
YEONG-JU SONG
YONG-SU SONG
JOSEPH SOPAK
CHARLES R SOPER
DEAN R SORENSON
GEORGE A SORENSON
CAYETANO SOSA
WILLIAM E SOSEBEE
JOHN N SOTELO
JOSE SOTO
PETER S SOTO JR
ALVA L SOUERS
WILLIAM SOUKUP JR
ERNEST C SOUTH
JAMES L SOUTHERLAND
GARLAND R SOUTHWOOD
ROY H SOUTHWORTH
DEWEY L SOWARD
RICHARD V SOWDERS
BENJAMIN F SOWERS
RICHARD J SPAAR
CHARLIE J SPAIN
ROBERT L SPAIN
DEMPSEY SPAINHOUR
WILLIAM C SPALDING
GEORGE L SPANGENBERG
DONALD E SPANGLER
DONALD G SPANGLER
JOSEPH F SPANN
BOBBY C SPARKS
JOHN E SPARKS
ROBERT H SPARKS
WALKER J SPARROW
WARREN W SPAULDING
DONALD E SPEARS
HENRY F SPEARS
LEONARD L SPEARS
CHESTER F SPEICHER
ROBERT A SPEICHER
DONALD B SPENCE
GROVER C SPENCE JR
JOHN W SPENCE
JOSEPH SPENCE
PETER SPERNYAK
FRED F SPERTZEL
JOHN A SPIDAL
ELMO M SPILLER
JACK L SPILLMAN
FREDERICK G SPINDLER
RUDOLPH J SPISKO
BRYAN SPITLER JR
JAMES R SPITZER
PETER SPONTIK
HERBERT M SPOONEMORE
GLEN L SPOONER
CLARENCE H SPOONHOUR JR
BEAR I SPOTTED
CECIL A SPRADLIN
CLYDE D SPRADLIN
WILLIAM G SPRADLIN
EARL F SPRADLING
SHERWOOD M SPRATLIN
ALVIN SPROCK
DONALD J SPRONG
JESSE E SPROUSE
STANLEY J SPYCHAJ
JAMES S SPYRE
VICTOR J STACCONE
PATRICK J STACK
RALPH S STACKIG JR
HERBERT STACY
LENOX STACY
ROLAND B STACY III
FRANK G STAFFEN

46 ARMY

RICHARD STAFFORD
THOMAS C STAGG
WILLIAM F STAGNOLI
CLIFFORD STALKFLEET
HAROLD E STALLSWORTH
NASON D STALNAKER
LEE R STANCIL
CURTIS STAND
RICHARD STANDAERT
JESSIE STANDRIDGE
EDWARD J STANEK
RAYMOND D STANFILL
JAMES C STANFORD
HARRY STANG JR
WILLIAM E STANGL
EDWARD J STANICKI
JOHN R STANKOVIC
THEODORE STANKS
FRANK K STANKUS
JAMES J STANLEY
KENNETH STANLEY
RICHARD L STANLEY
DOCK L STANPHILL
FRANK I STANSEL
EARL D STANTON
GORDON R STANTON
HARTSWELL STANTON
AUSTIN STAPLETON
JOSEPH W STAPLETON
THOMAS P STAPLETON
WILLIAM F STARIC
KENNETH R STARK
LOUIS K STARK
JUNIOR D STARKEY
LEWIS B STARKEY
RUSSELL STARKEY JR
RAYMOND S STARNES
NORMAN F STARR
WALTER R STASKIEWICZ
FRANK STATEN JR
ANGELO STATHES
LAVERN D STATLER
ROBERT L STAUFFER
HOWARD A ST BERNARD
DAVID A ST CLAIR
GEORGE A ST CLAIR
JOHN A STEARNS
DANIEL A STEDMAN
LARRY R STEED
JAMES B STEEL
CHARLES H STEELE
JOSEPH STEELE
LLOYD E STEELE
NATHAN STEELE JR
RONALD E STEELE
C J STEELMAN
OTTO STEEN JR
EDWARD STEFFAN
ALVIN J STEFFENSEN
ROBERT J STEIN
ANTHONY G
STEINHAUSER JR
OBED N STEININGER
DALE C STEINMETZ
PAUL B STEMRICK
JOHN F STENGER
HARRY E STEPHENS
HARVEY STEPHENS JR
JEROME STEPHENS
RALPH STEPHENS
ROBERT D STEPHENS
RUSSELL L STEPHENS
ALBERT E STEPHENSON JR
JAMES E STEPHENSON
NICHOLAS STEPHNO
HARLAN L STEPP
MERMON J STEPP
FRANK S STERCZEK
ALTON G STERNER
WALTER W STERNER
GLENWOOD A STETTLER
BARNARD STEVENS
CLEVE R STEVENS
FRANK L STEVENS
JAMES STEVENS
JAMES A STEVENS
LIONEL F STEVENS
ROBERT STEVENS JR
ROBERT L STEVENS
WILLIAM T STEVENS

BILLIE G STEVENSON
BOBBY R STEVENSON
CHARLES STEVENSON
JEFFERY STEVENSON
ROBERT E STEVENSON
WILLIAM L STEVENSON
DAVID L STEWART
DONALD STEWART
GEORGE E STEWART
HAROLD E STEWART
JAMES E STEWART
JAMES W STEWART
JOHN E STEWART
KENNETH C STEWART
LEON S STEWART
RICHARD H STEWART
ROBERT F STEWART
RUDOLPH STEWART
THOMAS K STEWART
UDELL V STEWART
WILLIAM L STEWART
LIONEL J ST GERMAIN JR
ARNOLD E STIBELMAN
WILLIAM W STICKLER
CARL STIDHAM
ERNEST J STIEFEL
GEORGE W STIMPSON
BOB F STINNETT
EDWARD N STINNETT
HERMAN E STINNETTE
CHARLIE STINSON
ELLWOOD C STIRM JR
JOHN A STIVER
RICHARD W STOCKMAN
CECIL R STOCKTON
LEE E STOCKTON
ROY L STOCKWELL
GEORGE STOECKL JR
CLAUDE L STOKES
GLENN R STOKES
JOE L STOKES
BERTRAM L STOLZE
BOB G STONE
CHARLES A STONE JR
FREDERIC E STONE
PAUL H STONE
RICHARD M STONE
JAY R STONER
JOSEPH D ST ONGE
CURTIS W STOOKEY
WILLIAM E STORCK
DALLAS R STOREY
ALVA J STORK
HAROLD A STORMS
DONALD R STORY
MARTIN L STORY
CHARLES H STOTLER
ISAAC D STOTLER JR
BEVERLY R STOTT
FRANK A STOUT
JAMES H STOUT
JOHN H STOUT
PHILIP D STOUT
JOHN R STOVALL
JOHN R STOVALL
RALPH STOVER
PHILLIP C STOWERS
MARVIN E STOY
ROGER A ST PIERRE
GEORGE A STRAIGHT
CHARLES D STRAIN
FOSTER R STRANGE
JOSEPH L STRANGE
EDWARD L STRATTON
TEX R STRAUB
DERYLE G STRAUGHN
LLOYD F STRAUSER
ROBERT L STRAWSON
JOHNNIE STREET
DONALD N STREIGHT
THOMAS S STRETSBERY
GEORGE M STRICKLAND
JOHN C STRICKLAND
JOHN M STRICKLAND JR
TERRELL STRICKLAND
CHARLES E STRICKLEN
RICHARD F STRICKLER
CLARENCE STRICKLIN
JOSEPH W STRIEGEL
PAUL W STRINE

LEONA STRINGFELLOW
WILLIAM F STRITZKE
CHARLES O STROEMER
FREDERICK W STROHM JR
DALE H STRONG
WILLIAM A STRONG
KEITH A STROTMAN
WAYNE A STROUD
JACK D STROUP
CLINTON J STROUSE
CLIFFORD D STROUT JR
FRANK STROZIER
HENRY M STRUEMPH
ROBERT ST THOMAS
DONALD L STUCKEY
STANWOOD STUFFELBEAM
GEORGE R STUHAN
RICHARD D STULL
JAMES T STUMP
CHARLES STURDIVANT
RALPH C STURGILL
RONALD G STURM
WILFRED A STUSSE
ANGEL L SUAREZ
JOHN R SUCICH
JOHN E SUGGS
PETER P SUKLEY
JOHN L SULAK
FRANK SULIER
HUGH L SULLENS
CHARLES P SULLIVAN
CHARLES R SULLIVAN JR
EDWARD T SULLIVAN
JAMES A SULLIVAN JR
JAMES C SULLIVAN
JOHN L SULLIVAN
LACY L SULLIVAN
ROBERT A SULLIVAN
THOMAS A SULLIVAN SR
WAYNE SULLIVAN
JAMES E SULSER
NORBERT C SULZER
ALLEN SUMMERS
JOHN F SUMMERS
JERRY M SUMMIT
MARVIN J SUMMITT
DELBERT L SUMPTER
HARRY W SUNDAY
LEONARD E SUNDBERG
LARRY D SUNDQUIST
EDWARD I SUNKEL
ROY L SUNSDAHL
EARNEST E SURBER
JAMES A SURBER
ROBERT SURPRENANT
PAUL J SUTER
KENNETH W SUTHERLAND
RAYMOND SUTHERLAND
CHARLES T SUTLIEF
CONRAD E SUTPHIN
HAROLD A SUTPHIN
GEORGE C SUTTON
WILLIAM F SUTTON JR
ROBERT J SVACHA
HENRY SVEHLA
VINCENT SWAIN JR
STANLEY H SWALM
EDWARD J SWAN
ERNEST SWANN
RICHARD P SWANSON
JAMES R SWARTZENTRUVER
WILLIAM F SWEARINGEN
JOSEPH V SWEAT
ERRETT L SWEENEY
WILLIAM C SWEITZER
EDWARD H SWIECHOWSKI
THOMAS C SWIFT
OSCAR B SWINDALL
CLARICE C SWINNEY
ROBERT L SWISHER
HERMAN T SWOFFORD
THOMAS G SYKORA
JAMES SYLVESTER
ALBERT L SYMON
ROBERT L SYNDERGAARD
EDMUND SYNSKI
EDWARD SZAFLARSKI
ELPIDIO TABANGCURA
BENNIE E TABB
DONALD J TABELLION

WILLIAM H TABERT
CHARLES A TABOR
HORACE S TABUSA
ROCCO TACCIO JR
HAROLD G TACKE
WILBUR T TACKETT
CHARLES E TADLOCK
ESTEL V TADLOCK
DONALD L TAETS
MARVIN TAFT
MELVIN E TAGGART
RUDOLPH A TAINIO
CHARLES T TAIT
JAE-BONG TAK
SANG-DEOK TAK
FRANK J TAKACS
MITSUGI B TAKAMOTO
NOBUYUKI TAKESHITA
JACK H TAKTAKIAN
BERNARD D TAKVAM
CESARA A TALAVERA
EDWARD A TALBERT
CLAUDE E TALBOT
EDGAR H TALBOT
CHARLES J TALBOTT
GLEN J TALKINGTON
DOYAL TALLEY
JAMES W TALLEY
SIDNEY D TALLEY JR
GEORGE R TALLMAN
CLARE TALLWHITEMAN
MATTHEW TALLY
DOMINIC A TAMBERINO
DAREL E TAMPLIN
HERBERT E TAMPLIN JR
CHARLES M TANNEHILL
BOBBY D TANNER
GEORGE H TANONAKA
KIYOSHI TANOUYE
PAUL J TANSKI
MORRIS E TANTON
LUIS E TAPIA
ANTONI TARNAS
FLOYD A TARPLEY
PHILIP P TARR
DOUGLAS E TARRY
EBB L TARRY
RICHARD TARTAR
MICHAEL R TATAR
DAVID A TATE
HARRY E TATE
JAMES R TATE
JOHNNY B TATE
MCNEAL TATE
WILLIE D TATE
TONY TAVARES
ARVIL L TAYLOR
BENNY C TAYLOR
BOBBY D TAYLOR
CHARLES S TAYLOR
EARL W TAYLOR
EARNEST A TAYLOR
EDWARD J TAYLOR
FRANCIS E TAYLOR
HARVEY TAYLOR JR
HOWELL TAYLOR JR
JAMES E TAYLOR
JAMES E TAYLOR
JAMES M TAYLOR
JAMES R TAYLOR
JOHN A TAYLOR
JOHN M TAYLOR
JOHN T TAYLOR
LEONARD E TAYLOR
LINNARD M TAYLOR
MICHAEL A TAYLOR
MURL L TAYLOR
OWEN R TAYLOR JR
RICHARD J TAYLOR
ROBERT V TAYLOR
WILLIAM F TAYLOR
WILLIAM K TAYLOR
GEORGE K TAYRIEN
HAROLD G TEAGUE
KENNITH J TEAGUE
WILLIAM J TEASLEY
GAIL R TEEGARDEN
CLAIR F TEETER
JOSEPH L TEETERS
FREDERICK TEFFT

AARON TEGAY
PAUL TEHERO JR
ROBERT J TELL JR
WESLEY E TEMPLE
JAMES E TENNILLE
EDUARDO T TENORIO
HENRY S TENZAR
FRANK TERCZAK
PETER TERNES
PETER J TERRANOVA
ANDREW J TERRELL
BENJAMIN F TERRELL
JOSEPH A TERRELL
LELMON J TERRELL
HERBERT R TERRY
LEWIS J TERRY
PAUL E TERRY
RALPH R TERRY JR
VAN N TERRY
LYLE C TERWILLIGER
ROGER C TESKE
RONALD R TESSIER
CHARLES S TETRO
WILLIAM J TEUCHERT
THEODORE M TEVLIN
BERNARD TEW
CHARLES B THACKER
ROY L THACKER
CHESTER E THARP
JAMES B THAYER
LEO W THAYER
KENNETH J THEISEN
SYLVESTER A THERIOT
JOHN R THEURER
ALLEN G THIBERT
GEORGE W THIBODEAU
IRVIN J THIBODEAUX
JOSEPH H THIBODEAUX
ANDREAS C THIEL
JACK H THIRD
HARLAND C THOEN
ALEXANDER A THOMAS
CALVIN L THOMAS
CHARLES F THOMAS
DONALD R THOMAS
ERNEST R THOMAS
FRANK W THOMAS
GARLAND R THOMAS
GEORGE W THOMAS
HERMAN L THOMAS
HOSEA THOMAS
HOWARD F THOMAS
ISSAIH R THOMAS
JACKSON THOMAS
JAKE R THOMAS
JAMES THOMAS
JAMES THOMAS JR
JAMES E THOMAS
JAMES F THOMAS
JAMES W THOMAS
JOHN F THOMAS
JOSEPH THOMAS
JOSEPH THOMAS
KENNETH W THOMAS
LELAND C THOMAS
MORRIS R THOMAS
NEAL E THOMAS
RICHARD F THOMAS
RICHARD N THOMAS
ROBERT A THOMAS
ROBERT C THOMAS JR
ROBERT V THOMAS
WALTER E THOMAS
WARDELL M THOMAS
WAYMAN L THOMAS
WILLIAM B THOMAS
WILLIE E THOMAS
WILLIS THOMAS
JOSEPH E THOMASON
FORREST J THOMASSON
ALBERT THOMPSON
ALBERT A THOMPSON
AMOS M THOMPSON
BERNIE E THOMPSON
CLARENCE E
THOMPSON
DALE D THOMPSON
EDWARD J THOMPSON
EDWARD L THOMPSON
EUGENE H THOMPSON

47 ARMY

EUGENE R THOMPSON
FLOYD THOMPSON
GENE A THOMPSON
HAROLD D THOMPSON
HAROLD M THOMPSON
HOWARD THOMPSON
J D THOMPSON
JAMES E THOMPSON
JAMES R THOMPSON
JAMES W THOMPSON
JOHN R THOMPSON
JOHN W THOMPSON
JOSEPH C THOMPSON
LEONARD THOMPSON JR
MAYNARD H THOMPSON
OLLIN Y THOMPSON
RALPH A THOMPSON
RALPH L THOMPSON
ROBERT E THOMPSON
ROBERT E THOMPSON JR
ROBERT F THOMPSON
THOMAS B THOMPSON
WAYNE L THOMPSON
WESTON H THOMPSON JR
WILLIAM THOMPSON
WILLIAM A THOMPSON
WILLIAM R THOMPSON
ALLEN E THOMSEN
BOBBY J THORNTON
DONALD M THORNTON
EDWARD D THORNTON
LONNIE THORNTON
RICHARD R THORNTON
ROBERT THORNTON JR
CALVIN THORPE
ERNEST L THORPE JR
ROBERT S THORPE JR
WALTER E THORPE JR
ROBERT C THRANE
BILLY L THRASHER
EDWARD J THRAUM
HOUSTON THROGMARTIN
GERALD E THROSSELL
ELTON E THUNANDER
ROLAND THUNDER HORSE
JAMES A THWEATT
MARVIN W TIBBITS
ROBERT W TICHNELL
DEWEY L TIDWELL
JAMES A TIDWELL
REUBEN W TIEGS
RAYMOND W TIEMAN
HENRY C TILDEN
WILLIAM L TILLEY
GEORGE D TILLMAN
THEODORE R TIMMERMAN
CLAUDE C TIMMONS JR
JAMES J TINDELL JR
PAUL L TINGLE
ARDEN L TINNEL
JULIO TIRADO-CORTES
AMADO TIRADO-SERRANO
EUGENE L TITSWORTH
JAMES R TITUS
ROBERT E TITUS
ROBERT O TITUS
STANLEY P TOBIAS
ROBERT W TOBIN
LOUIS TOCCI
DUANE H TODD
DONALD J TOGNI
IVAN TOKARTSCHUK
RICHARD R TOKUNAGA
WALTER TOLER
LOWELL H TOLLEFSRUD
RICHARD L TOM
HARUO TOMITA
ANDREW A TOMKOVICH
LAWRENCE TOMLINSON
SIMPSON E TOMLINSON JR
DANIEL D TOMPKINS
RICHARD A TOMPKINS JR
EDWARD E TONER
RAYMOND C TONER
WILLIAM H TONEY
DAVID A TONG
WILLIAM J TONKER
JOSEPH R TOOHEY
ORLIN R TOOHEY
CHARLES R TOOMBS

EDWARD F TORAITIS
GUY F TORCHIA
GEORGE TORHAN
LOUIS C TORIBIO
HOWARD P TORPY
FERMAN L TORRENCE
TITUS R TORRENCE JR
FERNANDO TORRENT
DESIDERIO TORRES
ERNEST E TORRES
ERNESTO J TORRES
JOSE TORRES
JOSE C TORRES
MARCELO TORRES
NICHOLAS TORRES
RALPH L TORRES
ROBERTO R TORRES
ANGEL R TORRES-FUENTES
JORGE TORRES-GREEN
ANGEL TORRES-LUNA
EMILIO TORRES-RAMIREZ
FRANK TOSETTI
MICAL M TOTLAND
LESTER E TOULMIN JR
JESSIE TOWE JR
JOSEPH N TOWELL
ELLIS E TOWERY
CHARLES E TOWNE
DELMAR A TOWNSEND
JAMES L TOWNSEND
JAMES M TOWNSEND
THOMAS S TOWNSEND
ALLAN L TRACY
BOBBY C TRACY
JOHN H TRACY
HENRY TRACZYKIEWICZ
JOHN W TRAIL JR
HENRRAINUM JR
JOSEPH L TRAMMELL
ELIJAH TRANNON
NELSON E TRASK
JOSEPH R TRAVERS
ARTHUR H TRAVERSO
CHESTER B TRAVIS
ROLLIN G TRAVIS
WILLIAM F TRAXLER
RICHARD A TREADWAY
WILLIAM A TREECE
REFUGIO TREJO
AUREL N TREMBLAY
DAVID K TREMBLEY
DONALD M TRENT
JEBRU TRENT
ARTHUR A TRENTT
GABRIEL TREVIS
RICHARD S TRIBBLE
JOHN A TRICOMO
GREGORY W TRIGGS
JOE B TRIMM JR
JAMES J TRIONE
RAY TRIPP
MAXIMO A TROCHE
VANCE E TROGDON
GEORGE TROMPAK JR
EUGENE F TROSS
ROBERT A TROUFIELD
EARL M TROUT JR
BILLY R TROW
CARL K TROY
LAWRENCE E TROY
CECIL S TRUAX JR
HUBERT P TRUEBLOOD
BOBBY L TRUELOVE
HAROLD TRUESDALE JR
RAY E TRUETT
HOWARD E TRUITT
JOHN D TRUJILLO
MELECIO H TRUJILLO
GLENN E TRUMAN
WILLIAM E TRUMBO
ARTHUR E TRUSLOW
NICKOLAS J TSAKNIS
JAMES TSITSINOS
EMILIO L TUBENS
NICOLA A TUCCI
WILLIAM C TUCK
DANIEL H TUCKER
DONALD H TUCKER
HERBERT TUCKER
J D TUCKER

JOHN L TUCKER
RAY D TUCKER
ROBERT L TUCKER
STANLEY R TUCKER
WILLIE L TUFTS
RICHARD J TUGMAN
JOHN TUIN
JAMES G TULIP
RALPH E TULL
CARL D TUMLINSON
MICHAUX TURBEVILLE
CLARENCE TURCOTT
GEORGE E TUREK
DANIEL A TURGEON
DORSEY V TURLEY
JAMES E TURLEY
BILLY A TURNER
CHARLIE TURNER
CORBET L TURNER
EUGENE C TURNER
GERALD O J TURNER
HERBERT TURNER
HOWARD L TURNER
JAMES W TURNER
JOSEPH L TURNER
LORENZO TURNER
MELVIN L TURNER
RONALD L TURNER
SAMUEL E TURNER
THOMAS J TURNER
WILLIAM H TURNER JR
WILLIAM H TURNER
WILLIAM T TURNER
JAMES P TURNEY
LLOYD C TUTTLE
OLAI J TWENGE
WALLACE TWITCHELL
LEONARD E TYE
BENJAMIN M TYLER
KENNETH E TYLER
ROBERT L TYLER
JOSEPH E TYNAN
AVERY B TYNDALL JR
JOHN T TYNER
NOAH H TYREE JR
STANLEY L TYRELL
BONG-DAL U
BYEONG-OK U
IN-HA U
SAM-CHAE U
LESTER J UBER
EDWARD UGUCCIONE
JERRY E UHLS
JOSEPH W UJEK JR
WILLIAM L ULBRICH
WILLIAM F UNDERDOWN
DONALD A UNDERWOOD
GUY L UNDERWOOD JR
HOMER H UNDERWOOD
RALPH F UNDERWOOD
ROY S UNDERWOOD
KENNETH W UNGER
HENRY J UNKEL JR
AKIRA UOTA
WILLIE D UPTAIN
JOHN W UPTEGROVE
TAKAYA URAGAMI
EDWARD M URBANOWSKI
DAROLD D URBANSKI
JOE D URIBE
JOHN URIBE
WILLIAM URICK
FAUSTINO URRO
JAMES E USELTON
WILBUR E UTTER
JOSEPH VAILLANCOURT
LEO J VAILLANCOURT
BENITO V VALDEZ
BERNARD T VALDEZ
MANUEL VALDEZ
ROBERT VALDEZ
SOLOMON VALDEZ JR
ANGEL M VALDIVIEZ
ANTONIO VALENTIN-
IRIZARRY
ALFREDO VALENZUELA
TONY L VALENZUELA
CARLTON C VALLIERE
WILBUR L VAN BREMEN
LEO F VAN CAMP

DORAL A VANCE
ZEB W VANCE JR
CHARLES C VANDERKOOI
WILBUR R VANDIVER
DALE E VAN DRASKA
WILLIAM G VAN DUNK
ELBERT D VAN GRUNDY
JULIUS L VAN GUNDY
JOSEPH J VAN HOOK
ROBERT E VAN HOOK
ROBERT G VANHOOSE
ROBERT L VAN HORN
THEODORE VAN NATTA
JAMES J VAN NESS
MARVIN G VAN NINGEN
ROBERT L VANOVER
WILLIAM O VAN PELT
ROBERT VAN QUAKEBEKE
CALVIN VAN WINKLE
JULIO S VARELA
FLOR VARGAS
GUILLERMO VARGAS-
RIVERA
CHARLES A VARKETT
EDMUND S VARNER
THOMAS H VARNER
GERALD L VARNEY
JON D VARNEY
BALINT VASH
JOHN V VASQUEZ
JOSE VASQUEZ
RUMALDO R VASQUEZ
H T VAUGHAN
WILLIAM E VAUGHAN
AUBREY D VAUGHN
DONALD C VAUGHN
GRAYSON S VAUGHN
THOMAS H VAUGHN
BILLY D VAUGHT
JOSEPH T VAZQUEZ
JUAN R VAZQUEZ
EPIFANIO VAZQUEZ-
DE JESUS
PABLO VAZQUEZ-DIAZ
HERBERTO VAZQUEZ-
RIVERA
RICHARDO VEGA
VICTOR M VEGA
VINCENT A VEGA
JOSE A VEGA-RIVERA
MANUEL N VELA
JORGE VELAZQUEZ
JORGE N VELAZQUEZ
RICHARD VELD
LEMUEL A VELEZ-
SANTIAGO
MIGUEL A VELEZ-
SANTIAGO
RICHARD G VELLES
CHARLES D VENDER
VINCENT VENEZIA
MARCIAL T VERA
TONY S VERA
RAYMOND A VERNON
ELLIS R VERRET
STEVE J VERTCNIK
CURTIS E VESTAL
GEORGE E VESTAL
CECIL T VESY
DONALD H VETOWICH
MAURICE L VIAENE
DALLAS W VIAN
STEVE VICH
GORDON R VICK
IVEY E VICKERS
ROY M VICKERY
MARVIN E VIEL
FRANK VIERA JR
ARTURO VIGIL
PABLO J VIGIL
RUDOLPH F VIGIL
HENRY F VIGNEAU
JAKIE J VIGNES
ABRAHAM VILA-LOPEZ
HERMAN F VILLA
DARIO VILLAFANE-
DAVILA
JOAQUIN VILLANUEVA
ALFONSO P VILLAREAL
RAUL S VILLAREAL

JUAN L VILLARREAL
PETER VILUTIS JR
LEROY D VINAR
DONALD F VINCENT
EDWARD C VINCENT
FRANK H VINCENT
WILLIAM E VINCENT
MURRAY N VINEYARD
ROBERT J VINEYARD
JOHN VINGIONE JR
JOHN P VINKENBERG
FREDERICK A VIOLA
DAVID G VIRAMONTES
PETER A VISCUSO
ROBERT J VITELLO
HERBERT D VIZENA
MITCHELL P VLAHOVICH
OSMAN VOGA JR
JOHN E VOIT
JOSEPH C VOLPE
ROBERT L VONALLMEN
VICTOR G VOORHEES
CARL F VORBECK
HAROLD B VORTHERMS
HARVEY R VOSS
JOHN W VOUGHT
HERBERT H VOWELL
EUGENE R VOYLES
WILLIAM E VOYLES
ROBERT S VOZAR
ANTHONY VRANIC
JAMES C VREELAND
GUS H
WACHENSCHWANZ JR
THOMAS G WACHTMAN
DONALD L WADDOUPS
ALEXANDER WADE JR
DUERELL WADE
JOHN G WADE
MEARL L WADE
TROY H WADE
VERNON L WADE
BILLY F WADKINS
EVERETT W WAFORD
FLOYD R WAGAMAN
JAMES J
WAGENSHUTZ JR
DAN H WAGERS
BILLE E WAGGONER
CARL R WAGNER
MILES E WAGNER JR
NICHOLAS J WAGNER
OSCAR W WAGNER
PAUL R WAGNER
ROBERT B WAGNER
SIM WAGNER
THEODORE A WAGNER
HOMER L WAID
WILLIAM H WAID
ARDEAN R WAILES
DANIEL E WAIN
ELMER G WAINMAN
BILLY J WAINWRIGHT
JAMES H WAITES
ROLAND A WAKENIGHT
JOE R WALBECK
CASIMIR F WALCZAK
ARNOLD R WALDBILLIG
ROMAN J WALDKIRCH
WILBUR E WALDON
JACK N WALDRUP
JOHN L WALENTY
BOBBY G WALKER
CHARLES WALKER JR
EDDIE WALKER
EMIL J WALKER
FRANCIS J WALKER
GLENN R WALKER
JACK O WALKER
JAMES WALKER
JAMES T WALKER
JAVY C WALKER
JOE W WALKER JR
LEO WALKER
LLOYD B WALKER
RALPH B WALKER
ROSS M WALKER
TEDDY J WALKER
TOMMY C WALKER
WILLIAM E WALKER

48 ARMY

TELMA W WALL JR
ALVIN L WALLACE
CARL E WALLACE
CHARLES A WALLACE
ELBERT P WALLACE
J I WALLACE
MALCOLM R WALLACE
PENDLETON W WALLACE
RAY E WALLACE
WILLIAM D WALLACE
DAVID WALLACH
WILLIAM W WALLACK
JAMES T WALLEN
HAROLD R WALLENDER
FREEMON C WALLER
WILLIAM D WALLER
WILLIAM WALLGREN JR
WILLIAM M WALLS
DONALD E WALSH
ROBERT F WALSH
DAVID F WALTERS
FRANK B WALTERS JR
KENNETH E WALTERS
WILLIAM F WALTERS
CEDRIC W WALTMAN
BOBBY B WALTON
CARL E WALTON
CURTIS L WALTON
HAROLD L WALTON
MARTIN E WAMPLER JR
LEROY WANDS
TAE-SEOP WANG
HAROLD N WANNED
HENRY A WARBLOW JR
BURLIN W WARD
CHARLES H WARD
DELMER R WARD
DONALD K WARD
FRANK M WARD
HERBERT WARD
JAMES B WARD
JAMES E WARD
JAMES F WARD JR
JOHNNIE T WARD
LOWELL M WARD
MAYO WARD
MELVIN R WARD
ROBERT A WARD
SAMUEL E WARD
THOMAS J WARD
VIRGIL E WARD
JOSEPH J WARDA JR
JOSEPH S WARDYNSKI
HAROLD G WARE
RAYMOND O WARE
ROBERT L WARE
EDWARD F WARFIELD
LAWRENCE WARFIELD
LLOYD R WARFIELD JR
JAMES P WARING
ALFRED E WARMOUTH
DEWAYNE H WARNER
PAUL C WARNER
TROY A WARNER
WILLIAM WARNER
DONALD A WARNING
DAVID W WARNOCK
CLARENCE J WARREN
EDGAR O WARREN
JAMES O WARREN
JAMES R WARREN
LARRY D WARREN
VALENTINE T WARRICHAIET
VAN WARRICK
DILLON E WARTHAN
GEORGE H WASHBURN
CHARLES L WASHINGTON JR
CURTIS N WASHINGTON
ISAAC WASHINGTON JR
JOHN M WASHINGTON
JOHNNY WASHINGTON
WALTER H WASHINGTON
WILLIAM WASHINGTON
EDWIN F WASIELEWSKI
RICHARD J WASKO
NICK WASYLYSHYN
RICHARD M WATANABE
GLEN E WATERMAN
EUNIS G WATERS
HAROLD L WATERS
CALVIN C WATKINS
DAVID D WATKINS
HAROLD B WATKINS
MELVIN WATKINS
RANDALL J WATKINS
SAMUEL K WATKINS
WOOSTER WATKINS
DONALD R WATSON
EUGENE F WATSON
GLEN L WATSON
HAROLD L WATSON
HARRY WATSON
KENNETH R WATSON
LEO WATSON
WAYNE T WATSON
LAWRENCE J WATT
FRED L WATTERSON
IRVING D WATTERSON
BOBBIE E WATTS
CLEVELAND E WATTS
FRANKLIN H WATTS
HUGH WATTS JR
ISHMAEL WATTS
ORVILLE L WATTS
ROY H WATTS JR
WILLIE WATTS JR
LEO J WAWRO
GEORGE WAY
HENRY L WEATHERFORD
LEROY W WEATHERFORD
WILLIAM R WEATHERMAN
CHARLES A WEAVER
DAVID L WEAVER
JAMES M WEAVER
WADIE WEAVER JR
DANNA L WEBB
DELNO V WEBB
DONALD E WEBB
DONALD F WEBB
DONALD K WEBB
DONALD W WEBB
HENRY L WEBB
JAMES F WEBB
JONAS B WEBB
SHIRLEY R WEBB
STANLEY S WEBB
GUILLERMO WEBER
JOHN F WEBER
MURRAY WEBER
ROBERT J WEBER
GEORGE W WEBSTER JR
JACK M WEBSTER
LEE R WEBSTER
WILLIAM E WEBSTER
ROY WEEKS
PAUL D WEGLEITNER
CHESTER J WEGRZYN
JEROME H WEHAGE
JOHN J WEHINGER
WILLIAM H WEHLAND
JESSE WEIDNER JR
MERLE R WEIDNER
ARTHUR A WEIGAND
WALTER A WEIGAND
WILLIAM J WEIGESHOFF
CHARLES E WEIMER
MITCHELL S WEINBERG
MELVIN WEINRAUB
CLARENCE H WEISS
IRVING S WEISS
STANLEY J WEISSMAN
JULIUS WEISTER
WILLIAM R WEITMAN
CHARLES W WEIZEL
DILLON F WELCH
EUGENE J WELCH
GOBEL J WELCH
HARRY E WELCH
ROBERT L WELCH
HAROLD D WELDON
ERNEST V WELKER
HAROLD M WELKER
JERRY L WELLER
BERNARD WELLS
CALVIN D WELLS
CARL F WELLS
CHARLES F WELLS
ELMER L WELLS
HARRY I WELLS
THOMAS J WELLS
WILLARD D WELLS
WILLIAM L WELLS
NEAL W WELSH
ROYCE A WELSH
RAYMOND D WENDELL
ERNEST A WENDLING
WILBERT W WENDRICKS
ARLIN H WENDT
DAVID C WENTLY
CARL R WENTZELL
EDWARD W WENZEL
JAMES F WERBER
FORREST R WERLEY
HERMAN R WESLING
DONALD F WESSEL
EDWARD H WEST
HENRY F WEST
HOWARD J WEST
KENNETH WEST
LEONARD L WEST
WALTER E WEST
WARREN WEST
ELIOT R WESTCOAT
JACK R WESTEL
PERVIS WESTER
KENNETH WESTERMAN
WILLIAM WESTMORELAND
ROBERT J WESTON
JAMES P WESTRY
HOWELL G WETHINGTON
MICHAEL T WHALEN
RICHARD D WHALEN
RICHARD V WHALEN
HENRY N WHALEY JR
NORMAN L WHALEY
ITHIEL E WHATLEY
DONALD W WHEELER
HARRY F WHEELER
JAMES G WHEELER
JAMES J WHEELER
ROBERT N WHEELER
SEBASTIAN WHEELER
FRANCIS E WHELAN
RALPH J WHETSTINE
HOWARD K WHIPKEY
ROBERT L WHISLER
WILLIAM L WHISLER
JAMES L WHISMAN JR
DONALD L WHITAKER
ODELL WHITAKER
ARLO L WHITE
BILLY R WHITE
CARL L WHITE
CARL W WHITE
CHESTER A WHITE
DANIEL M WHITE
ELVIS J WHITE
HARLAN A WHITE
JAMES A WHITE
JAMES B WHITE
JAMES S WHITE
JIMMIE M WHITE
KENNETH R WHITE
MARTIN E WHITE
PATRICK A WHITE
PERRY O WHITE
RICHARD E WHITE
RUDOLPH A WHITE
THOMAS P WHITE
WADDELL WHITE
WILLIAM K WHITE
WILMER C WHITE
WESLEY L WHITED
DANA L WHITEHEAD
WALLACE WHITEHEAD
WILLIAM WHITEHURST
MARTIN H WHITEMAN JR
RICHARD D WHITEMAN
JOSEPH E WHITESIDE
HOWARD A WHITLEY
LEEROY WHITLOW
BOBBY H WHITMAN
HAROLD W WHITMER
GEORGE H WHITNEY
WALTER E WHITSETT
ROBERT M WHITSON
ALTON WHITTAKER
IVAN D WHITTENBURG
WALTER WHITTINGTON
WORTHAW WHITWORTH
JIN-HWAN WI
PAUL J WICHMAN
ROBERT L WICKHAM
DONALD I WIDNER
WILLIAM L WIDNER
THADDEUS J WIEGEL
CHRISTIAN C WIELAND
JAMES E WIELERT
CHESTER W WIERZBICKI
THEODORE W WIESEKE
ROBERT L WIGEN
FREDERICK H WIGGINS
SAMUEL WIGGINS
HOWARD WIGLEY
JAMES W WIKE
JULIAN D WILBOURN
CHARLIE WILCHER JR
THOMAS R WILCOSKY
RALPH S WILCOX
HAROLD D WILDER
JAMES B WILDER
LUTHER M WILDES
JOHN M WILDY
IRWIN D WILENSKY
ROSSIE E WILES
ALBERT L WILEY
DONALD E WILEY
JAMES C WILEY
ROBERT N WILEY
WILLIAM W WILEY
ORON T WILHITE
CHARLES W WILKES
DAVID C WILKES
RALPH C WILKINS
FRANCIS T WILKINSON
WILLIAM H WILKINSON JR
EDWARD E WILKOSZ
GEORGE W WILLETT
RICHARD R WILLETT
ROBERT M WILLETT
ALEXANDER WILLIAMS
ALVIN C WILLIAMS
ANDREW D WILLIAMS
ARTHUR A WILLIAMS
BOB H WILLIAMS
CARL WILLIAMS
CHARLES D WILLIAMS
CHARLES E WILLIAMS
CHARLES J WILLIAMS
CHARLES L WILLIAMS
CHARLESTON WILLIAMS
CLARENCE WILLIAMS
CLYDE WILLIAMS
COLEMAN B WILLIAMS
DELMONT WILLIAMS
EARL E WILLIAMS
EDDIE WILLIAMS JR
EDDIE WILLIAMS
EVERETT L WILLIAMS
FLEMING WILLIAMS
FLOYD B WILLIAMS JR
FRANKLIN A WILLIAMS
FRED WILLIAMS
GEORGE H WILLIAMS
GERALD R WILLIAMS
HENRY L WILLIAMS
HENRY M WILLIAMS JR
HERBERT H WILLIAMS
HURA K WILLIAMS
IVAN F WILLIAMS
JAMES A WILLIAMS
JAMES C WILLIAMS
JAMES E WILLIAMS
JAMES I WILLIAMS
JIM E WILLIAMS
JOHN H WILLIAMS
JOHN N WILLIAMS JR
JOHN R WILLIAMS
JOHNNY WILLIAMS JR
JOSEPH H WILLIAMS
KENNETH B WILLIAMS
KENNETH E WILLIAMS
KENNETH P WILLIAMS
LAWRENCE H WILLIAMS
LEE G WILLIAMS
LEO H WILLIAMS
LUIS F WILLIAMS
MARVIN R WILLIAMS
MCKINLEY WILLIAMS
MORRIS WILLIAMS
NELSON E WILLIAMS
OTIS C WILLIAMS
PERCY E WILLIAMS
RALPH B WILLIAMS
REYNOLDS WILLIAMS
ROBERT H WILLIAMS
ROBERT K WILLIAMS
ROBERT L WILLIAMS
ROBERT L WILLIAMS
SAM D WILLIAMS
SAMUEL WILLIAMS
SAMUEL WILLIAMS
WILLIAM P WILLIAMS
WILLIE WILLIAMS JR
WILLIE V WILLIAMS
CHARLES T WILLIAMSON
CLAUDE H WILLIAMSON
HERBERT WILLIAMSON
JAMES WILLIAMSON
MELVIN L WILLIAMSON
RICHARD W WILLIAMSON
ROBERT A WILLIAMSON
ILA J WILLIE
BILLIE WILLINGHAM
ADAM M WILLIS
FLEMING G WILLIS
FRANK WILLIS
GEORGE W WILLIS
JESS E WILLIS
PAUL J WILLIS
SYLVESTER WILLIS
JAMES E WILLISON
LEE E WILLMSEN
RAY WILLOUGHBY
GENE W R WILLRICH
EARL E WILLS
ROBERT W WILMOTH
FRED D WILMUTH
CHARLES WILSON JR
CHARLES B WILSON
CHARLES E WILSON
CHARLES L WILSON
DAVID H WILSON
DONALD E WILSON
DONALD J WILSON
EARL T WILSON
FRANK WILSON JR
GARY R WILSON
GEORGE F WILSON
GEORGE W WILSON JR
GILMER W WILSON
HARRY L WILSON
HOMER C WILSON
J W WILSON
JAMES C WILSON
JAMES H WILSON
JAMES M WILSON
JAMES R L WILSON
JAMES W WILSON
JERRY WILSON
JESSE E WILSON
JOHN D WILSON JR
KENNETH R WILSON
LEROY E WILSON
LESLIE G WILSON
LINWOOD F D WILSON
RICHARD G WILSON
ROBERT E WILSON
ROY S WILSON JR
SAMUEL A WILSON
SHIRLEY A WILSON
WILLIAM E WILSON
WILLIAM G WILSON
WILLIAM H WILSON
WILLIAM H WILSON
ALBERT J WILTROUT
JOHN W WIMBLEY JR
LEROY H WINANS
CHARLES L WINCHELL
EDDIE WINCHESTER
GORDON WINCHESTER
WILLIAM J WINCHESTER
JAMES F WINCKLER
MAX E WINDLE
EDWARD G WINE
GEORGE H WINES
LEROY C WINFIELD
ELMER V WING JR

49

ARMY

WILLIAM WING
LEWIS M WINGARD
CHARLES R WINGFIELD
JACK M WINICK
HORACE T WINSLETT
JAMES R WINSTON
ARTHUR F WINTER
WILLIAM T WIROTZIOUS
JOHN E WIRTZ JR
ARTHUR F WISE
BRUCE P WISE
ESLEY WISE
GORDON L WISE
HAROLD A WISE
PAUL WISE
DONALD G WISEMAN
PAUL E WISEMAN
ALBERT WISHER
FELIX J WISNIEWSKI
ROBERT L WITHERS
ALOYSIUS WITSCHEN
HAROLD H WITTE
WILLIAM WITTENMYER
WILLIAM J WITTREICH
JACK J WITWER
CLAYTON J WIXSON
JOHN S WOHLFORD
WALLACE L WOLD
MELVIN G WOLF
PAUL C WOLF JR
THOMAS W WOLF
DAVID L WOLFE
EDWARD WOLFE
GEORGE E WOLFE
GLENN H WOLFE
LLOYD E WOLFE
SAMUEL L WOLFE
BILLY WOLFORD
EVERETT WOLFORD JR
RANSOME WOLFORD JR
JOSEPH J WOLK
BRYANT H WOMACK
EDWARD R WOMACK
ROBERT W WOMACK
WILLIAM K C WONG
ARLTON H WOOD
CHARLES E WOOD
GERALD S WOOD
HAROLD H WOOD
JOE F WOOD
JOSEPH E WOOD
JUNIOR R WOOD
PAUL E WOOD
ROBERT M WOOD
TOM J WOOD
HAROLD L WOODARD
HAROLD D WOODBURY
HARRY WOODFOLK JR
RUSSELL H WOODMAN
DAVID WOODRUFF
GEORGE H WOODS
ROGER L WOODS
TOMMY WOODS
WILLIAM J WOODS
GUY WOODSON
LEWIS B WOODSON
MORRIS WOODSON
RICHARD H WOODWARD
WILLIAM K WOODWARD
BOBBY J WOODY
EVERETT H WOODY
JAMES M WOOLSEY
LOWELL W WOOLSEY JR
CLAIR D WOOMER
EDWIN E WOOTEN
FRANKLIN D WOOTEN
RAY D WOOTEN
ARTHUR J WORDEN
CHARLES WORKMAN
DONALD G WORKMAN
DONALD B WORLEY
FOREST E WORLEY
FRANK WORLEY
JACK E WORLEY
LEONARD E WORRELL
MELBERN W WORRELL
WARREN W WORSTER JR
MARCELLUS D WORTH
PHILIP L WORTH
HOLLY WORTHY

FRANK J WOZNIAK JR
WILLIAM M WOZNIAK
ALLEN WRIGHT
DONALD WRIGHT
EMERSON J WRIGHT
FRED L WRIGHT JR
GERALD WRIGHT
HOWARD A WRIGHT
JAMES A WRIGHT
JOHN B WRIGHT
JOHN H WRIGHT
JOHN L WRIGHT
KENNETH W WRIGHT
LEWIS C WRIGHT
MARVIN L WRIGHT
MELVIN G WRIGHT
PRESTON A WRIGHT
RAYMOND WRIGHT JR
RICHARD E WRIGHT
ROBERT J WRIGHT JR
ROY E WRIGHT
ROY N WRIGHT
WILLIAM J WRIGHT
JOHN R WULF
MARVIN WUNDERLICH
ANDREW G WUTZ
DUANE WYATT
HERBERT G WYATT
JAMES W WYCHE
HOMER H WYLES
GEORGE R WYLIE
ROY F WYNN
EDWARD L WYSZCELSKI
FRANK A YABLONSKI
ARMOUR R YAHN
MUNEO YAKA
TSUGIO YAMAGUCHI
YEIJI YAMAGUCHI
JOICHI YAMASHITA
ROBERT G YANCEY
BEOM-SEOK YANG
DONG-MUN YANG
GEUM-DOL YANG
JAE-GWANG YANG
JAE-SU YANG
JONG-GEUN YANG
MU-TAK YANG
SIN-GEUN YANG
YONG-SIK YANG
YONG-UN YANG
JAMES A YANISCH
HAROLD L YARBROUGH
GERALD V YARRISH
JOHN P YARUSSO
DONALD T YASKO
GARY K YASUNAKA
BEN J YATES
EDWARD J YATES
GORDON C YATES
WILEY A YATES
WILLIAM J YATES
RALPH F YEAGER
RAYMOND E YEARGLE
LAWRENCE O YEATER
ANGELO B YECCO JR
V S YELVERTON
JAMES E YENOR
DANG-BOK YEO
JEONG-CHUL YEO
JO-HYEON YEO
JO-HYEON YEO
SEUNG-HWAN YEO
YONG-TAE YEO
JOHN YLINEN
DALTON B YOKEM
KATASHI YOKOTAKE
JACK W YON
CHANG-HUI YONG
STANLEY W YOPPINI
BLAINE G YORK
JOE L YORK
MELVIN D YORK
ELMER J YOSHIHARA
THOSHIHAR YOSHIKAWA
TATSUO YOSHINO
LEROY T YOST
OSCAR C YOST
VERNON R YOST
DONALD P YOUNCE
CARLTON H YOUNG

DONALD R YOUNG
EDWARD YOUNG
ERWIN C YOUNG JR
EUGENE YOUNG
FRANCIS E YOUNG
GILBERT F YOUNG
JACK L YOUNG
JAMES C YOUNG
JAMES T YOUNG
JOHN R YOUNG
KENNETH YOUNG
L D YOUNG
LEROY C YOUNG
NELSON E YOUNG
ORVILLE T YOUNG
PAUL H YOUNG
RAYMOND A YOUNG
RAYMOND C YOUNG
RICHARD W YOUNG
ROBERT L YOUNG JR
RUSSELL V YOUNG
THEODORE YOUNG
CHARLES R YOUNGBLOOD
DONALD D YOUNGER
WILLIAM R YOUNGER
CHAN-JO YU
GANG-UI YU
GU-BOK YU
IN-GEUN YU
SANG-EUL YU
WON-SEOK YU
JONG-HA YUK
YONG-JUN YUK
BONG-HYEON YUN
BYEONG-RYONG YUN
CHANG-HYEON YUN
CHEOL-JIN YUN
DAL-GU YUN
EUL-SEOK YUN
GAP-CHEOL YUN
GEUM-SEOK YUN
GI-SEOP YUN
GI-SU YUN
GI-YEONG YUN
HYEOK-GEUN YUN
JAE-HWAN YUN
JEONG-GEUN YUN
JONG-CHEOL YUN
JONG-YEOL YUN
SANG-DAE YUN
SE-O YUN
SEOK-WON YUN
WON-SAENG YUN
YEONG-GWAN YUN
YEONG-GYUN YUN
YEONG-SIK YUN
GEORGE YURITIC
MANDELL YUSTER
MICHAEL B ZACZYK
KENNETH F ZADE
JAMES H ZAHORIK
ANTHONY C ZAHRA
FLOYD F ZAKRZEWSKI
RICHARD V ZAKRZEWSKI
JOSEPH A ZALAR
TEDDY A ZALBA
GEORGE E ZALESKI
PAUL E ZALESKI
RICHARD J ZALETEL
ANSELMO ZAMORA
LOUIS E ZAMORA
ALPHONSE ZAMPIER
PRIMO A ZANNI
DONALD L ZANOVICH
SAMUEL V ZANTEN
VICTOR J ZAPATA
ANTHONY J ZAPPETTI
THOMAS E ZARADA
HENRY ZAREMSKI
PAUL ZATZEK
CHARLES P ZAWADSKI
JORGE ZAYAS-PEDROGO
DONALD D ZEA
RALPH ZECCO
DONALD F ZEDNIK
DONALD J ZEINART
CHARLES ZEITLER
JAMES J ZELEZNIK
EUGENE G ZELKOWSKI
ROBERT E ZELLARS

DONALD E ZENTNER
FRED C ZERK
ROBERT L ZEUMAULT JR
JOSEPH R ZICH JR
HARRY H ZICKEFOOSE
ROLF L ZICKEL
WILLIAM F ZIDELSKI
LAVERNE J ZIEBARTH
RAYMOND R ZIEMECKI
JACK R ZIEMER
DONALD J ZIMDAHL
RAYMOND J ZIMMER
CARL H ZIMMERMAN
EUGENE H ZIMMERMAN
LUTHER B ZIMMERMAN
ROBERT ZIMMERMAN
WALTER L ZIMMERMAN
CHARLES E ZINKAN
JACK A ZIRKLE
WILLIAM M ZOELLICK
JACK R ZOLLER
ALOYSIUS L ZONCA
HAROLD W ZOOK
DARRELL W ZORN
SALVATORE J ZUCCA
IGNATIUS S ZUPPARO
EDWIN J ZUREK

CORPORAL

LEONARD E AARONS
AUGUSTUS A ABBEY
JOHN D ABBOTT
WILBUR E ABBOTT
WILLIAM R ABDERHALDEN
WHERRY L ABERCROMBIE
BRUNO F ABLONDI
LESTER W ABSHIRE
VINCENTE G ACEDO
HENRY L ACEVES
PRESTON E ACOCK
ISMAEL A ACOSTA
RUBEN ACOSTA
MARVIN D ACTKINSON
FLOYD N ACTON
ANGEL L ACUNA-OTERO
JOSEPH J ADAMO
ALFRED B ADAMS
ANGUS B ADAMS
BOSIE A ADAMS
CHARLES W ADAMS
CLIFFORD L ADAMS
FRANCIS V ADAMS
GARNETT J ADAMS JR
HARRY L ADAMS
JAMES D ADAMS
JAMES O ADAMS
RAYMOND A ADAMS
ROBERT C ADAMS
ROGER K ADAMS
RONALD H ADAMS
WILBUR J ADAMS
ROBERT E ADDISON
HAROLD ADELMAN
COLIE J ADKINS JR
JAMES H ADKINS
VERNON E ADKINS
FORREST D ADKISSON
ROBERT C AGARD JR
CARLETON V AGRELL
LUCIO R AGUILAR
RICHARD AGUILAR
SAUL AGUILAR
BENITO R AGUINALDO
FRANK B AHERN
LOUIS AH LET
RAYMOND J AIZEN
BOBBY E AKERS
HERBERT D AKERS
VICTOR AKERS JR
LLOYD E AKINS
WALTER R AKRIDGE JR
RAMON ALBA
ABRAHAM ALBALADEJO
ROBERT H ALBERS
DONALD ALBERSON
ELMER J ALBRECHT
EUGENE D ALBRECHT
JOHN A ALBRECHT

GILBERT R ALCANTAR
GERARDO R ALDANA
MARVIN B ALDERMAN
BEN R ALDRIDGE
HARRY L ALECOCK
ANTHONY C ALEXA JR
ALFRED L ALEXANDER
BILLY B ALEXANDER
CHARLES E ALEXANDER
JACK D ALEXANDER
JOHN B ALEXANDER
LONNIE V ALEXANDER
LUCIUS ALEXANDER
OTTIS F ALFORD
DAN O ALFRED
DONALD N ALLAN
ARTHUR S ALLARD
PERCY ALLEMAND
ARTHUR W ALLEN
CHARLES C ALLEN
CHELCIA A ALLEN
DAVID ALLEN
DOUGLASS A ALLEN
HENRY L ALLEN
KENNETH R ALLEN
LEO ALLEN
OREALL L ALLEN
PHILLIP P ALLEN
RICHARD L ALLEN
ROBERT H ALLEN
WALTER E ALLEN
JAMES L ALLEY
JOHN C ALLEY
RICHARD O ALLIE
JACOB W ALLMARAS
DANIEL R ALMANZA
MAXIMINO ALOMAR-RUIZ
FRANCISCO ALONZO JR
HELMUT ALTERGOTT
RUFFUS B ALTHISER
MIGUEL T ALVARENGA
AGUSTIN ALVAREZ
ARMANDO ALVAREZ
HERMOGENES ALVERIO
ARTHUR L ALVESHERE
JOHN C ALVIS
LESLIE R AMANN
LUIS AMARO-GARCIA
JOSEPH D AMATO
KARL A AMBERG
HUMBERT J AMBRIZ
THOMAS AMBROSE
WILLIAM H AMES
MARVIN B AMIOT
HAROLD L AMUNDSON
JACK K AMYX
BYEONG-GIL AN
CHANG-HUI AN
DEOK-SANG AN
DONG-YEOL AN
GI-JO AN
IK-JU AN
JONG-I AN
JONG-SU AN
NAM-JUN AN
SANG-SU AN
SANG-TAE AN
SEOK-CHEON AN
SEOK-SI AN
TAE-WON AN
UK-IN AN
YEONG-HWAN AN
YEONG-SEOK AN
CHRISTOPHER C ANCELET
AUSTIN J ANDERSON
BILLY D ANDERSON
BOBBY G ANDERSON
CHARLIE M ANDERSON
CLYDE E ANDERSON
DONALD E ANDERSON
DWAIN ANDERSON
ELLIS L ANDERSON
ELLSWORTH L ANDERSON
EUGENE A ANDERSON
EUGENE C ANDERSON
HERBERT A ANDERSON
JACOB G ANDERSON

50 ARMY

JAMES ANDERSON
LOUIS D ANDERSON
M C ANDERSON
NORBERT O ANDERSON
RAYMOND G ANDERSON
ROBERT D ANDERSON
ROY G ANDERSON
ROY H ANDERSON JR
WALTER C ANDERSON
WESLEY A ANDERSON
WILLIAM C ANDERSON
WILLIAM P ANDERSON
RAYMOND ANDRADE JR
JOHN S ANDRESEN
CHARLES L ANDREWS
EARL R ANDREWS
EDWARD R ANDREWS
LEON E ANDREWS
ARNOLD V ANDRING
TITO J ANGARANO
EUGENE L ANGELL
GEORGE J ANGLES
JOSEPH ANTROM
TATSUO ARAI
CHARLES ARCE
DONALD E ARCHAMBAULT
RICHARD J ARCHAMBEAULT
FRANCESCO ARCHANGELI
ROBERT G ARCHER
DAVID O ARCHULETTA
ERNEST ARELLANO
STANLEY P ARENDT
FRANK V ARIAS
MILTON ARIAS JR
LYMAN H ARIONUS
CLARENCE E ARMBRISTER
BYRON K ARMSTRONG
JAMES A ARMSTRONG
JERRY W ARMSTRONG
CLYDE B ARNOLD
DAVID ARNOTT JR
ISIDORE C ARREDONDO
MARIANO ARREDONDO
ELBERT ARRINGTON JR
JAMES F ARRINGTON
FRANCISCO ARTEAGA
LEONARD L ARTHUR
JOHN ARTIS JR
ARTHUR A ARVESON
RECIL P ARWOOD
HIROSHI ASADA
JAMES W ASBURY
ALEXANDER ASCHENBRENNER
BILLY E ASH
JAMES V ASHBAUGH
JOHN E ASHBY
ROBERT J ASHE
RUSSEL ASHENFELDER
JACK D ASHER
ALFRED B ASHLEY
FLOYD J ASHLEY
HUEY ASHWORTH
JOHN J ASPDEN
WILLIAM ASPELL
NICK ASPROMIGOS
MICHAEL ASTARY JR
RALPH E ATCHISON
FRED W ATEN
ROBERT H ATHA
HAROLD J ATHERTON
KENNETH E ATHERTON
CHARLES R ATHEY
WALTER M ATKIN
IRVIN L ATKINS
CRUZ AULI-OSORIO
LEO R AULT
EDWARD J AUMACK
C J AUSTIN
LEON AUSTIN JR
WAYNE D AUSTIN
ALBERT G AUTRY
JOE T AVANT
BILLY R AVEN
DAVID AVENT
JACK A AVERY
JAMES L AVERY
PETER R AVILA
JERRY AVINA
HECTOR H AYOTTE

PAUL E BABIN
ALEXANDER A BACA
LIBBY H BACAYLAN
IVY O BACCUS
JOHN H BACKSTROM
DAL-YONG BAE
HONG-YEOL BAE
HYEON-BI BAE
I-HWAN BAE
IM-JONG BAE
JEONG-HOK BAE
JONG-YEOL BAE
YEONG-HYO BAE
YONG-HWAN BAE
JAMES L BAECHLE
CHEOL-GI BAEK
HO-SANG BAEK
IN-HO BAEK
JA-SEON BAEK
DONALD L BAER
JOHN R BAGGI JR
ALBERT G BAGLEY
ELMER C BAILEY JR
HUGH H BAILEY
JAMES A BAILEY
JAMES M BAILEY
MAX L BAILEY
R V BAILEY
RAYMOND E BAILEY
WILLIAM J BAILEY
WILMER BAILEY
JAMES R BAIR
JOSEPH BAK
ALVIN D BAKER
ARTHUR L BAKER
CLIFTON G BAKER
FLOYD K BAKER
FRANK A BAKER
JAMES A BAKER
LAWRENCE M BAKER
LEROY BAKER
LEROY L BAKER
RALPH E BAKER
RAYMOND L BAKER
THOMAS L BAKER
VIRGIL K BAKER
WALTER C BAKER JR
WALTER R BAKER
DONALD L BAKIE
JOSEPH A BALBI
RUFUS BALCH
EAGLE B F BALD
ELMER E BALDOCK
JOE R BALDONADO
WILLIAM C BALDWIN
WALTER BALEJA
RALPH B BALENTINE
PHILIP E BALFE
GEORGE F BALFOUR
MARVIN G BALHORN
HAYWARD C BALL
JAMES B BALL
KENNETH BALL
JAMES L BALLANTYNE
HARVEL L BALLARD
FREDERIC D BALLENTINE
KENNETH M BALLINGER
HOWARD L BALLOU
JAMES H BALLS
RICHARD C BALOGH
EDWARD J BALUTA
BONG-SIK BAN
EDWARD B BANCROFT
BILLIE B BANES
IK-SEOP BANG
SEONG-SIK BANG
LOYD K BANGS
JOHN J BANISH
EARL BANKS
SAMUEL BANKS
STARL L BANKS
WILLIAM R BANKS
ALBERT BANKSTON
BOB R BANNISTER
ROBERT A BARANEK
LAWRENCE E BARBARIN
FRANKLIN M BARBER
RAYMOND H BARBER
DIEGO BARBOSA-VELEZ
BALDWIN B BARCLAY JR

DONALD A BARE
WILLIAM J BARFIELD
DONALD L BARKER
EARL R BARKER
NORBERT L BARKER
CARLTON L BARLEY
SALVATORE J BARLOTTA
ARTHUR L BARLOW
DUANE F BARLOW
EDMUND J P BARLOW
KENNETH W BARLOW
CARL M BARNES
HERBERT R BARNES
JOE E BARNES
KEITH W BARNES
WILLIAM M BARNES JR
BILLY E BARNETT
RAYMOND E BARNETT
FREDDIE BARNEY
DALE K BARNHART
JEROME F BARNWELL
FRANK R BARON
JOHN BARON
CLIFFORD J BARR JR
NORMAN F BARR
ANDREW H BARRETT
THOMAS J BARRETT
CHARLES H BARRINGER
EDWARD P BARRIOS
JACK L BARRONS
ARTHUR A BARRY
DAVEY H BART
HARRY J BARTH
GERALD H BARTHOLOW
ERNEST P BARTLETT
HORACE B BARTLETT JR
HOWARD R BARTON
JOHN L BARTON
JAMES C BARTRAM
ROOSEVELT BASCO
KENNETH R BASHAM
DANIEL J BASSARAB
WELDON L BASSETT
JESSIE E BAUER
LESTER W BAUER
LOUIS A BAUER
RICHARD C BAUMGARTNER
ROBERT A BAUR
CHARLES R BAWDEN
BILLIE C BAYNE
BOB L BAYNE
WILLARD A BAZEMORE
BENJAMIN R BAZZELL
CHARLES R BEACH
EDWARD N BEAL
JAMES E BEALS
RICHARD M BEAM
CHARLES L BEAMS
HENRY H BEAN
ELMER BEAR
HUVILLE E BEAR
DAVID BEARD
HAROLD E BEARD JR
HOWARD BEARD JR
DANIEL E BEARDSLEE
DAVID W BEATTY
THOMAS W BEATTY
ERNEST R BEAUBIER
JOSEPH BEAULIEU
RICHARD J BEAULIEU
JAMES I BEAVERS
BRUCE BECK
JACK A BECK
JAY E BECK
CLARENCE R BECKER
CLARENCE W BECKER
LARRY E BECKHAM
CHARLES L BECKMAN
ARTHUR E BECTON
CHARLES J BEDORE
VINCENT V BEDOYA
JOHN H BEEBE
CARL BEECHWOOD
ELDERT J BEEK
THOMAS L BEELMAN
WILSON J BEENE JR
JAMES E BEGLEY
CHARLES BEISSWANGER
WEDRO C BELARMINO
SAMUEL L BELASKY

CLAUDE H BELCHER
CARROLL E BELENSKI
ANDREW BELEY
JOHN L BELHUMEUR
ROBERT L BELILLE
BULO BELL JR
DELBERT C BELL
FLOYD K BELL
JOHNNIE G BELL JR
JOSEPH T BELL
MELVIN R BELL
RICHARD A BELL
ROBERT E BELL
ROBERT G BELL
WILLIAM BELL JR
WILLIAM E BELL
EDWARD M BELLFLOWER
DONALD P BELLIS
FRANK J BELSKIE
ROBERT J BELT
GAROLD E BELTON
RALPH BENDER
WILLIAM C BENDORF
BOBBY L BENNETT
CLEMMETT BENNETT JR
GEORGE G BENNETT
KEITH E BENNETT
LEO F BENNETT
LEONARD H BENNETT
STANLEY K BENNETT
WILLIAM A BENNETT
ANDREW BENOIT
NORMAN E BENSINGER
GERALD B BENSON
RUSSELL D BENTLEY
OBBIE M BENTON
HAROLD G BENTZ
GERARD P BERGER
JOSEPH E BERGERON
WILLIAM D BERGMANN
EDMUND J BERGUM
MILO A BERKE
ANTHONY C BERLINGHIERE
ANTONIO BERMUDEZ
ALFRED J BERNARDY
FRED W BERNEBURG JR
STEPHEN L BERNIER
MATTHEW R BERRES
FRED C BERRY JR
HENRY W BERRY
JEROME G BERRY JR
RAYMOND H BERRY
ROBERT H BERRY
RICHARD D BERRYHILL
LEO B BERTRAND
FREDRICK W BERTRANG
JOHN I BEST
ROBERT A BEST JR
AUTREY J BETAR
JAMES A BEVERIDGE
JOHN H BEVERLEY JR
ROGER A BEVILLE
DONALD G BIAS
WAYNE C BIBEAU
GLENN W BICKELL
GERALD R BICKHAM
ALOYSIS C BIENKOWSKI
JAMES E BIERWIRTH
RONALD S BIES
GLYNN R BIGGS
SAMUEL W BIGGS
ROBERT G BIGLEY
WALTER H BILLIEL
HERMAN BINAM
CHARLES F BINGE
MARVIN H BINGGELI
EDWARD E BIRCHFIELD
DELBERT W BIRD
ENRIQUE BIRD-ROSADO
PETER A BIRKEL
JOHN BIROCHAK
ARTHUR L BISHOP
JAMES W BISHOP
JOHN K BISHOP
LESTER E BISHOP
TRAVIS A BISHOP
CHARLES H BISSELL
FRANKLIN E BITTNER
THOMAS M BIXLER
LAWRENCE L BJELLAND

ALFRED D BLACK
CLYDE E BLACK
DARWIN M BLACK
JAMES W H BLACK
NORMAN S BLACK
NELDON E BLACKETT
ARTHUR I BLACK HAWK
CHARLES J BLAIR
EUGENE S BLAIR
JAMES A BLAIR
MERVIOL W BLAIR
TED BLAKE
ROBERT E BLAKELY
RICHARD J BLAKENEY
GERALD E BLAKESLEE
JAMES C BLAKESLEY
ROBERT W BLANCHFIELD
BENNIE BLAND
ELLIE B BLAND
CLINTON L BLANKENSHIP
FERDINAND T BLECHINGER
JOHN R BLENKINSOP
CHESTER BLEVINS
GALLIEHUE BLEVINS
JOHNNY H BLEVINS
WILLIAM E BLICKENSTAFF
CLYDE A BLISARD
ARNOLD L BLOCK
KENNETH R BLOCK
CLARENCE E BLOODSWORTH
DAVID F BLOSSER
JACKEY D BLOSSER
ADELBERT T BLUE
HENRY BLUE
SAMUEL T BLUE
SHIRLEY K BLUHM
RICHARD L BLY
STANLEY A BLYE JR
MILTON BLYTHE
STUART A BOARDMAN
HERBERT L BOAZ JR
JAMES E BOBOVNYK
THADDEUS S BOBOWIEC
FRED B BOCKLEMAN
MELVIN J BODILY
RICHARD W BOER JR
ELDEAN E BOESE
BRUCE D BOETTCHER
MARTIN BOGART JR
LEONARD J BOGER
JOHN BOGERT JR
EARNEST H BOGGESS
VIRGIL BOGGS
NEIL H BOHM
C G BOLDEN
RAYMOND M BOLDEN
JAMES E BOLEN
ROBERT A BOLEN
JAMES H BOLIN
ROSS L BOLINGER JR
JOHN F BOLL
THOMAS E BOLLING
RAYMOND E BOLLMAN JR
RICHARD L BOLOGNANI
JAMES T BOLSUM
ROBERT E BOLTON
HERBERT F BONAS
WILLIAM E BONAWITZ
DATHRON BOND
ELIHUE BOND JR
JOHN H BOND
RAYMOND I BOND
WILBUR L BOND
ISAAC BONDAR
CHARLES E BONE
JESSIE C P BONE
JOHN W BONETTI
ROBERT W BONEY
DEUSDEDITES BONILLA-DAVILA
WILLIAM N BONNER
JACOB H BONSHIRE
CLEM R BOODY
ALEXANDER BOOKER
JOSEPH BOOKER

51 ARMY

EUELL C BOOTH JR
ROBERT W BOOTH
ALBERT E BOOTHROYD
FELIX V BOR
ROBERT S BORAS
SALVADOR BORBON
EDWARD L BORDERS
ROSCOE BORDERS JR
PAUL E BORING
WILLIAM J BORLAND JR
RALPH E BORNES
WILLIAM J BORTOLOTTI
JAMES BORUM
ROBERT E BOSHEARS
CHARLES P BOST
ELVIN L BOSWELL
PHILIP A BOTSFORD
HENRY BOTT
ARTHUR A BOUCHARD
LUCIEN J BOUCHARD JR
FELIX BOUDREAUX
RALPH S BOUGHMAN
NORMAN L BOUNDS
ERNEST H BOURASSA
GEORGE L BOURDEAU
A D BOURLAND
LUCIEN J BOURQUE
BEN R BOWEN
CHARLES E BOWEN
CHARLES L BOWEN
ROBERT A BOWEN
WILLIAM J BOWERMAN
HAROLD C BOWERS
HARRY L BOWERS SR
JAMES E BOWERS
LAWRENCE BOWLING
MASON J BOWMON
LEMUEL R BOWSER
DONALD W BOYD
LONZO BOYD JR
SAMMY J BOYD
MELVIN BOYDEN
ANDREW P BOYER
HOWARD E BOYER
WILLIAM S BOYER
TERRANCE F BOYLE
JOHN F BRABANT
FERDINAND O BRABOY
ARTHUR BRACKNELL
ISAAC M BRADBURN JR
DAVID BRADFORD
DENNIS B BRADFORD
EDGAR N BRADLEY
ELDON R BRADLEY
FREDERICK T BRADLEY
GEORGE C BRADLEY JR
JERRY D BRADLEY
RONALD G BRADLEY
CLARENCE BRADSHAW JR
DENNIS H BRADY
ANTHONY BRAGA
REUBEN R BRAGG
MELVIN BRANCH
NATHAN L BRANCH JR
CARROLL G BRANDT
LYLE H BRANDT
WALTER J BRANDT
WILMER BRANNON
EDWIN L BRANSCOME
SAMUEL R BRANSTEITTER
ALBERT W BRANT JR
DUANE F BRANT
BILLIE L BRASWELL
CLAUDE BRAUD
ELDRED L BRAUER
SYLVESTER A BRAUN
HAROLD L BRAXTON
ROBERT L BRAY
FERMAN T BREAKER
RAYMOND J BRECH
CHARLES BREEDEN
ERNEST J BRENDEL
FREDERICK W BRENDLEY JR
FRANCISCO E BRENES-
VALENTIN
ODELL C BRENNA
GEORGE C BRENTS
LLOYD H BRESETT
KENNETH J BRESLIN
HOWARD G BREWER

MORRIS D BREWER
ROBERT L BREWSTER
JAMES A BRICKER
ANICE D BRIDGES
JAMES N BRIDGETT
WILLIAM J BRIERE
CARLTON R BRIGHT
WILLIAM H BRIGHT
DANIEL L BRIM
ZEPHRY BRIM
DARREL R BRIMBERRY
BERTHIER W BRIMM JR
DONALD P BRINGE
ALFONSO S BRINKSMEYER
GILBERT D BRINSON
ROBERT O BRISTOL
MELVIN L BRISTOW
LAWRENCE BRITT JR
CARL F BRITTIAN
PAUL L BRITTINGHAM
MICHAEL J BROADERICK JR
DENNIS BROCK
NORVIN D BROCKETT
CLARENCE BROCKMAN
GORDON BROCKMAN
ELWYN G BROEGE
CARL H BROERS
ROBERT L BROGNA
MERVIN G BROMFIELD JR
CHARLES H BROOKS
DONALD BROOKS
J L BROOKS
JAMES E BROOKS
JOHN H BROOKS
LEWIS F BROOKS
LLOYD K BROOKS
LOUIS P BROOKS
MARVIN R BROOKS
RICHARD H BROOKS
OTIS L BROOME
PATRICK R BROPHY
PAUL W BROUCHET
GEORGE BROUSSARD
EDWARD A BROUSSEAU JR
ANDREW B BROWN
ARTHUR L BROWN
BEN L BROWN
BILL E BROWN
BOBBY C BROWN
BRUCE F BROWN
CALVIN D BROWN
CHARLES BROWN
CHARLES A BROWN
CHARLES L BROWN
CHARLES O BROWN
CHARLES P BROWN
CHARLES R BROWN
CHARLES W BROWN
DALE E BROWN
DAVID O BROWN
DELMAR H BROWN
DONALD C BROWN
DOYLE R BROWN
EARL A BROWN
EDDIE D BROWN
EDWARD L BROWN
EDWARD R BROWN
EDWIN E BROWN
ELGIE D BROWN
EUGENE D BROWN
FLOYD M BROWN
FRED G BROWN
FREDERICK O BROWN
HAROLD G BROWN
HENRY BROWN
ISAAC BROWN
JAMES C BROWN
JAMES H BROWN
JESSIE BROWN
JIMMIE L BROWN
JOHN C BROWN
JOSEPH S BROWN
KENNETH L BROWN
KENNETH O BROWN
LAWRENCE L BROWN
LELAND G BROWN
LEROY L BROWN
LOYD O BROWN
MORRIS E BROWN
MURIEL G BROWN

ORVILLE R BROWN
OTTO V BROWN
PAUL M BROWN
RAYMOND H BROWN
RICHARD E BROWN
ROBERT A BROWN
ROBERT A BROWN
ROBERT B BROWN
ROBERT E BROWN
THOMAS G BROWN
THOMAS J BROWN
WILLIAM C BROWN
WILLIAM E BROWN JR
WILLIAM F BROWN
WILLIAM L BROWN
JOHN J BROWNE
ALBERT M BROZELL
DEWEY F BRUCE
JAMES O BRUCE
KENNETH C BRUCE
RICHARD C BRUCKER
RUDOLPH T BRUGGNER
WALTER R BRUMMETT
PAUL BRUNDA
HERBERT S BRUNER
FLOYD L BRUNETTE
ROBERT F BRUNKE
NICHOLAS M BRUNO JR
ROBERT P BRUNO
RAYMOND E BRUSH
JACKIE M BRUTON
CLIFFORD W BRYAN
JAMES C BRYAN
RICHARD A BRYAN
GLADEN B BRYANT
HAROLD F BRYANT
JAMES E BRYANT
JOE H BRYANT
PAUL C BRYANT
RUSSEL BRYANT
VERNON L BRYANT
WILLIAM E BRYANT
WILLIAM L BRYANT
OSCAR H BRYCE
MIRKO BUBALO
ELDON R BUCHAN
ELSON BUCHANAN
CLARENCE V BUCKLAND
DENNIS D BUCKLEY
JAMES W BUCKLEY
PAUL F BUCKLEY
BUDDY E BUCKMASTER
TOMMY BUCKNER
ANDREW P BUCKO JR
GEORGE BUCKSON
THEODORE J BUCOLO
JAMES BUDLOW
LEO T BUEHLER
THOMAS M BUELL
BERNARD C BUETTNER
CHARLES S BUFFALANO
CARLOS S BUITRON
CLIFFORD G BULL
JERAL H BULLARD
MILTON T BULLIS
GERALD F BUMSTEAD
HUBERT BUNN
CHARLES E BURBA
ISAAC W BURCH
BOBBY G BURCHETT
DONALD V BURCHETTE
CLIFFORD BURCHFIELD
OBIE R BURDEN
ROBERT M BURDETTE
BOBBY L BURFORD
JACK R BURFORD
BURTON E BURGESS
ALFRED T BURGETT
LORETO BURGOS
DONALD L BURK
FRANCIS BURKE
JAMES E BURKE
ROBERT H BURKE
ROLAND L BURKE
THOMAS J BURKE
CLARENCE BURKES
DANIEL W BURKES JR
EUGENE B BURKETT
CARL J BURKHARDT
BILLIE R BURKHART

ALVIN C BURMAN
DUANE J BURMEISTER
DONALD J BURMINGHAM
ROBERT E BURNER
AVERY E BURNETT
JACK E BURNETT
RAYMOND M BURNETT
HENRY W BURNETTE
JAMES I BURNETTE
CHARLES P BURNS
JOHN J BURNS
PAUL J BURNS JR
PETER J BURNS
RALPH W BURNS
RICHARD N BURNS
ROBERT L BURNS
EARL F BURRIS
JESSE C BURRIS
BILLY B BURSON
GEORGE R BURTON
ROBERT C BURTON
SAMUEL R BURTON
JAMES E BUSBY
BILLY J BUSH
JOHN F BUSH JR
JOSEPH C BUSH
ROBERT E BUSH
ROBERT G BUSH JR
THOMAS BUSS
JESUS F BUSTAMANTE
JOHNNIE J BUSTER
JOHN P BUTCHER
BILLY J BUTLER
HOWARD A BUTLER
JOHN R BUTLER
NEHEMIAH E BUTLER
WILLIAM V BUTTREY
GEORGE F BUYENSE
DEOK-MAN BYEON
YEONG-BAEK BYEON
ROBERT L BYERLY
KENNETH G BYNUM
BILLY R BYRD
FRANK BYRD JR
HUBERT F BYRD
TOMMY BYRD
WILLIAM BYRON
CLARENCE H BYRUM
WILLIAM D BYWATER
EDUARDO M CABALLERO
PEDRO CABALLERO
ARAMIS CABALLERO-
MORENO
THEODORE S CABANBAN
LLOYD R CABE
NICHOLAS C CACCESE
LIBERATO B CADIZ
EUZELL E CAGLE
CHESTER CAHILL
FRANCIS X CAHILL
EDMUND H CAIN
SIDNEY G CAIN
TOMMY J CAIN
ORLANDO J CALABRESE
ANTONIO CALAUSTRO
WILLIAM E CALAWAY
DOMINICK P CALDARELLA
JUAN CALDERON-OSORIO
DONALD D CALDWELL
JOHN B CALDWELL JR
WILLIAM S CALDWELL
RALPH L CALE
CHESTER J CALHOUN
HAROLD CALHOUN
CARL CALLAHAN JR
FRANCIS J CALLAHAN
JACK W CALLAHAN
WILLIAM F CALLAHAN
HAROLD A CALLAWAY
HENRY O CALLIS
ALBERT CALLON
ADOLPH C CALLOWAY
CONSTAN CALOGIANES
JESUS A CAMACHO
RUBERTINO P CAMACHO
ANASTACIO CAMILLO
BOOKER T CAMPBELL JR
DEWITT CAMPBELL JR
FORREST R CAMPBELL
GEORGE H CAMPBELL

HOWARD L CAMPBELL
JACKIE A CAMPBELL
JAMES F CAMPBELL
LOUIS L CAMPBELL
VERNON L CAMPBELL
LEONARD R CAMPISI
GREGORY O CANAN
ROY C CANBY
PAUL CANDELARIA
LEE L CANFIELD
RONALD A CANFIELD
KENNETH J CANN
LEROY CANNON
NICHOLAS CANTELLA
CECIL D CANTRELL
ODES I CANTRELL
RODE C CANTRELL
RAYMOND D CANTU
ROBERT H CANUPP
JAMES E CANYOCK
JOSEPH A CAPANO
JOHN N CAPIZZI
FRED CARAWAY
EDWARD C CARDENAS
ROBERT R CARDOZA
ROSENDO P CAREARA
HENRY R CAREY
JAMES L CAREY
EDWARD M CARICO
PETER P CARLINO
WILLIAM S CARLISLE
LEONARD D CARLSON
LYLE H CARMAN
ROYAL G CARMAN
PRIMO C CARNABUCI
HARRY Z CARNES
JOHN M CARNES
BILL CARNETT
JAMES R CARNEY
CHARLES S
CAROTHERS JR
JERRY F CAROTHERS
BENNY CARPENTER
HARVEY E CARPENTER
XAVIER O CARPENTER
CHARLES CARR
CLIFTON M CARR JR
GEORGE D CARR
HARRY L CARR
JOHNNIE CARR
RICHARD C CARRIGO
CARMEN CARRILLO
JAMES A CARRINGTON
FREDERICK CARRINO
MIGUEL A CARRION
CHARLES L CARROLL JR
JAMES R CARROLL
JAMES W CARROLL
JOSEPH S CARROLL
PERCY C CARROLL
RALPH N CARROUTH
MAYNARD E CARSON
GORDON B CARSRUD
THOMAS CARTALINO
ALBERT CARTER
ALBERT R CARTER
DANIEL J CARTER
DONALD E CARTER
DOUGLAS E CARTER
DUDLEY CARTER
EMMETT J CARTER
FRED C CARTER
J B CARTER
JAMES E CARTER
JAMES R CARTER
JOSEPH F CARTER
LLOYD L CARTER
LOUIS A CARTER
ROBERT X CARTER
WILLIAM J CARTER
PAUL K CARTY
CARMEN F CARUSO
HERMAN R CARUSO
ALFRED P CASARES
RAYMOND J CASEY
WILLIAM D CASEY
DAVID J CASHION
CHARLES D CASPER
THOMAS H CASSENS
BOYD W CASSIDY

52 ARMY

MELVIN M CASTILLE
LEOPOLDO V CASTILLO
DONALD R CASTONGUAY
FREDERICK CASTRATARO
ANTONIO CASTRELLON
ARMANDO CASTRO
ARTURO C CASTRO
PEDRO O CASTRO
DOMINIK CATALDO JR
FRED S CATLETT
DAVID L CATLIN
WAYNE R CATON
MERLIN L CATTELL
JAMES A CAUDILL
JAMES C CAUDILL
WALTON M CAUDILL
ALTON M CAUSEY
ROBERT E CAUTHERS
JOHN S CAVAGNARO
JAMES E CAVE
JOHN C CAVIL
LEE R CAWLEY
DONALD C CAYAN
EDWARD CEARLOCK
JAMES CEASOR
EDWARD J CEBULA
GEORGE A CECCHEL
GEORGE T CECIL
JESSE L CECIL JR
WILLIAM CECKOWSKI JR
ROBERT A CECOT
RAUL M CENISEROZ
MANUEL C CENTENO
JOHN R CERVI
DU-SIK CHA
HAENG-JIN CHA
JIN-YONG CHA
SANG-HYEON CHA
SEONG-GI CHA
YONG-HWAN CHA
RICHARD E CHADWICK
BYEONG-HONG CHAE
CLIFFORD R CHAFFIN
JAMES A CHAFFIN
HENRY L CHAMBERS
CLARENCE CHAN
CHARLES G CHANDLER
ELMER M CHANDLER
MELVIN H CHANTRE
CHARLES F CHAPLIN
HAROLD S CHAPMAN
MELVIN C CHAPMAN
RAYMOND B CHAPMAN
RICHARD A CHAPMAN
SAMUEL A CHAPMAN
RICHARD A CHAPPEL
BARTLEY S CHAPPELL
EVERETT F CHAPPELL
GENE A CHAPPELL
JAMES O CHARLES
SAM CHARLESTON JR
HOWARD CHARTE JR
RAYMOND CHATMON
ALBERT J CHAVEZ
ELOY A CHAVEZ
GEORGE E CHAVIRA
JOHN CHEEVES JR
JAMES E CHENAULT
HAN-SU CHEON
JEONG-HWAN CHEON
SEONG-JUN CHEON
MARTIN M CHEPKE
MICHAEL CHEPPA
ALBERT J CHERCONIS JR
AUGUSTUS W CHERRY
R B CHERRY
GEORGE J CHESMORE
CHARLES A CHEW
JAMES F CHEZEK
GERALD CHIEPPO
ROBERT N CHILCOTE
HAROLD D CHILDERS
CHARLES L CHILDRESS
ROBERT L CHILDS
OWEN D CHILTON
HARRY M CHINEN
CANDIDO CHINI
GIBBS CHISHOLM
HOWARD E CHIVVIS
GERLAD A CHOATE

JOSEPH D CHOATE
BYEONG-GYU CHOI
CHA-DOL CHOI
CHANG-GWON CHOI
CHAN-SAENG CHOI
DEOK-JU CHOI
GI-HWAN CHOI
HAE-YONG CHOI
HAN-GYO CHOI
HEUNG-SU CHOI
HONG-GEUN CHOI
HWA-SIK CHOI
JAE-CHEON CHOI
JAE-GYO CHOI
JONG-CHAE CHOI
JONG-SU CHOI
JONG-SU CHOI
JUNG-GI CHOI
MAN-OK CHOI
MUN-SU CHOI
SAM-GYEONG CHOI
SANG-BOK CHOI
SANG-HUI CHOI
SANG-SU CHOI
SU-HAK CHOI
SU-HYEON CHOI
SUN-GEUN CHOI
SUN-JO CHOI
UN-GAP CHOI
UN-GU CHOI
YEONG-DEOK CHOI
YEONG-MO CHOI
YEONG-SUL CHOI
YONG-I CHOI
YONG-SIK CHOI
YONG-SU CHOI
CLEMENS N CHOJNACKI JR
KENNETH CHRISENBERY
ANDREW J CHRISTIAN
JAMES W CHRISTIAN
JIMMY L CHRISTIAN
JOHN B CHRISTIANA
ALTON CHRISTIE
ROSARIO J CHRISTINA
LAWRENCE W
CHRISTOPHER
BYEONG-SAM CHU
LORIN D CHURCH
VERNON J CHURCH
PETER P CIACCIO
RUDY CIENEGA
MIGUEL A CINTRON
TEODULO CINTRON
VINCENT CIPOLLA
JACK J CIRIMELE
GREGORIO CIRINO-
PIZARRO
THOMAS CISKITTI
AUGUST D CITRONE
GEORGE L CIUCCI
WILLIAM H CLAMPITT
JOHN N CLANTON
ROBERT W CLANTON
WILBERT W CLANTON
GEORGE B CLARIDY
ALBERT CLARK
CHARLES W CLARK
CHARLES W CLARK
CLINTON CLARK
EDWARD CLARK
GEORGE E CLARK
GEORGE F CLARK
JAMES H CLARK
JOHN J CLARK
JOHN M CLARK
ROBERT E CLARK
VIRGIL D CLARK
WALTER L CLARK
WILLIAM E CLARK
HARRY B CLARKE
THOMAS S CLARKSON
TROY CLARKSON JR
CARL J CLAUS
DOMINIQUE CLAVERIE
GEORGE T CLAY
OLIN S CLAY
RICHARD F CLAY
PHILLIP A CLAYTON
RUSSELL CLAYTON
DAVID F CLEAR

ROBERT D CLECKNER
KENNETH A CLEM
ARDEN M CLEMMER
FRANK E CLENDENING
GIOVANNI CLEVA
EUCLID L CLEVELAND
HEREFORD W CLEVELAND
LEON E CLEVENGER
LESLIE D CLICK
GEORGE W CLICKNER
CLYDE R CLIFFORD
ARTHUR Z CLIFTON
OBIE CLIFTON
ROBERT L CLIFTON
WILLIAM L CLIFTON
NATHAN O CLIMER
WILLARD L CLINCH
CHARLES J CLINE
HAROLD C CLINE
OTIS H CLINE
WILLIAM H CLINE
CYRUS CNOSSEN
BARTON COALSON
ROMAN W COATES
DONALD S COBB
WILLIAM L COBB
ARTHUR C COBBS
ROBERTO COCIO
CARLOS P CODINA
CHARLES G COFFMAN
CARL L COGGIN
THOMAS E COGHLAN
FLOYD E COHICK
WILLIAM S COHOWITZ
EDWARD F COITEUX
CECIL A COKER
RICHARD D COKER
JAMES A COLASANTI
EDWARD L COLBY
WILLIAM COLBY
CHARLES H COLE
DONALD B COLE
JACKIE L COLE
JAMES C COLE
RALPH R COLE
SCHUYLER B COLE
THOMAS E COLE
WALTER E COLE
CHARLES L COLEMAN
ELMER L COLEMAN
GILBERT T COLEMAN
LEROY R COLEMAN
RICHARD F COLEMAN
WILLIAM N COLEMAN
RAYMOND W COLFLESH
ERNEST J COLLETTI JR
EDWARD L COLLIER
JOHN W COLLIER
CLARENCE H COLLINS
EDWARD J COLLINS
HARVEY N COLLINS
JACK L COLLINS
JAMES R COLLINS
JAMES R COLLINS
RAYMOND J COLLINS
THOMAS C COLLINS
AUGUST E COLMENARES
MANUEL COLON-APONTE
FRANCIS COLONNA
JOSE S COLON-PEREZ
CHARLES T COMPTON
EDWARD W COMSTOCK
JOHN J CONAHAN JR
JOSE J CONCEPCION-LOPEZ
BOYD E CONDER
JACK G CONGER
STANLEY J CONHARTOSKI
CHARLES G CONLEY
PETE CONLEY
ROBERT H CONLEY
OWEN H CONLON
HENRY D CONNELL
JOHN M CONNELL
EDWARD J CONNELLY
LOUIS B CONNELLY
CONNIE M CONNER
DONALD E CONNER
GEORGE W CONNER
GERALD W CONNER
ROBERT K CONNER

KARL F CONNICK
PATRICK E CONNOLLY
DAVID R CONRAD
NORMAN P CONRAD
JOHNNIE E CONTARIO
LUPE CONTRERAS
CARL W COOK
CHARLES W COOK
CHARLIE C COOK
GERALD V COOK
HARRY W COOK JR
JACK L COOK
JOHN T COOK
JOSEPH J COOK
THOMAS H COOK
BOBBY G COOKE
GLEN L COOKE
VINCENT M COOKE
FRED E COOKSON JR
WILLIAM COOLEY JR
FREDERICK E COONS
BURL L COOPER
CLARENCE A COOPER
GILBERT R COOPER
JAMES M COOPER
JAMES R COOPER
JOHN W COOPER
LEROY COOPER
MELVIN J COOPER
PAUL D COOPER
ROBERT COOPER
ROBERT E COOPER
RUSSELL A COOPER
GEORGE W COPAS
WALTER W COPENHAVER
THOMAS E COPPINGER
ROBERT T COPPLE
JUNIOR K CORAM
JAMES W CORBIN
CHARLES P CORDANI
THOMAS E CORDELL
LEWIS K CORDER SR
PHILIP H CORDIER
FREDDIE C CORLEY
MARTIN N CORMAN JR
FERMAN CORMIER
JOHN J CORNACCHIA
LLOYD E CORNELIOUS
PATRICK E CORNELIUS
CROWDEN CORNETT
DONALD F CORNWALL
DAVID CORRALES
JOSHUA CORRUTH
RAYMOND W
CORTWRIGHT JR
JOHN H COSKEY
FRANCISCO COSME-BAEZ
CHARLES W COSSABOON
JOHN COSTA JR
CHARLES W COSTELLO
HENRY G COSTELLO
WILLIAM J COSTELLO
ROLAND E COSTON
WAYNE K COTHREN
GERARD F COTTER
ROBERT E COTTRILL
SAMUEL H COUCH
WALTER R COUCH
FRANK J COUGHLIN
PAUL R COUILLARD
LEON S COULTER
DARREL D COUNCIL
WILLIAM E COUNCIL
BILLY E COUNTS
CHARLES M COUNTS
WOODROW W COUNTS
FRANCIS J COURTNEY
REGINALD J COUTANT
JOSEPH A W COUTURE
EDWARD COVINGTON
DON A COWAN
WILLIAM D COWAN
BRUCE P COWDEN
DONALD C COWGER
BILLIE W COX
BOYD E COX
EDWARD COX
WALTER J COX
WILLIAM O COX
DEAN R CRABB

IVAN E CRABTREE
PORTER F CRABTREE
CLIFFORD P CRADDOCK
CHESTER J CRAFT
DONALD F CRAFT
NOAH W CRAFT
GORDON M CRAIG
JOHN F CRAIG
PAUL E CRAIG
ROBERT P CRAIG
BILLY W CRAINE
LEBANON CRANE
WILLIE CRATER
CLIFFORD H CRAW
CHARLES A
CRAWFORD JR
CLINE S CRAWFORD
EDWARD G CRAWFORD
HAROLD E CRAWFORD
HOOVER CRAWFORD
LAWRENCE CRAWFORD
NORMAN E CRAWFORD
ROY W CRAWFORD
FRANCIS E CRAWLEY
JIMMIE M CRAWLEY
JAMES H CRAYTON
THOMAS V CRAZE
PATRICK H CREAGAN
DEWEY W CREECH JR
WILLIAM T CREEL
WILLIAM D CREGGER
DEAN W CREMEENS
JEFF CRENSHAW
CHARLES J CREWS
CHARLES E CRISS
REED A CRISWELL
PAUL P CRITTENDEN
CHARLES B CROFTS
JOHN R CROLEY
FRANK H CRONCE
CLIFFORD J CRONK
AUGUST B CROSS JR
WILLIAM H CROW
DONALD G CROWDER
PAUL E CROWDER
MARSHALL CROWE JR
RICHARD E CROWE
LEROY CROWELL
JAMES E CROWL
JAMES O CRUISE
MARION N CRUMP
FLOYD T CRUMPTON
ROY S CRUTCHMAN
EARNEST P CRUZ
JESUS CRUZ-BELTRAN
JOSE A CRUZ-CARRERO
ANGEL L CRUZ-SANCHEZ
JOHN J CULBERTSON JR
JOHN J CULLEN
ROBERT G CULLERS
RALLEIGH D CULLISON
JAMES R CULP
BOBBY R T CULPEPPER
JACK B CUMBIE
ROGER D CUMMINGS
RONALD C CUMMINGS
ZOLTON CUMMINS
ELIDIO A CUNHA
CARSE J CUNNINGHAM
CONZAADO E
CUNNINGHAM
ERNEST J CUNNINGHAM
JAMES O
CUNNINGHAM JR
JOHN F CUNNINGHAM
LUTHER CUNNINGHAM
WILLIAM R
CUNNINGHAM
WILLIAM S
CUNNINGHAM
CARL S CURL
JOHN W CURRIE JR
WILLIE L CURRIN
HENRY L CURRY
JACK CURTIS
LLOYD L CURTIS
RONALD D CUSHING
PETER J CUSUMANO
ROBERT G CUTLER
RAY A CUTSFORTH

53 ARMY

BERNARD Z DABROWSKI
BYRON B DAER
RUI M DA FONSECA
DELOREN D DAGE
MANVILLE DAGENHART
HAROLD J DAGNON
RAYMOND F DAHLGREN
DONALD E DAHMS
ELMER C DAHN
JOSEPH R DAIGLE
LIFFORD J DAIGLE
ROBERT G DAIGNAULT
FRANCIS J DAILEY JR
MAURICE L DAILEY
RALPH DAILEY JR
RICHARD L DAILEY
RAYMOND G DAKE
DELFORD M DALBERG
DOUGLAS DALE
ROBERT P DALESSANDRO
RICHARD A DALEY
WILFRED S DALLAS
HOWARD D DALTON
LLOYD DALTON
JOSEPH F DALY JR
ANTHONY DAMELIA
CHARLES W DAMERON
LOUIS A DAMEWOOD
GEORGE A DAMICO
ROBERT S DAMPIER
JAMES O DANCE JR
RICHARD L DANEL
ASHER DANIEL
ROBERT A DANIELL
BUSTER L DANIELS
THOMAS W DANIELS
ERVIN J DANNEMILLER
WILLIAM E DANTA JR
JAMES P DARCY
KENNETH P DARDEN
WILLIAM L DARK
LAURENCE L DARMSTADT
W D DARNELL
LESLEY W DARTING
J C DAUGHERTY JR
CHARLES E DAUGHTRY
MELVIN J DAVE
CURTIS DAVENPORT
CURTIS J DAVENPORT
MARVIN J DAVENPORT
WARREN DAVENPORT
CLOPHAS J DAVID
RICHARD L DAVID
JOHN DAVIDOVIC
HAROLD J DAVIDSON
RICHARD C DAVIDSON
CHARLES E DAVIS
CLAUDE L DAVIS
DAVID L DAVIS
EDWARD J DAVIS
GEORGE P DAVIS
GORDON E DAVIS
HARVEY DAVIS JR
JAMES E DAVIS JR
JAMES R DAVIS
JIMMIE L DAVIS
JOHN J DAVIS
JOSEPH L DAVIS
MARVIN L DAVIS
NICHOLAS DAVIS
NORMAN R DAVIS
RONALD W DAVIS
SAM H DAVIS
WILLIAM E DAVIS
WILLIAM E DAVIS JR
LESLIE E DAVISON
THOMAS R DAVISON
FRANCIS M DAWKINS
JAMES G DAWSON
HORACE W DAY
JAMES E DAY
JOHN W DAY
NATHAN O DAY
ROBERT H DAY JR
WARREN C DAY
WILLIAM F DAY
GEORGE A DEACON
FRANK L DEADERICK
FRAZIER DEAL
ALVIN C DEAN

CHARLES A DEAN
DANIEL DE ANDA
JAMES D DEARMAN
CLARENCE E DEARTH
GEORGE DEASON JR
AREND DE BOER
RAYMOND D DEBUSKE
ALFRED H DECHANT
CLELLAN H DECKER
FRANK E DECKER JR
LLOYD M DECKER
EUGENE DEDMAN
HAROLD D DEDMON
ROBERT F DEEM
DAVID N DEFIBAUGH
CARL E DEFORD
ROBERT L DE FRIER
CHARLES W DE GRAFF
FRANK DEGREGORIO
JOHN DE GROOT JR
KENNETH L DEGROOT
JOSEPH N DEHAAN
MELVIN L DEHART
GEORGE J DEINHARDT
TRINIDAD DE LA FUENTE
FRANCISCO T DELANEY
ROY C DELAUTER
PETRO J DELEONARDO
CARLOS DELGADO-RIVERA
NICHOLAS S DELLOLIO
THOMAS J DELOHERY
CLAYTON C DELONG
DENTON K DELONG
GUY W DELONG JR
HARRY F DELOSH
GENE A DEL PERCIO
LESLIE J DELUCA
FELIX L DELUDE
ROMEO J DEL VILLANO
RICHARD L DEMERS
DALE A DEMMIN
EDWARD DEMOSKI
FREDERICK J DEMPCY
ROBERT DEMPSEY
CECIL M DENBY
ANTHONY M DENICOLA
RAY A DENNARD
JAMES V DENNING
ROGER L DENNY
HARRY R DE NOFIO
LYNWOOD L DENSON
ROBERT DENTON
LEONARD DEPERMENTIER
SALVATORE DEPONTI
OSCAR L DEPRIEST
ANTHONY J DERRICO
HAROLD E DESCAMP
NICHOLAS DESIMONE
JEAN A DES ROBERTS
ROBERT G DETAMORE
ALAN A DETTLOFF
WILLIAM C DEVAUL
BILLY R DE VOLL
GEORGE D DEVONE
DELBERT F DEWEY
ROBERT C DEWITT
GROVER C DEWOLFE JR
GILBERT L DEXTER
VINCENT V DIAZ JR
EMILIO DIAZ-SANCHEZ
GENE A DI BATTISTA
DONALD L DICK
WILLIAM B DICK
JOHN N DICKENS JR
CLARENCE D DICKERSON
NORMAN E DICKERSON
WILLIAM H DICKERSON
PERCY E DICKINSON
CHARLES R DICKISON
DONALD A DICKSON
LOUIS A DI CROCE
JOHN W P DIEDEMAN
JAMES H DIER
GLENN I DILL JR
FLOYD N DILLARD
CHARLES L DILLION
LAHUE B DILLION
EVERETT E DILLON
FRANK A DILLON JR
TENNIS DILLON

JOSEPH S DIMARIA
JOSEPH N DI NARDO
WALDO M DINGUS
FRANK J DIPINO
LEON D DIRKS
ABRAHAM DIRKSEN JR
ROBERT DITTLER
HORACE J DIVENS
CHARLES R DIXON
CLYDE G DIXON
DERRYL D DIXON
OSBORNE J DIXON
ROGER J E DIXON
WILLIE F DIXON
JAE-IL DO
HARRY R DOBBINS
RAYMOND A DOBBINS
J B DOBBS
EDMUND F DOBEK
VOLNEY F DOBYNS
EARL DOCKERY
AUBREY W DOCKINS
LELAND E DOCKUM JR
JOHN E DODD
ROBERT R DODD
FURMAN A DODGENS JR
BILLY J DODSON
DAVID I DODSON JR
RANCE H DODSON
CORNELIUS H DOHERTY
CURTIS W DOHERTY
JOHN C DOHERTY
DALE A DOLLENBACHER
LIONELL DONNELL JR
BEARL DONNELLY
JAMES J DONOHUE
JAMES T DOODY
MICHAEL J DORAN
N J DORCH
HARVEY E DORFF
JIMMIE L DORSER
HAROLD W DORSEY
GILBERT DORTCH
HERMAN C DOSS
THEODORE R DOSS
WILLIAM H DOSS JR
EDWARD W DOSSIE
ROLAND J DOSTIE
ROBERT F DOTSON
THOMAS S DOTY
ANTHONY C DOUCETTE
THOMAS L DOUFEXIS
WILLIAM M DOUGAN
BERNARD P DOUGHERTY
WOODY L DOUGLAS
WILLIAM E DOUGLASS
RUPERT L DOUGLESS JR
HENRY L DOVE
ROBERT F DOVENBARGER
WILLIAM J DOWD JR
DONALD D DOWELL
RICHARD L DOWELL
JAMES A DOWER
HENRY E DOWLING
RICHARD L DOWLING
THOMAS R DOWNIE
CLARENCE C DOWNING JR
WALTER W DOWNING
WILLIAM R DOWNS
CLYDE G DOYLE
ELDON E DOYLE
JOHN J DOYLE
JOHN W DOYLE
LAURENCE A DOYLE
JOHN D DRAINER
CURTIS T DRAKE
DELBERT R DRAKE
DALE E DRAYER
ELMER E DRESS
CHARLES F DREW
DONALD D DREW
KENNETH H DREW
CHARLES D DRINKWATER
DONALD D DRINNEN
BILLIE C DRIVER
FRED F DRIVER
STEPHEN W
DROCHOWSKI JR
ARTHUR W DRONSE
HAROLD E DROWN

SAUL A DROZ-CARTAGENA
GEORGE A DRUM
LEONARD W DRUMMOND
WILLIAM R DUARTE
GERARD L J DUBAY
TIMOTHY J DUBLIN
LEO E DUBOS
CLYATT R DUBOSE
ISREAL C DUBOSE JR
FRANK J DUCHARME
RICHARD E DUCHARME
EDWARD S DUCHNEVICH
CHARLES B DUDLEY
WILLIAM J DUERR
DARRELL M DUFF
GEORGE A DUFF
JOHN J DUFFEY
THOMAS A DUFFEY
ALFRED P DUFFY
THOMAS J DUFFY
THOMAS W DUFFY
HERMAN A DUHAIME
ARTHUR J DUKE
JOSEPH J DUKE
ROBERT DULD
DANIEL DULIN
ROGER A DUMAS
ROBERT E DUMMERMUTH
GILMAN DUMOND
ALVIN D DUNCAN
CLEO L DUNCAN
EARL W DUNCAN
LESTER A DUNCAN
ROY E DUNCAN
WILLIAM E DUNCAN
DONALD I DUNDORE
HERMAN DUNGEN
ALVA F DUNLAP
DELCHER F DUNLAP
DUANE V DUNLAP
GERALD P DUNLAP
JOHN G DUNLAP
FRANCIS DUNN
JAMES L DUNN
LARRY D DUNN
RONALD L DUNN
RAMON H DUNNIGAN
EDWARD D DUNPHY
ROBERT H DUPERRE
LOUIS J DUPLESSIS
DONALD L DUPONT
LYLE R DUPONT
DEWEY J DUPUIS
PEDRO DURAN
ANDREW L DURBIN
GERALD D DURBIN
HAROLD L DURBIN
RICHARD H DURBOROW JR
WILLIAM T DURHAM
JOHN P DURKIN JR
EDWARD J DURNEY JR
ROBERT G DUROCHIN
DONALD G DURST
J D DUSHANE
EDWARD DUSHAW JR
WILLIAM A DUSTER
JOHN L DUTRA
ADGIE DUVALL JR
ALFRED E DUVERNAY
MILTON F DVORAK
BILLY DWIER
STANLEY T DYBAL
ARNOLD G DYE
ARCHIE W DYER
JOHN J DZIENIS
WILLIAM T EADE JR
CHARLES L EADES
BEN EAGLE
WILBUR C EAGLE
LEONARD EARHEART
JAMES L EASON
WILDON C EAST
WILLIAM C EASTE
CHARLES W EASTERDAY
EUGENE G EASTMAN
GEORGE R EATON
JOHN O EATON
ROBERT EATON
BOBBY W EAVES
CLARENCE W EBENSPERGER

CLARENCE A EBERLY
GERALD D EBNER
CARL F ECKARDT
JOSEPH H ECKHART JR
JOHN W EDDINS JR
EDWARD C EDGE
CARL W EDGEMOND
JAMES EDMONDS JR
MARVIN M EDMONDS
J C EDSON
ROY H EDSTROM
CARROL EDVALSON
CHARLES P EDWARDS
DWIGHT W EDWARDS
EUGENE EDWARDS
JAMES A EDWARDS
PAUL K EDWARDS
VICTOR M EDWARDS
DONALD C EFLAND
DONALD L EHELER
DONALD A EHLERT
LEWIS C EIKNER
DURWARD S EILAND
BERNARD J EINUM
DELBERT G ELDER
HARRY F ELDREDGE
RONALD T ELDRIDGE
SAMUEL ELEY JR
FRED D ELLEN
OVA E ELLIOT
JAMES C ELLIOTT JR
DAVID M ELLIS
DONALD D ELLIS
JAMES E ELLIS
MARTIN R ELLIS
WANDAL R ELLIS
COLEMAN C ELLISON
CONWELL G ELLISON
J C ELLISON
R M ELLSWORTH JR
ROBERT R ELMER
EVERITT L ELMORE
JOHNNIE ELMORE JR
DONALD L ELSNER
PAUL D EMEOLA
ROBERT K EMERICK
AMOS EMERSON JR
JAMES L EMERSON
PHILIP EMERSON
GERALD R EMMANS
CLIFFORD O EMMONS
WILLIAM E ENAS
HARVEY G ENGELMAN
MYRON J ENGER
RUSSELL J ENGLADE
ROBERT M ENGLEHART
DALE T ENLOW
FRED L ENLOW
ORMELL L ENOS
HAE-YEONG EOM
JAMES ERDOS
ALBERT C ERICKSON
HERBERT L ERICKSON
REUBEN C ERICKSON
JACK ERICSON
KNUTE O ERIKSEN
JAMES D ERODDY
ELDON W ERVIN
CHARLES ERVINS
ERASMO ESCOBAR
ROBERT E ESHENBAUGH
MALCOLM J ESKINE
ENZO ESPOSTI
LIBRADO E ESQUER
JOHN ESSEBAGGER JR
ELWOOD R ESSLER
EDWARD E ESTES
FELIX J ESTES
ROBERT C ESTES
ROBERT V ESTES
ALBERT J ESTRADA
ANDREW EVANICH
B J EVANS
BRYANT EVANS JR
DUDLEY L EVANS
EDWARD J EVANS
EVERETTE R EVANS
FLOYD R EVANS
GENE E EVANS
HAROLD A EVANS

54 ARMY

HOWARD H EVANS
JIMMIE R EVANS
OWENS B EVANS
PHILLIP J EVANS
ROBERT E EVANS
ROBERT M EVANS
VIRGLE J EVANS
WALLACE EVANS JR
WILLIAM F EVANS
WILLIAM V EVANS
FRED E EVERETT
CLARENCE A EVERETTS
LEONARD V EVERHART
JOHN B EVERING
WILLIAM B EVERSON
LOYD W EVERTS
EDWARD F EWENS
GRANT H EWING
JOHN M EWING JR
DEROYCE H EZZELL
JOSEPH P FAGAN JR
KERMIT C FAHRMEYER
J C FAIN
JOHN W FAIN JR
MATAGISA S FALANAI
EUGENE H FALCON
ROBERTO FALCON
PIVO FALLORINA
GEORGE A FALLS
HAROLD S FANCHER
JAMES W FARMER
JOSEPH F FARMER
PAUL C FARMER
WILLIAM L FARMER
ROBERT E FARNESI
GLENN W FARNHAM
CHARLES E FARR
FELIX D FARRELLY
ALVIN R FARRIS
CHARLES L FARRIS
GERALD A FARRIS
ROBERT FARTHING
CHARLES R FARUS
WILLIAM F FASICK
CHARLES J FAST
FLOYD N FAULCONER
VERNON O FAULKENBERRY
ALFRED B FAULKNER
CHARLES C FAULKNER
LOUIS P FAUSONE
JAMES F FAVALORO
DANIEL V FAVELLA
RICHARD R FAWLEY
CARROLL R FEAGANS
HARLEY A FEAGIN
T J FEAGINS
RICHARD J FECKO
ROSARIO FEDE
BERKLEY S FEESE
WILLIAM J FEHRING
HARMON C FELDER
LEO D FELS
STEPHEN J FEMINO
THOMAS FENDYA
WILLIAM D FENWICK
JOSEPH FERENCE
ANTHONY M FERENTINE
BOBBY H FERGUSON
CARLOS E FERGUSON
CHARLEY FERGUSON
JAMES T FERGUSON
THOMAS D FERGUSON
JAMES E FERN
JOHN A FERNANDES
JAIME R FERNANDEZ-
CASIANO
RAYMOND FERREIRA
ROBERT S FERRELL
CARL M FERRER
ELWOOD FERRY JR
RICHARD P FERRY
LEO E FETZER
WILLIAM J FEURY
ROBERT F FEYEREISEN
CHESTER P FIBICH
ROBERT J FICK
CLIFFORD W FIELDING
GEORGE D FIELDS
KENNITH G FIELDS
LONNIE FIELDS
JESSE F FIERRO
JOSEPH G FIGARO
FRANCISCO FIGUEROA
JAMES A FIKE
MICHAEL J FILA
ROBERT T FILBIN
CECIL W FILLINGAME
RICHARD D FILLOON
LAWRENCE G FILOSENA
OSCAR FILYAW
STANTON E FINCH
RICHARD O FINDLEY
RICHARD M FINE
ROY C FINK
KENNETH C FINLAYSON
EDWARD FINLEY
RICHARD H FINLEY
WILHO O FINNILA
GEORGE H FINSTAD
CLYNE C FISCHER
HORACE R FISCHER
JAMES F FISCHER
WILLIAM R FISCHER JR
WILMER R FISH
AMOS FISHER
ARLIS H FISHER
EDWARD R FISHER
RALPH G FISHER
WALTER F FISHER
WILLIAM H FISHER
LESLIE J FITTS
ROBERT G FITZER
EDWARD F FITZGERALD
JOHN J FITZGERALD
THELBERT R FITZPATRICK
ROBERT L FITZWATER
ALAN D FLACK
ERIC N FLACKMAN JR
COLEMAN J FLAHERTY JR
MICHAEL W FLAHERTY
KENNETH FLAMER
DONALD F FLANAGAN
THOMAS E FLANAGAN
JOHN D FLANDERS
WAYNE V FLANNIGAN
ERVIN J FLAUGER
ROBERT D FLEAR
FRED FLEENER JR
CECIL L FLEMING
ISAAC FLEMING
ORANZEL FLEMING
CHARLES C FLENER
JOHN E FLETCHER
MORRIS W FLETCHER
ROBERT S FLETCHER
LEONARD J FLETT
WILMER G FLEURY
BOBBY D FLINN
ROBERT F FLOOD
GRADY H FLOOK
ALFRED S FLORES
FRANK G FLORES JR
JESUS C FLORES
MANUEL H FLORES JR
JAMES A FLORY
ARTHUR S FLOWER
ALFLORANCE FLOWERS
RONALD W FLOWERS
ANDREW J FLOYD JR
PETER P FLUHR JR
JOHN A FLYNN
PATRICK J FLYNN
DONALD G FOCHLER
IRVIN E FOCHT
WARNELL A FOGLE
CHARLES T FOLEY
HONG FONG
ROBERT L FONTANA
JOSEPH W FONTENOT
ALBERT P FORAND
BILLIE J FORBES
CLYDE S FORD
DONALD R FORD
EMMITT M FORD
FRANK D FORD
JOE L FORD
KENNETH E FORD
JOHN E FORE
KENNETH R FOREMAN
RUSSELL J FOREMAN
KENNETH R FORMAN
CONRAD F FORMICA JR
CHARLES D FORREST
EMMETT E FORRESTER
CARL L FORSYTH JR
WALTER C FORT
JESSIE L FORTE
PETER R FORTE JR
GEORGE A FOSHEE
DELBERT J FOSNAUGH
BEVERLEY H FOSS
EUGENE A FOSS
GEORGE H FOSS
GLEN E FOSS
OLIVER R FOSS JR
DONALD K FOSTER
ROBERT B FOSTER
ROBERT G FOSTER
ROBERT H FOSTER
THOMAS H FOSTER
VIRGIL L FOSTER JR
ROBERT O FOUNTAIN
KENNETH L FOUSE
ALWYN F FOWLER
DARRELL L FOWLER
THOMAS O FOWLER
ELDON E FOX
GORDON R FOX
GROVER J FOY
DAVID D FRACK
GILBERT S FRAIZE
JAMES C FRANGELLO
WILFRED G FRANKENBERG
HIRAM FRANKLIN
JEFF FRANKLIN
JULIUS C FRANKLIN
PRESTON FRANKLIN
TEDDY L FRANKLIN
THOMAS S FRANKLIN
WILLIAM D FRANKLIN
JACK M FRANS
WILLIAM R FRASER
JAMES J FRATTAROLI
ARTHUR J FRATUS JR
GEORGE E FRAY
CHARLIE FRAZIER JR
EDWARD M FRAZIER
JOHN A FRAZIER
CHARLES J FRECHETTE
JOHNNY J FREDERIC
BILLY E FREEMAN
DONALD R FREEMAN
ELMER FREEMAN
GRADY L FREEMAN
HARRY W FREEMAN
JAMES A FREEMAN
JIM C FREEMAN
JOHN H FREEMAN
JOHN N FREEMAN
JOHN W FREEMAN
THERON H FREEMAN
WALTER H FREEMAN
WILLIAM F FREEMAN JR
ARTHUR W FREGEAU
HARTWICK T FRENCH
HUEY P FRENCH
RAMON M FRESCAS
ARTHUR D FRESHOUR JR
KENNETH J FREY
LOUIS B FREZZO
WILLIAM P FRILEY
SAMUEL E FRISCO
ROBERT D FRISK
DON E FRITZ
WAYNE J FROMBACK
JACK L FRYE
NORBERT W FRYMAN JR
HOBART FUGATE JR
EDWARD F FUHRMAN JR
HITOSHI FUJITA
HARUO FUKAMIZU
ALBERT W FULK JR
LESTER E FULK
IRA J FULKS
TERRELL J FULLER
EVERETT E FULTZ
JOHN F FUNA
JOSEPH R FUNES
ROBERT D FURLOW
NORMAN J FURMAN
HAROLD R GABERDIEL
BENNY G GABLE JR
PETER J GABRISH
ANDREW J GADDIS
ROBERT H GAEDEKE
PATRICK J GAFFEY
ARNOLD G GAGNON
BILLIE H GAINER
LAWRENCE W GAINES
OBIE M GAINES
W J GAINEY
JESSE M GAITAN
EDWIN L GALARNEAU
PAUL S GALLA
JACK J GALLAGHER
JEROME E GALLAGHER
RAYMOND X GALLAGHER
ROBERT J GALLAGHER
ALBERT L GALLEGOS
JOSEPH E GALLITZ
GEORGE GALLO
DAVID L GALLOWAY
CYRIL A GALLUP
JUSTUS P GALLUS
ROBERT L GALT JR
BARTHOLOMEW GALVIN
JAMES L GAMBILL
SELESTINO M GAMBOL
WAYNE GAMMON
BYEONG-JIN GANG
CHEOL-SANG GANG
DAE-YUN GANG
DONG-SU GANG
GU-I GANG
GWON-HYEOK GANG
HAE-YEONG GANG
HONG-UK GANG
IM-SEOK GANG
IN-SUL GANG
JEOM-BONG GANG
JEONG-PAL GANG
KWAE-CHUL GANG
SANG-GU GANG
SEONG-GWON GANG
SEON-HYEONG GANG
SIN-MUN GANG
YEOM-WON GANG
YEONG-JUNG GANG
YONG-SU GANG
MICHAEL GANNON
WILLIAM J GANNON
WILLIAM W GANTT
ROBERT C GAPINSKI
ALFONSO GARCIA
BENNIE GARCIA
GUADALUPE GARCIA
GUILLERMO G GARCIA
HILIBERTO GARCIA
ISHMAEL GARCIA
LEONARD P GARCIA JR
ROGER B GARCIA
VICTOR I GARCIA
JOSE GARCIA-MARRERO
RANDALL G GARDIEN
CURTIS C GARDINER
CHARLES E GARDNER
ELMER D GARDNER
HENRY L GARDNER
LAWRENCE N GARDNER
MAURICE P GARDNER
MERRITT H GARDNER
JOHN F GARGAN
FLETCHER R GARLAND
JAMES L GARLAND
GEORGE D GARMAN
AUSTIN L GARNER
HUBERT L GARNER
MAURICE M GARNER
CHARLES J GARNETT
GEORGE R GARRETT
JOHN H GARRETT
LONNIE O GARRETT
NATHANIEL GARRETT
LLOYD G GARRETTE JR
DALE R GARRISON
GLENN T GARRISON
JERRY M GARRISON
JOHN L GARTRELL
CHARLES E GARVER
JOHN H GARVIN JR
GILBERTO GARZA
JOHN H GARZA
MAURO GARZA JR
RUBIN F GARZA
ANDREW J GASQUET JR
WILLIAM K GASTON
DONALD W GATELY
DONALD L GATES
CURTIS C GAULDIN
CHARLES E GAUMER
BILLY E GAY
JOHN S GAY
RICHARD E GAY
RAMON GAYA-ARCE
JAMES D GAYHART
ALVIN GAYLES
JAMES E GEBHART
WILLIAM S GEBOU
ALBERT F GECKLE
RICHARD P GEER
WILLIAM R GEER JR
GILBERT R GEHRKE
ROBERT E GEIGER
JAMES F GENDILO
MORRIS C GENSCH
ARCHIE C GENTRY
ARGLISTER A GENTRY
JAMES D GENTRY
EARL W GEORGE
NICHOLAS J GEORGE
ROBERT L GERHART
GEORGE J GERIG
ANTHONY GERSOSKEY
JOHN H GERSTNER
REGINALD E GERVAIS
ALVIN B GESSNER
MAURICE S GETCHELL
M C GEURIN JR
FRANK GFROERER
MARIO R GHINAZZI
ANTHONY J GHIOZZI
RALPH GIANNOTTA
EDDIE GIBBY
AUBREY L GIBSON
CARL A GIBSON
CHARLES V GIBSON
CLARENCE E GIBSON JR
GEORGE D GIBSON
JOHNNY W GIBSON
ROBERT L GIBSON
JAMES GIDRON
QUILLIE S GIGGER
THOMAS E GIGLIO
ROBERT D GILARDI
ARTHUR J GILBERT
CHARLES M GILBERT
DENNIS A GILBERT
FRANCIS GILBERT JR
FRANCIS GILBERTSON
WILLIAM F GILBOE
ROBERT J GILFORD JR
BOBBY R GILL
HARLES GILL
WAYNE B GILL JR
JAMES W GILLASPY
CHARLES W GILLES JR
RICHARD GILLETT
DARRELL G GILLEY
BUFORD C GILLIARD
EDMUND B GILLIGAN
DELMAS W GILLIKIN
WILLIE J GILLS
BERNARD J GILROY
WILLIAM A GILSON
REX D GINGLES
FLOYD A GINN
CONRAD M GITZEN
EDGAR S GLAISE
HENRY H GLASHOFF JR
FLETCHER GLASSCOX
BRUNO GLAZERS
LESTER E GLENN
ROBERT L GLENN
PATRICK R GLENNON
PAUL H GLORIA
CHARLES C GLOVER
RICHARD H GLOVER
THOMAS GLOVER JR
BOK-SEON GO
BONG-GYU GO

55 ARMY

GWANG-BAEK GO
HYEON-SU GO
JIN-YEONG GO
SEOK-GU GO
YEONG-HWA GO
YONG-DEOK GO
PRYOR GOBBLE
CHARLES A GODCHAUX
AUBREY GODWIN
CHARLES W GODWIN
HOWARD GODWIN JR
JOHN F GOEKEN
KENNETH E GOFF
DEAN R GOFORTH
PAUL R GOHLKE
MARTIN L GOINS
WILLIAM E GOLDEN
PAUL D GOLDSBOROUGH
LEONARD W GOLDSMITH
LEROY GOLDSTON JR
ARLYN R GOLTER
FELIPE C GOMEZ
RUBEN J GOMEZ
BENJAMIN GOMEZ-MORENO
CHESTER H GONSE
ANDREW L GONZALES
ARMANDO GONZALES
HENRY C GONZALES
JOSE GONZALEZ
JUAN A GONZALEZ
MANUEL E GONZALEZ
PABLO GONZALEZ-COLON
CLAIR GOODBLOOD
NELSON B GOODENOUGH
WILLIAM E GOODRUM
CONNIE GOOSBY
EDWARD J GORDON
JOHN R GORMAN
ROBERT F GORMAN
JAMES W GORMLEY
JAMES V GORZYNSKI
GEORGE C GOSS
HAROLD L GOSS
THEODORE L GOSS
RICHARD C GOSSELIN
BENJAMIN J GOSSMAN
GERALD G GOTHE
LOUIS P GOTHMAN
STERLING C GOWER
MASAO GOYA
PAUL A GRABER
ALFRED E GRABLEWSKI
EULIS G GRACE
ROBERT W GRACE
EDDIE GRACIA-SANCHEZ
ALEXANDER W GRACKI
HERMAN L GRAFF JR
JAMES H GRAGG
ALEXANDER GRAHAM
ARTHUR L GRAHAM
FLOYD E GRAHAM
JOHNNY C GRAHAM
ROBERT P GRAHAM
JUAN GRAJALES-ROSARIO
MARTIN L GRANILLO
ROBERT L GRANT
VIRGIL GRANT
DON JUAN W GRAPHENREED
FREDERICK H GRAVES JR
FREDERICK W GRAVES
FREDERICK M GRAY
GOLDEN L GRAY
MARION D GRAY
MERRETT G GRAY
ROBERT A GRAY
WOODROW GRAY
JACK R GRAZIER
HOWARD J GREAVER
ROBERT L GREAVER
EDWARD L GRECO
CHARLES A GREEN
CRYSTAL M GREEN
GEORGE L GREEN
HERBERT W GREEN
JOHN M GREEN
JOSEPH T GREEN
ROBERT A GREEN
WARD M GREEN
WENDELL H GREEN
WILLIAM G GREEN
GORDON A GREENE
HOWARD B GREENE
LARRY O GREENFIELD
BERNARD A GREENLEAF
DONALD R GREENWOOD
IVAN J GREENWOOD
LESLIE F GREER
FRANK GREGG
IVAN E GREGG
WILLIAM T GREGG
EDWARD GREGORCZYK
JOSEPH GREGORI
ALFRED R GREGORY
LESLIE GREGORY
ROBERT E GREGORY
TYREL J GREMILLION
EUGENE H GRENIER
HENRY O GREYBUFFALO
CHARLES G GRICE
KENNETH G GRIDER
ANTHONY J GRIECO
DOWER L GRIFFIN JR
JOHN T GRIFFIN
NELSON H GRIFFIN
CHARLES E GRIFFIS
BOBBY E GRIFFITH
GEORGE H GRIFFITH JR
HAROLD W GRIFFITH
RANDOLPH F GRIFFITH
RONALD R GRIFFITH
WILLIAM G GRIFFITH
STANLEY GRIFFITHS
GEORGE P GRIFFORD
CLIFFORD B GRIGGS
HARRY GRIGGS
ROBERT J GRIGGS JR
GEORGE T GRIMES
KEITH H GRIMES
PAUL K GRIMES JR
WILLIS F GRIMM
EVERETT V GRIMSLEY
ROBERT L GRIMSLEY
LOWELL R GRISER
DAVID H GRISHAM
FREDDIE C GRISSION
DELMER R GRISSOM
JOHNNIE A GRIZZLE
FRANK A GROACH
RAYMOND A GRODHAUS
EUGENE L GRODZKI
ROBERT G GROLEAU
CHARLES J GROLL
IVAN W GROOM
CARL A GROSS
JOHN O GROTTE
ALVA C GROVES
CARL R GRUBB
CHARLES H GRUBB
VICTOR A GRUBEN
CLARENCE E GRUBER
LAVERNE A GRUBER
RAYMOND F GRUHOT
HENRY T GRUNA
OSWALD GRUNIG
FRANK S GRYKIEWICZ
EDWIN C GRZECA
GAP-SEO GU
JAE-SEO GU
EDWARD A GUDE
JULIAN A GUERRERO
THOMAS S GUERRERO
JUAN GUERRERO-ORONA
RAY M GUESS
HERBERT E GUFFEY
ALFRED GUGLIELMONE
CHARLES J GUILE
LISBON GUINN JR
HARRY J GUINTHER
JORGE L GUIOT
RAYMOND B GUNDERSON
JAMES R GUNION
GEORGE P GUNKEL
JAMES T GUNNELS
MARVIN L GUNNS
FRANK GURCHIK
JAMES F GUSCOTT
SYLVESTER L GUSZREGEN
CHARLES GUTGESELL
ISADOR GUTIERREZ
EDWARD S GUYER JR
JOHN E GUYNN
BYEONG-GWANG GWAK
BYEONG-HUN GWAK
BYEONG-IL GWAK
DAE-SIK GWAK
GEUN-SEOK GWAK
GIL-SU GWAK
MAL-CHUL GWAK
PAN-SEONG GWAK
TEUK-YEONG GWAK
BYEONG-JUN GWON
HYEOK-JU GWON
HYEOK-SU GWON
JONG-GUK GWON
MUN-YONG GWON
SEUNG-CHEOL GWON
WAN-I GWON
YEONG-HONG GWON
YEONG-OK GWON
YU-MYEONG GWON
HAROLD E GWYNN
BAN-TAEK HA
JAE-MAN HA
JAE-UN HA
JANG-SU HA
JUNG-TO HA
TAE-UNG HA
RUSSELL N HAAKENSON
BUSTER HAAS
FRANK D HAGAN
JAMES E HAGAN JR
HALLIE E HAGER
BILLY M HAGGARD
GEORGE C HAGIE
HIROSHI HAGINO
R V HAGLE JR
ALEXANDER R HAGNER III
JAMES J HAGUE
RAYMOND C HAIGH JR
WILLIAM T HAIR JR
ROBERT L HAIRE JR
IRVIN D HAIRSTON
GERALD J HAKER
GEORGE R HALBERT JR
ALLEN L HALL
FRED C HALL
FRED G HALL
GLENN M HALL
HAROLD L HALL SR
HAROLD T HALL
JOHN HALL JR
LESTER J HALL JR
RAYMON F HALL
RICHARD L HALL
STANLEY F HALL
DAVID J HALLAHAN
W T HALLFORD
WESLEY I HALLOCK
CLARENCE V HALTON
HAROLD R HALVORSON
JONG-GAP HAM
CLEO D HAMBY
LARRY P HAMBY
MARVIN G HAMELIN
RUSSELL G HAMERSHY
BOBBIE S HAMILTON
EDWARD J HAMILTON JR
GENE E HAMILTON
HOWARD B HAMILTON
JAMES H HAMILTON
ROBERT T HAMILTON
RONALD W HAMILTON
CARL P HAMMER
WILLIAM G HAMMERLE
GLYNN R HAMMOCK JR
LESTER HAMMOND JR
ROBERT T HAMMOND
HERMAN HAMPTON
FLAVY C HAMRICK
BAEK-BONG HAN
GI-SIK HAN
PAN-SIK HAN
SANG-MUN HAN
WON-DEOK HAN
ALVAN M HANAVER
NORMAN W HANCE
GEORGE R HANCOCK JR
MANLEY R HAND
NORMAN C HAND
JOSEPH E HANDL
MELVIN L HANDY
ROBERT M HANDY
LLOYD L HANE
ANDREW J HANEY JR
JACK HANEY JR
GUY J HANFORD
FRED A HANKAMER
TOMMIE T HANKS
FRANK HANLON
JOHN W HANLON
MORGAN H HANNAH
THOMAS F HANNAN
ARTHUR T HANNON
WILLIAM T HANNUM
EARL H HANSEL
CARL E HANSEN
JOHN J HANSEN
MACCA P HANSEN
MEIDEL HANSEN
REED H HANSEN
LELAND HANSON
LEROY R HANSON
MELVIN F HANSON
RAYMOND W HANSON
ANTHONY T HARALSON
JAMES J HARCHENHORN
HORACE HARDIMON
JOHN D HARDIN
THOMAS HARDING JR
DONALD P HARDINGER
ELMER E HARDY
JAMES S HARDY
ROBERT F HARDY
THOMAS R HARDY
CLEMENT J HARE
JAMES R HARE
OSCAR H HARGROVE
WALTER R HARLESS
EARL M HARLEY
HUBERT HARMON
JAMES E HARMON
JOHN W HARMON
LAWRENCE A HARNAGE
GEORGE N HARNER
JAMES A HARRELL
LUCIOUS L HARRELL
CLIFFORD R HARRIES
WILLIAM E HARRIGAN
ROBERT J HARRINGTON
ARTHERIA M HARRIS
EDDIE V HARRIS
ELMER HARRIS JR
EUGENE S HARRIS
HOUSTON HARRIS
HOWARD K HARRIS
JOHNSON S HARRIS
LOVIEL S HARRIS
MAJOR M HARRIS
ODIS M HARRIS
ROBERT L HARRIS
ROBERT S HARRIS
SAMUEL C HARRIS JR
SYLVESTER HARRIS
WILBUR F HARRIS
ARTHUR HARRISON
BANNIE HARRISON JR
DICK HARRISON
FRED HARRISON
MARSHAL L HARRISON
PHILIP T HARRISON
J D HARROWER
EUGENE F HART
EVERETT W HART
MICHAEL J HART JR
REX R HART
ROBERT H HART
LOREN D HARTJEN
EDWIN E HARTLAUB
CHARLES W HARTLEY
GEORGE W HARTLEY
ALFRED B HARTMAN
JOHN R HARTMAN
WARREN P HARTNEY
CHARLES W HARTSFIELD
ARTHUR L HARTSHORN
FRANKIE HARVEY
BILLIE J HASH
ELDON E HASH
HAROLD L HASLEY
ANDREW HASSAGE
LAMAR F HASSEL
ROBERT A HASTINGS
GORDON M HATCHER
JAMES E HATCHER
JAMES A HATCHETT
JEROME D HATFIELD
RAYMOND L HATFIELD
ROBERT L HATFIELD
JOHN A HATT
GEORGE C HATTON
ARNOLD E HAUGEN
ROBERT G HAUSER
JULES HAUTERMAN JR
ERWIN A HAVRANEK
BILLY C HAWKINS
EDWARD HAWKINS
RALPH E HAWKINS
ROBERT W HAWKINS
CLIFFORD B HAWLEY
GEORGE L HAWLEY
JESSE V HAWLEY
KENNETH V HAY
EDWARD B HAYDEN
ORVILLE L HAYDEN
DULANEY R HAYES
HARRY G HAYES
JAMES HAYES
LOUIE R HAYES
RANDOLPH HAYES
JAMES R HAYMAN
THOMAS O HAYMORE
JOHN L HAYNES
ROY C HAYNES
WALLACE A HAYSLIP
MINEFORD L HAYWOOD
CLIFFORD HAZWOOD
ARTHUR D HEALD
PAUL E HEALD
JAMES L HEARD
MARVIN W HEARD
RICHARD L HEARD
CHARLES J HEARN
EDWIN F HEARN
JOHN E HEARN
EDWARD F HEATH JR
LESLIE R HEATH
WILLIAM E HEATH
RAYMOND E HEATON
JOHN J HEAVEY JR
MAURICE A HECK
DOLLIE HEDGEPETH
RALPH J HEDGER
EDWIN G HEDGES
ROBERT S HEDMAN
RALPH HEDRICK
IVAN F HEFNER
WILLIE M HEIDELBERG
ERNEST L R HEILMAN
RICHARD H HEIMBIGNER
JOHN E HEINCHON
MERLIN J HELBACH
IRVING HELLMAN
CARL F HELMAN
EDWARD A HELMES
HARRY R HELMICK
EUGENE HELMS
HENRY L HELMS
ROBERT E HELTON
WILBURN HELTON
THOMAS F HEMA
JOHN HEMBREE JR
WILLIAM J HEMSKEY
DELBERT E HENDERSON
EDWIN R HENDERSON
HAROLD HENDERSON
HAROLD L HENDERSON JR
HERBERT HENDERSON
JACK H HENDERSON
LESTER V HENDERSON
RICHARD L HENDERSON JR
TRAVIS E HENDERSON
WILLIE M HENDERSON
EDWARD L HENDRICKS
FRANK B HENDRICKS JR
GEORGE H HENDRICKS JR

DONALD R HENDRICKSON
JACK K HENDRICKSON
FRANCIS B HENIG
HAMILTON C HENLEY
LOUIS R HENN
JAMES K HENNINGTON
NORMAN R HENRICKSEN
FRED S HENRY
JOHN F HENRY
JOSEPH P HENRY
LEO HENRY JR
RICHARD A HENRY
ROBERT M HENRY
WILLIAM F HENRY
ELDRED J HENSLEY
LEE HENSLEY
FREDDIE L HENSON
GEORGE HENSON
IL-HWA HEO
JUN-GU HEO
VALENTINE W HERBERT
MARCEL HERMAN JR
PAUL O HERMAN
WALLACE B HERMANN
ALBERTO HERNANDEZ
HENRY S HERNANDEZ
JESUS HERNANDEZ
JESUS HERNANDEZ
JOHN HERNANDEZ
MANUEL B HERNANDEZ
BENJAMIN HERNANDEZ-TORRES
THOMAS D HERR
PABLO HERRERA
ROBERT N HERRINGTON
WILLIAM J HERRINGTON
WESLEY H HERRMANN
RICHARD L HERROLD
CURTIS W HERRON JR
RAYMOND J HERRON
WAYNE M HERRON
MURRY G HERSHKOWITZ
CLAUDE R HESS
CHARLES G HESTER
HARRISON L HESTER
LOREN HESTON
PAUL F HEUSS
FRANCIS L HEWETT
ALLEN S HEWITT
EDWARD HEYNOSKI JR
JAMES W HIBBS
PETER T HIBMA
DELBERT D HICKMAN
HAROLD L HICKMAN
BUEL G HICKS
CHESTER S HICKS
FRANCIS P HICKS
JAMES E HICKS
LUTHER HICKS
VESTER HICKS JR
YUTAKA HIGA
KENNETH J HIGBEE
BILLY R HIGGINBOTHAM
FREDERICK A HIGGINS
JOHN S HIGGINS JR
ROBERT HIGGINS
CARLIS E HIGH
CHARLES C HIGHSMITH JR
CECIL O HIGHTOWER
WILLARD F HILBERT
ROSCOE L HILDEBRAND
THURLE L HILEMAN
KENNETH C HILGART
BILLY C HILL
CHARLES R HILL JR
CLARENCE H HILL
DALE C HILL
EDWARD O HILL
FRED G HILL
GEORGE T HILL
HAROLD E HILL
JAMES C HILL
JAMES H HILL
JAMES L HILL
JAMES O HILL
KENNETH J HILL
LEWIS W HILL
MELVIN R HILL
RICHARD E HILL
ROBERT H HILL

ROBERT L HILL
THOMAS L HILL
CHARLES HILLANBRAND
GERALD G HILLIARD
CARL G HILT
CHARLES E HILTIBRAN
BILL G HILTON
LEO E HILTON
RICHARD E HIMELHAN
CHARLES W HINES
EDWARD F HINES
GEORGE H HINES
JOHN R HINSON
CHARLES E HINTE
RIN HIRAOKA
LOUIS M HIRATA
JIRO HIROKANE
ROGER E HITTLE
DONALD L HITZ
RAYMOND HIXENBAUGH
JAMES F HLAVAC
ARNOLD A HOAG
CHARLES R HOAK
RICHARD H HOBART
ELVEN J HOBBS
HOWARD L HOBBS
DONALD E HOBIN
CARLTON L HOBSON
LESTER E HOBSON
WILLIAM R HOBSON
FLOYD L HODGE
HERMAN H HODGE
VIRGIL L HODGE
JAMES A HOELSCHER
DALE A HOERR
EARL L HOFFMAN
EUGENE G HOFFMAN
HOWARD B HOFFMAN JR
JOHN A HOFFMAN JR
LAWRENCE E HOFFMAN
PATRICK M HOFFMAN
RICHARD E HOFFMAN
SAMUEL E HOFFMAN
LYNN G HOFFMASTER
CHARLES L HOGAN
JOSEPH G HOH
MARVIN J HOHEIMER
JACK HOHMAN
DONALD J HOLCOMBE
JOHNNIE R HOLDER
BILLY E HOLDMAN
DONALD F HOLDWAY
JOSEPH P HOLENCIK
RAYMUNDO E HOLGUIN
EARL HOLIDAY
DEAN M HOLLAND
EVERETTE HOLLAND
FRANK J HOLLAND
WILLIAM K HOLLAND
OWEN HOLLAR
JOSEPH F HOLLE
J T HOLLEY
JOHN F HOLLEY
PAUL A HOLLINSHEAD
ALBERT C HOLMAN JR
FREDDIE W HOLMES
JOHN R S HOLMES
PERVIS S HOLMES
SONNIE L HOLMES
OLIVER HOLT
ROBERT F HOLTMAN
CHARLES E HOLTZCLAW
JOHN M HOLTZCLAW
WALTER HOLYNSKYJ
WAYNE M HOLZER
CHARLES H HONEA
JAMES B HONEYCUTT
DO-HEUM HONG
DU-HONG HONG
GI-YEONG HONG
GWAN HONG
GWANG-HEUM HONG
JONG-MYEONG HONG
JU-HWAN HONG
SAM-HUI HONG
SEONG-YEON HONG
SUN-DEOK HONG
GEORGE C HOOD
WALTER B HOOD
BRUCE A HOOK

FLOYD E HOOPER
JOE HOOPER
PAUL E HOOTS
ROBERT E HOOVER
THEODORE H HOPKE
ALBERT HOPKINS
CHARLES G HOPKINS
DONALD W HOPKINS
WILLIAM E HOPKINS
JOSEPH J HOPPER
ROY J HOPPER
CHARLES W HOPSON
ROLAND E J HORN
JAMES H HORNBACK
ARVEL C HORNE JR
HAMILTON P HORNER
HERBERT M HORNER
JACK A HORNER
WILLIAM J HORNING
JOHN B HORTON
LEROY W HORTON
WALLACE R HORTON
WILLIAM R HOSKINS JR
ROBERT E HOUCHIN
NORVEL F HOUCK
ROBERT B HOUNCHELL
DOUGLAS V HOUSE
JOHN C HOUSER
JAMES L HOUSTON
RONALD B HOUSTON
RUFUS HOUSTON
JOHN HOVEL
JOHN I HOVEN
GLENN A HOVEY
EDWARD M HOWARD
JAMES L HOWARD
JOE W HOWARD
LEWIS P HOWARD
OLIN HOWARD
OLIVER M HOWARD
RALPH A HOWARD
ROBERT C HOWARD
SOLOMON C HOWARD
JAMES H HOWDYSHELL
JACK D HOWE
JAMES W HOWE
ROBERT L HOWE
CLIFTON O HOWELL
JAMES HOWELL
JOSEPH A HOWELL
MARTIN L HOWELL
BRUCE D HOWES
EDWARD F HOWLEY
DUANE A HOYLE
JURIJ B HRAB
JOHN R HRONEK
GLEN M HUBACK
RALPH E HUBARTT JR
WALTER C HUBBARD
SAMMIE HUBBELL
BILLY R HUCKABEE
CLAYTON M HUCKINS
GEORGE HUDDLESTON
BILLIE R HUDSON
FRANK C HUDSON
LESLIE D HUDSON
ROBERT L HUDSON
ALFRED A HUFENDICK
HERBERT D HUFFMAN
WILLIAM R HUFFMAN
JOHN O HUGG
JOHN E HUGHES
JOSEPH L HUGHES
LUCIUS W HUGHES
RICHARD K HUGHES
BARNEY M HUGULEY
RAY D HULSEY
JANS H HULZEBOS
JAMES E HUMERICK
DONALD L HUMISTON
JEROME V HUMMEL
JOSEPH HUMMEL
RICHARD D HUMPHREYS
HERBERT D T HUNG
KENNETH P HUNSICKER
CARL V HUNT
DALLAS W HUNT
ORA HUNT JR
ROBERT R HUNT
THOMAS A HUNT

WILLIE R HUNT
DONALD B HUNTER
GEORGE HUNTER JR
JOHN L HUNTER
JOSEPH HUNTER JR
ROBERT E HUNTER
WILLIAM HUNTER
CHARLES M HURST
FRANCIS J HURST
ROY L HURST
GARRISON G HURT
NORBERT G HURT
ROBERT F HUSS
WILFRED K HUSSEY JR
WILLIE J HUSTON
AMOS R HUTCHINS
WILLIAM P HUTCHINSON
RAYMOND E HUTCHISON
WILLIAM P HUTH
ALBERT C HUTTO
LOUIE E HUTTON
RICHARD E HUTTON
WILLIAM HUTZEL
AUBREY E HUX
BILLY C HUXHOLD
BYEONG-YONG HWANG
CHA-GAP HWANG
GWAN-HOE HWANG
GYU-SEONG HWANG
IN-HAK HWANG
I-SANG HWANG
JONG-GU HWANG
SANG-HO HWANG
U-GEUN HWANG
YEONG-GIL HWANG
YEONG-HO HWANG
YONG-AN HWANG
YONG-GAE HWANG
LESTER T HYATT
VERNON D HYDE
SANG-UK HYEON
LONNIE B HYLTON JR
ALVIN H IAEA
CLAUDIO ICMAT
WILBERT R IDLE
HERBERT K IDOL
ANTONIO H IGNACIO
STEVEN R IHLY
ARTHUR R IKKALA
CHAE-YEONG IM
GI-HWAN IM
HAN-SU IM
HO-JUN IM
JAE-TAEK IM
JONG-ROK IM
JONG-SIK IM
JONG-YUN IM
NAK-JIN IM
SANG-BONG IM
ROBERT K IMRIE
WARREN J INGLAND
GLENN R INGRAM JR
HAROLD G INGRAM
HUBERT D INGRAM
RICHARD D IRVINE
RICHARD ISBELL
MITSUYOSHI ISHIDA
RAUL R ISLAS
CHARLES E IVEY
JOHN R IVEY
WOODSON L IVY
ISAMU IZU
ALBERT JACKSON
ARNOLD R JACKSON
COMER JACKSON JR
ELWOOD L JACKSON
HOWARD T JACKSON
JAMES H JACKSON
JAMES H JACKSON
JAMES H JACKSON
JAMES H JACKSON
JIM H JACKSON
KENNETH R JACKSON
LEONARD L JACKSON
LEVI JACKSON JR
MARION E JACKSON
R D JACKSON
RICHARD D JACKSON
ROBERT G JACKSON
WILLIAM L JACKSON JR

WILLIE JACKSON
WILLIE J JACKSON
ARTHUR F JACOB
ERNEST J JACQUES
ROBERT D JACQUES
EDWARD J JAGER
GEORGE T JAMES
HOWARD E JAMES
JOHN C JAMES
LUTHER J JAMES
HUGH D JAMISON
WALTER P JANECZKO
HARLAN S JANEKSELA
ROY W JANES
PETER M JANETTAS
BYEONG-GWON JANG
DO-SIK JANG
EUN-DEUK JANG
GEUNG-YUN JANG
GI-O JANG
HONG-YEOP JANG
JAE-BOK JANG
JANG-HWAN JANG
JUN-DEOK JANG
SANG-MUN JANG
SEONG-TAE JANG
SEON-SUN JANG
TAE-SU JANG
YEONG-DAE JANG
YEONG-SEON JANG
RICHARD J JANKOWSKI
EARL A JANOSKY
DOMINICK JANUZZI
ANANIAS JANVRIN
ROBERT V JARDINE
HAROLD JARMON
ERVIN R JARMUSEK
RONALD L JARRELL
CARL E JARRETT
JOHN W JARRETT
ROLAND J JARVEY
FREDERICK C JARVIS
JOE JASO
HAROLD D JASPERSON
FRANCISCO G JAVIER
PAUL A JEANPLONG
DARWIN I JEFFERSON
JAMES JEFFERSON JR
RAYMOND J JELNIKER
CLIFFORD L JENKINS
GROVER G JENKINS
HUGH JENKINS
JESSIE R JENKINS
WILLIAM H JENKINS
DALTON M JENKS
ROBERT L JENNINGS
DAVID G JENSEN
GORDON W JENSEN
PAUL T JENSEN
BYEONG-O JEON
GYEONG-BAE JEON
OE-TAEK JEON
SAM-SIK JEON
SEONG-GI JEON
SEONG-SEOK JEON
YONG-BU JEON
BONG-HWA JEONG
CHIL-SU JEONG
DEOK-SU JEONG
DONG-HUI JEONG
GEON-YONG JEONG
GWANG-DEOK JEONG
GWAN-SIK JEONG
GYU-SEON JEONG
HAE-YUN JEONG
HAK-BONG JEONG
HAN-GIL JEONG
HONG-SIK JEONG
IL-YONG JEONG
IN-OK JEONG
JAE-HWA JEONG
JAE-SU JEONG
JUN-GI JEONG
SAM-YEONG JEONG
SANG-GU JEONG
SE-JIN JEONG
SEON-DONG JEONG
SEONG-JO JEONG
SEONG-MO JEONG
TAEK-SU JEONG

57 ARMY

UN-HEUM JEONG
WON-GAP JEONG
WON-JIN JEONG
WON-MO JEONG
YEO-CHUL JEONG
YEONG-GYU JEONG
YEON-SAENG JEONG
YONG-JU JEONG
BILLY JERKINS
JOHN M JERRED
LAWRENCE E JERRELL
THADDEUS J JERZ
HOWARD L JESSUP
WILLIAM R JESTER
DONALD E JETER
ROBERT M JETER
DONALD T JEWELS
IL-SEON JI
YEONG-DONG JI
JOE V JIMENEZ
VICTOR P JIMENEZ
ANGEL M JIMENEZ-MERCED
MIGUEL JIMENEZ-TOSADO
BILLIE J JIMERSON
KWAE-CHEOL JIN
YONG-CHUL JIN
LEONARD W E JINKS
BONG-SIK JO
BYEONG-MUN JO
DEOK-HWA JO
DONG-SIK JO
EUNG-RAE JO
GIL-SU JO
GYEONG-SEOP JO
HAENG-GI JO
HAK-ROE JO
HUI-RYONG JO
HYEON-CHIL JO
HYEON-SIK JO
JA-CHUL JO
JEONG-HYEON JO
JONG-SEON JO
SEON-JONG JO
SU-GYU JO
SU-JE JO
SUN-MYEONG JO
YONG-MO JO
YU-JO JO
JOSE JOAQUIM
VERNON D JOBE
EDWARD C JOHANSEN
THEODORE T JOHNSBURY
ADRIAN R JOHNSON
ANDY C JOHNSON
ARNOLD JOHNSON
ARTHUR R JOHNSON
BENJAMIN JOHNSON
CARLIS E JOHNSON
CECIL L JOHNSON
CHARLES E JOHNSON
CHARLES L JOHNSON
CHARLES W JOHNSON
CLARENCE A B JOHNSON
CLAUDE L JOHNSON
CLIFFORD S JOHNSON
DEWITT W JOHNSON
DONALD R JOHNSON
DONALD R JOHNSON
EDWARD A JOHNSON
EDWARD L JOHNSON
ELDRIDGE JOHNSON
ELIJAH G JOHNSON
FRANCIS E JOHNSON
FRANK H JOHNSON
GEORGE A JOHNSON
GRANVILLE N JOHNSON
GUDMUND C JOHNSON JR
HAROLD A JOHNSON
HARRY C JOHNSON
HENRY F JOHNSON
HERBERT JOHNSON
JAMES J JOHNSON
JEFFERSON JOHNSON
JOHN P JOHNSON
JOHN R JOHNSON
JOHN R JOHNSON
KENNETH C JOHNSON
LEWIS H JOHNSON
LOWELL W JOHNSON
MARVIN J JOHNSON

MCKINLEY JOHNSON
MEARL E JOHNSON
MELFORD JOHNSON
MERLIN E JOHNSON
MILTON JOHNSON
NORMAN H JOHNSON
PHILLIP B JOHNSON
REX G JOHNSON
RICHARD M JOHNSON
ROBERT L JOHNSON
RONALD H JOHNSON
RONALD M JOHNSON
ROY L JOHNSON
VARNELL JOHNSON
WALTER H JOHNSON
WILLIAM D JOHNSON
WILLIAM E JOHNSON JR
WILLIAM O JOHNSON
EDWIN E JOHNSTON
ADOLPH JONES
ALLIE C JONES
BERTRAM E JONES
BOBBY J JONES
CARL R JONES
CHARLES JONES
CHARLES W JONES
CLYDE A JONES JR
CONNIE W JONES
DALE R JONES
DAVID JONES
DENNIS M JONES
DOYLE T JONES
EDWARD M JONES
GEORGE J JONES JR
GUS J JONES
HERBERT H JONES
JACK E JONES
JAMES W JONES
JOHN R JONES IV
JOHN W JONES
JOSEPH N JONES JR
JOSEPH W JONES
KASSIDY K JONES
KENNETH L JONES
LINWOOD G JONES
LUCIUS JONES
ODIS F JONES
RALPH G JONES
RAYMOND L JONES
RICHARD A JONES
ROBERT A JONES
ROBERT C JONES
ROBERT N JONES
ROBERT S JONES
SAMUEL R JONES
THOMAS C JONES
THOMAS D JONES
WALTER L JONES
WALTER L JONES
WILBUR JONES
WILLIAM JONES
WILLIAM J JONES
ACE JORDAN
ARTHUR JORDAN
CHARLES E JORDAN
ARTHUR JOSEPH
CLAYTON W JOSEPH
RALPH A JOSEPH
DONALD A JOYCE
WILLIAM H JOYCE JR
WILLIAM L JOYNER
JEOM-SUL JU
MYEONG-SI JU
PAN-AM JU
SAM-BONG JU
SEON-GI JU
JAMES I JUBB
WILLIAM A JUDD
VIRGIL R JULIAN
RAYMOND A JUMP
RAYMOND C JUNG
ROBERT A JURSCH
FRANCIS J JURY
GERALD W JUSTEN
WILLIAM A JUSTICE
LEON P JUSTIN
JOHN K KAAKIMAKA
BYRON KACHERIS
JOE KACZMARCZYK
PAUL M KAFER

VINCENT P KAFTON
WILLIAM F KAHRHOFF JR
ROBERT W KAILIANU
JOSEPH C KAINZ
CARLOS S KAKAR
WILLIAM W KAMEKONA
WASIL M KAMIERZIA
ALFRED R KAMINSKY
DEROY F KAMMERER
BUFORD E KANE
HAROLD J KANE
HAYATO KANESHIRO
GORDON W KANTER
VASILIOS KARAGIOZIS
FRANCIS A KARALEWICZ
CHARLES H KARCHER
ALVIS E KARR
EVERETT M KARR
DENNIS K KARTY
ERNEST C KAUER
CLARENCE J KAUFFMAN
ALFRED L KAUFMAN
LEROY S J KAUHINI
SIDNEY K KAUI
DAVID W KAUL
FRANK M KAUTMAN
ROBERT W KE
FLOYD A KEACHER
WAYNE V KEE
JOHN W P KEELEY
RONALD O KEELEY
JAMES F KEENAN
JOHN J KEGLOVITZ
BILLY A KEHOE
CHARLES M KEITH
CLOYCE KEITH
EDWARD L KEITH
NELSON KEKIWI
MATTHEW K KELII
FRANCIS KELLEHER
JOHN J KELLEHER
FRANCIS W KELLER
GERALD J KELLER
LAWRENCE B KELLER
BERNARD B KELLEY
DAVID J KELLEY
HOBERT G KELLEY
JOHN M KELLEY
KENNETH E KELLEY
RUSSELL E KELLEY
WILLIAM A KELLEY
RAYMOND F KELLUM
CURTIS C KELLY
DANIEL F KELLY
DONALD E KELLY
GEORGE E KELLY
JOE KELLY
RAYMOND KEMICK
CLAUDE KENAN JR
WARREN O KENDALL
JOHN P KENDIG
MICHAEL J KENNEALLY
CLYDE S KENNEDY
ELLIS D KENNEDY
FRANKLIN P KENNEDY
JOHN E KENNEDY
LARRY KENNEDY
LEONARD M KENNEDY
RICHARD T KENNEDY
SAMUEL K KEOMAKA
JACK L KEPHART
WILBERT B KEPHART
JOHN A KERNS JR
LEE O KERR
ROBERT L KESHICK
VERNON L KESLER
GEORGE E KESSLER
ANDRE J KETELE
DAVID N KEYES
JOHN R KIBBE
EARL E KIBBEY
EUGENE B KICZEK
BILLY L KIDD
ELMER C KIDD
EDWARD KIERNAN
EDMUND KIEZANOWSKI
CALVIN L KIGER
GEORGE D KILE
ROBERT L KILLINGSWORTH
CHARLES J KILLORAN

RICHARD W KILMER
ROBERT J KILPATRICK
BONG-DO KIM
BONG-MUN KIM
BYEONG-CHEOL KIM
BYEONG-HO KIM
BYEONG-HUI KIM
BYEONG-HWAN KIM
BYEONG-JU KIM
BYEONG-SEOK KIM
CHA-GU KIM
CHA-MUN KIM
CHANG-MAN KIM
CHANG-SEON KIM
CHANG-SIK KIM
CHEOL-GYU KIM
CHEON-HUI KIM
CHEON-O KIM
CHI-SU KIM
CHI-SUL KIM
CHUNG-GEUN KIM
DAE-BONG KIM
DAE-IK KIM
DEOK-JIN KIM
DEOK-JO KIM
DEOK-MAN KIM
DEUK-YONG KIM
DO-GEUN KIM
DOL-I KIM
DO-MYEONG KIM
DONG-DAL KIM
DONG-HWAN KIM
DONG-SEON KIM
DO-YONG KIM
DU-YONG KIM
GAP-JUN KIM
GAP-SEONG KIM
GAP-SI KIM
GEUN-O KIM
GEUN-SU KIM
GI-BONG KIM
GI-DO KIM
GIL-SIK KIM
GUK-HEON KIM
GWANG-HUI KIM
GWANG-MU KIM
GWANG-YEOL KIM
GWI-YEONG KIM
GYEONG-DO KIM
GYEONG-O KIM
GYEONG-SIK KIM
GYEONG-TAE KIM
GYEONG-TAEK KIM
GYE-SU KIM
GYU-TAE KIM
HA-CHANG KIM
HAE-DONG KIM
HAE-GON KIM
HAENG-BONG KIM
HAK-YEONG KIM
HAN-SU KIM
HEON-HO KIM
HONG-JO KIM
HYEON-DAL KIM
HYEONG-SEOP KIM
HYEON-GUK KIM
HYEON-SIK KIM
JAE-BAEK KIM
JAE-CHEOL KIM
JAE-CHEON KIM
JAE-GUK KIM
JAE-GYEONG KIM
JAE-HA KIM
JAE-HAN KIM
JAE-HO KIM
JAE-NAM KIM
JAE-SU KIM
JANG-HO KIM
JEOM-GU KIM
JEONG-GI KIM
JEONG-SU KIM
JEONG-UNG KIM
JIN-SU KIM
JIN-TAE KIM
JONG-BAE KIM
JONG-DO KIM
JONG-DU KIM
JONG-GUK KIM
JONG-HAE KIM
JONG-HYEON KIM

JONG-IL KIM
JONG-OK KIM
JONG-SEOK KIM
JONG-SIK KIM
JONG-WON KIM
JUNG-GEUN KIM
JUNG-GI KIM
MAN-I KIM
MUN-GYU KIM
MYEONG-SIK KIM
MYEONG-SIK KIM
NAM-GYU KIM
NO-IN KIM
PAN-AM KIM
PAN-SU KIM
SA-DEUK KIM
SA-JIN KIM
SANG-DONG KIM
SANG-GYEONG KIM
SANG-GYEONG KIM
SANG-HUI KIM
SANG-IK KIM
SANG-SU KIM
SANG-TAE KIM
SANG-TAEK KIM
SANG-YUN KIM
SE-CHAN KIM
SEOK-MAN KIM
SEOK-MAN KIM
SEONG-DEOK KIM
SEONG-GU KIM
SEONG-HO KIM
SEONG-JIN KIM
SEONG-MYEONG KIM
SEONG-TAE KIM
SEONG-UN KIM
SEON-MO KIM
SO-DEUK KIM
SONG-RIM KIM
SO-SEOK KIM
SU-JIN KIM
SUN-DEOK KIM
SUN-DO KIM
SUN-GYU KIM
SU-TAEK KIM
TAE-HO KIM
TAE-HYEON KIM
TAE-SIK KIM
TAE-SIK KIM
TAE-SU KIM
TA-GWAN KIM
U-GON KIM
UI-GWAN KIM
UI-MAN KIM
UI-SEOK KIM
U-MYEONG KIM
WOL-HO KIM
WON-DO KIM
WON-GIL KIM
YEONG-BOK KIM
YEONG-CHEOL KIM
YEONG-GI KIM
YEONG-RYONG KIM
YEONG-SIK KIM
YEONG-TAEK KIM
YONG-BAEK KIM
YONG-HWI KIM
YONG-SEOK KIM
YONG-TAE KIM
YU-JONG KIM
YUN-HAN KIM
YUN-HO KIM
YUN-JO KIM
TIMOTHY E KIMBALL
JOHN W KIMBERLIN
KENNETH R KIMBERLIN
DAVID KIMBROUGH JR
JAMES E KINCAID
JAMES M KINCAID
RICHARD H KINCAID JR
ALBERT KING JR
CHARLES E KING
CHARLES E KING
CHARLIE R KING
DAVID M KING
DENVER KING
EARL L KING
EDWARD J KING
FRANK KING JR
FRANKLIN D KING

58 ARMY

HAROLD O KING
HARVEY KING
HERBERT KING
HUBERT R KING
JOSEPH R KING
MARTIN A KING
RALPH E KING
RICHARD H KING
RICHARD M KING
ROBERT D KING
THOMAS W KING
VERNON L KING
WILLIAM J KING JR
WOODROW W KING
GENE D KINGSTON
DON F KINSEY
PAUL R KIRKBRIDE
OLAND H KIRKLAND
ARDELL KIRKPATRICK
WARREN E KIRTLAND JR
DEMARET M KIRTLEY
ROY R KIRTON
RICHARD P KIRWIN
THOMAS W KIRWIN
TRAVIS N KISER
ROBERT J KISHBAUGH
JAMES E KISOR
ROBERT A KISTLER
MAXWELL O KITCHEN
MATTHEW KITT
PETER KITT
JAMES J KITTLE
ALLAN F KIVLEHAN
AMOS E KIZER
ANDREW KLATKO JR
LESLIE F KLEES JR
LOUIS J KLEIN
HAROLD L KLEINFELDT
HOWARD F KLEINKAUF
ERWIN W KLEINSCHMIDT
ARTHUR W KLEPPE
RICHARD E KLIMBACK
HARRY W KLINE
AUSTIN L KLINEKOLE
EUGENE H KLING
HARRY J KLING
BOBBY B KLUSMEYER
CLYDE E KNAGGS
ROBERT L KNAPP
ROBERT P KNAUS
FORREST N KNICH
BURL KNIGHT
DAVID C KNIGHT
NEAL M KNIGHT
ROBERT M KNIGHT JR
WILLIAM C KNIGHT
FRANCIS D KNOBEL
JEROME R KNOLLE
JEROME W KNORR
VIRGIL L KNOWLES
ALLAN L KNOX
PAUL C KNUTSON
ANDREW J KOBAGE
ANTHONY A KOCH
THADDEUS C KOCIENCKI
MARLIN P KOEHRING
FLOYD W KOEPKA
CLIFFORD L KOEPPEL
FREDERICK J KOGEL
WILLIAM O KOLB
WILLIAM V KOLBERG
MICHAEL KOLSON
ANTHONY KONZE
LEONARD J KOPICKI
JACK KORAKIAN
GEORGE KORBE
MIKE M KOROLIA
RICHARD R KOROSER
DONALD D KORTE
LEONARD J KOSCIELAK
TOIVO W KOSKI
STANLEY KOST
JULIUS H KOSTER
JEROME W KOTTMER
WILLIAM KOTWASINSKI
EDWARD R KOWALSKI
LEONARD P KOWALSKI
GRANT W KOYLE
ROMAN V KOZAK
STEPHEN F KOZLOWSKI
ROGER J KRAFT
FREDRICK H KRAMER JR
ELMER H KRANZ
RAYMOND V KRASINSKI
HENRY KRASZEWSKI
ADOLPH J KRAUS
FRANCIS J KRAUSE
JOHN G KREBS
CLARENCE E KREÍ
PETER KREITER JR
RICHARD G KREML
RICHARD W KREPPS
EARL B KRESEN
WALTER B KRETLOW JR
STEPHEN KRISCHAK
JOSEPH F KRISHEFSKI
GLEN E KRITZWISER
PAUL E KROEN
EDMUND A KROL
STANLEY S KRUKOWSKI
NORMAN J KRULL
JEROME M KRUMPOS
ADOLPH A KRUPICKA JR
FRANCIS J KRYGOWSKI
EDWARD KUBES JR
ALEX H KUBOVICH
HERMAN KUHN
DAVID A KUIKAHI
DAVID H KUIPER
ROBERT M KULA
MASARU KUMASHIRO
ARTHUR R KURTZ
WALTER J KUSPER
WILLIAM KUTTERS
BENJAMIN F KUZMINSKI
ALEFREDDIE A KV
JOHN KYLE
ROLAND L LABELLE
EDMOND P LA BRECK JR
RAYMOND H LACOSTE
HARRY D LACOUR
MOISE J LADNER
FERNANDO LAGRIMAS
ROBERT M LAGRUTH
JEROME LAHOOD
HAROLD L LAIRD
JOSEPH M LAMB JR
ROBERT R LAMBERT
ROLAND LAMBERT
FRANK A LAMBERTI
JOHN W LAMM
FREDERICK E LAMPORT
JOSEPH LANDA
DONALD A LANDECKER
DELOY J LANDERS
ROBERT A LANDMESSER
AVERY M LANDRY
ROLLAND P LANDWEHR
THEODORE LANDY
ELMER L LANE
GEORGE A LANE
JOHN LANE JR
THOMAS D LANE
TYLER E LANE
LEO D LANG
MELFORD H LANG
ROBERT G LANGLEY
LAMAR M LANGSTON
GEORGE LANGWISER
WALTER J LANKEN
L P LANKFORD
GEORGE B LANSBERRY
JAMES M LANSING
JOHN N LAPOINTE
SANTO J LAQUATRA
RUDOLPH LARA
JAMES N LARKIN
JACK C LARSON
PAUL A LARSON
ROBERT V LARSON
WAYNE L LARSON
WENDELL L LARSON
ALONZO L LARWOOD
LAURENT J LASANTE
ROBERT A LASHIER
JOSEPH J LASKOWSKI JR
PAUL E LASLEY
BILLY J LATHAM
WILLIAM R LAUGHLIN JR
DONALD L LAUGHRAN
OTHELLO LAURY JR
DONALD LAUTZENHEISER
ALFRED LAVALLIE JR
LOUIS J LAVASSEUR
ARNOLD J LAVIN
WAYNE E LAW
DONALD C LAWHORNE
CHARLES S LAWLER
ROBERT F LAWLER
EMORY T LAWRENCE
FRANCIS A LAWRENCE
ROBERT T LAWRENCE
AARON A LAWSON
HARVEY LAWSON
JAMES A LAWSON
JAMES I LAWSON
ROBERT E LAWSON
VENSON LAWSON
ROBERT P LAYDON
JULIAN LAYMON
ROY L LAYNE
HOWARD J LAYTON
WILLIAM M LAYTON
JOHN LAZAR
LAZAROS LAZAROU
MAPLE L LEADER
ROBERT B LEARY
HARRY F LEATHERS
RICHARD S LEBIODA
LAWRENCE J LEBOEUF
JOSE J LEBRON
HARVEY L LEDBETTER
STAFFARD LEDBETTER
ARNOLD LEDERER JR
ERNEST W LEDGER JR
WILLIAM F LEDINGTON JR
ALFRED C LEE
BONG-JEOM LEE
BONG-SEOK LEE
BU-YEOL LEE
BYEONG-UK LEE
CHARLES E LEE
CHARLES E LEE
CHEONG-GYU LEE
CHIL-GYU LEE
DONG-CHO LEE
DONG-GAE LEE
DONG-HWAN LEE
DONG-SU LEE
EMIL E LEE
EOK-MAN LEE
EUL-CHUL LEE
EUN-BAE LEE
GANG-CHAN LEE
GEORGE W LEE
GI LEE
GI-BYEONG LEE
GIL-YONG LEE
GI-SEONG LEE
GWANG-HO LEE
GYEONG-JEONG LEE
GYU-SEUNG LEE
HAROLD LEE
HARRY F LEE
HENRY A LEE
HO-DEUK LEE
HO-DONG LEE
HONG-CHAN LEE
HUI-SAENG LEE
HYEON-SEUNG LEE
HYEON-TAE LEE
I-HO LEE
IL-GYU LEE
IL-SEOK LEE
IN-SEOK LEE
IN-U LEE
JAE-DEOK LEE
JAE-HYO LEE
JAE-OK LEE
JAE-YONG LEE
JANG-SU LEE
JEOM-JO LEE
JEONG-HUI LEE
JIN-HO LEE
JIN-U LEE
JONG-BIN LEE
JONG-DAE LEE
JONG-GAP LEE
JONG-GAP LEE
JONG-GEUN LEE
JONG-HYEOK LEE
JONG-SIK LEE
LEONARD G LEE
MAN-TAE LEE
MYEONG-SU LEE
MYEONG-U LEE
NAM-JO LEE
OK-JIN LEE
PAN-AM LEE
PIL-GEUN LEE
RICHARD J LEE
ROBERT LEE
ROBERT A LEE
SAM-GYU LEE
SANG-BEOM LEE
SANG-BONG LEE
SANG-DEUK LEE
SANG-GWAN LEE
SANG-GYU LEE
SANG-HO LEE
SANG-MUN LEE
SANG-O LEE
SANG-RO LEE
SANG-SEOK LEE
SANG-SIK LEE
SANG-U LEE
SANG-WON LEE
SANG-YUL LEE
SAN-OK LEE
SE-DONG LEE
SEOK-GON LEE
SEONG-GI LEE
SEONG-YONG LEE
SEUNG-JUN LEE
SIL-GEUN LEE
SUN-GYO LEE
SU-SEONG LEE
SU-YONG LEE
TAE-IN LEE
TAE-JUNG LEE
U-GIL LEE
UI-U LEE
U-SU LEE
WILLIAM T LEE
WILLIE LEE JR
WON-CHEOL LEE
WON-HO LEE
WON-MAN LEE
YEONG-BAEK LEE
YEONG-OK LEE
YEONG-SEOK LEE
YEON-SUL LEE
YONG-HAK LEE
YONG-JU LEE
YUK K D LEE
YUN-SEUNG LEE
YUN-U LEE
ARNOLD L LE FEVRE
EVERETT W LEFFLER
HARRY E LEFLER
FRANK E LEFORT
JOHN A LEGALL
FRANK R LEGG
HARRY O LEISURE
JESSE L LEISURE
TRUE J LEMANSKE JR
DONALD G LEMATTY
ERNEST L LEMAY
GEORGE J LENNON
RICHARD N LENNOX
GERALD L LENTZ
ROBERT G LENZ
ELI LENZY JR
DAVID A LEONARD
JEAROLD D LEONARD
FRANCIS P LEPAGE
JOHN W LESCALLETT JR
JEROME LESHAW
FRANK LESNIEWSKI
MICHAEL E LEVERCOM
NORMAN R LEVESQUE
HARVEY N LEVIN
DAVID D LEVLEIT
HAROLD LEVY
A D LEWIS
ALFRED J LEWIS
ATLAS E LEWIS
BILLIE E LEWIS
CONRADE E LEWIS
ELWOOD LEWIS
GUY LEWIS
HAROLD LEWIS
HENRY P LEWIS
JACK W LEWIS
JOHNNIE L LEWIS
JOSEPH E LEWIS
LYMAN E LEWIS
PETE H LEWIS
ROBERT I LEWIS SR
SAMUEL B LEWIS
NORVAL L LIDDICOAT
ROBERT W LIEBEG
CLETUS R LIES
JAMES M LIGGETT
ARTHUR LIGON
CHARLES R LILLIE
RAY K LILLY
ERNEST C K LIM
DALE E LIND
STUART R LINDAHL
JOSEPH L LINDER
EDWARD W LINDSEY
FREEMAN LINDSEY
NATHAN L LINDSEY
LEONARD LINK
ADAM LINKEWICZ JR
BASIL C LINKINOGGER
HARRY LINNEMAN JR
RICHARD R LIPES
KENNETH W LIPPERT
CHARLES D LIPSCOMB
HERBERT E LIPSCOMB
WILLIAM LIPSCOMB
JOHNNIE B LISENBY
WILLIAM J LITMAN
THOMAS E LITTELL
OSCAR L LITTLE
PAUL E LITTLE
ROBERT H LITTLE
CHARLES J LITTLEJOHN
JOHN A LIVINGSTON
FRANK V LOCKEFER
LEWIS A LOCKERSON
ISAAC W LOCKETT JR
LINDSEY C LOCKETT
JOHN H LOCKLIN
EARLE M LOCKWOOD JR
DONALD A LOEFFLER
CLIFFORD A LOFTIS
ALVIN LOFTON
ROBERT E LOGAN
LLOYD A LOGUE
SILVESTER LOGWOOD
ROBERT F LOHR
FRANK LOIACONO
DONALD E LOIRE
MELVIN E LOKKEN
LUCA J LOMURNO
WILLIAM S LONCAR
CARL R LONG
CHARLES E LONG
DONALD G LONG
JACKIE D LONG
JOHN W LONG
LEROY W LONG
THOMAS A LONG
WARREN G LONG
WILLIAM F LONG
CHESTER LONGMIRE
JUAN M LONGORIA
ALFRED LOPES JR
ARTURO LOPEZ
GUILLERMO P LOPEZ
MARIO G LOPEZ
MILTON LOPEZ
RAY W LOPEZ
RAYMOND P LOPEZ
RICHARD E LOPEZ
CHARLES H LORD JR
JOSEPH L LORD
GEORGE H LORIMER JR
DAVID C LORREY
ARTHUR G LOSH
JAMES N LOSSETT
COSIMO S LOTEMPIO
THOMAS D LOTIS
JACK E LOUTZENHISER
GILBERT LOVATO
FRED LOVE JR
GUY R LOVE JR

59 ARMY

EDWARD G LOVEJOY
EMERY E LOVELAND
NILES S LOVELAND
RICHARD L LOVELESS
THOMAS D LOVELL
REX LOVELY
CHARLES E LOVETT
JOHN M LOVETT
CHARLES R LOVING
WILLIAM N LOVING
LAWRENCE C LOWE
MILFORD G LOWE
RALPH E LOWE
WILLIAM T LOWREY
FERMIN P LOZOYA
GEORGE S LUBLINSKI
HARRY R LUCAS
HERBERT LUCAS
JAMES R LUCAS
JIMMY LUCAS
STEVEN LUCAS
HOWARD J LUCE
HARVEY J LUCHIES
ANDREW J LUCKETT
JOHN B LUCKETT
JAMES H LUDLOW
RICHARD W LUDWICK
WALTER L LUFT
INEZ G LUGO
GEORGE LUJAN
JUAN LUJAN
HENRY N C LUKE
JOHN J LUKITSCH
LIBRADO LUNA
CHARLES L LUNDQUIST
ARTHUR C LUNDY
VIRGIL E LUNDY
LOWELL D LUNT JR
CARMINE LUPINACCI
REMI G LUSSIER
FRANK LUTZ
JOHN W LUTZ
ROBERT B LYALL
JOHN S LYCAN JR
EUGENE M LYDON
WILLIAM F LYELL
EARL P LYKINS
OZZIE LYNAH
ELWIN R LYNCH
JOHN A LYNCH
JOSEPH H LYNCH
PHILIP C LYNCH
ELMER L LYNN
TRENTON R LYON
J C LYONS
MARSHALL F LYONS
JOSEPH W LYSAGHT
JAMES W LYTLE
FIRMINIO MABENIS
FRANK J MACEK
WILLIAM A MACHEN
LAWRENCE K MACHIDA
HARRY MACHNICKI
JOHN A MACIAG
LOUIS I MACK
GABRIEL M MACKALL
ROBERT D MACKEY
WILLIAM A MACKLIN
DONALD V MACLEAN
HECTOR MACNAIR-RAGA
CHARLES E MACNEIL
DANIEL L MADDEN
DAVID E MADDEN
DONALD MADDEN
ROBERT F MADDEN
DONALD MADDOX
WALTER E MADDY
BENJAMIN G MADRIGAL
JOE L MADRIL
FRANK J MADSEN JR
PETE G MAGALLANEZ
JOHN H MAGGARD
DONALD F MAGNUS
CHARLES E MAHAFFEY
ELDEN E MAHANNAH
ANDREW W MAHON
JOHN T MAHONEY
THOMAS R MAHONEY
JOHN W MAINES
JAMES T MAINHART
EDWARD A MAJEWSKI
CHARLIE L MAJOR
RICHARD F MAJSZAK
CHARLES K MAKAENA
CHARLES D MAKELA
ANTHONY J MAKOSKY JR
ALLEN B MALACHI
CECIL A MALCOLM
WILLIAM J MALCOLM JR
FRANK M MALCZEWSKI
JOSE B MALDONADO-GARCIA
ROBERT D MALKIEWICZ
ROBERT J MALLOY
WILLIAM H MALLOY
J B MALMAY
JAMES F MALONEY
CANDIDO MALONZO
JOHN W MANASCO
GERARDO R MANDIA
HORACE M MANER
JOHN L MANIER
ROBERT S MANIER
EVERETT D MANION
HERBERT L MANION
ROBERT W MANLEY
RICHARD H MANN
WILLIAM C MANN
JOHN J MANNING
THOMAS M MANROSS
FREDERICK A MANSHIP JR
DELMER R MANUEL
WARREN R MAR
QUINTIN MARAVILLO
GLEN V MARCHANT
LEONARD J MARCINOWSKI
GEORGE I MARCKS
CHARLES E MARCO
ALLEN MARCOTTE
CARL MARCUM
LEE ROY J MAREK
RAYMOND W MAREK
ROLLAND W MARIER
FRANCIS J MARION
ROBERT G MARION
NYE MARK JR
HAROLD A MARKEY
ELBERT O MARKHAM
EARLE H MARKLE
HARVEY L MARKS
DONALD L MARLATT
WALTER L MARLER
WILLIAM E MAROLD JR
JOHN MARONI
CARMEN MARQUEZ-CRUZ
RAMON MARQUEZ-DE LEON
MIGUEL A MARQUEZ-QUINONES
CHARLES L MARR
JOSEPH MARRELLI
PABLO A MARRERO-BOCCHECIAMP
ALFREDO MARRERO-RIVERA
GEORGE A MARROCCO
DOUGLAS R MARSH
ALFRED MARSHALL
DONALD M MARSHALL
EUGENE D MARSHALL
JACK E MARSHALL
JAMES T MARSHALL
PAUL J MARSHALL
RONALD D MARSHALL
WILLIE F MARSHALL
RICHARD E MARSLAND
ALBERT F MARTIN
ALBERT L MARTIN
ARTHUR F MARTIN
BOBBIE G MARTIN
CHARLES C MARTIN
CHARLES R MARTIN
EDWARD J MARTIN
EDWIN C MARTIN
JAMES MARTIN
JAMES F MARTIN JR
JOEL R MARTIN
JOHN A MARTIN JR
JOHN P MARTIN JR
LEANDER MARTIN
OSCAR D MARTIN
ROBERT G MARTIN
SILTON J MARTIN JR
ANTERO MARTINEZ
BENITO MARTINEZ
CARLOS M MARTINEZ
DELORES MARTINEZ
FELIX MARTINEZ
JOSE MARTINEZ JR
JUAN J MARTINEZ
LOUIS MARTINEZ
MANUEL MARTINEZ
MANUEL H MARTINEZ
MANUEL J MARTINEZ
PRIMERO R MARTINEZ
RICHARD J MARTINEZ
JOHN MARTINS
ZIGMUND M MARUK
LOUIS A MARYOTT
FRED MARZLOFF
MICHAEL MASCARA
NICK J MASIELLO
JOHN E MASKO
ALWIN L MASON
CHARLES W MASON
EARL H MASON
GEORGE H MASON
JIM H MASON
JOSEPH E MASON
RALPH E MASON
ROBERT L MASON
WILLIAM J MASTERS
DONALD V MATEER
JOSEPH T MATEJ
AURELIO MATEO
JACK D MATHENY
HOWARD W MATHEW
NORMAN C MATHEWS
J L MATHIS
JOSEPH M MATHIS
HENRY D MATHUS
DONALD E MATNEY
FRANCESCO A MATOS-GONZALES
RAMON P MATOS-IRIZARRY
CHARLES F MATSON
JUN MATSUSHIGE
JACK H MATTHEWS
JAMES A MATTHEWS JR
JAMES J MATTHEWS
OLIVER W MATTHEWS JR
CHARLES E MATTINGLY
ALFRED W MATTON
CLARENCE A MATTSON
DALE I MATTSON
MICHAEL S MATUSIK
GRAHAM W MAUGHMER
ROBERT C MAURER
ROBERT S MAURO
EDWARD O MAURY
JOSEPH R MAUSER
ERVIN E MAUTZ
GEORGE A MAX
DONALD R MAY
HARLEY D MAY
RUSSELL D MAY
WARREN E MAYBERRY
THOMAS E MAYE
DONALD J MAYERHOFER
GORDON E MAYES
JAMES E MAYFIELD JR
GEORGE E MAYLE
GENE R MAYO
JAMES J MAYO
MARVIN MAYO
MELVIN J MAYO
ANDREW G MAYS
WALTER J MAZIARZ JR
JAMES W MAZZU
JAMES E MCABEE
WILLIE S MCADOO
KENNETH K MCAFEE
RAYMOND D MCAFEE
HAROLD R MCALISTER
JOHNNY L MCALPHINE
HAROLD E MCAVOY
GEORGE MCBATH
LEE R MCBRAYER
BOBBY G MCBRIDE
JOE D MCBRIDE
JOSEPH MCCABE
WILLIAM H MCCAFFERY
BERNARD D MCCAFFREY
JOHN W MCCAIN
DOUGLAS F MCCAINE
EDWARD L MCCALL
FRANKLIN L MCCALL
RUFUS A MCCALL
JOHN L MCCANN III
GORDON D MCCARTHY
CHARLES L MCCARTNEY
FRANK W MCCARTY
WAYNE W MCCASLAND
DONALD E MCCLELLAN JR
JAMES L MCCLENATHAN
JOHN R MCCLINTOCK
JAMES E MCCLOY
CLEO L MCCLURE
JAMES L MCCLURE
JEROME E MCCLURE
LAWERENCE J MCCOLLIM
WILLIAM J MCCOLLUM
WILLIS D MCCONNAUGHEY
ALBERT L MCCONNELL
CHARLIE E MCCONNELL
JAMES W MCCONNELL
CORDIS B MCCORD
ROY D MCCORD
ARTHUR G MCCORMICK
LAFAYETTE M MCCORMICK
JAMES A MCCOTTER
CONLY MCCOY
GLENN MCCOY
JOHN R MCCOY
PAUL E T MCCOY
ULYESS E MCCOY
KENNETH W MCCRACKEN JR
JAMES W MCCRAW
VERNE L MCCREA
ADDISON R MCCREARY
JAMES M MCCUBLIN
CHARLES H MCCULLERS
JOEL F MCCULLOUGH
JOSEPH C MCCULLOUGH
CHARLES B MCDANIEL
MERLE A MCDANIEL
RAYMOND O MCDANIEL
ROBERT P MCDERMOND
CHARLES L MCDONALD JR
DAVID N MCDONALD
FLOYD J MCDONALD
JOHN D MCDONALD
JOHN J MCDONALD JR
NATHAN U MCDONALD
VELTON R MCDONALD
JACKIE C MCDONNOUGH
DONALD P MCDOWELL
EDMOND M MCDOWELL
LEONARD MCDOWELL
WILLIAM C MCDOWELL
BENJAMIN J MCELROY
CLYDE E MCELROY
FOREST E MCELROY JR
JAMES C MCEVOY
JAMES L MCEVOY
STANLEY J MCEVOY
EDWARD N MCGAFFIC
ROBERT E MCGEE
WILLIAM R MCGEE
MALCOLM I MCGEOCH
RICHARD D MCGHEE
CREO C MCGILL
DONALD MCGINNIS
HARRY T MCGONIGLE
EUGENE H MCGOVERN
JAMES J MCGOVERN
RONALD F MCGOVERN
EUGENE MCGOWAN
ROBERT L MCGRAW
CHARLES L MCGUIRE
CLYDE A MCGUIRE
JAMES C MCGUIRE
OLIVER MCGUIRE
THOMAS J MCGUIRE
JAMES H MCHARGUE
LORN D MCHENRY
PAUL H MCHENRY
ROBERT W MCHENRY
LAMAR M MCINTOSH
BILLY M MCINTYRE
CLIFTON MCINTYRE
JAMES T MCINTYRE
JAMES M MCJUNKINS
JOSEPH R MCKAY
LEWIS MCKAY
HARRY H MCKEE
JOHN M MCKEE
LEO T MCKEE
JACK D MCKEIGHEN
ROBERT D MCKELL
GILBERT W MCKENNA
JOHN W MCKENZIE
NORMAN M MCKENZIE
HARRY A MCKIE
GERALD J MCKIERNAN
LYLE C MCKIM JR
THOMAS H MCKINLEY
JOHN V MCKINNEY JR
KENNETH G MCKINNEY
RICHARD H MCKINNEY
RONALD E MCKINNEY
VANDERBERG MCKINNON
FRANK D MCKLUSKY
ARTHUR L MCKNIGHT
JOSEPH MCLAUGHLIN JR
JOHN MCLAWS
BILLY E MCLEMORE
WILLIE P MCLENDON
JOE F MCLEOD
JOHN J MCMAHON
RAYMOND F MCMAHON
EUGENE MCMASTERS
WILLIAM R MCMORRAN
ALONZO J MCNATT
JOHN R MCNAUGHTON
STEWART MCNEIL JR
DEAN R MCNEW
CHARLES W MCPHERSON
FRANKLIN D MCPHERSON
WILLIAM E MCQUIEN
KENNETH A MCQUILLIAM
JOHN M MCQUINN
WILLIAM T MCSPADDEN
ALFRED C MCWHIRTER
CHARLES J MEAD
BILLIE W MEADORS
CARL J MEADOWS
HOBERT E MEADOWS
ROBERT H MEADOWS
SAMUEL K MEAGHER
HOYT F MEALOR
WILLIAM L MECKLEY
JOE S MEDINA
RAUL C MEDINA
FLOR MEDINA-RAMIREZ
BOBBY J MEDLIN
WALTER R MEDVED
JOSEPH J MEEHAN JR
OWEN J MEEHAN
FRANK MEEK JR
WILLIAM E MEEKER
CHARLES E MEEKS
GLENN D MEFFERT
DUANE B MEGARD
JACOB J MEIER
DAVID H MEIERS
JOHN L MEISS
ROBERT P MEISTER
GERARDO MEJIAS
LAUREANO MEJIAS-MARTINEZ
HUEY P MELCHER
JOSEPH D MELCHIORRE
ALBERTO MELENDEZ-MELENDEZ
JAMES R MELLINGER
ENRIQUE H MELLO
EARL W MELSNESS
GEORGE D MELTON
JOHN T MELTON
FERNANDO MENA
ARTURO MENCHACA
ALVIN R MENDES
BARON MENDEZ III

60 ARMY

JOE C MENDIBLES
ALFONSO L MENDOZA
JULIAN L MENDOZA
GEORGE MENESES
ROBERT R MENGES
DONALD L MENKEN
RAFAEL V MERCADO
SALOME MERCADO-HERNANDEZ
CLYDE T MERCER
EARL S MERCER
FOSTER M MERCER
ROBERT A MERCER
ALBERT MERGENDAHL
CHARLES A MERJANIAN
HOWARD P MERKLE
GERALD F MERRILL
LARRY O MERRILL
RALPH T MERRILL
RALPH E MERRIMAN
MAX H MERRITT
ALONDA L MERRY
ROBERT B MERRYMAN
MORRIS MESHULAM
OWENNEIL D MESSERSMITH
WILLIAM G METCALF
ALPHEGE M METIVIER
EDGAR A METLER
ALLEN L METTLER
JAMES H METZ
RAYMOND K W MEW
JOSEPH MEYER
OTTO T MEYER
GLENN D MEYERS
ROBERT E MEYERS
WILLIAM A MEYERS
WILFRED S MICHAUD
JOSEPH W MICK
MORRIS S MICKELSEN
HENRY E MIDDLEBROOKS
JAMES E MIDDLETON
LEONARD J MIKLOVICH
JOSEPH C MIKRONIS
ARTHUR A MIKULA
DAVID B MILANO
WILHELM F MILBRANDT
JOHN G MILES
WILLIAM H MILES
WILLIAM T MILES JR
CHARLES L MILLER
DARDEN D MILLER
DONALD C MILLER
EDWIN E MILLER
ELDEN L MILLER
EVERETT H MILLER
EVERETT L MILLER
FREDERICK J MILLER
GEORGE W MILLER
GEROLD M MILLER
GRADY H MILLER
HAROLD J MILLER
HARRY V MILLER
HENRY A MILLER
JESSE L MILLER
JOE R MILLER
JOHN B MILLER
JOHN M MILLER
JOSEPH E MILLER
MAX H MILLER
NORMAN MILLER JR
ORVILLE D MILLER
POSEY L MILLER
RAYMOND H MILLER
RICHARD K MILLER
ROBERT F MILLER
ROBERT G MILLER
ROGER G MILLER
ROGER L MILLER
RONALD R MILLER
RUSSELL R MILLER
THEODORE R MILLER
WALLACE A MILLER
WILLARD J MILLER
WILLIAM E MILLER
GERARD G MILLETTE
RICHARD MILLIGAN
RICHARD E MILLIS
ALBERT D MILLS
ALBERT E MILLS
WALTER B MILLS

JAMES R MIMS
BYEONG-SEON MIN
HONG-SIK MIN
WAYNE E MINARD
EDWARD W MINIKUS
JACK R MINKIN
DONALD T MINKLER
ROBERT G MINNIEAR
LLOYD S MINTER JR
CHARLES L MINYARD
CARLOS J MIRANDA-COTTO
ANTONIO MIRANDA-VAZQUEZ
MACARIO MIRELES
GEORGE MISARAS
EDWARD J MISCAVAGE
LUKE T MISCIAGNO
LOUIS F MISKAVAGE
JOSEPH J MISKO
JAMES J MISLOSKY JR
ALBERT L MISS
MICHAEL J MISSENTZIS
FRANCISCO MISSERI
VICTOR C MISTRETTA JR
JEROME A MISURACO
CHARLES L MITCHELL
DONALD K MITCHELL
EDWIN L MITCHELL
FREDERICK M MITCHELL
FREDERICK W MITCHELL
HARRY D MITCHELL
JESSE L MITCHELL
LINDSAY W MITCHELL
RAYMOND E MITCHELL
RUDUS MITCHELL JR
TOMMY F MITCHELL
WILLIAM L MITCHELL
THOMAS P MITCHELSON
ARNOLD S MITCHEM
PAUL MITCHEM
RALPH R MITOLA
GERARD J MITTEN
WILBERT Y MIYASATO
TOMOYOSHI MIYASHIRO
HARRY Y MIYATA
SHIGEO MIYAZAKI
JOSEPH A MLYNARSKI
WILLIAM J MOAK
RICHARD G MOCKSFIELD
GEORGE L MODGLIN
ARTHUR A MOELLER
TRUMAN O MOEN
ROBERT V MOFFETT
WESLEY K MOHAGEN
LOUIS W MOHR
RAYMOND T MOKIAO
LOUE J MOLAR
WENDEL R MOLES
ROBERTO MOLINA-GARCIA
MAXIMINO MOLINA-GERENA
ROLV MOLL
JAMES E MOLTON
ARNOLD L MON
VINCENT H MONDRAGON JR
EUGENE P MONFORTON
ALBERT V MONK
BILLY J MONROE
EMERY L MONROE
FRED B MONROE
JAMES H MONROE
CHARLES J MONTAGNA
EARLE E MONTAGUE III
ERNESTO MONTANEZ
SIXTO E MONTANEZ-FRANCO
ALBINO C MONTES
HERMAN MONTGOMERY JR
JAMES R MONTGOMERY
ROBERT W MONTGOMERY
JAMES R MONTLOUIS
PAUL MONTOYA
HENRY A MONZO
J R MOODY
ALLEN E MOONEY
BERT MOORE
BOBBY M MOORE

BOOKER MOORE
CHARLES E MOORE
CHARLES G MOORE
CHARLIE W MOORE
DAVID N MOORE
DEXTER MOORE
DORIS T MOORE
EUGENE K MOORE
GARFIELD R MOORE
HAROLD B MOORE
IRVINE W MOORE
JAMES L MOORE
JOHN T MOORE
LAYMON MOORE JR
LEON MOORE
LEON M MOORE
LEROY L MOORE
ROOSEVELT J MOORE
T S MOORE
TOMMY D MOORE
WAYNE T MOORE
WILBUR D MOORE
ROBERT E MOORMAN JR
ANGEL R MORA
BEN R MORALES
GILBERT MORALES
JOSE D MORALES
RICHARD J MORAN
CAROL J MOREAU
EUGENE M MORELLI
ALBERT MORENO
ALEXANDER M MORENO
GILBERT T MORENO
RAYMOND M MORENO
RUDOLPH MORENO
ARTHUR W MORGAN
DONALD MORGAN
FRANKIE K MORGAN
HILLARD G MORGAN
MELVIN H MORGAN
ROGER L MORGAN
DONALD R C MORIN
FERNAND A MORIN
THEODORE E MORIN
CARMEL MORINA
AKEJI MORINAGA
EIJI MORISHIGE
HARUO MORIYASU
GEORGE J MORREALE
MARTIN G MORRILL JR
ALPHA L MORRIS
ARVELL H MORRIS
BILLY G MORRIS
DAVID W MORRIS
JAMES MORRIS JR
JAMES F MORRIS
JOE MORRIS
JOHN W MORRIS
NORMAN M MORRIS
RAY M MORRIS
RAYFORD C MORRIS
BUSTER E MORRISON
ELBERT MORRISON
J A MORRISON
LLOYD V MORRISON
RAYMOND G MORRISSEY
PAUL L MORRISTELL
JACK L MORROW
JOHN W MORROW
WILLIAM B MORSE
DEAN A MORTIMER
BENJAMIN J MORTNER
RAEFORD L MORTON
ROBERT H MOSER
BILLY MOSIER
EDWARD MOSKOWITZ
W M MOSLEY
ALONZA MOSS
MANUEL MOTTA
HAROLD V MOTZKO
ROBERT J MOULAISON
LEWIS C MOULTON
CARLOS B MOYA
JAMES A MOYA
TONY MOYA JR
GLYNDON E MOYER
SYLVIAN A MOYERS
LAWRENCE M MROTEK
ELMO R MUDGE
ANTHONY J MUDICKA

WILLIAM R MULCRONE
DELANO B MULDER
ROBERT MULHOLLAND
WAYNE A MULHOLLAND
ALFRED E MULLEN
JOHN L MULLEN JR
ADAM J MULLER
BURL MULLINS
CEBERT W MULLINS
KENNETH MULLINS
MALCUM MULLINS
MYLES L MULLINS
PAUL S MULLINS
THOMAS H MULLINS
JAMES D MULLOY
ERWIN R MUMFORD
DEOK-CHIL MUN
HUI-SIK MUN
PAN-OK MUN
GEORGE MUNIZ JR
RAFAEL MUNOZ
MOISES MUNOZ-VAZQUEZ
FREDERICK T MUNSELL JR
JOSEPH MURA
JOSEPH A MURCHISON
ORLIN T MURCHLAND
CHARLES D MURDOCK
RAMON MURGA-AMADOR
HARRY T MURPHY
JOE L MURPHY
JOHN M MURPHY
LESLIE O MURPHY
ROBERT J M MURPHY
RONALD L MURPHY
THOMAS F MURPHY
WALTER L MURPHY
BERNARD M MURRAY
BOBBY L MURRAY
HAROLD L MURRAY
JAMES MURRAY
JAMES E MURRAY JR
JAMES S MURRAY
NEIL A MURRAY JR
HAYWOOD MURRELL
EARL L MUSE
ARTHUR R MUSGRAVE
CHARLES M MUSGROVE
ALVIN D MUSSER
LOUIS P MUTTA
GENE MUTTER
WILLIAM H MYER JR
MARTIN P MYERING
CHARLES D MYERS JR
FRED H MYERS
MAX L MYERS
PAUL E MYERS
PAUL H MYERS
RAYMOND MYERS JR
THOMAS MYERS
JEONG-YONG NA
TAE-SUL NA
ROBERT G NAATZ
SAM L NADAI
FADALLAH N G NADER
EDWARD J NAGEL
DALE B NAGLE
PAUL A NAGY
ADAM L NAHODIL
HIDEO NAKAMA
SEINOJO R NAKATANI
RAYMOND E NALL
GI-JEONG NAM
GUNG-SIK NAM
GUNG-YONG NAM
SANG-BEOM NAM
JIMMIE P NANCE
PAUL R NANCE
ROBERT C NANCE
WALLACE R NANCE
GEORGE R NASET
JAMES T NASH
WILLIAM L NASH
NAPOLEON NATHAN
RONALD A NAUGLE
JULIO Q NAVARRO
ROBERTO NAVARRO
STANLEY R NAWROCKI
ARDELL N NEAL
JOHN E NEAL
RICHARD A NEARY

CHARLES R NEDVED
FREDERICK E NEDVED
PAUL E NEECE
ANGEL L NEGRON
JORGE NEGRON-MARTINEZ
JAMES B NEHOWIG
GEORGE G NEIL
THOMAS W NEISWINGER
MIKE E NEISZ JR
RAYMOND E NELLE
FREDDIE NELLOMS
TENDELL R NELMS JR
HERBERT C NELSON
JOHN V NELSON
ROBERT NELSON
ROY R NELSON
WOODROW W NELSON
STEPHEN P NEMEC
BEN S NEMETH
MARVIN D NEMITZ
LEONARD D NESTOR
EDWARD D NETHERY
RUDY T NETRY
HAROLD L NEUBOLD
HARLAN R NEVEL
DALLAS L NEWBERRY
BERNARD E NEWBY
HERSHELL E NEWELL
JOHNNIE C NEWELL
CLIFTON D NEWMAN
CHARLES J NEWPORT
CHARLES W NEWTON
CHARLIE G NEWTON JR
EARLE C NEWTON JR
FOSTER E NEWTON JR
JOHN R NEWTON
WILLIAM A NEWTON
JAMES L NIBLICK
WAYNE NICEWANNER
CHARLES E NICHOLS
DALE L NICHOLS
DAVID H NICHOLS
ROBERT A NICHOLS
WILLIS J NICHOLS JR
DONALD G NICHOLSON
FRANKLIN A NICHOLSON
RICHARD L NICHOLSON
WILLIAM D NICHOLSON
DONALD E NICKEL
MELVIN H NICKEL
MILTON E NICKS
WILLIAM E NICOL
CARLOS A NIEVES
PEDRO NIEVES JR
MARTIN L NIGERVILLE
LAWRENCE Y NIHEI
CHARLES K NISHIMURA
FREDERICK M NITTA
FORREST C NIX
MYEONG-RAE NO
DONALD A NOBLE
JAMES B NOEL
ROBERT L NOEL
VIRGIL NOLEN
ROBERT N NONELLA
DAVID T NORDIN JR
IRVIN NORFLEET
RAY G NORLING
CARL R NORMAN
CLYDE L NORMAN
HARLEY NORMAN
JOHN T NORMAN
ROGER E NORMAN
ADIN C NORRIS JR
CECIL C NORRIS
GEORGE NORRIS
JOSEPH C NORRIS
CHARLES NORTHCUTT JR
WILLIAM C NORTHCUTT
HERBERT M NORTON
JOSEPH F NORTON
MILTON A NORTON JR
JOSEPH M NOWICKI
KASMIR E NOWICKI
ERNEST G NOWLIN
REGINALD NUNN
JAMES H NUSBAUM
ERWIN R NUSSBAUMER

61 ARMY

GEORGE NWRANSKI
STANLEY NYHLEN
ROBERT NYKVIST
KENNETH R NYLANDER
CHANG-SU O
DONG-SU O
JUN-GEUN O
SU-HWAN O
SU-MAN O
SU-NAM O
JAMES OAKLEY
CHARLES A OBERDORF
RAY W OBERLIN
RAYMOND J OBRIEN
ROBERT J OBRIEN
WILLIAM J OBRIEN
CARL OBRINGER JR
OLADIO OCHOA
ALPHONSUS OCONNELL
THOMAS E OCONNELL
JOHN D OCONNOR JR
LAWRENCE ODEA
KIRKLAND ODES
LLOYD B ODOM
WILLIAM J ODONNELL JR
JOHN H OETJEN
CHARLES O OGBURN
JOHN R OGILVIE
L G OGLE
ALFRED D OGLESBY
LEO D OGLESBY
PAUL F OHARA
THOMAS J OHARA
WILLIAM T OHARA
RICHARD C OKEEFE
KENNETH H OLDHAM
DARRELL OLDS
ROBERT D OLESINSKI
ALLEN K OLESON
ELMER B OLINGER JR
ROMAN A OLINGER
LUIS A OLIVA
JOSEPH OLIVAS
JAMES G OLIVE
EDWARD L OLIVER
JAMES C OLIVER
LUCIANO F OLLERO
AUGUSTIN I OLNAGAN
WILLIAM E OLSEN
CHARLES M OLSON
HAROLD B OLSON
KENNETH L OLSON
ROBERT A OLSON
CLARENCE E OLSZEWSKA
MARVIN E OMANS
HENRY R ONEAL
RAYMOND G ONEAL
EDWARD F ONEIL
VERNON J ONION
KENNETH W ONKA
TIMOTHY ONTAYABBI
CLARENCE E OPPERUD
JAMES A ORBACK
ALLEN L ORD
ANTHONY G ORLANDI
ALEX ORNELAS
ISHMAEL OROZCO
ERNEST L ORR
ELADIO M ORTEGA
EDWARD J ORTEGO
JAMES D ORTEGO
EDMUND E ORTIZ
ERIBERTO ORTIZ
ISMAEL ORTIZ
YSABEL A ORTIZ
CARLOS J ORTIZ-BERRIOS
RUFO ORTIZ-RODRIGUEZ
LUIS ORTIZ-ROSA
ROBERT H ORTLOFF
DICK E OSBORNE
OWEN H OSBORNE
DONALD C OSBOURN
WESLEY B OSLER
EDMUND J OSOSKI
DONALD E OSTERKAMP
ALVA C OSTROM
JACKIE T OSWALD
RICHARD B OSWALD
THOMAS N OTAGURO
HAROLD A OTIS

RAWLAND N OTTERSTROM
AMEN P OTTO
GEORGE W OTTO
ROBERT F OTTO
WENDELL H OTWELL
ALBERT J OUELLET
EDWARD A OULMAN
EDUARDO OUSLAN
CHARLES M OUTLAND
GEORGE N OVERFIELD
BILLY OWEN
BILLY A OWEN
CHARLES B OWENS
FRANKLIN A OWENS
LAWRENCE J OWENS
PERRY D OWENS
ROBERT L OWENS JR
JOHN D OXFORD
JOHN A PABON
HORACE PACE
JAMES O PACE
JAMES F PACHECO
NARCISSO PACHECO
WILLIAM R A PACKARD
IRVIN H PACKO
MICHAEL H PACZOCHA JR
ROOSEVELT PAGE
THOMAS A PAGE JR
SERGIO PAGUIA
JOSEPH T PAHLE
JAMES E PAIGE
JOSEPH PAIVA JR
ALFREDO PALAD
EMIL L PALENIK
SALVADORE J PALLADINO
FOREST M PALMER
HENRY P PALMER
JAMES R PALMER
RONALD J PALMER
THOMAS F PALMER
WILLIAM H PALMER
MARTIN PALOMO
STEVE PALUSKI
LOUIS J PANACEK
ESMENIO PANELA
JAMES A PANOSH
JOHN J PANOSSO
DOMINIC C PAOLUCCI
GEORGE PAPPAS
ALBERT C PAQUETTE JR
JOHN H PAREZO
EDWARD T PARHAM
BOK-CHUL PARK
BOK-SUL PARK
BONG-HYEON PARK
BONG-JUN PARK
BONG-MAN PARK
BYEONG-DON PARK
BYEONG-HO PARK
CHANG-JU PARK
CHANG-RAE PARK
CHAN-SU PARK
DEOK-JO PARK
DO-GAP PARK
DONG-GYU PARK
DONG-GYU PARK
DONG-JUN PARK
DU-GWAN PARK
GEUN-TAEK PARK
GI-HA PARK
GWANG-IL PARK
GYU-BYEONG PARK
HAE-SEONG PARK
HAN-UK PARK
HUI-SEON PARK
HUI-YEON PARK
I-GEUN PARK
IM-SU PARK
IN-HWAN PARK
IN-SUL PARK
JAE-GEUN PARK
JEONG-OK PARK
JEONG-SU PARK
JEONG-WON PARK
JONG-DU PARK
JONG-RAK PARK
JONG-SEON PARK
JONG-SEONG PARK
JONG-TAEK PARK
JU-MAN PARK

JU-SEOK PARK
MUN-SU PARK
O-DEUK PARK
OE-EOP PARK
PAN-YONG PARK
SANG-DO PARK
SEONG-BEOM PARK
SEONG-SU PARK
SEON-JIN PARK
SEUNG-HYEON PARK
SU-DONG PARK
SU-GEUN PARK
SU-MAENG PARK
TAE-SU PARK
YANG-GYU PARK
YEONG-DAL PARK
YEONG-GI PARK
YEONG-HWAN PARK
YEONG-JAE PARK
YEONG-RAE PARK
YEONG-SEOP PARK
YEONG-TAE PARK
YONG-SU PARK
YU-BONG PARK
YUK-NAM PARK
ANDREW PARKER
ERNEST G PARKER
GARY N PARKER
HENRY L PARKER
LEROY PARKER
MORRIS R PARKER
HENRY D PARKMAN
DAVID L PARKS
JOHN O PARKS
RICHARD W PARKS
WILLIAM E PARKS
RAFAEL PARRA-TORRES
CARL C PARRICK
WILLIE P PARRISH
CARL B PARSONS
CARL E PARSONS
TOM PARUNGAO
LOUIS PASCARELLA
RUDOLPH W PASCHBECK JR
MARVIN E PASCOE
PETER J PASERK JR
HARRY L PASK JR
WILLIAM E PASKETT
JOSEPH PATRICK
LEWIS D PATRICK
WILLIE PATRICK
CHARLES R PATTEN
JESSE W PATTERSON
JOE N PATTERSON JR
JOSEPH A PATTERSON
LINDLE E PATTERSON
ALBERT PATTON
JAMES W PATTON
MARVIN S PATTON
ANDRE A PATTYN
IGMEDIO PATUBO
ROBERT L PAULLEY
GEORGE H PAXTON
JESSE J PAXTON
LAWRENCE D PAXTON
BALTIMORE PAYNE
CARL W PAYNE JR
CHARLES R PAYNE
D F PAYNE
JOHN PAYNE
STERLING PAYNE JR
JOHN L PAYTES
HAROLD PEARCE
JOHN D PEARCE
GERALD P PEARO
LAWSON PEARSON
RAYMOND E PEARSON
WILLIAM A PEDIGO
FLORENCIO G PEDRAZA
EDWARD M PEDREGON
ANTIONIO A PEDRO
ERNEST K PEELER
JOHN A PEEPLES
THOMAS A PEET
JOSEPH N PELLETIER
JUAN PENA-ANDUJAR
CALVIN K PENBERTHY
CHARLES G PENCE
CHARLES F PENDLETON
ROY G PENDLETON

BILLY PENDLEY
JAMES R PENFIELD
TROY PENLAND
DOYLE D PENNINGTON JR
WILGUS PENNINGTON
SALVATORE F PENNISI
PERCY L PENROSE
PAUL M PENTECOST
ROBERT W PENTLAND
FRANK L PENWELL
LOUIS C PEPERA
JOSEPH C PERALTA
CAMERINO PEREA
JOSEPH W PEREIRA
FRANK M PEREZ
ISMAEL U PEREZ
JAIME R PEREZ
JOE C PEREZ
JOFFREY PEREZ
JOSE G PEREZ
MIGUEL PEREZ
TRANQUILINO G PEREZ
JUAN PEREZ-AVILES
PEDRO PEREZ-PEREZ
ARTHUR L PERKINS
DONALD J PERKINS
JESSE L PERKINS
JESSIE R PERKINS
OTTO T PERKINS
JAMES P PERNELL
GEORGE A PERREAULT
ALBERT C PERRERA
CLARENCE D PERRIN
DONALD B PERRIN
JULIO I PERRONE
AUGUSTINE PERRY
FLETCHER F PERRY
FRANK J PERRY
JACK L PERRY
ROSCOE E PERRY
SAMUEL G PERRY
WILLIAM S PERRY JR
WILLIE E PERRY
WALLACE E PETERMAN
FRED H PETERS
JAMES M E PETERS
WILLIAM F PETERS JR
CARL D PETERSEN
BRUCE A PETERSON
DONWIN R PETERSON
LELAND G PETERSON
LYNN R PETERSON
MYRON D PETERSON
PETER E PETERSON
RUSSELL D PETERSON
STANLEY F PETERSON
NICHOLAS A PETLUK
JAMES E PETRESS
JAMES H PETREY
LOUIS A PETRILLO
LOUIE J PETRO
MICHAEL C PETRUSKA
PHILIP M PETRY
JAMES PETTERESS JR
JOHN B PETTIGREW
GILBERT L PETTIS
EDWIN C PETTS
ALVIN R PETTY
EDWARD PETTY JR
CHARLES A PEUGEOT
WILMER R PFEIFLE
NICHOLAS A PFLIGER
WILBUR W PHARES
HARRY L PHELPS JR
WOODROW W PHELPS
GLENDON L PHILBRICK
BILLY M PHILLIPS
BRUCE K PHILLIPS
CHARLES A PHILLIPS
DARRELL J PHILLIPS
ELDA PHILLIPS JR
FRANCIS M PHILLIPS JR
HENRY L PHILLIPS
HOWARD D PHILLIPS
RAYMOND E PHILLIPS
ROBERT A PHILLIPS
ROBERT L PHILLIPS
ROBERT L PHILLIPS
WILLIAM D PHILLIPS
EDWARD J PHILLPOT

HARRY C PHIPPS
HERMAN R PHY
JONG-RYUL PI
MAXIE L PICKARD
RUSSELL B PICKEN
JAMES G PICKENS
WILLIAM H PICKENS
CLAYTON H PICKETT
GENE L PIELA
ALBERT C PIERCE
ARTHUR J PIERCE
FREDERICK E PIERCE
GEORGE C PIERCE JR
JAMES T PIERCE
RICHARD P PIERCE
HOWARD E PIERSEE
ROBERT W PIERSEE
ROBERT C PIERSON
ZIGMUND L
PIERZANOWSKI
HERMAN L PIETROWSKI
EUGENE H PIETRUS
ODIE T PIKE
TED PIKE
FLOYD A PILGRIM
WAYNE C PILLERS
WADE M PILLOW
WILLIAM T PILMER
FRANK J PINA
JOSEPH F PINDEL
CLIFTON F PINES
JAMES L PINKSTON
FREDERICK D PINNER
RANSOM D PIPER JR
JOHN F PIPPIN
ALBERT PISKOLTI
FRANK PITMAN
WILLIAM E PITMAN
ERNEST J PITRE
JOHN W PITTS
LOUIS PITTS JR
WALTER F PIVER
NICOLAS PIZARRO-
MATOS
CAMILLE PLAISANCE
THOMAS G PLANT
JUAN Z PLATA
ROBERT W PLAUNT
FRANK L PLOCHA
WILLIAM PLOTT JR
MARVIN S PLUE SR
HARRY R PLUMMER
ROBERT J POCZEKAJ
JAMES A POGUE
PAUL O POHLSON
SHIRLEY M POLAND
EDWARD M POLING
FOREST J POLING
PHILMORE POLK
CURTIS J POLLARD
EVERETT E POLLEN
CLAY H POLLEY JR
DAVID L POLLOCK
ROBERT F POLLOCK
ROBERT E POLZINE
WYATT H POMEROY
RAYMOND F PONTON
EDWARD POOL
JACK A POOL
BILLY R POOLE
CECIL POORE
LOWELL T POORE
GEORGE A POPE
JOSEPH POPE
MICHAEL POPOVICH
CARLOS PORTALATIN-
SANTIAGO
JOHN B PORTAS
ARTHUR L PORTER
FRANKLIN D PORTER
HAROLD B PORTER
HENRY M PORTER
OSCAR PORTER JR
RAYMOND S PORTER
ELDON G PORTSCHI
NOLAND D POSEY
RALPH POSNER
DALE A POSPYHALLA
FREEMAN POSTON JR
JOHN S POTORSKI

62 ARMY

JAMES E POTTS
RICHARD A POTTS
JOSEPH E POTVIN
GEORGE POULSEN JR
ERNEST F POWALISZ
BUFORD B POWELL
JACKIE L POWELL
JOE B POWELL
JOHN P POWELL
RAILEY L POWELL
REX W POWELL
WILLIE POWELL
BERNARD M POWERS
BURNICE D POWERS
ELBERT D POWERS JR
JAMES J POWERS
JOHN E POWERS
JAMES A PRATER
GLEN L PRATT
JOHN L PRATT
JOHN E PRATTER
CURLOUS M PREAS
HERBERT W PRENTICE
CHARLES L PRESLEY
VERNON D PRESSWOOD
DON R PRESTON
ROBERT J PRETTNER
HAROLD L PRICE
HERBERT L PRICE
WILLIAM P PRICE
MERLIN G PRIEST
JAMES R PRIESTER
GEORGE R PRITCHARD
WALTER C PRITCHARD
IRBY L PRITCHETT
CALVIN E PROCTOR
WILLIAM E PROCTOR
ARMAND H PROULX
WILLIAM J PROULX
ROBERT PROVOST
CLARENCE P PRUETT
J D PRUITT
OLIVER L PRUITT
BILLY PRZYBORSKI
RUDOLPH W PSCNERER
ERNEST E PUCKETT
WILLARD C PULLEN
JACK C PULLEY
GEORGE E PULLIAM
JOSEPH J PUOPOLO
DONALD E PURDY
WILLIS H PURDY
MICHAEL A PURGARIC
LEONARD V PURKAPILE
AMOS PURNELL JR
DAVID E PURSLEY
RICHARD L PURSLEY
ELWOOD C PUTT
RAYMOND E PUTTIN
DAVID H QUAM
CHARLES H QUASIUS
GILMER D QUEEN
JAMES P QUIGLEY
JOSE A QUINATA
ROBERTO QUINONES-DAVILA
MIKE J QUINTANA
JOHN A QUIROZ
BRUNO C QUITILEN
DONG-JU RA
THEODORE T RABAGO
STEVAN RADANOVIC
HARRY J RADANOVICH
MARION W RADECKE
EUGENE F RADEMACHER
EDWARD R RADEN
DONALD R RADER
GEORGE RADFORD
JOHNNIE E RADFORD
ROBERT P RAESS
WILLIAM J RAINEY
RICHARD F RAKE
KENNETH S RALPH
JOHN H RAMAEKERS
JAMES N RAMEY
ALBERTO S RAMIREZ
ARTHUR C RAMIREZ
GEORGE A RAMIREZ
REINALDO RAMIREZ-RAMOS

DANIEL T RAMOS
JOSEPH D RAMOS JR
FRANCISCO RAMOS-RIVERA
GERALD C RAMSAY
DONALD L RAMSEY
TROY O RAMSEY
DAN RANALLO
RUDOLPH M RANDALL
GEORGE H RANDOLPH
DAVID L RANKIN
DAVID A RANSOM
IRWIN G RAPAPORT
ARGUL D RAPIER
CLINTON D RAPLEE
RAOUL RAPOSA
ROLAND A RASMUSSEN
HAROLD RATLIFF
JERRY H RATLIFF
JOSEPH C RATTI
WILLIAM L RAU
EARL R RAY
JUNIOR L RAY
LEROY J RAYE
NATHANIEL RAYMOND
ROBERT F RAYMOND
FRED M REA
BILLY J REAGAN
THOMAS W REAGAN
HOWARD C REAMSNYDER
DAVID J REAVES
GARY E REBBIN
FRITZ J REBSOM
MITCHELL RED CLOUD JR
BILLY J REDD
BILLY F REDDICK
FRANK M REDDING JR
MICHAEL J REDMOND
LEON C REDUS
CHARLES L REECE
ARCHIE L REED
CECIL REED
HUBERT C REED
LAURENCE A REED
LEE B REED
RICHARD E REED
ROBERT D REED
ROBERT E REED
JAMES A REEDER
DAVID REESE
KENNETH F REESE
LAFAYETTE M REESE
RICHARD T REESE
HARRY J REEVE
CHARLES M REEVES
GEORGE R REEVES
ROBERT W REGAN
ALTON R REGISTER
HARVEY L REGISTER
ERNEST REGNEY JR
CLARENCE R REICH
GEORGE L REICH
ALFRED A REID
EDGAR L REID
THOMAS E REID
JAMES K REIDER
JOHN J REIHNER
ROBERT W REIGLE
ROBERT F REIL
CHARLES P REILLY
FRANCIS J REIMER
LEE F REIMERT
EDWARD S RENEY
ANTHONY RESTANTI
MONSERRATE RESTO-CRUZ
ROBERT L RETHERFORD
WILLIAM H RETTINGER
FERSON H RETTMANN
ROY RETZLOFF
HARLAN R REUTER
DEWEY E REWIS JR
GUADALUPE R REYES
ILDEFONZO REYES
BENIGNO REYES-RUIZ
ARNOLD V REYNA
BERNARD C REYNOLDS
JAMES H REYNOLDS
MERLE W REYNOLDS
STANLEY W REYNOLDS
THEODORE A REYNOLDS

WILLIAM L REYNOLDS
VERNON R RHINE
JAMES F RHOADES
VIVAN W RHOADS
ALVIN M RHODES
ROY D RHODES
VICTOR H RHODES
ALBERT R RHYNARD
ANTHONY A RICCI
CARL D RICE
CHESTER RICE
FRED L RICE
HOMER RICE
ROBERT E RICE
EARL J RICHARD
ELMER P RICHARD
ROBERT E RICHARD
EDWARD F RICHARDS JR
GEORGE I RICHARDS
MILFORD D RICHARDS
AMOS E RICHARDSON
C B RICHARDSON
EUGENE M RICHARDSON
JAMES N RICHARDSON
JOHN W RICHARDSON
ROLLAND L RICHARDSON
HARLEN E RICHERSON
JOHN RICHETTA
EDWARD G RICHMOND
LEROY A RICHTER
ROSS R RICKARD
ADAM L RICKENBACH
HARRY A RICKER
CORNELIUS L RICKERT
CLARENCE E RICKL
DOCK L RIDDLE
JAMES A RIDDLE
RICHARD A RIDDLE
KENNETH L RIDGE
JUNIOR V RIDGEWAY
ROBERT E RIDGEWAY
MAURICE D RIDGWAY
JOHN K RIFFLE
LIONEL W RIGAUD
CLIFTON R RIGGINS
WAYNE E RIGGLEMAN
GEORGE C RILES
CHARLES D RILEY
CLAUDE L RINER JR
LUTHER C RINER
RAYMOND F RINGO
HOWARD RINKES JR
KENNETH M RINKES
JESSE M RIOS
LEOPOLDO RIOS
GORDON RIPATRANZONE
JULIAN R RIPLEY
ROBERT L RISHER
GEORGE A RISING
VINEL RIST JR
HENRY J RITTENHOUSE
JACKIE L RITTER
JOEL N RITTER
WALLACE F RITTER
LUIS P RIVERA
JUAN RIVERA-CARRILLO
GILBERTO RIVERA-CRUZ
ISRAEL RIVERA-GALARZA
GUILLERMO RIVERA-OQUENDO
RAUL RIVERA-RODRIGUEZ
ROBERTO RIVERA-TAPIA
JOHN E RIVERS
REGINALD F RIVIERE
JAMES C RIX
CARROLL ROANE
DONALD E ROBARGE
CHARLES L ROBB
FLOYD J ROBB JR
EDWARD B ROBBINS
WAYNE ROBBINS
GEORGE J ROBENSON
EDWARD L ROBERSON
JOSEPH A ROBERTS
OMER ROBERTS JR
ROBERT E ROBERTS
RUSSELL H ROBERTS
CHARLES L ROBERTSON
DONALD L ROBERTSON
VERNON W ROBERTSON

JOHN J ROBICHAUD
EUGENE R ROBINETTE
FRANK O ROBINETTE
FRANK ROBINSON
GERALD G ROBINSON
GORDON P ROBINSON
JAMES B ROBINSON
JAMES E ROBINSON
JAMES H ROBINSON
JAMES W ROBINSON
JOHN W ROBINSON
JOSEPH C ROBINSON
JOSEPH W ROBINSON
KENNETH C ROBINSON
L J ROBINSON
ROBERT R ROBINSON
ROBERT W ROBINSON
JOHN ROBNETT
FRANK C ROCHA
ROBERT H ROCHEFORD
JAMES C ROCHELLE
DUANE F W ROCHESTER
FRANCIS J ROCHON
HAROLD A ROCHON
ARTHUR H ROCK
CLYDE T ROCKWELL
VERNON F RODEL
TRACY R RODEN
LEONARD T RODGERS
SAMUEL J RODKEY
DIEGO L RODRIGUEZ
EMILLIO C RODRIGUEZ
FELIPE RODRIGUEZ
LEONARDO F RODRIGUEZ
LUPE R RODRIGUEZ JR
MATILDO RODRIGUEZ
PEDRO A RODRIGUEZ
TONY P RODRIGUEZ
ALFONSO RODRIGUEZ-MARTINEZ
JOSE O RODRIGUEZ-NEGRON
ROBERTO RODRIQUES
JAMES B RODWAY
ROY E ROE
STEPHEN K ROE
CHRIS L ROED
ARTHUR H ROGERS
GEORGE S ROGERS
GERALD E ROGERS
HUEY F ROGERS
RAYMOND ROGERS JR
WALTER W ROGGOW
THEODORE ROGOSKY
LOUIS J ROHANNA
KENNETH L ROHRBACHER
LAWRENCE N ROHRBACK
RAYMOND A ROJAS
JUAN ROJAS-REYES
CLOTILDE ROJAS-RIVERA
FALLE T ROLLINS
LAURENCE E ROLLINS
EDWARD J ROMAN
JOSEPH ROMAN
RAMON ROMAN-CRUZ
STEPHEN J ROMANICK
RAYMOND J ROMANO
DANIEL F ROMEO
MANUEL J ROMERO
ARTURO ROMO
CRISTOBAL ROMO
FERNANDO V ROMO
JOSE ROMO
ROBERT J ROONEY
HENRY O ROOS
RICHARD E ROOSA
HOWARD L ROOT
LEO R ROOT
CHESTER J ROPER
RAMON ROQUE-PENA
GEORGE H ROSA
SANTIAGO ROSA
JOSE ROSADO-BRAVO
JAMES R ROSAMOND JR
FRANCISCO ROSARIO-MELENDEZ
ALBERT E ROSE
DAMON L ROSE
GILBERT G ROSE JR
JAMES S ROSE

PAUL E ROSE
SYDNEY C ROSE
WILLIAM H ROSELER
MICHAEL ROSEN
HERMAN J ROSENBLATT
THEODORE L ROSKY
CHARLES D ROSS
CHARLEY C ROSS
DONALD R ROSS
EARL O ROSS
FORREST S ROSS JR
GUY ROSS JR
HARRISON S ROSS
JAMES ROSS
TOMMY E ROSS
WALTER ROSTEUTSCHER
DOMINICK E ROSTINE
TEDDY E ROTEN
CLARENCE ROTENBERGER
JOSEPH H ROTH
THOMAS E ROTRAMEL
ARTHUR L ROUGHT
EDWARD P ROUNDS
CHARLES W ROUSE
DELBERT G ROUSE
ROBERT L ROUSH
ELMER A ROWE
JAMES R ROWE
LEWIS H ROWE
OTHEL H ROWE
JAMES E ROWELL
WILLIAM T ROWLAND
ARVIS F ROY
ELLIOTT ROY
ROBERT S ROY
JOHN M ROZEAR JR
CHARLES D RUBEL
THOMAS E RUBLE
OSCAR R RUCKER
THOMAS E RUDDOCK
JOHN F RUFENER
WALTER E RUFF
CIRO J RUGGERO
JOSE P RUIZ
LOUIS H RULON
CARLTON M RUMLEY
GLENN W RUNGE
FREEMAN C RUNNETT
ROBERT W RUPE
VICTOR R RUPNICK
DENNIS R RUSH
BILLY O RUSHING
CHARLES V RUSHING
ALVIN J RUSHTON
NORMAN D RUSS
BEVERLY E RUSSELL
ROCCO RUSSO
DENNIS A RUST
DANIEL H RUTHERFORD
WILLIAM K RUTLEDGE
CLAUDE E RUTTER
WAYNE C RUUD
DARRELL E RYAN
THOMAS F RYAN
VINCENT M RYAN JR
WILLIAM J RYAN
WILLIAM H RYMAN
THOMAS J RYNCAVAGE
GEUM-PIL RYU
SA-SU RYU
MARTIN A SAAR
ELMER J SABINO
WILLIAM R SADEWASSER
JOHN F SADLER
LEON R SADLER
JOSEPH J SADY
RALPH V SAENZ
JOSEPH H SAFFORD
ROBERT F SAGER
TSUGIO SAITO
CARLOS R SALAZAR
ENRIQUE A SALCIDO
ROBERT SALCIDO
CHESTER J SALECKI
BOOKER T SALLEY
JACK R SALMON
ALDIN B SALOWAY
ROBERT J SALVIE
JOHN D SALZBRENNER

63 ARMY

JOSEPH S SAMAYOA
PAUL SAMBOL JR
STANLEY J SAMCZYK
JACK C SAMMS
JOSE M SAMORA
GEORGE L SAMPSON
ORIE D W SAMPSON JR
RICHARD SAMPSON
RUDOLPH SAMPSON
DENZIL G SAMSEL
JESSIE A SAMSON
COLUMBUS SAMUELS
ANGEL S SANABRIA
GILBERTO L SANCHEZ
JOSE J SANCHEZ JR
ROBERT M SANCHEZ
ARMANDO SANCHEZ-HERRERA
RAFAEL SANCHEZ-LOPEZ
ELMER H SAND
HANS R SAND
MATHEW SANDER JR
BOBBY M SANDERS
CHARLES O SANDERS
JAMES D SANDERS
JOHN P SANDERS
OZELL SANDERS
FRANCIS P SANDERSON
GERALD R SANDERSON
FRANK L SANDOVAL
LEOPOLD SANDOVAL
GORDON SANDS
RUSSELL SANDS
WILLIAM T SANDS
NESTOR C SANDSTROM
WILLIAM H SANFORD
CASWELL L SANGSTER JR
JOSE E SANTIAGO-ORTIZ
EDWARD F SANTORA
DELMO SANTOS
NICOLAS SANTOS-ROSARIO
ISOLINO SANTOS-SALGADO
ROBERT D SANZI
JAMES S SAPACK
ELROY R SAPIA
STEVE SARAPA JR
ARTHUR S SARGENT
CLAUD C SARGENT JR
FELIPE SARMIENTO
JOHN E SARNO
MINORU SASAKI
MACK E SATCHER
NEIL M SATHER
FREEMAN D SATTERLEE
LEE SAUCIER
LEO R SAUL
WILLIAM A J SAULNIER
JOHN H SAUNDERS
LOUIS A SAUNDERS
NORBERT B SAUNDERS
CHESTER E SAWICKI
JOHN J SAWICKIS
GEORGE A SAWYER
LEO J SAWYER
PHILIP H SAWYER
CHARLES N SAYRE
FREDERICO SCACCHETTI
JOSEPH SCALESI JR
JOE R SCALF
WILLIAM M SCALF
ROBERT H SCANLON
DONALD O SCANZILLO
HENRY T SCARBORO
DARRELL SCARBROUGH
HARRY M SCHAAD JR
MARION F SCHAFFERT
RUSSELL D SCHANCK
PAUL R SCHANHOFER
WILLIAM M SCHARDEIN
CHARLES E SCHATZ JR
DOYLE SCHATZ
RAYMOND H SCHATZ
WILLIAM A SCHAUFLER
RICHARD H SCHEFFER
RAY W SCHEIBE
CARL J SCHEIDT
ROBERT G SCHEIRER
EVERETT D SCHENK

LEONARD SCHEPER
SEYMOUR SCHERER
ROBERT SCHERMERHORN
ROBERT J SCHIFANO
JAMES H SCHILLICUTT
FRANK L SCHLABACH JR
JOSEPH W SCHLETTE
CARL S SCHLOSSMAN
ROBERT H SCHLOTFELDT
DUANE C SCHMIDT
FRANK L SCHMIDT
HERBERT H SCHMITT
JOHN G SCHMITT
MAX R SCHMITT
JOSEPH F SCHMITZ
JAMES SCHMOLLINGER
FLOYD M SCHMOUDER
ARLEY B SCHNEIDER
GUS T SCHNEIDER
JOHN C SCHNEIDER
JOHN E SCHNEIDER
LEON J SCHNEIDER
WALTER O SCHNEIDER JR
PAUL W SCHNEPPER
ROBERT H SCHOEL
ROBERT G SCHOENING
JOHN D SCHOLES
LOUIS C SCHONBERGER JR
MYRON H SCHOONMAKER
DAN D SCHOONOVER
DELMAR L SCHOWENGERDT
EDWARD SCHRADER JR
GORDON W SCHRADER
FREDERICK O SCHRAMM
GLENN A SCHREINER
GUY M SCHROEDER
JOSEPH G SCHROEDER
FREDRICK E SCHROEN
HAROLD D SCHUBERT
EDWARD R SCHUH
RALPH H SCHULER JR
DANIEL J SCHULTZ
RICHARD J SCHULTZ
PAUL E SCHULZE
RICHARD T SCHUM
GERALD G SCHURING
KENNETH E SCHUTT
JAMES K SCHWACH
FRANCIS D SCHWAGER
DWAIN E SCHWARTZ
HAROLD A SCHWARTZ
HERMAN SCHWARTZKOPFF
WILLIAM T SCHWEIGER
HAROLD G SCHWEMER
WILLIAM J SCIULLI
LOWELL D SCOFIELD
A V SCOTT
BENJAMIN W SCOTT
EDWARD SCOTT JR
ELMER A SCOTT
FLOYD C SCOTT
GERALD L SCOTT
JAMES C SCOTT
JOSEPH W SCOTT
LAWRENCE H SCOTT
LEONARD SCOTT JR
OSA SCOTT JR
ROBERT G SCOTT
ROBERT W SCOTT
SAMUEL L SCOTT
WALTER C SCOTT JR
WILL SCOTT
WILLIAM G SCURR
RICHARD J SEADORE
ALTIE F SEAGLE
JOHN R SEAGLE
OTIS C SEALS
DELBERT G SEARLE
CLYDE H SEARS
ARTHUR L SEATON
LOGAN SEBASTIAN
DONALD R SECHMAN
DONALD G SEDLOW
ROBERT W SEIDEL
JOSEPH C SEIGLE
LEONARD T SELENSKI
ORVILLE C SELF
GAIL F SELLS
RICHARD SELOOVER

GEORGE J SEMETGES
VINCENT C SEMINARA
JOHN F SENAY
CHARLES H SENZ
DEOK-SU SEO
DONG-MAN SEO
GEUM-GON SEO
GI-CHEOL SEO
HYO-JONG SEO
JAE-OK SEO
SANG-GEUN SEO
SANG-GYU SEO
YONG-PAL SEO
CHEON-SIL SEOK
DEOK-AM SEONG
NAK-SUN SEONG
WOL-DO SEONG
YUN-HWAN SEONG
JOSEPH SERBACK
DONALD S SEREIKA
MARLIN F SERHAGL
DANIEL J SERRE
LEPE SESEPASARA
PHILIP K SESLER
MARVIN R SETTER
WILLIAM B SEVENING
WILFRED J SEVIGNY
TALMAGE J SEXTON
THOMAS B SEYMOUR
HOWARD SHACKELFORD
REGINALD F J SHACKLEFORD
GEORGE W SHAFFER
BILLY E SHAHAN
ROBERT F SHAMBAUGH
RICHARD H SHANE
RICHARD L SHANER
JOHN W SHANKLIN JR
THOMAS J SHANNON
HENRY C SHARLAND
JACK D SHARP
RALEIGH T SHARP
ALIN L SHARPE
MARTIN J SHARRON
BENJAMIN K SHAVER
ABNER V SHAW
CHARLES W SHAW
GLENACE H SHAW
JAMES C SHAW
CHARLES SHAY
JOHN B S SHAY
ANDREW B SHEA
PATRICK J SHEAHAN
RODNEY C SHECKLER
HAROLD SHEDD
ROBERT W SHEE
ROBERT L SHEED
GERALD D SHEEHAN
GORDON A SHEEKS
GLENN K SHEELY
JAMES L SHEFFIELD
DONALD F SHELDON
JAMES H SHELDON
GEORGE A SHELL
GLENN E SHELL JR
JOHN H SHELLY
JOHN SHELTON
PHILIP D SHELTON
PERRY SHEPHERD JR
ROBERT F SHEPHERD
GERALD I SHEPLER
CHARLIE C SHEPPARD
ROBERT F SHERBINEAU
GORDON R SHERTZER
CHARLES W SHERWOOD
HIROSHI SHIBAO
NOBUMI SHIBAO
HILTON G SHICK
ANDREW SHIELDS
CHARLES P SHIELDS
WILLIAM E SHIFFER
CHARLES W SHIFFLETT
DOYLE W SHILEY
KENNETH K SHIMOGAWA
JOSEPH E SHINE
EARL D SHIPERS
WILLIAM D SHIPMAN
CHARLES H SHIPPEN
CHARLES C SHIPPS
ALFRED O SHIRLEY

JOE E SHIRLEY
WILLIAM J SHOEMAKER
SIDNEY SHOIFET
ERVIN S SHOLES
JOHN W SHORT
PAUL H SHORT
R V LEO SHORT
THOMAS W SHORT JR
JAMES W SHORTER
WALTER SHORTS
EARL V SHUCKHART
HOMER H SHULTZ
HERBERT C SHUMAN
HENRY H SHY
EUGENE F SHYNE
JOHN A SIBLEY
CURTIS L SIEMERS
SIGMUND SIEMIES
DONALD J SIESKY JR
HARVEY B SIGERS
ROBERT L SIGGINS
WILLIAM R SIGLER
OLEN J SIKES
CHARLES E SILFIES JR
ENFRE SILVA
RAMIRO F SILVA
JOSEPH F SILVIA
JANG-HWAN SIM
JIN-HWA SIM
JONG-GYU SIM
SANG-SU SIM
GEORGE A SIMAN
ROBERT C SIMARD
ROFINO SIMBRE
JOE D SIMERLY
DOUGLAS N SIMMONS
ELDRED R SIMMONS
GENE SIMMONS
JOSEPH SIMMONS
LOUIS T SIMMONS
ROBERT J SIMMONS
ROY SIMMONS
WILLIAM A SIMMONS
STANLEY A SIMON
RANDOLPH SIMONS
DONALD H SIMONSON
CHARLES L SIMPSON
JAMES C SIMPSON
CARROLL J SIMRELL
ERNEST L SIMS
CHA-HYEON SIN
DONG-IL SIN
DO-SU SIN
GAP-DO SIN
GYEONG-TAE SIN
HAN-GYU SIN
HYEON-JAE SIN
HYEON-SU SIN
IK-GYUN SIN
IN-SU SIN
JONG-TAE SIN
MAN-HYU SIN
SE-HO SIN
SEONG-JIN SIN
SEONG-MAN SIN
SUN-CHEOL SIN
TAE-HYEON SIN
YONG-SIK SIN
JOHN P SINGLETON
JOSEPH W SINGLETON
CHARLES F SINNETT JR
LUTRELL M SINNETT
WILLIAM F SIRERA
HOMER L SISK JR
ROBERT W SISK
JOSEPH F SISSON JR
CHARLES E SIZEMORE
CLIDE E SKAGGS
JAMES H SKAGGS
CLARENCE R SKATES
LONALD D SKEENS
JOHN C SKELTON
GERALD A SKERRY
EARL L SKINNER
DONALD C SKOGLUND
STEVE SKORICH
PETER F SLANSKY
WAYMON SLATEN
JAMES A SLATER
LARRY E SLAUGHTER

MERLE T SLEDD
WILLIAM R SLUSS
JAMES E SLUTZ
WILLIE W SLY
MARVIN SMALL
RICHARD E SMALL
STEPHEN J SMALLBONE
GAIL W SMALLEY
WILLIAM A SMALLSTEY
OTTO W SMART
PAUL L SMART
WALTER A SMEAD
GLEN E SMETHERS
ALLEN W SMITH
ARCHIE SMITH JR
ARTHUR M SMITH
BENJAMIN F SMITH
BENJAMIN L SMITH
BILLY R SMITH
BOBBY H SMITH
BOBBY L SMITH
CECIL J SMITH
CHARLES B SMITH JR
CHARLES E SMITH
CHARLES J SMITH
CHARLES L SMITH
CHARLIE V SMITH
CRIST W SMITH
DANNY R SMITH
DAVID L SMITH
DAYLE L SMITH
DENVER J SMITH
DONALD F SMITH
DONALD G SMITH
DONALD L SMITH
DONALD L SMITH
DONALD L SMITH
DONALD R SMITH
DOUGLAS Y SMITH
DOYLE L SMITH
EDWARD A SMITH JR
EDWARD H SMITH
EDWARD J SMITH
EDWARD W SMITH
FRANCIS K SMITH
FRANK H SMITH
GEORGE C SMITH
GEORGE R SMITH
HAROLD A SMITH
HOWARD R SMITH
JAMES E SMITH
JAMES L SMITH
JAMES T SMITH
JERROLD R SMITH
JOHN C SMITH
JOHN R SMITH
JOHN W SMITH
JOSEPH A SMITH
JOSEPH L SMITH
LAWRENCE SMITH
LAWRENCE A SMITH
LELAND F SMITH
LLOYD G SMITH
MELVIN H SMITH
NELSON SMITH
PAUL H SMITH
PAUL V SMITH
RAY C SMITH
RICHARD F SMITH
ROBERT SMITH
ROBERT SMITH
ROBERT J SMITH
ROBERT J SMITH
ROBERT J SMITH
RONALD SMITH
RONNIE T SMITH
ROY E SMITH
ROY E SMITH
RUFUS A SMITH
SANFORD J SMITH
THEODORE G SMITH
THEODORE J SMITH
THOMAS O SMITH
WARREN C SMITH
WILLIAM D SMITH
WILLIAM D SMITH
WILLIAM H SMITH
WILLIAM L SMITH
WILLIAM L SMITH
WILLIAM S SMITH

WILLIE M SMITH
FERMAN T SMITHERS
JAMES N SMITHERS
ELTON E SMOAK
FRANK S SMOLINSKY
ADOLPH E SNARSKI
PAUL E SNAVELY JR
LAWRENCE L SNEAD
LAWRENCE A SNEDDEN
CARL G SNIDER JR
FLOYD W SNIPES
D C SNODGRASS
ROBERT C SNODGRASS
RONALD SNOW
CHARLES F SNYDER
DAVID L SNYDER
DONALD E SNYDER
EDWARD C SNYDER
GERALD D SNYDER
JOHN M SNYDER JR
ERNEST T SOCHA
JOSEPH J SOCHA
ADOLPH G SODEMANN
RUDOLPH W SOELLNER
RAYMOND C SOLIS
THOMAS F SOLOMETO
EDWARD J SOLWAY
JULIUS R SOMMER
WILLIAM H SOMMERS
DONG-DO SON
DONG-SIK SON
DU-BAEK SON
GI-GEUN SON
GI-HO SON
GYU-TAEK SON
SANG-SIK SON
DEOK-GU SONG
GAP-NEUNG SONG
GYEONG-BOK SONG
GYU-MAN SONG
HEUNG-DEOK SONG
HO-SAM SONG
HUI-SIK SONG
JAE-GWAN SONG
SANG-GAP SONG
SANG-YUN SONG
SEON-GEUN SONG
SU-SIK SONG
YEONG-GEUN SONG
YEONG-SEON SONG
LUIS A SONICO
LOUIS SONNIER JR
EDWARD SONS
GRIGORIJ SORIN
ANTHONY T SORRENTINO
LAWRENCE R SORUM
JOHN W SOTHERDEN
ANTONIO M SOTO
IAN SOUTAR
WILLIAM E SOUTHARD JR
FRANCIS B SPAETH
ANTONIO L SPAGNUOLO
WILLIAM C SPAID
FRANCIS E SPAIN
HORACE SPARKS
JAMES E SPARKS
RONALD C SPARKS
RONALD M SPARKS
WOODROE W SPEARS
HARRY E SPECK
CLIFTON T SPEICHER
JOHN C SPELLMAN
RICHARD L SPENCE JR
HAROLD G SPENCER
LLOYD SPENCER
CARL P SPERONDIO
ELMER G SPERRY
ORVILLE K SPICER
GEORGE E SPIEGEL
RICHARD H SPIRAT
EVERETT W SPITZER
BOBBY E SPIVEY
BERNARD SPLITTSTOESSER
PHILIP A SPOONER
OSCAR L SPRAGUE
HOMER J SPRANKLE
JOHN W SPRING
ROBERT W SPRINGBORN
WILLIAM L SPRINGER
THOMAS C SPROUSE

JOHN A SPRUELL
JESSE E SPRY
JOHN W SPURLOCK
JAMES W SQUIRES
RODNEY L SRB
GEORGE J SROGONCIK
JOHNNIE A SRONCE
DAYTON J STAFFORD
JACK N STAFFORD
WILLIAM C STAGGS
PAUL K STAHL
GEORGE K STAIRS
ERNEST E STALLINGS
CHARLES B STALNAKER
HARLAN W STAMP
JIMMIE STAMPLEY
DEWEY C STANLEY
JOHN STANLEY
PAT M STANLEY JR
WILLIAM H STANSBURY JR
FRANKLIN T STANTON
FREDERICK E STANTON
ARTHUR E STAPLETON
EDWARD D STAPLETON
CHARLES L STARCHER
ROBERT J STARK
JACK R STARKEY
ROBERT C STARLING
ARTHUR M STARR
RAYMOND STARZEE
LESTER C STAVOS
BENJAMIN F ST CLAIR
WILLIE A ST CLAIR JR
ALVIN L STEBBENS
RONALD C STEC
CLYDE D STEELE
HAROLD M STEELE
GERALD D STEEN
LOUIS T STEFANAK
WILLIAM R STEGER
EDWIN C STEIGERWALT
ROBERT E STEINLE
WILLIAM A STENGEL
GEORGE R STEPHENS
JAMES M STEPHENS
JAMES W STEPHENS
LEON B STEPHENS
RAYMOND G STEPHENS
DALLAS W STEPHEY
HAROLD W STERLING
JOHN T STERNAD
BILLY J STEVENS
CLAUD N STEVENS
J E STEVENS
BERNARD A STEWART
DUANE B STEWART
EDWARD F STEWART
HARRY M STEWART JR
ISIAH STEWART
JAMES E STEWART
ORESTUS M STEWART
ROBERT E STEWART
ROBERT J STEWART
ROY STEWART
RUSSELL D STEWART
VICTOR W STEWART
WALTER L STEWART
WARREN E STEWART
WELDON W STEWART
WILLIAM H STEWART
WILLIAM S STEWART
WILLIAM T STEWART
WILSON W STEWART
ALDON J ST GERMAIN
RENO D STICE
HENRY STIDHAM
LLOYD D STIDHAM
LAWRENCE H STIGGE
GEORGE W STILES
EDGAR H STILL
PERCY E STINE JR
GUYTON STINGLEY
BILLIE J STINNET
ROBERT STIREWALT
CHARLES E STOCKLEN
WALTER T STOEBER JR
FRED J STOKES
REGINALD H STOKES
ROBERT W STOKES
RICHARD W STOKUM

THOMAS H STOLIKER
BERNARD J STONE
CHARLIE A STONE
CHARLIE C STONE
EDWARD J STONE
JOHN F STONE
NEIL R STONE
ROBERT L STONE
WILLIAM H STONE
JAMES W STONER
JOHN L STORMENT
LUTHER H STORY
BILLY J STOTTS
JOHNNIE O STOUT
RICHARD L STOUT
JOHN J STRACK
DONALD F STRAUSER
PAUL P STRAWSER
JOSEPH M STREETMAN
DONALD O STREICHER
JOE F STRICKLAND
MARVIN B STRICKLAND
PETE STRICKLAND
WILLIAM W STRICKLAND
DONALD W STRICKLER
RICHARD J STRINGER
LAWRENCE H STROBEL JR
EDWARD D STROCKY
JOHN O STROM
RICHARD P STRONG
ROBERT G STRONG
ARTHUR H STROUD
JAMES R STROUP
ROY A STROUP
JOSEPH J STRUBCZEWSKI
HENRY T STRZELECKI
DONALD A STUART
JAMES F STUART
EVART R STUBBS
KENNETH R STUCK
WILLARD C STUFFELBEAM
ORVILLE L STUMBO
ROY STUMBOUGH JR
MARION F STUMPF
FRANCIS E STUTLIEN
ASHER B SUBLETT
MATHEW SUCICH
DENNIS P SUGRUE
DAVID C SULLIVAN
EDGAR SULLIVAN
HAROLD J SULLIVAN
HARRISON L SULLIVAN JR
JOSEPH J SULLIVAN
JOSEPH W SULLIVAN
PETER F SULLIVAN
ODIE F SUMRALL
JERRY D SUMROW
CELESTINE H T SUN
JAMES N SUND
MARSHALL C SUNTZENICH
HAROLD P SURBER
NORMAN G SUSICE
CONLEY R SUTHER
LAVERNE A SUTLIFF JR
ANDREW M SUTTON
LESLIE R SUTTON
RALPH W SUTTON
RAYMOND SUTTON JR
WALTER E SUTTON
ROBERT M SUVADA
TROY W SWAIN
ROGER G SWALM
JAMES E SWANEY
JOEL D SWANNER
FRANKLIN T SWARTZ
ROBERT L SWARTZ
KERMIT G SWAVELY
GEORGE L SWEARINGEN
QUINTON B SWEAT
WALTER M SWEATT
JOHN R SWEENEY
ROBERT J SWEENEY
LOWELL C SWEET
RANDALL R SWEET
RICHARD L SWEET
MELVIN A SWETT
ANDREW C SWIERS JR
CHAUNCEY W SWIGER
HENRY C SWINDELL
IVAN E SWINGLE

JAMES E SWINSON
JOHN SWISHER
CONTEE L SWITZER
WALLACE C SWOPE
ADAM SWORNOG
ADRIAN J K SYLVA
RICHARD E SYLVESTER
MAXYMILIAN A SZAFRAN
ANTHONY SZCZEPANSKI
FRANK SZELINSKI
EDWIN W SZWABO
ROBERT W SZWAJKOWSKI
HERLINDO TABARES
FLABIANO T TACAZON
RAYMOND TACKETT
STERLING D TACKETT
ALTON L TADLOCK
ALVIN R TADLOCK
MYEONG-RYONG TAE
ROBERT J TAIT
HYEON-SAM TAK
THEODORE S TAKAFUJI
RICHARD M TAKAHASHI
HARRY F TAKEBUCHI
ROBERT B TALLENTIRE
JOHN E TALLMAN
REFUGIO C TAMAYO
GLENN L TANGMAN
ARLOND M TANNER JR
DAVID H TANNER
NEIL F TANTORO
RICHARD L TARANTINO
HARVEY TARKOW
JOHN P TARO
RUDOLPH E TATALOVICH
JACK TATE
WILLIAM TAVRES
ARCHIBALD H TAYLOR
BILLY B J TAYLOR
CHARLIE TAYLOR
DEAN E TAYLOR
EARNEST D TAYLOR
EDWARD J TAYLOR
EVERETT W TAYLOR
GEORGE D TAYLOR
GERMAN V TAYLOR
HARRY L TAYLOR
HARVEY M TAYLOR
HENRY H TAYLOR
JACK O TAYLOR
JAMES K TAYLOR
JAMES P TAYLOR
JAMES P TAYLOR
JOHN J TAYLOR
JOHN J TAYLOR
LAWRENCE K TAYLOR
MARVIN L TAYLOR
NORMAN J TAYLOR
PORTER W TAYLOR
RALPH E TAYLOR
RAYMOND L TAYLOR
RILEY S TAYLOR
ROBERT E TAYLOR
ROBERT W TAYLOR
RODGERS H TAYLOR
TED C TAYLOR
VERL P TAYLOR
WILLIAM R TAYLOR
CLIFFORD K TEASEL JR
JOHN W TEDFORD
AUGUSTINE TELLEZ JR
RUDOLPH TELLEZ
MARVIN TEMPLE
RODERICK K TENAGLIER
FRANCIS H TENN
OLIVER TENNELL
RAMON B TENORIO
ROBERTO P TERAN
RAY TERRELL
WILLIAM TERRELL
BRYANT A TERRY
ESPY TERRY JR
GEORGE TERRY
JIMMIE TERRY
SIMON TERRY
ZACK D TERRY
CLAYTON TER WEE
DONALD B TESSENDORFF
JOSEPH J TETI
EDWARD A TEWS

COLUMBUS H THACKER
ROBERT L THACKER
GEORGE THAMEL
JAMES J THEBO
NICHOLAS E
THEODOROU
DONALD A THERKELSEN
DAVID L THERRIEN
ARTHUR J THIBAULT
JACK J THIEME
WILLIAM H THIEN JR
ALBERT E THOMAS
ARCHIE E THOMAS
CARL W THOMAS
CHARLES W THOMAS
CHARLIE N THOMAS
EDMUND R THOMAS
EVERETT E THOMAS
FREDDIE B THOMAS
GERALD S THOMAS
HARVEY H THOMAS
HAZEL THOMAS
JAMES S THOMAS
KENNETH D THOMAS
LLOYD E THOMAS
MARION L THOMAS
ORVILLE R THOMAS
PHILLIP THOMAS
REUBEN THOMAS
ROOSEVELT T THOMAS
ROY H THOMAS
ROY L THOMAS
WILLIE THOMAS
WILLIE M THOMAS
ARLIE O THOMPSON
CLEVELAND G
THOMPSON
DONALD W THOMPSON
FLETCHER THOMPSON
GERALD T THOMPSON
HARMON A THOMPSON
HARWOOD H
THOMPSON
JAMES K THOMPSON
JERRY A THOMPSON
KENNETH T THOMPSON
LEE J THOMPSON
NORMAN R THOMPSON
RONALD L THOMPSON
SEQUOYAH THOMPSON
SPENCER J THOMPSON
WILLIAM E THOMPSON
WILLIAM H THOMPSON
JOSEPH A THOMSON
MALCOLM M THOMSON
JOHN B THORN
CLAYTON H THORNTON
THEODORE THORNTON
JACKIE L THURMAN
JAMES B THURMAN
RALPH R THURMOND
RALPH G THURNER
CLARENCE E TIBBS
DON E TIBBS
ROBERT E TIBBS
CLINTON C TICE
STANLEY M TICK
EDMUND W TIERNEY JR
WESLEY E TIETGE
ANTONIO D TIJERINA
MELVIN H TILDEN
WILLIAM A TILGHMAN
ERNEST L TILLETT JR
HERBERT L TILLEY
CHARLES W TILLMAN
JOHNSTON C TILLMAN
DAVID TIMBERLAKE
JAMES E TIMMERBERG
EDWARD T TINDELL
CLARENCE H TINGLE
EARL G TINSLEY
GEORGE M TINSLEY
HOWARD TINSLEY
WALLACE A TINSMAN
DONALD E TIPPERY
HARVEY J TIPPING
ANDREW R TISCHLER
CHARLES E TISDALE
CLARENCE A TISH JR
GEORGE E TISHNER

65 ARMY

DALE M TJADEN
ANTHONY F TOBIO
PHILLIP J TODD
BARNEY A TOLBERT
HARRY C TOLLEY
ROBERT E TOLLIVER
SUN K TOM
HAROLD M TOMER
WILLIAM J TOMPKINS JR
RAUL A TONCHE SR
GEORGE A TONDREAU
JOSEPH F TONER
JEWELL A TOOMBS
GEORGE TORO
ANSELMO TORRES
ARACELIO TORRES
ELIAS E TORRES
ERNESTO TORRES
LUIS P TORRES
SAMUEL TORRES-RODRIGUEZ
REMI TORRES-TORRES
JAMES C TOTH
JOHN R TOTH
REGIS M TOUGAS
JAMES L TOWLES
JAMES H TOWNSEND
MERLYN F TOWNSEND
THEODORE P TRACY
LEROY A TRADER
EUGENE O TRASK
JESSE J TRAUGHBER
JOHN E TRAUTMAN
HENRY C TRAVIS III
JOHN T TRAVIS
PAUL E TRAVIS
JOHN E TREANOR JR
PAUL N TREMBLAY
RICHARD G TREMBLEY
JAMES L TRENT
JAMES E TREPANIER
JOSEPH TREPASSO
AGUSTIN TREVINO JR
ALFREDO T TREVINO
RAYFIELD A TREXLER
JOSEPH R TRIA
JAMES B TRIGGS
DELMER L TRIPLETT
CLARENCE W TRIVETT
BILLIE J TROBOUGH
GERALD D TROCCOLA
ALVA F TROMBLY JR
WILLIAM B TROMPICS
ROBERT D TRONCIN
ERNEST H TRONIER
HOWARD A TROUP
HARRY C TROUT JR
CORNELIUS TROWEL
LAMAR A TROXEL
DONALD O TROXLER
GEORGE F TROY
JOEL J TROY
KENNETH A TRUAX
REED A TRUAX
DONALD W TRUBEE
EDWARD D TRUEBLOOD JR
JOHN S TRUHAN
THOMAS TRUITT
DOMINGO TRUJILLO
TONY E TRUJILLO
WELTON P TRULL JR
GLEN K TRULOCK
JOHN H TRUSCKEWICZ
JOHN TRUTER
THOMAS T TSOUKRAS
JACK S TSUBOI
BOYD E TUCKER
GEORGE E TUCKER
LLOYD L TUCKER
ROBERT J TUCKER
WILLIAM F TUCKER
GEORGE A TULL
GEORGE E TUNIN
RAY C TURCOTTE
ARTHUR T TURINGAN
NED TURK JR
DONALD E TURNER
HALLIE K TURNER
LESTER S TURNER
MARVIN TURNER
RICHARD L TURNER
W D TURNER
WINSTON TURNER
WINSTON M TURNER
WALDO W TURNEY JR
JAMES K TUTTLE
MATHEW TUTTLE
BENJAMIN F TWIDDY
LLOYD D TWIDT
JAMES N TWITTY
CHARLES E TYLER
CHARLES R TYLER
ELMER J TYLER
MAXINE TYLER
JAKE TYNER JR
FREDERICK L TYRRELL JR
LESTER TYSON
BONG-GU U
HA-UN U
IN-GU U
JE-SEUNG U
YONG-HYEON U
JAMES E UDD
PAUL A UHERCHIK
YUKIO UJIMORI
RICHARD R ULREY
LOUIS M ULRICH
VIRGIL E UNDERHILL
ARCHIE M UNO
LAWRENCE A UNSELL
KONOMU URA
JOSEPH P URBANORWICZ
RICHARD M URMANSKI
BURDETT C URNESS
HUGHIE D URQUHART
WILLIAM R USNIK
TERAH A USRY
JOSEPH H UTARD
MANUEL J UVALLE
ALFRED S UYEHARA
DANIEL J VACCARO
FREDRICK W VACH
ELPHEGE VADENAIS
LLOYD C VAJEN
RUDY E VALDEZ
CONCEPCION VALENCIA
WELLINGTON C VALENTINE
WILLIAM VALENTINE
ANGEL R VALENTIN-FRED
ADOLPHO A VALENZUELA
CHARLES G VANALLEN
JOACHIM C VAN AMEYDE
JOHN K VANBRUNT
RICHARD B VANBUSKIRK
ASA E VANCE
WILLIAM R VANCE
RICHARD VAN CLEAVE
DONALD L VANDEN BERGHE
HAROLD N VANDENBURG
GORDON J VANDENBUSH
JACOB VANDERLAAN
GEORGE VANDERLOOP
CHARLES A VAN DEVENTER
PATRICK W VANDEWERKER
EDWARD L VAN DUSEN
WALLACE W VAN DYKE
RICHARD VANEEKHOVEN
KENNETH H VAN HAGEN
MARSHALL I VAN HOESEN
WILLIAM B VANHOY
POMPEY J VANICOLA
JOHN E VAN LOH JR
RICHARD VAN NEWHOUSE
THOMAS B VAN NORDEN JR
JAMES M VANNOY
EUGENE R VAN STEENVOORT
RONALD D VAN WEES
CLAYTON VANWINKLE
CLAYTON E VAN WYK
FRANK P VARGA
JAMES O VARNELL JR
BASIL VARNEY JR
BILLY F VARNEY
ALBERT M VASQUEZ
ALBERT S VASQUEZ
JOSE J VASQUEZ
ROBERT E VASS JR
HOBERT J VAUGHAN
WILSON H VAUGHAN
BILLIE V VAUGHN
CARL D VAUGHN
GLENN W VAUGHN
IRA L VAUGHN
WALTER F VAUGHN
WINFORD L VAUGHN
JOSEPH S VECKOV
WALTER C VEDAA
THOMAS P VEGA
PEDRO VELAZQUEZ
LUIS VELEZ-MONTES
VINCENT P VELLA
GEORGE VELLIAS
ANTONIO VELO
ROBERT J VENETZ
FRED L VERANT
JUAN A VERA-RAMOS
ELISEO C VERGARA
LAMBERT T VERVOORT JR
NICK VEZAKIS JR
WILLIAM A VEZZOLI
JAMES E VIARS
ROBERT VICALDO
CALVIN C VICK
OLEGARIO VIDAURRI
PAUL B VIDOCK
ISIDORO VIERA-RODRIGUEZ
HAROLD A VIERRA
ISAAC L VIGIL
JUAN B VIGIL
PAUL VILLA
JULIO VILLARREAL
ERNEST VILLAVERDE
LUIS VILLOT-NAZARIO
ALBERT A VINCENT
EARNEST L VINSON
BOBBY D VINYARD
JOSEPH C D VIOLETTE
DELBERT E VOGELI
RICHARD VOISINE
LOUIS T VOLK
SAM A VOLPE
HAAR J VONDER
ARTHUR R VOSSEN
ANDREW I VOYLES
DANIEL VUKASOVICH
CLEO F WACHEL
EVERETT H WADE
JIMMIE L WADKINS
LAGRANT L WADMAN
JOHN W WADSWORTH
GENE L WAGNER
JAMES R WAGNER
REX E WAGNER
WILLIAM WAGNER JR
JAMES C WAGONER
MELVIN J WAGUESPACK
LLOYD E WAINSCOTT
REX L WAITE
LOUIS E WAIWAIOLE
FRANKLIN G WAKEFIELD
ROBERT E WALDMAN
ALBERT J WALDO JR
ARNOLD E WALK
JOHN H WALK
ARCHIE WALKER
DON WALKER
GUY J WALKER
JACK L WALKER
JAMES Y WALKER
JOHN A WALKER
JOHN W WALKER
WALTER A WALKER
WILLIE A WALKER
DOYLE B WALL
DONALD E WALLACE
EARL WALLACE JR
GEORGE W WALLACE
GLEN Z WALLACE
GRADY WALLACE
HARRY R WALLACE
JACK D WALLACE
JAMES M WALLACE
WILLARD D WALLACE
WILLIAM K WALLACE
ZECHARIAH H WALLACE JR
JAMES A WALLEN
WILLIAM J WALLER JR
VINCON WALLING
MAX E WALLS
ROBERT W WALLS
ROBERT C WALSH
WILLIAM R WALSH
JESSE E WALSTON
FRANCIS G WALTER JR
JOHN G WALTER
WILLIAM H WALTER
CHARLES R WALTERHOUSE
BILLY WALTERS JR
DALE E WALTERS
DALLAS J WALTERS
EARNEST L WALTERS
FRED T WALTERS
GEORGE N WALTERS
GEORGE W WALTERS
LELAND R WALTERS
LLOYD R WALTON JR
ELMER E WALTZ
FRANK P WANCOSKI JR
EUGENE J WANKOWSKI
DONALD J WARD
ETSEL E WARD
JOSEPH L WARD
KENNETH C WARD
LEON WARD
NORMAN L WARD
DOYLE R WARDEN
BENNIE R WARNER
CARL J WARNER
WALTER W WARNKE
HAROLD T WARP
EVERETT WARREN
GEORGE A WARREN
GEORGE J WARREN
JOHN N WARREN
MAURICE D WARREN
RALPH E WARREN JR
WILLIAM J WARREN
RAYMOND P WARRICK
JAMES D WARRINER
RUFUS C WARRIOR JR
BILLIE F WARWICK
ROBERT WASHBURN
HANSEL W WASHINGTON
JOSEPH WASHINGTON JR
R A WASHINGTON
TIMOTHY WASHINGTON
RICHARD L WASIAK
RICHARD C WASINGER
JOHN L WATERS
LOUIS WATKINS
WILLIAM L WATKINS
CHARLES W WATSON
CLARENCE R WATSON
HAROLD WATSON JR
LEONARD WATSON
ROBERT E WATSON
THOMAS H WATSON
VERNON WATSON
WILLIAM W WATSON
DAVID E WATTERS
DELMER C WATTERSON
EDDIE WATTS
JACK K WATTS
SAMMY A WATTS
WILLIAM F D WATTS
RAY O WAUER
ROBERT I WAX
DONALD E WAXLER
CHARLES W WAY
ARTHUR J WEAVER
EDWARD P WEAVER
PAUL D WEAVER
WILLIAM G WEAVER
EDWIN F WEBB
JAMES D WEBB
JERALD C WEBB
RALPH B WEBB
JAMES K WEBBER
RICHARD A WEBER
CALVIN A WEBSTER
FLOYD D WEBSTER
MARVIN L WEBSTER
HENRY J WECKERLY
BERL D WEEKLEY
HOMER G WEEKS
RANDALL M WEEMS
ROBERT W WEGNER
WILLIAM R WEIAND
BERNARD E WEICHMAN
BENJAMIN D WEIDNER
NORMAN WEIDY
GEORGE C WEINGARTNER
DONALD G WEIR
WILFRED A WEISHEIT
JAMES R WEISINGER
HERMAN WEISSMAN
ARTHUR R WELCH SR
LONNIE F WELCH
ELBERT WELDON
JAMES C WELDON
RANDOLPH W WELLER
WINFRED N WELLER
CURTIS J WELLS
JAMES W WELSCH
HARLEY WELSH
ROY W WELSH
JAKE F WENG
CHESTER WENTKO
DURWARD E WENTZ
FRANK J WENZEL
GLEN E WERHAN
JAMES W WERKMAN
RICHARD J WERME
FRANCIS E WERTZ
GERALD E WESCOTT
LEE C WESSON
CHARLES E WEST
CLEVELAND WEST
DONALD L WEST
GEORGE WEST JR
DAVID C WESTBROOKS
ROBERT WESTER
EARL K WESTFALL
VIRGIL E WESTLUND
PHILLIP B WESTPHAL
BOBBY T WETHINGTON
EUGENE V WETZEL
FRANKLIN W WETZEL
JOSEPH WETZIG
RAYMOND WEWASON
CLIFTON A WEYERMAN
FREDERICK W WHALEN
ROY L WHALEY
CHARLES W WHEATLEY
JOHN H WHEELER
ORDIS J WHEELER
CHARLES V WHEELING
RICHARD G WHIBLE
WILLIAM H WHIGHAM
JAMES M WHIPPER
NOIS L WHISENANT
FRANCIS WHITAKER
GILBERT WHITAKER
EARL A WHITBECK
BURL D WHITE
CARL WHITE JR
CHARLES A WHITE
DALE I WHITE
DELBERT L WHITE
DONALD C WHITE
EDWARD F WHITE
FRANKLIN H WHITE
KENNETH D WHITE
ODELL WHITE
RAYMOND P WHITE
RICHARD A WHITE
ROBERT L WHITE
ROY WHITE
STANLEY H WHITE
WALTON R WHITE
WILLIAM A WHITE
WILLIAM F WHITE
ARTHUR J WHITEBEAR
LEE WHITEHEAD JR
MARVIN L WHITEHEAD
MINTER W WHITEHEAD
FLOYD R WHITEMAN
COLE E L WHITESIDE
SAMUEL E WHITFIELD

DONALD E WHITING
LANKFORD L WHITMAN
WALTER M WHITMAN
BILLIE WHITTAKER
JAY R WHITTEN
ROBERT D WICKLINE
LEIGH W WIDEL
DON M WIGGINS
MERVYN L WIGGINS
CONRAD D WILCOX
HARLAND N WILCOX
HARRY K WILCOX
VERNON A WILDE
JESSE WILDMAN
ARVILLE E WILFONG
ALBERT P WILHELM
CLARENCE E WILHELM
JOHN A WILKERSON
THOMAS H WILKES
CHARLES L WILKINS
JOSEPH H WILKINS
PAUL W WILKINS
JAMES H WILLIAM
JOHNNIE L WILLIAM
ALBERT WILLIAMS
ARTHUR I WILLIAMS JR
BASIL A WILLIAMS
BILLY J WILLIAMS
BILLY J WILLIAMS
BUCK WILLIAMS
C LEE WILLIAMS
CHARLES A WILLIAMS
CHARLES J WILLIAMS
CHARLES K WILLIAMS
CHARLES O WILLIAMS
CLAUDE M WILLIAMS
CLYDE S WILLIAMS
DONALD R WILLIAMS JR
HAROLD G WILLIAMS
HARVEY C WILLIAMS
HERMAN WILLIAMS
HUBERT T WILLIAMS
ISIAH WILLIAMS
JAMES O WILLIAMS
JAMES R WILLIAMS
JOHN D WILLIAMS
JOHN J WILLIAMS
JOSEPH WILLIAMS
LAWRENCE J WILLIAMS
MARVIN WILLIAMS
MCKINLEY WILLIAMS
MILTON L WILLIAMS
ROBERT WILLIAMS
ROBERT H WILLIAMS
ROBERT L WILLIAMS
ROOSEVELT WILLIAMS
SIMMUEL L WILLIAMS
THOMAS B WILLIAMS
WALTER N WILLIAMS
WILFORD H WILLIAMS
WILLARD F WILLIAMS
WILLIAM M WILLIAMS
JOSEPH WILLINGHAM
CHARLES A WILLIS
LOUIS R WILLIS
RICHARD A WILLIS
EARL C WILLOUGHBY
ELBERT F WILLS
EUGENE E WILLS
VICTOR L WILLS
WILLIAM H WILNER
AUBREY WILSON
BENJAMIN WILSON
BERNARD O WILSON
CHARLES E WILSON
CHARLES L WILSON
CLARENCE O WILSON
DONALD W WILSON
ELMER T WILSON
FOREST M WILSON
GEORGE W WILSON JR
GERALD N WILSON
HALLIE W WILSON JR
HURLEY WILSON
JUAN B WILSON
LEROY W WILSON
LOUIS R WILSON
RICHARD L WILSON
RICHARD R WILSON
ROBERT L WILSON

RODNEY H WILSON
RUBIN B WILSON
THOMAS WILSON JR
WALLACE WILSON
WINSTON G WILSON
JOHN T WILT
ALVIN A WINDER
ROBERT E WINDER
CLIFFORD J WINDOM
RALPH E WINFIELD JR
SAMUEL F WINFIELD
RICHARD L WING
GENE L WINIECKI
MARSHALL WINKFIELD
RICHARD A WINNIE
HOWARD W WINRADER JR
HAROLD G WINSOR
GERALD A WINTER
SAMUEL G WINTER
CLARENCE R WINTERS
VAN W WINTERS
RALPH E WINTHROP
DAVID WIREMAN
SAMUEL WIRRICK
CLARENCE J WIRSCHINGER
RAYMOND E WIRTH
JAMES D WISE
ERNEST J WISENOR
DAVID J WISHON JR
FRANCIS K WITHERELL
EARL L WITHEROW
DONALD M WITHERSPOON
STANLEY WITKOWSKI
PAUL E WITT
RAY WITT
ROBERT V WITT
WALLACE D WITT
BRUCE J WODA
HENRY A WOELK
DONALD I WOITAS
ALEX WOJCIECHOWSKI
FRANK P WOJNOWIAK
NORMAN F WOLBERT
DON WOLFE
RONALD C WOLFE
DONALD C WOLFF
ROY A WOLFF
JOHN C WOLFORD
CLARENCE WOMACK
KING S WOMACK
MARION M WOMACK
EDWARD W WONTKOWSKI
BOBBY J WOOD
DONALD K WOOD
HAROLD E WOOD
JOHN P WOOD
MARVIN R WOOD
WILLIAM E WOOD
WILLIAM G WOOD
CHARLES A WOODALL JR
CECIL V WOODARD
WILLIAM R WOODHALL
ALPHONSO WOODLIEF
CLARENCE C WOODMAN
RAYMOND L WOODRING
ROBERT W WOODRUFF
DONALD L WOODS
GEORGE C WOODS JR
JAMES E WOODS
JIMMIE D WOODS
JOSEPH H WOODS
LUTHER J WOODS
RESTEEN WOODS JR
THOMAS B WOODS JR
D W WOODSON
HARRY H WOOLLEY
DOW F WORDEN
DONALD B WORLEY
ELY E WORLEY JR
THEODORE WORLEY
CLARK E WORLINE
RICHARD C WORMWOOD
EDWARD J WOROSZ
HENRY H WORTHINGTON
JACK WORTHY
FRED B WORZALA
PAUL D WRATHER
C W WRIGHT JR
CHESTER A WRIGHT
DALE W WRIGHT

DONALD D WRIGHT
JAMES H WRIGHT
JAMES W WRIGHT
PAUL L WRIGHT
PAUL T WRIGHT
ROBERT L WRIGHT
ROY C WRIGHT
THEODORE J WRIGHT
WILLIAM G WRIGHT
JOSEPH C WRZESNIEWSKI
CLYDE A WURTZ
ALFRED E WYATT
CARL D WYATT
ROY A WYATT
JOHN P WYDA
MARTIN D WYNALDA
JAMES E WYNN
OLIVER WYNNE
RAMOND A YAFRATE
RICHARD F YAGAC
TAKETO YAMANE
HAROLD S YAMASAKI
EDWIN D S YANG
GIL-MAN YANG
HWI-SU YANG
JAE-HYEOP YANG
JAE-JUN YANG
JAE-SEONG YANG
SEUNG-GYEONG YANG
TAE-YUN YANG
WON-SEOK YANG
CHARLIE C YARBROUGH
CARL W YATES
RAY B YATES
BILLY G YAW
BRUCE J YAX
RICHARD YEE
JAMES H YELEY
CHUL-DONG YEO
YEONG-HYEON YEO
IN-SEOP YEOM
IN-SU YEOM
SO-DOK YEOM
GYU-SEOK YEON
WALTER L YETTER
WILBURN R YIELDING
THOMAS H YOKOMICHI
VINCENT A YONTA
ARTHUR A YORK
CLEBRON M YORK
RAY A YORK
WILLIAM E YORK
KANJI YOSHIDA
EDWARD F YOST
CURTIS R YOUNG
DAVID R YOUNG
GEORGE A YOUNG
GERALD E YOUNG
JACK R YOUNG
JOE C YOUNG
LEE R YOUNG
ROBERT H YOUNG
WALTER R YOUNG
WILLIAM J YOUNG
WILLIAM T C YOUNG
CURTIS YOUNGER
WAYNE R YOUNGQUIST
LAWRENCE R YOVINO
DONG-JUN YU
HYO-DAL YU
MAL-DOL YU
MIN-GEUN YU
YEONG-GU YU
YEONG-MOK YU
YEONG-YUN YU
TONY F YUHASZ
JOHN C YUILL JR
DON YUMORI
BYEONG-YUN YUN
CHANG-BAE YUN
GA-SUN YUN
HUI-GAP YUN
HWA-WON YUN
IN-JUNG YUN
JUNG-GYUN YUN
SEONG-CHAN YUN
SEONG-SU YUN
SU-MAN YUN
WON-SIK YUN
EDWARD A ZABILOWSKI JR

LESTER ZABRISKIE JR
OBIDEE ZACKERY
GEORGE ZALEHA
NICHOLAS G ZATEZALO
FREDDIE ZAVALA
MIGUEL A ZAYAS
JOHN W ZEBROWSKI
VICTOR P ZECCHIN
BERNARD M ZEKUCIA
RICHARD G ZERBIAN
EDWARD E ZIMBELMAN
THOMAS E ZIMMER
GLEASON L ZIMMERMAN
JOHNNIE F ZIMMERMAN
SEBASTIAN M ZIMMITTI
SIEGFRIED ZIMNIUCH
ANTHONY ZINGARELLA
FRANCIS J ZINKUS
RONALD M ZIRBEL
WALTER L ZOPF
ROBERT J ZULKE
ROGER E ZUNK
BILLY G ZUSPAN
LOUIS J ZWILLING

SERGEANT

FRANCIS H ABELE
ROBERT P ABELE
ARTIS ABNEY JR
HOMER R ABNEY
JACK W ABNEY
ISAAC ACEVEDO
SALVADOR ACEVEDO
ALBERT A ACKERMAN
FRANCISCO ACOSTA
WILBERT V ADAMICK
BILLIE F ADAMS
HOLLIS J ADAMS
JOHN D ADAMS
ROBERT ADAMS
ROBERT E ADAMS
THOMAS ADAMS
WILLIE G ADAMS JR
HAROLD F ADKINSON
CHARLES L AGARD
HENRY N AGUEL
JAMES E AINSCOUGH
CLARENCE H AKI
FRANK T ALANIZ
ROBERT G ALANIZ
GILBERT W ALBERT
RAY ALBERT
JAMES A ALDERDICE
DENNIS ALEXANDER
FLOYD N ALEXANDER
JAMES W ALEXANDER JR
WALLACE ALEXANDER
RAYMOND A ALLARD
ALONZO ALLEN
CHARLES ALLEN
EARNEST ALLEN
ENGLISH W ALLEN
JAMES ALLEN
JAMES L ALLEN
PAUL L ALLEN
RAYMOND L ALLEN
WILLIE ALLEN JR
LOUIS D ALTIERI
GORDON H ALTON
LLOYD A ALUMBAUGH
HUGO H ALVAREZ
ANDRES ALVAREZ-MERCADO
R C ALVERSON
CLEMENT A AMBROSE
HARRY L AMIGH
GAYLORD AMOS
MORRIS AMOS
JOSEPH O AMPON
GU-SEON AN
JONG-WON AN
PAN-GIL AN
SANG-BONG AN
GERALD R ANCTIL
BILLY W ANDERSON
CHARLES E ANDERSON
DEWEY R ANDERSON
OMER L ANDERSON

RICHARD A ANDERSON
TERRELL ANDERSON
HERBERT C ANDREAS
EARNEST M ANDREWS
ISSAC ANDREWS
NICK W ANGELAKOS
ROBERT H ANGEVINE
JAMES R ANGUS
HENRY C ANISZEWSKI
GEORGE ANSPAUGH
JAMES L ANTLE
JOSE A ANTUNA
BALDOMERO ANZALDUA
MITCHELL G ARAMAN
EUGENE E ARBOGAST
JOHN R ARMAN
JAMES S ARMENTROUT
KENTON W ARMSTRONG
BLOYCE C ARNOLD
LINCOLN C ARNOLD
WILLIAM M ARNOLD JR
RAY L ARPKE
WILL ARVANGLE JR
ALTON M ASHWORTH
WILLIAM W ATKINSON
WALTER ATTWOOD
WILLIE J ATWATER
CLYDE B ATWOOD
OPAL D AULDS
CLARENCE M AUNCHMAN
EUGENE AVANTS
CLIFTON F AVERY
JOSEPH P AVERY
ARTURO D AVILA
ROY D AXTON
HARMON H AYERS
GEORGE H BABCOCK
RUSSELL L BACA
RICHARD B BACH
VIRGIL BACH
RICHARD E BACHUS
ARTHUR D BACK
DONG-GI BAE
JONG-GAP BAE
JONG-GUK BAE
JONG-SU BAE
GI-BONG BAEK
TAE-GU BAEK
DAVID J BAERMANN
CECIL R BAGWELL
EDWIN H BAILER
CHARLES V BAILEY
EARL T BAILEY
EDWARD J BAILEY
OTIS C BAILEY
RENFREW D BAILEY
JOHN J BAIN
EDMON S BAINBRIDGE
ALLEN BAKER
CHARLES E BAKER
DENNIS L BAKER
DONALD L BAKER
GASTON R BAKER
HENRY BAKER
JAMES M BAKER
ROBERT L BAKER
JOSE BALALONG
JACK L BALDWIN
LAWRENCE BALDWIN
BONG-SIK BAN
CHAE-SIK BAN
CHARLES J BANKS
DANIEL E BANKS
RUDOLPH P BAQUET
WILLIAM A BARBER
GEORGE M BARBIERE
PASQUALE E BARBIERO
CHARLES D BARCAK
BILLY L BARDER
EDWARD W BARGFREDE
ROBERT W BARKER
RONALD R BARKER
WILLIAM A BARKER
WILLIAM C BARKER
WILLIAM T BARKER
THOMAS J BARKSDALE
DONALD L BARNES
FRANCIS J BARNES
GEORGE E BARNES

KENNETH W BARNES
LEN BARNES
WILLIAM F BARNES
MURRAY W BARNETT
MICHAEL J BARRA
ROBERT F BARRATT
RUSH W BARRETT
LAWRENCE H BARRON
EDWARD M BARRY
RICHARD H BARRY
FREDERICK W BARTH
LEO R BARTOLO JR
CHARLES W BARTON JR
DWAYNE W BARTON
THOMAS A BARTON
HORACE J BARWICK
ERNEST E BASHEM
JAMES W BASS
HAROLD H BATES
LONZO BATES
THOMAS W BATES
BOBBIE J BATTE
GEORGE E BATY
WILLIE J BATY
MELVIN A BAUERFIELD
DONALD T BAXTER
WILLIAM A BAY
STANLEY E BAYLOR
FREDERICK B BEAN
STANLEY W BEAR
CLIFFORD D BEASLEY
CLIFFORD L BEASLEY JR
CHARLES E BEATY
HUBERT W BEAUBIEN
JEFFERSON BEAVER
BILLY W BEAVERSON
WAYNE E BEBB
ROY W F BECK
DONALD R BECKER
HAROLD L BECKERT
MELVIN C BECKWITH
FRANK J BEDNARA JR
JAMES L BEEMAN
NORMAN L BEEN
FRANK E BEGLEY
RUBEN BEJARANO
JAMES H BELCHER JR
HOWARD R BELDEN
ROBERT E BELIVEAU
GEORGE P BELKOM
CHARLIE BELL
JAMES M BELL
JESSIE S BELL
THOMAS L BELL
TIMOTHY BELL
VERNARD G BELL
MORGAN V BELLAH
BENNIE E BELLAR
NICOLAI BELLEGARDE
WILLIAM H BELLINGER
ARTHUR L BELT
ENRIQUE BELTRAN
CLYDE L BENNETT
JOHN R BENNETT
KENNETH F BENNETT
PERCY L BENNETT
WILLIAM A BENTHIEN
FRANCIS C BERGER
EARL J BERLING
ELTON J BERNARD
WILLIAM N BERNET
WILLIAM A BERNIER
ANTHONY BERNOSKY
BILLY A BERRY
ROBERT L BERTRAM
ROBERT L BESEMER
ALVA L BESHEARS
JOHN J BETANCOURT
JOHN S BETTEM
CHARLES C BETTS SR
DEWITT BETZ
IRVIN N BETZ
MICHAEL J BEVACQUA
CHARLES M BEVELS
FLOYD T BEY
ROBERT R BIANCHI
ROBERT E BIENZ
LYMAN W BIGELOW III
JOSEPH C BILLICK
MILTON P BILLIGMEIER
MARION D BILLS
ADRIAN L BILODEAU
CHARLES C BINNION
JAMES P BIRD
LOUIS H BIRD
MILO W BIRD
LEO R BIRDSALL
AVERY G BISHOP
JAMES R BISSELL
PAUL A BLACK
THOMAS J BLACKBURN
FOREST W BLACKFORD
TURNER F BLACKWELL
VIRGIL A BLAKELEY
WILLIS BLAKELY
JOHN E BLAKEMORE
LELAND F BLAKESLEE
WALTER M BLALOCK
ADRIAN G BLANCHARD JR
JOSEPH L BLANCHARD
ARCHIE L BLANCHETT
OMER R BLANCHETTE
JOE I BLEVINS
GERALD V BLOCK
WILBERT G BLOCK
ALFRED M BLOTZ
CLYDE D BLOUNT
ORMAR G BLOWERS
GEORGE J BLUE
JOHN W BOBBS
ROBERT C BOCKEY
LEONARD G BOGUSZ
JOHN P BOISVENUE
ALBERT W BOLAND
LOYD D BOLING
RICHARD T BOLTON
EARNEST H BOMAN
DONALD J BOMBARDIER
GUY E BOND
CARLOS BONET-MORALES
CLARENCE BONNER
JAMES E BOOHER
GERALD R BOOK
LEROY BOONE
GUY R BOOTH
ROBERT E BOOTH
CHARLES H BORDERS
ALFRED G BORKLAND JR
WALTER O BORROR
DONALD J BORTNER
MARVIN BOSCHEE
DAVID BOSTIC JR
ALFRED M BOTELHO
ROBERT H BOTKIN
SIDNEY J BOTTS
EDWARD M BOWEN
JACK L BOWEN
JAMES R BOWEN
JOSEPH A BOWEN
BENNY BOWSTRING
HAROLD R BOYD
CHARLES E BOYER
JOSEPH G BOYER
VIRGIL W BOYER JR
WAYNE J BOYK
LINSEY BRADEN
REGINALD O BRADFORD
OSCAR S BRADLEY
THOMAS B BRADLEY
WILLIAM C BRADLEY
GEORGE D BRADO
ROBERT C BRADY
FRANCIS BRAMANDE
ELMER H BRANDANGER
KENNETH BRANDENBURG
RALPH BRANDENBURG
DONALD S BRANDER
ROBERT D BRANDES
EWING A BRANDON
BENNY L BRANDVOLD
WILLIAM E BRASHEAR
LOUIE D BRASHERE
JOSEPH J BRAUN
ARLIN S BREDESON
FURMAN T BRENDLE
HENRY E BREW
NICODEMUS BREWER
JAMES L BRICE
VICTOR A BRICE
LOLAN O BRIDGES
HARRY K BRIGGS
JAMES T BRIGMAN
RAY A BRILEY
LARRY C BRIMHALL
ROBERT L BRINGHURST
DALE E BRINGLE
LEO R BRISENO JR
ROBERT E BRITT
JAMES B BROCK
JOSEPH H BROCK
DONALD C BROEMELING
GILBERT B BROOKS
JEWELL BROOKS
RAYMOND BROOKS
EUGENE T BROPHY
ALFRED R BROWN
CHARLES W BROWN
CLARENCE J BROWN
ERA H BROWN
FLOYD E BROWN
GEORGE BROWN JR
HARRY L BROWN
JAMES B BROWN
JOSEPH C BROWN
SAMUEL BROWN
WILLIAM L BROWN JR
RICHARD A BROWNE
CHARLIE M BROWNING
CLIFFORD G BROWNSON
DONALD G BRUDY
EUGENE O BRUHN
AUBRY L BRUMFIELD
JEROME BRUNSON
JEAN W BRUSO
JOHN P BRYAN
DAVID BRYANT
VIVIAN D BRYANT
WILLIE N BRYANT JR
BERNARD F BRYK
WILLARD BUCHANAN
ARTHUR D BUCKLEY JR
JOHN F BUDKE JR
MAURICE A BUECK
PHILEMON S BUHISAN
EARL J BUKU
FRANK W BULLOCK
JOHNIE B BULLOCK
CHARLEY C BUNCH
PAUL T BUNCH
FRANK BUNCHUK
CLAUDE F BUNN
ISAAC BUNN JR
WILLIE G BUNN
WORTH L BUNTING
PETE BURBAGE JR
LOUIE F BURCH
TRAVIS BURCHAM
DONALD BURDETTE
CHARLES E BURGESS
PRESTON M BURGESS
HARVEY W BURKE
SIDNEY J BURKETT
RODNEY F BURKHAM
FRED E BURKS
DALE S BURNETT
ROBERT R BURNETT
FRANCIS T BURNS
JOHN J BURNS
JACKSON E BURNSWORTH
DONALD K BURR
MATTHEW BURRELL
JOHN E BURT
MELVIN D BURTON
WALTER A BURTON
JOHN R BUSH
GLEN D BUTLER
VIRGIL E BUTLER
OSCAR H BUTTS JR
CURTIS P BYRD
DELBERT A BYROM
JOSEPH B CABINESS
ROBERT P CAFFREY
DANIEL E CAHALAN
BERNARD J CAIONE
JOHN W CALDWELL JR
THOMAS T CALDWELL
WILLIAM L CALFEE
ERNEST M CALHAU
CECIL O CALHOON
HAROLD D CALKINS
FRANCIS E CALLAHAN
LEWIS R CALLAHAN
ROBERT R CALVERT
RAUL O CAMACHO
DONALD B CAMERON
JACK CAMP
CHARLES C CAMPBELL
DAVID L CAMPBELL
HOWARD V CAMPBELL
JAMES E CAMPBELL
JAMES L CAMPBELL
JOSEPH N CAMPBELL
ROBERT D CAMPBELL
CARLOS C CAMPOS
CLAUDIE B CANDLER
JOSEPH M CANTRELLE JR
FREDERICK CAPALLIA
JOE B CAPEHART
ALBERT C CAPOZZI
GERALD B CAPWELL
RAYMOND V CARAWAY
LELAND A CARDER
JAMES R CARDILLO JR
KENNETH J CAREW
GALE CAREY
DONALD C CARLSON
NORMAN G CARLSON
RALPH W CARLSON
WILLIAM J CARNAHAN
DONALD E CARNES
DOUGLAS D CARPENTER
ROBERT E CARPENTER
ROBERT E CARPENTER
WESLEY B CARPENTER
LEROY F CARR
LEOPOLD M CARRILLO
NIEVES CARRILLO
JAMES A CARROLL
DONAVON R CARSON
ANDREW CARTER
CARL E CARTER
DAVID W CARTER
GEORGE CARTER
OWEN M CARTER
LLOYD A CASE
ROBERT M CASEY
HOYT B CASH
JAMES R CASH
PRINCE A CASON
RALPH A CASTLE
ROBERT E CASTLE
WILLIAM B CASTLE
VICTOR E CASTRO
CLIFTON CATCHINGS
ROY M CAUDELL
RALPH K CAUDILL
ROBERT L CAUDLE
CARSON B CAULDER
GEORGE W CAULEY
WILLIAM E CAVENDER
RICHARD E CEGLOREK
BERNARDO D CENTENO
JOSEPH CERTA
REYNALDO CESENA
JONG-SU CHA
LAWRENCE F CHALIFOUX
HARVEY CHAMBERS
ALBERT S K CHANG
DELBERT CHANSLER JR
ALFRED E CHAPMAN
RAYMOND L CHAPMAN
BENIGNO CHARBONIER-DIAZ
RICHARD B CHARLAND
MADISON F CHARLES
CORNELIUS H CHARLTON
WADE J CHATAIGNIER
FRED T CHATFIELD
JOE CHATMON JR
CELESTINO CHAVEZ
DANIEL CHAVEZ
JOHN B CHEATAM JR
JAMES CHEATHAM JR
JOSEPH CHEE
BYEONG-HO CHEON
CHEON-SIK CHEON
WALTER W CHERRY
BENNIE F CHILDREE
LOUIS O CHINN
FRANCIS N CHOATE
DONG-SU CHOI
DONG-WON CHOI
GAE-MUN CHOI
HYEON-GU CHOI
IL-SONG CHOI
JAE-EOP CHOI
JEONG-GAP CHOI
JONG-GU CHOI
JONG-TAEK CHOI
MYEONG-HA CHOI
SEONG-TAK CHOI
SEONG-YONG CHOI
TAE-IN CHOI
VICTOR J CHOINIERE
BERNARD A CHOPEK
VAL D CHRISTENSEN
WARREN C CHRISTIANSEN
LLOYD E CHRISTMAS
RONALD N CHRISTOPHER
JA-JUN CHU
WON-DAE CHU
JOHN CHUDO
ALPHONSO CHURCH
RAY CHURCH JR
JOHN W CHURCHILL
JOSEPH K CIESLAK
VAN E CLAGG
DONALD J CLAIRMONT
GENE F CLARK
GEORGE A CLARK
GLEN J CLARK
HALLIE A CLARK JR
HERBERT F CLARK JR
JAMES R CLARK
JAMES V CLARK
LEWIS C CLARK JR
ODELL CLARK
ROBERT M CLARK
WALTER B CLARK
WILLIAM J CLARK
THOMAS CLARKSON JR
RAYMOND L CLARY SR
CARLETON B CLAY
CHARLES L CLAYTON
EDWARD L CLEGG
ROBERT D CLEMENTS
KENNETH D CLEMMONS
TEDDY V CLEMMONS
JAMES E CLINE
PARKER L CLINE
ROBERT L CLINE
KENNETH H CLOUGH JR
BERNARD C CLOUSE
EARL S CLOUSER
ROBERT J CLOUTIER
LAWRENCE CLOVER
ALGERNON S CLOWE
ERNEST L COAKLEY
JESSIE COATS JR
BILLY G COCHRAN
JACK W COCHRAN
JOHN E COCKRELL
HERBERT COHN
JAMES A COLBERT
BURRELL B COLE
MATHEY G COLE
RICHARD V COLE
ALAN R COLEMAN
GROVER W COLEMAN
LAWRENCE Q COLEMAN
RICHARD R COLEMAN
ROBERT COLEMAN
RAYMOND H COLLER
GILBERT G COLLIER
ROY D COLLIER
EDWARD R COLLINS
FREDERICK J COLLINS
HARRY P COLLINS
JAMES E COLLINS
LOUIS E COLLINS
WILLIAM H COLLINS
MICHAEL V COLONNELLO
BOBBY V COMBS
FERRICE G COMBS
CLORAL L COMER
LOUIS B CONDE
JOHN L CONDIT

68 ARMY

STEPHEN A CONDON
HERBERT R CONFER
EUGENE J CONIS
JAMES P CONNELLY
JEFFERSON L CONNOR
NORMAND P CONNOR
RALPH J CONOVER
JOSEPH P CONROY
MELVIN E CONSTABLE
FREDERICK A CONTI
THOMAS P CONWAY
ALFRED COOK
BERNARD D COOK
CAMPBELL D COOK
MCKINLEY C COOK
JOHN COOLEY JR
VIRGIL COONTZ
BILLIE J COOPER
JOSEPH COOPER
LAWRENCE E COOPER
STEPHEN P COOPER
WINSTON R COOPER
JILES P COPELAND
GRADY COPLIN
ERNESTO J CORDERO
RAYMOND F CORL
LOUIS E CORNELIA
FREDERICK R CORNELL
TROY CORNETT
JESSE B CORNETTE
SAMUEL CORNEY
VINCENT CORONA
LORNE W CORROW
ROBERT R CORY
DELBERT L COSNER
ANTHONY E COSTA
JAMES E COSTELLO
ELMER K COSTIGAN
HOMER R COSTNER
CYRENUS E COTTIER
RAYMOND A COTTRELL
RALPH L COUFAL
JOSEPH M COULOMBE
CALVIN COULON JR
GEORGE W COUNTS
THOMAS H COURT
CHARLES C COWART
LINTON J COWART
LARRY T COX
LESTER A COX
ROBERT C COX
THOMAS F COX
GARRETT COYNE
KENNETH L COZAD
ALBERT COZART JR
MORGAN L CRABTREE
WILSON CRADDOCK JR
HOWARD V CRAFT
RAYMOND CRAFT
JOHN E CRAIG
JOHN R CRAIG
JAMES B CRANE
DEWITT CRAWFORD
ELLIS CRAWFORD JR
JESSE M CRAWFORD
NOLAND F CRAWFORD
BENJAMIN R CRAWLEY
MYRON G CREVELLING
ASA J CRIMIN JR
WILLIAM W CRIST
JAMES A CROFT
MAYNARD A CRONIN
JOHN B CROOK
ARCHIE T CROOM JR
HARRY H CROSBY
FREDERICK D CROSS
RICHARD E CROTTY
WILLIAM F CROUSE JR
LORENZO D CROWDER
DONALD E CROWELL
JAMES W CRUCE
RUSH F CRUM
ROY K CRUSE
CHARLIE H CRUTCHER
GRAVES B CRUTCHFIELD JR
WILLIAM R CRUZAN JR
NICOLAS CRUZ-PEREZ
EDWARD F CUEVAS
WILLIAM D CULHANE
DONALD P CULLEN

THOMAS W CULLITON
CLAYTON J CULP
LONNIE CULPEPPER
LAWRENCE C CUMBO
ROBERT R CUMMINGS
JACK J CUNNINGHAM
JAMES C CURCIO JR
WILLIAM K CURRAN JR
HAROLD L CURTIS
LLOYD W CURTIS
WILLIAM J CUSICK
MYRON L CUTLER
JOSEPH DAGASTINE
ROY W DAIGLE
ROBERT C DAKIN
ROBERT A G DALOISIO
THOMAS W DALTON
LOUIS T DAMITZ
HANSEL DANIELS
PAUL L DANIELS
PAUL M DANIELS JR
WILLIS L DANIELS
EDWARD L DANN
PHILIP F DANNOLFO
KENNETH DARNALL
JOHN H DARNELL JR
CHARLES W DARR
DUNCAN N DAUGHERTY
ELTON DAUPHINEY
BETHEL DAVENPORT
WELLINGTON DAVENPORT
GERALD J DAVEY
JOSEPH DAVIDOSKI
ESAU E DAVIES JR
HOWARD M DAVIES
ARNOLD G DAVIS SR
AUSTIN DAVIS
BERNARD N DAVIS
BILLY G DAVIS
EDGAR E DAVIS JR
EDWARD H DAVIS
FREDERICK F DAVIS
HOWARD DAVIS
ISAAC S DAVIS
ISAIAH DAVIS
ROBERT C DAVIS
ROBERT M DAVIS
ROSS H DAVIS
SAMUEL DAVIS
STANLEY J DAVIS
WALTER V DAVIS
WILLIAM D DAVIS JR
WALLACE J DAWSON
GERALD F DAY
MORRIS N DAY
EUGENIO DE ALBA-RODRIGUEZ
TULON V DEAN
ATTILLIO M DE CARLI
PAUL W DECKARD
FOREST D DECKER
WILLIAM T DECKER
JOHN DEDON
GEORGE R DEEMER
ROY A DEES
EDWARD W DEETER JR
ROBERT F DE HAAN
WILLIAM W DEHNER JR
TOMMY DE LA PENA
NICHOLAS DELGADO
NORMAN J DELONG
STANLEY C DEMELLO
BILLY E DEMENT
STEVEN DEMETER JR
WILLIAM E DENNEY
HARRY C DENNIS
WILLIAM C DENSON
JAMES L DENTZ
STANLEY T DEPKI
PEARL G DEROSSETT
RICHARD G DESAUTELS
NORMAN E DESJARLAIS
ROY C DESPAIN
ALFRED DEVANNO
JACK B DE VENY
AARON W DEVINE
RICHARD K DEVOE
JAMES D DEWEY
JACK L DEWITT
STANLEY L DEWITT

HOMER F DIAL
EDUARDO DIAZ-JIMENEZ
DONALD E DIBBLE
RONALD W DIBBLE
JAMES A DICKENS
MARTIN L DICKERSON
THOMAS M DICKEY
MARK W DICKMAN
BEN H DICKSON
HAROLD F DIEKMAN
LESTER H DIEKMANN
JAMES L DIGGS JR
CLIFFORD A DILLEY
WILBERT I DINGMAN
GILES C DINGUS
JOHN W DINSMORE
AGOSTINO DIRIENZO
CHARLES E DISMUKES
ELWOOD L DITMER
JOHN C DITNER
ROBERT W DITTBENNER
JAMES W DIXON
MELVIN L DIXON
BYEONG-HO DO
ENOCH A DOBBINS
KING D DOBIE
ALFONZO DOBY
CARL DODRO
GEORGE W DODSON
MARVIN M DODSON
ROBERT T DOHERTY
STEPHEN DOMBROWSKI
HAROLD D DONAHOO
ANTHONY J DONATELLI
JOHNIE DONKERS
PAUL K DONLON
EUGENE J DONNELLY
WILLIAM F DONNELLY
ALFONSO DONOFRIO
JOHN H DONOVAN
BERNARD DORAN
WILLIAM DORAN
GEORGE DORMAN
NEIL K DORRION
HAROLD D DORRIS
EDWARD G DOSCH
LAWRENCE DOTSON
HERBERT J DOUGHTY
WILLIAM H DOUGHTY
HAROLD DOUGLAS
TONY W DOUGLAS
JAMES M DOYLE
THOMAS J DOYLE
LAWRENCE D DOYON
BARTO H DOZIER
ROBERT V DRAGOO
ROBERT E DRAKE
THERON W DRAKE JR
ALBERT W DRAPER
JAMES L DRENTH
RICHARD R DREW
HAROLD J DRISCOLL
BERNARD J DROUILLARD
ARCHIBALD B DRYSDALE
STEVIE J DU BOISE
JOHNNIE J DUES
PAUL E DUEZ
RUSSELL C DUFFER
JAMES D DUKE
CHARLES L DULANEY
CHARLES H DUNLAP
DANIEL U DUNN
HAROLD U DUNN
JOSEPH W DUPART
JOHN C DUPEEY
RICHARD DUPONT
JOSEPH N DUPUIS
ROGER L R DUQUESNE
EDWARD F DURBOROW JR
GEORGE B DURHAM
JESSE DURHAM
WADE L DURHAM
GERALD O DURRETT
ARTHUR DUSSAULT
ERNEST F DWIGHT
ARTHUR DWYER
FRANCIS W DWYER
CECIL G DYE
RICHARD DYE
BOBBY L DYER

HAROLD DYSON
AVON E EADS
ELBYRNE O EARLY
EDWARD D EATON
CALVIN C ECHOLES
MARION M ECK
LESTER R ECKARD
ROGER F ECKERT
THOMAS R ECKERT
NOEL J EDGAR
WILLIAM T EDGAR
LESTER E EDMONDS JR
CLIFTON R EDMONSTON
ALBERT EDWARDS
COLEMAN EDWARDS
DONALD A EDWARDS
ROBERT L EDWARDS
THOMAS D EDWARDS
TY C EDWARDS
FLOYD EELLS JR
KENNETH F EHLERS
JOHN EIDE
KENNETH C EIRICH
BOYD W ELAM
HOWARD G ELDER
KENNETH G ELEY
JUNIOR E ELLEFSON
BILL ELLIOTT
ANDREW J ELLIS
EMANUEL ELLIS
JAMES H ELLIS
JULIUS L ELLIS
RAYMOND C ELLIS
RICHARD W ELSASS
JACOB A ELY
FOREST EMBRY
WILLIE B EMERSON
ROBERT P EMMOTT
RICHARD ENAENA
RICHARD C ENCINAS
CARY J ENGLAND
LEONARD ENGLISH JR
VERNON R ENGLISH
GORDON F ENOS
MARIO M ENRIQUEZ
JEUNG-YEONG EOM
ALBERT M EPPLEY
VERNON J ERBY
ROGER L ERICKSON
DOMINIC ERITANO
ANDREW ERNANDIS
JOHN A ERNDT
CLARENCE J ERNEST JR
DOUGALL H ESPEY JR
JAMES ESPITA
ANTHONY D ESPOSITO
DAVID ESSBERG JR
CLESTON B ESTES
WILLIE N ESTRADA
HERBERT J ETIE JR
ALEXANDER EVANS
ARTHUR J EVANS JR
EDWARD R EVANS
HAROLD L EVANS
HENRY E EVANS
WALTER R EVANS
ELMER EVERHART JR
JAMES R EVERLING
ALBERT R EYTCHISON
WILLIAM D EZELL
LESLIE L FAIRCHILD
JOHN FALLAT
ORSON D FALLIS
PASQUALE FAMULARO
CLYDE A FANNING
JOHN W FARBER
LAWRENCE B FARFAN
CLARENCE L FARMER
JOHN N FARMER
KENNETH L FARMER
KENNETH W FARMER
ROBERT P FARMER
DONALD H FARNHAM
WILLIAM M FARONE
THOMAS F FARRELL JR
WILLIAM F FARRELL
STEPHEN J FARRIS
LIONEL R FAVREAU
FRANK G FAY
ROBERT L FELIX

ELLERY A FENSTAMAKER JR
HUGH W FERGUSON JR
DAVID A FERIEND
LAWRENCE J FERKOVICH
GERALD J FERREIRA
WILLIAM J FICKER
CHARLES E FIDDLER
PAUL G FIELD
BUDDY R FIELDS
CHESTER A FIELDS
JULIO FIGUEROA
GERMAN FIGUEROA-SEDA
RONALD FIGUREID
EDWARD J FILARECKI
JACK R FINCH
EDWARD H FINDLAY
DAVID L FINNIE
VIRGIL L FISCHER
BERNARD J FISHER
CHARLES V B FISHER
CLARENCE R FISHER
DALE L FISHER
GEORGE T FISHER
JAMES R FISHER
JOHN W FISHER
VIRGIL L FISHER
CONRAD G FISLUL
JAMES E FITZHUGH
FRANCIS J FITZPATRICK
CAMERON M FLACK
HOWARD C FLAVELL JR
CLAUDE B FLEMING
RICHARD E FLEMING
JAMES A FLETCHER
ROY L FLETCHER
DAVID H FLIGHT
PAUL E FLORA
WILLIE S FLORES
CLYDE FLOWERS
ARTHUR L FLUCKER
MARTIN C FLUEGEL
MOZELL FLUELLIN
JAMES B FOGGIN
BILLY G FOGLE
EARL W FOLEY
RAYMOND P FOLEY
WILLIAM C FONNER
NORMAN R FONTAINE
CHARLES M FORBES
JAMES R FORD
LORNEL FORD
NORMAN R FORD
WILBERT S FORD
CHARLES E FOREHAND
IRA L FOREMAN
CHARLES R FOREN
ROBERT N FORSYTHE
WILLIAM H FORTNER
DELMAR L FOSTER
ELMER E FOSTER
JOSEPH M FOSTER
KIMBLE H FOSTER
SIDNEY E FOSTER
ARTHUR J FOUST
WILLIAM T FOWLER
FRANK C FOX
FRANK W FOX
LOUIS D FOX JR
NOE FRANCO
ELMER N FRANK
HOWARD M FRANKEL
NORMAN FRANKS JR
HUGH R FRAZIER
BILLY L FREEMAN
JOHN FREEMAN
OSWALD B FREEMAN
LYLE A FREGO
CECIL W FRENCH
HAROLD J FREYMUTH
HARRY D FRICK
ERVIN A FRICKE
JAMES F FRIDAY
JOHN P FRIEL JR
ARMAND A FRIGON
JAY W FRISBEY
MARLAND E FRITZ
EMIL FROEHLICH
THOMAS Y FUNAKOSHI

69 ARMY

JOHN M FUORE
WALTER C FURTADO
ISAAC FURUKAWA
CHARLES M FUSON
ARVOUS FUTCH
WILLIAM C GABOS
ROBERT G GAILEY
CHARLES GAINS
WILLIAM J GALIVAN
DONALD J GALLACHER
PATRICK J GALLAGHER
ERNEST E GALLATIN
FRANK R GALLEGOS
VICTOR I GALLERANI
NICKOLAS R GALLO
WILLIE V GALVAN
ALBERT R GAMACHE
JAMES E GAMMANS
HAE-SU GANG
JANG-WON GANG
MAN-YEONG GANG
RALPH E GARBISCH
CHARLES M GARCIA
CRESENCIANO GARCIA JR
JOSEPH G GARCIA
MOSE GARCIA JR
ROBERTO GARCIA
GLENN GARDNER
TENNIE GARDNER
WILLIAM GARDNER
MELVIN R GARLETS
HERMAN C GARNER
TED GARNER
RICHARD F GARRELS
CHARLES GARRIGUS
VERNON T GARRISON
BILL B GASS
HENRY A GASTELO
JAMES D GAUSNELL
PETER L GEANNOPULOS
ANTHONY GEBBIA JR
DONALD B GEISLER
RICHARD J GEISSLER
ROBERT M GENEREUX
EDWIN GENTRY
RAY GENTRY
CARL B GEORGE
FRANK M GERAGHTY
JOHN L GERHEART
ALBERT J GEVARA
DONALD W GIBSON
EDWARD B GIBSON
MAXIE L GIBSON
WILLARD M GIBSON
ALBERT E GIDDINGS
MERLE C GIFFORD
MILES R GIFFORD JR
NATHAN GILBERT
CHAMP G GILLESPIE
LAWRENCE T GILLESPIE
RUBIN W GILLESPIE
CLAUDE S GILLETTE
JOHN F GILLETTE
HOMER B GILLEY
VOLNEY H GILLIAM
CHARLES E GILLINGHAM JR
DANIEL E GILLIS
JOHN R GILMORE
MELVIN G GILMORE
DOMINIC J GIORDANO
PETER R GIULIONI
ALPHONSE F GLADKOWSKI
ALFRED B GLASS
GERALD W GLASSER
EDWARD J GLEASON
CHARLES F GLENN
RALPH L GLOVER
SAMUEL H GOATS
JULIUS R GOC
RALPH J GODBOUT
LIONEL GODEAUX
ROBERT E GODWIN
ROBERT G GOERLICH
MARVIN GOETZ
RONALD W GOIK
DONALD L GOLDEN
ENRIQUE G GOMEZ
WILLIAM R GOMEZ
U-GAP GONG
HENRY P GONSOULAND
LAURO R GONZALEZ-HERNANDEZ
PAUL R GOODSON
CLARENCE J GORDON JR
DAVID C GORDON
GEORGE T GORDON
PAUL M GORDON
ROBERT H GORDON
ARTHUR C GORMAN
FRANK G GORMAN JR
ALBION J GORRIS
THOMAS B GORUP
ERVIN P GOTHIER
PAUL J GOTNEY
DAVID J GOUDLOCK
JOHN J GRACAN
JOHN H GRADY JR
ARNOLD W GRAHAM
DAVID L GRAHAM
WILLIAM L GRAHAM
WILLIAM M GRAHAM
DUFFIE C GRANT
GEORGE H GRANT JR
RICHARD E GRAUMAN
BEN H GRAVES
ROBERT E GRAVES
LORENZO L GRAVINA JR
GLEN L GRAY
LEMUEL T GRAY
WALTER L GRAY
B L GRAYSON
THOMAS J GRAYSON
JOSEPH P GRECO
CHARLES M GREEN
JAMES L GREEN
ROBERT B GREEN
CECIL L R GREENWALL
CARROLL D GREENWOOD
EUZZIAH GREER
WALTER M GREER
JOHN L GREGG
LEVERN GREGG
ROBERT S GREGORY
ROSSLYN E GRESENS
NORMAN J GRESSENS
EDWIN E GRIENKE
JACOB T GRIFFITH
EUGENE GRIMES
ALLEN E GRIMM
CECIL W GROOM
MARVIN L GROOM
BILLY L GROSS
MALVIN L GROSS
ROBERT L GRUBB
BROCK D GRUETZNER
RICHARD A GRUNDMAN
CHEOL-SU GU
MYEONG-U GU
SEONG-HWA GU
JOSEPH D GUDGER
ROBERTO GUERRA
ALBERT D GUIDELLY
JOSEPH GUIDRY
LESLIE GUILL JR
CECIL H GUITER
FRED E GUMMOW
ARTHUR S GUNNELL
JIMMIE GURR
LOUIS G GUSSINE
ROGER W GUSTAFSON
MELISENDEO GUTIERREZ
VIRGEL GUY
VANCE W GWINN
EOK-SU GWON
GI-HYEON GWON
HYO-SEOK GWON
YONG-DEOK GWON
CHEOL-JIN HA
ELVIN W HAASE
RUSSELL D HAGER
JOHN T HALCUM
CARL V HALCUMB
MORRIS E HALEY
ARTHUR P HALL
GEORGE A HALL
JOHN W HALL
ROBERT B HALL
ROBERT R HALL JR
LAWRENCE H HALVORSON
GARNETT K HAMBRIGHT
DONALD S HAMILTON
PAUL W HAMILTON
DONALD L HAMM
JESSE T HAMMACK JR
RAYMOND D HAMMEL
WILLIAM J HAMMEL JR
CARL A HAMMER
HAYWARD HAMRICK JR
BOK-GYU HAN
GWON-BOK HAN
RICHARD L HANCOCK
JAMES F HANER JR
JOSEPH B HANEY
DARRELL G HANGER
JACK HANLEY
KENNETH R HANSEN
CARL H HANSON
LEROY E HANSON
JULIUS F HARDEMAN
GEORGE R HARDIN
KERMIT M HARDIN
JOSEPH W HARDING JR
CLIFFORD F HARDMAN
GUY G HARDMAN JR
KESTER B HARDMAN
DAVID E HARDY
JAMES HARGET
DAVID J HARGRAVE
EDWARD W HARPER
RAYFORD H HARPER
RICHARD S HARPER
WILLIAM L HARPER
JAMES F HARRINGTON
JON G HARRINGTON
HENRY C HARRIS
JAMES HARRIS
JOHN T HARRIS
PAUL HARRIS
RACHELL HARRIS
ROBERT C HARRIS
ROBERT G HARRIS
THOMAS R HARRIS
WALTER HARRIS
MAXIE G HARRISON
HOWARD F HART
CHARLIE HARTLEY JR
RICHARD M HARTMAN
CLIFFORD J HARTNECK
JAMES HARTZER
CLYDE M HARVEY
ROSCOE L HARVEY
WILLIAM R HARVEY
CHESTER L HARWOOD
MORRIS D HASKINS
GEORGE J HASSELL
WILLIAM R HATAWAY
GENE N HATCH
J P HATCHER
PERRY R HAWORTH
WILBUR A HAWORTH JR
CORNELIUS E HAYES
JAMES E HAYES
JAMES W HAYES
JOHN J HAYES
JAMES F HAYNAM
CURTIS G HAYS
RAY E HAYS
LAVERNE HAYTON
CALEB W HAZEL
JIM T HAZELWOOD
CHARLES W HAZLETT
JAMES E HEAD
DANIEL E HEALY
BOOKER T HEARD
ROBERT R HEATON
ROBERT J HEBERT
HENRY A HECHT
FREDERIC R HECK
BENNIE J HEDGCOTH
ROBERT P HEFLIN
KENNETH HEFTA
JOSEPH J HEIDER
EUGENE L HEINZ
GERALD G HEITHER
HAROLD J HELBING
WILLIAM C HEMBREE
CLIFFORD D HENKLE
LLOYD J HENLEY
LEE D HENRY JR
RAY F HENRY
WILLIAM F HENRY
ALFRED HENSON JR
CHAN HEO
SAM-DO HEO
SEON-HAK HEO
DAVID A HERENDEEN
LUIS HERNANDEZ
ISIDRO HERNANDEZ-DONES
VIRGIL B HERRICK
DONALD R HERRIN
GARLAND HERRINGTON
DONALD H HERTRICK
HERBERT A HESSELTINE JR
CHARLES V HEWITT
EARL S HIBBARD
DOUGLAS F HICKENBOTTOM JR
JAMES L HICKEY
GERALD E HICKMAN
CHARLES E HICKOX
TOMMY V HICKS
JACK R HIDAY
CHARLES HIGGINS JR
ELIJAH T HIGGINS
JAMES T HIGGINS
JOHN A HIGGINS
ODIS HILBURN
CARL L HILL
FRANK L HILL
GEORGE N HILL
GEORGE W HILL
JESSE D HILL
THOMAS H HILL
WILLIAM G HILL
WILLIE D HILL
XAVIER W HILL
JOSEPH F HILLARD
LEONARD HINES
WENDELL D HINES
LESTER C HINGSBERGEN
CLYDE J HITE
GEORGE B HITTNER
JACK A HIWATASHI
MARTIN F HOCHENBERGER
ELMER HODGE
JAMES L HODGES
GEORGE M HOEFELER
WALTER W HOELTJE
HERBERT W HOFF JR
ERNEST HOFFMAN
KURK HOFMANN
ASHTON S HOGAN
ISHMAEL D HOGSTON
FRANCIS J HOHN
JAMES J HOHN
JULIUS J HOLBROOKS
ALFORD L HOLDEN
RALPH S HOLDER
PRESTON HOLEMAN JR
FRANK E HOLLAND
GERALD L HOLLAND
ROBERT E HOLLAND
BILLY E HOLLIDAY
G D HOLLINS
MONROE J HOLLIS
RALPH R HOLLY
CHARLES W HOLMES
DANIEL L HOLMES
EDWARD E HOLMES
WALLACE HOLMES JR
WILLIAM C HOLMES
CLAUDE D HOLT
CHARLIE B HOLTZCLAW JR
JAMES W HOMAN
ALFREDO C HOMAWAN
ROY J HONEYCUTT
GWAN-I HONG
JONG-SEON HONG
CHARLES E HOOD
JAMES L HOOD
LEONARD HOOD
PETER M HOOKANO
CHARLES E HOOKS
MAYNARD A HOOPER
ANDREW L HOPKINS
FRANCIS J HOPKINS
LEONARD M HORENDER
RUSSELL T HORNE
ROBERT J HOSSLER
OLIVER W HOTTENSTEIN
BRISON HOWARD
CORDELL HOWARD
ROBERT W HOWARD
ROBERT G HOWE
DALE R HOWELL
ELMER HOWELL
ROY L HOWELL
RUEL L HOWELL
ROSS L HOWEY
RUSSELL S HOYER
WILLIAM C HOYES
HARRY A HUBBS
HENRY L HUBER
RAYMOND E HUCK
ROBERT J HUDAK
LEONARD G HUDDLESTON JR
JOHN E HUDSON
RUFUS F HUDSON JR
GEORGE F HUETGER
EARL J HUFF JR
GLENN HUFF
HORACE W HUGGINS
ARTHUR L HUGHES
CLIFFORD HUGHES
DORMAN D HUGHES
JOHN P HUGHES
MICHAEL J HUGHES
ROBERT J HUGHES
WALTER N HUGHES
HARRY R HUGHEY
ERVIN HULETT
LEONARD C HULL
THOMAS J HULSEY JR
ROBERT A HUMES
ALEXANDER HUNT
WILLIAM E HUNT
CARSON HUNTER
JAMES E HUNTER
MARRION L HUNTER
CLARENCE A HURT SR
THOMAS E HURT
LOUIS B HUSTON
JOHNNIE R HUTCHINS
OTIS E HUTCHISON
ROBERT N HUTCHISON
DANIEL H HUTTNER JR
DONALD J HUTTON
BOK-JEUNG HWANG
CHAN-IK HWANG
SI-HEUM HWANG
EDWARD HYATT
D T HYDE
JAMES H HYDE
MU-JAE HYEON
BILLY E HYLTON
YOSHIO IKEDA
CHEON-DAE IM
MAN-GI IM
MYEONG-GWAN IM
NO-BOK IM
ROY H INBODEN
LEON C IRVING JR
ROBERT W IRWIN
BILLY J ISBELL
EUGENE J ISBRANDT
RAYMOND ISERN-ORTIZ
HARRY ISHEM
ALBERT A ISHIMOTO
ROLLIN J ISLER
ELMER C ISSACS
YEIKICHI B ITOKAZU
THEODORE A IVEY
MARVIN L IVIE
PHILIP J IYOTTE
CHARLIE L JACKSON
DAN JACKSON JR
EDWARD M JACKSON
EUGENE A JACKSON
FLOYD J R JACKSON
HERBERT H JACKSON
RALPH V JACKSON
GEORGE J JACOBS
JAMES E JACOBS
ROBERT L JACOBSEN
CLARENCE A JAMES
DAVIS E JAMES
LAWRENCE B JAMES JR
ALLAN E JAMIESON
JAMES R JAMISON

70 ARMY

JIN-HWI JANG
OK-SEONG JANG
SANG-GAP JANG
GEORGE JANGULA
STANLEY W JANSEN
CHARLES E JARRELL
JOHN JASINSKI
LAURENCE R JASMER
ALAN R JASTRAM
HENRY JEANJACQUES
WILLIAM R JECELIN
ROBERT L JEFFERSON
JAMES C JENKEL
PAUL L JENKINS
VERNON D JENKINS
WILLIAM C JENKINS
ALFRED S JENNINGS
JOHN E JENNINGS JR
WALTER V JENSEN
WILLIAM L JENSEN
STANLEY C JENSON
DU-SEOK JEON
JIN-CHEOL JEON
MU-TAEK JEON
BYEONG-UK JEONG
CHA-TAE JEONG
CHUN-HO JEONG
DONG-DEOK JEONG
GI-BONG JEONG
GYU-HYEON JEONG
GYU-HYEON JEONG
HAE-SIL JEONG
IL-JO JEONG
JAE-BOK JEONG
JAE-YEON JEONG
JEONG-GIL JEONG
JONG-I JEONG
SEONG-DAE JEONG
SEONG-GYU JEONG
CARL O JERNIGAN
WILLIAM T JESSUP
JOSEPH S JETT
CHARLES L JETTON
JAE-GU JI
PETE JIMENES
AMADOR JIMENEZ
CANDIDO JIMENEZ
ISMAEL JIMENEZ-HERNANDEZ
ANTONIO JIMENEZ-OLIVENCIA
GWAN-I JIN
JEOM-JUNG JIN
SAM-SIK JIN
TAE-RYONG JIN
BONG-SIK JO
CHEONG JO
GYEONG-YUN JO
HAK-GYU JO
HAN-OK JO
HEON-JUNG JO
HO-JE JO
JUNG-BOK JO
SEONG-GU JO
YEONG-RAE JO
YEONG-SU JO
YONG-WON JO
JOHNNIE E JOHNS
WILLIE L JOHNS
ALBERT S JOHNSON
DONALD T JOHNSON
EUGENE A JOHNSON
GEORGE B JOHNSON
GEORGE W JOHNSON
GERALD D JOHNSON
JAMES E JOHNSON
JAMES V JOHNSON
JOE E JOHNSON
JOSEPH E JOHNSON
LAWRENCE D JOHNSON JR
LEROY JOHNSON
LEROY JOHNSON
MAJOR A JOHNSON
MELVIN L JOHNSON
NORMAN R JOHNSON
ORVEL J JOHNSON
OTTIS D JOHNSON
RANDLE JOHNSON
RAY JOHNSON
RICHARD A JOHNSON
RICHARD B JOHNSON
ROSS JOHNSON
ROY C JOHNSON
SAMUEL JOHNSON
THOMAS M JOHNSON
VERNON G JOHNSON
CARL F JOHNSTON JR
JAMES F JOHNSTON
ARTHUR M JONES
BILLY B JONES
CALVIN S JONES
CARL R JONES
CLYDE JONES
DONALD JONES
FRANK L JONES
ISAAC JONES
JOHN W JONES
LESLIE J JONES
MACK D JONES
MARVIN W JONES
MELBER J JONES
MILES H JONES
MOISE JONES JR
RICHARD L JONES
ROBERT JONES
ROY V JONES
W R JONES
WILLIAM P JONES
WILLIE D JONES
FRED O JORDAN
WILLIE E JORDAN
LUTHER B JORDON
ADOLPH JOSEPH
DALE E JOSLIN
HERBERT R JOSLYN
RAYMOND C JOYNER
JOHN C JUDD
VERNON R JUDD
JIMMIE JUMBO
J D FLOYD JUNIOR
LEO JURASZ
ROBERT J JURKOWSKI
BASIL K KAAPANA
JAMES KABALEN
THEODORE E KAISER
STEVEN C KAPITAN
MILTON J KASARDA
JEROME J KASIULIN
DONALD P KATZENBERGER
ROBERT P KAUFMAN
EDWARD L KEALLY JR
CLARENCE KEARNEY
WILLIAM H KEARNS
GERALD P KECK
WILLIE F KEE
DAVID L KEEL
EDWARD J KEELER
BAILEY KEETON JR
RALPH E KEGLEY
CORNELIUS KEIRNAN
JAMES E KELLEHER JR
JAMES H KELLER
PAUL L KELLER
CLEMENT KELLERMAN
CHARLES W KELLISON
BERNARD L KELLY
ROBERT N KELLY
WILLIAM C KELLY
GAYLORD W KENFIELD
ARTHUR M KENNEDY
GILBERT C KENNEDY
ROBERT E L KENNEDY
ROBERT G KENNEDY
ROBERT L KENNEDY
J VANN KENT
ARTHUR M KENTY
JAMES H KERKLIN
LEO P KERN
JOHN C KERSKA
LESTER M KESLER
RUFUS L KETCHUM
HAROLD L KETNER
ROBERT J KETTLEWELL
WILBER J KEY
RICHARD D KEYSOR
CHARLES KICKLIGHTER
CHARLES A KIDD
HARRY D KIEFER
HERBERT M KIEK
ROBERT KILAR
HUGH C KILLAM
BEOM-YUN KIM
BONG-SU KIM
BONG-SUL KIM
BYEONG-GYU KIM
BYEONG-GYU KIM
BYEONG-GYU KIM
CHA-MUN KIM
CHI-JUNG KIM
CHIL-GYU KIM
CHIL-JONG KIM
DEOK-JIN KIM
DO-I KIM
DONG-CHEOL KIM
DONG-HUN KIM
DONG-JO KIM
DONG-SIK KIM
DONG-SUK KIM
DONG-WON KIM
EUNG-GWON KIM
EUNG-SU KIM
GEUN-SU KIM
GI-HONG KIM
HAK-CHUL KIM
HAK-SUL KIM
HAN-GON KIM
HA-SIK KIM
HEON-GYU KIM
HO-CHUL KIM
HYEONG-GU KIM
HYEONG-JIN KIM
HYEON-SU KIM
IN-JUN KIM
IN-SU KIM
JAE-BONG KIM
JANG-GON KIM
JEOM-DO KIM
JEONG-DAE KIM
JEONG-HO KIM
JEONG-MAN KIM
JEONG-SU KIM
JO-HO KIM
JONG-DAE KIM
JONG-GYU KIM
JONG-HWAN KIM
JONG-YUN KIM
JU-HAK KIM
MAN-CHUL KIM
MAN-GIL KIM
MAN-HO KIM
MYEONG-SIK KIM
NO-HYANG KIM
SA-GON KIM
SANG-IL KIM
SEOK-GI KIM
SEOK-GU KIM
SEONG-BOK KIM
SEONG-JIN KIM
SEONG-PYO KIM
SEUNG-CHAN KIM
SIL-GYEONG KIM
SUN-DOL KIM
SUN-SAENG KIM
TAE-DONG KIM
TAE-GYU KIM
TAE-HO KIM
TAE-UK KIM
TA-SU KIM
WON-GYU KIM
YEONG-CHEOL KIM
YEONG-GEUN KIM
YEONG-GU KIM
YEONG-SU KIM
YEONG-SU KIM
YEONG-SU KIM
YONG-DEUK KIM
YONG-GAP KIM
YONG-HWA KIM
YONG-HWA KIM
YONG-TAE KIM
YUN-GEUN KIM
YUN-HO KIM
DONALD J KIMBALL
WILLARD KINCHELOW
BOBBY R KING
ELDRED H KING
GEORGE R KING
JAMES E KING
JIMMY E KING
LEROY F KING
ROLAND L KING
TOM KING
WILLIAM L KINMAN
ROBERT E KIRBY
KENNETH R KIRCHHEFER
WILLIAM KIRSHFIELD
JOSEPH G KISELA
GEORGE J KISH
CALVIN H KITZMILLER
TETSUO KIYOHIRO
MARINUS G KLARENBECK
ROBERT N KLAUS
MERTEN G KLAWITTER
BILLIE F KLINE
JOE KLUSS
WILLIAM J KLYMN
ANTHONY L KNAPKE
HOWARD H KNIERIEM
JIMMY KNIGHTON JR
FRANK H KNOWLES
EDWIN H KNUTSON
ROBERT S KOBASHIGAWA
CLARENCE KOCH
KARL J KOCHANOWICY
FRANK J KOEHLER JR
JACK M KOENIG
CLARENCE W KOKE
CARL W KOLHAGEN
ROBERT E KOLLER
FRANK KOLONICH JR
RICHARD R KOPERSKI
GERALD KORNREICH
ARNIE V S KOSKI
WILLIAM J KOSKI
JOSEPH J KOSTUCH
ANTHONY E KOSTURA
CHESTER F KOTOWICZ
DELBERT D KOVALCHECK
JOHN KOVALESKI JR
STANLEY M KOWALSKI
MICHAEL P KOZER JR
RICHARD W KRAHL
ANDREW P KRALICK
EUGENE B KRAMER
RONALD L KRAMER
EDWARD C KRATZER JR
LEIGHTON G KREIDER
WILLIAM P KRELL
GRAHAM H KREUNEN
JASON D KRIEDLER
EUGENE A KRONBECK
DONALD A KRUGER
HENRY KUBICKI
SUMNER J KUBINAK
ARNOLD O KUHLMAN
JOSEPH J KUPRAITES
DONALD N KURTZ
SHIGETOSHI KUSUDA
RICHARD KWIATKOWSKI
DALE L KYLE
ALBERT L KYMER
ROGER F LABEAU
MAXIMIANO LACSAMANA
DON M LA FOREST
ROB R LAIRD
AUSTIN K LAKE
JOHN G LAKIN
PHILLIP LALONDE
EUGENIO L LAMARROSA
ELMER H LAMBERT
HAROLD L LAMPSON
EDWIN LAND
LAWRENCE E LANDER
HORACE LANE
ANTHONY L LANGONE
CLAUDE LANIER
ROBERT L LANIER
MELVIN E LANSING
TONY LAPPAS
WILLIAM A LARKINS
BILLY J LAROUE
ROBERT J LASSEN
LAWRENCE P LASUA
JAIME LAUGIER
HARRY J LAURENCE
LOUIS E LAUTENBACHER
MARK D LAVELLE
TOMMY K LAW
DONALD F LAWLIS
JACK L LAWRENCE
RAY L LAWRENCE
ALVIS D LAWSON
CARL B LAWSON
FRED A LAWSON
JAMES L LAXTON
JOHN C LAZALDE
STANLEY LAZARUS
CLOYD E LEACH
JAMES M LEAVINS
ADRIEN LEBEL
JOSEPH LEBIEDZ
RAWFORD E LE BLANC
RENE R LECLAIR
HUGH G LEDBETTER
VERNON S LEDFORD
WILLIAM H LEDFORD
BOK-GI LEE
BOK-GI LEE
BU-HYEONG LEE
BYEONG-HWA LEE
CARSON LEE JR
CHA-BOK LEE
DAL-HO LEE
DO-HUI LEE
DO-SIK LEE
GEON-SU LEE
GYUN-HUI LEE
HO-JUN LEE
HO-JUN LEE
HUI-BOK LEE
HUI-SU LEE
HYO-HYEONG LEE
JACK LEE
JAE-SANG LEE
JAMES D LEE
JEOM-CHAE LEE
JEONG-CHUN LEE
JEONG-HO LEE
JEONG-YEON LEE
JIN-HWA LEE
JONG-MAN LEE
JONG-SIK LEE
KWAE-DEOK LEE
MYEONG-SAENG LEE
OK-PYO LEE
ROBERT P LEE
SA-DONG LEE
SAM-AM LEE
SANG-GYU LEE
SANG-JO LEE
SANG-JU LEE
SANG-SEOP LEE
SANG-YEOL LEE
SEONG-HO LEE
SEUNG-DEOK LEE
SU-DONG LEE
SUNNIE S M LEE
YEONG-HWAN LEE
YEONG-SIK LEE
HENRY LEENSTRA
DALTON LEFTWICH
MEREDITH L LEHMAN JR
CLIFFORD L LEIGHTON
EDMOND G LEIGHTON
KERMIT J LEJEUNE
WARREN LEJEUNE
JAMES E LEMASTER
GEORGE R LEMAY
LOUIS B LEMONS
JOHN LENKO
JOHN H LENO
ALBERT N LEONARD
CARLOS LEPIZZERA
JOHN J LEPP
THOMAS M LESPERANCE
GEORGE E LESTER
MELTON LESTER
GORDON J LEVAHN
LEE G LEVERING
ARTHUR I LEVINE
LAWRENCE J LEVIS
ALBERT A LEWIS
BLAIR J LEWIS
DAVID W LEWIS
DAVIS LEWIS
EARL LEWIS
EUGENE D LEWIS
WILLIE N LEWIS
RAYMOND M LHOMMEDIEU

71 ARMY

VINCENT LIBASSI
GEORGE D LIBBY
AMOS LIGE
RICHARD E LIGHTNER
KERMIT K LILYROTH
MIGUEL S LIMA JR
HERMAN L LIMBERG
ALFRED B LINDLEY
DONALD C LINDQUIST
FRANCIS E LINDSAY
JOHN W LING
KEITH L LINGLE
WILLIAM J LINGLE
EDGAR M LININGER
RICHARD J LINKLETTER
BILLY D LIPE
KENNETH C LIPSHITZ
WILLIAM R LIST
GILBERT J LITCHAUER
HERMAN H LITTLE
GARY E LITTLEFIELD
I LINDLEY LITTLETON
CHARLES W LIVING
JAMES R LOCKLAR
EDWARD N LOGAN
NORMAN J LOISELLE
LESLIE V LOKKER
AUBERY C LONG
CHARLES M LONG
CHARLES R LONG
WILLIAM C LONG
NORMAN L LONGDON
THOMAS A LONGWELL
JOHN W LONGWITZ
MANUEL A LOPEZ
PETER R LOPEZ
WILLIAM J LOPEZ
JOSEPH LOPICCOLO
ANDREW P LOPUHOVSKY
WILLIAM A LORD
RALPH E LORENZ
JOHN LOSCHIAVO
PAUL J LOTTI
JAMES E LOTZ
GIBSON LOUDIN JR
PHILIP J LOUGHMAN
RAY V LOUVIERE
BRUCE I LOVDOKKEN
WILLIE LOVE JR
WALLACE R LOVELADY
JUNIOR B LOWE
ROBERT L LOWERY
CARL LUCAS
VINCENT LUCIO
FRANK L LUDWIG
EDWARD F LUISSER
BLAS W A LUJAN
LEE F LUKE
RICHARD L LUKE
EDWARD G LUNA
KENNETH LUNDBERG
WILLIAM E LUNDQUIST
ALLAN E LUOMA
WALLACE R LUSK
MORTIMER E LUX
JAMES H LYNCH
THOMAS J LYNCH
MELVIN D MAAS
ALBERT C MAASS
FRANK E MABEY
JAMES MABRY
JOHN R MABRY
ROBERT D MACDONALD
GEORGE L MACISAAC JR
ALVIN L MACK
ALLEN T MADDY
RICHARD MADEJ
KENNETH E MADSEN
MARLIN O MADSON
THOMAS M MAFFETT
MORRIS R MAGNAN
ROBERT D MAHAN
KENNETH R MAHON
CLARENCE F MAIDEN SR
STANLEY E MAJESTIK
BERNARD E MAKI
MORGAN J MALANEY
ANGELO S MALANGA
HOWARD G MALCOLM
DONALD J MALLETTE

RICHARD L MALLETTE
RICHARD R MANCEBO
THOMAS R MANCHESTER
TONEY MANDINO
BILLY C MANGRUM
LENZIE H MANGRUM
LLOYD L MANGRUM
BOB R MANKIN
WILLIAM J MANLEY
DONALD W MANN
ALBERT MANNING JR
LEE H MANNING
RICHARD L MANSFIELD
JOHN R MANUEL
PASTOR B MANZANO
YANDAL H MARABLE
JOSEPH MARANCHE
DONALD E MARCELLI
MARTIN J MARCHOWSKY
THOMAS D MAREK
NATHERENE C MARETT
JUAN J MARIN-DE LA ROSA
FLOYD A MARKLE
RUDOLPH MARQUEZ
FRANK O MARS
CLOMA MARSHALL
ALFRED J MARTIN
CHARLES R MARTIN
DAVID J MARTIN
ELWIN C MARTIN JR
JAMES E MARTIN
JAMES H MARTIN
JAMES R MARTIN
JOHN A MARTIN
JOHN R MARTIN
ROBERT A MARTIN
ROBERT L MARTIN
VERNELLE T MARTIN
WILLIAM R MARTIN
ARTURO B MARTINEZ
RAYMOND R MARTINEZ
ANGEL MARTINEZ-OQUENDO
ANDRES MARTINEZ-OTERO
PEDRO MARTINEZ-OTERO
LAWRENCE A MASESIE
JOE R MASICH
RAYMOND E MASON
HOMER E MASSON
CLAVIS C MATHER
ROY E MATHEWS
GRAYSON L MATHIS
ROBERT K MATHIS
CRISANTO MATOS-SANTIAGO
ISMAEL MATOS-TORRES
ARTHUR A MATSON JR
HOLLEY T MATSUDA
JOSEPH J MATSUNAGA
DONALD F MATTHEW
JAMES F MATTHEWS III
RICHARD L MATTHEWS
BILLIE T MAUPIN
EDMUND R MAURY
WESLEY M MAWSON
BILLY J MAXWELL
ROBERT L MAY
JIMMIE MAYEMURA
JOHN J MAYERHOFER
DALE W MAYES
ELBERT J MAYNARD
DONALD L MAYO
JOHN MAYS JR
WILLIAM J MCALLISTER
PHILIP D MCAUGHAN
CORNELIUS J MCAULIFFE
JULIUS J MCCALL
TERRY S MCCALL
ROBERT V MCCAMMACK
JAMES J MCCANN
WILBUR C MCCARTHY
JAMES C MCCARTY
ROBERT J MCCAUL
EARL E MCCLAIN
RICHARD MCCLAIN
ALTON L MCCLANAHAN
ROBERT A MCCLAVERTY JR
MAURICE N MCCLELLAN
JIM MCCLURE
CHESTER E MCCOLLEY

ROBERT C MCCORD
LONNIE MCCOY JR
RAYMOND H MCCOY
PAUL T MCCRACKEN
MILES E MCCRAW
JOHN MCCULLOUGH
BUSTER MCCURTAIN
JAMES J MCCUTCHEN JR
CHARLES H MCDANIEL
HOMER M MCDANIEL
WILLIAM F MCDANIEL
GEORGE W MCDIVITT
WILLIAM E MCDONALD
HARRY G MCDONOUGH
GARNET W MCDOUGAL
JOHN R MCDUFFEE
JOSEPH A MCELROY
ROBERT J MCFEE
JOHN M MCGINITHEN
GEORGE F MCGIVNEY
DOUGLAS H MCGOWAN
WILLIAM G MCGOWAN
JAMES P MCGUIRE
WILLIAM M MCGUIRE JR
HENRY MCINTOSH JR
ROBERT H MCINTYRE
WARREN H MCINTYRE
CLARENCE H MCJUNKIN
WILLIAM C MCJUNKIN
JAMES E MCKENNA
MARION D MCKENZIE
ANDREW J MCKINLEY
BILLY R MCKINNEY
EUGENE L MCKINNEY
HENRY C MCKINNEY
JULIUS E MCKINNEY
MACKEY D MCKINNON
WILLIAM J MCKNIGHT
EDWARD T MCKOTCH
EDWIN E MCLAUGHLIN JR
DAVID J MCLENDON
ROBERT E MCLEOD
WILLIAM F MCLEVIS
GEORGE T MCMAHON
JOHN E MCMAHON JR
RICHARD B MCMANUS
ROBERT L MCMANUS
JOSEPH W MCMASTER
JOSEPH L MCMURRY
BURTON E MCNAUGHTON
GUY W MCNEELY
WILLIS F MCNIEL
FRED R MCNULTY
G W MCNUTT
CARL E MCPHERSON
GERALD J MCQUERRY
BILLY M MCQUINN
JAMES Z MCREARY
CORNELIUS MCREYNOLDS JR
KENNETH J MCRITCHIE
LEON MCSWAIN
CARL R MCVOY
NEIL W MEAGHER
WILSON MECKLEY JR
LUIS MEDINA
ALFRED E MEIKLE
EDMUND MEKHITARIAN
MARCIAL MELENDEZ-NEGRON
NICHOLAS MELILLO
RICHARD D MELTON
DONALD J MEMMER
LUIS A MENDEZ-HERNANDEZ
LEROY A MENDONCA
JOSE MENDOZA
RICHARD L MENNINGER
LAWRENCE A MEREDITH
LOUIS A MERINO
EARL W MERRIMAN
RALPH L MERRITT
PHILIP F MERTH
ROBERT L MERVICKER
ORACE J MESTAS
EDWARD METKOWSKI
RAYMOND E METTERT
GEORGE P METZKER
LAVERN MEUFFELS
ALBERT W MEYER

FREDERICK R MEYER
AL MICHAELIS
RAYMOND MICHAELS
JAMES C MIKELL
HUGH J MIKKELSEN
RONALD F MILBRATH
THEODORE J MILCZARCZYK
DEWITT C MILES
JAMES O MILES
BRUNKO R MILJUS
CHARLES P MILLAR
ARTHER L MILLER
CHESTER MILLER
CLIFFORD J MILLER
DONALD M MILLER
DONALD N MILLER
EDWARD D MILLER
EDWARD J J MILLER
GEORGE J MILLER
HARRY MILLER
JOHN R MILLER
JOHNNY J MILLER
LLOYD E MILLER
LOWELL L MILLER
NORMAN B MILLER JR
REUBEN MILLER
ROBERT F MILLER
ROTHELL MILLER
SETH S MILLER
THOMAS C MILLER
WILLIE MILLER
JERRY MILLOFF
CARROLL E MILLS
EDWARD F MILLS
EZEKIEL C MILLS
GEORGE C MILLS
JOHN W MILLS
EDWARD R MILOS
VICTOR MISEKOW
STANLEY MITALOVICH
ARCHIE F MITCHELL
FRANK R MITCHELL
PAUL R MITCHELL
WILLIAM A MITCHELL
HERMAN L MIXON
SAMUEL S MIYAHIRA
AUBREY W MIZE
HOWARD R MIZELL
WILLIE E MODENA
WILLIAM W MONAGHAN
FRANCIS C MONFETTE
JOSE MONTERO
JOSE A MONTESINOS
DANIEL MONTGOMERY
BERNIE MONTOYA
ENOCH P MONTOYA
ERNEST MONTOYA
LOUIS MONTOYA
EUGENE J MONVILLE
CHARLES R MOODY
JAMES A MOODY
SAMUEL M MOODY
BILLY G MOONEY
CUSTER F MOONEY
CARL C MOORE
JOHN D MOORE JR
LEONARD MOORE JR
LEROY MOORE
LESLEY A MOORE
LESLIE D MOORE
MILLER E MOORE
ROBERT L MOORE
WILLIAM T MOORE
FRANK M MORALES
ALFREDO MORALES-REYES
MELVIN W MORE
NELSON MORENO-ROSA
LEON C MOREY
AARON MORGAN
ARNOLD L MORGAN
CLARENCE E MORGAN
EDWIN L MORGAN
ELBERT L MORGAN JR
ENOCH E MORGAN
JAMES P MORGAN
JAMES P MORGAN
PETER J MORIN JR
ALBERT E MORRIS
GEORGE A MORRIS
JOHN C MORRIS III

NORMAN F MORRIS
RUSSELL A MORRIS
RUSSELL F MORRIS
STAFFORD L MORRIS
TOM J MORRIS
WILLIAM A MORRIS
JAMES W MORROW
ARTHUR J MORSE
EDWARD J MORSE JR
HERMAN E MORSE
GEORGE E MORTON JR
VICTOR MORTON
LOUIS R MOSES
ROBERT L MOSES
LEONARD L MOSIER
WILLIAM R MOSS
CARL R MOSSON
JAMES O MOUSER
JOSEPH F MOUZER
LEWIS D MOWERY
DUDLEY G MOYLE
GERALD J MUELLER
CARL H MULLER
VERLON L MULLINAX
ELMER MULLINS
ROY L MUNSEY
TADAO MURAKAMI
HEROLD F MURDOCK
JOSEPH H MURGA
CHARLES P MURPHY
DONALD L MURPHY
JAMES D MURPHY
KENNETH D MURPHY
LEONARD A MURPHY
MICHAEL D MURPHY
WILLIAM MURPHY
WILLIE B MURPHY
FLOYD A MURRAY
JOHN F MURRAY
LEE R MUSICK
ORVILLE D MUSICK
ANGELO A MUSONE
WILLIE E MUSSELWHITE
RONALD D MYERS
STEPHEN A MYERS
MILTON W NABER JR
EDWARD NADIR
HIROSHI NAGAMINE
ARNOLD NALLEY
PHILIP R NAONE
NORMAN C NARDICK
WILLIAM R NASH
ROBERT E NAULT
MANUEL NAVARRA
ADOLFO NAVARRO
WILMA R NEAL
PAUL A NEALE
JOHN W NEARHOOD
EDWIN J NECKERS
JOHN NEEDHAM
TONY A NEELEY
PABLO NEGRON
JOSE A NEGRON-ORTIZ
JAMES NELMS
CHARLES W NELSEN
CHARLES T NELSON
GEORGE W NELSON
GILBERT NELSON JR
GORDON C NELSON
JOHN L NELSON
PAUL W NELSON
RICHARD P NELSON JR
ROBERT A NELSON
ROLAND L NELSON JR
RHINOLD NEUMILLER
CHARLES W NEWBERRY
MELVIN E NEWILL
CECIL A NEWMAN
CECIL G NEWMAN
IRA NEWMAN
MYRON E NEWMAN
JAMES A NEWTON
EVERET C NICHOLS
JAMES D NICHOLS
RICE M NICHOLS
DAVID L NICHOLSON
JOE B NICHOLSON
CORBETT NICKELL
ROY J NICOLAI
ANTHONY J NICOWSKI

72 ARMY

HARRY L NIEBEL JR
MELVIN E NIEDENS
RUSSEL H NIELSEN
CHARLES R NIEMI
ARCADIO NIEVES-LARRY
RICHARD A NIXON
WILLIAM H NIXON
DAL-HWAN NO
HAK-YONG NO
JAE-SIK NO
DONALD D NOEHREN
RALPH J NORD
ELWYN D NORDYKE
ELMER R NORTON
JOHNNIE NORTON
PAUL R NORTON
JOHN F NOWAK
RICHARD R NOWICKI
LAWRENCE NUMKENA
THOMAS F NUNES
JAMES E NUTT
CHI-SAM O
HUI-CHEOL O
JEONG-SEOK O
SEONG-ROK O
DELBERT W OAKLEY
RONALD R OAKLEY
JAMES M OBOYLE
EDWARD J OBRIEN
THOMAS J OBRIEN
LUTHER ODUMS
HOWARD W OGDEN
EDWIN C OHARA
OTTO A OHME
WILLIAM R OILER
HUBERT E OLACH
ESEQUIEL A OLACHIA
FREDDY J OLAKER
JAMES P OLEARY
MICHAEL F OLESHKO
JOHN A OLIVEIRA
ARLANZA OLIVER
BERNARD J OLSOVSKY
WILLIAM T OMALLEY
WALTER J OMEARA JR
HOWARD L ONSTOTT
NELS OPHEIM
BASCOMB M OPPERT
JESSIE W OQUINN
JOHN H ORR
JOSEPH M ORR
CHARLES V ORRIE
RAYMOND E ORSETTI
RUFUS M ORTIZ
THOMAS A ORTIZ
RAFAEL ORTIZ-ORTIZ
ANTONIO ORTOGERO
JOHN G ORZECHOWSKI
JAMES W OSBORN JR
CURTIS G OSMER
CHARLES M OSTRANDER
MICHAEL J OSULLIVAN
EUGENE J OSWEILER
MITSUYUKI OTA
ROBERT T OTT
EUGENE L OTTESEN
BYRON M OTWELL JR
JOSEPH G OUELLETTE
JAMES A OUSLEY
CHARLES M OVERBAY
ELWOOD E OVERGARD
ROBERT E OVERTON
JACK C OWEN
CHARLES H OWENS
RICHARD K OWENS
WILLIAM H OWENS
RALPH D OWINGS
GERMAN OYOLA
WILLIAM L PACE
SZENTFULOPI Z PACK
RAYMOND E PADEN
EULIA PADGETT
JAMES A PAGE
RAY S PAIGE
GEORGE H PAINE
JOHN M PAINE
LINCOLN R PAINTER
NORMAN E PAINTER
STERLING G PAINTER
ELPEDIO P PALCAT
PASQUALE B PANZINI
CHESTER J PAPINEAU
HARVEY M PARDEE
ANGELO C PARISE
GEORGE W PARISH
BYEONG-YEOL PARK
CHANG-GIL PARK
CHEON-I PARK
DEOK-HWAN PARK
DEOK-MAN PARK
DONG-CHIL PARK
DONG-SU PARK
DU-HYEON PARK
GEUN-BOK PARK
GEUN-YEONG PARK
GI-HO PARK
GU-SU PARK
GYEONG-UN PARK
HUI-CHEOL PARK
IL-JE PARK
IN-SANG PARK
I-SIK PARK
JAE-GYU PARK
JAE-JU PARK
JEONG-SU PARK
MARMER J PARK
MI-SEONG PARK
MUN-GAP PARK
NO-YEONG PARK
RAYMOND PARK
SANG-BONG PARK
SANG-GU PARK
SO-HO PARK
WON-HYEON PARK
YANG-SEON PARK
YEONG-HO PARK
YONG-HWAN PARK
YONG-I PARK
YONG-MUN PARK
DAVID D PARKE
JERRY W PARKER
KENNETH W PARKER
MILTON L PARKER
JOHN W PARKEY
RALPH L PARKS
RAYMOND F PARKS
ROY PARKS
CHARLES L PARLE
CHARLES E PARLIER
ROBERT E PARNOW
JAMES D PARRENT
WATSON F PARRISH
HENRY A PARRON
CLENT E PARSONS
JAMES PARSONS
WALTER R PARTRIDGE
HENRY N PATE
WILLIAM PATERNOSTER
PETER A PATETE
LEIGHTON H PATRIQUEN
JAMES E PATTERSON
BILLY R PATTON
LAWRENCE A PAULY
CARROLL W PAYNE
CLEO O PAYNE
OLIVER E PAYNE
MILO G PAYNOVICH
DONALD A PEACH
DUANE N PEASCHEK
KESLEY S PECK
DAVID D PECOR
HARVEY L PEDERSEN
WILLIAM J PEIFER
RICHARD F PEINADO
LEWIS J PELFREY
ROBERT L PELLETIER
EVERETT H PENDARVIS
BENJAMIN E PENDELL
ALDEE H PENNER
BARTIE E PENNINGTON
JOHN B PEPPARD
GEORGE PEREZ-CRESPO
EFRAIN PEREZ-RODRIGUEZ
FRANK PERKINS
ERVIN A PERMANN
CLEVELAND PERRY
FRANKLIN R PERRY
JOHN C PERRY
JOHN C PERRY JR
LONDON L PERRY
RUSSELL L PERRY
JOHN PESKE JR
FREDERICK N PESTANA
HERBERT D PETERMAN
MARVIN V PETERS
RUSSELL F PETERS
CLARENCE A PETERSEN
DAVID J PETHEL
JOHN S PETRAS
CLYDE E PETRI
JOHN PETROFF JR
FRANK H PETRONE
EDWARD H PETRUNYAK
JOHN W PETTIT
FIRMAN E PETTUS JR
HOWARD A PETTY
WILLIAM F PFANN
WILLIAM F PFLEEGOR
DONALD E PHILLIPS
ORVILLE P PHILLIPS
ROBERT PHILLIPS
VIRGIL L PHILLIPS
VINCENT A PIATTELLI
CLAYTON M PIERCE
RAYMOND PIERCE
RAYMOND O PIERCE
RICHARD O PIERCE
WALTER PIERCE
PAUL M PIERI
DONALD A PINA
WILLIAM E PINER
LEONARD L P PIORUNSKI
ARNOLD PITMAN
JOHN PITTERSON
IRVIN W PITTMAN
CARL W PITTS
LEON PIWONI
JOSEPH PLATZKOESTER
PAUL W PLUMMER
RICHARD D PODESTA
STEVE A PODPLESKY
MARCEL C POELKER
RUFUS C POINDEXTER JR
WILLIAM A POMEROY
BENJAMIN A PONCIANO
LOVELL POOLE
WILLIAM POOLE
WILLIAM J POOLE
FRED C POORE
WILBER G POPWELL
DONN F PORTER
ELMO PORTER
HENRY N PORTER
JASPER M PORTER
RICHARD E PORTER
LAWRENCE W POSEY
MICHAEL J POSIVAK JR
WILLIAM POSTLEWAIT
RONALD L POSTON
HARRY E POTTER
BERNACE F POTTS
RICHARD POTTS
WILLIAM B POTTS
JULIAN H POUND
CHARLES E POWELL
DONALD W POWELL
EARNEST T POWELL
ROY L POWELL
JOSEPH L POWENSKI
EDWIN E POWERS
KERMIT Q PRATHER
JAMES T PREECE
LUVERNE C PRESCOTT
ROBERT H PRESSLER
DOUGLAS W PRESTAGE
RICHARD L PRICE
WILLIAM T PRICE
BARNARD V PRIEST
DUWARD H PRINCE
FLOYD PRINCE
GENE C PRINCE
RICHARD E PRIOR
HAROLD E PRISK
WILLIE G PRITCHETT
CLIFFORD C PROFFITT
NEWMAN C PRUITT JR
HARRY C PRUNIER
FLOYD W PRYOR
DEWEY R PUCKETT
KENNETH A PUGH
JOHN J PULLIAM
ODREN R PULLIN
JOSEPH S PURCELL
LEANDRO L PURGANAN
JOSEPH R PURSLEY
EUGENE H PUTNEY
JAMES H PYLATE
HURSHEL QUALLS
JOSEPH R QUARESMA
JOHN F QUIGG
CHARLES D QUINN
JOHN M QUINNAN
PEDRO A QUINONES-VELEZ
CHARLIE D QUINTANA
EARNEST E RACKLEY
GERALD RAEYMACKER
JOSEPH W RAILEY JR
THOMAS E RAILLING
ALFORD B RAINES
ALTON B RAINEY
HAROLD P RAKKE
EPIFANIO C RAMIREZ
FIDEL RAMIREZ
MAX D RAMSEY
SAM RAMSEY
ELGIN V RANDALL
RAYMOND R RANDOLPH
RICHARD C RANFRANZ
EULALIO N RANGEL
GRIFFITH J RATCLIFFE
LEWIS W RATZEBURG
CHARLES L RAUSCH
CHRISTOPHER J RAUSCH
HERBERT L RAWLS JR
FLOYD J RAY
JAMES W RAY
LOYD C RAY
ROBERT L RAYBURN
CARL E REABE
LELAND O REAGAN
GRAHAM L REAMS
CHARLIE E REAVES
JAMES C REECE
ELVIE J REED
FRANCIS REED JR
GEORGE E REED
JOSEPH E REED
PLES REED JR
ROBERT A REED
SYLVANUS F REED
MARTIN L REEDER
STANLEY G REEDER
CLAUDE E REEDY
EUGENE S REESE
WILLIAM G REGAN
JOE A REGMUND
ALEXANDER REID JR
NORMAN L REID
THOMAS A REID
RAYMOND N REIFERS
WALTER F REIMER
WARREN M REINBOLD
WALTER REMUS JR
CHARLES A REPKIE
LOYD A RESCH
ARTHUR E RESSOR
LEANDER J RETTLER
GUILLERMO REYES
JOHN A REYNOLDS JR
WILLIAM G REYNOLDS
KENNETH R RHOADS
EUGENE C RHODE
NORMAN N RHODES
CLIFTON M RHOLETTER
CLIFTON L RICE
DONALD R RICE
JIMMY M RICE
BAYARD W RICHARDS
FLINT B RICHARDS
ISIAC E RICHARDS
JOICE C RICHARDS
CHARLES RICHARDSON JR
GLEN C RICHARDSON
JACK RICHARDSON
JAMES F RICHARDSON
LESLIE K RICHARDSON JR
SAMMIE J RICHBURG
ALFRED D RICHNER
N L RICKARD
JAMES W RIDDLE
JAMES R RIDDLEY
FLOYD A RIDGLEY JR
GEORGE RIGGINS
JOHN F RIGGS JR
KEITH B RIGNEY
FRANCIS A RILEY
JOHN F RILEY
JOSEPH F RILEY
WILLARD A RINEHART
ROBERT D RITTER
ROBERT M RITTER
JULIO RIVERA
PAUL RIVERA JR
DARCY M RIVERS
NORMAN O RIVERS
JOHN RIZZO JR
NORMAN J ROBARE
ROBERT J ROBERGE
EUGENE ROBERSON
ERNEST R ROBERTS
GEORGE E ROBERTS
RANDALL C ROBERTS
RAYGER G ROBERTS
SAMUEL R ROBERTS
DEWEY E ROBERTSON JR
EARNEST R ROBERTSON
JAMES R ROBERTSON
LAWRENCE J ROBIDOUX
BILLY J ROBINSON
ERNEST ROBINSON
JASPER ROBINSON
MAX E ROBINSON
STANLEY E ROBINSON
WALTER G ROBINSON
ROBERT L ROBISON
DONALD G ROBSON
HUGH J RODDY
HOYE L RODEHEAVER
BILLY V RODGERS
EDWARD RODRIGUES
ARTHUR RODRIGUEZ
GREGORIO RODRIGUEZ
ROBERTO RODRIGUEZ
SAMUEL RODRIGUEZ-LOPEZ
GEORGE E ROEHRICH
CHARLES L ROGERS
JONE ROGERS
WILLIAM J ROGERS
PAUL L ROHR
ALEX ROLEK
WILLIAM G ROLL
DONALD E ROLLS
FRANCIS M ROMANO JR
EARNEST I ROMANS
VINCENZO D ROMEO
ANTONIO ROMERO
JOSE L ROMERO
WILLIAM L ROQUES
JAMES E RORIE
JAMES C ROSAMOND
WILEY D ROSEBERRY
HERSHEL H ROSELL JR
EDWARD E ROSLOF
EDWARD F ROSS
ARMAND G ROSSI
NORMAND S ROSSIGNOL
ROBERT L ROSZEK
DONALD G ROTHLAUF
EMANUEL ROUT
RODNEY R ROWE
WILLIE ROWE
CARL W ROWLAND
LOUIS ROWLETTE
MARVIN ROYAL
CHARLES B ROYER
DONALD J RUBIDEAUX
JAMES C RUBLE
CHARLES A RUBLEE
JOSEPH RUFFULO
ARMANDO RUIZ
LEOPOLDO L RUIZ
RONALD P RUKA
LAWRENCE G RULE
CRAVON O RUSSELL
EARL RUSSELL
ROBERT G RUSSELL
JOSEPH F RUSSO
JOHN R RUTH

73 ARMY

ALVIN N RUTHERFORD
LAWRENCE V RUVOLO
ARTHUR A RYAN
ROBERT W RYAN
JOHN P RYHTER
HYEON-SU RYU
IN-MO RYU
AGAPITO SABANDO
CLARENCE C SAIN
RICHARD SALAZAR
SASTINES SALAZAR
ARMADO L SALCIDO
FRANK SALGADO JR
FLOYD B SALLEE
JOSEPH S SALONY
SCOTT W SALYER
GEORGE SAMUEL JR
JAMES E SANBORN
GERALD E SANDERS
JOHN H SANDERS
LEONARD C SANDERS
WELDON SANDERS
WILLIAM L SANDERS
LEWIS O SANDERSON
JAMES E SANDLIN
ISAAC SANDOVAL
PHILLIP G SANDOVAL
DEALTON H SANFORD
DONALD A SANGSLAND
PEDRO SAN MIGUEL
NORBERTO SANTOS-RIVERA
ALBIN P SARAFIN
CLARENCE SAUERBREI
EDWARD SAUNDERS
JOSEPH V SAVARESE
WILLIAM A SAWYER
HARVEY F SAXTON
HERMAN SAYLOR
HERBERT G SAYRE
ARTHUR SAZO
PAUL E SCHAD
JAMES W SCHAFFER
RAYMOND P SCHAFFER
CARLTON F SCHANKIN
ERVIN A SCHELLER
VERNON SCHERMERHORN
GEORGE R SCHIPANI
LYLE E SCHIRO
CHARLES B SCHLEGEL
CLEMENT J SCHLINGEN
JOHN G SCHMENGER
MYRON L SCHMIDT
ANDREW SCHNEIDER
DONALD E SCHOLTEN
OLAN B SCHRANK
JAMES R SCHROEDER
RONALD R SCHUCHERT
JOHN H SCHUMAN
LON SCHWARTZ
HERBERT B SCHWATKA
DANIEL F SCIANNAMEO
DOMINIC N SCOCCHERA
BILL SCOTT
CHARLES L SCOTT
GERALD F SCOTT
JIMMIE SCOTT JR
JOHN J SCOTT
ROBERT D SCOTT
BERNARD E SCOVELL
ARTHUR J SCOWCRAFT
DONALD T SEABOURN
KEITH D SEAMAN
HENRY H SEBASTIAN
RAYMOND W SEEGERT
ROBERT E SEIDEL
FRANCIS R SEIJO-SAENZ
GEORGE D SEILER
BENJAMIN J SELL
FLOYD H SELLERS
OSCAR SELTZER
ROBERT B SENELL
JEOM-TAE SEO
MUN-HO SEO
IN-PYO SEOK
CHEON-PIL SEON
HA-DO SEONG
PAN-SIK SEONG
ALLEN A SEQUIN
LEON J SEVERAN

DAVID R SEWARD
DAVID C SEWELL
NATHUL SEWELL
ROMUS SHADID
ANDREW B SHANE
ROBERT D SHANKS
ROBERT E SHANNON
JAMES W SHARP
RICHARD M SHARROW
RALPH L SHAW
ROBERT E SHAW
ROBERT E SHEFFIELD
WILLIAM B SHELTON
CLARENCE E SHEPARD
OLLIE E SHEPARD
ROBERT A SHEPARD
THOMAS A SHEPHERD
ROBERT L SHEPPARD
JOSEPH D SHEPPERSON
CARL E SHERADEN
ROBERT J SHIMABUKURO
DALE D SHINABARGER
ROBERT M SHINDE
TRUMAN O SHIPP
HENRY G SHOOP
IRA W SHORE JR
JAMES R SHORTELL
RAYMOND A SHORTINO
JOHN P SHOTT
CHARLES D SHREEVE
HAROLD R SHREVE
HERBERT D SHUCK
HOWARD R SHUCK
ALFRED H SIDNEY
EARL V SIEGMUND
PABLO SIERRA
MARVIN M SIHRER
JESUS A SILVA
ALBERT E SIMMONS
LEON F SIMMONS
THOMAS SIMMONS
WILBERT SIMMS
FRANK P SIMON
HOMER I SIMPSON
ROBERT W SIMS
GYEONG-U SIN
IK-GEUN SIN
JEONG-SU SIN
JIN-YEONG SIN
SEON-GI SIN
GENE H SIPPEL
HENRY M SIPSEY
ERNEST SIUDZINSKI
BILL T SIZEMORE
MELVIN D SKIDMORE
JOSEPH J SKWIERAWSKI
ROBERT W SLAICK
LUM L SLAUGHTER
ALFRED C SLITER
HAROLD SLOAN
NORBERT J SLOMBA
MARTIN H SLUTSKY
GEORGE L SMALLWOOD
ANDREW K SMELIK
ARTHUR B SMITH
BILLY G SMITH
CALVIN SMITH
CALVIN L SMITH
CLAUDE E SMITH
CLIFTON E SMITH JR
EDGAR E SMITH
EUGENE W SMITH
FRANCIS T SMITH
GERALD L SMITH
HAROLD E SMITH
HOWARD F SMITH
JACK O SMITH
JAMES C SMITH
JAMES E SMITH JR
JAMES M SMITH
JOHN H SMITH
JOHN H SMITH
LEONARD J SMITH JR
LEWIS B SMITH
LOUIS L SMITH
RALPH F SMITH
RAY SMITH
RICHARD E SMITH
ROGER A SMITH
SHADRACH B SMITH

STEVE SMITH JR
VERNON D SMITH
WALTER B SMITH
WALTER L SMITH JR
WILLIAM E SMITH
WILLIAM S SMITH
WILLIE SMITH
DONALD SMITHSON
BILLIE A SMOOT
LOYD SMOTHERS
WILLIAM R SMYTH
JOSEPH M SNOCK JR
DAVID B SNYDER
MERVIN B SNYDER
WILLIAM H SNYDER JR
JOHN G SOLLIE
RICHARD W SOLOMON
CHARLES L SOMERS
PAUL H SOMMER
EDWARD SOMMERFIELD
BYEONG-SU SON
JONG-SU SON
CHANG-SU SONG
HYEONG-HO SONG
IL-HO SONG
JONG-JAE SONG
MAN-HO SONG
YEONG-JU SONG
WILLIAM SONNAMAKER
JOSEPH A SOPKO
DOMINGO SOTO
JAMES W SOUTHARD
ROBERT G SOWDER
ARTHUR H SPANGLER
DONALD D SPARKS JR
HAROLD SPARKS
JAMES R SPARKS
COLUMBUS S SPEARMAN
ELTON M SPEARS
PAUL SPEARS
ROBERT P SPECHT
WILFRED G SPECHT
RUSSELL L SPEGAL
CHAPMAN T SPENCER
FLOYD S SPENCER
LEWIS F SPERDUTO
WILLIAM R SPILLER
WILLIE F SPINKS
EUGENE SPINOSA
GERALD K SPONSLER
DAVID J SPRAGGS
CURTIS B SPROW
RAYMOND A STAATS
ALTON R STACEY
CLYDE T STACY
REX F STACY
KENNETH R STADLER
JACK J STAI
THEODORE A STAINBROOK JR
ROY G STALLARD
WALTER E STALLARD
HAROLD C STAMM
ROY STAMM
WAYNE E STAMPER
OSCAR E STANFORD
FRANK J STANKEVICH
GRADY STANLEY
JAMES O STANTON
JAKEY F STAPLES
WILLIAM R STARKEY
JOHN C STAUCH SR
DEAN A STEELE
JAMES A STEELE
WALTER W STEELE
JOHN E STEINSON
ROBERT T STENSON
PAUL E STEPHAN
MOSE STEPHEN JR
CLEO STEPHENS
WESLEY STEPHENS
ERNEST H STEVENS
LEO STEVENS
WILLIAM STEVENS
CHARLES L STEVENSON
KENNETH E STEVENSON
ALEXANDER STEWART
HOWARD STEWART
EARL C STILES
ROBERT J STIM

GEORGE C STITH III
WALTER STODOLSKY
SHERMAN M STOKES
OLIVER STONEY JR
HARVEL M STOOKSBERRY
JOSEPH E STORTI
LEROY A STORY
JACK STOVALL
HARRY C STRINGER
CORNELIUS STRONG JR
ARMOUR D STROTHER
DAVID J STROWIG
RALPH A STRUEWING
JAMES N STRYKER
RICHARD L STUCK
ROLAND S STUDLEY
CHARLES E STULLER
DONALD P STUMP
JOE D STUTTS
MICHAEL P SUCHAR JR
EDMUND W SUHREN
FRANK J SULIMAN
FRANK E SULLIVAN
JAMES D SUMMY
WILLIAM G SUMNER
JAMES E SUMNERS
BILL S SUMPTER
JOHN E SUMRALL
JAMES E SWAINBANK
GENE E SWANGER
FLOYD C SWEATT
CHARLES O SWEETWOOD
HAROLD M SWIHART
CLARENCE W SWINEY
JOHN O SYMONS
THADDEUS T SZWEDA
RICHARD TABLANTE
RALPH F TACHENY
ALVIN J TADLOCK
LUKE B TAINPEAH
TOHORU T TAKAI
CHARLES E TALIAFERRO
RUSSELL D TALLEY
JAMES M TALLON
PRUDENCIO TALON
CHARLES Y TAMARU
JAMES H TANNER
JOHN H TAPPER
GEORGE G TATARAKIS
JAMES R TATE
GLEN W TATEM
CLARK E TAYLOR
DOUGLAS L TAYLOR JR
ELBERT M TAYLOR
HERMAN R TAYLOR
JAMES L TAYLOR
JOHN A TAYLOR
RAYMOND S TAYLOR JR
JAMES W TEAGUE
LUIS A TELLEZ
SHINJI TENGAN
BILLY E TENNISON
DONALD W TERRY
HAROLD L TERRY
HUBERT TERRY
ROBERT W TERRY
LYLE K THALLER
GEORGE W THARP
KENNETH A THEIS
JOSEPH L THIBAULT
ARTHUR E THIBEAULT
CLEMENT THIBODEAUX
LUCIAN J THIBODEAUX
BOBBY J THIELE
DONN H THOMAS JR
FRANCIS D THOMAS
GERALD THOMAS
JOSEPH THOMAS JR
LLOYD THOMAS
AUBREY E THOMPSON
BEKAY THOMPSON
BENJAMIN F THOMPSON
DUANE THOMPSON
ELMORE M THOMPSON
JOHN E THOMPSON
LESLIE C THOMPSON
PAUL D THOMPSON
RICHARD D THOMPSON
HAROLD V THORNHILL
BOBBY O THORNTON

WALLACE THORNTON
WILLIAM B THORNTON
JAKE R THORPE
CHESTER T THRAILKILL
RUBEN THURMAN JR
JOHN H TICER JR
RICHARD H TILLMAN
JARED E TILLOTSON
CLARK M TILTON
LEO J TINDALL
CECIL E TINSLEY JR
LEONIDAS L TITCHNELL
ALEXANDER TOATLEY
WALTER H TOBIN JR
ALBERT E TODD
BLANTON TODD
LEO C TODD
MARION H TODD
OWEN M TODD
RICHARD H TODD
ROBERT S TOLER
WILLIAM E TOMLINSON
EDWARD B TONANDER
ARNOLD E TOOLE
FRANK W TORIGIAN
CASEY N TORIKAWA
GEORGE TORRES
JOE TORRES
PHIL TORRES
ROSELIO J TORRES
RUSSELL G TORRES
WALTER TORRES
EDWARD J TOTH
GENE D TOTTEN
IRVING TOURTLELOTTE
KENNETH L TOUSIGNANT
HUGH A TOWNSLEY
JOSEPH H TRAIL
JAMES TRAMMELL
ANDREW L TRANO
W ARREN G TRANTHAM
WILLIAM S TRAVERS
EDWARD J TRAVIS
DONALD C TRENT
ROBERT G TREVINO
GEORGE C TREXLER JR
ROBERT M TRIVETT
ROBERT C TROTMAN
NORMAN F TRUDEAU
ROGER TRUDEAU
PAUL H TRUEHEART V
ELWOOD M TRUSLOW
SUEO TSUNODA
HARRY N TSURUOKA
JOSEPH T TUCKER
JUNIOR R TUCKER
THOMAS W TUCKER
THOMAS J TULLO
STANLEY TURBA
JAMES D TURNBULL
CLEMON TURNER
ERNEST K TURNER
ALLEN H TUTTLE
FREDERICK H TUTTLE
HARRY G TWIFORD
ANTHONY J TYRALA
YEONG-DEOK U
SEIHO UEJO
MITSUO UEMURA
ROBERT E UMBEL
ALFRED UNDERBAGGAGE
TROY D UNDERWOOD
WALTER UNRUH
ROBERT F USTICK
RALPH J VALENTIN
CELESTINO D VALERA
MARIO F VALLE
LOYD A VAN ALLEN
FRANK G VAN ANTWERP
VERNON E VANDER BURG
JOHN G VAN GOETHEM
HERBERT L VANMETER
CHARLES E VAN OSDOL
SAMUEL VAN SADERS
ALVIN L VARNER
CHRISTOPHER Y VARS
JOSEPH A VAUGHAN
CLEVELAND VAUGHN
ORVILLE L VAUGHN

74 ARMY

FRANK A VELASCO
HAROLD W VENSON
ROBERT M VETTER
WENDELL VICKERS
GEORGE H VILLACRES
GREGORIO VILLAFANE-VAZQUEZ
CRISTOBOL VILLARREAL
ANTONIO B VILLELA
OTHA R VINCESON
JACK L VINING
LAWRENCE E VINK
HERBERT F VINYARD
BRUCE O VOGEL
WILLIAM VOGEL JR
PAUL T VOIGHT JR
FRED W VOLKMAN
DALLAS VOWELL
RAY F VOYLES
EDWARD R VYDRA
EDWARD L WADDELL
TIM E WADE
VINCENT M WADE
RICHARD H WAGNER
CHARLES E WAITS
CHARLES J WALDEN
MAX M WALDHERR
LLOYD L WALDRIP
CLIFTON W WALDRON
RAYMOND S WALIGORSKI
EARL W WALKER
HENRY L WALKER
HUGH W WALKER
JAMES K WALKER JR
JAMES W WALKER
KENNETH E WALKER
WENDELL H WALKER
CLARENCE M WALLACE
MITCHELL A WALLACE SR
ROBERT L WALLACE
W O WALLACE
BERNARD J WALSH
STEPHEN E WALSTON
MARVIN O WALTERS
LEONARD M WALZ
HAROLD E WANDOVER
JESSIE WARD
WILLIAM F WARD
JOHN N WARNY
ERNEST G WARRAM
ROBERT P WARREN
SAMUEL WARREN
JOHN E WARRICK
JUNIUS E WASHINGTON
ANDREW R WATADA
RAYMOND L WATERS
WILLIE WATERS
BILLY S WATFORD
CECIL H WATSON
CLARENCE E WATSON
JAMES D WATSON
LEONARD S WATSON
ORREN S WATSON
ROBERT B WATSON
WALTER J WATSON
GEORGE W WATT
WILLIS WATTERS
GEORGE F WATTS JR
JAMES E WATTS
ELMER C WEAR
DALE E WEARS
ROOSEVELT J WEARY
CURTIS H WEAVER
GENE E WEAVER
JASPER P WEAVER
ROBERT R WEAVER JR
ROBERT S WEAVER
ROGER J WEAVER
ROGER L WEAVER
LOUIS A WEBB
DONALD W WEBBER
LEONARD F WEBER
JACOB WEBSTER JR
HAROLD J WEED
OTIS B WEEKS
GEORGE E WEHAGE
RONALD J WEIDER
COOK WEIKLE JR
HOWARD R WEINGARTH
ELTON WELCH
JAMES L WELCH
HARVEY J WELCOMER
EUGENE P WELKER
RAYMOND B WELLBROCK
JAMES R WELLS
CHARLES WENN
WALTER H WESLEY
DALLAS G WEST
DAVID L WEST
JOHN W WEST
RICHARD T WEST
MELVIN P WESTER
ROY R WESTMORELAND
JONNIE WESTPHALL JR
DELBERT J WHALEN
DONALD L WHEELER
FRANCIS D WHEELER
ROBERT W WHEELER
NORMAN L WHITAKER
CYRUS J WHITBY
DAVID J WHITE
DONALD R WHITE
JAMES H WHITE
JOHN H WHITE
LONNIE R WHITE
RICHARD C WHITE
ROBERT J WHITE
ROBERT L WHITE
SHERMAN H WHITE
ORBIA WHITECOTTON
ROY N WHITED
WILLIAM F WHITEMORE
CHARLES P WHITLER
BENCE G WHITLEY
ROBERT M WHITMIRE
MELVIN T WHITTAKER
JACK D WHITTLE
ROBERT J WICHMAN
MORRIS J WICK
WILLIAM C WIENER
JOSEPH J WIERZBICKI
JAMES M WIEWEL
HAROLD WIGGINS
JAMES M WIGLEY
DUANE W WILCOX
WILLIAM J WILEY
LEEMAN D WILFONG
CLEOPHAS WILKINS
LOUIS V WILKOWSKI
FRANCIS J WILL
GEORGE WILLARD JR
BERTRAM E WILLIAMS
CHESTER L WILLIAMS
CURLESTER WILLIAMS
DONALD E WILLIAMS
ELLIS E WILLIAMS
EZRA WILLIAMS
JACK R WILLIAMS
JAMES E WILLIAMS
JOHN WILLIAMS JR
JOHN H WILLIAMS
KENNETH O WILLIAMS
LEWIS D WILLIAMS
NATHANIEL WILLIAMS
ROBERT H WILLIAMS
ROMAN J WILLIAMS
STEVENS WILLIAMS
TALMAGE C WILLIAMS JR
THOMAS W WILLIAMS
BENNIE M WILLIAMSON
DANIEL J WILLIAMSON
JOHN WILLIAMSON JR
CECIL M WILLIS
ERNEST A WILLIS
GAYLORD B WILLIS
HOWARD WILLIS
ROBERT WILLIS
AMOS WILSON
EARNEST G WILSON
GARVIN WILSON
HAROLD F WILSON
JAMES WILSON
JAMES V WILSON
JESSE WILSON
JOHN B WILSON
JOSEPH F WILSON
JOSEPH G WILUSZ
ROYCE W WINARSKI
WILLIAM W WINBUSH
HENRY J WINDECKER
WILLIE E WINDHAM
CARL O WINDLE
HORACE WINGFIELD
FRANK N WINKLE JR
BILLIE G WINKLER
ARCHIE D WINN
HENRY G WINSTEAD
EDWARD R WINSTON
HUSTON WINSTON
WILBERT L WINTER
EARL E WISE
CARL E WISECUP
JACK V WISEMAN
RICHARD L WOJESKI
GEORGE L WOLDIKE
MELVIN E WOLFE
ROBERT O WOLFE
THOMAS F WOLFE
ALFRED S WOMER
JONG-GYU WON
HARVEY J WOOD
LYLE E WOOD
WYATT L WOOD
CHARLES R WOODALL JR
WILLIAM T WOODALL
RUSSELL E WOODARD JR
ALBERT D WOODCOX
THURMAN K WOODLIEF
JAMES J WOODMANSEE
FLOYD A WOODRING
ROBERT WOODS
WILFRED E WOODS
WILLIAM L WOODWARD
EVERETT J WOODY
WILLIAM L WOOLFORD
DOUGLAS S WOOLMAN
WALTER WORHACH
PHILIP W WORM
GERALD E WOTRING
RICHARD J WOZNIAK
JOHN G WRAY
BENJAMIN H WRIGHT
EDWARD C WRIGHT
GAINES WRIGHT
JAMES B WRIGHT
ROBERT WRIGHT
THEODORE WRIGHT
WILLIAM H WRIGHT JR
RICHARD S WYATT
WILMER T WYATT
JERRY M YANCEY
JOHN A YANECKO
GI-HWAN YANG
IL-GYU YANG
LIGE YARBROUGH
MIKE J YBARRA
MANUEL YDROGO
CORBETT YEATER JR
BERNARD YELSKY
DALE YENGER
JAE-HWAN YEOM
GYU-WON YEON
RICHARD A YERNAUX
EARL D YINGER
ITSUO YONESHIGE
LYLE F YONGE
KEITH P YORK
EUGENE W YOST
BEAR J YOUNG
CHARLES H YOUNG
FREDDIE W YOUNG
GERALD R YOUNG
JAMES E YOUNG JR
LESLIE YOUNG JR
THOMAS YOUNG
DAE-HO YU
GWANG-SIK YU
JIN-GI YU
JONG-SIK YU
YEON-JUN YU
JEONG-GEUN YUN
JIN-SU YUN
JONG-GUK YUN
JONG-TAE YUN
JUNG-GI YUN
ROBERT W ZAK
ALBERT A ZALNER
RUPERT ZARIN
FRANK J ZAWACKI
CHARLES E ZEPP
MYLES W ZIMMERMAN
FELIX J ZOLKOWSKI
RALPH ZONTA
ROBERT L ZUBROD
ANTHONY J ZUKAS
HARRY R ZUPKE
VERNIE A ZURN
JACK C ZUVER

SERGEANT FIRST CLASS

RAYMOND J ACOSTA
JOHN R ADAMS
WILLIAM A ADAMS
HATTEN ADKINS
HILLREY B ADKINS
LITISONI AETONU
W T AKINS
WINSTON L ALBERS
JOSEPH ALDRETE
ELLIS L ALDRIDGE
BILLY J ALLEN
GEORGE H ALLEN JR
HAROLD E ALLEN
NEIL E ALLEN
MORRIS ALLUMS
CLARENCE E ALSPAUGH
ROBERTO ALVA
LOUIS A ALVES
YUTAKA AMANO
BYEONG-GU AN
SANG-BOK AN
CHARLES E ANDERSON
JAMES T ANDERSON
THOMAS E ANDRZEJEWSKI
HERMAN ANTHONY
HARRY A ARCENEAUX JR
LAWRENCE L ARIAS
BILLY J ARMSTRONG
MELVIN C ARTHUR
PATRICK J ARTHUR
LOUIS W ASHFORTH
GEORGE ASHTON
DONALD B ATHERTON
BENNY C ATKINSON
JOSEPH P AUCOIN
SEOK-GEUN BAE
SO-O BAEK
HARRY B BAGNELL
CHARLES M BAILEY
MILTON W BAILEY
CHARLIE C BAKER
FRED E BAKER
ISAAC E BAKER
JACK B BAKER
JAMES K BAKER
RALPH W BAKER
MARCELO A BALANG
JOSE A A BALTOLOMEI
CHARLES M BANKS
EARL BANKS
WILLIAM P BANKS
ANTHONY J BARBER
LESTER V BARCHESKY
VERNON R BARKER
EDWARD J BARNAK
MACK R BARNES
GEORGE J BARNETT JR
ALVIN J BARRETT
GEORGE C BARROW
HENRY G BARROW
LOUIS E BARTNING
CLYDE H BATEMAN
ELMORE C BATES
GEORGE F BAUER JR
EARL R BAXTER
LOUIS M BAXTER
FRANKLIN E BEATTIE
BENJAMIN L BEATY
CLARENCE C BEAVER JR
JOSEPH L BECKER
RICHARD R BECKER
MILTON M BEED
JAMES E BEEVER
JAMES H BELL
PETER C BELL
RALPH BELL
FRANCIS A BELLASINO JR
HAROLD D BELLVILLE
WYATT H BELTON
EDWARD BENAVIDEZ
VICTOR Y BENDER
BOYD J BENNETT
HAYDEN BENNETT
ROBERT C BENNETT
ALFRED G BENSINGER JR
DANIEL F BENTON
ALFRED P BERNARD
BILLY J BEST
CHARLES A BETSWORTH
ERNEST D BETTENCOURT
ERSEL BEVILOCK
DONNIE L BIAS
CLARENCE A BILLHEIMER
DAVID K BIRCH
GEORGE T BISSELL
DOMINIC F BIZZARRO
ROBERT R BLACK
WILLIAM M BLACK
ROGER BLACKBURN
CHARLES E BLACKLEY
JAMES R BLACKWOOD
LAURENT R BLAIN
ROBERT E BLAIR
WARREN BLAKE JR
DOUGLAS W BLANKSCHEN
JOSEPH A BLISSENBACH
THEODORE J BOCKHOFF
DIXIE F BOGGESS JR
BISH BOGGS
ANDREW G BOOK
ROBERT L BOOKER
JOE J BOOKOUT
JOSEPH BORLA
ADOLPH M BOSSHARDT
ANTON BOTEK JR
ROLLAND BOUCHARD
LUDWEST J BOUILLION
ROBERT L BOUNDS
TRAVIS O BOUNDS
NORMAN A BOURQUE
GERALD B BOWDEN
WILLIAM L BOWDEN
THOMAS N BOWERS
W F BOWERS
PHOM BOWIE
JAMES L BOYCE
LEONARD G BRADFORD
JAMES BRADLEY
GEORGE H BRAINARD
J W BRANTON
ROBERT A BRATTON
ELLIS M BREWER
CARL BREWINGTON
HOWARD BREWINGTON
LEWIS G BRICKELL
GEORGE BRICKER
CLYDE W BRINDEL JR
NELSON V BRITTIN
BERNIE B BRITTON
WENDELL I BROAD
WALTER T BROADDUS
MERLE D BROADSTON
BILL M BROOKIN
BRUCE E BROOKS
WILEY B BROOKS
SIMON W BROUSSARD
PHILIP F BROUSSEAU
GEORGE T BROWER
CARLTON H BROWN
CLARENCE G BROWN
CLYDE U BROWN
DANIEL K BROWN
HAROLD M BROWN
MALCOLM J BROWN
MARION A BROWN
WILLIAM E BROWN
SAM R BRUCE
LAWRENCE A BRUNO
ROBERT BRYANT
NORBERT A BRZYCKI
ROBERT C BUCHEIT
WILLARD L BUCHOLS
MARTIN E BUDACK
JAMES E BUDD
JERRY E BULLARD
DEAN C BUNDSCHUH

HUBERT K BUNNELL
BILLIE BURCH
RILEY BURCHFIELD
ROBERT G BURCIAGA
DAMON BURGESS
JOHN D BURGESS
ELROY F BURGETT
JOHN S BURKE
FLOYD K BURKHART
WILLIAM T BURNS
TONY K BURRIS
MYRON H BURT
DONALD K BURTON
WALTER R BURTON JR
JOSEPH S BURZYNSKI
LOUIS G BUSCH
BRUCE E BUSHRE
GILBERT J BUTLER
WALLACE V BUTLER
OWEN G BUTTRESS
JOSEPH S BUZYNISKI
JAMES T BYRNE
JOHN L CABLE
RICHARD J CABRAL
JOHN A CAHILL
CARLOS M CAJERO
JOE J CALAMAN
ALVIN O CALDWELL
JAMES C CALDWELL
EDWARD J CALLAHAN
OWEN J CAMERON
CHARLIE A CAMPBELL
JIMMIE R CAMPBELL
ANGELO CAMPO
NEAL P CANTRELL
MILTON L CAOUETTE
PAUL V CARDER
CYRIL E CARMICHAEL
THOMAS G CARR
WINSTON A CARR
LEE C CARRAWAY
JAMES A CARRIGAN
ZINN CARRIGAN JR
CHARLES F CARROLL
RAYMOND B CARROLL
JAMES B CARTER
JOE D CARTER
ROBERT L CARTER
DANIEL L CARTWRIGHT
JEREMIAH CASEY
JAMES E CASON
AGAPITO R CASTANEDA
EUGENE T CASTELLONE
MARTIN CASTILLO
DOMINADOR G CATALON
ALVA E CATT
WILLIAM E CAUTION
JOHN J CAVENDER
JOSE A CEBALLOS
WILLIAM A CECIL
JOHN B CHAN
GUY CHANCEY
DEAN D CHANEY
CYRIL G CHAPPEL
JOSEPH CHARLES JR
GEORGE E CHASTAIN
LEROY CHATMAN
GEORGE L CHEATEM
JOSEPH G CHESS
WILLARD CHILDRES
ERNEST A CHILDRESS
EDWARD J CHMELKA
JOHN E CHOATE
BOK-MAN CHOI
BYEONG-SAENG CHOI
JIN-GYU CHOI
JONG-CHIL CHOI
SEONG-JO CHOI
SU-JIN CHOI
TAE-GEUN CHOI
LEONARD M
CHRISTIANSON
HERMINIO CINTRON
BASIL L CLARK
ELDRED B CLARK
JESSE F CLARK SR
ROBERT L CLARK
WESLEY H CLARK
ROLAND W CLATTERBUCK
PATRICK J CLEARY

CHARLES E CLEMONS
CLIFFORD J CLEMONS
NED J CLEVELAND
JAMES M CLEVENGER
ROY M CLIFTON
WILLIAM E COALE
ORLAN G COBB
LESLIE K COBER
WALTER R COBLE
VALENTIN COCA
HAYDEN D COCKRUM
JOHN F COCO
PHILIP L COINER
DELMAR P COLE
HERBERT COLEMAN
JAMES A COLEMAN
EUGENE J COLLEY
EDWARD H COLLINS
JOHN M COLLINS
JOSEPH E COLLINS
CANDIDO COLON-
FONSECA
JUAN A COMA
ALBERT K COMP
JAMES M CONGER
CHARLES W CONKLIN
BILLY J CONNOR
ROBERT D CONRAD
JAMES D COOK
OSBORN H COOK
WILLIAM A COOKE JR
OCIE W COOKSIE
ELLIS COON
BOYD L COOPER
OREN S COOPER
WILLIAM E COOPER
EARL L COPPLE
JAMES H CORNELL
STANFORD O CORNER
FOLTON COSBY
CALIXTO COTTO-LUYANDA
MELVIN L COTTON
GEORGE COUTTS JR
WILLIAM R COVERSTONE
ARTHUR W COX
CALVIN M COX
CLARENCE V COX JR
DURWIN J COX
DONALD D CRAFT
JAMES A CRAWFORD
PAUL D CRAWFORD
WILLIAM H CREAMER
JAMES B CREECH
IRVINE T CREWS
RICHARD F CRONIN
HAROLD R CROOK
WILLIAM C CROOKHAM
LLOYD B CROSBY
HAROLD R CROSS JR
HOWARD M CROSS
WILL T CROSS
DONALD E CROUSE
CLIFTON M CULVER
JAMES L CUMMINGS
WILLIAM H CURRAN
WOODROW W CURTIS
RICHARD G CUSHMAN
HAROLD CUTLIP
GOODRICH I DAHLIN
FRED J DAILEY
MURLIE DAILEY
WALLACE J DALY
CLAUDE H DANIELS JR
EARL L DANSBERRY
ROBERT E DARE
GARLAND E DARTER
CLAIR C DAUBERMAN
JACK R DAUPHIN
BILLY R DAVENPORT
ARCHIBALD DAVIDSON
DONALD E DAVIDSON
LESLIE H DAVIDSON
HARRIS N DAVIS
HENRY W DAVIS
LEROY DAVIS
REUBEN J DAVISON
HAROLD D DAY
LAMON M DAY
CLARENCE W DEAL
GLEN R DEALE

ERCEL W DEAN
GEORGE DEAN
DAVID J DE BOLT
JIMMIE DEBORD
JOHN DECERNO
CLAYTON E DECKER
FLOYD DECORREVONT
WILLIAM DEJOHN
EDWARD E DELAND JR
ANTONIO DE LA ROSA
LORETO DELATOBA
DANA A DELLINGER
MODESTO P
DE LOS SANTOS
JOSEPH J DE LUCA JR
ALFRED L DEMAIN
JUSTIN M DEMELLO
CASIMIRE T DEMOLL
EUGENE A DESAUTEL
JOSEPH A R DESLOGES
GERALD J DE SOUSA
ROBERT E DEWITT
MYRON G DICK
PAUL DICKERSON
ROBERT H DICKERSON
WOODROW L DIEBOLD
GEORGE H DILLARD
ROOSEVELT DIXON JR
SU-IL DO
THOMAS V DODSON
ERNEST C DOEPNER
JAMES F DOLAN
DAVID DOMINGUEZ
JOHN F DONLIN
NORRIE C DOOLITTLE
JAMES L DORRANCE
MORGAN L DOWNS
PAUL DOXIE
JAMES A DRAPER
CARL W DRESSLER
HENRY A DUDLESON
DONALD L DUFF
WILLIAM A DUNAVANT
WILLIAM E DUNCAN
JAMES R DUNN
ROBERT C DUNN
HENRY F DUPLEASE
VERGIL DURHAM
EDWARD M DURKIN
JAMES E EARL
CHARLES D EASON
JOHN W EBERT
HARRY ECKERT
HAROLD M EDGINGTON
JUNIOR D EDWARDS
RAY EDWARDS
PATRICK J EGAN
DUANE E EGE
VERNON A EGGENBURG
JACKSON C ELLIOTT
JOHN Y ELLISON
VINCENT N EMMETT
EDGAR ENFINGER
HORACE S ENGLAND
WALTER S ENGLEHART
LLEWELLYN J ENSTROM
LAWRENCE W ERDMAN
GERARDO ESCONTRIAS
GUY T EUBANKS JR
JOHN H EVANS
JOSEPH K EVANS
ROBERT L EVANS
WALTER D EVANS
WILLIAM J EVANS
BOBBIE EVANTS
CECIL W FAGG
CURTIS A FAIR
ROBERT W FARMER
RUDOLPH FARMER
GUSS R FARR
CLOFUS O FARRIS
RAYMOND FEENSTRA
ISAAC FENNELL JR
CLYDE J FERGUSON
JAKE L FERGUSON
RAYMOND A FERGUSON
SAM W FERGUSON
DWAINE E FIELDS
OLIVER M FIELDS
FRANK R FIGUEROA

JAMES W FINK
EUGENE H FIRNGES
DONOVAN L FISHER
LAWRENCE E FLACK
HENRY C FLANDERS
FREDERICK E FLEMING
ROBERT P FLEMING
ROBERT L FLINNER
BRAULIO FLORES
HENRY E FLOWERS
WILLIAM J FLYNN
WELDON S FOGLEMAN
WILBUR W FOLCK
ERNEST J FONTAINE
ALVIN FONTENOT
JOHN W FORD
ROBERT E FORD
CHARLES G FORNUFF
HENRY J FOURACRES
LOUIS M FRANK
DONALD E FRANKLIN
RICHARD L FRANKLIN
HARRISON M FRASER
HERBERT W FRAZIER
JEAN FREEMAN
LEONARD FREEMAN JR
OTHAR C FRENCH
ALOYSIUS J FREUND
REUBEN W FREYTAG
TEDWARD E FRIAR
DAVID FRYE
NORRIS FUGATE
DANIEL W FULKS
GERALD W FULLBRIGHT
ROBERT R FUNKE
MARVIN C FUNKHOUSER
FRED FUQUA
JOHN A FURST
JOSEPH E GAGNE
HUGH E GALIGHER
ROSALIO GALIUS
ARMAND J GALLI
ARNOLD C GALLOWAY
WILLIAM E GALLUP
HENRY C GAMBLE
HUI-CHEOL GANG
JOSEPH E GANTT
JOHN J GARCIA
WILLIAM B GARDNER
WILLIAM L GARRETT
WILLIAM M GARRETT
ALBERTO B GARZA
WEBBER J GASKINS
HERBERT L GAY
ROMIE R GAY
WILLIE G GENTRY
GORDON J GETTMAN
CHARLES GIANNETTO
EDWARD GIBSON
GRADY W GIBSON
KARL H GIBSON
LEO G GILL
THOMAS E GILLIAM
JIM GIPSON
EMIL J GIRONA
JAMES L GLIDEWELL
CHARLES H GLOVER
JOSEPH E GLOVER JR
PAUL R GLOVER
CARL L GODING
DONALD H GONANO
OSCAR GONZALEZ
JAMES C GOODMAN
WILLIAM L GOODMAN
ELMORE B GOODWIN
GEORGE GOODWIN JR
HOWARD C GOODWIN
JAMES E GOODY
WILFRED F GORDANIER
KENNETH J GORMAN
CLIFFORD E GOTHARD
ALFRED V GOULDMAN
DONALD J GOUVEIA
EDWARD GRACE
ROBERT M GRACE
BURTON A GRACEY
ALFRED L GRAHAM
EARLON V GRANT
DAVE GRASS JR
WINSTON GRAVES

RICHARD J GRAY
CAREY GREEN
JOHN L GREEN
KENNETH L GREEN
WILLIAM S GREEN JR
EDWIN A GREENE JR
CHARLES W GREGORY
SIMON GRIEGO
ALONZO GRIER
VIRGIL L GRIGGS
NORMAN A GRIMM
WALTER H GRUEBBELING
ALEXANDER T GRUNOW
GIROLAMO J GUERRISE
LEWIS D GUILDS
DONALD E GUNSTROM
MATTHEW F GURA
ROBERT H GUTHRIE
RODRIGO Q GUZMAN
GAP-SUL GWON
SEUNG-U GWON
HERMAN C HAASE
ORLIN K HAGEN
JOSEPH F HAGERTY
CHARLES F HAINES
JOHN J HALAMUDA
ALFRED B HALE
COOPER K HALL
GEORGE L HALL
HOWARD W HALL
RAYMOND E HALL
MERLIN J HAMILTON
WILLIAM W HAMILTON
ROBERT J HAMLIN
EMMETT T HAMMOND
GORDON L HANNAH
WILLIAM H HANNAH
DARREL D HANSEN
FLOYD M HANSEN
BOOKER T HARDEWAY
ERNEST B HARKEY
HARRY E HARKNESS
RICHARD G HARLESS
JOHN HARMON
ROBERT D HARMON
SHELDON L HARRIMAN
ELDRIDGE HARRINGTON
CHARLES M HARRIS
JOHN E HARRIS
MAX E HARRIS
RICHARD L HARRIS
THEODORE J HARRIS
WAYNE E HARRIS
GLEN O HARRISON
LEONARD G HARSY
CLAYTON D HART
RUSSELL C HART
BEVERLY T HASKELL
ROBERT E HATCH
HAROLD P HAUGLAND
EDDIE V HAWKINS
JULIUS W HAWKINS
ROLAND HAYES
BOBBY L HAYNES
EARNEST HAYNES
LEWIS E HAYS
RAYMOND L HEARREN
WAYNE D HEATH
JOSEPH L HEFLIN
MERLIN A HEINECKE
THEODORE HEMPHILL
HAZEN C HENDRICK JR
PAUL E HENDRICKS
BRUNO R HENKE
BENNIE HENSON
HARRY L HENSON
WILLARD F HERITAGE
PEDRO E HERNAEZ
FLORENTIN G
HERNANDEZ
RODOLFO L
HERNANDEZ
JAMES F HERRIMAN
BERNARD R HEWITT
NORVAL L HICKS
OSCAR A HICKS JR
RICHARD C HICKS
ANSEL C HIERS
EDWARD D HIGGINS
EARL E HILGENBERG

76 ARMY

JESSE E HILL
OWEN T HILL
PHILIP J HILL
HARRY HILLENBRAND
ROBERT R HILLYER
KENNETH E HINES
TALMAGE A HINSON
AXEL HIRSCHBERGER
ALBERT S HLOUSEK
EVERETT A F HO
RAYMOND H HOGARTH
CLARENCE S HOGUE
THOMAS E HOGUE
JOHN K HOLBURN
ELMER E HOLCOMB
RAY E HOLDER
THOMAS E HOLLEY
ROBERT L HOLLIS
JOHN H HOLMAN
PAUL E HOMIER
JOHN HOMOLA
EVERETTE T HONAKER
WALTER L HOOD
JOHN G HOPE JR
DANIEL D
HOPFENSPERGER JR
WILLARD H HOPKINS
HERMAN J HORN
JOSEPH H HORNER
HOWARD HOSKINS
PATRICK J HOULIHAN
ALFRED O HOVE
ALBERT HOWARD
WALTER R HOWARD
RAMON L HUBER
WILLIAM F HUBERT
DOVER C HUDSON
HARRY C HUDSON JR
ACY HUFFMAN
GERALD L HUFFMAN
JOE A HUFFSTUTLER
GEORGE L HUGHES
COLEMAN C HUNDLEY
JAMES A HUNNICUTT
CHARLES W HURD JR
IRWIN M HURST
DONALD J HURT
LAWRENCE W HUTCHENS
ROSS E HUTCHINSON
WILLIAM F HUTTON JR
JOSEPH W HYNES
JOE D IBANEZ
CLAYTON G IBBOTSON
BYEONG-CHUN IM
BYEONG-HWA IM
GWANG-SU IM
JIN-YONG IM
CHARLES H IMHOF
SAMUEL D INGHRAM
DONALD J JACKSON
ELMAN JACKSON
HENRY A JACKSON
JAMES R JACKSON
NEWTON C JACKSON
OTIS L JACKSON
ARTHUR C JAGNOW
EDWARD JAKUBOWSKI
HENRY P JAMES
JESSIE J JAMES
EUGENE C JAYNES
ROBERT L JENNINGS
CHEON-SU JEONG
HAN-GI JEONG
ARTHUR F JEWETT
BYEONG-SEOP JIN
CHANG-GYU JO
YEONG-JE JO
CORNELIUS A JOCHIM
JOHN E JOENS
DUKE JOHNSON
JOE L JOHNSON
JOHN E JOHNSON
JOHN E JOHNSON
ROBERT F JOHNSON
ROBERT H JOHNSON
ROY L JOHNSON
WILLIAM F JOHNSON
JACK A JOLLIFF
LOVELL P JOLLYMORE
CHARLIE F JONES
DONALD J JONES
DWIGHT D JONES
EARL E JONES
EMERSON L JONES
LESTER O JONES
SAM JONES
WILLIE M JONES
ALFRED S JORDAN
BARNEY H JORDAN
JACK M JORDAN
LOUIS J JORDAN
TAEK-JUNG JU
JAMES W JUST
ELDEN C JUSTUS
CASIMER P KACZOR
EMIL L KACZROWSKI
KENNETH KAISER JR
HERBERT KALAMA
JOSEPH R KAMBIC
DAVID T KANESHIRO
CLYDE W KAPPUS
BENJAMIN KASMEROVITZ
THEODORE A KATSOOLIAS
LOREN R KAUFMAN
RICHARD A KEAGLE
RICHARD E KEANE
JAMES C KEATHLEY
JAMES W KEITH
ROBERT B KELDER
JOHN C KELLER
DOUGLAS F KELLY
GUY B KELLY JR
OBIE L KELLY
VIRLEN E KELLY
GILBERT A KEMNITZ
DON L KEMP
JESSE R KENDRICK
CHARLES R KENLEY
EDWARD L KENNEDY
DUANE E KENT
WILLIAM J KEPPEL JR
JOHN J KERBY
JOSEPH J KEREKES
EDWARD M KEYS
GEORGE D KEYS
GERALD E KEYSER
GENINE KIDD
JOHN H KILROY
DEOK-TAE KIM
DONG-JU KIM
GI-SEOK KIM
GWANG-TAE KIM
IN-HAN KIM
JEON-GON KIM
JI-TAE KIM
JONG-CHEOL KIM
MAN-JIN KIM
PAL-YEONG KIM
SANG-JUN KIM
TAE-WON KIM
YEONG-DONG KIM
YEONG-GEUN KIM
YEONG-GWAN KIM
YEONG-SIK KIM
YEONG-SUK KIM
YONG-DEUK KIM
COLONEL J KIMBROUGH
FLOYD KINARD
ARTHUR S KINDER JR
ANDREW W KING IV
JAMES E KING
WILLIAM J KING
CARLIE P KIRBY
HENRY G KISER
CHARLES M KLEIN
WILLIAM L KLEIN
CHARLES KLUGE
JOHN KLUNK
RAYMOND KLUSSMANN
GEORGE N KNECHT
HARRY J KNICKERBOCKER
GEORGE J KNIGHT
HARRY H KNOTTS
ALBERT KNOX JR
DALE L KOBBEMAN
JOHN G KOHL
GEORGE W KOON
PAUL KOSCO
HARRY A KRAUSS
JOHN KRIMSKY
GEORGE A KRIZAN
JOSEPH KRUPA
LADDIE KRUPA
WAYNE A KUEHN
ADAM KULOVICH
MINORU KUNIEDA
EDWARD J KUZNIAR
ROBERT E LABORDE
IVAN E LACY
JAMES T LADD
HOWARD D LADIEU
ARNETT LAMB
RUDOLPH J LAMBERT
ROBERT E LANDES
DONALD R LANE
HOWARD L LANE
LEE W LANGEBERG
LYLE M LANGLITZ
ANTHONY J LANZE JR
FREDERICK E LARKIN
VERNON G LARMAN
FLOYD R LARNEY
ROBERT J LAROSE
BERTIL S LARSON
MIKE LATANATION
ROBERT M LAUER
DAVID R LAWSON JR
ROBERT R LAWSON
WESLEY C LAWSON
MAX L LEAR
JOHN N LEARY
JOSEPH F LEBOW
ALFRED B LEDBETTER
AUBREY LEDFORD
THEODORE W LEDOUX
GEUN-SIK LEE
GYEONG-U LEE
HYO-GAP LEE
IN-DAL LEE
RAYMOND H LEE
WILLIE E LEE
YEONG-JUN LEE
YUN-HO LEE
GEORGE S LEIBRAND
LELAND P LEMAY
CLIFFORD E LEMERE
JOSEPH J A LEMIEUX
GRANT W LENEAUX
FRANK J LEWANDOWSKI
ARTHUR E LEWIS
EARL C LEWIS
GORDON P LEWIS
JAMES M LEWIS JR
JOE D LEWIS JR
OLEN LEWIS
ERNEST A LIGGETT JR
FRANK M LINN
HENRY LIPSHAY
BILLIE G LITCHFIELD
EARL LITTLE
JOHN P LITTLE
THOMAS R LLOYD
LLOYD M LOCKE
VERNON H LOCKLAR
CARTER B LOGAN JR
JOHNNIE R LONG
VAN W LONG
OTIS W LOOMIS
EVANGELIO LOPEZ
WILLIAM J LOVILL
THEODORE E LOWERY
HAROLD S LUND
JAMES E LUNSFORD
EDWARD J LUTY
DEAN LYLES
DAN G LYNCH
JACK W LYTLE
KERMIT A MAASS
DEWEY F MACCLINTOCK
DELBERT U MACE
LENTON L MACK
WILLIAM A MACKEAN
JAMES W MADDOX
GERALD D MADEL
FRANK Y MAHER
PHILIP F MANIS
ALPHONSE
MANITOWABI
J W MANN
ANTHONY J MANNINO
HECTOR A MARIANI-
PERALTA
CHRISTOPHER C
MARION JR
JAMES F MARLAR
HENRY A MARNEY
BERNARD H MARQUARDT
HARRY A MARSHALL
EDWARD W MARTIN
HENRY C MARTIN
JOHN R MARTIN
LELAND M MARTIN
TERRY C MARTIN
HENRY MARTINEZ
BURKE J MASON
ROBERT L MASSENGALE JR
GEORGE C MASSEY JR
EDWARD W MATCHETT
LEONARD J MATHERS
ROY L MATHIS
HOWARD K MATLACK
DONALD L MATTINGLY
WALTER A MATTSON
WILLIAM F MAUS
HOMER I MAY
LINCOLN C MAY
MAX E MAYNARD
NORMAN K MAYNARD
JOHN F MCALLISTER
KENNETH A MCALLISTER
JOHN H MCCALL
KEITH V MCCASLIN
CARL E MCCLAFLIN
FREDERICK F MCCLAIN
HARLAN E MCCLELLAN
STEVE MCCLOUD
JOHN S MCCLURE
TOM N MCCLURE
WILLIAM E MCCORMICK
WILLIAM F MCCOWN
CURTIS C MCCRARY
MARK F MCCREARY
RICHARD C MCDOLE
KENNETH J MCDONALD
JOHN M MCDONNELL
THOMAS L MCDONOUGH
LESLIE D MCDOUGAL
JUNIOR R MCDOWELL
CLAY J MCGARRITY
DEWEY E MCGEHEE
JOHN F MCGOVERN
THOMAS A MCINNIS
NEIL S MCKENZIE
ARNOLD E MCKINNEY
EDWARD MCKINNEY
BRUCE D MCKOWN
KENNETH R MCLEISTER
JOHN W MCLELLAN
JAMES E MCLEROY
ARTHUR MCMILLIAN
RAYMOND K MCMILLIAN
DELMAS MCNEAL
BILLIE W MCNUTT
ELLIS G MCPHERSON
VANCE R MCQUISTON
ROY MCROBERTS
BERNARD V MCSORLEY
JOHN L MEAD
EMMETTE S MEADOWS
JAKE MEFFORD JR
EDWARD H MEHMEN
NICK A MEICK
ARNOLD MEIER
KENNETH N MELLICK
ERNEST J MELZER
JOHNNIE V MENA
JAMES L MENATOLA
PHILLIP C MENDOZA
RAYMOND MENDOZA
PAUL G MENTZOS
DONALD H MENZ
ATANACIO MERCADO
WILLIAM N MERCER
RICHARD H MERVIN
KENNETH M MESEL
EDGAR E MICHALEK
ANDREW P MIHOVCH
CHARLES W MILAM
WILLIAM T MILES JR
ALBERT H MILLER JR
GEORGE D MILLER
GRANT S MILLER
JACK H MILLER
MILAN E MILLER
OSCAR W MILLER
QUINTON E MILLER
ROBERT E MILLER
ROY W MILLER
THOMAS F MILLER
BENJAMIN H MILLIKEN
LAWRENCE W MILLS
JESSE L MIMS
CHARLES W MINARD
ROBERT W MINCH
WALLACE T MINNICH
ALBERT MINTZ
ALVIN C MITCHELL
HILTON L MITCHELL
HOWARD L MITCHELL JR
JOHNNIE MITCHELL
LINUS D MITCHELL
SHIRLEY MITCHELL
WILLIAM P MITCHELL
KERMIT M MITCHELTREE
GEORGE MOLENAAR
PAUL MONACO
ANGELO MONGIARDO
HAROLD W
MONTGOMERY
CHARLES V MOODY
JOHN I MOODY
GEORGE MOOIKI
ARTHUR L MOORE
CARL MOORE
CHESTER H MOORE
GEORGE H MOORE
HENRY F MOORE
JACK S MOORE
JOHN H MOORE
JOHN U MOORE
WILLIAM E MOORE
WILLIAM R MOORE
WILLIE L MOORE
LLOYD W MOREAU
ALBERT MORGAN
CHARLES C MORGAN
RALPH E MORGAN
TOMMIE L MORGAN
CLARENCE A MORRIS
NEAL M MORRIS
NICHOLAS MORRIS
PRINCE H MORRIS
EDWARD W MORTON
SAMUEL L MOSELEY
EMMETT D MOSS
WILLIAM H MOSS
EARL D MOULTON
WILLIAM C MOXLEY
DONALD R MOYER
JOHN T MOYNIHAN
CLIFFORD B MUIR
BERNARD MULLEN
JESSE MUNCY
MIKE H MUNDY
GRAHAM B MUNGER
MERLE C MUNSON
FRED MURPHY JR
RICHARD H MURPHY
MELVIN R MUSGRAVE
ARTHUR E MUSGROVE
GEORGE MUSICK
EUGENE L NABOZNY
KENNETH D NADEAU
CHARLES NAPIER
RICHARD L NASH
WALTER E NAUGLE
FRANK A NEAL
KENNETH E NEFF
JOHN H NELSON
ROBERT C NELSON
GORDON P NESS
JOEL C NEWBERRY
JAMES A NEWMAN
CHARLES L NIBERT
EDMUND H NICHOLS
WILLIAM H NICHOLSON
JAMES R NICODEMUS
KENICHI NISHIYAMA
DONALD G NITZ
JOSEPH J NOKES

77 ARMY

LAWRENCE T NOLAN
RICHARD C NONEMAKER
CARL L NORMAN
WADSWORTH A NORREN
MERVIN G NORRIS
DONALD R NORTHRUP
CHARLES G NORTON
RICHARD A NOYES
HENRY C NUNNERY
LEWIS N NUTTER
ROBERT B NYE
ORVILLE J NYQUIST
CHEOL-HU O
NICHOLAS OBROVAC
PAUL H OCONNELL
NEWMAN R ODOM
JEROME L OLEARY
CARL C OLSEN
PAUL OLSON
PAUL ONDREY
CLIFTON C ORR
CLYDE ORR
WARD B ORR
EDISON M OSBORN
PAUL H OSHIRO
GEORGE M OUTLAW
ANDREW H OWENS
HEBER R PADGETT
ROLLYN E PALM
ANDREW S PALSA
RICHARD E PANN
GLENDON J PARENTI
EDMOND G PARISH
GIL-SU PARK
IL-GYU PARK
JAE-YONG PARK
JONG-MUK PARK
PAN-AM PARK
U-HYEON PARK
U-SAM PARK
YANG-GEUN PARK
YEONG-GYU PARK
CLIFFORD A PARKER
HERBERT F PARKER
JOHN W PARKER
JOSE M PARRA
EARNEST B PARRIS JR
LEVANT S PARSELL
CARSON L PARSONS
FARRELL PARTON
ROBERT W PASKE
ALFRED J PATNAUDE
JOHN W PATON
JAMES J PATRICK
EDWARD PAVLAK
CHARLIE W PAYNE
FERNANDO S PENA
RAYMOND D PENLAND
EDWARD L PENN
EUGENE PENNINGTON
JUAN A PEREZ
ALBERT A PERRY
ERNEST H PERRY
THOMAS H PERRY
ALFRED M PERSON JR
FORREST L PETERS
EARL W PETERSON
EDWARD J PETERSON
JOHN H PETERSON
MICHAEL J PETRO
GEORGE E PETT
VERNON L PETTIGREW
THOMAS P PETTIT
RAY T PEVEHOUSE
JOHN P PHILLIPS
FREDDIE F PICKENS
CHARLIE F PIGFORD
HAROLD L PINNELL
RUSSELL C PINNELL
JOHN Z PLANT JR
FRANCIS POLKA
MAJOR E POOLE
JOHN W POOR
FRED L POPPELL
EARL G PORTER
ENOCH S PORTER
OLIVER PORTER
THOMAS R PORTER
JACK K POST
CLARENCE E POSTETHWAIT

EDWARD M POULSEN
FORREST E POWELL
GEORGE POWELL
JAMES M POWELL
JAIRUS E POWERS
ROBERT F PRATER
LAWRENCE H PRATHER
PAUL E PRATHER
EDWARD J PRATT
DANIEL E PRESTON
ALBERT L PRICE
WILLIAM E PRICE
ROY D PROBST
PRESTON J PROFFITT
ROBERT F PRUE
JAMES T PRUEITT
ALEXANDER P PRZYBYSZ
GASTON PUGH
HENRY PUGH JR
CHARLES D QUARLES
MARION A QUILLEN
JOHN RACICH
WILLIAM C RADFORD
ISRAEL RAMOS
PABLO RAMOS
ROLAN D RARICK
CHARLES H RAY
DUAARD L RAY
HAROLD C RAY
HAROLD R RAY
LOUIS A RAYMOND
ROBERT REAGER
ROBERT C REASOR
MARK REDD
FRANK T REDDICK
FRANK M REDMON JR
CLIFFORD M REEVES
JAMES A REICHARD
EUGENE A REID
WILLIAM B REINHARDT
HARRY W REITZE SR
RAY REMORIN
DONALD G RENSTROM
JAMES O REPLOGLE
GERARD L RESTEL
JOHN T REYES
JAMES C REYNOLDS
VAN W REYNOLDS
GEORGE M RHOADMAN JR
HAROLD L RHODES
BARTOLOME S RIBAC
JOHN R RICE
RONALD D RICH
CHARLES A RICHARDS
ALEXANDER RICHARDSON
HOYLE T RIDDLE
NORMAN A RIDDLE
CHARLES RIDDLEBAUGH
WILLIAM G RIDEL
ROBERT J RIDINGS
OLIVER P RIELS
LOUIS RIVARDO
ANDREW C RIVERA
ANGEL H RIVERA
ADOLFO RIVERA-ORTIZ
MARION RIVERS
MELVIN C RIVERS
MICHAEL ROBANKE
EUGENE A ROBENOLT
GORDON G ROBERTS
MARION O ROBERTS
ALLAN R ROBERTSON
HERBERT E ROBERTSON
WILLIAM J ROBERTSON
JAMES ROBINSON
WALTER R ROBINSON
WILLIAM ROBINSON
MARVIN L RODMAN
ROBERT J RODMAN
JOHN RODRIGUEZ
ALEXANDER ROESSLER
BENNY D ROGERS
CLYDE N ROGERS
DONALD C ROGERS
RAYMOND C ROGERS
WYLLIS P ROGERS
JOSEPH J ROMAN
CARLOS R ROMAN-BRULL
DONATO ROMAN-
REICHARD

PETER R ROMEO
ADAM M ROMERO
MARTIN Z ROMERO
MIGUEL A ROMERO
LUTHER V ROMINGER
NILS O RONNQUIST
FRANK D RORRER
JUAN ROSARIO-MORALES
EDWARD M ROSE
GEORGE F ROSECRANTS
EMANUEL ROSS
HAROLD E ROSS
ROBERT E ROSS
WALTER A ROSS JR
DAVID C ROUSE
RICHARD B ROUSSEL
DON E ROWLEY
WAYNORD W ROWLEY
CHARLES A ROY
FLOYD A ROY
LEFF V ROYAL
WILLIE ROYAL
WILLARD A RULE
EMMITT RUSSELL
ERNEST F RUSSELL
GORDON C RUSSELL
HELMAR O RUSTH
FOSTINE R RUTLEDGE JR
LEEROY R RYAN
ELPIDIO M SAGISI
JAMES W SAMPSON
DONALD D SANBORN
EARL C SANDERS
JOHN W SANDERS
CONCEPCION SANTANA
LUIS F SANTANA
JUAN SANTIAGO
RAMON SANTIAGO-
ROSARIO
HARRY J SAUNDERS
THEODORE A SCHIERMAN
HARVEY T SCHINKAL
EUGENE O SCHMID
GEORGE C SCHMIDT JR
WILLIAM R SCHOOLCRAFT
JAMES A SCHOOLER
DAVID A SCHREFFLER
ROBERT C SCHREIBER
DARRELL H SCOTT
JEROME F SEARS
OSCAR G SEGOBIA
RAY D SELBY
LARRY E SELL
ELLIS SELLERS
PEDRO SEMIDEY
DONALD W SENTZ
IN-SU SEO
CUSTER SERBASCEWICZ
LUTHER D SERWISE
FRANKIE W SHAFFIER
GEORGE J SHANK
HARRY M SHARPLESS
JOSEPH C SHATTAS
LYLE L SHAUL
CLARENCE H SHAW
ERNIE C SHAW
NEALON C SHAY JR
THOMAS E SHEMWELL
RAY A SHEPHERD
JAMES W SHEPPARD
JAMES H SHERRELL
ALTON L SHIRTZ
FRANCIS E SHOEMAKER
JAMES P SHUNNEY
WAYNE C SHURBET
JOHN M SIEWIELSKI
ALBERT W SIGLEY JR
JOSEPH C SIKORA
BILLIE L SIMMONS
CLARENCE A SIMMONS
JAMES B SIMON
PETE W SIMON
HERMAN I SIMPKINS
LEWIS SIMPSON
WILLIAM W SIMPSON
ROBERTO SIQUEIROS-
GAMEZ
ANDREW SISSACK
WILLIAM S SITMAN
LESTER R SITTON JR

LEONARD P SLAGLE
OLIVER W SLAUGHTER
HERBERT N SLEETH
JAMES C SLEMP
WALLACE L SLIGHT
LOUIS E SLUSARSKI
EARL W SMALL
JAMES R SMILEY
ALBERT D SMITH
BILLY R SMITH
DELBERT W SMITH
DELMA B SMITH
EARL K SMITH
ERNEST E SMITH
HARRY S SMITH
HOWARD A SMITH
IRA B SMITH
JOHN SMITH
JOHN E SMITH
JOHN F SMITH
LAWRENCE J SMITH
LEOTIS Q SMITH
RICHARD W SMITH
ROBERT K SMITH
RUDY B SMITH
TRAVIS SMITH
WILLIAM L SMITH
WINFORD D SMITH
HARVEY H SMOAK
CLARENCE O
SMOTHERMON JR
COMER SMOTHERS
ROBERT I SNIDER
JOHN SNIPE
LEON S SNIPES
MILNOR L SOLBERG
LESLIE H SOLOMON
RAYMOND SONEILLAN
RALPH E SOOY
LEWIS W SOWLES
GOVAN L SPELLS
WAYMON SPENCE
RICHARD SPON
JOHNNIE H SPRUELL
JOHN M SQUIER
VIRGIL L STAMBAUGH
MACK STAMPER JR
JOSEPH E STANCEL
ORLIN C STANCHFIELD
GERALD L STANTON
RODEY D STAPP
GAYLORD W STARK
GERALD F STEDMAN
JOHN W STEELE
JOSEPH D STEINBERG
HENRY J STEPHANY
CHESTER G STEPHENSON
JAMES F STEVERSON JR
JAMES W STEWART
PAUL E ST JULIEN
JEROME H STOFFEL
CHARLES A STONE
RICHARD T STONE
BENNY R STOVER
KARL J STREETER
JAMES S STREETMAN JR
FORREST T STRONG
BILLY O STUBBLEFIELD
DONALD R STURM
HENRY R STUTTE
JOHN P SUGGS
WILLIAM W SULLIVAN
L D SUMMERLIN
EDDIE C SUMMERS
CLEVE SUMPTER
MARVIN J SUMPTER
DANIEL H SUTTON
HARRY C SUTTON
LLOYD L SUTTON
WILLIAM R SWARMER
DONALD W SWEETALL
STANLEY B SWINSINSKI
DONALD L SYBRANT
MICHAEL G SZOLLOSY
JAMES L TABOR
ROBERT B TAGGART
CHARLES S TAHARA
GEORGE TAKAHASHI
JACK F TALBOT
MARCIAL M TANGENTE

HERBERT TARNOPOL
HERSHEL L TATE
RAYMOND W TATRO
NICHOLAS R TAWEEL
MASAO TAYAMA
IRA N TAYLOR
JAMES H TAYLOR
JAMES H TAYLOR
MOTT TAYLOR JR
HOWARD C TENLEY
CHARLES D TENNISON
THEODORE M TERKOS
WILLARD N TESSIN
GEORGE L THAYER
CALVIN M THEIS
ROMEO G THERIAULT
CHARLES C THOMAS
WILLIE L THOMAS
EULIS D THOMASSON
HERBERT THOMPKINS
JACK S THOMPSON
JAMES R THOMPSON
OGDEN N THOMPSON
PHILIP R THOMPSON
RAYMOND R THORNTON
GEORGE S THORSEN
THOMAS J TIGHE
WILEY J TIPTON
EUGENE L TIRADO
HERBERT R TISON
JAMES O TRENT
KENNETH W TREPTAU
WILLIAM A TRIPP
JOHN J TRUAN
ISIDRO E TRUJILLO
WILLIAM J TSCHUSCHKE
CHARLES W TURNER
JAMES L TURNER
LEON H TUTT
JACK O TYE
EDWARD M UHL
ONIS L ULERICK
CURT W ULRICH
RAY C UNDERWOOD
JOHN W VAGG
JOHN VAILLANCOURT
ERNEST VALDEZ
JOSEPH F VALENCOURT
NICHOLAS J VALENTINE
LEONARD J VANATA
JAMES VANDERGAST
DONALD F VAN DINE
CLARENCE L VANHOOSE
IRVING VAN HORN
HENRI J VASCHETTO
ROBERT T VAUGHN
JOSEPH F VAVROCH JR
JORGE L VAZQUEZ
JOAQUIN
VAZQUEZ-CRUZ
ALBERT W VEENSTRA
CECIL T VEIT
FRANK G VEJAR
RODOLFO VELEZ
ALBERT L VERCOLEN
JOSEPH E VIATOR
EDRIS A VIERS
RUBEN VILCHES
JESUS VILLARREAL
RAUL Q VILLARREAL
DONALD C VINSON
JOSEPH C VOGEL
RUFUS E VOIGT
VIRGIL H VOLK
EDDIE G WADFORD
BURTON A WAGNER
DANNY L WAGNER
KENNETH E WAITE
EUGENE L WALDO
EDWARD S WALDOCH
ARTHUR T WALDROP
EARL F WALKER
JESSE L WALKER
LESTER R WALKER
PAUL A WALL
CALVIN E WALLINGFORD
JAMES J WALSH
JAMES C WALTERS
GENE C WARD
JESSIE T WARD

78 ARMY

CLARENCE E WARE
KENNETH F WARNER
T P WARREN
FRED WATERS
WILLIE J WATKINS
MICHAEL R WATSON
SAMUEL E WATSON
CECIL H WATTERS
JEROME H WAX
N D WEARY
JOHN E WEBER
WILLIAM J WEBER
DONALD L WEBSTER
DONALD N WEBSTER
JOSEPH O WEBSTER
WILLIAM A WEBSTER
WILLIAM P WEHRLE
JAMES R WEINGARTNER
OLEBIA B WELDON
BOBBY L WELLS
RAYMOND G WELLS
DAVE W WENTZEL
CARL WEST
PAUL R WEST
WILLIAM H WEST
JOHN F WESTFALL
VERNON C WESTON
VERNON D WHEELDON
JOHN N WHEELER
CHARLES E WHITAKER
CLYDE E WHITAKER
GRACEON H WHITE
ALFRED WHITSON
JAMES A WHITTEN
WILLIE C WILBANKS
ROBERT W WILBURN
ROBERT B WILCOX
BEAUFORD E WILKINS
JAMES L WILKINSON
DALE E WILLIAMS
DAVID WILLIAMS
GAYLON S WILLIAMS
HARDY L WILLIAMS
JAMES H WILLIAMS
JAMES J WILLIAMS JR
RELDA H WILLIAMS
ROBERT M WILLIAMS
STANLEY R WILLIAMS
BERT L WILLIS
CHARLES R WILSON
GENERAL J WILSON
HENRY C WILSON
JAMES E WILSON
JERRY D WILSON
ROBERT F WILSON
EARL V WISE
JOHN L WISKOSKI
GORDON WITHERSPOON
ALBERT J WITTMANN JR
LAWRENCE R WOFFORD
EUNG-SIK WON
JAMES L WOOD
KENNETH E WOOD
PAUL L WOOD
EARLE L WOODARD
JOEL G WOODARD JR
FRED WOODBURN
RICHARD H WOODS
ERNEST A WOODWARD
AUDREY H WOOSTER
ARTHUR J WOOTEN
CECIL L WOOTEN
WALTER E WORTHEN
MILLARD R WRIGHT
DAVID H WUSTRACK
RUBLE W WYATT
EDWARD T YACKENT
DONALD E YAHNKE
NOBUJI YAMAGATA
NELSON W YARGAR
JACKIE C YATES
BRUCE J YEAGER
FLOYD J YELL JR
LEO B YELLE
ROBERT B YONTS
JOHN D YOUNG
MERLE W YOUNG
NORMAN YOUNG
GI-SEON YUN
HA-DAL YUN

JOSEPH ZAGAR
LEONARD F ZAHORIK
MANUEL G ZARAGOZA
JOHN C ZAVALICK
MICHAEL F ZIMMERMAN
RALPH L ZINCK
GORDON J ZORN

MASTER SERGEANT

J C ABBOTT
RICHARD F ABBOTT
RAYMOND J ADAMS
ROBERT A ADAMS
ROBERT E ADAMS
TROULIUS ADAMS
RICHARD AGUAYO
HYPOLITE A ALEXANDER
ERNEST R ALLEN
JOHN P ALLEN
ALFRED H ALONZO SR
JOHN ANDERSON
LEONARD W ANDERSON
ROBERT E ANDERSON
CHARLES W ANTHONY
ALEXANDER D ARICK
JAMES L ARMOUR
DONALD W ARNESON
FREDERICK B ARNOLD
DOMINO T AVELINO
EVERETT J AXTELL
DONALD J AYEN
RAY C BAILEY
LEON BAIRD
CLAUDE F BAKER
BENJAMIN B BALDWIN
EDWARD BALL
RAFAEL E BALZAC
CHARLES M BAMFORD
GEORGE R BANKS
NORMAN L BANNISTER JR
ALBERT L BARBER
JAY T BARE
WILLIAM R BARKER
ROY E BARROW
JOSEPH T BASS
STANLEY R BATOR
ALLEN A BAUGHMAN
RICHARD R BEARD
JOSEPH C BEAUCHEMIN
ALFRED BEAUCHESNE
CLYDE N BECKETT JR
RUSSELL F BEHRINGER
JOHN A BELAVIC
HERBERT D BELL
ARCHIE K BELLON
CLAUDE C BELT
A D BERRY
GEORGE W BERRY
JOHN BESKID JR
LEONARD J BEST
BRUNO D BEVIVINO
ROBERT P BIBB
JAMES A BIRCH
WILLIAM W BJORK
JAMES M BLACK
WINFIELD M BLACK
EUGENE O BLACKSTON
THOMAS W BLANCHARD
CLOIS M BLUE SR
JAMES V BOGGS
ROBERT H BOHL
ROSARIO J BOISSE
HERBERT E BOLEY
GEORGE O BOOS
EVERETT H BORLEY
WILLIAM A BOST
JOHN G BOUCHER
RICHARD E BOWMAN
MARVIN L BOYCE
WILLIE C BOYCE
RUSSELL BRACKEN
GEORGE W BRADLEY
ELDRIDGE BRADY
CLIFTON C BRAGG
CHARLES S BRANCH
MELVIN L BRANT
HARRY BRASSFIELD

LOUIS W BRATTON
GORDON L BRAXTON
RAYMOND I BRIGGS
PAUL BRINSON
IVAN P BRISTOW
HERMAN L BROTHERS
WOODROW W
BROUSSARD
ANTHONY E BROWN
CHARLES J BROWN JR
GARLAND S BROWN
WILLIE L BROWN
PAUL J BROWNING
OSCAR E BRUNER
MORRIS N BRYANT
WILLIAM J BRYANT
EDWARD J BUCHOLTZ
EUGENE BUCKALEW
JACK Y BUFF
LEE A BUFFINGTON SR
ROBERT J BUNNELL
STERLING M BURDICK
RAYMOND L BURKE
JOHN J BURKETT
WADUS H BURNAMAN
CHARLES E BURNS
JAMES L BURNS
GUENTHER A BURRER
KENDALL BURROUGHS
CHARLES BURTON
KENNETH BUTCHER
CHARLES C BUTLER
CONLEY E BYRD
EDWARD H CAINE
CARLIS J CALLAHAN
ROSCOE C CAMPBELL
ARTURO CANTU
JESUS R CANTU
HERBERT G CAPERTON
RONALD L CAPTAIN
LOUIS CAPUTO
LOUIS J CARIATI SR
JOHN H CARLSON
BENJAMIN F CARR
RALPH R CARR
RAYMOND E CARROLL
FRANK M CASSETTA
ROMEO J CASTONGUAY
JAMES G CATES
CARLTON R CATON
LEWIS W CHAMBERS
HERMAN CHAPMAN
SAM CHAPMAN
WILLIAM M CHAPMAN
LEONARD K CHINN
HERBERT W CHIPMAN
FLOYD V CHITWOOD
ALPHONSU CHOLEWSKY
EARL A CHRISTENSEN
JERRY C CHRISTENSEN
RAYMOND C S CHUNG
JOSEPH P CIDADE
JAMES S CLAYBORNE
OWEN L CLAYCOMB
RUSSELL E CLAYMON
CLAUDE A CLAYTON
THEODORE C CLAYTON
RAYMOND T CLEMENT
CLARIEL M CLEVENGER
JAMES M COCHENOUR
ROBERT M COFFMAN
KENNETH C COGDILL
JOHN M COLE JR
JOSEPH L COLEMAN
WALTER COLLETT
DENNIS J COLLINS
DONALD W COMINS
ROBERT E CONANT
LESTER CONARD
HARVEL L CONE
ULYSSES CONELY
THOMAS J CONNORS
JESSE R COOKSEY
HAROLD R COOPER
MATTHEW R CORY
RAYMOND V COSTELLO
METRO COSTON
RICHARD C COULTER
JOHN J CRAIG
RUSSELL L CRAMPTON

CHARLES E CRAWFORD
ROBERT L CRAWFORD
THOMAS CRAYTON
LEONARD O CREECH
ALBERT N CURTIS
KENNETH H DALLY
CARL J DANIELSON
ALEX DANOWSKI
WILLIAM P DARAH
CHESTER DAVIDOWSKI
ALFRED L DAVIS
BANARD R DAVIS
FINLEY J DAVIS
JOHN G DAVIS JR
MADISON L DAVIS
RICHARD DAVIS
RICHARD F DAVIS
TIMOTHY DAVIS
WILLIE M DAVIS
SALVATORE DE COSTA
ERNEST D DENHAM
VIVAN DENNIS
THEE O DERRICK
JOSEPH G DEWS
JAMES K DIONNE
WILLIAM R DIXON
ROBERT B DOBBIE
LAVERNE H DODGE
BILLY G DONAHOE
TELLIS W DONALDSON
GEORGE T DONOVAN
ROBERT V DOWLING
DAVID B DRAWDY
HUGH J DRENNEN
HAROLD F DREWS
RICHARD F DROWN
JACK DUDLEY
RAY E DUKE
WYATT G DUNCAN JR
BYRON R DUNHAM
BERNARD A DUNLAP
J T DUNN
JOSEPH DURAKOVICH
LAMONT J DURFEE
RAYMOND R DYKES
ALBERT W DZINKOWSKI
JERRY J EADS
DONALD E EDWARDS
ROY E ELLIOTT
JAMES H ELLIS
CHARLES E ELMORE
PAUL T EMBREY
BERTRAM F EMERSON
WILLIAM C ENNIS
HOSEA L EVANS
MURL R EVANS
ROBERT L EVANS
LEONARD EVERS
CHARLES A FALK
WILLIAM G FARMER
MICHAEL C FASTNER
HAROLD M FAWCETT
LINO FELICIANO
GRANT R FETROW
MOJMIR P FICEK
WILLIAM W FINNER
GEORGE FIRMENT
JOHN M FISH
CHARLES E FITZGERALD
ROBERT J FITZGERALD JR
JOHN M FLEMING
HORRIE FLOWERS JR
THOMAS FLOYD
ELMER FLUELLEN
GERALD E FONDRY
ARTHUR F FORD
ISAAC D FORD
LEONARD FORD
THOMAS A FOREHAND
CARL F FOSTER
DAVID W FOSTER
RICHARD K FOSTER
ANDREW F FOUNTAIN
RAYFUS FRANKLIN
JOYCE E FREDERICKSEN
WILLIE L FREDRICK
RICHARD D FRESEN
AMADIO J FRIZZI
JESSE L FRY JR
JOHN FULTZ

THOMAS L GAINEY
ANDREW C GAVURNIK
ROBERT E GENTRY
WILLIAM D GERALD
JOHN O GIBSON
EUGENE C GILL
NORMAN L GLEATON
CLYDE GOE
GEORGE R GOETZ
ALPHONCE GOLDEN
JAMES L GOODIN
JOSEPH T GOYETTE
LUTHER GRACE
ERNEST W GRAINGER
LAWRENCE C GRAY SR
ELWOOD GREEN
JAMES D GREEN
NORMAN GREEN
JOHN GRIDLEY
CHARLES W GRIFFIN
THOMAS E GRISARD
JOE GULLEY
DALE R GUSTAFSON
JUN-HA GWON
WILLIAM L HACKNEY
HARRY G HAINES
RAYMOND
HALDENWANG
RICHARD A HALEY
ARTHUR J HALL
JOHN F HALL
ROBERT D HALL
BERNARD W HALLORAN
ROBERT L HAMMOND
RENE HAMMONDS
BILLIE HANCE
CHARLES L HANCOCK JR
MELVIN O HANDRICH
IRVIN E HANKEL
ARTHUR P HANKS
ROBERT T HANSEN
ELLWOOD F HANSON
WILLIAM W HANSON
IVON H HARDIN
EDGAR W HARDY
MARCUS L HARMON
STANLEY W HARMOR
ALTON E HARPER
RUSSELL D HARRINGTON
EDGAR H HARRIS
RUDOLPH HARRIS
JAMES HART JR
GEORGE E HARTWELL
MICHAEL HAVRILLA JR
WALTER R HAYES JR
JOHN E HAYNES
SANDY HAYS
ROY E HEAD
CLARENCE M HEADLEY
DELBERT E HEARD
RICHARD C HEATH
WALTER L HEE
CHARLES J HEMPHILL
JASPER N HENSLEY
EDWARD W HERETH
EUGENE H HERKLESS
PEDRO HERNANDEZ
JAMES M HEROLD
JOHN O HERRING
JOSEPH C HESTER
DONALD C HEWINS
IRVING W HEY
HENRY E HICKMAN
KENNETH A HICKS SR
NATHAN L HILL
CLYDE R HILTON
ROBERT N HINKEL
EDWARD L HLUBOKY
ANDREW D HOCKADAY
CHARLES W HOCKMAN
PAUL H HOKOANA
ARTHUR J HOLLAND
JIMMIE HOLLOWAY
CLARK L HOLMAN
JACK H HOLT
ROBERT G HOOVER
GEORGE R
HOUSEKEEPER JR
CALVIN C HOUSTON
HOWARD C HOVEY

ARNOLD L HOWARD
RAYMOND J HOWARD
WILLIAM G HOWARD JR
JAMES R HOWE
CHARLES C HUGHES
ERNEST D HUGHES
SPENCER V HUSKEY
ANDREW HUSZAR
VICTOR M IGLESIAS
PETER IMMORDINO
JAMES L INGRAM
JOHN R INYARD
CHARLEY B IRELAND
WILBUR A ISAACS
EDWARD M ISHIBASHI
EMMIT M IVY
DONOVAN J JACKSON
IRVIN L JACKSON
NORVAL E JACOBS
LEO J JAMES
ROY F JAMES
LEONARD D JANICKI
JOHN W JEAL
HOWARD R JEFFREY
FRANCIS R JENKINS
JOSEPH F JENNINGS
JAE-OK JIN
YONG-BOK JO
LAWRENCE O JOCK
ELMA H JOHNSON
ERVIN M JOHNSON
EUGENE P JOHNSON
FREDERICK W JOHNSON
GAYNOR T JOHNSON
LOUIS C JOHNSON
MELVIN M JOHNSON
RAYMOND R JOHNSON
THOMAS C JOHNSON
WILLIAM W JOHNSON
GEORGE J JONES
HERBERT C JONES
NATHANIEL G JONES
MICHAEL KARPINECZ
GEORGE R KAY
HIRAM L KE
FLOYD C KEENEY
CECIL D KELLEY
ERNEST M KELLY
JAMES C KELLY
WALTER J KELLY
ELVA L KEOPKE
BILLY M KERSHNER
JACOB M KEYSER
RALPH KIDD
KENNETH KILPATRICK
HYEON-GYU KIM
LIONEL KING
REGINALD W KING
SAMUEL L KING JR
WILLIE L KINGSLEY
JOHN D KINGTON
GEORGE H KINNEY
CLARENCE E KIRKNER
ERNEST S KNIGHTON
ALEXANDER S KNOX
DONALD L KOZLIK
LEO J KRAFT
LESTER E KRIHA
RAYMOND KRZYZANIAK
FRANCESZEK J KULIK
WILLIAM M KUNKEL
GEORGE L KYZER
ROBERT L LACEY
JAMES W LA FORGE
DELMAR J LA FRANCE
DITLEF J LAGONI
HARRY LAMBING JR
GEORGE H LAMITIE
CHARLES R LANDON
LAWRENCE A LANE
FRANKLIN J LASKOWSKY
JACK D LAWVER
ROBERT V LAYTON
ARTHUR LEE
CLARENCE O LEE
GYU-SEOP LEE
PAUL W LEGG
ELOIE D LEJEUNE
BENNIE Z LEMMONS
EDWARD W LEWIS JR

HAROLD W LEWIS
RALPH G LILLARD
MERITT T LILLEY
DAVID E LINDENAU
QUINTON E LINDLER
CARL H LINDQUIST
JOHN G LINKOWSKI
ERNEST LITTLE SR
HAROLD S LOEWENKAMP
JAMES W LONG
TOMMIE L LONG
CARLOS LOPEZ
DONALD H LOUDON
FREEMAN W LOUDON
EUTIQUIO J LUJAN
RICHARD S LUNA
LEO LUPTON
JESSE M LUSK
EDWARD T LYDON
ROBERT A MAAS
JOHN V MAGEE
ROBERT L MAGOON
HAROLD L MAIN
ISRAEL MALARET-JUARBE
ROBERT V MANN
ARTHUR E MANNING
GEORGE C MANRING
CHARLIE J MARES
EDWARD F MARES
OTTIS P MARK
DOMINIC F MARROCCO
HAROLD L MARSH
CARL D MARTIN
CLARENCE F MARTIN
ERNEST K MARTIN
FLOYD W MARTIN JR
JAMES M MARTIN
AMBROSIO MARTINEZ
DIONISIO MARTINEZ
WILLIAM J MARTIS
HAROLD A MASTERSON
ROY C MATHESS
WARD F MATHEWSON
ANTONIO MATOS-RIVERA
CLARENCE MATTHEWS
JAMES L MATTHEWS
RICHARD F MATTHEWS
JAMES MAXWELL
JAMES MAXWELL
MARSHALL M MAYES
HENRY L MCAFEE
JAMES D MCCAIN
ALBERT A MCCARTHY
ROBERT L MCCOLE
JOHN E MCCOY
CHARLES H MCDANIEL
EDWARD J MCDONALD
WARREN B MCDONALD
FRANCIS J MCDONNELL
MARSHALL H MCGEE
JAMES R MCGREW
GROVER J MCGRIFF
JOHN R MCINNIS
MILLARD E MCINTIRE
ARTHUR E MCLAUGHLIN
JOHN J MCLEOD
JOSEPH L MCNALLY
PRENTISS E MCPHATE
WILLIAM M
MCPHEETERS JR
RALPH A MCPHERSON
JOHN P MCQUADE
NORMAN MCQUEEN
JOHN L MCTAGGART JR
FREDERICK J MEDRANO
SELIA M MEEK
ED F MERCER
FELIX MICHAELISKI
GORDON G MICHEAU
ROBERT E MIDDLESWORTH
REX H MILES
EUGENE N MILLER
FLOYD MILLER JR
GERALD E MILLER
JAMES E MILLER
JAMES L MILLER
JOHN A MILLER
ROBERT E MILLER
JOHNNY A MILLON
MOSCO MILLS

IRA V MISS JR
JOHN H MITCHELL
GILBERT D MONTENEGRO
IVAN L MONTGOMERY
THOMAS C MOON
ALBERT MOORE
FRANK MOORE
ROBERT B MOORE
ROLAND A MOORE
WALTER L MOORE
CARMELO MORALES
DONALD S MORAN
ROBERT C MORRISON
WILLIAM R MORRISON
JOHN J MORROW
JAMES B MOTHERWAY
LESTER C MUELLER
ERVIN L MULDOON
JOSEPH F MUNDA
UVALDO M MUNGUIA
JACK MURPHY
FRED W MURRAY
JACK M MYERS
ROBERT H MYERS
IRVINE M NASON
LEWIS J NAYLOR
MICHAEL T NEGRICH
EDMUND W NEILSON
JOHN J NEJMAN
ROBERT C NELSON
EARL W NEWELL
ROBERT E NEWSOME
MARION M NEWTON
CARL W NIESTADT
WARREN T NISHIHARA
JOHN NOLAN
RICHARD NOLEN JR
ROBERT P NONEMAN
GERALD D NORDER
ANGEL L OCASIO
WILLIE E ODEN
CHARLES A OGDEN
FRANK J OLEYAR
DEMPSEY R OLIVER
NORMAN E OLSON
THEODORE OMALLEY
ANGEL L ORTIZ
JAMES E OVEREND
EDWARD V OWEN
PAUL PADGETT
MARK G PAGE
BERNARD M PALADINO
ZINO M PAMPANIN
THOMAS O PAPE
SEOK-JU PARK
JOHN F PARKER
ROBERT L PARKS
RONALD R PARKS
DONALD L PATCH
IRVING A PAYLOR
EDWIN E PEARSON
JOHN F PECKHAM
GROVER C PEGG JR
MIKE C PENA
LEON B PENDERGRASS
EDWARD F PERRY
GRAY P PETE
CLARENCE A PETERSON
OSCAR P PEVELER
DONALD R PHELPS
HUGH W PHILPOTT
DESMOND PIERCE
BERNARD S PINTER
GEORGE A PIXLEY
JAMES PLUMP
WAITCELL PLUNKETT
RAY POINT
RICHARD J POLLARD
JOSEPH POSTICK
HOLLIS POWELL
JOSEPH C POWELL
JOSEPH F PRAST
MERRITT L PRATT
FORREST L PRICE
THOMAS J PRICE
JAMES L QUONG
CLEON RABURN
EZEQUIEL H RAMIREZ
NOLAN R RAMSEY
FRED RANDLE

JOHN B RAPEE
JOHN J RASCHER
RAY R RAUGHT
ROBERT H REAMES
MICHAEL J REARDON
THOMAS P REILEY
GEORGE E RELIHAN
MANUEL J RENDON
JACK RENFRO JR
THOMAS R RENNER
CHARLES M RHODES
HAROLD P RICE
KENNETH S RICHARDS
WILLIAM H RICHARDS
VINCENT R RICKMAN
PAUL E RIESS
BRYAN K RIGGS
OSCAR V RIKKE
HOWARD C RILEY
RAY O RILEY
HAROLD L RINARD
CHARLES E ROACH
GORDON A ROBERTS
HOBSON J ROBERTS
JAMES P ROBERTSON
EMMETT ROBINSON
CLIFFORD R RODRIGUEZ
ALBERTO RODRIGUEZ-
LOZADA
JAMES E ROGERS JR
JOHN V ROMANEK
JACK F ROOT
ARTHUR ROSS SR
JOHN H ROSS
ULYSSES ROSS
RAYMOND E ROZYKA
BENJAMIN RUBIO
GEORGE E RUCHTY
LEO P RUSSAVAGE
JAMES P RUSSELL
JOHN W RUSSELL
CLIFFORD L RYAN
CHARLES SANCHEZ
BARNIE L SANFORD
JACK SAUM
THEODORE L SAUNDERS
ADDISON SCHANTZ JR
CHARLES V SCHEESER
WILLIAM H SCHELLENGER
RICHARD W SCHIM
HENRY SCHMIDT JR
WESLEY J SCHMIDT
RALPH H SCHOOLEY
GEORGE E SCHOONOVER
FLOYD M SCHROEDER
EMANUEL R SCHUBERT
EUGENE SCHULER
SAMUEL E SCOTT
ALBERT A SELF
HAROLD SELLS
CLYDE M SETTLEMYRE
CHARLES L SEWELL
WILLIAM F SHAW
J M SHEPHERD
EARL W SHERMAN
WILLARD H SHIPP
ALTON E SHIRLEY
GERALD R SHIRLEY
GLEN R SHISLER
JAMES G SHORMAN
HOWARD M SHUPP JR
LESTER G SIMERAL
ALLEN W SIMMONS
WALLACE SIMMONS JR
CLEMMIE SIMMS
FRANK SIMS
HENRY J SKINGER
DEWITT L SLAUGHTER
DAVID P SLUDER
CLARENCE D SMITH
CLAUDINE E SMITH
DAVID B SMITH
EARL J SMITH
GARRARD L D SMITH
JESSE C SMITH
JOHN D SMITH
LUIS SMITH
WENDALL C SMITH JR
GLENN A SNIDER
JAMES F SNODGRASS JR

HOMER L SNOWDEN
CHARLES R SOHLER
JOSEPH J SOLEM
CHARLES S SPARKS
KELTON SPEEGLE
MANUEL J SPOON
FRANCIS H STAMER
JAMES R STAPLETON
CLYDE M STARKEY
ROBERT A STEIN
JOHN J STEMPOWSKI
WILLIAM M STEPHENS
GEORGE STEPINA
GRAHAM STEWART
JAMES T STEWART
RICHARD H STEWART
NEALE S STINNER
KENNETH H STOKES
WALTER C STOKES
LLOYD H STONE
NARCISSE D ST ONGE
WOOLARD F
STRICKLAND
BRITTON R STRUBLE
EDWARD C STRYLOWSKI
HAMER S STUMBO
JOHN L STUMPF
JACK D SUMRALL
JOHN R SUTTON
ROBERT J SWEEZEY
BENNY S SWINIARSKI
JOSEPH SYSAK
IVA B TADLOCK
LEONARD M TALLEY
IRA N TAYLOR
ROBERT A TEDFORD
JAMES C TEIXEIRA
ROBERT N THACKER
EZELL THOMAS
REUBEN THOMPKINS
BEN THOMPSON
HOWARD S THOMPSON
JAMES O THOMPSON JR
CLYDE THORNBURG
FRED THREET
WILLIAM E TIMMONS
BIONDINI S TIRABOSCHI
PETER V TODARO
CHARLES R TODD
TED L TOLLESON
MARVIN E TOMLINSON
THOMAS F TONER
SIGMOND L TOTH
EDWIN R TRACY
DANIEL J TRAHAN
JAMES M TRAYLOR
JULIAN TRIBBLE
COOPER T TURNER
CHARLES C TWIGG
LESTER L UDENBERG
ALBERT VAILLANCOURT
CIRILDO VALENCIO
BOB S VALERA
RALPH J VANGSNESS
HARVEY T VANN
THOMAS R VANTRE SR
SAMUEL L VAUGHAN
ROY VIZUETE
JOSEPH P WAGERS
LEROY M WALKER
OTIS E WARD
JACOB H WARMBRODT
HAL B WARNER
JACK W WARREN
JOHNNIE T WARREN
LEONARD E WARREN
MARTIN W WARREN
CARL W WATERBURY
JACK G WATKINS
TRAVIS E WATKINS
JOHN W WATLINGTON
HAROLD B WATSON
WILLIAM G WATSON
WILFORD W WEAVER
ROBERT E WELKER
JOSEPH WELLS
ERNIE E WESCOTT
JOHN W WESKE
CLARENCE WEST
WILLIS N WEST

TONY WESTON
JOHN R WHALEN
KENNETH J WHALEN
WILLARD J WHALEY
HUGH D WHITACRE
DONALD H WHITE
CHARLES H WHITFORD
WILLIAM J WIDENER
JAMES M WIGHTMAN
PHILIP J WILKES
OMER T WILLETTE
JAMES B WILLIAMS
OLEN B WILLIAMS
WINSTON W WILLIAMS
JAMES H WILLIAMSON
VIRGIL V WILLS
JAMES L WILMOTH
HAROLD D WILSON
JOHN R WILSON
JOHN R WILSON
RAY WILSON
SILAS W WILSON
LUTHER WISE
WILLIAM L WISE
ALBIN J WISNESKI
SIEGFRIED A WOLF
ROBERT E WOLFE
RONALD C WOOD
EDWARD C WOODROOF
GEORGE WOODS
ISAAC T WOODS
RICHARD A WOODWORTH
DILLARD C WYATT
MERRITT L WYNN
HOWARD W YOUNG
CHANG-BOK YUN
GI-BONG YUN
GI-HYO YUN
SEOK-GU YUN

SERGEANT MAJOR

JIN-GU KIM
SUN-YEONG KIM

WARRANT OFFICER

ALFRED H AUGER
JOSEPH S BERNA
JAMES J BOLTON
GEORGE W BOOHER
CHARLES C CACKOWSKI
ROSCOE M CALCOTE
WILBERT W CATO
SAMUEL W COMER
EDWARD J COONEY
JAMES D DE ROULE
COLIN C ECCLES
WILLIAM ESSMEIER
EINO E FALLS
PHILIP C FARNHAM
CLEMENT D FRYMARK
GEORGE D GILLESPIE JR
HAROLD S GLAUDER
LEE A GRAVES
OLAF R HANSEN
WILLIAM M HARRELL
LYLE B HARRIS
RICHARD W HOLLENBECK
RALPH H HUMBOLDT
SIDNEY C HUNT
JAMES W KEELY
ARNOLD R KOLDEN
RUSSELL E KORB
JOSEPH C LACKNER
BRUCE B LANGFITT
LEO J MANEGRE
CHARLES D MCALISTER
ADOLPHUS NAVA
STEPHEN J OLEKSIUK
JOSEPH W PAULL
LEWIS C PERRY
MARVIN H PETERSEN
WILLIAM R PORTER
WILLIAM F RAY
ROBERT D REGNIER

JAMES E STEVENS
RAY W TAYLOR
FRANK D TRUMAN
CARL W VAWTER
MARVIN WILSIE
RALPH E WILSON JR

SECOND LIEUTENANT

WILLIAM E AARON JR
WHERRY L ABERCROMBIE
JAIME ACOSTA-GARCIA
ROBERT E AFFLERBACH
HOWARD G AIRINGTON
JOE W AKINS
ACE ALLEN
COMER L ALTLAND
JOHN F ARCHER
WILLIAM W ASBURY
FRANK V ASTON
VIRGIL M ATWOOD
KELLIS B BAKER
STEWART M BAKER JR
DALE E BALL
ROBERT L BALTZ
TRAVIS L BANKS
WORTH H BARBER
JOHN C BARBEY
CECIL A BARNETT
COURTENAY L BARRETT JR
GEORGE M BARRICK JR
JERRY BARRY
PHILIP F BAUER JR
WILLIAM M BENEFIELD JR
BRUCE BEVERIDGE JR
STUART M BLAZER
ROBERT F BLOHOWIAK
FRANK E BLOOMENSHINE
GERALD P BONNER
ALVIN A BOXLER
STEWART S BOYDEN
JAMES L BOYDSTON
THOMAS D BOYLE
HARRY C BRADLEY JR
ROBERT E BRAITHWAITE
RYAN A BRESSLER
JOHN B BRISTOW
LEWIS BROGENS
HOWARD G BROWN
JAMES F BROWN
WILLIAM K BRUCE
RALPH M BUFFINGTON
DOYLE J BURKE
JOHN F BURTON JR
JAMES T CARLTON
NORMAN R CARNES
JOHN E CAROLAN
MICHAEL P CARRINGTON
ROBERT C CARROLL
JACK W CASE
JOSEPH M CASTRO
JOE V CERRI JR
HO-SUN CHA
EARL F CHAMBERS
JOHN L CHILDRESS
FRANK P CHRISTENSEN JR
CURTIS W CHRISTOPHER
JOHN CLENDINNING III
WILLARD H COATES
JOSEPH A COCHRAN JR
WILLIAM L COCHRAN
FRANCIS A CODD
PAUL C COFFIN
RANDALL E COINER
DONALD E COLGROVE
JOSEPH R COLLETTE
HURDER F COLSON
EDWARD A COLTON
DAVID W CONNOLLY
DALE R COPELAND
FRANK J COSNAHAN
CHESTER H CRAMTON JR
WILLIAM H CROWE
HERBERT C CUMMINGS JR
PAUL A CUOZZO
RALPH E CURTIS
JAMES V H DALE
EARL J DAVIES

COURTENAY C DAVIS JR
MERVIN H DAVIS
CYRIL E DELAY
LIONEL J DELCAMBRE JR
CHARLES H DETWEILER
PATRICK A DEVIVO JR
ALFRED P DIANDA
PETER P DIMARTINO
GENE M DITTBENNER
KENNETH R DIXON
THOMAS A DODSON
JAMES N DORLAND
HERMAN L DRISKELL JR
JOHN J DUGAN
RALPH E DUGAN
ROBERT W DUNCAN
FREDERIC N EATON
ROBERT D EBERT
CARL W ELLIOT
JOHN D ELMORE
GREGORY F ERLACH
HENRY B FARINHOLT
JOHN W FARRAR
LYLE E FASSETT
CHARLES G FERGUSON
RONALD R FERRIS
ROGER L FIFE
CLYDE W FLETCHER
JERRY P FLYNN
JAMES E FORD
MAURICE E FORD
ANDREW H FORNICA
FREDERICK P FORSTE
CALVIN R FREEMAN
JACK C GAINER
JOHN E GANDY
LUIS G GARCIA
CHARLES D GARNER
CHARLES E GARNETT
THOMAS F GAULE
JOSEPH H GEIS III
EUGENE L GETTIG
OWEN J GIBLIN
ELBERT E GILDER JR
JOHN H GILLES
DAVID R GILLESPIE
FRANCIS T GLASGOW
JONAS W GLASSGOW
DONALD S GOODMAN
RAYMOND T GOTO
WILBUR J GRAVES
ROY A GRAYSON
HARRY H GRIFFIN
HOWARD J GRIFFIN
JEROME H GRIGAL
HERBERT B GROSCHE
JOSEPH W GUPKO
CARTER B HAGLER
ROBERT G HALAY
VAN L HALFERTY
WILLIAM H HALL
GEORGE E HANNAN
RICHARD M HANNON
ANDREW G HANSEN JR
DARRELL J HANSEN
JOHN L HANSEN
THOMAS G HARDAWAY
CLARENCE A HARRIS
RICHARD E HARRIS
PAUL C HART
JESSIE M HARTLE JR
GEORGE W HARVEY
RICHARD HAWKES
FREDERICK S HAYS JR
VERDUN E HEADLEY
CHARLES B HINSON
DOUGLAS C HOEKSTRA
JAMES R HOLLAND JR
ROBERT J HOPKINS
JOHN A HORONY
PHILIP J HOWARD
ROBERT N HOWE
JOHN B HUCKIN
JACK G HUDSPETH
KENNON A HUGGINS JR
ALFRED O HUTCHISON
DAVID W IMEL
RICHARD G INMAN
WILLIAM M IVES
FRANK J IWANCZYK

CHARLES J JAMES
ROBERT L JANES
ALBERT H JAY JR
DONALD C JENKINS
KEITH A JENSEN
CHANG-HO JEONG
VERNON JERNIGAN
RICHARD G JEWETT
LEWIS E JOBE
CHARLES F JOHNSON
HERBERT W JOHNSON
MAYNARD B JOHNSON
MELVIN E JOHNSON
WARREN G JOHNSON
ARTHUR O JONES
MARTIN J JORDAN
THEODORE R JOYNER
DANIEL F KAMPS
DAVID O KENDRICK
JOHN E KERRY
JAMES J KIERNAN JR
FRANK W KILGORE
JIN-SU KIM
FRANK H KING JR
JASON R KING
CARL F KNOBLOCH
GEORGE KOPSCICK JR
MELFERD L KOSTOFF
NICK KRAWCION
MITCHELL KRUSZEWSKI
ROGER R KUHLMAN
DARWIN K KYLE
ROBERT J LAHEY
HAROLD J LAKE
LEON E LANCASTER
FRED M LANG JR
JASON C LARSON
JACK E LAY
GERALD C LEBLANC
ELVIN M LEE
JASPER W LEE
SU-CHANG LEE
GORDON D LEESCH
CHARLES W LENDER
EDMUND J LILLY III
DONALD A LITTLE
WARREN C LITTLEFIELD
THOMAS W LIVINGSTON JR
KENNIS E LOCKARD JR
JOHN B LONG
GEORGE R LONGENECKER JR
FRANK R LOYD JR
RICHARD F LUCAS
MILTON S F LUM
RODERICK MACDONALD
ROBERT K MACKEY
MUNRO MAGRUDER
THOMAS A M MAHER
JAMES R MAHON
EDWIN F MAHONEY
ROBERT A MANN
ROBERT J MANUEL
JAMES E MARSHALL
HERBERT E MARSHBURN JR
KARL L MARTIN
ODVIN A MARTINSON
STEPHEN MATE JR
GREEN B MAYO
JOHN M MCALPINE
RUSSELL J MCCANN
AUBREY C MCCLUNG
RICHARD R MCCULLOUGH
FRANCIS J MCGOVERN
JOHN N MCGUIRE
CLAUDE L MCINTYRE
ROBERT E MCINTYRE
CONNIE C MCKAY
WILLIAM W MCKELLAR
JACK M MCKINNEY
WILLIAM H MCLELLAN
CHARLES M MCMILLAN JR
GEORGE A MCNERNEY
JOHN J MEADE
THOMAS A MEDINGER
CARLETON A MILLER
ROBERT B MILLER
ASA B MINER
FRANKLIN MITCHELL

DAVID H MOCK
WILLIAM E MOMENT
ROLLAND P MORNEAULT
THOMAS C MORRISON
ROBERT W MORTON
JOHN W MULLANEY
DANIEL P MURPHY
JOHN B MURPHY JR
KENNETH J MURPHY
WAYNE A MURPHY
DIXON H NABORS
STANLEY E NEFFENDORF
CECIL E NEWMAN JR
MILTON E NICHOLS
CHARLES L NIXON
WILLIAM E NORTON
FENTON M ODELL
PAUL A M OECHSLE
JAMES N OGLESBY
DON E OLMSTEAD
RICHARD O OLSON
HAROLD H OSBORNE
WILLIAM E OTIS JR
HAROLD F OVERTON
HAROLD W PARLIER
DAVID L PARMER
MURRAY L PAYNE
THOMAS P PEARCE JR
TREVOR J PERRY
EARL K PETERS
ARNOLD E PETERSON
ALAN F PLUMMER
ROGERS PORTER
KENNETH W POWERS
WILLIAM C PREACHER
WILLIAM W PRIVETT
ERVIN H PURE
RALPH H QUEEN
GLENN F QUINLIVAN
DAVID V RADCLIFFE
FRED M RAMOS
DIETER W RAMPENDAHL
ROBERT L RAMSAUR
JAY B RASH
EDWARD R RAVENEL III
GRANVILLE E REED
KENNETH F REIMER
WILLIAM F RILEY
ALFRED L RIST
DAVID A RIVES
JORGE F ROACH
ROBERT W ROBINSON
BURT A ROBSON
GEORGE W RODGERS
GLENN R ROGERS
HARVEY W ROGERS
GILBERT J ROMERO
GEORGE ROTHENBERGER
KENNETH E SAWYER
EDWARD J SCHWARTZ
DAVID W SCOGIN
FREDERICK M SCRIBNER JR
JERROLD R SCRIBNER
WALTER J SCROGGIN
JOHN A SEARS
JAMES F SEITZ
NATHANIEL M SHARP
TALLY J SHEPPARD
CHAUNCEY E SHICK
MARK L SHIELDS
ROBERT N SHIPE
DAVID W SHUTE
RUSSELL A SIEDER
DONALD E SLOUGHFY
CHARLES H SMITH JR
HAROLD L SMITH
MYRON D SMITH
ROBERT N SMITH
SMITH S SOMERVILLE
PAUL M STAVNITZKY
DAVID C STEPP
L V STEWARD
CARROLL A ST MARTIN
JOHN M STOKES
LYLE D STUCKER
ROBERT B STUDNICK
JEROME A SUDUT
THOMAS J SUMMERS

81 ARMY

MARVIN E TAYLOR
MARK TAYNTON JR
WILLIAM E TEMPLIN
HOWELL G THOMAS JR
HEREFORD P THOMPSON
JAMES L THOMPSON JR
ROBERT K THOMPSON
JOHN W TIMMINS JR
ALFRED J TITONE
DAVID B TITUS
CHARLES R TOMLINSON
ALBERT E TOON
GEORGE W TOW
JOHN C TRENT
FRANCIS A UZZO
WILLIAM M VALACHOVIC
MARTIN D VANOY
FRED J VENNER JR
DAVID VON ESCHEN
WILLIAM M WADSWORTH
CHARLES P WALTHOUR
HARRY W WARE JR
NUMA A WATSON JR
THEODORE S WATSON
JOHN F WATT JR
ROBERT F WEAVER
KEITH W WEEKS
RICHARD G WELCH
ROBERT D WELCH
HENRY WELLING JR
RICHARD D WEST
JOHN C WESTCOTT
CECIL W WHITE
WILLIAM E WHITE
JOHN S WHITTEMORE
WILLIAM H WILBUR JR
GORDON M WILKERSON
FRANKLIN J WILKINSON
GERALD F WILLIAMS
JAMES L WILSON
WILBUR S WING
THEODORE R WOO
ROBERT H WOOD
THOMAS D WOOD
THOMAS F WOOD
FRANK E WOODCOCK
CHARLES L WORLEY JR
HENRY F WRIGHT
ALEXANDER YAROSKY
ERNEST A ZECHA JR

FIRST LIEUTENANT

EDWIN E ADAMS
ROBERT I ADAMS
WILLIAM H ADAMS
WILLIAM R ADAMS
RICHARD A AKERS
TEDDY B AKINS
BOYD K ALDERDICE
MALCOLM E ALDRICH
EDWARD F ALDRIDGE
MARION L ALES
HILARY F ALLEMEIER
THOMAS E ALLEN
JOSEPH R ALLISON JR
WILLIAM J ALLISON
DONALD R ALLMON
ROBERT W ALLYN
RICHARD C AMES
ORIS W AMY
JAMES A ANDERSON
MELVIN F ANDERSON
RUSSEL E ANDERSON
STANLEY A ANDERSON
HORACE B ANDERTON
OKEY M ANKROM
GABRIEL C ANSELMO
LOUIS L ANTHIS
ARTHUR M APMANN JR
JOSEPH F APPENFELDER
LOUIS W ARMSTRONG
DONALD D ARNOLD JR
ALFRED H ASH
VERNON R ASHLEY
CLARENCE N AUST
HAROLD S AVERY JR
SOLOMON A BACHRACH
JOHN G BACON JR
BROWNELL E BAKER JR
JAMES J BALDUZZI JR
WOODROW W BALDWIN
ARNOLD L BAMBURG
THOMAS J BARNES
DONALD D BARTLEY
ELIAS G BASA
JAMES E BASS
JOHN O BATES JR
NEIL B BAXTER
MERL A BEACH
ROBERT A BEARD
RAMON C BEARSE JR
JAMES M BECKER
WILLIAM L BENGSTON
THOMAS W BENSON
DONALD E BERGER
WILLIAM BERGMAN JR
ROBERT O BERGMANN
FELIX R BEVERAGGI
ROBERT A BICKNELL
THEODORE C BISHOP
DAVID R BLAKELOCK
ROBERT T BLAKEY
DOUGLAS K BLAND
HERMAN W BLANKENSHIP
CLARENCE B BLISS
RAYMOND U BLOOM
JAMES R BLOUNT
JESSE B BOLLING
WARNER T BONFOEY JR
ARTHUR H BOOKS
BOYCE J BOONE
GLENN R BOTHWELL
JULES T BOUCKHUYT
PETER H BOWDEN
HERBERT L BOWMAN
RONALD C BOWSHIER
THOMAS W BOYDSTON
ROBERT M BOYER
JAMES W BRACKEN JR
CHARLES E BRANNON
BILLY B BREWSTER
RODNEY M BRIGGS
MAX BRITO
J D BROADWAY
ROBERT G BROBST JR
LEE D BROCK
BRUCE BROMLEY JR
JACK E BROOKS
NEILSON V BROUILLETTE
EDGER B BROUSE
FRANK L BROWN
LAWRENCE R BROWN
ROBERT C BROWN
WILLIAM E BROWN
DEXTER W BROWNE
WILLIAM J BROWNING
MARINUS BRUINOOGE
ALAN L BRUNO
GEORGE J BUCKLEY JR
MCKINLEY G BUCKNER
HARRY L BULLINGTON JR
STANLEY E BULLOCK
MORGAN L BULMAN
LAWRENCE V BURKE
SHERMAN K BURKE
FORREST S BURNS
JOHN K BURROWS
FRED BURTON
THOMAS H BURTON
LEONARD W BUTTON
WILLIAM H BUTTS
ROGER F BUXMAN
JAMES W BYRD
MABRY E CAIN
HOWARD O CALDWELL
JAMES L CALDWELL
GERALD M CAMP
HENRY C CAMP JR
HOWARD W CANTRELL JR
FRANCIS T CARLSON
ROBERT W CARNEY
BALDWIN R CARR
WILLIAM A CARTIER
WILLIAM W CASHOUR JR
JOHN L CHAMBERLAIN
PETER F CHARNETSKI
R E CHASTAIN
THURMAN J CHASTAIN
JOHN J CHAUVIN
EDWIN D CHAVOUS
DONG-GYU CHOI
PIERRE C CHRISSIS
WILLIAM K CHRISTIE
JEROME B CHRISTINE
THOMAS C CLARE
PAUL E CLAWSON
DALLAS E CLAYTON
WILLIAM R CLUFF
RICHARD B COKE JR
ROBERT B COLEMAN
ROGERS B COLLIER JR
JOHN COLLINS
PAUL D CONLIN
JOSEPH P CONROY
JOHN R COOGAN
WILLIAM W COOK
ROLAND E COOPER
RICHARD A COPE
WILLIAM E COPLEY
SAMUEL S COURSEN
JANSEN C COX
MALCOLM R COX JR
RICHARD G COX
CARL E CRAIG
WILLIAM B CRARY
DALE F CREGER
GEORGE S CRISP
JOHN O CROCKETT
AVON H CROOK JR
STANLEY W CROSBY JR
ROBERT H CROSS
WILLARD W CROWELL JR
BARNARD CUMMINGS JR
THOMPSON CUMMINGS
DANA A CURTIS
JOHN N DALE
STANLEY R DANKOWSKI
DANIEL D DANN
OSCAR F DANNER JR
HARRY P DARBY
FRANK T DAVIDSON
HARRY P DAVIS JR
LOUIS H DAVIS
M L DAVIS
JAMES E DEFRAIN
THEODORE R DELPLAIN
RICHARD W DENNER
MAX L DEROSSETT
PHILLIP E DE SHAW
MILTON H DE VAULT
GENE M DEYOUNG
GEORGE H DICKINSON JR
JACK L DINKEL
WILLIAM J DOLAN
JAMES A DOLLINGS
DALLAS M DOTSON
HAROLD F DOUGLAS
EARLE S DOWNES
DOUGLAS L DRINKARD
DALE B DRINKO
RAYMOND C DRURY JR
MCCLELLAN A DUBOIS
CLIFFORD G DUFFNER
JOHN H DUNN
JAMES R DUPUIS
CORNELIUS C DUYF
EDWARD A EDNIE
RICHARD O EILER
RALPH J ELLINGSEN
JAMES H ELLIOTT
SHERMAN L ELWOOD
DONALD C ENGH
LEMUEL L ENGLISH
MARCELO O ENZINGER
TIMOTHY T S EUM
LEO E EUTSLER
EARL EVANS
EUGENE L EVANS
HARFORD C EVE JR
JAMES F EXLEY
HERMAN L FALK JR
CHARLES K FARABAUGH
WILLIAM M FARRIS
NELSON E FENWICK
WENDELL E FERGUSON
ROBERT A FINCH
WILLIAM J FINLEY
ROBERT A FINNEY JR
WILLIAM E FITZPATRICK
JOHN W FLAHERTY
JOSEPH L FLAHERTY
EDWARD G FLANAGAN
CHARLES H FLEMING
BEN E FORD
HENRY A FORIS
GEORGE E FOSTER
EUGENE B FRANCOVICH
ALBERT G FRANTZICH
JOHN FRECH JR
AUTREY W FREDERICK
ARTHUR N FREEMAN
RICHARD L FRIEDLUND
JUNIOR F FROCK
WILLIAM R FROST JR
ALAN D FRY
ROBERT L FULLEN
VERNON B FUNKHOUSER
WILLIAM G FUSS
GEORGE A GALION
JAY M GANO
KOELING B GARDNER
OTIS L GARRISON
ROBERT M GARVIN
WILLIAM C GATES JR
ROBERT A GAVIN
MARTIN J GAVIO
JOHN L GAYHART
RILEY C GAZZAWAY
RICHARD E GERRISH JR
LENNARD E GEWIN
MALCOLM A GIBBS
DAVID W GIBSON
HAL T GIBSON
JOSEPH A GIDDINGS JR
RAYMOND B GILBERT
CHARLES L GILL
PHILIP K GLENN
WALLACE E GOFF
BAILEY H GOLDBERG
PETER T GOLDEN
SAMUEL GOUDELOCK
MARVIN P GOULDING
JOSEPH G GOVAN
ALBERT W GRADY
LESLIE O GRAGG
CHARLES W GRAHAM
WALTER R GRAHAM
BERNARD M GRAMBERG JR
JAMES W GRAMS
JOHN H GREEN
RALPH H GREENE
THOMAS P GREENE
THOMAS W GREER
JACK T GRIDER
JOHN D GRIEVE
JAMES R GRIST
RALPH S GUSTIN
HARRY J GUTTERIDGE
CHANG-IL HA
DOUGLAS H HAAG
JOHN H HADDOCK JR
WILLIAM C HADLEY
BURT HAFKIN
ROY A HAGEN
HARVEY R HAGER
CARL M HAGMAN
LEONARD C HALEY
JOHN C HALL
WILLIAM C HALL
ROSCOE E HALLIDAY JR
DONALD E HALVERSON
ALONZO R HAMMOCK
BELTRON R HANCEY
JACK HANCOCK
MARVIN A HANEY
MORGAN B HANSEL
RICHARD D HARDING
DOUGLAS D HARRELL
JAMES A HARRIS JR
LEWIS T HARRISON JR
ALBERT L HART
LEE R HARTELL
ROGER W HARTMAN
JOHN J HARTONG
MARVIN H HAYNES JR
MAYO S HEATH
THOMAS H HEATH
CHARLES K HEBERT
JAMES H HEFFRON
ROLLAND HEINTZELMAN
JE M HELT
WILLIAM K HENDERSON
ALLAN M HENSLEE
RICHARD C HENSON
JOHN F HERDLICK
ALFRED H HERMAN II
MERLE A HESS
JAMES G HICKERSON
JOHN H HIGGINS
WALTER N HIGGINS
GEORGE E HILL
FRED D HILLIARD
LESLIE B HILLS
HAROLD G HIPPIE
JAMES M HOBAR SR
JAMES R HODSDON JR
HENRY HOFMEISTER
PAUL E HOGAN
CHARLES J HOLLERAN
DALE G HOLLINGSWORTH
RICHARD G HOOTEN
CHARLES T HOPPER
DANIEL H HOPPING
FREDERICK L HORNUNG III
WILLIAM H HOTCHKISS
WILLIAM H HOTT
JAMES D HOUGHTON
VERNON N HOYT
ROBERT W HUDSON
HAROLD W HUMPHREY
ROBERT G HUNT
JUDSON P HURD
EARL T HUTCHINS
JAMES C HUTCHINS
JACK R HYRE
JOHN P IMBER
JAMES F INGELSBY
AMOS J JACKSON
ARTHUR JACKSON
BRUCE D JACKSON
CHESTER A JACKSON JR
JERRY JACKSON JR
MELVIN R JACKSON JR
LEON J JACQUES JR
HOWARD F JAMES
WILLIAM B JAMES
STUART R JELLY
DAVID B JENNINGS
HAROLD L JENNINGS
WILLIAM F JESTER
CARL J JOHNSON
FRANKLIN D JOHNSON
JAMES B JOHNSON
WESLEY H JOHNSON
EDWARD P JOHNSTON
CLIFFORD M JONES
GEORGE W JONES
JOHN H JONES
LEON S JONES
SAMUEL L JONES
CECIL F JORDAN
HERBERT L JORDAN
WARREN H JORDAN
DORAN L JURGENSEN
BERT W JUSTUS JR
DANIEL K KEALALIO
PATRICK H KELLEY
WILLIAM H KELLUM
CARL L KELLY
ROGER J KELLY
WILLIAM S KEMPEN JR
THOMAS E KILBY III
MYRTH J KILLINGSWORTH JR
DAVID A KIMBALL
HUNTER H KIMBALL JR
ALLEN D KING
CLIFFORD B KING
EDMUND KING
ELSTER R KING
RAYMOND F KING
ROGER B KIRCHOFER
DWIGHT A KIRK
LESLIE W KIRKPATRICK
HARRY A KLEBO JR

82 ARMY

JOE T KLINEFELTER
LEWIS C KLUTTZ
WILLIAM C KNAPP
ALBERT J KNECHTEL
BERNARD KNIZNICK
KARL G KOENIG JR
EDWARD L KOLESSAR
PAUL E KREMSER
STANISLAU KURDZIEL
HAROLD O KUUTTILA
DONALD E LAMB
JAMES O LAMBERT
CLYDE E LAMKINS
BENJAMIN S LANCASTER
JOHN F LAND
JAMES F LANE JR
OTIS O LANE
ALFRED L LANGSTON
SALVATORE T LAROCCA
GEORGE A LASASSO
JACK K LAUGHLIN
RUBEN LAUREANO
PAUL LAVERGNE
WILLIAM H LAWSON
EDWARD T LEACH
JACK W LEDBETTER
OFFIE L LEEPER JR
LUKE D LEFEVRE
DENNIS LEITE
LOUIS W LESTER
WARREN G LEWIS
RAYMOND J LIEB
HENRY A LIND
JAMES J LINDSAY
ROBERT T LINDSEY
GEORGE D LIONBERGER
CHARLES A LIPPHARDT
JAMES B LOFTIS
THOMAS A LOMBARDO
MELVIN I LONG
GEORGE W LOTT
LEROY LOVETT
ALFRED N LOWDER
JACK C LOWE
HARRY G LOY
CHARLES W LUTHER
SAMUEL A LUTTERLOH
LEONARD G LYON
ROBERT D MACDONALD
ARCHIBALD S MACFARLANE
HENRY T MACGILL
DUNCAN A MACLEOD
JOHN J MAGUIRE
MELVIN E MAHAR
MARK W MAIRICH
MILTON L MAJETTE
JACK C MANIS
WILLIAM G MARTIN
LAVON MARTINEAU
CHARLES A MATLACH
JOSEPH MATONIS
ELMY L MATTA
HENRY T MATTHEWS
GEORGE A MATTISON III
PAUL F MAURICIO
EDWARD W MAYNARD
CHARLES E MAYRAND
ANTHONY R MAZZULLA
JAMES W MCBRIDE
NEELY T MCCALEB JR
LESTON R MCCALL
FRANK L MCCARTHY JR
PHILIP A MCCARTHY
MICHAEL W MCCLONE
HAROLD MCCORMACK
JAMES R MCCOY
EDMUND MCCULLOUGH
JOHN J MCDONALD
WILLIAM E MCDONALD
CHARLES C MCDOUGAL
DENNIS O MCFARLAND
CHARLES F MCGEE
THOMAS W MCGEEVER JR
LEONARD E MCGHEE
BRIAN D S MCGLYNN
ROBERT M MCGOVERN
ALFRED K MCILQUHAM
DAN I MCKEITHEN JR
RICHARD E MCKINSTRY
TERENCE J MCLARNON

FRANCIS J MCLAUGHLIN
RICHARD N MCLEOD JR
PATRICK J MCMULLAN
JAMES J MCMULLEN
VANCE B MCWHORTER
ROGER F MEAGHER
RICHARD H MEALOR
JOHN W MEEKINS JR
NORMAN A MELANDER
JOHN A MERCER JR
DONALD L MERRILL
JOHN N MERRILL JR
HENRY C MERRITT
JAMES D MICHEL
FRANK S MIKULSKI
WILLIAM M MILLAR
HOWARD A MILLER
JAMES B MILLER
ROLLY G MILLER
GUY E MITCHELL JR
PHILIP C MITCHELL JR
EDWARD J MOLONEY
PETER H MONFORE
FRANCIS J MONTAGNOLO
TROY E MOODY JR
HENRY M MOORE
WILLIAM K MORDECAI
JAMES R MORENCY
CYRUS L MORGAN
DALE C MORGAN JR
THOMAS D MORGAN
CLYDE C MORRISON JR
HARRY S MORRISON JR
CARL N MORROW
JARED W MORROW
LAWRENCE D MOSS
EDWARD J MUELLER JR
ALLEN C MUHLBACH
GERALD N MULHOLLAND
GUNTHER T MULLER
ARTHUR F MULOCK
ARVID O MUNSON
HENRY G MURPHY JR
MARVIN S MURPHY
RAYMOND B MURPHY
JOHN C MYERS
IRVIN E NACHMAN
ROY T NAKASHIMA
RICHARD C NEIDINGER
JOHN M NELSON
ROLF W NELSON
WILLIAM F NELSON
ROBERT C NIEMANN
ROBERT L NORTON
JOHN W NYSTROM
RONALD E OAKES
ALWIN D OAR
JOSEPH T ODONNELL
CHARLES R OLSON
RICHARD J ORMISTON III
CARLO J ORTENZI
STANLEY D OSBORNE
BILL M OTOMO
WILLIAM E OTTMANN
CHARLES E OVERSTREET
JAMES B OWEN
MARVIN P OWEN JR
JEROME J PADEN
CLYDE P PADGETT JR
EDMUND C PALLESEN
RICHARD C PAPPIN
WON-SUN PARK
CHARLES E PARKER
DIXIE S PARKER
JAMES N PARKER
PATRICK E PARKES
PAUL O PARKHURST
HAROLD G PARRIS
ARTHUR J PATTERSON
DOUGLAS W PAYNE
GILBERT B PEARSALL
RAYMOND E PEARSON
EDWIN A PEART JR
ROBERT L PECK III
WILLIAM R PENINGTON
JAMES B PERCIVAL
WILLIAM C PERRY
TILLMAN O PETERS
MAUN T PETERSEN
CHARLES W PETSCHE

BENJAMIN W PHILLIPS JR
JAMES R PIERCE JR
JACK D PIERSON
WILLIAM PLOTNIK
ROBERT D PONTIUS
JAMES B PORTER
SYLVESTER V PORUBSKY
HUBERT W POTTS
CHARLES W POWER
MAYLON D PRICE III
RICHARD M PRICE
RICHARD E PROHL JR
JAMES E RADCLIFF
CHARLES H RADCLIFFE
JOHN J RAGUCCI
PABLO RAMIREZ
JAMES C RAMSEY
SAMUEL J RANGATORE
ALFRED J RASKIN
EDWARD J RAVEN JR
THOMAS J REDGATE
WAYNE W REED
EMERSON L REFFNER
ROBERT M REHOR
ROBERT A RENNEMAN
JAMES T REYNOLDS
JOHN R RHODES JR
CLARK M RICHARDS JR
GEORGE E RICHARDS
LESTER R RICHARDSON
MARLIN L RICHARDSON
JULES A RICHE
ROY T RIGGS
KENNETH V RILEY JR
STANLEY K RISNER
ROBERT B RITCHIE
CARLOS E RIVERA
GERALD T ROBBINS
ROBERT S ROBERTS
EDWARD ROBERTSON
SAMUEL F ROBINSON
MALCOLM A ROBISON
WILLIAM J RODGERS
ADAM B RODRIGUEZ
MANUEL RODRIGUEZ-
RODRIGUEZ
ROBERT M ROESSLER
KENNETH G ROGERS
WILLIAM ROLLINS
ROBERT V ROOD
ROBERT E ROOKSBERRY
MELVIN G ROSKELLEY
TENNEY K ROSS
CHARLES ROSSTEUSCHER
BERNARD F ROTH
JOHN D ROUSE
OTIS G RUCKER JR
CHARLES R RUSSELL
HENRY W RUSSEY
JAMES J RYAN
JULE C RYBOLT
RAYMOND A RZEPECKI
RANDALL G SAMMONS
JACK D SANDERS
HENRY B SARRAIL
JACK J SAUNDERS
WILLIAM C SCHEMMEL
HENRY A SCHENK
MAYNA SCHERMERHORN
PAUL E SCHICK
VERNON G SCHIEFFER
CARL J SCHLITZ
CARL P SCHMIDT
EDWARD SCHMITT
ROBERT G SCHMITT
JOHN R SCHMUTZ
CHRISTOPHER L SCHNEIDER
PAUL R SCHULZE
MELVIN A SCOTT
KEITH L SEALS
HOYT L SEALY JR
EARL M SEAY
ROBERT J SEBACHER
JOHN H SEIP
LOUIS G SELIG JR
JAMES M SELZER
ALAIN L SETTLE
JACK R SEXSON
RICHARD T SHEA JR
JOHN G SHEEHAN

RICHARD B SHERIDAN
JOHN W SHOEMAKER
BION Q SHUTTS
THOMAS E SIFLING
CORYDEN J SIMMONS
DERWOOD W SIMS
JOHN R SJODIN
ROLLIN W SKILTON
EVERETT F SMALLEY
RAYMOND SMALLWOOD
ALBERT W SMITH
CHARLES SMITH
JOSEPH S SMITH
JOSEPH W SMITH
WILLARD E SMITH
RICHARD T SMOCK
DAVID M SNIDERMAN
EDGAR T SNIPES JR
LOUIS M SORMRUDE
DAVID B SPELLMAN
HARRY W SPRAKER JR
JACK W STALLINGS JR
JOHN B STANTON
KENNETH G STAUFFER
JOSEPH STDKO
JAMES E STEPHENSON
LYNN STEVENS
WILLIAM E STEVENS
VICTOR L STEWART
ALLEN A STITELER
JAMES W STOLL
EDWARD M STONE JR
LOUIS J STORCK
MAX R STOVER
JOHN D STRANSKY
GORDON M STRONG
ROBERT C STYSLINGER
JAMES F SULLIVAN
HARRY E SUTTON
MERLIN R SWEET
CARROLL W SWEIGER
WILLIAM U SYKES
STANLEY E TABOR
KENNETH A TACKUS
JACK G TAPSCOTT
WILLIAM S TAWES
DAVID F TAYLOR
GLENN D THOMAS
MITCHELL C THOMAS
GEORGE M THOMPSON
ROBERT E THOMPSON
CORDUS H THORNTON
DELMER R THREADGILL
FRANK S TOMAN
WACLAW A TOMASZEWSKI
MAURICE R TOMLINSON
JOSEPH D TOOMEY
JOSE TORRES-CABAN
ROBERT A TOTTY
RANDOLPH TOWNSEND
ROGER N TRALL
DONALD W TREDER
WILLIAM P TRINEN
GRANVILLE H TRUITT
JACK L TUCKER
EDWIN P TURNER
JAMES H TURNER
BRADFORD E TYNDALL
JOHN F UMLAUF
WILLIAM F VAHLSING
MONELL VAN
FRADENBURG
ROBERT E VARNEY
FERNANDO VASALDUA
GEORGE E VINNEDGE JR
ALPHARD R VISMOR
ALEXANDER VOROBEY
ROBERT A WAGNER
JOHN K WAINWRIGHT
STANFORD M WAIT
FRANK M WALKER
THOMAS S WALKER
CLYDE L WALLACE
ROBERT J WALLACE
NORMAN C WANLESS
CHARLES L WAPLES
WILLIAM D WARE
CHARLES L WARNER
LEONARD K WARNER
RICHARD L WARREN

JOHN R WASSON
LUTHER N WATERS
JOHN E WATKINS
ROY R WATKINS JR
LOGAN C WEATHERS
JOHN L WEAVER
ST CLAIR WEBB JR
GERHARDT H WEBER
WARREN WEBSTER III
RAYMOND P WEDDLE
ALAN R WERNDLI
E GEORGE WEST
SAMUEL V WESTERMAN
REGINALD W WHIDDON
DAVID N WHITE
EDWARD A WHITE
JOHN G WHITE JR
WILLIAM L WHITE
WALTER C WIECKOWSKI
ROBERT L WILLIAMS JR
WILLIAM WILLIAMS
ALBERT E WILLIS JR
DOUGLAS C WILSON
ROBERT D WILSON
THOMAS P WILSON
HARLAN R WINKLER
WALTER W WINKLER
WILLIAM W WINTERS
FRED W WOOD
WALTER R WOOD
WILLIAM M WOODRUFF
CARL S WRIGHT
GEORGE M WRIGHT
VIRGIL A WYATT
MIKE YANOVIK
BILLY A YOHNER

CAPTAIN

MELVILLE E ADAMS
ALDEN D ALLEN
DOUGLAS R ANDERSON
PETER G AREND
DAVID W ARMSTRONG
BEVERLY I ARNOLD
ANTONIO L BACA
CLIFFORD E BAKER
CLARENCE C BALLARD
MALCOLM G
BANNERMAN
TED U BARNES
GEORGE D BARNETTE
CYRIL B BARTHOLDI
HAROLD B BAUER
HAROLD R BEAVERS
WILLIAM F BIVENS
JOHN D BLEVINS JR
PAUL R BLEW
HARRY W BORGIA
WILLIAM Q BOYD
ULYSSES H BRADFORD
JOHN R BRIDGES
JOHN J BROCKMAN
CHARLES W BROWN
EDWARD O BROWN
KENNETH E BROWN
RALPH G BROWN
TURNACE H BROWN
JOHN A BRUCKNER
LAWRENCE F BRUNNERT
GEORGE BULKOWSKI
WALT W BUNDY
JOHN H BURKE
ROTHWELL W BURKE
WILLIAM C BURKIT
WILLIAM R BURN
FRANK H BURWELL JR
WENDELL F BYRD
ELDRIDGE CARTER
TAYLOR K CASTLEN
JACOB W CHAPIN
SEONG-YONG CHOI
JOHN T CICUR JR
JAMES W CLANCE
SAMUEL G CLARK
RODNEY F CLOUTMAN
GEORGE R CODY
MARTIN A COKER
NORRIS L COLEMAN

83 ARMY

JOSEPH F CONCANNON
JAMES W CONNER
JEAN R CONYERS
WALTER G COPE
FRANCIS X COPPENS
JOSEPH J CORDONE
RUPERT J COSTLOW
REGINALD L COWEN
JOSEPH D COX
ODEAN T COX
LEO P CRAIG
ROBERT M CRANE
GARLAND D CRAWFORD
FRANK W CURTIN
ANTHONY DANNUCCI
ONLEY T DAVIS JR
RAYMOND S DAVIS
CHARLES M DAY
GLENN R DEAN
THOMAS W DECOSTE
RAYMOND C DENCHFIELD
FRED P DEPALMA
KENNETH DESCHENEAUX
REGINALD B DESIDERIO
ALEXANDER DIDUR
PAUL N DILL
FRANK H DOHONEY
THOMAS E DOWLING JR
STEPHEN DUBINSKY
LOREN G DU BOIS
EDWARD R DUNCAN
ROBERT B DUNHAM
JAMES E EARLY
HOMER R EDDY
WILLIAM H EDER JR
DELBERT V EDGETTE
EDWIN G EKLUND JR
ORIN B ELLIOTT
JOHN F ELLIS
THOMAS T EMERTON
JOSEPH A ERRIGO
COLEMAN L EVERETT
HARRY S EVERETT JR
HERMAN G FELHOELTER
FRED G FERRIS
JOHN H FIELDS
ARNOLD R FLOOK
WILFRED S FORD
SAMUEL R FOWLER
HERSCHEL E FUSON
WILLIAM H GIBBENS
CHARLES G GIBSON JR
FREDERICK J GIROUX
JOHN J GLEASON
WILLIAM J GLUNZ
NICHOLAS N GOMBOS
WILL H GORDON JR
ERNEST L GRAVELINE JR
WILLIAM E GRAVES
HAROLD GRAY JR
RICHARD H GROB
MORTIMER G GUINN
REX C GUNNELL
ALLAN P HACKETT
TAE-SIK HAN
OSCAR E HANSEN JR
ROBERT M HANSEN
WARNER H HARMS
WILLIAM R HARRIS
CHARLES V H HARVEY
JOHN C HASTIE
CHARLES J HASTINGS
RAYMOND D HATFIELD
RICHARD D HAUGEN
ROBERT F HAYNES
DAVID C HEARN
ROBERT W HEMENWAY
FREDERICK F HENRY
MICHAEL HERKO JR
ISHAM C HEWGLEY JR
WILLIAM H HICKMAN
JOHNNIE M HIERS
CARTER D HILGARD
HAROLD L HODGE
BILL J HOLLAND
CRENSHAW A HOLT
WILLIAM R HONE
ROBERT M HORAN
ELON L HOUSE
LOUIS W HOWE

EDWARD D HOWELL
BARNEY W HUGHES JR
KENNETH W HUGHES
FRANK E HULA
EDWARD W HUNN
JOSEPH A HURD
RUFUS J HYMAN
KENNETH C HYSLOP
CLINTON H JACKSON JR
ELWOOD F JAMES
JOHN N JOHNSON
WILBER G JONES JR
PAUL H JORDON
THOMAS JOYCE JR
ELMER J KALLMEYER
EMIL J KAPAUN
ROBERT G KEENE
CHESTER L KEMP
JOHN N KENNEDY
YEONG-GYEOK KIM
JOHN E KINGSLEY
CHARLES J KLING
GEORGE KRISTANOFF
ANTHONY P KRUMPACH
EDWARD C KRZYZOWSKI
ROLAND W KUBINEK
THOMAS C LAMAR
MARTIN J LARKIN
BYRON D LEE
U-BEOM LEE
ALLEN K LEGGE
EARL E LUNDBERG
WILLIAM E LUZADDER
WILLIAM J LYMAN JR
WAYNE B MACOMBER
LEROY E MAJESKE
OSCAR W MARASKA JR
ELDON L MARKUM
AUBURN MARR
NATHANIEL MASIN
ALBERT K MATHRE
RAYMOND B MAXWELL
FELIX J MCANDREWS
ALFONSO T MCARTHUR
RAYMOND J MCCARRELL
STUART MCCASH
WILLIAM K MCCURDY
RAYMOND J MCDONIEL
DALE W MCDOWELL
JOHN P MCELMURRY
EDWARD R MCELROY
LAWRENCE K MCKINNEY
R MAURICE METZCAR
JAMES T MILAM
HUGH P MILLESON
JAMES L MITCHELL JR
RUSSELL Y MITCHELL
ROBERT M MOORE JR
HARRY D MORELAND JR
DOUGLAS E MORROW
HENRY S MORTON
LESTER J MUHLE
MERLIN M MULCAHY
LORENZO T MURRAY
DONALD E MYERS
ARTHUR J NEALON
JOHN H NELSON
WARD O NEVILLE
WALTER M NILES
JOHN J OCONNOR
LEONARD K OLVIS
PHILIP J ONEILL
LAWRENCE S C OVERTON
JUN-HWA PARK
ROBERT E PARKE
ALFRED G PEIFFER
BERNARD M PEPPER
GEORGE W PETERBURS
FRED N PETERSEN JR
LEON A PINGENOT
VICTOR M PIROWSKI
ROBERT L POMERENE
JOHN D PORTERFIELD JR
EDMUND D POSTON
PARKER H PRATT
COLEMAN L PRESCOTT
THEODORE A PUSHNIG
ROBERT S RAITH
MARION A RAMAGE
JAMES W REAVES

CLARENCE REED
PATRICK C REID
ARTHUR C RICHARDS JR
KENNETH K RISTE
ROBERT H RIVET
FRANK J ROBERTA
EDMUND C ROBERTS JR
HERMAN W ROESCH
ADOLPHUS W ROFFE
ORMA E ROUSE
MURPHY ROY
JAMES C RUDDELL JR
LESTER R RULIK
THOMAS K RYAN
CATESBY E SCHIELE JR
EDWARD B SCULLION
JAMES E SEAMON
BROWN SEBASTIAN
IRVING L SEEBERG
DALE L SEEVER
JACK B SHANAHAN
MOLTON A SHULER JR
DONALD H SIDDELL
ROY L SIDENER
EDWIN P SIEDLER
SAMUEL R SIMPSON
YUN-SU SIN
PAUL L SINGLETON
GEORGE D SLACK
DEWITT R SMITH
WILLIAM J SMITH
LYNDEL M SOUTHERLAND
HARRY SPEIGHT
JOHN K SPENCER
MELVIN R STAI
WILLIAM H STANBERY
ROBERT I STARR
ARTHUR J STEELE
ERNEST W STEINBERG
CHARLES M STRUTHERS
ROLAND V SUND
KENNETH L SUTHERLAND
ROY W SWANSON
KENNETH SWENSON
SAM O TAKAHARA
JOHN A TATE
DANIEL W TAYLOR
GEORGE W TERRY
RICHARD E THOMPSON
ROBERT L TIMMONS
LAWRENCE S TOHILL
JIM S TRIMBLE
ARTHUR H TRUXES JR
FRANK B TUCKER
WALLACE W TURNER
ISIDRO D URBANO
RICHARD VANDERPLOEG
HAROLD E VAN LEHN
JOHN W VESTER
BENJAMIN M WALKER
ROBERT B WALKER
RALPH R WANCE
JAMES K WARNER
HOWARD H WEBB
JOHN T WELLS III
STEN E WESTIN
FRANK M WHITE
JOSEPH C WHITEHEAD
MAURICE E WILHELM
CHARLES E WILHITE
DONALD S WILKINS
HAROLD E WILLECKE
FREDERICK B WIRT
ERIK F YDE
CHARLES L ZMESKAL

MAJOR

BARRY E ALBRIGHT
CLAUDE E ALLEN
RICARDO T ARCA
JAMES BAIDO
BAXTER L BAKER JR
CHARLES T BARTER
FREELING W BELLAMY
WILLIAM M BOLTON
FRANK M BROWN
WAYNE H BURDUE
ARTHUR B BUTLER

JOHN CALLUM
MARVIN W CARIUS
CHARLES L CARRIER
HUGH B CASEY
CHARLES L CECIL
FRED D CHESNUT
PAUL F CONKLIN
PAUL R CONRAD
JOHN M COOK
CLIFTON Z COUCH JR
HORACE E DONAHO
DONALD L DRISCOLL
ARTHUR H EARNSHAW
ROBERT J FARTHING
LONNIE B FLOWERS
WILLIAM H FRAZIER JR
BILLY E FRITTS
THEODORE C FROIS
JAMES O GARDNER
ROBERT E GODFREY
RAYMOND C GREIS
JACK D GRIFFITHS
ROBERT S HAMILTON
MILTON L HANNER
WILLIAM D HARALSON
WILLIAM F HERRINGTON
OMAR T HITCHNER
BYRD W HOPPES
HENRY W HOUSE JR
FRANK B HOWZE
SAM HUMPHFUS
WILLIAM P HUNT JR
RICHARD J KARNOS
JAMES F KEENAN
MELVIN B KING
DURFEE LARSON
ROBERT T LATTA
GEOFFREY LAVELL
FELIX S LEE
JONG-SU LEE
KARL LEONBERGER
HOMER F LINDSAY
LAWRENCE E LOOS
BYRON D MAGEE
FRED E MARLOWE
NORMAN F MARSHALL
CLARENCE A MARTIN JR
FRANK J MARTINEZ
DONALD J MAUS
PLOTT M MEDFORD
EUGENE P MILLER
LEON F MORAND JR
MAX A MORRIS
EDMUND J MURPHY
PAUL M NESTLER
CHARLES A NEWMAN
OWEN R ONEILL
ROBERT J ORMOND
FRANK M PARKER JR
HELGE E PEARSON
LELAND R PELLERIN
JOHN J PHILLIPS
FRED D PICKERING
GERALD POTTS
WAYNE E POWELL
FREDERICK C PRICE JR
PAUL N ROBARGE
JACK W RODARME
DANIEL F ROOKS
BOONE SEEGERS
HAROLD W SHOEMAKER
ALBERT C STANDISH
MARSHALL W STARK
SIMON J STEVENS
HARVEY H STORMS
ROBERT B STRAIGHT
JOSEPH W TERMAN
OSBORNE R THOMPSON
STEPHEN T UURTAMO
MAXWELL W VAILS
HAROLD A VIZINA
JACK W WALKER
WILLIAM H WALKER
HENRY L WAMBLE
FREDERICK A WELLS
ELWIN I WHALEY
AVERY W WILLIAMSON
KENNETH C WILSON
FREDERICK W WINTER
SAMUEL M WITHERS JR

LIEUTENANT COLONEL

CHARLES S ALLEN
OREN C ATCHLEY
ROBERT A BELL
ARNOLD N BRANDT
JOHN C BRINSMEAD
CLARK G CAMPBELL
BURT N COERS
GEORGE W CONNAUGHTON
WILLIAM T DAVIS
EMIL W DELU
DONALD D DIAZ
WILLIAM E DRESSLER
HOWARD A DUCK
LELAND R DUNHAM
OSCAR E ESPELIN
JESS E EVANS
DON C FAITH JR
CARL G GOERING
GEORGE B HAMILTON
HENRY J HAMPTON
EMERY M HICKMAN
JAMES F HILL
HOMER C HINCKLEY
THOMAS A HUME
WILLIAM H ISBELL JR
CARL C JENSEN
THEODORE JOHNSON
WILLIAM T MCDANIEL
FRANKLIN W MCVAY
ALBERT L MONK
JOHN U D PAGE
LLOYD A PARKER
ORVILLE W PIERCE
HUBERT W SHURTZ
CALVIN O SMITH
SAMUEL E SPITZER
JEREMIAH F VAN WAKEMAN
OTHO T WINSTEAD
JOHN C YOUNG

COLONEL

FRANK H FORNEY
JOHN W KEITH JR
ALLAN D MACLEAN
EARL H MARSDEN
ROBERT R MARTIN
EDGAR J TREACY JR
CHARLES H UNGER
CHARLES S WARE

BRIGADIER GENERAL

LAURENCE K LADUE

MAJOR GENERAL

BRYANT E MOORE

GENERAL

WALTON H WALKER

84

ARMY

UNITED STATES MARINE CORPS

PRIVATE

NICHOLAS M ARCURI
BOB L ARLEY
HERBERT L BAZLEY
THOMAS R BERRYMAN
STANLEY D BLACK
PAUL BLEVINS
WARREN BOWLING
CLAUDE M BROADHURST JR
KENNETH W BROCK
WILLIAM R BUCEY
GENE R BURKMAN
GERALD J CARMICHAEL
VINCENT A CASSANO
JOSEPH J CITERA
NORMAN H CLAPPER
ANTHONY D CLUFF
GLEN R CRAMER
JAMES J CRIBBEN
DANIEL V CURLEY
ZANE E DELONG
ROBERT L DELP
MICHAEL J DOLAN
DON J DOREMUS
DONALD M FENNER
JACK S FISCHER
RICHARD M FITZGERALD
ROQUE I FLORES
DALLAS L FOLKNER
RUSSELL S FORGRAVE JR
SHERMAN E B FOWLER
MELVIN P GAMACHE
LELAND C GODFREY
ARMANDO P GONZALEZ
JAMES T HAMILTON
HAROLD E HANCOCK
WOODROW R HAUSERMAN JR
JOHN L HEILMAN
ASTOR R HENDRY
ROSS D HESSER
DON P HEUBEL
FRANK O HOLLOWAY
WILLIAM R HORRIGAN JR
ALEX D JAMES
DALE E JENSEN
IRA W KANTNER
CHARLES E KEATING JR
JACK W KELSO
RICHARD W KOUNTZ
MILAN KRAINOVICH
ROBERT O KRIDER
ROY M KUYKENDALL
GUY L LAINE
GEORGE W LAWRENCE JR
GENE A LAWS
ERVIN LEMASTER JR
LUPE LEYVA JR
FRANCIS B MAHONEY
JOHN MARTIN
JAMES C MASSIE
EDWIN D MAYS
WILLIAM MCALLISTER
BILLIE J MCCARRELL
CHARLES A MCCOSKEY JR
EDWARD J MCGRATH JR
JEROME P MIGALA
PEDRO MORENO
ANTHONY G NERO
JAMES W OCONNOR
CARL H OWENS
GONZALO T PACHUCA
THOMAS PAIGE
RAY E PARKS
LEON E PATCHEN
MAIKA PELE
KENNETH O PERRY
SALVATORE A PILERI
CAROL C PREJEAN
JOHN J R RADSEWITZ
BOB M ROACH
JACK A ROBERSON
PINKNEY ROBERTS JR
BERNARD J RODGER
PHILIP S ROMANO
OTTO L RONEKER JR
FRANCIS SCHERMAN
JOSEPH G SEDLAK
FLOYD SHAHAN
WILLIAM C SHORES
ARNOLD N SILVERSTEIN
GERALD N STANKO
LOREN STATON
AUTHER R STEELE
VIRGIL E STEPHENSON
DENNIS L TALIAFERRO
JAMES F TAYLOR
OLIN J TAYLOR
HERMAN L THERIOT
ALONZO T THOMAS
EMETERIO TORRES-RODRIGUEZ
LOUIE D WALKER
FRANCIS J WHIDDEN
JOHN B WHITSON JR
JOE E WHITTEN
JIM P WIGGINS JR
JEROME F WILLIAMS
NEIL R WILLIAMS
PAUL E WILLIAMS
HOLLIS G WILSON
JAMES M WILSON
CHARLES K YORK
DAVID M G ZERBACH JR

PRIVATE FIRST CLASS

DAVID H ABERNATHY
ALBERT S ABRAM
RURIE T ABSHIRE JR
PABLO ACOSTA
RUBEN S ADAME
ELNO ADAMS JR
JOHN E ADAMS
ROBERT W ADAMS
WARREN E ADAMS
RICHARD C AGUIRRE
SANTIAGO AGUIRRE
LUSIO C AHUMADA
HOMER R AINSWORTH
DEWILLIS L ALBERT
HENRY J ALBERT JR
JOHN S ALBERT
RICHARD S ALBERT
ROBERT L ALDRIDGE
JAMES T ALEXANDER
ROBERT E ALEXANDER
EDDIE C ALFARO
HORACE ALFORD JR
THOMAS R ALIFF
ROBERT T ALILOVICH
ROGER H ALLE
ALFONZIA D ALLEN
DAVID F ALLEN
FRED M ALLEN
GEORGE W ALLEN
JACK L ALLEN
JOHNNY L ALLEN
RAYMOND C ALLEN
RICHARD L ALLEN
HOWARD A ALLENDER
JOHN W ALLISON JR
ARMANDO ALMARAZ
DONACIANO B ALMAZAN
HERMAN ALSUP
JOHN S ALTON
ROBERT E ALTOSINO
RICHARD L ALVARADO
GILBERT ALVAREZ
RICHARD J AMANN
DOMINICK M AMBROSINO
NORMAN R AMENDT
AMOUS L AMEY
DONALD P AMIDON
MONDAL R AMMONS
JACK D ANDERBERG
CLYDE E ANDERSON
FRED L ANDERSON
LOREN E ANDERSON
MILTON A ANDERSON
RICHARD N ANDERSON
GARY G ANDREWS
ROBERTO APONTE-DELGADO
BILLY R APPLEBY
JAMES S ARAKAI
CHARLES E ARCH
RONALD R ARCHER
JOAQUIN A ARMENTA
LEWIS H ARMENTROUT III
WILLIAM J ARMSTRONG
JOHN R ARNALL
RALPH E ARRINGTON
BOBBIE R ARTHUR
JAMES L ASHBROOK
BILLIE J ASHBY
OLLIE R ASHER
EUGENE L ASHLEY
RONALD E ASHLINE
THERON C ASKEW
CHARLES A ASTLEY JR
VICTOR W ATWELL
ROWAN D ATWOOD
DELBERT F AUSTIN
MONROE AUSTIN JR
BERNARDO R AYALA
RAMON L AYMERICH-GONZALEZ
LORENZO BACA
HUGO V BACCARI
HAROLD E BADGLEY
PAUL G BAENEN
CLARENCE M BAILEY
HAROLDENE BAILEY
LAWRENCE A BAILEY
BOBBY G BAIZE
DONALD H BAKER
EUGENE J BAKER
PAUL T BAKER
WILLIAM K BAKER
HERBERT W BALBONI
LOUIS W BALDWIN
RALPH E BALL
JOSEPH J BALLARD JR
BOBBIE R BANKSTON
MARVIN W BARBER
DANIEL C BARCAK
JOHN B BARDWELL
WILLIAM V BARFIELD
PHILLIP P BARHAM
EDWIN J BARMAN
DANIEL W BARNES
HOWARD J BARNES
CHARLES R BARNETT
DAVID E BARNEY
ROBERT C BARNHART
PAUL C BARNHOUSE
JIM B BARNS
WILLIAM C BARR
ORA E BARRATT JR
JOHN P BARRETT JR
THOMAS G BARRETT
VALENTINE N BARSOUKOFF
ROGER P BARTHOLF
GILBERT BASHE
LEROY R BATEMAN
MARLYN BATEMAN JR
WILLIAM A BATES
REGINALD J BATTEN
ERWIN G BAUER
GEORGE C BAUERFEIND
WILLIAM B BAUGH
EDWARD W BAUMGARD JR
KEITH R BAYLEY
DONALD BEAM
JOHN L BEAN
KENNETH L BEASLEY
LAVERN H BECHER
ROBERT R BECKER
KENNETH E BECKLEY
EDWARD R BELARDI JR
BERNARD J BELFE
JAMES H BELL
EDGAR L BELLEFLEUR
OLLIE J BELT
DAVID L BELTZ
PAUL BENAVIDES
FRANK J BENENATI
BENNIE BENNETT JR
RAYMOND R BENNETT
JOSEPH P BENOIT
ROBERT C BENTLEY
CESAR I BENZONI
JOHN A BERG
RICHARD W BERG
CHARLES F BERGERON
GORDON F BERGREN
PATRICK J BERKLEY
RALPH L BERNHARDT
DENNIS J BERRY
FLOYD E BERRY
MICHAEL D BETTHAUSER
ROBERT J BETZ
PERRY M BEVENS
LEO E BEVER
FRED G BEVFODEN
JAMES E BEVILLE
HAROLD A BEYER
DAVID R BICKLEY
PETRO BILECKYJ
DWAYNE L BILES
FRANK B BILLINGS JR
DONALD S BILLS JR
MORGAN E BINET
THEODORE F BINETTE
ALFRED D BIRCH JR
LEO A BIROSS
FRANK L BIRRELL
WALTER L BIRT
DAVID E BISHOP
STEPHEN A BITNER
PAUL E BLACK
TILMER H BLACKSMITH
PAUL L BLAIR
RONALD BLAKE
GLEN BLAKLEY
DONALD R BLANCHARD
DONALD K BLANKENSHIP
EDWARD F BLASKO
STANLEY A BLAZEWICZ
JOHN D BLINN
HARRY E BODENHAMER JR
EDWARD J BOGLIN
THOMAS BOHATCH
EDWARD J BOHNAS
HERMAN C BOHNKE JR
WILLIAM F BOLDUC
DENVER H BOLING
HOWARD G BOLING
GEORGE C BOLOTAS
RUDOLPH BONINCONTRI
JOHN C BONINO
GERALD R BOOKAMIRE
WILLIAM E BOOTH JR
KENNETH J BOOTHE
FREDERICK W BORN JR
JOHN P BORSETI
DONALD L BORUFF
CHARLES BORUM
EDWARD R BOSCH
MERLYN E BOSHAW
GEORGE L BOSWELL
EARL E BOTTOMS
ALLAN J BOUQUIN
WILLIAM A BOUQUIN
THOMAS J BOURG
GERARD A BOURRET
EUGENE W BOWDEN
WILLIAM E BOWDEN
RICHARD L BOWER
ROBERT L BOWERS JR
RICHARD M BOWMAN
CHARLES W BOYD
HUGH W BOYD
THOMAS J BOYLAN
PALMER S BRAATEN
ALFRED P BRADSHAW
BILLIE F BRADSHAW
CHARLES W BRADSHAW
FREDDIE L BRADSHAW
ROBERT H BRADSHAW
JAMES R BRALY
RICHARD Q BRAMAN
CLIFTON BRANDENBURG
BERNARD L BRANDFASS
CHARLES N BRANDNER
CLYTHELL BRANSON
WILLIAM R BRENNAN
EDWARD W BREUTZMANN
ELMO R BRIDGES JR
CHARLES R BRIGGS
MERTON E BRIGGS
SETH E BRITT
MARTIN C BRIZIUS
SAM BROCATO JR
JOHN W BRODIE
PHILIP R BROHEN
VERNON L BROKKE
DORIES W BROOKS JR
MELVIN D BROOKS
RICHARD A BROOKS
ROBERT G BROOKS
LANEY B BROOME
JOHN C BROSSARD
BOBBY L BROWN
DONALD R BROWN
GEORGE E BROWN
STANLEY BROWN
DONALD C BROWNE
RICHARD W BRUCE
THOMAS C BRUCE
HENRY L BRUDER
GAETON A BRUNO
JOHN R BRUNS
THOMAS W BRUNSON
JOHN C BRYAN
FLOYD G BRYANT
JAMES C BRYANT
JERRY R BRYANT
WALTER J BRYDON
ROMOLO A BUCCI
THOMAS M BUCHANAN
JACK J BUCHL
WILBURN D BUCKNER
JAMES W BUDDENBURG
JOSEPH M BUDESKY
ELBERT BUNCH
JACK E BUNNELL
ELMER V BURGER JR
TED C BURGESS
CARL M BURKE
JOHN E BURKE
RAYMOND B BURKE
WILLIAM R BURKE
RAYMOND R BURKHOLDER
AARON S BURNAN
THOMAS G BURNAUGH
IRA E BURNETT
CHADWICK O BURNS
WILLIAM J BURREY
KENNETH C BURROUGHS
LESTER M BURROWS JR
WILLIAM T BURTYK
GEORGE B BURZOTA
GEORGE W BUSCH
MARSHALL L BUSH
RICHARD E BUSTLE
JAMES E BUXTON
GLENN H BYRD
OWEN C BYRD
WILLIAM E BYRD
FROILAN CABRERA-GONZALEZ
JAMES D CADDELL
JAMES B CAILLOUET
JAMES E CAIN
TOMAS CALDERON-COSME
ERNEST T CALDWELL
GERALD K CALDWELL
JAMES E CALLAWAY
VINCENT W CALVANICO
BOBBY L CAMERON
FLOYD D CAMERON
HENRY V CAMIRE
DONALD E CAMPBELL
RAYMOND B CAMPBELL
JOSEPH S CAMPO
RICHARD A CAMPOS
BOBBY C CANTERBERRY
LOUIS M CAPUTO
MARIO J CARDILIO
LARRY A CARELLA
WALTER F CAREY

85 MARINE CORPS

WILLIAM CAREY
DOUGLAS B CARICO
VICENTE CARLO-PEREZ
ROBERT E CARLSON
JAMES C CARNEY
CLAYTON W CARON
BILLIE C CAROTHERS
CHARLES F CARPENTER
ROBERT J CARPENTER
SAM J CARPENTER
MARVIN D CARR
ALFREDO CARRIZALES
AUBREY D CARROLL
CHARLIE P CARROLL JR
PATRICK J CARROLL
ROBERT J CARROLL
BOBBY R CARTER
DOYLE CARTER
HORACE J CARTER
LEONARD P CARTER
JOSEPH E CARUSO
ROBERT E CASAGRAND
ALEX CASANOVA
PETER F CASEY
MANUEL G CASILLAS
PAUL CASTIGLIONE
ERNESTO P CASTILLA
FELIX A CASTILLE
RAMON CASTILLO
LEON L CASTINO
JOHN L CAVENDER
BENITO A CECILIA
VINCENT S CERITELLO
HOWARD H CHANCEY
BOBBY J CHANDLER
CHARLES D CHAPMAN
CURTIS E CHAPMAN
THEODORE W CHAPMAN
ALFREDO P CHARLES
GERALD CHARLESWORTH
HOWARD F CHASE JR
ROBINSON CHASE
ALFREDO G CHAVEZ
HERMAN CHAVIRA
STANLEY J CHECKI
GEORGE CHEGAY
VICTOR A CHENEY
THOMAS J CHERF
JOHN S CHERSKOV
STANLEY A CHOCIAN
ARTHUR G CHOQUETTE
BORIS R CHRIST
WARREN E CHRISTIAN
STANLEY R CHRISTIANSON
RALPH E CHUTE
MITCHELL J CIEPLAK
LARRY R CIMINO
LOYD V CLAPP JR
BOB E CLARK
BRUCE L CLARK
EDWARD L CLARK
JOHN P CLARK
JOHN T CLARK JR
RICHARD D CLARK
ROBERT L CLARK
WALTER H CLOE III
MERLE D CLYMER
TERRILL O COATS
HARLAN R COCKERHAM
GILBERT CODDINGTON
DENVER C COGER
PURL L COGHILL
FRANK J COGINGS
CHARLES N COLBERT
DAVID T COLEGATE
DONALD L COLEMAN
JACK COLEMAN
JOHN B COLEMAN JR
GROVER COLEY
DONALD R COLGETT
RAYMOND F COLIN
DONALD R COLLIER
ALBERT H COLLINS
CALVIN R COLLINS
DAVID COLLINS
DOYLE COLLINS
EDMOND COLLINS JR
JUNIOR R COLLINS
RAFAEL COLON-MARQUEZ
JOHN C COLONNA

RICHARD J COLPAERT
JOHN T COMPTON
DONALD R COMTOIS
CLYDE L CONFER JR
JOHN J CONLON
PAUL M CONNOLLY
HARRY R CONNORS
ROBERT E CONNORS
BERNARD J CONSIDINE
DEHAVEN L CONWAY
JAMES L COOK
THOMAS R COOK
MICHAEL E COOLEY
MARVIN H COON
FLOYD COOPER JR
ARNOLD L COPITZKY
JOHN E CORBETT
JOHN J CORCORAN
FELIPE CORDERO-CANTINO
VICTOR CORDES III
ANDREW CORDOVA
JAMES H CORDOVA
JUAN B CORDOVA
ERNEST J CORIN
DON L CORLEY
CONRAD L CORNMAN
JOHN T CORREA
BOBBY D CORRELL
CHESTER L CORRELLO
HERBERT L CORRIGAN JR
RICHARD A CORSIGLIA
WILLIAM H CORTWRIGHT
PASQUALINO J
COSTANTINO
JAMES C COSTELLO JR
EUGENE COTA
MAURICE P COTE
ANTHONY J COTRONEO
LAWRENCE E COTTEN
DARRELL R COTTIER
CLIFTON C COTTON
WILLARD A COUTANT
ROGERIO L COUTO
WILLIAM N COWAN
RAY W COWLES
FLOYD S COX
GEORGE M COX JR
JAMES C COX
ROBERT J COZZALIO
GRADY J CRAWFORD
NOBLE L CRAWFORD
VERNON J CRAWFORD
CHARLES S CRISP
FRANK W CROCKER JR
GEORGE A CROCKER
GEORGE L CRONAUER
POWELL CROSLEY IV
JOHN C CROSS
ROY E CROSS
JACK D CROUCH
HAROLD M CROW
CHARLES S CROWLEY
JOHN J CROWLEY JR
GUILLERMO CRUHIGGER-
RODRIGUEZ
ROBERT J CRUSER
ESEQUIEL E CRUZ
RUBEN C CRUZ
DONALD J CUBRANICH
JAMES V CULLEN
JOSEPH C CULLIGAN JR
JOHN CUPRYNA
JAMES H CURNEAL
CHARLES M CURRY
DONALD A CUSHMAN
WILLIAM K CUSTER JR
WADE L DADE
ANGELO DALCOLLO
DANIEL J DALIER
JEROME M DALY
LOUIS J DANA
RAY T DANIEL
GRADY G DANIELS
NORMAN DANIELS
ARTHUR L DANZER
EDWARD D DARCHUCK
HUBERT E DARR
DOUGLAS E DAVIDSON
BILLIE H DAVIS
DAN R DAVIS

DONALD D DAVIS
JACK S DAVIS
JOHN R DAVIS
RICHARD C DAVIS
ROBERT E DAVIS
ROBERT T DAVIS
ROGER R DAVIS
WILLIAM E DAVIS
JOHN L DAWBER
WILLIE L DAWKINS
RICHARD D DAWSON
CHARLES E DAZEY
PAUL D DEAN
WILLIE R DEASON
JOHN A DE FRANCHESI
HENRY DEISS JR
CHARLES K DELAFIELD
ERNEST A DE LEON
GILBERT M DELIZ
ISAAC DEL TORO
JOSEPH DE MASE
JOSEPH A M DEMERS
GEORGE E DEMPSEY
BERNARD A DEMSKI
JOHN H DE MUNDO
ROY J DE NIKE JR
ALBERT F DENT
GEORGE DEQUIRE
ROBERT K DERBY
FRANK D DERMILIO
ROCCO W DEROSE
WILLIAM J DESBRO
ROGER L DESCLOS
JAMES J DEVLIN
PAUL N DE VRIES
HUGH D DIALS
DONALD J DIDIER
JOHN DI DONNA
HAROLD M DIEDERICH
JOHN W DIEMER
WILLIAM F DIEMLER
DUGALD A DILL
EDWARD V DILLON
DOMENICO S DI SALVO
EUGENE E DODGE
RICHARD A DODGE
JOSEPH E DOHERTY
BOBBY J DOLEN
JESSE P DOMINGUE
JAMES H DONAHUE
WELDON C DONALDSON
JAMES C DONHAM
DONALD W DONNELL
JOHN J DOPAZO
ANTHONY V DORAZIO JR
CONRAD E DORN
GERALD E DOTY
VERNON J DOUCETTE
PAUL DOUGHERTY
VINCENT P DOUGHERTY JR
WILLIAM J DOUGHERTY
CHARLES A DOW
JAMES A DOWD
RAY E DOWLER
DONALD F DOWLING
PAUL E DOWLING JR
JACKIE D DOYLE
JOHN A DOYLE
JOHN M DRAKE JR
DONALD M DRAKULICH
ROBERT E DRENNAN
WILLIAM C DRISKILL
ROBERT L DROYSEN
ALBERT E DRUMMOND JR
JOHN G DRUZIANICH JR
GREGOR DUBAS JR
CARL L DUE
DANIEL J DUGGAN
THOMAS A DUGGER
ALBERT J DUMBECK
HERSHEL D DUNAGAN
RAYMOND E DUNCAN
DONALD E DUNHAM
DONALD C DUNKLE
KENNETH W DUNLAP
THOMAS J DUNNE
RICHARD W DURHAM
HARRY M DUSTERHOFF
DOUGLAS T DUSTIN
LEE E DUTCHER

KENNETH E DVORAK
JAMES DWYER
DAILEY F DYE
DONALD W EADS
JAMES S EARLES
JACK R EATON
EDWARD E ECCLESTON
MELVIN EDENS
ALVIN L EDGINTON
PATRICK J EDMUNDS
DONALD E EDWARDS
GEORGE N EDWARDS
ROBERT B EDWARDS
THOMAS J EGAN
WALTER R EICHHOLZ
DONALD E EICHSCHLAG
RICHARD H EIDAM
JAN R EIKE
LEONARD D EISMIN
ROBERT M ELLARS
RICHARD H ELLENBERGER
ROBERT J ELLIOTT
HENRY E ELLIS
THEODORE C E ELLIS
HAROLD E ELLISON
KENNETH L ELLISON
GEORGE W ELMORE
WILLIAM T ELROD
JOHN B ELWELL
ROBERT L ELZE
FRANK EMANUEL JR
GEORGE R EMHOFF
MILTON C ENDICOTT
DANIEL J ENG
DONALD ENGLEHART
JOSEPH W ENNIST
ROBERT E ENRIGHT
WILLIAM G EPP
CHARLES R EPPLEMAN
ROBERT L EPPERSON
FRANKLIN H EPPLEY
RICHARD W ERDENBERGER
WILLIAM K ERDMAN
WILLIAM C ERNST
BURT ERVIN
ROBERT H ERVIN
BENJAMIN B ESTRELLA JR
JOHN A EVANS JR
JOHN L EVANS
KENNETH O EVANS
MELVIN L EYE
ALEXANDER FACCHINI
BILLIE R FAILE
RAY P FAIRCHILD
THERON FAIRLEY
RAY L FAISON
FELIX R FAJKUS
ANTHONY J FALATACH
ANDREW L FARIE III
LOUIS G FARLEY
DONALD A FATICA
PAUL D FAULCONER
THOMAS O FAUST
LEO S FAUTSCH
PRESTON S FAY JR
DONALD G FEENEY
GERALD FEINSTEIN
THEODORE FELLIS
CHARLES H FELLOWS
JOHN A FELTON
CHARLES C FERGUSON
MARVIN D FERGUSON
RONALD P FERGUSON
LEONARD J FERKO
KERMIT M FERRELL
ERICH R FICHTER
WILLIAM R FICKE
JAMES T FIEDLER
REUBIN FIELDS
WALTER M FIFE
ALEX G FILOMENO
DARRELL E FINE
JOHN E FINN
PATRICK T FINN
ROBERT J FINNEGAN
DONALD L FISH
WILLIAM FISH
ROBERT J FISHER
ROBERT S FITCH
ROBERT C FITTS

ERNEST FITZGERALD JR
ROBERT J FITZGERALD
THOMAS J FITZGERALD
GEORGE F FITZPATRICK
MICHAEL J FITZPATRICK
DONALD E FLAGG
RUSSEL W FLAGLORE
PAUL H FLAMAND
JAMES E FLANAGAN
STANLEY M FLEENOR
SAM FLEMING JR
DAVID R FLOOD
RICHARD A FLOOD
CHARLES K FLORA
FIDEL G FLORES
FLORENCIO G FLORES
FROELAN FLORES
HENRY V FLORES
WILLIAM B FLORES
DANIEL W FLOREY
JOHN F FLOREZ
DONALD W FORBES
FRANCIS E FORD
NOLAN E FORD
PAUL L FORD
RUSSELL H FORD
GEORGE G
FORNELIUS JR
EDSEL G FORRESTER
EUGENE R FORSGREN JR
JAMES FORTE
WILLIAM H
FORTENBERRY
WILLIAM E FORTIN
RODGER D
FORTINBERRY
ROBERT S FOUNTAIN
DONALD R FOURMAN
FRANK A FOUST
KEITH B FOWLER
MURRY N FOWLER
LANTY R FRAME
ANTHONY P FRANCIS JR
WILLIAM FRANCIS
JOSEPH L
FRANCOMANO
DEWAYNE N FRANK
ANTHONY E FRANKLIN
GLEN E FRAZIER
JUNIOR E FRAZIER
WILLIAM R FRAZIER
NORMAN P FRAZZINI
WILLARD N FREDERICK
ANTON J FREER
JIMMIE E FRENCHMAN
CLEO B FRIESS
JAMES N FRISBIE
WILLIAM A FROELICH
VAN J FRONEFIELD
LYMAN FRY
WILLIAM L FRY
WILLIAM D FUGIT
RICHARD O FUKA
ANTHONY H
GAGLIORMELLA
CHARLES GAHM
JAMES E GAISFORD
FRANCIS C GALL
MORRIS L GALLANT
RAYMOND H GALLANT
CHARLES GANGL
FERNANDO L GARCIA
FREDIE GARCIA
OSCAR GARCIA
RALPH GARCIA
RAMIRO GARCIA
RALPH H GARDNER
RICHARD J GARGUILLO
DONALD E GARMAN
WILLIAM E GARNETT
FRANKLIN D GARRETT
RICHARD C GARZA
BERT J GASPORD
TOMMY GATEWOOD
GILBERT R GAUDET
NORMAND GAUTREAU
WILLIAM L GAYHART
WILLIAM H
GAZAWAY JR
JAMES W GEBHARDT

86 MARINE CORPS

NELSON R GEDDES
ANTHONY GENOVESE
JOHN S GENTRY
WALTER W GEORGE
JOHN G GERGELY
ARTHUR J GERSEBECK
LOUIS O GERUE
CHARLES S GETZ
BASIL W GEWVELLIS
BERNARD J GEYGAN JR
REX D GIBSON
GEORGE GIEDOSH
JOHN GIESEKING
MICHAEL J GILBRIDE
JAMES C GILCHRIST
WILLIE A GILCHRIST
JAMES L GILLAM
DURSTON D GILLEAN
LEROY GILLISPIE
EDWARD E GILMORE
TIMOTHY J GILMORE
LEON R GINGLEWOOD
RALPH J GIPSON
GILBERT G GOEPEL
HERBERT H GOETZ
CHARLES C GOFF
ARNOLD J GOLDBERG
RICHARD M GOLDEN
HILLIARD M GOLDORF
MELVIN E GOLDSMITH
FRED GOLDSTEIN
ALBERT E GOLDY
WILLIAM R GOLL
EDWARD GOMEZ
JAIME O GOMEZ
ROY GOMEZ
ALEJANDRO A GONZALES
ALVIN J GONZALES
DONALD P GONZALES
LEO R GONZALES
PEDRO V GONZALES
ROGER GONZALES
RUDOLPH V GONZALES
HERSHEL B GOODING
GLENN H GOODLANDER
DALE E GOODMAN
EDWARD H GOODMAN
GERALD K GORDY
DIONICIO J GORENA JR
WILLIAM H GORSUCH
RICHARD H GOSS
JOE B GRADY
RONALD T GRAHAM JR
HANS W GRAHL
DWYER D GRANT
FREDERICK E GRANT
GERALD C GRAVEEN
WILBUR B GRAY
ROBERT GREAVES JR
RALPH GRECO
RONALD W GREEB
ANTHONY J GREELEY
JAMES L GREEN
JAMES T GREEN
JOHN F GREENE
WILLIAM J GREENE JR
WILLIAM R GREER
JAMES A GREGORY
CARL H GRESSMAN
HOMER F GRIBBINS
CLARK W GRIBBLE
LOUIS F GRIEGO
JULIAN F GRIFFIN
WALTER L GRIFFIN
CHARLES E GRISE
HARRY E GRISWOLD
JAMES T GRISWOLD
EDMUND P GROH JR
WILLIAM C GROVE
RICHARD L GRUNEBERG
RICHARD F GUILES
CHARLES H GULLEDGE
DAVID L GUNTER
ADOLFO M GUTIERREZ
RUDOLPH R GUTIERREZ
CHARLES B GUY
JOSE D GUZMAN-RODRIGUEZ
RICHARD S GZIK
RICHARD A HAAGENSEN

DARRELD D HACKBARTH
HARRY J HADEN
LEO J HADLEY
GERALD L HAERR
JAMES A HAFFEY
CARL J HAGLE
HOWARD J HAHN
DWAIN L HAIGWOOD
JOHN B HALL
QUINTON V HALL
RICHARD W HALL
RONALD G HALL
STEPHEN C HALL
ROBERT H HALLAWELL
THOMAS J HALLMARK
FELIX B HALTER
DAVID E HALVERSON
PHILIPPE E HAMANN
WILLIAM H HAMBLIN
KENNETH C HAMILTON
WILLIE HAMILTON
RONALD R HAMMETT
HUGO HAMMOND
JAMES D HAMMOND
PHILLIP O HAMMOND
HOMER M HAMMONDS
LLOYD W HAMON
RICHARD E HANCOCK
GEORGE E HAND
IRWIN HANDLER
ALVIN R HANEY
JERALD J HANKINS
WOODROW I HANKS
JACK L HANNAH
LAWRENCE D HANSEN
ROBERT G HANSEN
ROBERT E HANSLER
RICHARD B HANSON
ROBERT J HANSON
HOWARD R HARBRIDGE
EDWARD C HARDCASTLE
JAMES W HARDY
MAYNARD L HARGO
FLOYD H HARKINS
ERVIN E HARKNESS
RICHARD L HARLOW
EDGAR F HARMAN
HOWARD H HARMAN
GILBERT L HARMON
CLAY HARNESS
EDWARD HARPER
FLOYD HARRIS
JAMES M HARRIS
RICHARD G HARRIS
ROBERT L HARRIS
JIMMIE M HARRISON
ROY E HARRISON
DONALD R HARRYMAN
AMON F HARVEY JR
NORMAN F HARVEY
ELTON J HARWELL
OTIS M HARWELL
DONALD G HASTY
THEODORE L HATFIELD
BILLY D HATLEY
ELLSWORTH J HATT JR
ALLAN P HATTON
JOHN M HAUSEMANN
EDWIN B HAVENS JR
DAN B HAWKE
EARL C HAWTHORNE
JAMES A HAYDEN
JOHN B HAYDEN
KENNETH D HAYEN
DONALD A HAYES
HORACE HAYES
KEITH M HAYES
LADDIE L HAYES
RICHARD V HAYES
ALBERT W HAZELTON JR
ROBERT C HEALY
CHARLES W HECKMAN
LEONARD A HEDRICK
JOHN J HEGARTY III
CARL J HEIGL
THOMAS W HEINZEN
RAYMOND F HEJNY
JAMES W HELLEM
J B HELM
HENRY E HELTON JR

RICHARD R HELTSLEY
DEARL L HEMPHILL JR
JOSEPH F HENDERSON
RICHARD E HENDERSON
WILLIAM P HENDERSON
DARRELL T HENDRICKS
DONALD E HENDRICKS
DONALD J HENDRIX
LAWRENCE J HENGY
LEO J HENKENIUS
RAYMOND L HEPLER
RAYMOND L HERGERT
J W HERLSTON
WALTER HERMANSEN
CARLOS HERMOSILLO
RONALD A HERSON
IRVIN W HESS
JAMES C HESTER
CHARLES M HIBBERT
DALE D HICKS
JOHN D HICKS
GEORGE C HIGGINS
THOMAS R HIGGINS
CARL HIGGS
ERNEST J HIGHTOWER
ROBERT H HILGENBERG
EARL R HILL
GRISWOLD M HILL JR
JAMES M HILL
WILLIAM F HILL
ROBERT W HILTON
ROBERT L HINDS
WILLIAM B HINKLE
DAVEY L HINSON
WILLIAM J HINTON
THEODORE B HIRSCH
DARRELL B HIRSCHBACH
KYLE A HOFFMAN
DAVID D HOFRICHTER
WILLIAM H HOILES III
ROBERT J HOLBROOK
CARL H HOLDER
FRANCIS E HOLLAND
IVAN L HOLLAR
JAMES L HOLLEY
JACK S HOLLOWAY
NORBERT F HOLTER
HENRY A HONZA
GERALD D HOOPER
JAMES H HOPPER
JOHN R HORAN
CHARLES E HORN
JACK HORN
WAYMOND L HORNE
JAMES W HORNING JR
HERMAN L HORTON
LONNIE E HORTON
EVERETT J HOWARD
LLOYD L HOWARD
DAVID K HOWCROFT
JOHN T HOWELL
ROY F HOWINGTON
JOHN A HOY JR
THOMAS S HOY
GEORGE J HRIC
RAYMOND C HUBBARD
PAUL E HUBBS
WILLIAM A HUBERT
BENJAMIN R HUDSON
NORMAN R HUGHES
LEONARD J HUNDSHAMER
JOHN D HUNSBERGER
FREDERICK S HUNT
ROBERT J HUNT
HERBERT F HUNTER
WILLIAM B HUNTER
JANS F HURSEY
FLETCHER M HUTCHINS
LORENZER HUTCHINSON
THOMAS J HUTSON
BENAB HYATT
BENJAMIN A HYMEL JR
LUIS J IBARRA
CHARLES L IGEL
JOHN J IMBERT
NICHOLAS C INCONTRERA
KENNETH R INGMAN
MARTIN V INGOGLIA
GERALD E INGRAHAM
HAROLD J IOTT

FRANK IPPOLITO
JUAN R IRIZARRY-OLIVER
THEODORE R IRVIN
ROBERT C ISBESTER
DAVID D IVENS
NICK S JACK
JACKIE D JACKMAN
DONALD R JACKSON
HOWARD L JACKSON
JAMES D JACKSON
JAMES E JACKSON JR
JEREMIAH JACKSON
R A JACKSON
ROBERT E JACKSON
VIRGIL A JACKSON JR
JOSEPH T JACOBS
JOHN T JAGEACKS
ANDREW R JAKUSZ
JESSE E JAMES
WILLIAM R JAMES
JAMES R JANCA
ADRIAN D JANISZEWSKI
PAUL J JANOWSKY
LONNIE R JARRELL
CHARLES E JARRETT
FRANK J JEFFS
THOMAS K JENKINS
HENRY D JENSON
RAYMOND E JESKO
WILLARD G JIRICEK
EDWARD H JOACHINSON JR
RICHARD A JOHANNSEN
NORMAN D JOHNSEN
BILL E JOHNSON
BILLY E JOHNSON
CHARLES E JOHNSON
CHARLES L JOHNSON
ERIC JOHNSON JR
FRANK JOHNSON
HARRY JOHNSON
JOHN L JOHNSON
JOHN W JOHNSON
LEONARD L JOHNSON
MERLYN JOHNSON
RANDOLPH A JOHNSON
RICHARD JOHNSON
RICHARD G JOHNSON
ROBERT W JOHNSON
TOM H JOHNSON
HAROLD M JOHNSTON
JIMMIE C JOHNSTON
MARVIN H JOLLIFF
BERNARD C JONAS
CLANTON C JONES JR
DENNIS JONES
EUGENE V JONES
GLENN I JONES
JAMES E JONES
JAMES E JONES
JOHN W JONES
JOSEPH H H JONES
LUCIAN M JONES
ODELL JONES
RALPH D JONES
THOMAS E JONES
THOMAS L JONES
TILFORD R JONES JR
WALDO B JONES
WILLIAM E JONES
WILLIAM H JONES
WOODROW D JONES JR
JOHN D JORDAN JR
LAMBERT A JORDAN JR
WILLIAM S JOSEPH
ROBERT A JUHL
JOHN M JULLIEN JR
VITO J JUNEVICUS
EDWIN G JUSTICE
HERBERT JUSTICE
THOMAS M JUSTICE
MICHAEL C KAAIHUE
ARTHUR C KAHUE
RAYMOND R KAISER
HOWARD W KAIUWAILANI
WILLIAM K KALEO
OLIVER W KAMM
DELBERT R KAMPHAUG
THOMAS KARADEEMA
CONRAD W KASSELMANN

WALTER F KASTERKO
EDWARD K KAUFMAN
LLOYD D KAUL
WILLIAM P KEERY
ROLAND T KEESEE
PAUL O KEETH
FRANCIS W KEEVER
ORREN R KEEVER
JOHN C KEISER
HAROLD W KELLER
IRVIN R KELLEY
JOHN D KELLY
DONALD L KELSCH
BILLY E KELSO
HARVEY D KEMP
WILLIAM J KENIGSEDER
GEORGE Q KENNEDY
RICHARD M KENNEDY
JOSEPH R KENNEL JR
ROBERT E KENNEY
WILLIAM R KENNEY
DONALD A KENWORTHY
JOHN R KERIVAN
JERRY J KERNS
WILLIAM C KETTRICK
EDWARD KIEDROWSKI
YALE S KIEFER
JOHN J KIGGINS
JACK C KIGHTLINGER
JOHNNY KILBURN
RICHARD B K KIM
JAMES E KIMBALL
WESLEY KINARD
LONNIE H KINCAID
ROBERT B KINDER
BLAINE D KING
GEORGE F KING
GEORGE R KING
JAMES D KING
JAMES P KING
JAMES V KING
RALPH E KING
ROBERT KING
WILLIAM A KING
JAMES R KINNEY
SALVADORE D KINNEY
KENNETH W KINSEY
WILLIAM M KITCHENS JR
PETER H KIVALOS
CLIFFORD J KLEBER
PALMER KLINE
EDWIN J KLINGER
HENRY F KLINZING
ARTHUR F KLOPPENBURG
PAUL A KLUG
EDWARD D KLUSKY
MELVIN T KNICKERBOCKER
REGIS R KNORR
WALTER D KNOTT
JOSEPH J KNOX
JEROME F KNUTSON
BUDDY N KOEHLER
DOUGLAS J KOEHNEN
ROY E KOENIG
EDWARD KOKOTT
JOHN KOROLY
JOIE KORTE
DONALD R KOSEL
FREDERICK J KOSHKO
FABIAN T KOTARA
DANIEL B KOTT
JOSEPH E KOWALSKI
ARTHUR M KOZUKI
MORRLYN D KRANZLER
JOSEPH C KREMINSKI JR
LYLE H KRIENKE
FLOYD T KRIGBAUM
CHESTER A KROLAK JR
EDWIN J KRUCIAK
ROBERT C KRUEGER
REGIS E KRUG
ROBERT L KUBISTY
ANTON J KUCSERA
HARVEY E KUDICK
ROBERT A KUENY
MARYLYN D KUESTER

87

MARINE CORPS

EDWARD D KUHN
RICHARD C KUHN
THOMAS R KUNTZ
LAWRENCE J KUNZWEILER
JOSEPH F KURZAWSKI
LOUIS P KWADER
DONALD E LABARGE
JIMMIE D LABOGEN
ARTHUR R LABONTE
JOHN E LABORG
ATNORY LABOY-COLLAZO
CLARENCE R LABRIE
ROLAND E LAFLEUR
JOHN J LAIVELING JR
JOHN T LAMBERG
JOHN N LAMBERT
MARVIN R LAMBERT
EDWARD F LAMERS
JOHN E LAMMERS
EDWARD J LANAHAN
JOHN H LAND
ARTHUR L LANDACRE
HOMER J LANDERS
JULES H LANDRY
JOHN R LANG
ROBERT D LANG
JOHN P LANGWELL
SHELTON LANIER
FAUSTINO LAPING
RICHARD R LARA
DONALD F LARE
RALPH W LARKINS JR
LOYAL G LASSLEY
WILLIAM C LASTINGER
JAMES P LAUGHY
JOSEPH LAUKAITIS
WILLIAM R LAUNDRY
LESTER C LA VOIE
PETER P LA VOIE
WILLIAM LAVORGNA
JOHN A LAW
MILTON R LAWHORN
ALFRED E LAWRENCE JR
JOHN P LAWRENCE
MILTON E LAWSON
WALTER K LAWSON
JOHN D LAWTON JR
ESIDRO A LAYCOCK
GENE H LEASE
HENRY T D LE BLANC
HUBERT J LE BLANC
BILLY S LEE
LAWRENCE J LEE
LEON LEE
WILFORD H LEE
JOHN W LEGG
KENNETH O LEHNUS
HOMER LEICHLITER JR
JOHN C LE MASTER
RAY F LEMMONS
EDWARD M LEMON
EDWARD C LENEVE
GUSS R LENON
PHILIP I LENZ
REUBEN LEONARD
ROBERT A LEONBERGER
BARNEY LERNER
EARL W LESTER
RICHARD C LESTER
WALTER T LESTER
JOSEPH J LESZCZYNSKI
RUSSELL A LETHBRIDGE
RONALD N LEVASSEUR
HARVEY F LEVINE
LOUIS H LEVINE
JOHN A LEWCHUK
DONALD R LEWIS JR
EDWARD L LEWIS
JACK H LEWIS
JAMES M LEWIS
JOSEPH LEWIS JR
LAWRENCE L LEWIS
WILLIAM R LEWIS JR
WILLIAM T LEWIS JR
WILLIAM W LEWIS
RICHARD M LEWRY
PHILLIP A LIERSE
RONALD D LILLEDAHL
JAMES A LILLY
JOSE M LINARES-ORTIZ
EARL O LINDEMANN
ROBERT J LINTON
LAWRENCE M LISTON
GORDON A LITTLEFIELD
HERBERT A LITTLETON
JOSEPH M LIVICH
JIMMIE B LIVINGSTON
CARL H LLOYD
SAMMIE LOCASH
JIMMIE E LOCKHART
EARL W LOGAN
MARTIE D LONG
STEWART W LONG
NORMAN P LOOKER
ALFONSO E LOPEZ
GERALD A LOPEZ
JOE M LOPEZ
PEDRO A LOPEZ JR
SALVADORE L LOPICCOLO
ROY L LORAH
ROY B LORD JR
JOSEPH P LOSTETTER
WILLIAM M LOVE
ARTHUR R LOVINS
MICHAEL LOVRA
ROY LOYD
EDWARD S LUCARZ
BOBBY D LUCAS
CHARLES R LUCAS
EARLAND L LUCE
RAY F LUCKENBILL
RAFAEL LUGO JR
PAUL V LUHRS
HARVARD E LUICK
JOHN E LUKE
GILBERT F LUNA
DARYL D LUND
DAVID L LUNDBERG
RONALD D L LUNSFORD
ATTILIO M LUPACCHINI
TOM E LUSK
WILLIAM H LUTZ
ROBERT F LYNCH
ELVIN H LYONS
PATRICK A LYONS
LESLIE D LYTLE
MALCOLM A MACASKILL
HENRY B MACHADO JR
ALFRED L MACHMER
ROBERT J MACKISON
KENNETH C MACLEAN
ALLEN H MACQUARRIE
GEORGE E MADRESS
LUCIANO E MADRID
ROBERT B MADRID
STANLEY W MAEDKE
HENRY J MAGOLAN
JOSEPH MAHALAK
VERNON MAHAN
JAMES J MAHONEY
MICHAEL J MAHONEY
RAFAEL MALDONADO-CORTADA
FRANKLIN C MALKEMES JR
ROBERT A MALLETT
JAMES J MALLOY
JOE W MALONE JR
CHARLES H MANGIN
JEROME M MANGNER
JAY MANN
WILLIAM R MANNING
WILLIAM A MANNS
WILLIAM G MANUELLO
CHARLES E MARBURGER
ANTHONY MARCATANTE
DAVID T MARCHANT
ALEXANDER J MARCHESE
JOHN A MARCHESE
NICHOLAS J MARCIANO
ALFRED R MAREK
DAVID C J MARIER
WAYNE A MARKER
AMAR D MARKS
GEORGE J MARKUS
BOBBY G MARLER
CHARLES MARLOW JR
JOSEPH MARRYOTT
HOWARD M MARSH
ROBERT L MARSH
WILLIAM B MARSHALL
RICHARD W MARSON
ROBERT C MARTELL
GERALD F MARTIN
JEWEL R MARTIN
GEORGE P MARTINEAU
ARNULFO MARTINEZ
DENNIS D MARTINEZ
OLIVER G MARTINEZ
PAUL MARTINEZ
JOHN E MARZEC
WALTER E MASON
VERLIN D MASTON
FRANCIS J MATASOVSKY
JOHN D MATEJOVICH
LAFE H MATERNE
KENNETH J F MATHEWS
RAYMOND C MATHONY
JOHN R MATTEI
GEORGE M MATTHEWS JR
STANLEY R MATTIER
ROBERT J MATUSOWSKI
ROY L MAXWELL
DONALD L MAY
LEVERT MAY
JAMES H MAYFIELD
EARNEY A MAYO JR
ROBERT E MCALLISTER
CHARLES A MCANDREWS
DONALD MCBETH
CHARLES H MCBRIAR
KENNETH E MCCAMIE
DONALD E MCCARTY
WILLIAM L MCCARVER
RAY A MCCLASKEY
HERBERT H MCCLELLAND
AARON J MCCOMBS
JAMES R MCCONNELL
DONALD W MCCORD
TERENCE F MCCORMACK
HOWARD MCCORMICK
THOMAS J MCCORMICK
FLOYD MCCOY
BILLY J MCDANIEL
CLAUDE C MCDANIEL
MARION E MCDANIEL
MICHAEL A MCDERMONT
MARTIN MCDERMOTT JR
WILLIAM C MCDONALD
RICHARD E MCDONOUGH
CLYAMON G MCDOWELL
POWELL H MCELHENNEY
HALLETT E MCGAFFIGAN
ROBERT L MCGEE
WILLIAM A MCGINNIS
WILLIAM R MCGLENNON
JAMES V MCGOVERN
KENNETH E MCGRADY
LLOYD J MCGRAW
JOHN J MCHUGH
DELTON MCINNIS
ALFRED MCINTOSH JR
KENNETH E MCINTUSH
MURDOCK MCKAY
MERLIN M MCKEEVER
ESQUE MCKEITHAN
HAROLD M MCKENNA
HUGH P MCKENNA
JOSEPH A MCKENNA
ROBERT J MCKENNA
HENDERSON D MCLEAN
RICHARD C MCMICHEAL
CHARLES R MCNELLY JR
JAMES R MCNEILLEY
RUBY L MEADE
EMMETT L MEAGHERS
WILSON M MECHE
ROBERT D MEDFORD
BILLIE J MEDLIN
JAMES J MEEHAN
VIRGIL S MEENACH
RICHARD J MEINZ
MOISE MELANCON JR
ROLAND J MELBYE
SPENCER C MELDRUM
WALTER A MELLER
CECIL G MELLINGER
BURL D MELTON
ROY G MELTON
CHARLES W MELVOLD
NELSON J MENARD
MANUEL T MENDOZA
JOSE H MERCADO
PERRY J MERCER
STANLEY B MERCHANT
EDWARD A MERCURIO
CLIFFORD S MERONK
WILLIAM M MESKOWSKY
PHILIP J MESS III
JOSEPH B MESZAROS
LAURENCE L METTLIN
KENNETH E METZGER
WILLIAM C METZGER
CHARLES A MEUSE
JAKE R MEYER
JOSEPH J MEYER
HENRY M MICHELL
ROBERT F MICONI
WILLIAM A MIDYETT
SAMUEL H MILANDER
FRANK MILES
GERALD D MILES
HARRY R MILES
ALLEN I MILLER
CHARLES R MILLER
ELWYN J MILLER
FLOYD G MILLER
GEORGE S MILLER
GORDON A MILLER
JOSEPH J MILLER JR
JOSEPH R MILLER
RAYMOND T MILLER
ROBERT J MILLER
THOMAS E MILLER
VERNON E MILLER
WILLIAM J MILLER
KENNETH J MILLIGAN JR
HUBERT MILLS
ROBERT J MILLS
JAMES H MINOR
KENNETH A MISAKI
NORBERT J MISORSKI
ALFRED E MITCHELL
LAWRENCE T MITCHELL
RAYMOND L MITCHEM
SEBASTIAN MITRANO JR
BOBBIE F MOCK
JAMES R MOFFITT
EUGENE F MOHS
JACK H MOLIN
EARL P MOLLERUD
GEORGE E MONCRIEF
WALTER C MONEGAN JR
ROOSEVELT MONETTE
THURMON W MONEY
FRANCIS F MONGONE
JEROME N MONNEY
TRACY W MONROE JR
HORACIO N MONTEZ
JAMES A MONTOYA
THOMAS MONTOYA
ROBERT P MOONEY
EDGAR E MOORE
OREN R MOORE
PHILIP T MOORE
SAMUEL E MOORE
WILLIAM D MOORE
WILLIAM L MOORE
BROOKS E MOORHEAD
MARVIN D MORE
ALVARO J MOREIRA
WHITT L MORELAND
ISAAC P MORENO
MANUEL H MORENO
ANDREW J MORGAN JR
HERBERT F MORGAN
LLOYD E MORGAN
ROY E MORGAN
CLARENCE T MORRIS
GEORGE F MORRIS
JAMES G MORRIS
JAMES F MORRISON
JESSIE MORRISON
RICHARD E MORRISSEY
GEORGE MORROSIS
BILLY J MORROW
ROBERT L MORROW
EUGENE M MOSCICKI
MARVIN E MOSELEY
WILLIAM H MOSER
JOSEPH D MOSS
FRENCH MOUNTS JR
ROBERT A MOZER
LEO W MRYNCZA
KENNETH A MUDGE
WILLIAM G MUIRHEAD
KENNETH J MULLEN
EDWARD J MULLIN JR
CHARLIE MULLINS JR
EMIL W MULLINS
THOMAS G MULLINS
LUMAN E MUNGER
DAVE L MUNSON
WARREN L MUNSON
EDWARD A MUNTZ
JOSEPH E MURPHY
RALPH J MURPHY
ROBERT E MURPHY
RONALD D MURPHY
HAROLD D MURSCH
DONALD W MYERS
FRED L MYERS
JESSE L MYERS
OLEN F MYERS
TOM W NANEY
GOLDEN NAPIER
WALTER G NAPIER
WILL E NASH III
PETER M NASSETTA
WALTER S NASTAWA
PHILIP P NEARY
JOE E NEELY
RONALD E NEES
WILLIAM H NEFF
PEDRO J NEGRON-RODRIGUEZ
CHARLES V NEJEDLY
WOODROW NELLONS
ENEAS J NENEMA
LYLE L NESBIT
ALBERT O NESSI JR
ALVIN NEUSTADT
JOHN NEVERS JR
CHARLES NEWELL
LEO A NEWHOUSE
JAMES E NEWTON
JOHN E NEWTON
LOUIS F NICHOLS
JAMES A NICHOLSON
RONALD L NICKEL
DONALD W NICKERSON
JAMES E NICKERSON
DONALD J NICKEY
RICHARD L NICKLES
DAVID M NICOLL
JAMES E NIEPORTE
CARL F NIX
CHARLES R NORMENT
WALTER M NORRIS JR
NORMAN P NORTH
MARVIN E NOTHSTEIN
CARL A NOWOCZYNSKI
DONALD G NUCKEL
RAMON NUNEZ-JUAREZ
RONALD J NUNGESSER
ALAN R NYE
AUBREY N OAKES
STANLEY T OBANION
ARTHUR L OBERMAN
EDWARD J OBERSHAW
EUGENE A OBREGON
JOHN P OBRIEN
RICHARD P OCONNEL
EDWARD M OCONNER
RICHARD J OCONNOR
TIMOTHY P OCONNOR
JIMMIE L ODELL
THOMAS J ODONNELL
ROBERT S OFSONKA
RICHARD F OGBURN
FRANK S OGDEN
JAMES W OGDEN
EDWIN P OGRODNIK
JOHN J OKANE
HAWORD D OKELLEY
SECUNDINO V OLIVARES
ENRIQUES J OLIVAS
CARL D OLIVER
JACK G OLIVER
SAMUEL R OLIVER JR

88

MARINE CORPS

EUGENE P OLSEN
WILLIAM T OLSON
JAMES M OMELVENY
EDWARD J ONTKO
WILLIAM K OPULAUOHO JR
ROGER H ORE
CHARLES D ORR
LOYDE R ORR
HARRY ORTEGA
JESUS M ORTEGA
GUILLERMO ORTIZ-OCASIO
LEWIS R ORVIS
CHARLES R OSBORN
RICHARD G OSBORNE
JOSEPH B OSTERGAARD
JAMES W OTOOLE
RICHARD F OUTTRIM
TED OVBEY JR
FORREST L OVERALL
ALBERT C OWEN
JOHN J OWENS JR
BERT OYA
FORD E PACE
LOUIS M PACELLE
RANSOM PACK
ALVIN E PAINTER
JOHN PALLAGI JR
RICHARD E PALMER
RALPH J PAPA
BILLY J PARDUE
ARTHUR G PARKER
CHARLES W PARKER
RICHARD A PARKER
RICHARD V PARKER
LARRY L PARMENTIER
ARKIE B PARRISH
CHARLES W PARRISH
JOHN C PARRY
DEAN W PARTIN
HERBERT J PASSER
GUERINO PASSERO JR
RAYMOND J PATIN
FRANK PATRICK JR
BILLY L PATTERSON
BRUCE R PATTERSON
MASON N PATTERSON
WALLACE I PATTERSON JR
EDWIN M PATTON
GOTFRIED PAULSON JR
JOHN C PAVLAK
BILLY J PAYNE
WILLARD D PAYNE
BRUCE W PAYTON
EUNIS O PAYTON
BILLY E PEACOCK
SHELLIE PEAK JR
MERLE D PEARSON
RAYMOND D PEARSON
ALFRED J PECHIN
WALTER G PEHLING
JOHN E PELFREY
ALBINO S PENA
GEORGE A PENCE
GLENN R PENDERGAST
BILLY D PENNISTON
CLAUDE PEOPLES
PEDRO J PERELES
JESUS J PEREZ
SIMON M PEREZ
MANUEL PEREZ-PIZARRO
JOHN L PERKINS
BRADLEY G PERRY
RAYMOND J PERRY
WILLIAM PERRY
JACK D PETERS
LOYD M PETERS
ROBERT W PETERSEN
GORDON A PETERSON
LARRY L PETERSON
UDELL L PETERSON
HAROLD L PETREE
PHILIP N PETTERSON
JAMES A PEVETO
ALLEN L PHILLIPS
CHARLES A PHILLIPS
CHARLES J PHILLIPS
JAMES E PHILLIPS
MARVIN E PHILLIPS
LOY A PHILPOT

JAMES T PICKETT
ROBERT E PICKETT
JOSEPH W PIERCE
ROBERT E PIERROUX
HAROLD L PIESIK
ALPHONSE R PILOSI
LLOYD A PINNER
WESLEY L PIPER
PATRICK D PITTILLO
DUANE C PLACE
CAMILLO PLACENCIA
REED E PLUMB
JUSTYN C PLUTA
BOBBY R POARE
NORMAN I PODOS
GEORGE J POE
JIG B POLAND
WALTER M POLLARD
EPIFANIO POMALES-SANTIAGO
ALVIN PORTER
HOMER L PORTER
KEITH M PORTER
WILLIAM B PORTER
JONATHAN R POSEY JR
WILLIAM P POSTEN
BOBBY L POTHAST
WILLIAM R POTTER
JOHN B POWE JR
ARTHUR D POWELL
HARRY A POWELL
WILLIAM N POWELL
MATTHEW G POWERS JR
MAURICE W PRENDERGAST
DUANE F PRICE
JOHN W PRICE
KENNETH D PRICE
LAURENCE P PRIDDY JR
RAYMOND R PRIETO
HARRY J PRINCE
MILFORD H PRITCHARD
WALTER O PRITCHARD
GERALD PRYHODA
RAYMOND K PUA
JAMES D PUCKETT
JOSEPH L PUFFER
JESSIE E PULLEY
WILLIE B PURNELL
GEORGE H PYATT V
JAMES E QUILLEN JR
JOHN P QUINLAN JR
JEROME W QUINN
LLOYD B QUINN JR
ANASTACIO QUINTANA JR
FRANK P RACHOU
CHESTER R RADZISZEWSKI
GEORGE W RAE
ROBERT W RAGLAND
JAMES D RALSTON
ROBERT C RAMAKER
EMILIO A RAMIREZ
SANTOS RAMIREZ
GILBERT R RAMSDELL
LINDY J RAPHIEL
PAUL M RAPP
WARREN J RARICK
ALLEN E RASMUSSEN
HARRY L RAU
KAYE E RAUCH
ALTON G RAY
DURWARD A RAY
EDWARD G RAY
JAMES E RAY
WILLIAM A RAY JR
DONALD R RAYMOND
ARTHUR H RAYNOR
WILLIAM D RAYNOR
GORDON J READ
LAVERN E READLE
JOHN K REAGAN
KYLE REASOR
RALPH E REAVES
LAWRENCE P REBAGLIATI
CHARLES L REBESKE
RALPH E REBMAN
PHILIP A REDIGONDA
HUGH I REDMON
HENRY R REDNER JR
MYRON H REED
THOMAS E REED

RICHARD G REESE
JACK B REESOR
HUMBERTO REGALADO
JOHN L REGAN
WILLIAM E REGAN JR
JOHN R REGULSKI
THOMAS E REIFSTECK
EDMUND H REILLY
LAWRENCE L REINKE
JACK W REINSMITH
GEORGE J REITMEYER
HERIBERTO L REYNA
ARTHUR R REYNOLDS
CHARLES J REYNOLDS JR
PROMUS F REYNOLDS
VIRGIL L REYNOLDS
WILLIAM R REYNOLDS
WILLIAM D RHODES
DANIEL RICCI
JOSEPH J RICE
RONALD RICE
DEWAYNE F RICHARDS
ARDYS L RICHARDSON
JOE B RICHARDSON
LUE D RICHARDSON
ROBERT J RIES
EDWARD J RIGLEY
ROGER B RIGNEY
DONALD F RINEER
WILLIAM E RINEHART
LAWRENCE T RIPLEY
WALTER J RISK
HARST RISTER
LEOCADIO RIVERA
WILLIAM P RIVERA
RUFINO RIVERA-CORTEZ
VICTOR M RIVERA-DIAZ
JOHNNY L RIVERS
FRANK V RIVIELLO
LEO A RIZZUTO
JAMES J ROACH
HAROLD S ROADENIZER
GERALD H ROARK
ROBERT F ROBBINS
JOHN H ROBERSON
WILLIAM M ROBERTS
CORBETT B ROBERTSON
WILLIAM L ROBERTSON
EDWARD ROBINSON JR
GEORGE N ROBINSON
REX F ROBINSON
ROBERT W ROBINSON
RICHARD L ROBISON
RAMON C ROBLEDO
CARLOS L ROBLES
ROBERT E ROBLING
LAWRENCE M ROCHA
ROBERTO D ROCHA
JOSE D ROCHE-TORRES
DAVID L RODDEN
EARL F RODERICK
GARY L RODGERS
ELPIDIO RODRIGUEZ JR
JOSE R RODRIGUEZ
JOSEPH R RODRIGUEZ
RUBEN RODRIGUEZ
RUBEN C RODRIGUEZ
ROSS E ROE
LEON ROEBUCK
EMANUEL G ROEHM
EUGENE H ROERING
JOSEPH L ROGERS
ROBERT J ROGERS
VINCENT F ROGERS
WARREN W ROGERS
JOHN E ROLAND
LOUIS H ROMAN
RAPHAEL ROMAN
RICHARD ROMANCHIK
JAMES J ROMEO
JAMES J RONE
ROY F ROOFFENER
ROBERT F ROONEY
WILLIAM ROSE
GLOYD E ROSEN JR
WARREN S ROSENBERGER
NORMAN M ROSENBLATT
HARVEY ROSENBLUM
JEROME C ROSENTHAL
VICTOR J ROSETTO

ARDEN D ROSS
ARTHUR L ROSS
HAROLD L ROSS
THOMAS REGAN ROSS
ANDREW ROSSETTI JR
MARVIN H ROSWELL
ROBERT L ROTHER
ALLEN L ROUNTREE
DONALD E ROWE
EDWARD E ROWE
LEONARD E ROY
BILL D ROYER
FRANCIS A ROZESKI
RICHARD B ROZNOWSKI
GENE R RUBY
EMIL J RUCKI
DUANE N RUID
JEROME A RUNCIE
FRANK J RUNNELS JR
EUGENE F RUSH
DAVID E RUSSELL
HERMAN RUSSELL
LOUIS E RUSSELL
TOM F RUSSELL
WILLIAM R RUSSELL
LAWRENCE J RYAN JR
RICHARD A RYAN
THOMAS J RYAN
TRAVIS L RYAN
JAMES SABO JR
GEORGE B SACSON
ROLF J SAGDAHL
SAMUEL S SAGE
HANS P SAKS JR
EUGENE M SALAZAR
JOHN M SALAZAR
JOHN S SALISKI
RICHARD SALOMON
ALBERT R SAMPSON
RICHARD SANCHEZ
VICTOR M SANCHEZ-VILLEGAS
ALBINO SANDOBAL
PAUL L SANDOVAL
DOMENIC J SANTA-MARIA
GILBERT SANTIAGO
SHOJI SATO
WILLIAM M SATTERFIELD
PAUL L SAVERY
JOHN P SAVITSKI JR
HERBERT L SCANLON JR
WILLIAM C SCARSELLONE
BRUCE A SCHAEFER
MALCOLM J SCHAEFFER
WALTER G SCHERER JR
HERBERT A SCHERZINGER
GERALD A SCHICK
ROBERT A SCHICK
ALBERT F SCHILDMEYER
ORIS J C SCHMIDT
RAYMOND F SCHMIDT
ROBERT H SCHMIDT
GORDON L SCHMIEDER
EDWARD SCHMITT
EDWARD C SCHNEIDER
EDWARD J SCHNEIDER
MYRON L SCHNEIDER
FRED J SCHNORR JR
HERBERT L SCHOLL
CHARLES E SCHOONOVER
DWAIN A SCHUH
FRED SCHULLER
JAMES R SCHULTE
COLIN SCHULTZ
EMIL SCHULTZ
ROBERT E SCHULTZ
CHARLES A SCHULZ
WARD SCHUPBACH
CLARENCE L SCHUSTER
JOHN J SCHWEGMAN
CHARLES L SCOTT
CONRAD W SCOTT
RICHARD C SCOTT JR
WILLIAM D SCOTT
BILLY SEALS
JOHN E SEAMAN
PHILLIP W SEELEY
THOMAS R SEGAR
RAYMOND G SEIDEL
JACK H SELLE

ROBERT R SENTER
JOHN F SENZIG JR
CLAYTON SEPULVADO
FRANK J SERNA
DEAN H SEVEY
RONALD E SHADDOCK
JACK G SHANYFELT
LAWRENCE C SHARPE
ROBERT V SHARPE
WILLIAM J SHAUF
WILLIAM L SHEBLOSKI JR
JOHN F SHEEHAN
VIRGIL C SHELLEY JR
GILMAN L SHELTON
ROBERT N SHEPHERD
BRIAN F SHEPPARD
JOHN L SHERIDAN
LEROY J SHERMAN
LARRY R SHINER
ROY E SHIREY JR
WILLIAM A SHIVEREE
RAYMOND R SHOCKLEY
EDWARD L SHOEMAKER
GEORGE A SHORE JR
RAYMOND U SHORT
PERCIVAL SHORTEN
JACK H SHRAMEK
CLARENCE E SHREVE
DORSE W SHRYOCK
JERRY L SHULLENBERGER
HARRY S SHUNKAMOLAH
JERRY E SHUP
RAYMOND J SHUTE
RICHARD J SHVONSKI
ABALARDO SIERRA-ORTIZ
JACKIE P SIKES
LEONARD SILEO
JAMES R SILK
CLARENCE P SILVER
BENJAMIN C SIMPSON JR
ISSAC SIMPSON JR
JOHN E SIMPSON JR
RICHARD E SIMS
WILLIAM L SITTIG
GLEN W SKAGGS
THEODORE M SKEALS JR
KENNETH L SKEEN
DOYLE R SKIDMORE
FORREST G SKIDMORE
LINDELL SKINNER
ROBERT B SKOWRON
JULIUS E SLAUGHTER
RICHARD S SLEBODA
DELBERT C SLIDER
ROBERT B SLOTABEC
IVAN B SLOTE
ROSCOE D SMALL
RICHARD F SMARTT
EDWARD E SMEDLEY
NICKOLAS SMERKAR
ARTHUR L SMICKLEY
ALFRED SMITH JR
ARCHIE L SMITH
ASA W SMITH
CLAUDE SMITH JR
DAVID J SMITH
DENFORD R SMITH
DEWAIN D SMITH
DONALD E SMITH
DONALD L SMITH
DONALD R SMITH JR
DOUGLAS E SMITH
ED L SMITH JR
GERALD J SMITH
GERALD K SMITH
GERALD L SMITH
HAROLD B SMITH
HERBERT L SMITH
HERBERT W SMITH JR
JAVERY E SMITH
JESSIE A SMITH
JIMMIE R SMITH
JOHN L SMITH
KENNETH L SMITH
LEONARD L SMITH
ORVIL SMITH
OTIS C SMITH

89 MARINE CORPS

RAYMOND T SMITH
ROBERT B SMITH
ROBERT E SMITH
ROY C SMITH
RUSSELL E SMITH
WILLIAM B SMITH JR
WILLIAM E SMITH
WILLIAM L SMITH
JOHN K SNIDER
ROBERT R SNODDY
CECIL A SNODGRASS
RONALD F SNYDER
WALTER H SNYDER JR
RAYMOND C SOLBERG
ROBERT G SOLOMON
EUGENE F SOMMER
WAYNE B SOMMERFIELD
GLEN A SOMSEN
JOHN E SONGER
EUGENE R SORENSEN
FRANCIS P SOUCIE
BOBBY G SOUTH
LESTER I SOWELL
HUIL D E SPARKS
THOMAS B SPEAKER
GEORGE SPEEDY JR
ALBERT W SPENCER
CHARLES R SPENCER
JOSEPH A SPINA
MYRON H SPRINGSTEEN JR
JOSEPH L SREBROSKI
ROBERT E STAFFORD
JOHN E STAMMEL
ALBERT W STAMPFEL
DAVID F STAPLETON
JAMES L STARR
DOUGLAS STATES
JOHN C STAUBER
ROGER N STAUFFER
BERNARD U STAVELY
CHARLES O STEELE
HOMER D STEELE
JOHN A STEELE
JOHN C STEFANAC
STANLEY J STEFANIAK
RICHARD J STEIN
JAMES A STEINER
HENRY J STELMASIAK
ALLEN G STENERSON
CARLTON C STEPHENS
JAMES L STEPHENSON
DONALD E STERN
CLAUDE O STEVENS JR
LEONARD R STEVENS
CARL N STEWART
PAUL G STILES
VERNON L STILES
DANIEL J STILLER
CHARLES R STILWELL
ROBERT C STOCKARD
BENNY G STOCKERT
EARL D STOLL
MARION H STONE
LEROY G STOREY
DONALD W STORY
DELMER E STRAWHORN
RICHARD S STREETER
RICHARD E STRIDER
JOHN T STRITCH
RONALD D STROMMEN
RAY C STROUP
JAMES W STRUTHERS
WILLIAM STURM
ROGER V D STURTEVANT
LLOYD S SULLIVAN
MAURICE P SULLIVAN
ROBERT P SUMMERIES
JERRY E SUMPTER
JOSEPH B SURETTE
GEORGE SVEC
ALFRED L SWARTHOUT
KENNETH D SWEARENGEN
EARL A SWEATT
PAUL D SWENSON
RICHARD L SWENSON
EDWARD D SWISHER
JAMES A SWISHER
JESSE C SWOAPE
FOREST D SYKES
RAYMOND SZYMOVICZ
EDWARD G TAASEVIGEN
GEORGE TAFOYA
EDWARD J TAGGART
JOHN C TALARICO
DONALD W TALL
ROBERT TALLEY JR
HOWARD TALLSALT
EUGENE D TANGEMAN
TILDON E TANKSLEY
JOSEPH G TANSEY
HAROLD M TARDIO
JOHN E TATE
RICHARD TAUZELL
ALAN C TAYLOR
ALTON E TAYLOR JR
CARL E TAYLOR
CHARLES A TAYLOR
ERVIN J TAYLOR
GENE S TAYLOR
GROVER C TAYLOR JR
LESTER R TAYLOR JR
MICHAEL U TAYLOR
PAUL K TAYLOR
WILLIAM E TAYLOR JR
BYRON C TEEL
DOUGLAS E TEMPLETON
VINCENT C TERINO
DONALD TERRIO
EARL C TEW
BILLY R THATCHER
DELMAR L THEVENET
JOEL A THINNES
FRANCIS R THOMAS JR
FRED THOMAS
JAMES G THOMAS
PHILIP R THOMAS
BILLY THOMPSON
FRANKLIN B THOMPSON
HARLEY G THOMPSON
LEONARD F THOMPSON
RICHARD H THOMPSON
EDWARD E THORN
DEVAUN L THORNBERRY
MARION E THORNHILL JR
BRIAN B THORNTON
JACK R THORNTON
KENNETH A THORNTON
JOHN W THURSTON
DONALD E THWAITES
AUSTIN J TIERNEY JR
PETER TILHOF
LOUIS H TILLEY
JOSE M TIRADO-GRACIA
ARNOLD R TOBIAS
JAMES E TOBIN
LEONARD V TODD JR
DANIEL T TOMA
WILLIAM R TOME
EDWARD J TOMLIN
PETER F TONELLATO
JOHN TOPOLANCIK
PABLO TORRES
EDWARD J TOTO
JULIAN T TOVAR
JACK D TRADER
JOHN TRAIN JR
ATLEE B TRAINER
DONALD C TRAUSCH
JOSEPH E TREADWAY
GORDON T TREOLAR
LAWRENCE J TROSCLAIR JR
BEN D TROUT
ALFRED J TROVILLO
TRUMAN D
TROWBRIDGE JR
PAUL T TROXELL JR
FURMAN M TRUETT
ROBERT M TRUJILLO
DREXELL E TUCKER
RICHARD F TUCKER
THOMAS E TUMEY
ELMER C TURNER JR
ROY F TURNER
RICHARD F TURPIN
RAYMOND J TUTTLE
RAYMOND L TUTTLE
HARRY D TUXHORN
HAROLD A TWEDT
ROBERT E TYKARSKI
JESSE TYRA
ROGER L UHLL
CHAUNCEY L ULLMAN
ROY D UNRUH
JAMES B UPSCHULTE
HUEY E UPSHAW
ANTONIO Y URBALEJO
RONALD C USHER
JOE M VALENZUELA
DAVID T VALLEJO
EUGENE S VALLO
DOUGLAS G VANDERMYDE
DONALD L VAN FRAYEN
CHARLES C VAN GORDEN
FREDERICK D VAN LEHN
RUSSELL E VAN NATTA
LESTER H VAN NORT
ROBERT D VAN NOTE
DONALD G VAN TIL
JULIUS J VARGO
JOHN W VARNER
MELVIN D VARNER
JACK D VAUGHN
WILLIAM C VAUGHN
JOHN VECKLY JR
JOSEPH H VEEVAETE
ALBERT J VEGAS
LOUIS D VEILLON
FREDDIE J VEIT
ANGELO M VELASQUEZ
JOSEPH P VELLA
FRANK J VENDITTI
ROBERT VERARDI
WILLIAM C VERBURG
RONALD L VERTZ
ARNOLD R VEY
ENRIQUE VIGIL
ROBERT L VILES
JOHN R VILLA
GELIO J VILLANI
GILBERT VILLANUEVA
THOMAS F VINES JR
WILLIAM E VIOLANTE
IRVIN F VIZENOR
CHARLES B VODICKA
EDWARD F VOIGHT
WILLIAM R VOORHEES
BERNARD W VOS
EUGENE F VOSS
GUSTAVE R VOSS JR
WILLIAM T WACKERMANN
DON E WADE
PAUL A WAGNER
RICHARD L WAHLERT
VINCENT E WAIDMAN
JOSEPH M WALCK
OWEN L WALGAMOTTE
DONALD M WALKER
JAMES D WALKER
LEONARD L WALKER
JOSEPH E WALLER JR
JAMES E WALSH
ROBERT K WALTERS
GUSSIE V WALTON
ROBERT L WANNER
DONALD E WANORECK
CALVIN B WARD
CHARLES E WARD
JOHN L WARD
WILLIAM D WARD JR
BRUCE H WARNER
GEORGE F WAROPAY
COURTNEY V WARREN
PAUL E WARREN
CLARENCE E WASHBURN
JOHN G WASHBURN
ALLAN J WATERMAN
BENJAMIN F WATKINS JR
GEORGE R WATKINS
BYRON E WATSON
FRANK WATSON
GEORGE R WATSON
GLENWOOD F WATSON JR
THOMAS F WATT
JEFF L WEAVER
RAYMOND E WEAVER
JOHN B WEBB
JACK E WEBBER
JOHN C WEBER
PAUL WEBER JR
WILLIE H WEDGEWORTH
CECIL WEDWORTH
MAURICE H WEIDEMANN
CHARLES A WEITEKAMP
WILLIARD M WELCH
JOHN E WELCHES
HARVEY F WELLMAN
ROBERT G WENSLEY
CHARLES E WERKMEISTER
LOWELL L WERLING
CARL A WEST
MILTON M WEST
DONALD E WESTON
WILLIAM R WESTWOOD
DANIEL T WHALEN
CHARLES L WHATLEY
CAROL G WHEELER
LEONARD J WHELAN
DALTON J WHITE
DEAN W WHITE
JAMES R E WHITE
JOHN P WHITE
ROBERT E WHITE
SIDNEY M WHITE
MARSHALL E WHITEMAN
DONALD R WHITMORE
RALPH H WHITNEY
JAMES D WHITTEMORE
JAMES L WIEDAU
LAWRENCE A WILCOX
JOHN H WILHELM
EDDIE W WILKERSON
CLARENCE WILLIAMS
CLARENCE WILLIAMS JR
DONALD R WILLIAMS
EDWARD A WILLIAMS
EVERETT L WILLIAMS
FRANKLIN L WILLIAMS
FREDERICK R WILLIAMS
JOHN M WILLIAMS
LAMSON P WILLIAMS
LESTER D WILLIAMS
OSCAR WILLIAMS
RICHARD G WILLIAMS
RONALD D WILLIAMS
WILLIE J WILLIAMS
PERRY W WILLIS
RICHARD E WILLOUGHBY
GLEN E WILLOW
ALBERT WILSON
FLOYD L WILSON
HERBERT WILSON
HUGH C WILSON
JAMES W WILSON
LOYD J WILSON
RUSSELL C WILSON
WILLIAM W WILT
THOMAS H WINES JR
PHILLIP R WING
WILLIAM P
WINNINGTON JR
KENELM N WINSLOW JR
PETER P WINTER
HOWARD S WIRTH
EDWARD L WISE
PHILIP F WISNESKI
ADOLPH D WISNIEWSKI
JOSEPH R WITHERSPOON
ROBERT H WITHERSPOON
ELBERT J WITT
RICHARD E WITTEKIND
LAURENCE
WOJCIECHOWSKI
MATHEW WOJTOWICZ
EUGENE A WOKATY
JAMES V WOLF
KENNETH F WOLF
CARL B WOLIN
JAMES F WOOD
OTTIE L WOOD
WILLIAM K WOOD
JAMES R WOODARD
ELMER J WOODRING JR
DENTON B WOODS
JULIGA WOODS JR
FRANCIS WOODWARD
THOMAS WOOLCOCKS
OMAR E WOOLDRIDGE
HARRY R WORDEN
RONALD WORLEY
VANCE O WORSTER
SAMUEL B WORTHY
CARLTON A WREN JR
DAVID V N WRIGHT
JASPER L WRIGHT
MORRIS B WRIGHT JR
SPURGEON WRIGHT
PAUL H WULF
ROBERT E WURTSBAUGH
KENNETH L WYMAN
ROBERT D WYMER
ROBERT D WYNN
KENNETH F YABLINSKY
DAVID YARBROUGH
MELVIN L YARBROUGH
BERTRAM J YAROCH
DONALD J YATES
ERNEST W YEHLE JR
JOHN P YELLEN
HAROLD E YELTON
MICHAEL YERCICH JR
RAY N YERDON
GEORGE R YERGER JR
GEORGE J YOHE
BERNARD M YOUNG
BOBBY E YOUNG
CLIFFORD L YOUNG
EARNEST M YOUNG
RALPH L YOUNG JR
ROBERT J YOUNG
JAMES L YOUNGBLOOD
JOHN J YOUNGSMAN
AMADORE YOUNT JR
BURL R YOUSE
RICHARD C ZAWLOCKI
JOHN J ZDYBEL
LELAND ZELINSKY
ROBERT W ZELLER
WILLIAM F ZELTMAN
DELBERT L ZENGARLING
CASEMIR J ZIARKO
WARREN A ZINN
LAWRENCE J ZINNER
GEORGE M ZUKOWSKI
RICHARD A ZUKOWSKI
ANTHONY P ZULLO

CORPORAL

CHARLES G ABRELL
JOHN G ADAMS
ROBERT A AGAR
JAMES F AKERS
JOHN W ALBERTS
COLBERT J
ALEXANDER JR
DURWARD F
ALEXANDER
HUBERT O ALLEN
ROBERT L ALLENDER
BUDDY E ALLISON
JAMES L ALLISON
CLIFTON L ALMONRODE
EULALIO ALVARADO
MANUEL G ALVARADO
EDWARD C ANDERSON
ROBERTO A ANDRADE
ROY J ANDRESEN
HUBERT E ANTES JR
JAMES ARAGON JR
RICHARD W ARNDT
DAVID ASPILI
ELROY J ATKINS
RALPH E AUTEN
CHARLES R AVARY
ROBERT W AVERILL
RUBEN G AVILA
RICHARD I BACKOFF
ROBERT F BAILEY
ODOM C BAIN
BILLY W BAKER
BORIS BAKER
JAMES E BAKSA
DANIEL J BALLEM
GUS G BALLIS
JAMES L BALOG
WILBUR T BARBEAU
JACK E BARBER
HENRY J BARBIERI
ALBERT P BARNES JR

90

MARINE CORPS

CALVIN P BARNETT
JOHN M BARRETT
JOSEPH J BATLUCK
WILLIAM M BAUGH JR
JACKSON R BEAN
HOWARD E BEASON
FRANCIS E BECKER
ROGER P BECKER
JOHN C BELL
HOWARD D BELLAMY
DAN F BELLES
ROBERT H BENCK
CLARENCE L BENTLEY
WILFRED J BERNIER
BRYAN D BERRYMAN
ROBERT C BETH
DONALD H BINEK
WILSON L BINGAMAN
ABNER S BLACK
JACK W BLACKLIDGE
ROBERT L BLAKE
WILLIAM S BLASDEL
ALVA L BLEAU
DANIEL L BLUBAUGH
MAURICE I BOGGESS
JAMES J BOLICEK JR
RICHARD L BOLYARD
TED BONCHEK
GONZALO BONILLA-ARCE
EDWARD J BOROWSKI JR
JOSEPH H BOUCHER
AMOS J BOUDREAUX
JAMES H BOVE
PAUL H BOVENSIEPEN
ARTHUR J BOWER JR
RAYMOND T BOWERS
ALLEN M BOWMAN
JOHN D BOWYER
EDWARD J BOYD
DONALD F BOYER
JOHN J BOYLE
CALVIN H BRACE
PERRY O BRADEN
GERALD P BRADLEY
KENNETH E BRADY
WILLIAM E BRANDT
CARL W BRASWELL
EARL B BRATBACK
JOHN C BRAVO
JOSEPH A BRAY
DERICK F BRINCKERHOFF
HARRY M BRINGES
JAMES R BRISTOW
RALPH A BRITTON
LEONARD C BROWN
OSCAR M BROWN
JEWELL C BRUCE
JOHN F BRUCE
EDGAR L R BUCHANAN
EDWARD J BUCHERICH
WILLIAM H BUCKLEY
FRANKLIN E BUCKNER
ROBERT J BURGWINKLE
ERMON R BURKE
FRANCIS B BURNS
FORREST E BURNSED
ROBERT A BUSH
RICHARD A BUTTERY
CHARLES D BUTTON
DAVID E CABRAL
CRAYTON L CALDWELL
TOMMIE L CALLISON
JONATHAN J CANCEL
FRANKLIN M CANTERBURY
JOSEPH J CAREY JR
WILLIAM J CARINE
HENRY F CARLTON
JOHN A CARPENTER
HAROLD CARTER
GILBERTO CASAS
WILLIAM A CASEY
LONNIE N CASSLE
GERALD E CASTAGNETTO
CLAUDE C CASTAING
RICHARD S CASTER
ALFRED F CATIMON
DAVID B CHAMPAGNE
THOMAS L CHANCELLOR
JAMES V CHAPMAN
DONALD M CHAPPLE

DEAN D CHARLES
DONALD R CHRISTIANSEN
DAVID B CHRYSTIE
ROBERT A CHURCHILL
JOSEPH E CICCHINO
ARTHUR L CLARK
THOMAS L CLARK
DONALD J CLAYTON
GEORGE H CLINE
ALVIS CLOWERS
DALE E CLUTTER
CLYDE P COATES JR
LEE R COLE
PAUL D COLLINS
DAVID P COLOPY
ALLEN W COLSDEN
HARRY L COLSON
CHARLES R COLT
ROBERT C COLVIN
CLINTON D CONN
ROBERT T CONNELL JR
GERALD J CONNOLLY
ROBERT W CONWAY
JEWEL D COQUAT
HOWARD T CORLISS
WILMER CORNN
GUIDO J CORSINI
WILLIAM E COTTOM
JOHN H COWGER
JAMES S CRAIG
FRANKLIN L CRANDALL
FRANK E CREGO
HERBERT E CRIBB
EVERETT L CRIST
CHARLES R CROCKETT
OWEN E CROCKETT JR
JOSEPH W CROOK JR
RAYMOND L CROSS
CHARLES P CRUIKSHANK
RICHARD S CRUZ
JOSE A CUETO
PAUL F CULLEN
ROBERT E CULLEN
WILLIAM F CULLINANE
DONALD J CUNHA
ALFRED H CUNNINGHAM
NORMAN S DAGENAIS
HOWARD W DAHART
GAYLE H DAHL
JAMES K DAMON
DONALD R DANIELS
JACK A DAVENPORT
JAMES L DAVIS JR
JEFFERSON F DAVIS
ROBERT D DAVISON
GERALD J DAY
GEORGE DEBAUN JR
ROBERT L DEHN
ONZEL C DEMENT
ANTHONY F DEMEO
MARVIN J DENNIS
STANLEY R DENNIS
LOUIE B DENTON
JOSEPH A DE SANTI
LOUIS J DESIMONE
RICHARD E DE VILLIERS
JOHN N DE VIRGILIO
THOMAS G DIER
MICHAEL W DILL JR
EDWARD A DI RUSCIO
ANGELO E DISTEFANO
PAUL A DIXON
RALPH W DOATY
ROBERT L DOBBS
RAYMOND E DOLAN
ROBERT H DOMINICK JR
HARRY W DONKERS
JAMES K DORAN
THOMAS P DORAN
GEORGE W DOTY JR
GEORGE R DOW
EDWARD F DREHER
JACK DREXLER
STANLEY J DROZDOWSKI
DONALD J DRUST
VERNON V DUFFY
FRANCIS X DUGAN
PAUL A DUGLE
KENNETH R DUHR
DAVID J DUNHAM

ANTHONY D DURAM
DAVID G DUREN
LEONARD J DWYER
ERNEST L EADS
FREDERICK W EDELMAN JR
GARY R EDWARDS
THOMAS A EDWARDS
THOMAS L EDWARDS
HENRY C EGGENBERGER
JOHN E ELLINGTON
JOHN M ELLIOTT
DONALD E ENGH
RALPH M ENGSTROM
RICHARD L EPPLEY
THOMAS C ESTWICK
DONALD R FAHRENHOLZ
KENNETH W FARE
JOHN D FARLEY
JOE R FARR
CLARENCE C FARRELL JR
THOMAS C FAVA
VICTOR E FEANY
DAVID E FELDMETH
LAWRENCE R FERGUSON
THEODORE G FERGUSON
FRED B FICKEL
BILLY G FIELDS
DENNARD M FIGG
DOUGLAS S FINLEY JR
ERSKINE D FINN
RALPH R FISCHER
JOHN T FISHER
HAROLD J FLARTEY
EDWARD A FLOM
PAUL C FLOWER
CHARLES L FLYNN
WALTER M FLYNN
ARTHUR A FOLEY JR
ALFRED D FOUST JR
HENRY R FOX
JAMES W FRANCHOW
VANCE N FRAZIER
BILL H FREEMAN
HARVEY J FRIEND
JAMES E FRIEND
GERALD K FRIZZELL
WILLIAM FULTON JR
LEON A GARCIA
RICHARD D GARCIA
ERNEST J GARNIER
CLARENCE E GASSMAN
VICTOR J GENRE
FELIX GIANGRANDE
FRANK J GILBERT
ROBERT H GILBERT
TOM A GILCHRIST
JAMES E GLASGOW
DONALD E GOEBEL
IGNACIO S GONZALEZ
WILBURN M J GOODMAN
FLOYD V GOODRICH
FREDERICK C GOSS
WILLIAM B GOSSETT
ROBERT B GRAHAM
LAWRENCE R GRASKE
GARLAND A GRASS
WILLIAM A GRAUMAN
HOMER GREEN
RALPH H GRIES
RICHARD J GRIFFIN
ROY L GRIFFIN
JOSEPH M GRIFFITH
JAMES F GRIZZARD
DONALD R GROSS
WILLIAM C GROSSMAN
MICHAEL C GRUBISICH
JOSEPH GUIDO
JAMES E GULLAGE JR
ORVILLE R HABER
DONALD F HADLEY
JOSEPH H HAGENEY
FRANK W HALLEY
DAVID L HAMILTON
CHARLES J HAMLIN
PAUL J HANNON
WILLIAM G HARDIN
CLODE M HAROLD
JEWEL W HARRIS
WELDON D HARRIS
JACK R HARRISON

ELLIS C HART
MELBOURNE C HART
ROSS A HARTWIG
DANIEL A HARVEY
DONALD D HASTINGS
CURTIS A HATFIELD
WILLIAM A HATHCOX JR
THEODORE F HAUSMAN
CARLIS D HAWKINS
GEORGE E HAWKINS
RICHARD E HAWLEY
JOHN C HAYES
LEONARD E HAYWORTH
MASON C HAZARD
HOWARD W HEATER
ERWIN G HEINZ JR
DONALD J HENDERSON
RICHARD R HENDERSON
J D HENSON
CHRISTIAN F HERTEL
WILLIAM G HEWITT
DOUGLAS L HEWLETTE
JOSEPH H HIGHLEY
MAYNARD L HIGHLEY
CLARENCE F HILE JR
LLOYD E HILL
RAYMOND F HILL
WAYNE R HILL
PAUL J HIMMELS
CHARLES H HINES
FLOYD E HINKLE
ALLAN B HOAGLAND
JACK D HOBBS
PHILIP N HOBSON JR
HENRY C HODDE JR
WESTON W HOEY
FRANK C HOFFMAN JR
RICHARD D HOGAN
RAYMOND L HOLLIDAY
KIRBY H HOLT
RAYMOND A HOLTHAUS
PATRICK W HOOLAHAN
JAMES R HOPKINS
HARROLD K HORN
RUSSELL HOUSE JR
GEORGE M HUDSON
CLARENCE H HUFF JR
BENJAMIN W HULSEY
VELOY G HUMPHREY
EUGENE H HUMS
CHARLES O HUNT
ALLEN E HUNTER
MILLARD H HUNTER
FRANKLIN D HURSH
SPENCER W HUTSENPILLER
DONALD G HUYCK
CHARLES R HYDE
HAROLD W ICETT JR
THOMAS M ILIC
JAMES A ILLA
RICHARD M ISLAS
JAMES E IVERSON
JAMES H JACK
KENNETH J JACK
CHRISTOPHER K JACOBS
HARRY R JACOBSEN
JOSEPH A JANCZAK JR
JOHN R JENSEN
WILLIAM C JEWELL JR
CHARLES B JOHNSON
DAVID L JOHNSON
JACK W JOHNSON
NORMAN J JOHNSON
OTIS S JOHNSON
REGINALD V JOHNSON
DONALD E JONES
JOHN L JONES
MELVIN H JONES
ROBERT C JONES
WILLIAM L JONES
LONNIE V JORDAN JR
CHARLES R KASTOR
JOHN J KAVANAGH
DEMAR D KEENER
RONALD L KELLER
DELBERT F KELLEY
GEORGE R KELLY
WARREN A KELLY
ELMER B KENDALL
RICHARD KENNEY

JAMES R KENNY
ALBERT J KEPPLER
CURTIS P KERN
GLENN M KETCHERSID
DAVID A KIENE
HAROLD KIEPKE
CURTIS J KIESLING
JOHN E KILDUFF
RALPH H KILNER
JACK H KIMBROUGH
JAMES R KIMBROUGH
ROBERT P KIPP
JOHN W KLINKERMAN
RICHARD J KNIGHT
MERRILL I KNOX
KENNETH J KOHLBECK
DONALD F KOLB
DONALD E KOLLING
RICHARD Y KONO
JOHN L KOOP
EDWARD J KOSTER
JOSEPH J KOTWICA
MARTIN J KRAGER
EARL V C KRONE
ALEX KRUK
DENNIS C KURTZ
HOBERT P LADNER
HUEY P LAFFOON
ELMER C LAKIN
CHARLES A LANGDALE
ERVIN W LANGLAS JR
WILLIAM LAUGHLIN
JOHN T LAVELLE
WILLARD E LAWRENCE
CHARLES R LEACH
DONALD W LEE JR
JAMES R LEECH
JOSEPH R LEEDS
CHARLES F LEHMAN
PHILIP C LEO
ROBERT V LEON
LAWRENCE E LETT
BURTON H LEVENSON
ALBERT D LEVIE
RICHARD S LEWIS
WILLIAM G LEWIS JR
FREDERICK A LEY
ARLAND D LINDBERG
FLOYD P LINNEMEIER
SANTOS LIVAS
ROSCOE H LOCKE
DAVID L LOMAN
JASPER C LOMAX JR
ROBERT P LONEY
ROBERT R LONG
DUANE E LONGBRAKE
ADALBERTO V LOPEZ
RAYMOND G LOPEZ
RICHARD S LOPEZ
DANIEL V
LOTRECCHAIANO
RUDOLPH LOVE
PAUL A LOWERY
THEODORE A
LUBOBANSKI
DUANE G LUCAS
JAMES F LUCAS
WILLIAM J LUDES
MIKE LUKAS
FRED E LUNA
WARREN A LUNDBERG
LLOYD R LUSHER
CLARENCE P
LUTTRALL JR
JAMES R LYNCH
JAMES H MACDONALD
JOSEPH A MACHANN JR
ALEXANDER
MACMILLAN
WILLIAM A MACMILLIN
JOHN L MADVIG
PELLEGRINO J
MAFFEO JR
LOUIS C MAID
WILLIAM W MAISCH
VICTOR MALACARA
JAMES W MALIFF JR
RONALD R MALONEY
MANUEL D MAMARIL JR
ROBERT S MANDICH

91

MARINE CORPS

JAMES L MANDREAN JR
GILBERT P MANTEY
FRED J MARCHERT JR
MARTIN MARCUS
WILLIAM J MARINO
HUBERT D MARK
LEO P MARKEY JR
ROBERT A MARKLE JR
ELIJA MARSH
JAMES H MARSH JR
CARL E MARTIN
PAUL E MARTIN
ALEX V MARTINEZ
ERNEST MARTINEZ
JACABO L MARTINEZ
EDWARD R MASIULIS
LAURENCE E MASTERS
FREDERICK H MATTHEIS
JOHN A MATTSON
JOSEPH S MATULICH
JOSEPH MAXWELL
RODOLFO A MAYBE
JOSEPH H MAYO
THOMAS C MAYS
CHARLES MCBRIAN JR
THOMAS F MCCARTHY
CLAUDE J MCCARTY JR
THOMAS P MCCLELLAN JR
ARTHUR W MCCLENAGHAN
JAMES F MCCORKLE
THEODORE E MCCORMICK
RAYMOND J MCCOUN
RALPH N MCCUAN
HOWARD A MCDONOUGH JR
JOHN F MCDOWELL
THOMAS L MCGINNIS
PATRICK T MCGONAGLE
EDWARD J MCGUINNESS
DONALD F MCKEEVER
HAROLD J MCKNIGHT
HAROLD J MCLAURIN
RUSSELL F MCNULTY
TERENCE J MCNULTY
CHARLES V MEARS
RICHARD L MECHANIC
ALBERT MEDAS JR
FRANK R MEDINA
PETER MEDUNIC
DALE B MEHLHORN
RICHARD M MEISWINKEL
CLAUDE S MELIORIS
WILLIAM R MELTON
JIMMIE L MENDENHALL
FERDINAND MENDONCA
DANIEL P MENDOZA
CLARENCE S MENGLER
MILAN MERVOSH
DONALD E MESHAW
RICHARD C METZ
EARL C METZLER
EDWARD J MEUSE JR
ALLEN D MEYERS
JOSEPH D MEYERS
LEVON MILES
CHARLES R MILLER
GEORGE W MILLER JR
LARRY E MILLER
RAYMOND M MILLER
THOMAS D MILLER
WESLEY D MILLER
JAMES B MILLINGTON
WILLIAM P MILLS JR
KENNETH L MILSTEAD
DONALD D MINER
FREDERICK W MINER
ROBERT A MINSER
HARVEY J MISENER
HARLEY M MISNER
MICHAEL MISOVIC JR
DONALD G MITCH
ROBERT C MOCK JR
PETER MONACO JR
THOMAS J MONAGHAN
RAY M MONTGOMERY
GORDON W MOONEY
JAMES W MOONEY JR
LOUIS B MOORE JR
EDGAR B MORK

NORMAN F MOSHER
VERNON D MOSSBERG
ANTHONY J MUCCI
JACK C MUELLER
DAVID L MURPHY
JOHN M MURPHY
RONALD B MURPHY
RAY E MURRAY
MICHAEL E MUSSATTO
JOHN A MUSZYNSKI
ROBERT A MUTH
JULIUS C NACCI
JAMES A NAOUR
WALTER L NELSON
CLAUDE Y NICHOLS JR
DONALD N NICHOLS
RONALD C NICKLOS
FREDERICK R NIXON
ROBERT H NOLEN
GRAYSON G NORBOM
HAROLD V NORTON
HAROLD N NOTSUND
DANIEL NOVACK
STANLEY NOWAK JR
JAMES P OBRIEN
CLIFFORD P OCHOA
MICHAEL J OCONNOR
WALTER G ODAY
KELLY C ODNEAL
JAMES L OGLETREE
DAVID J OHL
PAUL E OLENICK
ROBERT N OLIVER
FRANK E OMEIS
GERALD A OSTERBERG
NEIL R OSTERBERG
DAVID OSUNA
DONALD R OVERTON
RICHARD C OXBOROUGH
WILLIAM B PADGETT
BILLY J PAIGE
ANDREW V PANELLA
EDWARD PARHAM
CHESTER E PARIS
GUSTAVE PARR JR
CLAUDE T PARRISH
PATRICK O PARRISH
JACKIE E PARSONS
RICHARD W PATTILLO
JAMES R PATTON
HEINZ PAUTKE
THOMAS PEAKE
RICHARD A PEARCE
WILLIAM A PEARSON JR
CLIFFORD S PETERSON
FRANK F PHILLIPS
LEE H PHILLIPS
PETER G PHILLIPS
RICHARD H PHILLIPS
ROLLY L PIEPER
ZACHARY T PIERCY II
CLARK J PITTMAN
WAYFORD B PITTS
LOUIS P PLAGAKIS
ROBERT D PLATO
BILLY N PLAYER
EDWARD F POCZEKAJ JR
MAX O POINTER JR
HERMAN A POISSON
LAWRENCE E POLAN
WILLIAM B POLLARD
JOHN F POPP JR
HENRY B PORTILLO
MARION J POWELL
ROBERT E PRICE
MARVIN B PRIDDY
HOWARD C PRIDE
MARVIN E PRINCE
GEORGE S PUHR JR
JOHN V PULEO
GLEN K PULLINS
HERBERT PUTZEK
EDWIN J QUADE
NIELS I QVISTGAARD
LESTER D RADER
ALVARO RAMIREZ JR
CHARLES H RANDALL JR
ROBERT J RASPANTI
FRANK L RAWLINGS
WILLIAM H RAY

MAHLON L RAYMOND
HARLEY N REASONER
MARK F REDFORD JR
ROBERT D REDNER
HAROLD W REED
DONALD W REESER
FRANCIS A REGAN
ALVA L REID JR
JOHN P REILLY
GEORGE F REIS
JOSEPH W REMINE
JAMES E RENNER
JOHNNIE REYNOLDS
PAUL R REYNOLDS
PHILIP A REYNOLDS
PAUL R RHODES
LARRY D RIBBLE
SIRIO A RICCI
RALPH L RICHARDS
JAMES A RICHARDSON
GORDON F RICHMOND
HUGH A RIDENOUR JR
PAUL B RIFFLE
WILLIAM R RIGGS
JAMES F RILEY
PHILIP I RILEY
REGINALD A RILEY
IRVING RIPPEN
JACK D RITZ
ALBERT R ROBBINS
ALFRED G ROBINSON
JIMMIE ROBINSON
ROBERT E ROBINSON JR
MARTIN RODRIGUEZ
ALBERT J ROGALLA
EUGENE J ROGERS
PAUL H ROGERS
GAYLEN F ROHWER
TERRELL R ROULSTON
EUGENE E ROWLAND
JOHN D RUCKER
WILLIAM F RUHLMAN
WALDEMAR F RUPP
JOHN E RUSH
CLIFFORD V RUSSELL
ANTHONY L RUSSO
JOHN F RUSSO
CHARLES V RUST
WILLIAM H RYAN
FORTUNATO A SABATINO
CARLOS L SALAICES
ANTHONY R SALENA
ALEJANDRO E SALINAS
JAMES E SAMPSON
HARRY W SANDERS
ROY SANDVIK
ACHILLE C SARNO JR
PIETRO SATALINO
CARL L SCHAEFFER
GAYLORD L SCHAFFER
EDWARD P SCHEIDER
CHARLES F SCHEMMEL
EDWARD D SCHERER
PETER M SCHIRO
WALTER D SCHMID
JAMES A SCHNEIDER
GEORGE A SCHUCK
RICHARD F SCHUCKMAN
JOHN E SCHULTZ JR
CONRAD J SEABLOOM
EDWARD G SEATON
HERMAN J SEESENGOOD
JOHN P SEGREDE JR
MAYNARD A SELVOG
JOHN E SEMAR
ALBERT R SEMPLE
CAROL W SEXTON
ALAN M SHADIS
LEROY SHAHAN
FORREST S SHAMBAUGH
JOHN A SHAMMO
HAROLD W SHANKS
ROBERT J SHANNON
DONALD E SHAVER
EUGENE M SHAW
LEO C SHAWANESSE
WILLIAM J SHEEHAN JR
DOREN P SHEFFIELD
JOSEPH F SHEMELEWSKI
ALLEN D SHIPLEY

FREDERICK J SHIPMAN
WILLIAM D SHURTS
ARTHUR E SIAS JR
RICHARD H SIECKMANN
THOMAS C SILVA
BRYAN E SIMMONS
DENNIS O SISNEROS
CHARLES E SKINNER
RAY E SLASOR
DONALD D SLY
BOBBY J SMEDLEY
DONNELLY F SMITH
FRANCIS R SMITH
JOHN B SMITH
MYRON J SMITH
ROBERT E SMITH
PORTER J SMITHSON
WALTER J SMYK JR
NOLAN H SNELLING
DONALD W SOMERVILLE
JOHN E SOMSKY JR
DONALD A SORRENTINO
CHARLES O SPALLONE
HARRY L SPEARMAN
KENNETH H SPENCER
CLARENCE E SPITZ
CHRISTIAN J SPOERL JR
WILLIAM A STANLEY
CLYDE R STARLING
JOHN C STENGER
JAMES F STEPHENS JR
ASA D STIDGER
HENRY C STIDHAM
FELIX C STOCK
MILTON E STONER
LAWRENCE N STRAINIC
JOSEPH STRAZA
GUY H STREUVEN
ASA W STRICKLAND JR
JIMMIE A STRICKLAND
GENE A STURGEON
LOUIS G SULLIVAN
ARTHUR C SUMMS
CAESAR SYLVESTER
JAMES R TAFT
BILLIE E TAYLOR
WALTER R TESTERMAN
CONRAD W THERIAULT
GEORGE H THOMAS
GERALD THOMAS
LARRY G THORNTON
BILL D THORPE
JAMES E THRASH
HENRY T THURMAN JR
JACK TIERNEY
LEONARD M TISCIA JR
RAYMOND H TITLEY
DONALD G TITUS
ROY J TOBIN
AUGUSTUS E TODD
DONALD T TOLAND
ROBERT P TOOLE
JAMES E TORGESON
DONALD TORRES
DOUGLAS E TOTTEN
EDWIN J TOWN
EDWARD J TRAUTWEIN
JOHN E TROTTER
EMIL TRYNOSKI
LAWRENCE A TRYON
EARL J TUCKER
JOE H TURNER
RAYMOND A TURNER
ROBERT E UMHOEFER
EARNEST H UPMEYER
GILBERT U VALDENEGRO
LOUIS VALENCIANO
GERALD F VANDENHENDE
PAUL E VAN LOO
GILBERT A VAN NOSDALL
HAROLD A VAN NOSTRUM
KENNETH F VAN OST
ZANE M VASOLD
HENRY R VASSALLO
JOHN M VAYDICH
JOHN R VENDITTO
CARL J VERBANAC
JOHN S VICK
ROBERT J VIOLETTE
ANTHONY P VIRGADAMO

JOSEPH VITTORI
JAKE N VOERMANS
ANDREW E VOLLO
CECIL A WADDELL
FREEMAN M WADE
WILLIAM E WAGNER
EUGENE J WALLACE
RICHARD E WALLEN
HOWARD K WALLING
DAVID C WALSH
JAMES H WARD
WILLIAM A WARD JR
LEROY WASKIEWICZ
LAWRENCE J WATSON
WILLIAM B WATSON
ALBERT G WEBER
RICHARD L WEGNER
RONALD W WEIK
RICHARD M WEIL
MELVIN WEISS
DANIEL L WELCH
JAMES D WELCH
ROBERT S WELDING
FRANK P WELLER
ROBERT WELLS
JAMES D WELSH
JEROME D WENTWORTH
ROY L WEST
JAMES R WESTERMAN
JESSE J WHEELER
VERNON O WHEELER JR
JOHN E WHITE
ERIC WHITFIELD JR
OWEN C WIEDERHOLD
ROBERT D WILDER
FRANK B WILLHITE
ALBERT R WILLIAM
DONALD K WILLIAMS
GEORGE M WILLIAMS JR
GROVER L WILLIAMS
JACK V WILLIAMS
RAYMOND C WILLIAMS
ROBERT A WILLIAMS
RICHARD C WILLMANN
ROY C WILSON JR
HARRY WINN JR
LOWELL T WOLFE
DONALD O WOOD
HAROLD E WOODS
ROBERT E WOODS
CLYDE L WOOLERY JR
DEWEY E WRIGHT
RICHARD H WROBEL
RICHARD L YATES
FRANK E YEAGER
LEMASTER B YEARWOOD
CLAUD A YELTON
RICHARD W YORK
WALTER J YUSZKIEWICZ
ANTHONY M ZALEK JR
JERRY J ZANETTI
ALFRED ZELAZO

SERGEANT

DIRK R ABBAS
HOMER V H ANDERSON
WILLIAM L ANTONUCCI
DAVID M ARCHER
RAUL B BABASA
JOHN S BACZEWSKI
JOHN F BAGWELL III
DONALD BAILEY
GEORGE L BAKER JR
ROBERT R BARAJAS
JOHN BARNELLO JR
KENNETH L BARNES
FRANK R BARRETT
DONALD K BARTOLI
JOHN W BAUER
HARRY R BEAM
BEVERLY R BEARD
JOSEPH M BECKER
GEORGE E BEER
MARSHALL E BENNETT
JACK B BIGDEN
WILLIAM BINAXAS
ALFRED A BITTER

92

MARINE CORPS

JOHN L BITTERS
THOMAS W BLACKMON JR
JOHN A BLANKENBURG
THOMAS R BODELL
RICHARD F BOEHME JR
FRED W BOESIGER
LOUIS C BOLES
DUANE L BOLL
TED R BONES
ROGER R BONIN
ANTHONY S BORASKI
DONALD J BRADLEY
WALTER C BRAZILL
JOHN R BRENNAN
GEORGE C BROWN JR
JOHN R BROWN
DON R BUCHANAN
MALCOLM L BUDD
RICHARD D BUHS
CARL E BUMPUS
RAYMOND F BURHORST
ROBERT E BURTON
EDWARD W BYCZKOWSKI
THOMAS CANNIZZARO
PAUL E CANTRELL
ANTHONY M CAPPUCCI
JOSEPH CARMELLO
JESUS R CARRASCO
PETER M CARROZO
MATHEW CARUSO
WILLIAM L CASCELL
THOMAS H CASE
NEIL F CASEY
FRED CASTLE
FRED D CHADWICK
DENVER I CHAMBLISS
GEORGE L CHAPMAN
DONALD G CHRISTOPHERSEN
DOMINIC A CISCO
DOW J CLARK
HOWARD F CLARK
WILLIAM C CLARK
ROBERT L CORBETT
JOSEPH L CRAIG JR
OLIVER B CRAIN JR
LYMAN T CRANNELL
ELWOOD S CREWS JR
JAMES C CROUSE
WILLIAM C CROWE JR
CHESTER E CUMMINGS
EDDIE G CUNNINGHAM
DONALD M CUSTARD
ROBERT V DAMON
ROY DARDEN JR
WILLIAM B DAUGHERTY
GLYNN E DAVENPORT
GERALD O DAVIS JR
CHARLES R DE ARMON JR
GEORGE L DE FORGE
DOMINIC J DEL VECCHIO
LEONARD DENTI
ANTHONY J DE SCISCIOLO
JOHN A DES ROSIER
ROBERT E DEVANS
JOHN F DE WITT
URAL DORSEY
WILLIAM J DOWNS
GLEN R DRAPER
LOUIS D DRAZEY
ALBERT S DREON JR
ROBERT P DUBAY
ROBERT E DUFRENE
JAMES C DUGGAN
KENNETH L DUKE
GIFFORD E DUNN
LAVERNE DUQUENNE
CHARLES K DWYER
DONEL F EARNEST
LELAND E EHRLICH
FRED A ENNIS
WILLIAM C ENRIGHT
THEODORE R ERLER
ROBERT L ESSIG
EARL EVANS
ROBERT J EVANS JR
ALBERT H FANT
THURMAN L FARRIS
RALPH E FENTON
EDWARD P FITCH
JACK E FLACK
GEAROLD D FLEMING
RENE J FLORY JR
PAUL FOLEY
JOHN L FORD
CHARLIE FOSTER
RICHARD P FRAZURE
LEROY A FRICK
GERALD J GAGNE
JACK D GAINES
FRANK D GARCIA
WILLIAM M GAUL
NORMAN A GERTZEN
WILLIAM J GIDDINGS
MURRAY GOLD
JOSE L GONZALES
WILLIAM E GOODING
JOHN R GORDON
DAVID W GOWMAN
HARRY N GRAY JR
WILLIAM H GRAY
HAROLD E GREEN
GLEN F GREGG JR
CHARLES GRIGELIS
LAWRENCE L GROSS
LOUIS C HAIRSINE
CHESTER I HALL
RALPH H HALL
WILFRED E HALL
JACK HANCOCK
RICHARD J HANDING
DON G HANES
RICHARD C HARANG
FRANCIS M HARMON
JAMES V HARRELL
FRANK HARRIS
RICHARD E HARRIS
JOHN T HART
KENNETH D HARTLEY
GEORGE N HASKETT
ERNEST E HAUSSLER
OTIS S HAYNES JR
MERLE A HENDERSON
THOMAS C HENDRIX
ELTON T HENRY
ROBERT L HILL
JOHN C HOLLEY
MELBOURNE G HOLT
WILLIAM F HOTTINGER
JACK A HOUCK
SANFORD HOVDA
MICHAEL HRABCSAK
JOHN J HUGHES JR
LEE R HYCHE
JAMES H HYNES
JAMES P IMMEL
MARIANO JACQUES JR
OTTO C JANNUSCH
MARTIN L JEFFCOAT JR
ROBERT E JENNINGS
DAVID M JOHN JR
JAMES E JOHNSON
JAMES W JOHNSON
RAYMOND L JOHNSON
WALTER M JOHNSON
BRYANT E JUDSON JR
JAMES J KANE
ARTHUR R KAZMIERCZAK
MEREDITH F KEIRN
PAGE L KEITH
DONALD K KERRIGAN
JOHN C J KIM
KEITH D KING
MARION R KING
KENNETH R KIPP
ALBERTUS T KLEINTOP JR
JOSEPH A KOPCZAK JR
MARSHALL E KRANTZ
LOUIS C KRAUS
BERNARD J KREIDERMACHER
WALTER KURES
ADRIAN KUROWSKI
RAYMOND LACAVERA
DALE E LAFRANCE
RODERICK H LA FRANCE
MELVIN H LAMB JR
LLOYD W LANDERS
THEODORE P LANDRY JR
EDWIN LAPP
THOMAS J LEAVER
DOYLE L LEE
KENNETH R LEE
JOHN F LESKO
VIRGIL B LIENEMANN
GENE F LILLY
ROBERT L LINKE
HANSFORD D LONG
WILLIAM B LOURIM
FRANK E LOVETT JR
GORDON W LUEDKE
HAROLD J LUND
REGINALD MADISON
JAY E MAJOR
THOMAS O MALLERY
ROBERT H MALLOY
PHILIP V MANDRA
JOHN D MANDT
HOWARD L MARBLE
CHARLES MARTIN
LAWRENCE E MATHIS
DANIEL P MATTHEWS
FREDERICK W MAUSERT III
DELMAR E MAY
JAMES P MAYBERRY
JOHNSON MCAFEE JR
CLEON K MCCLELLAND
RAYMOND R MCCOMBER
ROBERT G MCCORMICK
CHARLES A MCCOY
CHARLES W MCCOY
WILLIAM E MCCREA
THOMAS C MCCULLEN
RICHARD E MCCUNE
WAYNE H MCCUSKEY
WILLIAM G MCDADE
JOHN W MCDERMOTT
ALTON G MCDONALD
ROBERT F MCGOWAN
DALE A MCGREGOR
JAMES M MCKAY
JOHN MCLAUGHLIN
PATRICK J MCWAIDE
PAUL G MECKSTROTH
DAVID C MENDELSOHN
NORBERTO N MESA
CHARLES A MILLER
JOSEPH E MILLER
SAM Q MILLER
ROBERT A MISSMAN
ANCIL A MITCHELL JR
CHESTER E MOLLNOW
WILLIAM R MOORE
ALVIN E MORRIS
SIMS F MORSE
DAVID D MUELLER
HAROLD E MUELLER
HOWARD W MURRAY
TOMMY J NEVES
DONALD S NICHOLS
ROBERT J NICORA JR
CHARLES D NORTON
WILLIAM P NOUD
WILLIAM J NUTTER
WILLIAM E OCKERT
PATRICK F OCONNOR
JOSEPH S ODONNELL
JOE R OLAGUE
JOSEPH T OLEJARKA
JESSE H OLIVER
FRANCIS J OLIVIGNI
ARTHUR J OMARA JR
JOHN F OSTICK
JAMES PADILLA
FRANK A PAGANO
ALBERT J PAGLIONE
VIRGIL H PARHAM JR
HAROLD L PARKER
MELVIN B PARKER
RICHARD S PARSELL
WILLIE PARTIN
KENNETH A PARTLOW
OLIVER PAUL
ROBERT J PAULSON JR
EUGENE J PAVEGLIO
WILLIAM F PAYNE
EARL F PEACH
JACK R PERIGO
ALFRED O PERRY
THOMAS L PERUGINI
ROBERT J PHELAN
JAMES B PICKWORTH JR
FRANK A PITRE
CLYDE T PITTS
ROY H PLOEGER JR
DONALD E PONTO
RAY POPE
HORACE H PORTER JR
JACK L POST
ARTHUR W POWELL JR
JAMES I POYNTER
ERNEST R PRINCE
PRENCE A PRISOCK
DONALD W PROCTOR
DENNIS A PRYZGODA JR
JAMES E PUTNAM
ARLIS W RAMSAY
ROBERT J RAYMOND
ROBERT L RAYMOND III
ADAM J REDMERSKI
LOREN D REED
LEON REESE
THOMAS F REILLY JR
HAROLD E RICE
LEONARD B RICHARDS
SUMNER E RICHARDS
JAKE R RICHARDSON JR
HAROLD E RIKER JR
FORREST D RISCH
CLAYTON L ROBERTS
RALPH E ROBERTS
BERT D ROBIRDS
EDWARD J ROCK
ANTHONY N RODRIGUEZ
WILLIAM B RONE
JERRY M ROOS
BOBBY J RUDDLE
HOWARD RYAN
HARRY E SCARBOROUGH
JOSEPH A SCHAEFER
PAUL G SCHICK
WALTER S SCHMIDT
WILLIAM A SCHNADER JR
ROBERT W SCHULTZ
WALTER L SEIVERS JR
ROBERT N SEVERSON
FREDERICK B SHENK
JAMES R SHEPARD
ELVIN B SHIELDS
WILLIAM G SHORE
MICHAEL SIKORA JR
WALTER L SKWIERCZ
ALFRED A SMALLEY
LLOYD B SMALLEY
DAVID E SMITH
DONALD F SMITH
ROBERT L SMITH
ROBERT W SMITH
JOSEPH R SOLLARS
GLEN J STANLEY
DONALD W STANTON
CHARLES W STAPP
ARTHUR R STEBNER
JAMES W STEPHEN
DAN STEPHENS JR
JOSEPH E STEWART
LEE C STOCKHOLM JR
JAMES J SULLIVAN
WILLIAM B SUMNER
WILLIAM H SUSONG
GEORGE A SVICAROVICH
ROBERT R SYPNIEWSKI
JOHN H TAYLOR
ALAN E TELLIN
JACK A THOMAS
FREDERICK B THOMPSON
JIM H THOMPSON
WILLIAM E THOMPSON
ROBERT L THOSATH
GERALD K TIBBIT
MELVIN TOHO
DAVID O TREJO
LARRY D TURNER
BILL M VAUGHN
CLARENCE H VERETT JR
SALVATORE VINCI
STEPHEN C WALTER
GEORGE A WARK JR
WILL WARLIE
PRESTON WASHINGTON
HENRY M WEEMS
JAMES R WELFARE
STANLEY R WEST
LESLIE E WESTBERRY
GRANVIL H WHALIN
ROBERT J WHERLEY
DONALD C WHITE
JAMES W WHITFORD JR
EDWARD H WHITTAKER
EUGENE WHITTAKER
ROBERT L WIEGMAN
DALE R WILCOX
HARRY J WILCOX
ROBERT B WILKINS
EDWARD W WILLIAMS
JAMES M WILLIAMS JR
JOHN D WILLIAMS
MELVIN E WILLIAMS
TOMMIE J WILLIAMS
FLAVIUS J WILLIAMSON
WILLIAM D WILSON
DONALD E WOLF
WILLIAM C WOLF
ROY W WOOD
THOMAS YESENKO
PAUL YOUNG
LEWIS W ZWARKA

STAFF SERGEANT

JOHN H ARTER
WARD O BARD
ROBERT F BONNETT
ARTHUR M BONWELL JR
HENRY A BORKOWSKI
ROLLINS M BRYANT
JAMES P BURKE
BUFORD L BURNS
JAMES A BUSH
ROBERT M CALLAGHAN
JOSEPH L CAMPBELL
JAMES J CARLSON
ORLANDO A CICCONE
JOHN A CIMA
LARRY L CLARK
JACK W CORNELIUS
BRUCE H CORSON
BUFORD L DALE
JAMES C DAVIS
EDWARD N DORMAN JR
ALBERT H DUNLAP JR
WAYNE A DYKES
CREED L EADS
JIMAYE K FARRAR
ROBERT FISHER JR
WAYNE F FISHER
DONALD S FOSTER
CHARLES J FRANKS
GORDON GARNER
CHESLEY G GILBERT
MELVIN J GILLEY
JOSEPH L GIOVENCO JR
HERBERT L GOLDING
JOHN L GOSSETT
MARVIN C GREGORY
AMBROSIO GUILIEN
WILLIAM H GUNTER
GEORGE F HAMILTON
ARNOLD G HANNUKSELA
EDWARD J HANRAHAN
WILLIAM R HARALSON
WILLIAM H HARLOW
CORNELIUS F HARNEY
HERBERT F Y HEU
EUGENE T HITE
JOHN T HOENES
HAROLD D HUGHES
LEONARD H HUGHES
HOMER W HULL
HARDY J HUTCHINSON
EUGENE B INGRAM JR
JOSEPH A JAGIELLO
ANTONIO JAIME
MANUEL J JIMENEZ
CLYDE W KEEL
CARL R KENNEDY JR

93 MARINE CORPS

ROBERT J KIKTA
JOHN D KIMMINS
WILFRED O LA ROCHELLE
CHARLES H LARSEN
EUGENE L LAWSON
WILLIAM S LIPE
JAMES E LOWE
JOHN E MADSEN
ABRAHAM I MANDEL
BRUCE MATHEWSON JR
RICHARD A MCINTYRE
CLAUDE A MOORE JR
JAMES A MORTON
WYNN T MOSS JR
GERALD NANCE
IRA F NICHOLAS JR
CHRISTIAN B NICOLAISEN
JOHN ONEILL
LAWRENCE W OVERMAN
MAURICE A PADWA
OLEN PARKER
BILLIE PAYNE
FRANK G PEIRITSCH
MALCOLM B PEVETO
JOHN A PILLAR
THEODORE G PROCTER JR
HAROLD E REINS
ALEXANDER D RIDER
ROBERT W RILEY
JUAN C RUBIO JR
JASPER V RUSSELL JR
ROBERT M RUSSELL
EDWARD F SCHAFENACKER
JESSE SERNA
HARRY SHELQUIST JR
HENRY H SHENK
WILLIAM E SHUCK JR
STEPHEN R SOMJAI
JOHN M SPUDICK III
JOHN J STENZ
DOUGLAS STOCKSTILL
RALPH E SURBER
JAMES B SUTTON JR
LEONARD E TANT
WILL A THOMPSON
GERALD D TILLMAN
WILLIAM ULLMANN
ERNEST J UMBAUGH
BERNARD E F VAN RAAY
GEORGE E WAGGONER
WILLIAM S WALKER
LEWIS G WATKINS
WALTER C WATSON
NILE L WELLS
WILLIAM H WESTBROOK
EDWARD J WILHIDE
HUBERT A WILLIAMS
JAMES R WILLIAMS
FRANCIS C WINDOVER
WILLIAM G WINDRICH
WILLIAM A C WOOD JR
EUGENE T WOOLRIDGE
JIMMIE D YOUNG
CHESTER ZECICISKEY

TECHNICAL SERGEANT

JOHN E ALBRING
WALTER H ALLEN
JAMES D BAKER
MATTHEW J BIEDKA
VINCENT C BOEHNERT
WALTER C BORAWSKI
JOE L BRAND JR
BERLIN CALDWELL JR
ROSCOE CARNES JR
MARION J CRAWFORD
CHARLES J DAVIS
MARIO A DE SANTIS
DONALD M DUNCAN
JOSEPH R ERRGANG
JAMES R EVANS
HENRY M FOSTER
NORMAN C FOWLER
CHRISTIAN P GAAEL JR
HUME A GILES JR
MICHAEL J GRANT III
JAMES W HARGIS
JOHN F HIGGS JR
EARL G HOPKINS
WALTER B HORNBEAK
FRED HUGHES
JESSE JOHNSON
WILLIAM G JONES
HERMAN C KAHL JR
LORAS J KEEGAN
JAMES A KING
KARL V KLUDT
EDWARD D KNECHT JR
LEO J KUBIAK
RAYMOND LAMB
CHARLES S LANGTRY JR
JACK N LOCKHART
DONALD J LUPO
ROBERT E LYNCH
WALTER A MACIOROWSKI
SHANNON L MEANY JR
PAUL E MEISTER JR
ROBERT J MONTEITH
JESSE E MORRIS
ROBERT E MORRIS
RICHARD E MULLETT
HUGH F NEWELL
JUNIOR J NIXON
BERNARD J OUSNAMER
DONALD L OWEN
WILLIAM P PURCELL
CHARLEY L RADFORD
JOHN F REVELL
JAY R RHODES
CHARLES P ROMERO
ERNEST W SCHOOLEY
GEORGE C UNDERWOOD
HAROLD L WAGNER
ROBERT L WHEELER
RAY WHITE JR

MASTER SERGEANT

JOSEPH P BABIN JR
WILLIAM T BAXTER
JAMES L BECKER
EDGAR CAMERON
DANIEL J CARROLL
GILBERT N CAUDLE JR
FLOYD E COMPTON
MAC R CORWIN
RALPH A DAVIS
LEON F DEVILLIER
JAMES M DUNN
CHARLES W EDWARDS
EDWARD FRISTOCK
WILLIAM R GOODALL III
CECIL S GRIER JR
WELDON E HARDIN
JULIUS G HARRINGTON
ROPER HENRY
JAMES W HERNDEN
HOWARD F HEYLIGER
ROBERT L KAPPELMANN SR
EDWARD L KIRKPATRICK
DON W KOONTZ
FRANK J LAWSON
JOHN F MCAVOY
WILLIAM J MCCLUNG III
ALBERT J MORTON
FRANCIS NIGRA
CHARLES J RHOADES
ERNEST ROESSNER
ROBERT J RUSSELL
VERNON I STANLEY
DALE L STROPES
BOYD T TEAGUE
WILLIAM E ZBELLA

WARRANT OFFICER

FLORENZ M BANJAVCIC
LOYD V DIRST
BILL E PARRISH

SECOND LIEUTENANT

JAMES L ABLES
HUGH D ADAIR JR
JOHN W ALLING JR
JOHN L BABSON JR
CORNELIUS J BAKER JR
JOHN E BAKER
JACK M BALLMER
JAMES W BANNANTINE
ROBERT J BAUMGART
JAMES D BEELER
ALAN BEERS
ROBERT K BENJAMIN
ORLE S BERGNER
JOHN J BISSELL JR
DOUGLAS H T BRADLEE
CARL H BRUGGEMEIR II
ROBERT E BUCHMANN
WALLACE S BUTLER JR
JOHN S CARSON
BYRON H CHASE
ERNEST A COBLENTZ
DONALD C COLBURN
GILBERT M CORDES
CAREY S COWART JR
MORTIMER W COX JR
ROBERT C CRAIG
FRANKLIN P DUNBAUGH
WENDALL C ENDSLEY
DAVID B EVANS
KENNETH J FACTOR
WILLIAM J FANO
WILLIAM P FINCH
JOHN T FITZGERALD
LAURIE FITZGIBBON JR
EDWARD J FLANAGAN
EDWARD T FOGO
HOWARD O FOOR
PAUL A FRANKLIN
MARTIN L GIVOT
RAYMOND D GODFREY JR
HARVEY A GOSS
FELIX W GOUDELOCK JR
DAVID C GREENE
BRUCE J GREENHILL
CLAUDIUS J R GREY
WILEY J GRIGSBY JR
JOHN N GUILD
WYCH E GUION
JOHN F HAMRICK
JOHN R HANIGAN
WILLIAM R HANSMAN
RAY HECK
ROBERT G HERLIHY
JOHN W HILL JR
THOMAS S HODGSON
WILLARD B HORN
THOMAS A HUBBARD
GORDON M HUGHES
DAVID L HYDE
THOMAS A JANELLE
SPENCER H JARNAGIN
AUSTIN C JENSON
THOMAS H JOHNSTON
STEPHEN H JUDSON
JERED KROHN
JOSEPH H KUNEY JR
CARL R LAFLEUR
DONALD F LAMBERT
JAMES M LARAMORE
DAMON J LARSON
GEORGE C LEE JR
JOHN J LEONHARD
JOHN M LINDSETH
JOHN R LINNENKAMP
ODYCE W LIVINGSTON
CHARLES H MATTOX
JOHN J MCCOY JR
THEODORE F X MCINTYRE
THOMAS L MCVEIGH
DANIEL G MELENDREZ
FREDERICK M MUER
ROBERT T MUNDAY
OWEN A NORTON
ARTHUR A OAKLEY
DONALD L PARKS
CHARLES A PEARSON
WILLIAM R PHILLIPS
ALEXANDER J PICONE
JAMES J PRIOR
GEORGE H RAMER
ROBERT D REEM
WALLACE J REID
MORRIS F REISINGER
DANIEL F ROGERS
RICHARD L ROTH
STANLEY J SEWARD
WALTER J SHARPE
DANA W SHELLEY
GEORGE A SINGER JR
SHERROD E SKINNER JR
DARREL O SMITH
ELMORE C SMITH
STUART L SPURLOCK
CARL W STAPLES
EUGENE W STEWART
DAWN J STOVALL
JEROME C STUART
BEDROS M TANEALIAN
WARREN H TAYLOR
DAVID C THEOPHILUS
GERALD G TIDWELL
WINFRED B TOONE
EARL L VALENTINE JR
SOLOMON L VAN METER III
EMILE A WALKER
CALVIN P WALSTON
WILLIAM D WHITE
ROBERT H WHITNEY JR
LYNN B WHITSETT
LESLIE C WILLIAMS

FIRST LIEUTENANT

GLEN ALLEN
GERALD P ANDERSON
THOMAS A BALDWIN JR
RAYMOND O BALL
ARTHUR R BANCROFT
RALEIGH E BARTON JR
ROGER B BEEM
DORSIE H BOOKER JR
ALVIN R BOURGEOIS
WAYNE E BOYLES
JOHN C BRECKINRIDGE
ALBERT A BRISCOE
JAMES M BROWN
PAUL C BURRUS
JAMES CALLAN III
JOHN M CHAMBERLAIN
THOMAS J COCHRAN
THOMAS B COLLINS
DONALD F COTTLE
ROBERT O CROCKER
WILLIAM F CURRY
HAROLD J DAVIS
WILLIAM H DEAN
ARTHUR D DELACY
ROBERT D DERN
FRANCIS X DONOVAN
RAYMOND E DUNLAP
CHARLES S DUNNE
JOHN M DUNNE
GRANT R ELLIS
REX D ELLISON
EDWARD D FISCHER
EDWARD L FRAKES
JAMES L FRAZIER
WILSON A FREASE
JAMES A GLEAVES JR
JOHN B GOERY
ROSCOE F GOOD JR
JOHN S GRAY
JOHN R HANCOCK
ALAN M HARRIS
HOWARD F HOELZEL
WALTER JUNG
FRANK L KECK JR
LAMAR A KNUDSON
WILLIAM H KULLER
JOSEPH R KURCABA
FREDERICK N LARIVEE JR
PAUL W LATHAM JR
RICHARD H LEWIS
CARL E LINDQUIST JR
ORVILLE J LIPSCOMB
ROBERT A LONGSTAFF
BALDOMERO LOPEZ
DONALD L MANN
NATHANIEL F MANN JR
MICHAEL L MCADAMS
JOHN J MCBRIDE III
STANLEY D MCELWEE
JAMES J F MCGOEY
ROBERT C MCGREGOR
CLARENCE E MCGUINESS
JOHN P MCLAUGHLIN
FRANK N MITCHELL
GRADY P MITCHELL JR
ADELORDE G MORENCY
JOHN D MORGAN
ANTHONY G MORRISON
THOMAS D ODENBAUGH
BRUCE W OTTO
CHESTER O PENNEY JR
ROBERT G PRICE
BURTON W RANDALL
RICHARD U RICH
BERNARD H ROSS
EUGENE R RUSSELL
MAGNUS D SCHONE
ROBERT F SCOTT
KARLE F SEYDEL
JUNIOR D SHARP
LESLIE T SHELTON JR
ARTHUR J SHROPSHIRE
LAWRENCE H SIMMON
MARSHALL E SIMONSON
HOW J SMITH
RICHARD Y SMITH
SAMUEL T STUMBO
GEORGE S SULLIMAN
WILLIAM SWANSON
DAVID S TAYLOR
LAWRENCE I TAYLOR
THOMAS L THOMSON JR
ALFRED J WARD
WALLACE L WILLIAMSON
WILBUR H YOUNGMAN JR

CAPTAIN

ALFRED H AGAN
HERBERT M ANDERSON
JOE D BAILES
CARL F BARLOW
WALTER D BEAN
LEON J BERNAL JR
JOSEPH E BLATTMAN
JOHN S BOSTWICK
JUDSON J BRADWAY
AUSTIN E E BRENNEMAN
JAMES B BROWN
WILLIAM P BROWN JR
BYRON M BURBAGE
LEWIS H CAMERON
HOWARD D CAMPBELL JR
LESTER T CHASE
DONALD H CLARK
RALPH R CLARY
WALTER A CLINNIN JR
GEORGE W COLE
LEROY M COOKE
THOMAS E COONEY
HOMER J CORNELL
GEORGE R D CROSS
CALVIN K CURRENS
STANLEY D CURYEA
WILLIAM L DE VINNEY
KENNETH L DODSON
DONALD W DORN
JAMES ENGLISH
NEAL R EWING
RICHARD A FLANAGAN
BOBBIE FOSTER
DONALD R FRANCE
WILLIAM K GARMANY

94

MARINE CORPS

JAMES L GARRISON JR
DAVID T GOODEN
HAROLD L GREEN
THOMAS D GRINNELL JR
LAWRENCE E HAYNES
RAYMAN G HEIPLE
HERSHEL F HERBERT JR
WILLIAM A HIGGINS
HAROLD HINTZ
EDGAR A HOLLISTER
CLYDE T HOLMES JR
JOSEPH JANUSZEWSKI
WILLIAM G KNAUF
ROBERT W LEBO
EDWARD R LEESON
WILLIAM E LESAGE
WALTER E LINDBERG
RALPH E LOWER
GUY A MACLAURY
CHARLES MARINO
GENE R MAULDIN
MORTIMER MAZUR
WILLIAM S MCCARSON
JAMES H MCROBERTS
CHARLES R MILLER
JERRY E A MILLER
CORNELIUS T MONTGOMERY JR
ROBERT F MOORE JR
ARTHUR R MORIN
VIVIAN M MOSES
JOHN D NADELHOFFER
FOREST A NELSON
JAMES W NELSON
RUPERT H NELSON
WILLIAM H NESS JR
ROBERT I NORDELL
ARNOLD E OLSON
BRUCE M PASS
EARL F PATRICK
WALTER D PHILLIPS JR
PAUL R PIANA
PERRY W PORTER JR
WILLIAM J RAINALTER
CHARLES I RICE JR
EDWIN E RIVERS
ALLEN W RUGGLES
VICTOR SAWINA
HENRY F SCHLUETER
LEONARD SCHNEIDER
CHARLES C SCHWARTZ
FREDERICK P SELL
JEREMIAH D SHANAHAN
JOHN C SHELNUTT
ROBERT W SHIRLEY
WILLIAM F SIMPSON JR
HERBERT D SMITH
HARRY S SOLADAY
MAINERD A SORENSEN
JAMES A STEVENSON JR
JOSEPH O L STONELAKE
PAUL N STORAASLI
FRANKLYN H STRATTON
JOHN STRICKLAND JR
DUANE A SWINFORD
KENNETH E TAFT JR
LOTE THISTLETHWAITE
RALPH H THOMAS
DONALD K TROTTER JR
WILLIAM A TULK JR
JOHN E VAN HOUSEN
MERCO J VERRANT
RALPH L WALZ
BIGELOW WATTS JR
ROBERT H WHITE
WALLACE N WOOD
LOREN W WOOLEVER
GEORGE W YATES
WARREN M YORK JR

MAJOR

DEANE M BARNETT
JOHN W BEEBE
MARVIN L BERG
EDMUND W BERRY
GROVER R BETZER
CHARLES W BUNTIN
JOHN J CANNEY JR
JAMES H CRUTCHFIELD
DANIEL H DAVIS
RAYMOND E DE MERS
HARROLD J EILAND
ROBERT FLOECK
SCOTT G GIER
JACK B GIFFORD
ROBERT W GILARDI
DONALD F GIVENS
NOLAN A GREEN
MALCOM C HAGAN
MAX H HARPER
GORDON E HASKELL
ROBERT D HAYES
EDWIN J HERNAN JR
FRANK S HOFFECKER JR
JOHN W JOHNSON
FRANCIS B KELLY
BENJAMIN G LEE
ARTHUR H LILLY
GEORGE MAJOR
MORGAN B MCNEELY
EARL C MILES
EDWIN G NELSON
ROBERT A OWENS
HYDE PHILLIPS
RICHARD A POLEN
MORRIS L POTTER
DORRANCE S RADCLIFFE
RAYMOND J RIGHTMYER JR
ROBERT R SCOTT
THOMAS M SELLERS
CARL E SOREIDE
DOIL R STITZEL
JAMES R TURNER
LEE P VANCE

LIEUTENANT COLONEL

JACK L BRUSHERT
JOHN L DEXTER
JAMES K EAGAN
DONALD P FRAME
EDWARD R GAGENAH
ALFRED N GORDON
EDWARD R HAGENAH
WILLIAM F HARRIS
WILLIAM L G HUGHES
WALTER E LISCHEID
HARRY W REED
BARNETTE ROBINSON
GEORGE U SMITH
ROBERT H THOMAS
RADFORD C WEST

COLONEL

ARTHUR A CHIDESTER
PETER D LAMBRECHT
CHARLES W MAY
WESLEY M PLATT

UNITED STATES NAVY

AIRMAN APPRENTICE

ROGER A FROST
ROGER C HAMMOND
CHARLES L HARRELL
RICHARD N HOGAN
SIDNEY M SANDERS
EVERETT R WILLHOITE

FIREMAN APPRENTICE

BENNIE J BERRYMAN
RAY A BRIGGS
JOHN D BRYAN
BRUCE L CARRINGTON
WILLIE H FISHER JR
BOBBY E FREEMAN
RUSSELL J GRAF
WILLIAM E JONES
JAMES J KRCIL
RAYMOND J MARLIER
BRATTON MCKINNEY JR
RALPH F MORTON
ROBERT S NAVIN
EUGENE R OWENS
OLIVER C SEXSON
GERALD L SWAN

HOSPITAL APPRENTICE

ROBERT F BROOKS
LAWRENCE J DOUCETTE

SEAMAN APPRENTICE

CHARLES L ALBRITTON
LEO D ANDREWS
ELMA I CHAVERS
WILLIAM R CSAPO
RALPH R GILES
EDWIN Y HOWE JR
JAMES R HUDGENS
GERALD J JAMES
THURMAN R JOHNSON
CAROL J JONES
RAY D KERR
MILTON J KOSAR
GENE K KRONGARD
FREDIE C KRUEGER
IRVIN R MCDANIEL
WILLIAM J MURPHY III
ROBERT H OESTERWIND
COMMIE E PRICE
CHARLES E RICKLEFS
FRANK J ROGERS
BENNIE SISNEROS
ALBERT E SMITH
DONALD E TAPIA
EUGENE J THOME
ALTON WALDROP
ALLEN WOODS
JOEY L ZALDAIN

AIRMAN

CHARLES R ALLEN
RUSSELL A BAKER
PHILLIP K BALCH
JOHN P CAPRIO
ELMER C COON JR
EDWARD J C FARRELL
JAMES F FINAU
ERNEST N FRANKLIN
FRANKLIN D GAUT
JOHN M GULDHORN
THOMAS H GUYN
HARLEY E HAIGH
VAN C INGRAM
LAWRENCE O LARSEN
FREDRICK C LYNCH
CLINTON B MACKLIN
THOMAS L MCGRAW JR
VERNON NETOLICKY
SHELBY V NEVILLE
HARRY D NUTT
ROBERT E OVERTON
EUGENE A PFEIFER
CLAUDE PLAYFORTH
DALE H POOLE
ROBERT A ROSE
THOMAS R RUSSELL
RALPH W STACY JR
THOMAS M YEAGER

DENTALMAN

THOMAS A CHRISTENSEN JR

FIREMAN

RAYMOND J BUNTIN
MELVIN F BYDALEK
STANLEY L CALHOUN JR
FRANK N CATALDO
ALFRED L COLEMAN
JAMES T CROSSMAN
JAMES C DOWELL
CHARLES J EVANS
HARRY E FERRELL
VERNON F FRANKENBERG
KENNETH E GALLEY
LEO HAMPTON
DALE L HOOVER
HOMER L KELLY
BRUCE C KIRCHER
NELSON J LANDON
WILLIS E LEWIS
RICHARD D MUSGROVE
ROBERT J NELSON
WILLIAM G RAPIEN
PAUL V SATTERFIELD
HAROLD J SAVOIE
GEORGE A SCHOFIELD JR
WILLIAM M SCHWEITZER
JOHN M SHERRY
THURMAN M SHULTS
GERALD G SMITH
FLOYD SNEED
WALTER E THIERFELDER JR
JOHN E WALKER

HOSPITALMAN

GENE E ANDERSON
ROBERT A BERGMAN
ROBERT M BERRY
GLEN E BIDDLE
JACK S BLANKENBAKER
HOWARD H BLANTON
MURRAY M BOWEN
COY M BREWER
JOSEPH H BURKS
RAYMOND C CHAPMAN
BARRY H CRESSMAN
DONALD J CUNNIFFE
RICHARD D DEWERT
CHARLES W DOERR
THOMAS A DUGO JR
JAMES R EMPFIELD
CHARLES A FJAER
PETER C FROSLEV
ROBERT GILLESPIE
THOMAS G GRECO
WARREN R HAMMETT
FRANCIS C HAMMOND
HARRY J HARPER
KENNETH G HOESCHEN
EDWARD JONES JR
MERLON L KILLAM
JOHN E KILMER
ANTHONY D LAMONICA
MONTY J LANE
PAUL J MCMAKIN
JAMES H MCVEEN
RUSSELL G MISHLER
GERALD E MONTGOMERY
DEANE W NORINGSETH
TERRENCE W ODONNELL
JOHN C REINHOLD JR
WALLACE R REUTER
JAMES D RYE
ARTHUR H SCHLANSKY
WYLIE P SHAFER
EARNEST N SLAGLE
BILLY D SMITH
DORIN S STAFFORD
IGNATZ J STROGIS JR
DONALD G SUMMERS
MERLE E SUTTON
STANLEY L SYPNIEWSKI
JOHN J SZWAJKOS
RICHARD S TAYLOR
GORDON W THOMAS
JACK E VAUGHAN
ROBERT R WELCH

SEAMAN

JOHN A ADAMS
DANIEL M ALVAREZ
WILLIAM M BARKER
DONALD N BARNETT
CHARLES R BASH
ALONZO G BLANTON
JOHN T BROCKMAN
DORIS F BROWN
FRANK B CARROLL
DENNIS L CHATELLIER
NORMAN E CLUPE
BOBBY J COLE
JAMES R COLLERAN
JOHN A COLLETT
THEODORE A COOK
JIMMY L DAVISWORTH
CREIGHTON F DONALDSON
ROY L ESTES
JAMES H FLETCHER
JOSE GALLEGOS JR
DONALD C GHEZZI
CLYDE M GIFFORD
FRANK C GRUBB
BENNIE W HAMILTON
THOMAS R HAMILTON
CLIFFORD M HENDERSON JR
CHARLES T HORTON
EARL G HUDSON
FRED C HUGHES
RONALD J HUNT
CURTIS L JOHNSON
GORDON E JOHNSON
PAUL H JUNE
JESSIE J KESTNER
JAMES H KING
EUGENE P KROUSKOUPF
WAYNE A KRUEGER
HENRY D LITTLE
MERLIN R LOWE
ROBERT H MANN JR
MARCUS L MINOR JR
WILLIAM R OVERMAN
JAMES D OVERSTREET
CARTER T PAGE
THOMAS A PERKINS
THEODORE B PRINGLE JR
THOMAS E RAMSEY
RICHARD W SCHUNKE JR
BRUCE E SCOTT JR
STEWART B SILVER
ROBERT S SMITH
LOUIS C STARK JR
WILBUR T TARWATER

95 NAVY

WILLIAM M TAYLOR
ARTHUR H WALL
WILLIAM S WEST
JAMES E WOLFE
VIRGILE L WOOD
BILLIE D WRIGHT

PETTY OFFICER THIRD CLASS

OSCAR R ANDERSON
RICHARD ARMSTRONG
JOHN L BABBICK JR
HERBERT A BAILEY
WALTER E BAILEY
WADE H BARFIELD
ELFRED E BAXTER
WILLIAM M BECKETT
EDWARD C BENFOLD
CARNELL E BOOTH
BENNIE G CARTER
CARL S CASE
BRENICE CAUTHEN
MARTIN L CEDENO
GORDON H CHANDLER
RICHARD A COLEMAN
GUY J DEANGELIS
OLIVER P DEHART JR
HERBERT E DEMAREST
JAMES W DONAGHE
JOHN DREITH
JAMES R DUFFIN
LOUIS S DUHAIME JR
JAMES J EGRESITZ
CARL EICHHORN JR
ROGER R ELLERD
STANLEY H EMOND
ARMAND E ESTRADA
VINCENTE Q FEJARAN
THEODORE E FINFROCK
GEORGE L FISHER
HAROLD L FITZ
CHARLES H FRANCIS
HAROLD GAYLE
HARLAN G GOODROAD
CLAUDE R GOODWIN
DALE P GRAY
DAVID M GRUBB
JAY L GUIVER
ELVEN N HANEY
CARL C HARCOURT
VIRGIL L HARRIS JR
GEORGE W HART JR
FRED D HELEMS
THOMAS L HORTON
DONALD J HOVATTER
BELVIN HUDSON
WILLIAM C HUSHION
LAURENCE B JACKSON
LOUIS N JARAMILLO
BUSTER B JONES
WILLIAM G JONES
ARNOLD W KARLIN
JOSEPH F KEENAN
JACK S KENNEDY
JAMES P KING
EDWARD KRAVETZ
EDWARD A LENOIR
JOSEPH E LILE JR
JACK D LIVELY
EDWARD G LOVELESS
JOHN L LOWE JR
JOHN F LYONS JR
FERNANDO MAGRI
ELIJA K MANNING
OSCAR H MARK JR
JOHN MARQUEZ JR
LIONEL E MATHEWS
CHARLES H MCINTYRE
LEROY MCMURRAY
MELVIN G MCNEA
HAROLD MEYERS
JOSEPH F MUNIER JR
ROBERT L NEWMAN
JOSEPH W PANCAMO
KENNETH A PERRAUT
KAY S PLATT
CHARLES E POPE
RONALD J PORTER
ROBERT J POTTS
BOBBY L PURDY
LOUIE J RIGHTMIRE
JAMES V ROONEY
ADLER E RUDDELL
ROBERT E SAWYERS
ROBERT E SCHAEFER
ALLEN F SCHLUETER
GEORGE G SHECKLEN
JOHN T SKELLEY
ROBERT T SLATTERY
ANTHONY K SMITH
JAMES A SMITH JR
JAMES E SMITH JR
MARCEL A SMITH
LYLE A SORENSEN
C B STACY
LLOYD H STARKEY
BILLY C STEPHENSON
CHARLES F STEWART
ROBERT N STONE
PAUL D STROHMEYER
GEORGE F THOMMES
JOHN N THOMSON
RICHARD B THORPE
LESTER P THURMAN
EUGENE L TIMMONS
JOHN E TRIMM
ROBERT D TRUELOCK
ROY D TURNER
ROBERT L UNDERSINGER
ARTHUR VOSS
JOHN L WALTON
JAMES V WARK
TUBBY B WATSON
ADON H WELCH
DONALD WILKES
BOBBY R WILSON
FREDRICK C WITTWER
PAT A WORSHAM
WILLIAM D WYNN
HARRY T YOUNG
GERALD G ZIMMERMAN

PETTY OFFICER SECOND CLASS

JAMES C BROWN
JOHN D CARMICHEAL
HAMPTON C CARTER
HARRY J CHEWNING
JOHN R CLEVELAND
FRANK A DAVIS
EDWARD DOMINQUEZ
LAWRENCE B FLOYD
ROBERT M FUNK
WILBA GREEN
JAMES L HAAS
JOHN A JAMES
JAMES F JAY
PAUL G JURIC
EDWARD O KREUTZ JR
LESLIE E LANG
JOHN MARCHESE
SERGIO M MARTINEZ
LAMAR H MCDANIEL
WILLIAM S MEYER
EDWARD L MILLS
RUFUS L MOUNCE
FRANCIS P MURPHY
MARTIN J NOWAK
MELVIN D OBEE
THOMAS J RICOTTA
CLEVELAND G ROGERS
RICHARD RONCZKOWSKI
LEO C SANCHEZ
JOHN R SCHMID
ROBERT E SMITH
BILLY G SODEN
CLYDE D STATON
JOSEPH T TENNENT
RALPH A WIGERT

PETTY OFFICER FIRST CLASS

JOHN D BAGALE
REUBEN S BAGGETT
ROBERT E BERTAIN
PAUL BLACKSTOCK
JOLLY W BRITTON
RICHARD E BROWER
JAMES B BURT JR
GEORGE G CLOUD
EDWARD J COALSON
BILLY G COOPER
GEORGE COSTA
NUBERN D DAVIS
ROY A DAVIS
SETH D DURKEE
PAUL R FOSTER
VERN H FULLER
ROBERT GARIEL
MEYER L GETZ
GEORGE E HAIGH JR
LEONARD H HANSEN
STEPHEN V HOSCHLER
LLOYD E HUGHES
ADRIAN W JOHNSON
JOHN H JORGENSEN JR
FRANK H KENNON JR
CHARLES H KUNSCH JR
JOSEPH A LINCOLN
RICHARD T MCCOY
REX B MIDDLETON
OTIS E MILAM
EARL J MOCKLIN
CHARLES J MOORE
EUGENE T MURPHY
WILLIAM G PAYNE
COLEY G PRIDGEN
ERWIN D RAGLIN
RAYMOND E REMERS
RAYMOND P SCHWERER
RICHARD D SCOTT
JAMES B SMITH
WILLIAM R STILL
EUGENE H SWANSON
WILL R THORPE JR
MARCK L TOOKER JR
JOHN R WARD
JOSEPH M WILKINS
MARTIN J WRIGHT

CHIEF PETTY OFFICER

JOHN D BEAGLES
ROBERT A BECK
HOWARD J CONNORS
WARREN H FAUBEL
JOHN FRANCHINO
WILLIS D GROGG
KERMIT K HATHORN
CHARLES C HILL
LESLIE R HUMISTON
AUSTIN W HURD
WILLIAM C KLAUS
ALLEN B LACY
JOHN M LINDSEY JR
NICK MILUS
WILLIAM D MORRIS
EARL K NEIFER
RAYMOND S PARRISH
RALPH W REED
DAVID J SCHMIT
WARREN M SHEPHERD
LINTON C SMITH JR
CARL C STEVENSON
WILLIAM J STEWART
ROBERT W TURNER
HAROLD E WHITE

ENSIGN

DONALD E ADAMS
RICHARD A BATEMAN
THOMAS C BIESTERVELD
LOWELL R BREWER
ELWOOD E BREY
JOHN R BRINKLEY
GERALD R BROWN
JESSE L BROWN
WILLIAM E BROWN
EDWIN N BROYLES JR
RONALD D EATON
LLOYD M FAVER
GORDON R GALLOWAY
JOSEPH W GARDINER
MORGAN K GROOVER JR
JOSEPH S HALL
ARTHUR W HANTON
EVAN C HARRIS
CLAUDE C HOWELL JR
RICHARD D JENSEN
JOHN F KAIL
RAYMOND G KELLY
GEORGE C KLIESER
ROBERT W LANGWELL
THOMAS F LEDFORD
RICHARD C LOOMER
GEORGE A MARTIN
WILLIAM W MARWOOD
ROBERT L MAYHEW
JOHN P MOODY JR
RAYMOND W MURPHY
CONRAD L NEVILLE
WILLIAM D NOONAN
JOHN H NYHUIS
FRANCIS E PAINTER
RONALD E PARIS
WILLIAM E PATTON
WILLIAM M QUINLEY
DONALD R QUINN
PHILIP S RANDOLPH JR
GLEN H RICKELTON
GLENN A RILEY
RICHARD M RUPPENTHAL
HUGO V SCARSHEIM
RANDOLPH T SCOGGAN
CHARLES H SELLS
JOHN R SHAUGHNESSY
CURTIS L SMITH
DONALD A SMITH
JAMES F STATIA
DON R STEPHENS
GERALD J SULLIVAN
FORREST D SWISHER
JOHN H THOMAS
KEITH E THOMSON
HAROLD TROLLE
MAURICE A TUTHILL
WILLIAM G WAGNER
ROBERT E WAINWRIGHT
HENRY K WALLACE
CLARENCE E WEST
JERRY D WOLFE

LIEUTENANT JUNIOR GRADE

JAMES J ASHFORD
WILLAM R BALL JR
WAYNE E BANCROFT
ROLAND R BATSON JR
ROBERT S BICK
ROSS K BRAMWELL
DONALD E BREWER
LEONARD R CHESHIRE
GROVER C CHICK JR
BOYERS M CLARK JR
ANDERSON M CLEMMONS JR
RICHARD C CLINITE
BILLY E COCHRAN
BAXTER H COOK
JAMES B C COUCH
RALPH CROSS
HOWARD M DAVENPORT JR
JAMES B DICK
ARTHUR DIXON
MARION T DRAGASTIN
LAWERENCE F EMIGHOLZ JR
HUBERT T EVANS
EUGENE L FRANZ
LEO T FREITAS
EDWARD I FREY JR
CHANNING GARDNER
KENDALL C GEDNEY
FRANCIS G GERGEN
JOSEPH H GOLLNER
DONALD H HAGGE
EUGENE B HALE
HARLEY S HARRIS JR
ROBERT C HAYS
JOHN W HEALY
JUDD C HODGSON
ALAN HOFF
CHARLES R HOLMAN
JAMES A HUDSON
JAMES C HUGHES JR
SCOTT M JULIAN JR
JOHN K KELLER
BOYD D KNOX
FRED L KOCH
JOHN K KOELSH
JOHN E KORDELESKI
RUSSELL J LEAR
BRUCE B LLOYD
ROSS M LOCKHART
DAVID A MCCOSKRIE
MARCUS P MERNER
WILLIAM H MERO
RALPH N MEW
LESTER L MISCHE
DANIEL L MUSETTI
EDWIN A NIXON JR
JOSEPH B PARSE JR
JACOB L PAWER JR
WARREN R PERSON
HAROLD R PODORSON
LAWRENCE L QUIEL
HENRY B RATHBONE
DONALD V RAY
FENTON B ROBBINS
SAM ROSENFELD
RICHARD C ROWE
PAUL L SCHAEFER
CLIFFORD E SEEMAN
JOHN W SHOOK JR
RICHARD G SIGG
FRANKLIN SMITH JR
LOREN D SMITH
CHARLES G STRAHLEY
DAVID H SWENSON JR
DAVID F TATUM
ROY TAYLOR
CORDICE I TEAGUE
JACOB TOROSIAN
HAROLD T WALKER
DONALD V WANEE
HOWARD W WESTERVELT JR
CASSIUS A WILLIAMS JR

LIEUTENANT

DALE W ANDERSON
FRANCIS C ANDERSON
MORRIS A ANDERSON
PETER E ARIOLI JR
DAVID A ARRIVEE
WILLIAM C BLACKFORD JR
GEORGE S BRAINARD
FRED V BRYAN
WILLIAM A BRYANT JR
JOHN Z CARROS
ROYCE CARRUTH
ORVILLE M COOK
EDWARD P CUMMINGS
THOMAS J EUSTON
WILLIAM M FRANKOVICH
CHARLES GARRISON
RICHARD E GARVER
GEORGE A GAUDETTE JR
CHARLES O GLISSON JR
JACK W GRIFFITH
LEONARD A GUNDERT
HORACE M HAWKINS
JOHN B HEDDENS
RICHARD B HULL
ROBERT J HUMPHREY
RICHARD L JACKSON

96

NAVY

EUGENE F JOHNSON
GEORGE W JOHNSON
JAMES F LEE
DONALD E LONDON
FRANK MARTIN III
JOHN P MCKENNA
ALFRED E NAUMAN JR
DANIEL R PAUL
JAMES T PORTERFIELD JR
WILLIAM E PULLIAM II
EUGENE D REDMOND
LELAND R RICHEY
RICHARD G RIDER
JOSEPH D SANKO
JAMES A SAVAGE
WILLIAM H SHAW
JAMES E SHROPSHIRE JR
FRANK SISTRUNK
RALPH A SMITH
ROBERT L SOBEY
DURWARD J TENNYSON
ALFRED W C THOMAS
ALBERT R TIFFANY
JAMES J VENES
WILFRID WHEELER III
OWEN F WILLIAMS
WILLIAM B WOERMAN
JOHN C WORKMAN
HULL L WRIGHT

LIEUTENANT COMMANDER

HERBERT L BASLEE JR
FREDERICK W BOWEN
THOMAS B BROOKS
GLENN F CARMICHAEL
EMORY R COFFMAN
LYNN F DUTEMPLE
ROBERT C HOPPING
CHARLES M JONES
JOHN J MAGDA
WALTER P NEEL
IRAD B OXLEY
BENJAMIN T PUGH

COMMANDER

HALBERT K EVANS
RICHARD C MERRICK
JOHN C MICHEEL
ROBERT J PERKINSON
DENNY P PHILLIPS
BRUCE T SIMONDS
CHARLES R STAPLER
RAYMOND W VOGEL JR

UNITED STATES AIR FORCE

AIRMAN

ORVILLE E ASHBAKER
EUGENE B BRAUNSDORF
CHAUNCEY E COLEMAN
ELEODORO R FERNANDEZ
JOHN A MATHEWS
WALLACE A MEBANE
DUWAYNE C MORTIMER
JAMES J RIVERS
CHARLES C SANDS
HOWARD W TILLOTSON

AIRMAN THIRD CLASS

EUGENE BAIDY
JOHN C BRENNAN
LEMON BUTTS JR
GRANT D CARTER JR
GEORGE T CULLEN JR
RICHARD A DE COSTA
ROBERT A DUNN
WILLIAM H FARRELL
JOHN J FAUGHMAN
GEORGE A FREEMAN
JOHN W GREENE
NORMAN C HARMON
ALONZO J HAUGH JR
JOHN E HICKEY JR
RALPH A HODGES
JACKIE L HULSE
GORDON R INGERSOLL
FRANKLIN N IZUO
FRANCIS L KYLE
JAMES A KYLE
EDWARD A LENT
RICHARD M LINDSEY
MONROE M MILLWOOD
JOHN PARKER JR
RAYMOND C REED
GENE S ROSE
WALTER K RUTLEDGE
FRANK J STEVENSON
GLEN F STORY
VALERIAN ULINSKI
HAROLD WOISKI

AIRMAN SECOND CLASS

DONALD L ABNEY
RAYMOND R BACON
JAMES J BARRETT
THOMAS H BEACHAM
CLYDE H BELLAMY
BILLY R BISHOP
DONALD H BUSS
REYNOLD G CAMPBELL
RONALD W CHESTON
HERMINO V CONTRERAS
CHARLES E DAVIS
DARIEL L DAVIS
EARL A DAVIS
ELLIS L DEIHL
JOHN G DE LANCY
NORMAN H DIERKS
JAMES A ELLIOTT
GERALD FIELDS
RONALD J FOGLIETTA
RICHARD C FULLER
KENNETH L GAGE
MARVIN L GAINEY
HARRY C GAMMAGE
RUSSELL B HAM JR
DONALD L HART
MELVIN B HAYS
JOHN M HICKEY
ROBERT Q HOPKINS
LEROY S HORTON JR
LLOYD W INGRIM
HIDEMARO S ISHIDA
MICHAEL L JACOBS
JOSEPH C JAMIESON
GERALD E JOHNSON
GEORGE D JONES JR
GERALD JONES
JIMMIE L KAHANEK
LEWELLYN K KALEPA
EDWARD KAZMIERCZAK
JOHN KOTORA JR
DUANE W LARSON
EDWARD R LOGSTON
JOHN W MASLIN
RICHARD MASON
JAMES MCCORMICK
BERNARD F MCEVOY
RONALD G MCGRATH
JOHN G MCMANN
DAVID E MILES
ARLEN J MORGAN
JAMES C NEWELL
JAMES J OMEARA JR
JESS A OSBORNE JR
WALTER H OVERBACK
WILLIAM H PATE
HARRY T PEOPLES JR
NORMAN W PETERSON
JAMES D POPE
JAMES C PRASNIKAR
HUGH A RHODES
DANIEL G RUBY JR
WARREN W SCHMITT
DONALD C SCHNEIDER
EDWARD A SCHWAB
CLIFTON E SCITES
THURMAN N SIMMONS
MORRIS A SOLEM
CHARLES O SPAIN
PERCY L STEUART
CLEM L STINNETT
AMOS C TEMPLES
LUKE J TUCKER JR
WILLIAM H VANWEY
CLIFTON N WATSON
WILLIAM J WATSON
CARL E WEST
DONALD H WILSON
MILTON V WOOD
KENNETH E WRIGHT
TIMOTHY S YAMAKAWA
MANUEL J YDUATE JR

CORPORAL

JAMES R AIKEN
NORMAN A AUER
MARVIN BICKLEY JR
RONALD F BRODEUR
HOWARD P BURGESS
LELAND L BUTTLER
RAYMOND L CLAYTON
ARTHUR G COFFEY
JOSEPH R COLSON
ROBERT R CREECH
ROBERT G CURRAN
WINFRED N DAWSON JR
JAMES A DAY
ROBERT P DOMALESKI
MILO G EARLS
WILLIAM J EXUM
CHARLES J FEDORKA
EDWARD R FERRIS
ANGELO B GALLO
KEITH J HARVIEW
DONALD J KIEFLING
BILLY L KING
DELORAINE M KINGSBURY
ROBERT M KNOTT
RONALD L LIEN
ANDREW L MILLER
JOSEPH R MORIN
JAMES B MURRAY
MARVIN J MYHRE
ARTHUR R PARIS
CHESTER L PARKER
CHARLEY O PARR
RICHARD J PEREIRA
VITO W PRANO
SAMUEL H RAINEY
DONALD L RILEY
DONALD M RINGER
WILLARD F ROBERTS JR
THOMAS G ROGERSON
EDMOND M ROHAN
HAROLD J ROVIRA JR
JOHN SPANN
ROBERT W TAYLOR
JERRY URSINI
KENNETH N VICK
JOSEPH R WALLMAN
WILLIAM F YARNELL
ALFRED O ZIEGLER

AIRMAN FIRST CLASS

ALFRED W ARRINGTON
DOUGLAS E ATTINGER
LEROY J BEER
JAMES L BELL
CHARLES L BILLINGSLEA JR
JAMES A CAVE
GEORGE L CHERRINGTON
EDWARD CHUMAK
RUSSELL L COLEGROVE
EDWIN W COLLINS
THOMAS J CONDRON
SPENCER R COOPER JR
VICTOR G CORONA
HOWARD L CROSHAW
JAMES DEGEORGE
DAVID E DEGOLYER
WILLARD M DENN
JAMES E EDWARDS
DEAN J ERICKSON
PAUL A ESQUE
JAMES M EVANS
THOMAS B EVANS JR
EDWARD J FLEMING
JOHN W GAHAN
JAMES A GALLANT
RONALD A GANOUNG
JOSEPH S GLINIAK
JOHN S GONTESKI
WALLACE D HANDE
ALVIN D HART JR
RUSSELL HAWKINS JR
ROLLO D HIBBS
HOWARD M HIGLEY
JIMMIE R HOBDAY
WILLIAM R INGOLD
DANIEL JACK
JAMES L JONES
JEROME KARPOWICZ
ROBERT P KELLEHER
PAUL K KELLSTROM
JAMES W KELLY
JAMES R LE BARON
WAYNE E LEWIS
LUDOLPH C LINGOHR JR
PERCY J MAPLES
ISREAL MARSHALL JR
ROBERT R MASE
LESLIE E MCHANEY
CHARLES F MCINTOSH
JAMES W MCLAIN
ROBERT J MCLOUGHLIN
JOHN W MCNULTY
FREDERICK MICHAELIS JR
RICHARD T MICHEL
PAUL L MILLER
JOHN C MOORE
IRVING MUNROE
JAMES L NICHOLS
RUDOLF NIKLES
ROSS L NORMINGTON
DAMIAN F OTOOLE
DONALD W OVERTON
LEONARD G OWENS
FREDDIE E PADGETT
CHARLES E PARHAM JR
THOMAS PETTIT JR
JAMES H PORTER
DALE R POST
LAWRENCE A REID
JOHN A ROBERTSON
DARYL E RODNEY
WILLIAM W ROSE
LUTHER L RUTTER JR
CALVIN G SANDROCK JR
JIMMY C SIDES
GLEN L SLAVICEK
WESTERVELT C STAGG JR
RONALD L STEWART
ROBERT R ST MARY
JAMES C THOMAS
JOHN E THURMAN
PHILIP W TILCH
JAMES O TROSCLAIR
TRAVIS L TULL
HAROLD M VERNON JR
FRED A WARD
EDWARD A WEBB
CHARLES W WHEELWRIGHT
KENNETH D WILEY
DESMOND R WILKERSON
MERLYN K WILLIAMS
WILLIAM H WIMBISH
GEORGE D WOODY

SERGEANT

ELMER V ALTON JR
ROBERT O BICHARD
DAVID BRUZELIUS JR
JOHN V CHITWOOD
REXFORD L COLOMBEL
ROY P COLVARD JR
JAMES P COOPER
OTHAR E ESTEP
LOFTON B FAIRCHILD
GERALD K FINDEL
ROBERT H GREENE
OSSIE M GUNTER
HENRY F HATFIELD JR
PHILIP C HILL
THEODORE J HOFFMAN
CARL A JACOBS
JAMES A JOHNSON
RICHARD LANG
IRA F LORD JR
ANDRE J MATTON
JAMES T MCAFEE
WILLIAM L MCHORNEY
PHILIP MCMANUS
JAMES H MILLER II
FRANK A RAIHL
JAMES R SCOTT
JAMES D SHELTON
JAMES A THROWER
RICHARD R UPTON
JOE B WHITENER JR
WILLIAM E WILLIAMS
DONALD E WITHERSPOON

STAFF SERGEANT

LARRY B AKINS
RICHARD L ALBRIGHT
ROBERT E ALLRED
LINFORD R ANDERSON
THOMAS C BAKER
JOSEPH L BARR
EDGAR F BARRINGTON
LOUIS H BERGMANN
ROBERT W BEVANS
VINCENT J BEVILACQUA
BUDDY J BONNEY
ARTHUR I BOWDEN
N Y BRANDON
ROY F BREITSPRECHER
DILLMAN L BRENDLE
DONALD E BRINE
ROBERT E BULLMAN
GEORGE W BUNN
HUGH M BURCH
RICHARD B CALDWELL
JOSE C CAMPOS JR
ROBERT L CARLSON
MARVIN CESSNA JR

HARRY L CHANT II
CLARENCE M CHERRY
ALVIN L CLARK
CHARLES W CROCKER JR
NORMAN G DAVIS
ROBERT A DEETER JR
ALLEN C DINGER
CARL J DORSEY
JOSEPH S DOUGHERTY
JAMES H DUNCAN
JACK DUNN
STACY EDWARDS
RALPH ELSMAN JR
CLAUDE M ENGLER JR
LAWRENCE J ENRIGHT
LEE E ERICKSON
WILLIAM P FAETH
JOHN F FLAHERTY
ROBERT W FLUKE
VICTOR G FOOTE
ALOIS A FUEHRER
WILLIAM H GISH
ROBERT T GLAKELER
WILLIAM J GOODWIN
ORVIS J GUNHUS
MARVIN L GUTHRIE
JAMES W HATHAWAY
BIRD HENSLEY JR
BROWN HENSLEY
EDWARD D J HERB
GEORGE HERR
GEORGE W HIGGINS
ARTHUR W HOULT
JESSE M HUGHES
MELVIN J HUNT
CARL A JENKINS
RAY L JENNINGS
WAYNE F JENSEN
CLARENCE S KATES
DEAN D KEHR JR
FRED S KIRBY JR
HAROLD L KUSEL
CHARLES A LAMBERT
ASA L LAW
GENE E LILLARD
RAY E LINDSEY
EDWARD A LYON
DOUGLAS J MACARTHUR
FRED E MACK JR
JOHN MADSEN JR
RAY W MANSHOLT
PHILIP W MANTOR
CLAUDE D MARTINEZ
CLIFFORD H MAST
ALBERT C MAY
ERNEST R MCADOO
CLAUDE D MCFEE
GROVER G MCGUIRE
LEWIS O MCNEILL
WILLIAM H MCNUTT
EARL S METZGER
BERNARD MITCHELL
WINFRED D MORGAN
FORREST M MUTSCHLER
FRANK OBZINA
NICHOLAS M PALMIOTTI
CARL J PANEPINTO
JAMES F PERONTO
RALPH L PHELPS
WILLIAM H RANES
GERALD W RAYMOND
ELBERT J REID JR
STANLEY T REMAR
CLARENCE E RENFROW
JOHN A RICE
HOUSTON N RICH
THOMAS W RITTER
VOORHEES S ROOT JR
RICHARD C ROSS
ROBERT L ROSS
THOMAS W ROWDEN JR
EUGENE E SHERWOOD
RAYMOND H SHOWALTER
PAUL A SMILEY
THADDEUS L SMITH JR
GEORGE J SOTO
OTHA P STANLEY
VERLYN L STANPHILL
FRANK STEFAS
EDWARD J STOLL
LEON C STRIEFF
JACK SULLIVAN
LEWIS A THOMAS JR
ELWOOD J THOMPSON
RAYMOND THOMPSON
OTTO C TRAKBERGER
HERBERT C TURMAN
MANUEL J VIVEIROS
CHARLES C WADE
KENNETH P WALLAN
GRADY M WEEKS
RAYMOND A WEESNER
MERLE E WHITE
WILLIAM H WHITMAN
JOSEPH H WILLSON JR
EDWARD J WOHLGEMUTH
GEORGE W WORTH JR
GEORGE T ZEIHER
ELLIOTT ZELLARS

TECHNICAL SERGEANT

LEONARD J BENDINSKY
WILLIAM J BOTTER
DANIEL CADENA JR
WILLIAM A CANNING
DONALD V CAPRON
JOYCE M DORSEY
JOHN H ERRINGTON
JOHN E GRABOSKY
KEITH E HAMMON
LEROY A HANEY
VIRGIL B HARRELL JR
RALPH R HEATH
SHIELDS T HENSON
ANDREW HERYLA
PAUL J HICKS
CARL C HOLLAND
JAMES R HOLLYFIELD
MORTON H JENSEN
DARWIN A LILLIE
FRANCIS J MARSTILLER
WILLIE J MATTHEWS
GEORGE M MCBRIDE
BERNARD L MCMANAMAN
WILLIAM A METCALFE
FOSTER C MILLER
JACK A MORRISON
JOHN MOSS JR
QUENTIN L NEWSWANGER
MAURICE A OLSON
ROBERT F PARKS SR
ROBERT L PROUD JR
CHESTER D QUIDER
JAMES R SANDERS JR
JOE Z SANDOVAL
MELVIN E SARKILANTI
ROBERT L SEESE
CLIFFORD O SLOPPY
CARL M SPENCE
KEITH D THOMAS
ROLFE M WATSON
KENNETH E WILLIAMSON

MASTER SERGEANT

JAMES O ARCHERD
FLOYD D ASHCRAFT
CHARLES T AVERY
MICHAEL A BAKICH
CLEO A BROWN
NELSON M BROWN
HERSCHEL L BUSHMAN
ALBERT B CARLSON
FRANK J CHESNOWSKY
ALVA B CONINE
JOHN DAVIS
PATRICK M DIFFER
WILBUR N FOSTER
WINIFRED R GEORGE
AVERY J GREEN
ROBERT F GROSS
ROBERT W HAMBLIN
AUGUST H HINRICHS JR
JOHNNY M JOHNSON
ROBERT W JONES
JACK E KENNEDY
WILLIAM D KING
JOHN W LAUSBERG JR
LESTER E LEMASTER
HOWARD T MACARTHUR
RALPH A MAVES
DAVID A POWELL
JAMES RUSKA
ARTHUR H SCHUMAN
RICHARD D SEAGOE
MARVIN E SLEPPY
GEORGE S SPRAGUE
HORACE N TILLER
DONALD B TOVSEN
EDWARD P WILLIAMS JR

WARRANT OFFICER

CARROLL M EASTMAN

SECOND LIEUTENANT

JAMES H ALLSTON
ALFRED J ALVERSON
MERLE T AYERS
HENRY R BAAS
RICHARD D BARTLEY
ROGER W BASCOM
THOMAS L BELYEA
MICHAEL BOCHNOVIC
DONALD L BROCK
JACK M BROCK
DAVID L BURWELL
BOB P CANNON
EDWIN A CAREY JR
JACK CARRARA
HARRY F CARTER
WILLIAM M CARTER
EDWARD C CAYEMBERG
BERTHOLD B CHRISTIAN
DAVID C CLEMENTS
MAX H COLLINS
BILLIE R CRABTREE
DAVID P DELL
MICHAEL F DINAPOLI
BURLEIGH V DOLPH
ROBERT L DUNNE
THEON O EASON
CHARLES M FAMILIA
JOHN F FAYMAN
JOHN C FLOYD
ROBERT S FLUHR
HAROLD S FORSTER
DEAN E FREDERICKS
DANIEL G FURY
WILBERT W GRAMMER
WILLIAM T HAINES JR
HARLAN P HALL
CHARLES A HARRIS
JOHN H HAUN
JACK R HELMS
WALTER C HERR
WILLIAM F HILL
BOBBY JOE HOEFER
WILLIAM J HUMMER
FRANCIS J HUNTER
ERNEST HUTCHENS JR
RICHARD L JOHNSON
PAUL J KEARNS
ROBERT G KEMMERER
WILLIAM R KIMBRO
GERALD W KNOTT
MICHAEL P KOVALISH
RAYMOND S KRENEK
ROBERT O LACEY
JACOB C LEHMAN
JOE A LOGAN
GEORGE W LOWDER
DON O LYND
RUFUS H MAHAFFEY JR
THOMAS MALONE
CHARLES MASON
ROBERT E MCCORMICK JR
DANIEL W MCKINNEY
PATRICK J C MCPHERSON
WALLACE R METZ
VERDO A MITCHELL
CECIL R MOHR JR
JOHN C MORTENSEN
PHILIP MOSCATELLI
RALPH D NESS
KENNETH L NOSK
MARQUIS H ORACION
GLENN PAYNE
ROBERT D PETERSON
KENNETH O POLENSKE
JOSEPH M QUAGLEY
WAYNE J RABUN
MALCOLM L RUSH
HARRY E RUSHING
ROY G RYDIN
HOWARD D SCHOONOVER
DONALD A SCHWARTZ
RICHARD L SCOTT
MYRON F SESTAK
HARRY H SHERMAN JR
WILLIAM S SMITH JR
BILL J STAUFFER
FLOYD A STEPHENSON JR
ROBERT E STERNARD
WALLACE D STEWART
WILLIAM H SUFFERN JR
JAMES E SWENSON
EDWIN F TABACZYNSKI
JOSEPH A TADDEO JR
ALLAN M TARR
ROBERT J THOMAS
HOWARD R THOMPSON
JOHN E THOMPSON
JOHN E THOMPSON
WILLIAM F UMBARGER
HARRY G VOSBURGH
HOWARD J WALKER
JAMES S WALKER JR
GORDON S WALLS
WILLIAM B WARWICK
CHARLES P WENZL
HAROLD G WILKIE
BRUCE S WILSON
ROBERT S WOODRUFF

FIRST LIEUTENANT

AARON R ABERCROMBIE
GEORGE E ADAMEC
ERNEST M ADLER
JUNIOR M ADLER
EUGENE G ALDRIDGE
JIMMIE H ALKIRE
CHARLES E ALLEN JR
EDWARD N ALPERN
JAMES J ANDERLE JR
ERIC W ANDERSON
GEORGE F ANDERSON
ROBERT E ANDERSON
CHARLES M ANDREWS
FORREST B ANGSTMAN
JAMES ARGETIS
CONRAD J ARMEL
JOHN W ARMS
DREXEL E ARNOLD
JAMES E ARNOLD
FRED F ATKINSON JR
HENRY G AUSBURN JR
CHARLES AVARELLO
JAMES F AYLWARD
ROBERT C BAETZ
GEORGE BAIN
ROBERT K BANCKER
DAVID P BARNES
CARL G BARNETT JR
LINDSAY S BARTHOLOMEW
ROBERT B BAUMER
THURSTON R BAXTER
FRANK D BAY
ALBERT W BEERWINKLE
AUSTIN W BEETLE JR
DONALD E BELL
WILLIAM J BELL
JAMES M BELLOWS JR
CLARENCE O BERGSTRAESSER
BERNARD BERMAN
ALLAN S BETTIS
JERRY D BINGAMAN
DOUGLAS R BITTERLE
MEDON A BITZER
SHUMAN H BLACK
CHARLES H BLOMBERG
JAMES W BONNER
CHARLES H BOONE
RICHARD W BORSCHEL
RALPH L BORUM
GEORGE B BOUGHTON
NORMAN E BOWEN
ROBERT C BOWERMAN
LLOYD P BOWMAN
CLARENCE E BOYLE JR
RALPH P BRADLEY
ROBERT C BRASWELL
JOHN J BREITKREUTZ
EUGENE A BRIGGS JR
JACK E BRINDLEY
WILLIAM R BRISCOE
RICHARD G BRISTOL
PETER J BRITTON
DONALD D BROWN
JOHN H BUCKLEY
OLIVER E BUCKLEY JR
ALBERT H BULL
ELMER T BULLOCK
ROBERT G BURNETT
FRANCIS P BURNS
JOHN R BURTIS
WILLIAM D BUSH JR
STERLING J BUSHROE
ROBERT D CANFIELD JR
JAMES D CAREY
ROBERT O CARTIER
THOMAS F CASSERLY III
MARK J CASTELLANO
NEIL A CHAPMAN
EDWARD S CHILD
JAMES E CLAY
JAMES G CLAYBERG
MELVIN E CLOVER
CECIL H CLYOTT JR
ROBERT G COFFEE
JAMES L COLLINS
JOHN S COLLINS
CARL E COMBS
CLAYTON CONLEY
ARCHIBALD H CONNORS JR
DAVID L COOK
CHARLES E COONS
SAMMY B COOPER
JOHN M CORBETT
JOHN R COULTER
RICHARD M COWDEN
AL B COX
ALVIN E CRANE JR
RICHARD E CRONAN JR
ROBERT M CROSLEY
RICHARD D CUNNINGHAM
RAYMOND J CYBORSKI
GERARD P CYR
JOSEPH L DALMON
PETER M DARAKIS
MIKE S DAVID
THOMAS L DAVIDSON
JAMES F DAVIS
RAYMOND A DECKER
ROBERT F DEES
LEONARD O DE LUNA
GENE A DENNIS
JOHN A DILLE JR
VINCENT J DI PALERMO
GILBERT M DOBBS
JAMES M DOLAN
HAROLD W DOWNES JR
DONALD J DRAMA
JOHN L DREESE
RICHARD S DREZEN JR
RAFAEL A DU BREUIL
MARCE P DUNN
EDGAR A EHRLICH
GEORGE B EICHELBERGER JR
JIMMY L ESCALLE
FRANCIS W ESCOTT
LOUIS T ESPOSITO
CARL J EVANS

98 AIR FORCE

DANIEL J EVANS JR
EMMETT O EVANS
BILL G FAIN
EDWARD L FEAKES
NOLAN H FERREE
WARREN M FICKLEN
ROBERT C FINCH
JACK A FISHER
JOHN M FITT
EDWARD D FLEMING
JAMES W FLEMING JR
JOHN J FLOURNOY
ROMA C FOGLESONG JR
DAVID A FORREST
JACK FORRESTER
ROBERT R FOSTER
ORRIN R FOX
EDWARD R FRANCIS
NED C FRANKART
GARY E FRASE
FRANK T FREY
RICHARD M FRIEDMAN
GORDON N FROISNESS
ORVAL FUNK
LUKE C FYFFE
LAWRENCE W GALLAGHER
WELDON D GARDNER
HARRY G GARMAN JR
LESLIE L GARROW
ANTHONY GARY
ROBERT P GAUDE JR
ROBERT A GEHMAN
JOHN M GILBERT
WALTER P GILLES
ROBERT W GILLESPIE
PATTESON GILLIAM
ROBERT H GILTNER
HEATH T GLASS JR
DONALD E GLIDDEN
IRWIN L GOLDBERG
NEWMAN C GOLDEN
GEORGE M GOODMAN
RICHARD L GOODMAN JR
BOBBIE A GOODWIN
WILLIAM C GORDON
JAMES B GORRAL JR
WILLIAM W GRAHAM
HERMAN H GRAMMER
EDGAR B GRAY
J RAY GREENWAY JR
GEORGE G GREENWELL
DONALD G GREY
EDWARD S GUTHRIE JR
GARFIELD W GUYER JR
BOYD B GWIN
RICHARD W HAAS
WILLIAM J HABERLE
THOMAS E HADLEY II
ROGER C HALL SR
ROBERT A HALLMAN
GEORGE H HANSEN
THOMAS C HANSON
CARL G HAPP JR
KENNETH A HARDIGAN
REMER L HARDING
CHARLES A HARKER JR
GRANT D HARKNESS
LEE A HARPER
RALPH L HARRIS
BENJAMIN F HARRISON JR
JOHN W HATCHITT
DONN H HAUGEN
RICHARD E HAWES
GERALD J HEAGNEY
DAVID T HEER
HARRY S HEINKE JR
STEWART G HELD
JOHN F HELM
DEWEY R HENRY
ROBERT E HENRY
ANDREW J HERBENICK
RAUL A HERNANDEZ
WARREN L HILDEBRANDT
GRADY L HINSON
CALVIN E HODEL
EMORY E HODGES
WARREN M HOFF
DONALD E HOFFMAN
CHARLES D HOGUE
JOHN D HOKE

WILLIAM L HOLCOM
FRANCIS A HOLCOMB
HAROLD R HOLMES
SCOTT A HOLZ
JOHN W HONAKER
JOHN J HORNER
RAYMOND B HOUSTON
ARNOLD S HOWARD
MARTIN F HOWELL JR
LAURENCE H HUDSON
ROBERT E HUDSON
ALLAN P HUNT JR
WILLIAM E JACKMAN
CHARLES P JACKSON
JOHN J JACKSON
HARRISON C JACOBS
RALPH E JACOBS
PAUL J JACOBSON
CARROLL L JAMES
RAY F JARDINE
DONALD R JENKINS
ARTHUR E JOHNSON
OLIN W JOHNSON
RAYMOND H JOHNSON
WILLIAM B JOHNSON
GEORGE D JONES
MARION M JONES
OLIVER E JONES
HENRY B KELLY
LAWRENCE B KELLY
DOUGLAS B KERN
ALFRED H KING
JOHN W KING
CHARLES F KIRK
DONALD S KOBEY
VICTOR A KOEHLER
EUGENE C KOHFIELD
FREDERICK R KOONTZ
FRANCIS J LABARGE
THOMAS C LAFFERTY
HOWARD J LANDRY
MARVIN E LANTZ
JOHN H LASKEY
BOB A LAUTERBACH
GEORGE A LAVOIE
LAURENCE C LAYTON
BERNARD S LEAVITT
ROLAND E LEE
WILLIAM J LEVI
BEN P LEVY
ROBERT C LEWIS
WILBUR E LEWIS
FREDDIE R LEWTER
DAVID E LEYSHON
JACK A LIGHTNER
VERNON A LINDVIG
BRADFORD LODGE
JOHN LOGOYDA
VINCENT F LOMBARDO
LAMAR B LONGSHORE
FRANK M LOPES
WILLIAM H N LORENZ
FRANK T LOUGHERY
ROBERT J LUCAS
GEORGE M LUKAKIS
JOHN S LUSH
WILLIAM R LYDEN
GRANT W MADSEN
DAVID MANDELL
NICHOLAS MANOS
PAUL N MARCO
DOMINIQUE K MARTIN
HORACE E MARTIN JR
ROBERT L MARTIN
KENNETH C MASON
DOUGLAS N MATHESON
JAMES I MATHIS
IRVIN W MAY
JOHN M MCALPINE
CHARLES L MCBRIDE
VIRGINIA M MCCLURE
JOSEPH E MCELVAIN
CLARENCE A MCGOWAN
JOHN B MCGUINNESS
WILLIAM F MCMURRY
RICHARD L MCNULTY
GERALD W MCPHERSON
DANIEL G METHA
EDWIN I METZGER
FRANCIS J MEYER

FREDERICK H MILHAUPT JR
HENRY D MILLER
HOWARD P MILLER JR
JOHN W MILLER
RALPH B MILLER JR
RAYMOND MILLER
WALDEMAR W MILLER
AYCHIE C MILLIGAN
ROBERT A MITCHELL
IRWIN MOLDAFSKY
MELVIN M MONTIE
DAVID A MOORE
LYLE E MOORE JR
CHARLES B MORAN
WARREN L MORGAN
DAVID H MORRIS
NORMAN E MORRISON
JOHN B MORSE JR
AUGUST W MOUTON
WILBUR J MUELLER
CHARLES E MUHLEBACK
WILLIAM D MULKINS
ARLIE D MULLET
SIDNEY R MULLIKIN JR
JOHN N MUNKRES
JACK L MURRAY
JOSEPH J MURRAY
RICHARD G NEILLANDS
RALPH A NEIS
LAWRENCE A NELSON
JOHN M NETTERBLAD
GUY H NEVINS III
LEO J NICAISE JR
ROBERT F NIEMANN
WILLIAM T NORRIS
ERIC F OBRIANT
WILLIAM T OCONNELL JR
RAY W OLCOTT
RICHARD L OLCOTT
ERNEST C OLIPHANT
ARTHUR R OLSEN
ALLAN J OLSON
LEONARD S OLSON
LOVENDER C OSBURN
LESTER F PAGE
HARRY R PAINTER
ALFORD C PALMER
DAVID H PARK
LONNIE L PARKER
ROBERT B PARKER
CHARLES R PARKERSON
CHARLES F PARKINSON
GEORGE V PATTON
JOHN R PENTECOST JR
CHARLES R PERRY
MARGARET F PERRY
SPIRO J PETERS
JAMES H PETTY
ROBERT F PHALEN
DUANE M PHILLIPS
WILLIAM K PHILLIS
RALPH I PHY
ROBERT L PIERSON
HERBERT PINCUS
DONALD L PITCHFORD
HAMILTON C PLATT
ALBERT E PLECHA
LEWIS P PLEISS
RAYMOND T PLEVYAK
WARREN F POLK
LEON W POLLARD JR
THOMAS L POTTER
JOHN E POUND
CON F POYNOR
CLIFFORD F PRATT
WILLIAM F PRINDLE
VAUGHN D PRUNIER
WILLIAM A PUGH
ROBERT J RAMSEY
JOHN B RANDOLPH
ALBERT E RASE JR
MICHAEL G REBO
RONALD W REED
EDWIN B REESER
ERNEST J REEVES JR
THIEL M REEVES
MELVILLE E REFFNER
HARRY M REHM
PAUL R REICHE
YALE R REILICH

CHARLES M REIN
DONALD R REITSMA
CHARLES W RHINEHART
PETER B RICHARDSON
DALE R RIES
ARNOLD D RIVEDAL
JOEL O RIVES
THOMAS M ROBB
JAMES R ROBERTS
MARTIN R ROBERTS
JOHN J ROESSEL
RICHARD B ROSENVALL
JOHN H ROUMIGUIERE
WILLIAM E ROY
WINFRED RUBLE
ALLAN K RUDOLPH
EUGENE L RUIZ
RICHARD G L RUSK
FRANK R SALAZAR
WILLIAM C SANKEY JR
ELLIOTT B SARTAIN JR
DERRELL B SAYRE
JAMES M SCHOOLEY JR
RICHARD J SEGUIN
REGIS A SELLERS
CLIFFORD G SELMAN
GEORGE A SENIOR
JOHN P SHADDICK III
JOHN H SHEPHERD
FRANK F SHERMAN
EVERETT L SHIELDS JR
MAXWELL J SHIPP
BILLIE J SHORES
ROBERT L SIMPSON
PRESTON SKINNER
WILLIAM B SLADE
CHADWICK B SMITH
DOUGLAS M SMITH
JAMES D SMITH JR
JAMES M SMITH
ROBERT L SMITH
MARION K SMOTHERMAN
CLEMENT R SOUSA
JOHN E SOUTHERLAND
MELVIN SOUZA
GLEN L SPRADLEY
WILBUR R SPRADLING JR
JOHN S STARCK
WARD L STARKWEATHER
JACK C STEINHARTER
RAYMOND A STEWART JR
DEWEY STOPA
EUGENE E STROPE
DAVE P SULLIVAN
MARSHALL J
SUMMERLIN JR
JOHN A SWANSON
LESTER K SWEAT
BRUCE A SWENEY
BEVERLY A SWINGLE
KENNETH P TALLANT
MARLIN A TANNER
CLAUDE R TAYLOR
IRVIN E TAYLOR
WILLIS W THATCHER
JOHN F THEES
CHARLES R THOMPSON
HUGH K THOMSON
ROBERT J THORP
ALLEN R TIERNAN JR
CHARLES R TIRCUIT
WILLIAM W TOOPS
DONALD R TORSTAD
JAMES E TOWLE
ALBERT M TOWNSEND
ARTHUR A TRAUTMANN
THOMAS W TRIMBLE
JOHN R TULLY
JACK H TURBERVILLE
JAMES N VALENTINE
CLAYTON W
VANDARWARKA
RAY J VAN DEN BELDT
JAMES A VAN VEEN
IRWIN L VICTOR JR
JEROME A VOLK
WILLIAM A VOSS
JAMES G VRETIS
STANLEY E WAFLE
JACK E WALKER

WILLIE J WALL JR
JOSEPH C WALLACK
LUCIUS P WALTON
JOHN A WANDS
HAROLD B WARD JR
DAVID WARFIELD
ROBERT H WARNER
BILLIE B WATSON
HENRY D WEESE
GEORGE T WELLS JR
THOMAS F WELLS
KENNETH L WEST
DIRCK D WESTERVELT
CLAUDE V WHITE
WILL C WHITE
STANTON G WILCOX
RAYMOND C WILK
BERTRAM D WILKINS
OLIVER S WILLIAMS
ROBERT A WILLIAMS
ROBERT J WILLIAMS
ROBERT R WILLIAMS
ROBERT V WILSON
WESLEY A WINSTON
WARREN B WISDOM
MILTON L WISEMAN
LELAND H WOLF
LAWRENCE E WOLFE JR
RUSSELL J WOLFGRAM
WILLIAM C WOMACK
WILLIAM F WOMACK
FERNIE WOOD
BENJAMIN H
WOODRUFF JR
THELBERT B WORMACK
GENE E WRIGHT
JACK M WRIGHT
FREDERICK E WYSOCKI
ARTHUR D YAICH
JOSEPH P ZEIGLER
FREDERICK O ZENTNER

CAPTAIN

GEORGE AARON
DONALD L ADAMS
JOHN H ADAMS
ROBERT ADAMS
ROBERT H ADAMS
JOHN P AHLERS
DONALD W AKERS
ROLAN M AKIN
JACK V ALLEN
LAURENCE E ANCTIL
BERIGER A ANDERSON
ROBERT B ANDREWS
ROY ANTHONY
LEROY E
ASCHENBRENNER
GILBERT L ASHLEY JR
ELLIOTT D AYER
JOSEPH M BABASA JR
STANLEY W BAILEY
GEORGE A BAKSANKAS
BERNARD E BARNES
EDWARD E BARROW
JAMES A BATEMAN
CLAUDE A BATTY JR
EUGENE E BAUWIN
SAMUEL C BAXTER III
HAROLD M BEARDALL
JACK M BEESON
CLYDE J BEHNEY
WALTER C BENEKE JR
CHAUNCEY A
BENNETT JR
RAYMOND J BENNETT
ELMER T BIGGS
DONALD G BIGHAM
ROBERT J BIRD
WAYNE F BLACK
FRED E BLOESCH
DONALD D BOLT
CECIL W BRANDSTED
WILLIAM BROCKMIRE
TAUNO O BROOKS
GERALD L BROSE
CHARLES J BROWN
WILLIS R BROWN

99

AIR FORCE

PHILIP W BROWNING
JOHN L BUCKNER
RICHARD G BULL
LAWRENCE E BURGER
JACKSON A BURRELL
WOODROW BURTON
ARTHUR D CALLAN
ROBERT T CANNON JR
OSBORNE T CARLISLE
RAYMOND J CARLSON
FRANCIS CARMODY
THOMAS M CARRAHER
LIBERO P CASACCIA
BARNEY P CASTEEL JR
BERNARD D CERNOSEK
ROBERT L CHERRY
LOUIS N CHRISTENSEN
ADRIAN L CHRISTENSON
JOHN J COLEMAN
HARRY L COLLINS JR
JOSEPH S COLLINS
WILLIAM J CONLON
ROBERT W CONNER
JAMES J CONNOLLY
WILFORD T COOK
TROY G COPE
RONALD R CREE
GEORGE J CROFT
WILLIAM D CRONE
RICHARD G CROSKREY
DEAN G CROWELL
GENE A CULBERTSON
FRANCIS J CUMMINGS
JAMES F DALE
WILBUR S DARBY
GLEN DARDEN
HOWARD J DAVIES
GEORGE A DAVIS JR
RAMON R DAVIS
PERRY A DAWSON
RAYMUNDO DELGADO
ALBERT P DEROSIER
ELZEARD J DESCHAMPS
HARRY W DINGLE
EDWIN R DISCHINGER
HENRY T DIXON
KENNETH L DOOLITTLE
FRANK A DOYLE
ERNEST H DUDERSTADT JR
VICTOR L DUER
WILLIAM S EARNS
MORTON G EDWARDS
RALPH A ELLIS JR
BILL ELSOM
JOHN H EMBACH
JOSEPH J ENGELBREIT
JOSEPH L FARBER
STEVE J FESTINI
WILLIAM R FISHER
DONALD L FLENTKE
JULIUS C FLUHR JR
JAMES A FOULKS JR
JOHN D FRAZER
DAVID J FRENCH
DAVID GANDIN
FRED H GARRISON
OSBALDO GARZA
ROBERT D GIBB
LOUIS P GORRELL
GENE W GOULD
RICHARD A GRABLIN
PAUL K GRAHAM
KENNETH J GRANBERG
VICTOR B GRAPER
GEORGE E GRAY
ROBERT L GREER
DAVID H GRISHAM
JOHN F GROSSMAN JR
CORNELIUS P GUILFOYLE
CHARLES W GUNTHER
JOHN L HAAS
WILBERT E HABAKANGAS
LEWIS G HAEFELE
EDWARD D HAGERTY
GEORGE E HAINES
STANLEY B HALADYNA
ALLEN L HALLUM
JEFF L HAMILTON JR
EUGENE R HANSEN
EARL H HARBOUR

WARREN G HARDING
GUY B HARRELL JR
CHARLES W HARRIS
ROBERT G HARVEY
WILLIAM T HASKETT JR
LUTHER R HAWKINS JR
NATHAN C HAYNES JR
JUSTICE K HAYTHORNE
JAMES D HEATH
ROBERT R HEBERT
JACK H HEDERSTROM
ARTHUR HEISE
THOMAS L HELTON
JOSEPH R HEWITT
JOHN J HIGGINS
RICHARD E HINES
WILLIAM O HOBBA
JACK M HOBBIE
LESTER A HOLCOMB
LOUIS D HOLLAND
WILLIAM K HOOK
JOHN L HORN
SAMUEL HOSTER JR
DAVID W HOWARD
MELVIN J HOWARD
HOWARD D HOWELL
JAMES H HOWELL JR
ROBERT N HOWELL
FREDERICK G HUDSON III
GORDON P HUMPHRIES
WILLIAM R HUNTER
ARTHUR E HUTCHINSON
DON HYATT
TEDRICK G IRWIN
WILBUR D JENSEN
ARTHUR J JOHNSON
FRANK S JOHNSTON JR
ASHLEY G JONES
GEORGE M JONES
RALPH N KALLOCK
HAROLD O KEISTER
FREDERIC S KELLEY
JOSEPH C KEPFORD
WALTER M KEPLEY
JOSEPH H KIENHOLZ
HUGH L KIENITZ
ROGER E KIMBALL
ROBERT C KLEIN
KINGDON R KNAPP
JACK A KNIGHT
RAYMOND J KNUEPPEL
JOSEPH L KORSTJENS
ROBERT M KRUMM
GORDON V KUEHNER JR
IVAN M LACHNIT
ROBERT E LADEN
ROBERT H LAIER
JOHN F LANE
GUY F LANEY
JACK C LANGSTON
HUGH F LARKIN
DE FORREST A V LAUFER JR
ROBERT H LAYTON
DANIEL B LEAKE JR
LESLIE W LEAR
JACK LEWIS
EMMETT N LONG
JAMES A LOWE JR
GARLAND E MADISON
JOHN S MANIATTY
JAMES D MARSHALL
ROBERT MARTIN JR
DAVID J MATHER
WILLIAM S MATUSZ
WILLIAM K MAULDIN
JOHN A MCALLASTER JR
ROBERT W MCANELLY
JOHN J MCCOLLUM
LEO F MCGEOUGH
JOHN C MCGINNIS
CHARLES F MCGUIRE
ROBERT E MCKEE
MARTIN J MCNAMARA
ALBERT MCNEELEY
CHARLES E MCWHIRK
DAVID MEREDITH
HARRY R MIDDLETON
FRANK E MILLER JR
JOHN R MILLER
ARA MOORADIAN

HARRY C MOORE
JOHN G MOORE
RICHARD D MOORE
LEROY A MORGAN JR
WILLIAM C MOSKOSKY SR
RALPH D MULHOLLEN
ARILD C NIELSEN
DAVID L NIELSEN
BRUCE K NIMS
MARLIN T NOLAN
LEO P NOWICKI
JOHN M NUTTING
WARREN E OBRIEN
CLARENCE B ODEL
HOWARD E ODELL
CARL H OELSCHIG JR
RALPH M OLSON
EDWARD J ONZE
JAMES R OVERSTREET JR
JASPER N OWENS
ERNEST R OYLER
ALEXANDER B PADILLA
ALBERT W PAFFENROTH
FREDERICK R PARTRIDGE
LAWRENCE E PAUL
BERNARD L PEARSON
JAMES K PECK
ROGER W PENNINGER
JAMES V PEUTER
JAMES J PICUCCI
LUTHER S PIERCE
WALTER E PITTMAN
JOE H POWERS JR
CHARLES W PRATT
BENJAMIN N RADER
ROBERT D RAMSEY JR
HOLMAN C RAWLS JR
DON R REMSNYDER
JOHN K RHOADS
EDGAR D RICE
HERBERT E RITTER
JOHN L ROBERTS
HARRY W ROCKLAGE JR
TALVIN J RORAUS
ALVIN S ROSENTHAL
PAUL C ROSS
WILLIAM M ROSS
FRED B ROUNTREE
TED G ROYER
FRED O RUDAT
EARL O RUHLIN
MICHEL B RUSSELL
WALTER R RUSSELL
FLOYD W SALZE
HARRY T SANDLIN
GILBERT J SCHAUER
ROBERT L SCHENCK
LEE G SCHLEGEL
NORMAN W SCHNEIDT
CORNELIUS E SCOTT
STANLEY V SCOTT
EDWARD H SEAVEY
ROBERT E SHEEHAN
JOHN W SHEWMAKER
THOMAS L SHIELDS
WERNER F SIEBER
GRANT W SIMPSON
RICHARD H SIMPSON
DONALD S SIRMAN
ZAMRIA V SIZEMORE
CARTER M SKARE
CLARENCE V SLACK JR
GORDON O SMITH
GRAHAM SMITH
HOWARD E SMITH
WILLIS P SMITH
CHARLES R SPATH
ROBERT E SPRAGINS
HAROLD R SPROUL
LEE ROY STANLEY
STEPHEN STAYSICH
ROBERT C STEELE
WILLARD R SUTTON
ERNEST C SWANSON
DONALD D TEGT
ALBERT G TENNEY
MINTER C TERRY
NORBOURN A THOMAS
JOHN F THOMPSON
MORRIS F THOMPSON

WILLIAM E THRELKELD
IRVIN M TINDALL
ARCHIE P TRANTHAM
JAMES L TREESTER
HAROLD P TURNER
HARRY M TYLER
HALBERT C UNRUH
LAWRENCE M VANDERWILT
JAMES A VAN FLEET JR
THOMAS L VAN RIPER
PAUL E VAN VOORHIS
HAYDEN G VAUGHN
JERRY D VOELM
LEONARD P VOGT
EDWARD C WAHLGREN
ROGER WALLIS
JOHN S WALMSLEY JR
CECIL O WARE
CARL L WASHBURN JR
NORMAN E WATKINS
HAROLD D WEBSTER JR
NELSON H WILKERSON
EDWARD J WILLIAMS
MARSHALL M WILLIAMS III
JAMES G WILLIS JR
JAMES W WILLS JR
HOWARD A WILSON JR
JAMES S WILSON JR
DONALD F WINTERS
MELVIN P WINTERS
CLELAND D WITH
ELLIOTT D WOLFSEN
JOHN G WOLIUNG
CHARLES W WOOLAM
CECIL R WRIGHT
CHARLES F WRIGHT
RALPH F YAROSH
JOHN H ZIMMERLEE JR

MAJOR

HERBERT W ANDRIDGE JR
FELIX ASLA JR
ARTHUR M AUSTIN
GEORGE T BARRENTINE
LAWRENCE W BEAL
JOSEPH W BOWMAN
MEADE M BROWN
DEWEY L CHAPMAN
ROBERT W COGSWELL
MURRIT H DAVIS
ANACLETHE P DECESARE
MALCOLM B EDENS
VERNON ELLIFRITZ
HUGH P FARLER
ARTHUR B FAUNCE
ERNEST C FIEBELKORN
DELTIS H FINCHER
MARLYN C FORD JR
WILLIAM J GREENE
GEORGE A HADLEY
WILLIAM H HIATT
KENNETH S HODGES
ZANE M HOIT
MAURICE JOHNSON
NEIL R JOHNSON
GORDON K KAHL
KASSEL M KEENE
THEODORE H KUCH JR
SAMUEL P LOGAN JR
JOSEPH S LONG JR
CHARLES J LORING JR
JOHN G MARTIN
FRANCIS N MCCOLLOM
CHARLES E MCDONOUGH
RICHARD A MCNEES
KENNETH E MIKALAUSKAS
SHELTON W MONROE
HORACE H MYERS JR
THOMAS E MYERS
ROBERT O NEIGHBORS
ROBERT R NEWTON
JOHN E ROBERTS
HILLIARD M ROPER
EARL J SANDERS JR
GLEN D SCHILTZ JR
LOUIS J SEBILLE
BERNARD K SEITZINGER
AMOS L SLUDER

MARVIN J SPENCE
CALVERT L STAIR
RICHARD E STECKEL
ROBERT A SYDNOR
THOMAS A
SYMINGTON JR
HAROLD J TITUS
JOHN F TULLOCH JR
ADAM P TYMOWICZ
FRANK L VAN SICKLE JR
JOHN J WALSH
GEORGE V WENDLING
ROBERT F WILLIS
WILLIAM P WINDUS JR
MELVIN C WOOD
ROGER C WOODARD
JULES E YOUNG

LIEUTENANT COLONEL

VANCE E BLACK
PAUL M BREWER JR
EDWARD E CAMPBELL
VINCENT C CARDARELLA
JAMES F CRUTCHFIELD
GEORGE A DAVIS JR
ARTHUR W GEBAUR JR
HOWARD A HAYES
WALTER S KING
ROBERT V MCHALE
PAUL B MILLER
LELAND P MOLLAND
GERALD E
MONTGOMERY
JULIUS E ONEAL
JAMES A RIPPIN
ROBERT E SCANLON
WALTER K SELENGER
MEECH TAHSEQUAH
SYDNEY W
WEATHERFORD
LEWIS F WEBSTER
RAY E WELLS
JACK P WILLIAMS
GEORGE H WYMAN

COLONEL

SHERMAN R BEATY
MILTON F GLESSNER JR
THOMAS B HALL
WILLIAM T HALTON
DOUGLAS H HATFIELD
PAYNE JENNINGS JR
JOHN R LOVELL
JAMES L MCBRIDE JR
GLENN C NYE
KARL L POLIFKA
ALBERT C
PRENDERGAST
THERON H
WHITNEYBELL

100 AIR FORCE

Starfield Library in Starfield COEX Mall. The public library is a popular destination among tourists and citizens of Seoul. *Photo courtesy of Getty Images/iStockphoto.*

CHAPTER 20

Korea Today — The Victory of Freedom

Korea's social, economic, and political transfiguration has allowed it to take a place among the world's leading nations.

Korean corporations such as Samsung, Hyundai, and LG are global leaders in their fields. Korean companies have earned particular renown in high-tech industries such as semiconductors, next-generation displays, and information technology. In recent years, Samsung has achieved international success as the world's largest producer of smart phones. The transformation of automaker Hyundai from late-night talk-show punchline to producer of globally reputable, high-quality cars mirrors the transformation of Korea itself. Hyundai Heavy Industries, Samsung Heavy Industries, and Daewoo Shipbuilding and Marine Engineering have made Korea the world's largest shipbuilder. In 2009, Samsung C&T finished work on Dubai's 163-story Burj Khalifa, the world's tallest building.

These are just a few of the many ways the Korean marketplace has become a launchpad for new technologies and innovative products. From mobile device technologies to home entertainment, Korean brands have set new global standards for quality, reliability, and availability. Today's Korea is uniquely poised to develop new and exciting technologies and bring them to a global market.

In recent years, Korea has also acted as a leader on the world's stage by successfully hosting several international economic and political events. In November 2010, the leaders of the world's largest economies converged on the Korean capital for the G-20 Seoul Summit. The Republic also hosted the 2012 Nuclear Security Summit and the 2005 APEC Summit. Korea's role as an international venue has extended beyond politics. In 1988, Korea hit another global milestone by successfully hosting the Summer Olympic Games. The eyes of the sporting world were once again fixed upon the nation in 2002, when it hosted the 2002 FIFA Korea-Japan World Cup that saw the Korean national soccer team pull off a miraculous run to the semifinals. The Olympic spirit returned to Korea once again when the town of Pyeongchang hosted the 2018 Winter Olympic Games.

With an expanding infrastructure and an educated population, Korea has all the necessary ingredients for sustained long-term socioeconomic growth. Today, South Koreans can look forward to a bright future as a global, economic, and political leader.

Korean Companies: Leaders in World Industry

In the decades following the Korean War, the Republic of Korea (South Korea) embraced free enterprise and international trade, making the nation one of the best business economies in the world. Driven by a highly educated and skilled workforce, it has the world's eighth-highest median household income—the highest in Asia—and its single citizens in particular earn more than their counterparts in all G7 nations.

Today, Korea is home to a growing number of globally recognized companies, including Samsung, LG, Hyundai, and Kia. The Republic of Korea was recently named the world's most innovative country by the Bloomberg Innovation Index, ranking first in business R&D intensity and in patents filed per GDP. In 2005, Korea became the world's first country to fully transition to high-speed internet and it currently has both the world's fastest internet speed and highest smartphone ownership, ranking first in ICT Development, e-Government, and 4G LTE coverage.

Many Korean brands are among the most recognized in the entire world, and the list of these successful brands will only continue to expand as time goes by.

HYUNDAI

KIA

SAMSUNG

LG

posco

Asiana Airlines

Hanwha

LOTTE

GS

SK

LIG Nex1

KOREAN AIR

KEPCO

Korean companies featured prominently on the lighted facade in Picadilly Circus, London, United Kingdom. *Photo by Mario Guti via Getty Images/iStockphoto.*

he art of seeing
GAP
beauty
midnight pharmacy
30% OFF DENIM

Some 1,100 students form the Seoul Olympic emblem. The 1988 Summer Olympic Games, hosted in Seoul, introduced Korea and its development to the international community. *Photo by Korea Tourism Organization.*

One of Korea's best-known sports stars, figure skater Kim Yu-na won gold in the women's single event in the 2010 Winter Olympic Games. Kim holds several international figure-skating records. *Photo by Yonhap News.*

South Korean short-track skaters (from left) Shim Suk-hee, Choi Min-jeong, Kim A-lang, Kim Ye-jin, and Lee Yu-bin pose with their gold medals during the medal ceremony in Pyeongchang. The team won the women's 3000m relay in short-track speed skating. *Photo by Yonhap News.*

A pagoda of prayer is displayed during the closing ceremony of the Pyeongchang Winter Olympics at the Olympic stadium. *Photo by Yonhap News.*

Olympic figure skating gold medalist Kim Yu-na lights the Olympic cauldron during the opening ceremony of the 2018 Winter Games at Pyeongchang Olympic Stadium. *Photo by Yonhap News.*

Speed skater Lee Seung-hoon of South Korea poses with his gold medal during the medal ceremony at the 2018 Pyeongchang Winter Olympics. *Photo by Yonhap News.*

Songdo International Business District is the centerpiece of the Incheon Free Economic Zone. One of the world's most technologically advanced cities, Songdo is the headquarters of the UN Green Climate Fund. *Photo by aomam via Getty Images/istockphoto.*

Gwangan Bridge shines above the waters of Busan. *Photo by Korea Tourism Organization.*

The KTX (Korea Train Express) operates high-speed train service (approximately 350 km per hour) via the Honam and Gyeongbu lines to South Korea's main cities: Daejeon, Gwangju, Mokpo, Daegu, and Busan. *Photo by Minseong Kim via Creative Commons license.*

In Korea and the U.S., SK is building a stronger tomorrow.

Double Bottom Line

SK's Double Bottom Line approach is shaped by the belief that strong financial returns and a positive social impact are mutually reinforcing and will grow simultaneously.

ESG Management

The commitment by SK and its businesses to meet Environmental, Social and Governance (ESG) principles has led to increased investments in renewable energy, alternative food sources and sustainable technologies.

Social Value

At SK, we recognize that companies are no longer solely accountable for the returns they generate for shareholders. They must also actively foster and promote values to benefit and strengthen the surrounding communities and the world at large.

Net-Zero Journey

SK companies are taking a leading role in helping address global climate change. Across its businesses, SK has pledged to cut 200 million tons of carbon emissions by 2030, or about 1% of the reductions needed to meet global climate change targets.

$30 Billion invested in the U.S. through 2025

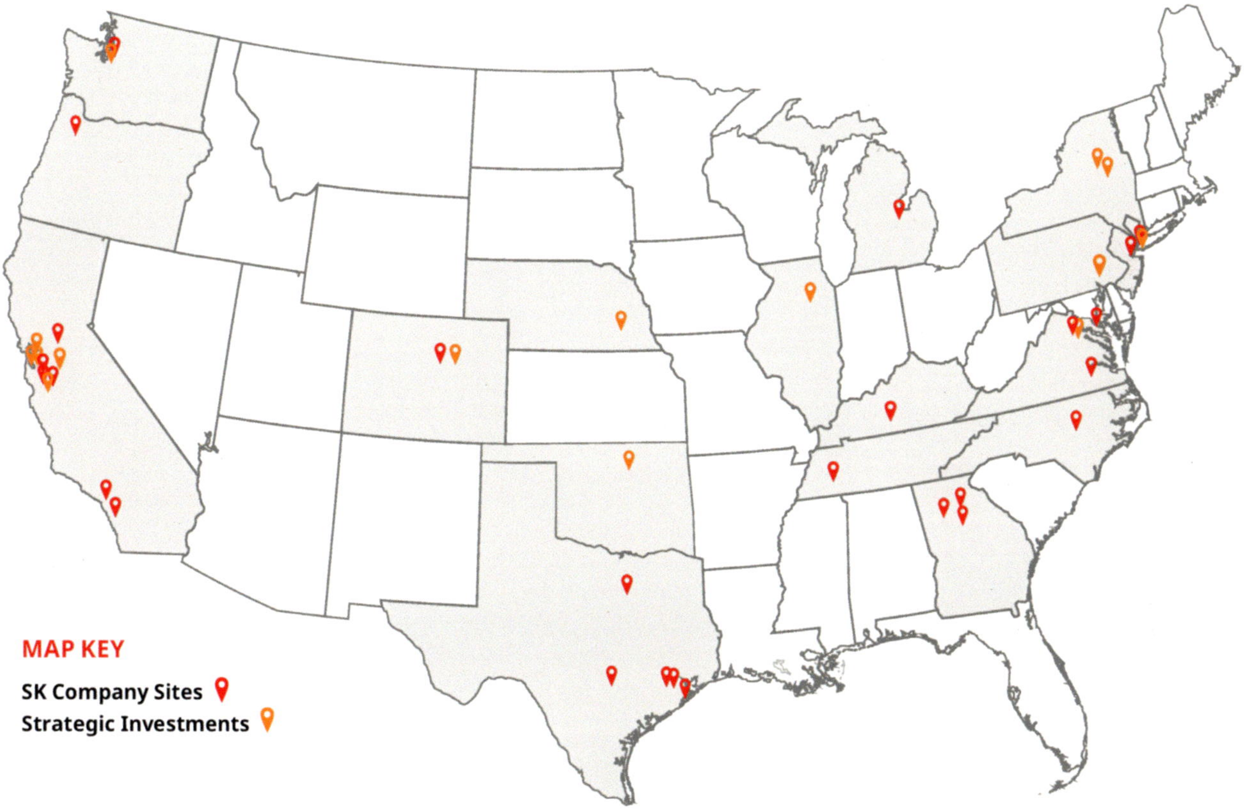

Born from the ashes of the Korean War

The bravery shown by the service members who fought for the freedom of the Korean people will not be forgotten. Their courage is directly reflected in South Korea's flourishing domestic economy, an expanding global presence, and a lasting partnership with the United States. SK has made great strides globally by creating jobs and investing in the U.S., which includes $30 billion of investments through 2025.

Key Milestones

- **$13 billion** in assets across the U.S.
- **4,000+** U.S. employees
- Additional **16,000 U.S. jobs** expected to be created through 2025
- Ranked **#129** on *Fortune Global 500*

CHAPTER 22

DONORS TO THE MEMORIAL

We are grateful to the following donors for their contributions to the Korean War Veterans Memorial project.

CHAIRMAN DONORS

($1M and above)

Ministry of Patriots and Veterans Affairs

The Government and the People of the Republic of Korea

SK Holdings

PRESIDENT DONORS

($100K up to $999,999K)

Mudang Gumpa
Korean American Society of Virginia
Sae Eden Presbyterian Church
National Unification Advisory Council
KWVA Foothills Chapter 301
State of Maryland
Community Foundation for Greater Atlanta
Korea–U.S. Alliance Foundation
Korean Veterans Association of the Republic of Korea

DIRECTOR DONORS

($50K up to $99,999K)

Sang Kwon Choi
Nae il Foundation
Yoido Full Gospel Church
KWVA Richard L. Quatier Chapter 321
KWVA Maryland Chapter 33
Richard Stosbery

ASSOCIATE DONORS

($25K up to $49,999K)

Far East Broadcasting Company
World Korean International Married Women's Association
Susan L. Hall
The Honorable James Mattis
TracFone Wireless
Washington Korean Women's Society
Jonathon Davies
KWVA General John H. Michaelis Chapter 327
Kukbo Design Co., Ltd.

FRIEND DONORS

(Up to $24,999K)

187th Infantry Regiment – Rakkasan Association
A&M Mobile Dustless Blasting
Jonathan Abbett
Matthew Ackerman
J.A. Adams
Tracy Adkins
Donna Adler
Advisory Council on Democratic and Peaceful Unification in Washington, D.C.
Leo Agnew
Peter Ahn
Richard Ahne
Richard Albregts
Eugene & Ileana Alim
Bill Alli
Nestor Alonso
Michele Altobelli
Moses Altsech
Rodie Alvare-Henson
Jenay Alvarez
Jill Amacker
Richard A. Ambrosoli
American Council of Engineering Companies of Metropolitan Washington
American Legion
American Legion Harford Post 39
American Legion Post 254
Gloria M. Amoroso
William Amos
Barbara Anderson
Ken Anderson
Jana L. Anderson
Rose A. Anderson
Scott Anderson
Suzanne Andreasen
William Andrews
Paul J. Angelina
Neil Aquino
Curtis Archambault
Jeanne Archambault
Felicia Arculeo
Karen Arestides
Martin Arling
Alfred Arno
Anne E. Arnold
Jack & Fran Arogeti
Geoffrey Arone
Daniel Arons
Neal Aronson
Benjamin Arriola
Michael Asato
Esther Ashton
Terry Atkinson
Atlantic Consulting Associates
Atlas Security Service, Inc.
Susan Ator
Patrick Attridge
Judith Aubin
Kyle Auger
Ann-Marie Autio
John S. Autry
Rudy K. Avadikian
Carlton Avant
Barry Avery
Lisa Azzarelli
Harold H. Baden
Suzanne Badyna
Chung Hyun Bae
Howard Baik
Carolyn Bailey
Michael V. Baio, MD
Cathy Bakalar
Franklin L. Baker
Jeanette Baker
Lois Baker
Joseph Baldwin
William L. Ball
Thomas Ballard
Jane Banister
Robert Banker
Roxanna Bankston
James A. Barbieri
Cynthia Barger
Edward Barnes
Barnes-Allison Labor Management COOP Committee
Peter Barnett
S. Barrantes
Barrett & Weber, LLC
Frank Barrie
Joe M. Barrios
Joseph Barry
Kari & Fred Barton Foundation
Marcella Basta
Santanu Basu
Rod & Gail Bates
Tracee Battis
Albert Bauer
Karen Bauer
Gregory & Sharon Baum
Toni Bauman
Gene Baynor
Gene C. Baynor
Linda Beaman
Trent & Lee Ann Beane
Donald C. Beck
Sidney Bedell
Victoria Bedo
Brian Beger
Beger Family
Scott Behnen
Kathy Bell
Sharen S. Bell
Bell Family
Gloria Bella
Barbara Bellamente
Gerilyn Bender-Rabinowitz
Holly Benfield
Julie Benjamin
Susan Benjamin
Robin Bennett
Loretta Benoit
Susan Benson
Bill Berg
Alex Berger
Arthur Bergeron
Gena Berkebile
Daryl Berman
Bridget Bernadette
Bernadt Family
Berne Chamber of Commerce
Harry Bernhard
Edward Bernosky, Jr
Mark Berny
Dr. Trevor Berry
Giles & June Berry
Vincent P. Berry
Martin Bershtein
Daniel Bertoldo
Alicia Beth
Bethel Korean Baptist Church
Bethel Korean Presbyterian Church
Poma Bho
Andrea Bickford
Mark & Kimberly Billek
Bruce Bingham
Michael Birsic
Central Acupunture & Herb Clinic
Mary K. Black
Patricia Black
Blake & Uhlig , PA
Robert W. Blakely
Elmer Blaney Parker
Mark Blankenship
Therese & Lee Block
Ashley Blumling
Zane Boatright
James E. Bockman
Kathryn Bodle
George A. Boinis
Antoinette Boisclair
Heather Boissonneault
J. Kevin Bokeno
Joseph J. Bolduc
Patricia Bolland
George H. Bolling
Colieen Bolte Murphy
Nancy Boore
Linda Boothby
Borough of Watchung
Mary Ann Borowiak
Brad Boutaugh
Brian Bouvier
Barbara Bowen-Tilghman
Columbia Pacific Building & Construction Trades Council
Margaret & Ed Boyer
Christie Boylston
Terry Brackman
Chris Bradley
Lewis R. Bradley
Frank Brady
Joanne Brady
John Bragg
David A. Bramlage
Kyle Brann
Marjorie Branson
Jennifer Brau
Cynthia Bredernitz
David Breece
Edeward Breehl
John K. Breese
Pam Brekas
Kevin Brennan
Diane Brenner
Marissa Brescia
Mary Lu Bretsch
Diane Brick
Teresa T. Brick
Bridgeway Community Church
Brighthouse
Monica Bringle
Lasalle Bristol
James J. Britt, III
Mary Ann Brockway
Joan O. Brodeur
Geri Brody
Robert Brogan
Carole Brookins
Alexis Brooks
Keith Brooks
Marlene Brooks
Amy J. Brown
Joseph L. Brown
Brownell Travel
Kelsey Brozek
Britt Brunke
BJ Brunner
Peter Bruno
Yvonne M. Bryant
Theresa Buckley
Lloyd Buechel
Jeni Buelow
Frederick J. Buffone
Betsy Burgess
Norma Burke
Johnnie W. Burkhead
Jack Burkman
Brian Burlant
Andy Burleigh
Burr & Forman, LLP
Michelle Burress
Mary Buskirk
Cynthia Butcher
Butcher Boys
James N. Butcher, PhD
Donna Butler
Angela Byrns
Marie Cabrelli
Cadiz-Trigg County Ladies Auxiliary, VFW #7890
James D. Cale
Ronald W. Camillo
Richard Campanale
Elizabeth Campbell
Francis Campbell
Gabrielle Campbell
Kathryn Campbell
Maria Campbell
Gilbert C. Canchola
Canton Union School District #66
Jaime Cantrell
Joseph Cantrell, Sr.
Melissa Capen
Capital Bank
Donald Caplan
Vincent Carbone
Colleen Carey
John C. Carlin, Jr.
Katie Carlson
Carnavicom Co., Ltd.
Brandalin Carnes
Carol Carr
Maureen Carr
Sylvia Carr
Kathy Carrier
Carruth Capital, LLC
Marcel Cartagena
Alyce L. Carter
Jim Cartlidge
Gene Cartwright
Thomas Cary, Jr.
Joyce C. Casey
Dianne L. Cashman
Richard Caslow
Joan Cassidy
James Castellotti
Tricia M. Casten
Barbara Castlow
John Castonia
Andrea Catala
Bernadette Catellanos
Jerry Catron
David A. Caudle
Jane Cauley
F. R. Cavin
Ray Cebrian
Central Baptist Church
Central Korean School
Allie Cerami
Jane Cerhan
Robert Chaffee
Steven Chalnick
Bernie Champoux
Ki Chang
Byrne W. Chapman
Doug Chapman
Mary Chapman
Steve Chapman
Amy Chasanoff
Nancy Jo Chatham
Shawn Chatterton
Arthur Cheek
Duanjie Chen
Julie Chen
Stephen A. Cheney

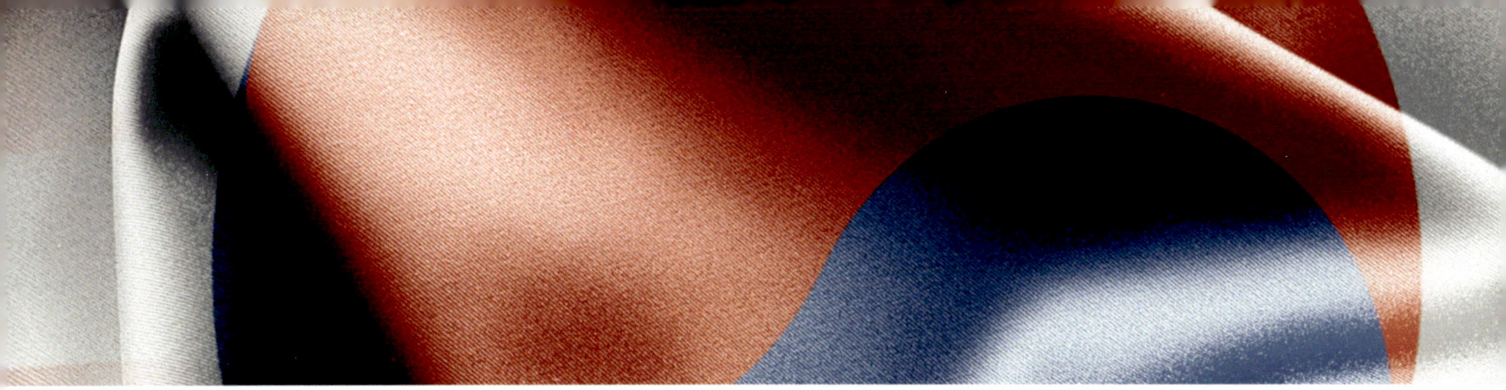

Cy Cherry
Sharon Chevalier
Jeffrey Chi
Brittany Chiaravallo
Karen Chilcote
Charles L. Chipley, Jr
Doris G. Chisholm
David Chivo
Dr. Gyu Wan Cho
James Cho
Johnathan Cho
Myung Eun Cho
Soo Hak Cho
Sung Jae Cho
Yongjoo Cho
Hyon Choe
Kichol Choe
Arthur S. Choi
Bill Choi
Byungsuk Choi
Heungsun Choi
Phile Choi
Chosin Few Michigan Chapter
ChoSun Hwaro Family
Tiffany Chow
Jennifer Christensen
Chu Family Foundation, Inc.
Chisuap Chung
Joseph Chung
Philip Chung
Young In Chung
John R. Church
Monica Ciavarella
Thomas J Ciccone, Jr.
Patricia Ciesla
Steven Cifelli
Charmaine Cigliano
Dolores Ciliotta
Oliver Cipollini, Jr
Dale Clark
Roland Clatterbuck
Nicole Clauburg
Marilynn Claus
Therese Claussen
Linda F. Clay
H. Dormant Clayton
Caryn Clements
Barry S. Clemson Family
CliftonLarsonAllen, LLP
Clines Social Club
Susan Clooney
Leon Cluts
Heather Coburn-Schill
Kathy H. Cochran
Bradford Cochrane, Sr.
Richard F. Cody
Margaret Coe
Barbara Coen
Susan Cohen
Jacob Cole
Mary Jane Cole
Molly Cole
John & Kathleen Coleman
Sarah Coleman
James L. Colgan
Donna Colla
Jessica Colucci
Columbia Pacific Building & Construction Trades Council
The Columbian
Matt R. Combs
Community Military Appreciation Committee
Elizabeth Comolli
Compass Call Big Safari Depot
Chris Connelly
Pam Connor
Contemporary Health Care, PC
Continental Poultry Group, Inc.
Wendell H. Coogan
Christopher R. Cook
Kimberly Cook
Lisa Coons
Christa Cooper
Karen Cooper
Lisa Corbett
Core BTS Leadership Team
Huey Cotton
Council of Korean Americans
Joyce & Lloyd Courtney
Claire Coverdell
Christina M. Cowan
Cowlitz Indian Tribe
Edward Cox
John Cox
Kathleen Cox
Ralph Crafton
Kelli Cragin
Irene Craine
Allen Crandell
Cresap's Rifles Post 78, 29th Division
Steven Cronk
Linda L. Cross
Harry Crumling
Dawn M. Crunden
Richard Cummings
Clay Cummins
Jack Curcio
Janis Curran
Daehan Seniors Association in Alaska, Inc.
Erin Dahlin
Sarah Daley
Joyce Dalton
Georgianna D'Amico
Mary T. Danehy
William H. Danforth
Dee Daniels
Joseph Dapello
Kelly Darmiento
Data Strategies, Inc.
Daugherty, Inc.
The Charles Sylvan Daun Family
Stanley Davidson
Betty Davis
Sherry B. Davis
Stephen Davis
Davison-O'Brien Family
Rudolph De Winter
Jennifer Dean
Richard W. Dean, II
Angela Deangelis
Christian Deangelis
Steven Deblieck
Jasinski, Deborah
Horace Dediu
Joseph A. DeFrancesco
Joyce Degruchy
George B. Delaplaine, Jr.,
Gioia Deleonardo
Deloitte Services, LP
Janet Demichele
Cynthia Dendinger
Darlene Denicola
Diane L. Dennis
Donna Denon
Janine Depenning
Margaret DeSantis
Anthony M. Deshiro
Frank Desiderio
Harold L. Devins
Donald & Martha DeWees Foundation
Armistead Dey
Robert Dickson
James F Dietrich
Doug Dillard
Elaine Dills
Daniel R. Dilts
Rick Dineen
James A. DiPerna
Disabled American Veterans Department of Ohio
Kimberly Ditommaso
Eugene Dixon
Jim Dixon
Wayne Doenges
Karen Doerfler
Kathleen Doherty-Hewins
Liam Donaher
David Donaldson
Deborah K. Donaldson
Jin Dong
Tom & Wanda Donkin
Michael & Genevieve Doody
Tom Doorley
Timothy Doran
Keith G Dorman
Reese Dorrepaal
Marie Dougherty
Robert Douglass
Robert Douglass
Vivian I Douglass
Allison Doyle
Kerry Doyle
Marie T. Doyon
Emily Drake
Sharon Dravecky
Harry Drier
David Driskell
Linda W Dube
Jane H. Dugan
William F. Dunaway
Maxine Dunn
Terra Durham
Marianne Dyer
T. Robert Eader
Mychal Eagleson
David Easley
Steve Eberly
Howard S. Edelstein
Sandra Edmonson
Earl Edwards
Kathleen Edwin
Christopher F. Egan
Paul Egbert
Mark Ehlers
Eisenhower Elementary School Sunshine Club
Bobby Ekers
John & Sandi Eliel
Edgar Elkins
Kristen Elliott
Charles D. Ellis
Peter V. Emanuele
Tanya Emanuele
Kevin Enad
Kathryn Engberg
Vicki Erazmus
Lisa Erickson
Jim Escalle
Harold Essex
Carmen F. Esteve
Marilyn Etcoff
Stacy Eubank
Eunpyeong First Presbyterian Church
Alan Evanish
Deborah Ewers
Lewis M. Ewing
Joette Fabbri
Mary Fagan
Jerry & Judy Fahl
Michael & Diane Fahrbacher
Chad Fahs
Satonya Fair
Ralph Fairman
Farm Credit of the Virginias, ACA
Hulyn Farr
Dinah Farrell
Kristi Farrington
Margaret Fasnacht
Marilyn F. Fasnacht
C. Fayette Staples Post No. 57
Federal Home Loan Mortgage Corporation
Federal Reserve Bank of Boston
Kimberly Feigley
Stuart Feinstein
Carol Feld
Albert M. Felix
Euenie Fenerty
Nancy A. Fenton
David Fenuccio
Mary Ferezan
Virginia Ferlan
Denise Fernandez
W.G. Ferrell
Leonard Feuer
Sam Fielder
Mitch Fields
Susan Fields
Kimberly Figlar-Barnes
Andrea Filla
Illa B. and Frank A. Filotei, Sr.
Stephen Finnegan
Robert L. Fisher
Fisher Family
Denise Fitzgerald
William Fitzgerald
Five Rivers Oil Inc.
Judith M. Flaherty
Joanne Flanagan
John Flanagan
Veronica Fleischmann
Laurel Fletcher
Sissi Fletcher
Susan Flett-Pomeroy
Constantine W. Flevares
Angelica Flores
Keith Flower
Patricia L. Foldetta
Betty Force
Lionel E. Ford
Mark J. Ford
Thomas Ford
John Forte
Gilbert Foster
Lynn Foster
Jeremy Fought
Elizabeth & Max Fowler
William G. Fowler
Alan Fox
Frame Frame
Judith Frankhauser
Alton Franklin
Giorgina Franklin
Robert Franklin
Fraternal Order of Police Munster Lodge 147
Richard Frazee
Deborah Freda
Robert Frey
Helen S. Fried
Barbara Friedman
Charles C. Frisina
Judith Frisone
Patricia Frobes
Frois Family Foundation

Eileen Fry-Bowers
Margaret W. Ftikas
Karen Fulbright
William Fulton
Edward R. Furie
Marian Gable
Peter Gage
Scott Gallopo
Arnold J Galloway
George Gambino
Melvin Gamble
Peter Gamer
Letitia A. Gamez
Jay Gano
Harry Garcia
Joe Garcia
Michael E. & Joanne Garcia
Melvin Garner
Edward Garone
Vivien Garrigues
Deborah Gaston
Susie Gatland
John Geier
Geisinger Inpatient Management Council
Verlon H. George
George Washington University U.S.-Korean Alumni Association, Inc.
Carole Gerrity
Monica Gessner
Nadine Gibb
Tonya Gietzen
Joseph & Lisa Giguere
Catherine G. Gillen
Robert Gilliam
Katharine Gillies
Gilman School
James Gilmer
Rowena Gilstrap
Gail Ginsburgh
George & Cheryl Girman
Douglas Gish
Wanna Glass
Michael Glazzy
Seth Glickman
Global Korean Affairs Committee of Washington, D.C.
Global Sun Investments, Inc.
Carol Glover
Loretta Gnade
Lawrence A. Goga
Deborah Gogliettino
Robin Gold
Tara Gold
Margaret Goloboy
Paula Gomora
John H. Gonzales
Diane Goodridge
Liz Gordon
Susan Gordon
James Gorski
William Goss
Nick Goucault
Gail G. Gouger
Dolores Goughneour
Kelly Gowin
Grace Community Church
Marianna Grady
G Richard Graham
Jeffrey M. Grahn
Gene Granger
Kathleen L. Grant
Melanie B. Grant
Merle B. Grant
Jeanne & John Grau
Mary Beth Graziano
Greater Cincinnati Water Works
Mary Green
Ruth G. Green
Robertson Greenbacker
Billie Greenberg
Karen Greene
Jaci Griffen
Hubert Griffin
Peter Griffin
Thomas J. Griffin
Sophia Gronnevik
Ellen Gros
Stephan Gross
Zelma L. Grostick
Lindsey Grove
William Grove
Alan R. Gruber
David E. Grus
Richard Grus
Nancy Gruwell
Rachel Guiry
Carole Guld
David C. Gum, Jr.
Kyle Gunby
Richard Haab
Shirley A. Haag
William G. Haase
Randy & Sara Habbe
Barbara Hagberg
Ralph Hager
Richard Hagge
Warren C. Haglund
Hairtistics
Lynne Hajjar
Linda Halfmann
Harold Hall
Doris B. Hallinger
Robert P. Hamburg
Hamill Manufacturing Company
Albert Hamilton
James B. Hamlin, Jr.
Susy Hammons
Imsik Han
Insup Han
Scott Han
Han Bit Foundation Inc.
Han Gang Corporation
John Hanley
Mary Hanney
Michael Hapgood
Angela Hargett
Darissa & Jason Harkey
Christina Harman
Mary Harmeyer
Amy Harper
Patrick Harrington
Winifred Harris-Allen
Chris Harrison
Debbie Harrison
Mollie Harrison
Theresa Hart
Harter Secrest & Emery, LLP
Stephen N. Hartig
Nancy Harton
John Hartsky
Harvey Anderson Funeral Home
Heather Hasemeyer
Barbara Hass
John Hauser
Brenda Hausman
William Hausner
Mini Haven
Hawes-Pediatric at Dartmouth-Hitchcock
Joy Hawley
Chad Hayden
Diana Healy
Robert Heidrich
Susan Heimann
Joseph Heinrichs
Anne Heipel
William Heiss
Helix Family
Scott Henderson
E.H. Hendron
Christine Henessee
John D. Henley
Rossanna Hennessey
Doreen Henning
S. Hensley
Ritz & Sandra Henze
Heriverto Herrera
Michelle B. Heyman
Pamela Hicks
Fred M. Hidary
HIHB Gas Co., LLC
Susan Hildebran
Family of John P. "Jake" Hill
Lunetta Hill
Timothy Hines
Nathan Hintze
John C. Hirsimaki
Laurie Hitchcock
Phyllis Hitt
Donald A. Hitzeman
John Hjorth
Ben Hoang Insurance Agency
Pat & Bill Hodgson
Elise Hoffman
Hoffman Family
Frank Hoffmann
John R. Hogan
Linda Hogg-Wood
Jeanne Hohl
Molly Hohn
Sally F. Holl
Mitchell Hollin
Marion J. Holly
Thomas Honemann
Steven Honigman
Honor Flight Network
Arthur Hood
Pamela Hood
Jim Hoodlet
Daryl Hoole
Keith Hopper
Peter Horkan
Brenda Hornbaker
G.K. Hornung
Arthur T. Horton
Michael Horvit
Rose Marie A. Houser
Chris Hovanec
Susan Hovanec
Ethel Hovde
Alice & Ed Howard
Cody Howard
Katie Howard
Melinda Howard
Barbara Howe
Charles Hoyt
Isabel & Tony Hughton
Hyang Mi Huh
Terry Hulse
Dawn Humphrey
Dennis Huner
George & Marcia Huner
Elfriede Hunt
Linda Hunt
Huron Consulting Group, Inc.
Robert H. Hurt
Jennifer Huskey
Nancy Hutchins
William Hwang
Hyang-Gun, TX Inc.
Phillip Hyland
Peter Hyun
Hyundai Motor America
Francis R. Iacobucci, Sr.
Meggan Iacona
Joel Iams
IBEW Local No. 48
IBM
Naomi S. Ichinose
Dorothy Iglinski
Donna Ikenberry
Therese Iknoian
Illinois Tools Works, Inc.
Joseph Imbrogna
Alice Ingle Krug
Inglewood Board of Realtors, Inc.
Mary A Ingman
International Brotherhood of Electrical Workers
Andrew Irwin
Italian-American Citizens Club
J. Edwards Insurance Agency, Inc.
Robert Jackson
Jane Jacobsen
Petter Jacobsen
Karen Jacobus
Renee Jaegers
Kathy & James Jakel
Diana R. James
Wonchul Jang
Matthew Jankowich
Lesley Jarolim
Elaine Jarzeboski
Deborah Jasinski
Penny H. Jasper
Jay & Young Kim Foundation
Michael Jelen
Linda A. Jenacaro
Alan W. Jenner
Carl G. Jennings
Lee Jensen
Eunae Jeong
Jinho Jeong
Brent W. Jett
Sandra Jetton
Christina Ji
JoeAnna Ministries
Stanley Joehlin
Amy Johnson
Dorothy C. Johnson
Patrick Johnson
Reginald Johnson
Wayne Johnson
Beverly Jones
Frank Jones
Greg & Carla Jones
Max H. Jones
Raymond W. Jones
Virginia Jones
James Jordan
Kathleen Jordan
Donald Jorgensen
Heechul Jung
Jinyoung Jung
Eric Junge
Seo, Jungmin
Ann Justice
K. H. Kim's Tae Weon Do
Jeanne Kadet
Marino Kain
Adam Kalb
Daeho Kang
Hyeon S. Kang
Ik Kang
Youngok Kang
Warren Kaplan
Freemont Karhu
Mary L. Karhu
Karlin & Karlin Law Offices
Ray & Ruth Karst
Ellie Kassab
William Kastroll
KATUSA Association
Stanley Katz
Linda Kazanecki
Lois Kaznicki
Thomas Keaty
Tim & Susan Kee
Lynn Keene
John W. Keep
James Keilman
Frank Kelemen
Keller Foundation
Erin Kelley
Michael E. Kelley
Catherine Kelly
Christine Kelly
Denice M Kelly
Michael E. Kelly
Richard Kelly
Rodney Kelly
Ed Keltner
Joseph M. Kendrick
Barbara Kennedy
Jennifer Kennedy
Kevin M. Kenney
Sharon Kenoski
Kentlands Book Club
Mary E. Kenworthy
Robert Kern
Ned Kerstetter
Arthur N. Kesselhaut
George Kessler
Margaret Ketter
Steven Kettler
Leslie Ketzu
George Key
KFF Hawaii
Jasmeen Khuban
J. Gordon Kiddoo
Amy Kiley
Byong Kim
Charles C. Kim
Chulha Kim
Ernest Kim
Eunjung Kim
Hae Lyeng Kim
Hannah Kim
Hong Kim
Hooja Kim
Hyung-Joo Kim
Jandre Kim
Jinho Kim
Kyung Kim
Kyungkeuk Kim
Luciana Kim
Mia Kim
Okhee Kim
Rachel Kim
Sara Kim
Seunghwan Kim
Sunwha Kim
T.J. Kim
Taewon J Kim
Thomas S. Kim
Won Kuin Kim
Yong Suk Kim
Yoon Hee Kim
Young Cheon Kim
Young Kee Kim
Ed Kimminaw
Greg Kimsey
Sarina Kimura
Sherry L. Kin
Larry Kinard
Addison & Sandra King
Gary N. King
J. King
Jeff & Carol King
John King
Julie King
Karina King
Sally King
Donald H. King, Sr.
Frances E. Kinkead
Catherine Kippert
Kathy Kirkland
Kirkland Development, LLC
Kathryn Kirsch
June Kisker
Henry Kisovic
Janet Kleban
Nathan Klein
Daniel Kleinrock
Jeanne B. Kline
Ruth Kline

Christina Klocke
Sheryl Klotz
KLS Martin, LP/North America
C.M. Knapp
Francis Knight
Della M. Knowles
Annette Ko
Bong Ko
Donghyun Ko
Stanley Kober
Mark Koch
Dan Kochensparger
James Koenighain
Janice Koepke
Katie Kohn
Ruth K. Kohn
W. L. Kohn
Keith Kopinski
Catherine Kopko
Meghan Korb
William Kordula
Korea Association of Virginia in Washington Metro Area
Korea Peace Sharing Foundation
The Korea Society, Inc.
Korean American Foundation of Greater Washington
Korean American War Veterans
Korean ROTC Federation of North America
Korean Veterans Association
Korean Veterans Association, Inc.
Korean-American Women's Association of the USA, Inc.
Korea-U.S. National Prayer Breakfast, Washington, D.C.
Laura Korn
Mary Ann Kovack
Edwin Kovarik
Roxanne Krape
George Kraus
Mindy Kraus
Ron Kraus
Peter Kravitz
Carl Kropp
Keith Kuchel
Norbert & Marcia Kulesza
Marsha Kuligowski
Dave Kumar
Jerome Kushner
Frank & Gail Kwolek
KWVA Akron Regional Chapter 138
KWVA Antietam Chapter 312
KWVA Arden A. Rowley Chapter 122
KWVA of Atlantic County, NJ Chapter 234
KWVA Auxiliary Missouri Chapter
KWVA Cape & Islands Chapter 1
KWVA Captain Paul Dill #2 Chapter 12
KWVA Carson City Chapter 303
KWVA CenLA Chapter 180
KWVA Central Jersey Chapter 148
KWVA Charles L. Gilliland Chapter 22
KWVA The Chosin Few Michigan Chapter
KWVA The Chosin Few Arizona Chapter
KWVA Colonel William E. Weber Chapter 142
KWVA Department of Maryland
KWVA Department of New Jersey
KWVA Department of Virginia
KWVA Eastern Oklahoma Chapter 177
KWVA Frozen Chosin Chapter 41
KWVA General James A. V an Fleet Chapter 267
KWVA General Matthew B. Ridgway Western PA Chapter 74
KWVA General Raymond G. Davis Chapter 19
KWVA General Walton H. Walker Chapter 215
KWVA Greater Danbury Area Chapter 11
KWVA Greater Rockford Chapter 272
KWVA Gulf Coast Chapter 1
KWVA H. Edward Reeves Chapter 311
KWVA Hawaii #1 Chapter 20
KWVA Indiana #1 Chapter 30
KWVA Kansas Chapter 181
KWVA Kansas City Missouri #2 Chapter 43
KWVA Kansas City Chapter 181
KWVA Lake Erie Chapter 112
KWVA Lieutenant Richard E. Cronan Chapter 17
KWVA Massachusetts Chapter 299
KWVA Maui No Ka Oi Chapter 282
KWVA Mountain Empire Chapter 289
KWVA Nature Coast Chapter 174
KWVA New Hampshire Chapter 320
KWVA Northeast Chapter 59
KWVA Northern California #1 Chapter 5
KWVA Northern Virginia Chapter 100
KWVA Northern Wyoming Chapter 307
KWVA Northwest Illinois Chapter 150
KWVA Northwest Ohio Chapter 131
KWVA Olympic Peninsula Chapter 310
KWVA Oregon Trail Chapter 72
KWVA Sam Johnson Chapter 270
KWVA Shenandoah Valley Chapter 313
KWVA South Suburban Chapter 23
KWVA Southern Oregon Chapter 315
KWVA Thomas W. Daley, Jr, Chapter 54
KWVA Tidewater Chapter 191
KWVA Treasure Coast Chapter 106
KWVA Tri-State Chapter 126
KWVA Ventura County Chapter 56
KWVA of Washington, D.C.
KWVA West Hawaii Chapter 279
KWVA Western North Carolina Chapter 314
KWVA Western Ohio-Lake Erie Chapter 71
KWVA Western Wayne-Washtenaw County Chapter 326
Helen Labelle
Lisa Laboda
Labor Roundtable of Southwest Washington
Laborers International Union of North America Local 335
LACAMAS Insurance Services
Bette Ladd
Nancy & Gene Lagerholm
Victoria Lague
Charles P. Lallo
Maryann Lallo Hutt
Joyce Lambert
Richard Lancia
John Landahl
Reid Langrill
Amanda Lannigan
Christophe Laroche
Joyce Larsen
William & Cindy LaRuffa
Judith A. Lasher
Roberta Lasley
Kathie Lauback
Pete & Maggie Lauria
Thomas Lavan
Brittney Lazaro
Christine Leary
Dawn Marie Lecklikner
Alex Lee
Angela Lee
Byung (Paul) Lee
Choonja Lee
Greg Lee
Hyun Chang Lee
James H. Lee
Jason Lee
John Lee
Joon Suk Lee
Junseok Lee
K. Freeman Lee
Kyunghee Lee
Myung H. Lee
Phil Woon Lee
S.H. Lee
Samuel K. Lee
Sang Hoon Lee
Sheila Lee
Sun Lee
Sun Young Lee
T.W. Lee
Tae Seup Lee
Wonjin Lee
Lee & Associates
Diane M. Leech
Richard LeFleur
George Legarreta
Harriet LeMaster
Jim LeMay
Carolyn & Gano Lemoine
Lenape District Education Association
Marilyn Leopold
Michael Levar, Jr.
Andrew Levchuk
Stanley Levin
Janet Levinson
Larry Levinson
Lisa Leweck
Kathy S. Lewis
Nancy Lewis
Virginia K. Lewis
Patricia Leyland
Denise Libke
Tim Liebman
Beverly A. Lievens
Kim Lilly
Paul Hyong Lim
Gay Lincoln
James Lindsey
H.N. Lisgar
Franlyn L. Litsky
Kathleen Littlefield
Anita M. Loar
Matthew E. Loar
Kristen M. Locastro
Kenneth R. Locklin
Elaine Loffredo
Timothy Logman
Scott Lombardi
Michele Lombardo
Stephanie Long
Nancy Longley
David Lopez
Elizabeth Loredo
Los Angeles Superior Court
Ryan P. Loser
W.E. Louis
Monty Loving
Jacob Loviska
Gilbert Lowery
Barbara Lowry
Robert H. Lowry
Ivan M. Lucas
Roland Lucas
Christina Luedke
Marie Lugo
Nicholas Luisi
Richard M. Luna, Sr.
Plyllis Lund
Charles C. Lunt
Douglas Lunt
Antonella & Robert Lynch
Michael Lynch
Thomas Lynch
Ronald Lynn
Carla Lyons
John Lyons
Pauline Lysko
MacArthur Foundation
Sharon MacDonald
Beth Mack
Clotilda Mack
James W. Mackley
James A. Maersch
Jolene Magerl
Magnolia Little League
Mike Mahaney
Dewanna Mahon
Maine State Troopers Foundation
Etta Malloy
Sarah Malneritch
Cynthia Manca
Susan & Rick Mancini
Nancy E Manderson
Faith Mangan
Richard Marcotte
Cindy Maressa
George Margolis
Tom & Leighann Markalunas
Donna Markley
Robert Marsh
Marshall Hair Salon
John Martignetti
Richard Martine
Pete Martinez
Eva Martino
Maryland, Baltimore County
Maryland, Baltimore County
Maryland, Calvert County
Maryland, Carroll County
Maryland, Cecil County
Maryland, Charles County
Maryland, Frederick County
Maryland, Garrett County
Maryland, Harford County Council
Maryland, Howard County
Maryland, Queen Anne's County
Maryland, Somerset County
Maryland, St. Mary's County
Maryland, Talbot County
Maryland Saltwater Sport Fishing Association
Maryland State Society Daughters of the American Revolution
Dr. Thomas A. Mascaro
Massachusetts Environmental Police Officers Association
Thomas J. Massimiani
Nancy Mathews
Robert Mathis
Dennis Matteo
John Matthews
Lynn L. Matthews
Katrina Mattingly
Mark Maurer
Paul Maxwell
Kyle May
Peter May
Dick & Jane Mayer
Nancy Mayer
Brenda D. Mays
Aubrey Maze
Dante Mazza
Kathleen McBlief
Jerry McBride
William McCabe
Pyllis McCarthy
Terri McClements
James McClure
Margaret J. McCormack
Carol A. McCormick
Ryan McCormick
William J. McCormick
Donna McCourt-McElroy
Alison McCoy
Thomas McCreesh
Barbara McDaniel
Elliott McDaniel
John E McDonald
Theresa McDonald
James McGinley
Charles McGovern
Jacob McGuigan
Beatrice & Daniel McGuire
Charles McHaney
Wesley McIndoe
Jeff McKay
Kelly McKeague
Thomas McKeel, Jr.
Marylen McKenna
Patrick McLain
Richard L. McLaren
John McLean
Wade McLean
James McNally
Mary Kay McNamara
Nancy McNeeley
Jeanita McNulty
Joseph McNulty
Sara McVicker
Homer Mead
Robert Medearis
Margaret Meeker
Raymond Meeker
Rhody & Carolyn Megal
Jill Mellman

Mellon Private Asset Management
John Menghini
Jane A. Mentzer
William Menz
Robert & Tori Merced
Mercer Prieto VFW Post 2043
Stephen F. Mershon
Milton Meshirer
Brian Mesko
James Michalowicz
Michiana Korean Association
Middletown High School Volleyball Program
Mid-Shore Community Foundation
Denise Miehle
Joseph A. Migatz, Sr.
Dennis Miller
Frank Miller
Jillian Miller
John Miller
Linda Miller
Pamela R. Miller
Ron Miller
Diana Mills
Michael Mills
Milwaukee Valve Company, Inc.
Bok Ki Min
Ki-shik Min
Timothy James Min
Paul E. Ming
Joe Minner
Sara Mirabilio
MIT Laboratory
LeeAnn Mitchell
Susan Mitchell
Janet Mitson
Eileen Mohlfeld
Mary Moler
Sue Ellen Monfra
Paul N. Montague, III
Virginia Montalvo
Roberta Montemurno
Darla Montgomery
John Montgomery
Lizabeth Montgomery
Montgomery County Association of Administrators & Principals
Nicole Montoney
Angel Moon
Virginia Moon
Joshua Moore
Kelley Moore
Robert Moore
Rosie Moore
David Morales
Clarissa Moran
Lucas Moran
Tonja Moran
Nicholas Morfogen
Christopher Morgan
Luella & Charles Morley
George Morrell
Janet Morris
Scott Morris
Stephanie Morris
Susan M. Morris
Butch Morrow
Moschetti Family
Mary R. Moser
Bruce Moskowitz
Sandy Moskowitz
Shelby Mowrey
Jan Moyer
Mtech Mechanical
Grace A. Mueller
Kurt Mueller
Stanley Mulfeld
Multhauf Foundation Ltd
Patricia Munley
Edward F. Murphy
John H. Murphy
Terry Murphy
Caitlin Murray
Kathleen Murray
Ryan Murry
Sae Bong Myoung
Kellie Nadell
Archie Nakamoto
Michio & Sachiko Nakano
Salvatore Nalbone
James Nappi
Meggan Nasrey
Margaret Nastro
Matteo Natale
National Information Solutions Cooperative (NISC)
National Philanthropic Trust
Helen B. Neal
Roberta Neel
Stanley Neely
Mark Nelson
Kristina Nemec
Joan Nemick
Nesheiwat Medical Practice, PC
David Neumann
Marilyn Neville
Allan Newbey
Fred Newhouse
Jeff Newman
Newport Lions Club
Frances Newton
Jamie Nichols
Alfred (Plug) Nickell
David Nielsen
David Nierenberg
Tammy & Pat Niesen
Deborah Nikolis
Dr. and Mrs. Frank Nisenfeld
Northwest Oregon Labor Council
Edward E. Nothstein Family
Eugene Novak
Patrick Nucciarone
Janice OBrien
Theresa A. O'Brien
Mark Ochsenfeld
John H. O'Connell, Jr.
Leonard C. Odom
Steven Odrezin
Richard Oertel
Miriam Oettinger
David B. Offer
Teren Ogle
John OHara
Robert O'Hare, Jr.
Maureen Oja
Kim Dong OK
Elise & Tom O'Keefe
Stacey Olhovskky
Cecelia J. Olinger
Janice Oliva
Kate Olsen
Patricia Olsen
Peggy & Howard Olsen, Jr.
Oncology Nursing Society
Meaghan E. O'Neel
Operation Patriot
Christie Ordway
Organization of Korean American Women, Inc.
Lincoln Orologio, III
Patricia Orozco
Jesse Ortiz
Stacy Osborn
Osceola County Property Appraiser's Office
Mike Ost
Anastasiia Ostroverkh
Michael Osvai
Katie Osweiler
Richard Ottinger
Robert Otto
Paul & Jan Overgaard
John Owen
Dawn Owens
Ron Owens
Linda Oxford
Darrell Pace
Joyce Pace
Renee Packel
Rebecca Padilla
Pat Pagnucci
Margaret Palaszeski
John Palla
Nicholas Pannes
George Panno
Antonios Pappantoniou
Paralyzed Veterans of America Bay Area & Western Chapter
Tina Paries
Dominick Parillo
Peter Parillo
Joan Pariso
In Young Park
Jae Park
Jae Hyun Park
Jane Park
Jean Park
Karen Park
Kathy Park
Namhi Park
Paula Park
Yang Soon Park
Gerard Parker
John Parker
Linda Parker
Parker VFW Post 4266
Parkview Regional Medical Center
Peter Parrinello
Gregory Parson
Daviid Parsons
Angela Partalas
Partisan Veterans Association of Washington, D.C.
Phillip A Pasteris
Lakshmi Patri
Dale Paulson
Maria Pavletic
James L. Pearsons
Karen Pease
Linda Pedersen
Joel Pedlikin
George Pelletier
Laurent Peltier
Michael K. Peltier
Peninsula Korean American Cultural Center
Doris F. Peracchia
Erica Perez
Robert Perillo
Anne Perina
Marianne Pesick
Leslie Petersen
Jennifer Peterson
Kathleen A Peterson
Merle Peterson
Linda Petri
Luigi Petuzziello
Deborah Phillips
Deborah Phillips
Shelby Phillips
Jeffrey Piazza
William Pickett
Melanie Pieczkowski
Piedmont Lace Guild of Virginia
Curtis Pilgrim
Ping Medvigy Family
Kara Pitou
Ed & Honey Pivirolto
Andrew Pleat
J. Pochert
Brian L. Poindexter
Royce Pollard
Pollard Family
Robert O. Pollock, Jr.
Michael Polsley
Sandra Pope
Emily Popovic
Norma Pordy
Vicki Powers
Betty Pratt
Louis J. Presenza
Gerald E. Price
Albert A. Prickel
Primus Technologies Corporation
Joe Princehouse
Larry Probst
Geoffrey & Debbie Prose
Judith Prose
Prove Inc.
James Puckett
Maria R. Puckett
Purely Mee, Inc.
Gregory Putnam
Carol R. Pyle
Quadra Productions, Inc.
Diane Quaid
Verlie Quinan
Natalie Quinn
Julia Rabadi
Matt Raby
David Raccagni
R.J. Radano
Lisa Radcliffe
Sandra Radulski
Melody Raglin
Della Mae Raguse
Charles Rajnai
Kimberly Rakos
Priscilla Rall
Maria Ramirez
Thomas Randall
James Randels
Geraldine Randolph
John Rapp
Amy & Joel Rathbone
Daniel Rea
The Real Estate Group
Timothy Reardon
Denise Records
Evelyn Reed
Tom Reed
Regional Cardiology Consultants
Euphazine Reid-Kendall
Margene A. Reif
Samantha Reif
Wiley Rein LLP
Richard W. Reinthaler
John Renard
John Renella
Carrie Reoh
Susan Revell
Judith A. Rezy
RFS Investments, LLC
Hoon S. Rhee
Frank Rhodes
Frank G. Rhodes
Jerry B. Rice
Tom Rice
Kimberly Rich
Patricia Richardson
Chris Riche
Ursula R. Richey
Clarine N. Riddle
Jennie & Gary Rider
Matthew Riello
Rosalia Riello-Viana
Frank Ring
Deborah Ripke
Sherry Rivera
Robert Rives
RJG Corp
Linda Roberts
Martha Roberts
Rachel Roberts
Jamal Robertson
Daniel Robinson
Joanne Robinson
Melinda & Gordon Robinson
Melissa Rocklen
Leola Rodarte
Kelli Rodenbo
Jerry Rodgers
Antonio Rodriguez
Carlos Rodriguez
Dona Rodriguez
Linda Rogers
Rogers Towers Attorneys at Law
Roy & Roberta Rohn
Patricia Rolfes
Walter Romano
Mary Romero
Michael Rood
Katharina Root
Gloria Roque
Gilbert Rosales, Jr.
David Rose
Melanie Rose
Monica Rosen
James D. Rosenthal
Louise P. Rossi
Sandra L. Roth
Sherman Rothberg
Lauren Rothenberg
Robert Rotunda
Roger & Linda Roux
RTC
Ron Rubek
David Rubert
James Ruble
Terri Ruchalski
John Rudd
John Rudi
Anne Rudman
Barb Rue
Mary Ann Ruehling
Leo Ruffing
Urban Rump
John Ruselowski
Anne Russell
Joseph W. Russo
Thomas Ryan
S & Y Prime Net Property, LLC
Raymond Sabbag
Henry Sacco
Dennis Sadler
Meena K. Sadyojathappa
Anthony W. Salem, M.D.
Salesforce.com, Inc.
Greg Salmon
Barbara Salyer
Michael Salyers
Sharon L. Sanborn
Joshua & Cheryl Sandleback
Paul Sangster
Santa Barbara Foundation
Samuel J. Santeusanio
Alexander Sapega
Craig Saunders
Larry J. Saunders
Marc Savare
Douglas Sawyer
Carol Scales
Jimmy Schaberg
Robert Schafer, P.C.
Virginia Schaffer
Shirley Schatz-Miller
Barbara Schemanski
Michael Schenk

Joseph P. Schirmers
Marcia Schlatter
David Schmidt
Eric Schmidt
Lisa Schmidt
Michael Schmidt
Robert Schmidt
William W. Schmidt
Joe Schneider
Karin Schneider
Clarence J. Schommer
Ingrid Schoppe
Marvin M. Schrage
Sara Schrimsher
James Schuck, II
Michelle C. Schulik
Cathy Schumaker
Janet Schupbach
Lenore Schwartz
Catherine Schwartzer
Fred L. Schwien
Joseph D. Scolis
David Scott
Merle & Sue Scott
Susan Scully
Gail Sease
Donald W. Sechrist
Kimberly Selber
Cheryl Selvage
Anna Semon
Scott Senour
Ronna Sepielli
Brett Sessums
David Shaffer
Robert S. Shaffer
Nancy L. Shaffner
Shangri La Marine Corps League
Kevin Shanley
Arthur Sharp
Todd Sharp
Shawnee Mission Chapter Kansas, Daughters of the American Revolution
Elizabeth Sheeran
Louanne Shelton
Adrian Shepard
Joel Sherman
Terra Shideler
Richard Shim
Hiroshi Shima
Ji Chul Shin
Tae Shik Shin
Shin Etsu Handotai America, Inc.
David Shutan
Tae Shynn
Helen M. Sidor
Michael Sidor
Ronald J. Sidor
Saul W. Siegel
Elizabeth Silfer
Patti & Jim Simchera
Joseph Simeone
Michael Simkins
Victoria Simmons
Joan Simon
Bernadette Simsic
Donna Sinclair
Gurpreet Singh
Maryann Siniscalchi
Carolyn Sinn
Select Sires
Robert Sisson
Scott & Maureen Skifano
Donald Skrdlant
Thomas Sliviak
William Slusarczyk
Richard Slutsker
Rosalie & Dick Slutsker
Barbara Smarsh
Scott Smiley
Craig & Elli Smith
David R. Smith
Donald O. Smith
Doris Smith
Gary Smith
Jeanne Smith
Joel & Janet Smith
Kimberly Smith
Margaret L Smith
Robert L. Smith, III
Rylla Smith
Samuel Smith
Sheila Smith
Stacy J. Smith
Suzanne Smith
Tyler D. Smith
Victoria Smith
Warren Smith
Dorothy Snedden
Margaret Snitzler
James H Snow
Frank & Cynthia Soares
Social Studies Department of Mepham High School
Ok Cha Soh, Ph.D.
Bokki Son
Kyunghwa Song
Paul Song, MD
Diane S. Sonneman
William T. Soper
Cindy Sortillo
Sondra Sortillo
Clayton Soule
Anne Soulia
Stan Sourlis
South Zanesville Alumni Association
Southwest Washington Central Labor Council
Cindy Sovran
Jack Spahr
Stephanie Speers
Mark Spence
Ron Spiegel
Bob Sprouls
Karen St. Claire
Chris St. Pierre
Christopher Stallman
G. Stanley
David Starling
Kerry Starr
Linda Starry
Joseph F. Stavola
Jane Steen
Paul Steen
Daniel Steenstra
Robert Stefanelli
Cynthia Stein
Joan Stemm
Gary Stephens
Bonnie Stephenson
Cynthia Stewart
James Stewart
Wallace T. Stewart
Bernard Stoehr
Samuel H. Stoltzfus
Barbara Stone
Kimberly Stone
Laurence B. Stone
Paula Stone
Samuel Storms
Charles Stover
Becky Strobel
Clifford Strovers
Christine Strubbe
Barbara Stuart
Thu Stubbs
Becky Strobel
Joseph R. Suchanek
Dave Suchorski
Choo-suk Suh
Eunkyung Suh
Jaehyoung Suh
Barbara Sullivan
Heather Summers
Robert Sumrill
Sun City Veterans Association
Suncoast Wood Carvers
Jill E. Susser
Brian Sutherland
Raymond H. Swan
Karla Swartz
Edward W. Swearer, Jr.
Systems Planning & Analysis
Duane R. Sywassink
Karen Szabo
Ellen Szalinski
Patricia Szarek
Christine Taborelli
Sal Talomo
Rebecca Tanzyus
Doug & Cathy Tarvin
Alexander Tateyama
Natalie Tatz
Marion & Richard Taxin
William Taylor
Patricia S. Taylor
Tonya Taylor
Brent Teal
Marie L. Teigen
Khoi Tennies
William Tennis
Ernest Tepper
Judi Tergeson
Thomas Terko
The Rakkasans Mason/ Dixon Chapter
William Thiesen
Kwon O. Thomas
Matt Thomas
Daniel Thompson
Jean E. Thompson
William Thompson
Trent Thompson
Kevin H. Tichenor
John Tierney
John Tilelli, Jr.
Gina Tilton
Elaine Tobita
Justin Todd
Barbara Tolan
Linda Tomaka
Donna Tomaszewski
Gerald & Denise Tomechko
Jonathan Tomell
Kiyomi Tomita
James Tomlinson
Catherine Toner
Tina Tong
Christine K. Toole Sidwell
The Toro Foundation
Judy Torre
Paul Toth
Neill W. Trask, III
Jack E. Tremain
Marcelle Tremblay
Nilda Trilhe
Rose Tronfo
Nancy Trotter
Trouts Towne Restaurant, Inc.
David E. Trus
Craig R. Tsukamoto
Adam Tuckman
Jonathan Turner
Mary Turner
Ron & Trish Twentey
UBS
Young J. Un
Charles Unger
Urbana Volunteer Fire Department & Rescue Squad
US Regional Funding, Inc
Lotte Vajda
Donald Vallee
Jean Valley
Scott Van Arsdale
Beverly Van Dam
Mary Van Muelken
Joe & Shirley Van Parys
Charles Varca
Nicholas Vaream
Joseph Varone
Matthew Varvaris
Steven K. Vasta
Edwin D. Vater
Tony Vaughn
Madeline Vavricek
Maria Veja
Carmen Velarde
Steven M. Veling
Steven M. Veling
Steven M. Veling
Victoria Velinski
John Vellucci
Ventura Harley-Davidson
Joseph T. Vercellone
Mark & Elena Veta
Veterans at Renaissance at Monroe
VFW Post 1526
VFW Walhalla, SC, Post 6830
Elaine Videto
Kerry Videto
Kimberly Videto
Victoria H. Viglione
Quintin Villanueva
Michelle Vitiello
Robert Vogelpohl
Roxanne Voira
Thomas Vollmuth
Douglas Voss
VPC Investor Fund B, LLC
Betty R. Wachtel
Mary J. Wachtel
Roberta Wade
Ann Marie Wagner
Jean Waite
Jeanie Wakeland
Clarence Walbert
Kari Walden
Deborah Walker
Traci Walker
Robert Wallace
Ann Walsh
Kristine L. Walsh
Walt Carpenter Sporting Collectibles
Mary Wamsley
Mary Wamsley
Ray E. Ward
Stephen L. Wasby
Jay Washesky
Washington Association for Korean Schools
Margaret Wasmund
Alan H. Watanabe
Cheryl Watkins
Patricia Webb
Janice Weber
Janice Weber
William & Annelie Weber
Allisha Weeden
Nancy Weigle
Alice Weinberg
Lyn Weinberg
Harry Weiser
Melvin Weiss
Kathleen M. Welch
Kerrianne Wendover
Sara Whelton
Doris H. White
Jennifer White
James B. White
Keith White
Mark E. White
June L. Whitmer
James M. Whitney
Dale Whitworth
Matthew Whong
Stacy Wiener
Glenn Wienhoff
Susan Wigdor
Betsey Wilder
Margaret R Wilkie
Christine Williams
David Williams
Ezra Williams
Marcia Williams
Rachel Williams
Suzanne Williams
Verna Williams
M. Susan Williamson
Melissa Williamson
Anell Willis
Daryl Wills
Joni Wilson
Patrick Wilson
Tom Wilson
Debra Winfield
Karen Winther
Rebecca Wise
Eddie Wisemon
David Wolfe
Women's Health Group, LLC
Changmin Woo
Jean Woodruff
Maxine Woodworth
David Wooldridge
Gerald Wooldridge
Nancy Workman
Valorie Worsley
Catherine Worth
Courtney Wrenn
Donna L. Wright
James Wright, PhD
Elisabeth Wrona
Yang's Taekwondo Academy, LLC
Diane S. Yannetta
Michelle Yellin
Song Yo
John A. Yohn
Heidi Yoho
Hyeyeon Yoo
Stephen Sunghan Yoo
Young Yoo
Barbara Youderian
R. A. Young
K Kale Yu
Tae Suk Yun
Walter Yung
Nancy Zaborowski
Marianne, Peter & Stephen Zalys
Ramona Zammetti
Sheila Zart
Wesley W. Zart
Richard D. Zaveta, Jr.
Kimberly Zazula
Charles R. Zemp
Joan M. Ziegelmayer
Paul E. Zielinski
William Ziemer
John Zimmerman
Teresie Zmyslinski
Dennis & Kristin Zook
Allison Zorn
Deborah Zupancic
KWVA Arizona Chapter 3

자유는
거저 주어지는 것이
아니다.
FREEDOM
IS
NOT FREE